Camillo Mapei

Italy, Illustrated and Described

Camillo Mapei

Italy, Illustrated and Described

ISBN/EAN: 9783741167928

Manufactured in Europe, USA, Canada, Australia, Japa

Cover: Foto ©Andreas Hilbeck / pixelio.de

Manufactured and distributed by brebook publishing software (www.brebook.com)

Camillo Mapei

Italy, Illustrated and Described

ITALY,

ILLUSTRATED AND DESCRIBED.

ITALY

ILLUSTRATED AND DESCRIBED,

A REVIEW OF ITS PAST CONDITION

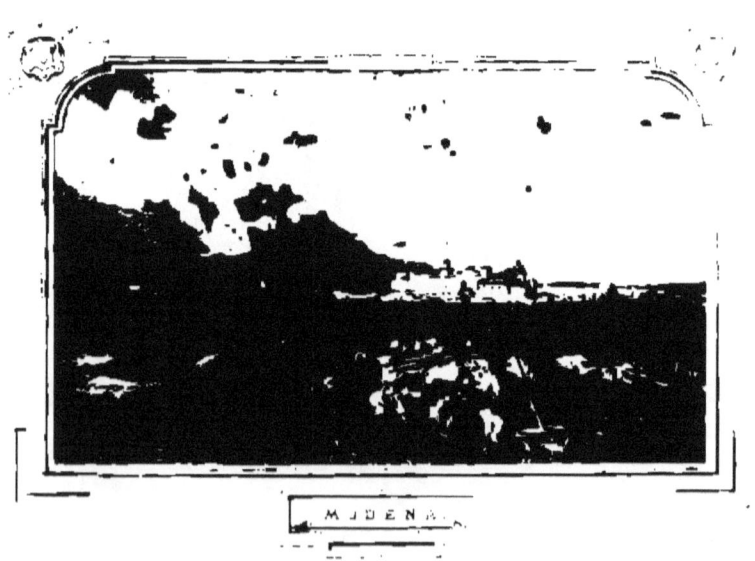

MODENA

ITALY,

ILLUSTRATED AND DESCRIBED,

IN A SERIES OF VIEWS,

FROM DRAWINGS BY

STANFIELD, R.A., ROBERTS, R.A., HARDING, PROUT, LEITCH, BROCKEDON, BARNARD, &c. &c.

WITH DESCRIPTIONS OF THE SCENES.

AND

AN INTRODUCTORY ESSAY,

ON THE POLITICAL, RELIGIOUS, AND MORAL STATE OF ITALY.

BY CAMILLO MAPEI, D.D.,

FORMERLY CANON OF THE CATHEDRAL OF PENNE, AND GRADUATE OF THE COLLEGE OF SAN APOLLINARE AT ROME.

AND A SKETCH OF THE

HISTORY AND PROGRESS OF ITALY DURING THE LAST FIFTEEN YEARS (1847–62),

IN CONTINUATION OF DR. MAPEI'S ESSAY.

BY THE

REV. GAVIN CARLYLE, M.A.

LONDON:
BLACKIE AND SON, PATERNOSTER ROW;
GLASGOW AND EDINBURGH.

MDCCCLXIV.

For ever and for ever shalt thou be
Unto the lover and the poet dear,
Thou land of sunlit skies and fountains clear—
Of temples and gray columns, and waving woods,
And mountains, from whose rifts the burning flood
Rush in bright tumult to the Adrian sea:
O thou romantic land of Italy!

      BARRY CORNWALL.

PUBLISHERS' PREFACE.

In whatever aspect Italy may be viewed, she is an object of interest. The student of history finds in her annals the most thrilling narratives and the most instructive lessons. To him her very dust is dear, whether attracted by the splendour of the old Roman Empire, the mercantile activity of a Venice or a Genoa, the phenomena of the Papal Power, the wars of a Napoleon or a Victor Emmanuel, or by those more recent struggles begun by the patriot Garibaldi, and resulting in that long sought for unity—a kingdom of Italy. The antiquary finds in her architectural and other remains the most ample field of investigation. The theologian, the Christian, never tires with contemplating the scenes where a Paul preached, where Christians were made a prey to wild beasts, where the Waldenses stood firm and suffered for "the faith as it is in Jesus," and earned for themselves the well-merited title of "The Israel of the Alps." The country of a Raphael, a Correggio, a Titian—of a Virgil, a Horace, a Dante, a Tasso, must possess a fascination for the painter and the poet, and for every man of cultivated tastes. While the tourist, bent merely on enjoying the beautiful, or on obtaining healthful relaxation, finds in her picturesque mountains, her fertile valleys, and her delicious climate, a combination which satisfies his most ardent desires.

To the features of lasting interest possessed by Italy, recent political events and changes have added others of a peculiar kind. The career of Garibaldi has added new lustre and new attractions to his native town Nice; the sufferings of Perugia have added a fresh though painful interest to that ancient Etrurian city; Turin, Milan, Florence, Genoa, Bologna, Ancona, Naples, Rome, has each in its turn come vividly before us, animated with the struggles of a noble people determined to be free.

ITALY, ILLUSTRATED AND DESCRIBED, was formerly published under the less appropriate title of "Italy, Classical, Historical, and Picturesque." It consists of a series of views of Italian Towns, and of River, Lake, and Mountain Scenery, engraved in the most finished manner, from Drawings by some of the leading landscape painters of Great Britain. The scenes selected for representation are all interesting, from historical, legendary, or poetical associations, or from their own natural beauties. Among them will be found views of various places seldom visited by the tourist, which come before the public with a pleasing freshness from never having been previously engraved in this country. The places that have been more frequently represented are in many instances pictured from new points of view, or shown under novel aspects.

A large proportion of the Engravings in this collection are from drawings by W. Brockedon, Esq., F.R.S., whose works, the "Passes of the Alps" and "Road Book to Italy," are so highly esteemed.

PUBLISHERS' PREFACE

In addition to the subjects furnished by Mr. Brockedon, and to contributions from many distinguished amateurs, whose names will be found acknowledged on the Engravings from their sketches, this work is also enriched from the sketch-books and portfolios of the following eminent artists:— Eastlake, Chantrey, Stanfield, Roberts, Harding, Prout, Leitch, and Barnard; and among the Engravers will be found the names of many whose works are generally recognised as being of the highest excellence.

The views are accompanied with Descriptive Notices, embracing the topographical features, the historical and classical reminiscences, and the legendary and poetical associations connected with the several localities depicted. The whole is preceded by an essay on the "Political, Religious, and Moral State of Italy," from the pen of the learned Dr. Mapei, formerly Professor of Divinity in Rome, written for the original edition of the work; to which is now added "A Sketch of the History and Progress of Italy during the last fifteen years (1847-1862), in continuation of Dr. Mapei's Essay, by the Rev. Gavin Carlyle, A.M."

GLASGOW, October, 1862.

LIST OF ILLUSTRATIONS.

	PAINTER.	ENGRAVER.	PAGE
TURIN........(*Frontispiece*)........	S. Bough............	W. Richardson........	164
MODENA..........(*Engraved Title*)......	S. Bough............	W. Richardson........	167
ITALIA..........(*Bastard Title*)........	H. Corbould..........	H. Adlard..........	xxlvi
NICE, GENERAL VIEW FROM THE HEIGHTS........	W. L. Leitch........	J. T. Willmore........	1
VINTIMIGLIA..............	G. Barnard..........	J. T. Willmore........	3
GENOA, THE TOWN AND PORT FROM NEAR THE NEW MOLE....	W. Brockedon........	R. Brandard........	5
LERICI, ON THE GULF OF SPEZZIA........	G. Barnard..........	R. Brandard........	12
CARRARA, AND THE SITE OF MARBLE QUARRIES........	W. Brockedon........	W. Richardson........	13
PISA, THE TORRE GUELFA AND PORTO A MARE........	C. Stanfield, R.A....	J. T. Willmore........	16
LEGHORN, FROM THE MONTE NERO........	W. Brockedon........	R. Brandard........	21
FLORENCE, FROM SAN MINIATO........	W. Brockedon........	J. B. Allen........	25
CERTALDO—VAL D'ELSA, TUSCANY........	W. Brockedon........	A. Willmore........	36
SIENA..............	W. Brockedon........	J. Cousen........	38
AREZZO—THE ANCIENT ARRETIUM........	W. Brockedon........	J. Cousen........	42
CORTONA..............	W. Brockedon........	T. Higham........	44
PERUGIA..............	W. Brockedon........	R. Brandard........	45
CHIUSI—THE ANCIENT CLUSIUM........	W. Brockedon........	A. Willmore........	46
RADICOFANI, AND THE CASTLE OF GHINO DI TACCO........	W. L. Leitch........	J. B. Allen........	49
BOLSENA—THE ANCIENT VOLSINIUM........	W. Brockedon........	R. Brandard........	52
VITERBO—THE ANCIENT VANUM VOLTUMNÆ........	W. Brockedon........	J. T. Willmore........	54
ORVIETO..............	W. Brockedon........	J. T. Willmore........	56
NARNI—RUINS OF THE BRIDGE OF AUGUSTUS........	W. Brockedon........	T. Jeavons........	58
TERNI—CASCATA DELLA MARMORA........	W. Brockedon........	J. T. Willmore........	59
CIVITA CASTELLANA............	W. Brockedon........	T. Jeavons........	61
CIVITA VECCHIA, THE PORT OF ROME........	W. L. Leitch........	J. T. Willmore........	63
ROME, FROM THE PINCIAN HILL............	W. L. Leitch........	J. Cousen........	65
ROME—SAINT PETER'S AND THE VATICAN FROM THE JANICULUS HILL	D. Roberts, R.A....	T. Higham........	80
ROME—BASILICA OF SAINT JOHN LATERAN........	W. Brockedon........	J. B. Allen........	84
PRATICA—THE ANCIENT LAVINIUM........	W. Brockedon........	J. B. Allen........	87
CASTEL GANDOLFO, ON LAKE ALBANO........	W. Brockedon........	J. Cousen........	97
OLEVANO—PAPAL STATES........	W. Brockedon........	R. Wallis........	98

LIST OF ILLUSTRATIONS.

TERRACINA—The Ancient Arx, Gulf of Gaeta	W. Brockedon	T. Jeavons	97
NAPLES, from the Santa Lucia	W. L. Leitch	J. B. Allen	100
NAPLES, from the Scoglio of Vergilio	W. Brockedon	J. Cousen	102
CASTELLAMARE, Bay of Naples	G. Barnard	J. T. Willmore	103
SORRENTO, the Eastern Gate from the Ravine	W. Brockedon	J. T. Willmore	107
META—near Sorrento, Bay of Naples	W. Brockedon	J. T. Willmore	110
AMALFI, on the Gulf of Salerno	W. Brockedon	J. T. Willmore	110
THE TEMPLES OF PÆSTUM	W. Brockedon	R. Brandard	113
REGGIO, the Straits of Messina and Mount Etna	W. Brockedon	W. H. Capone	114
BENEVENTO—The Ancient Beneventum	J. D. Harding	R. Brandard	116
ISOLA DI SORA, and Falls of the Liris, Abruzzi Mountains	W. L. Leitch	J. Cousen	117
SUBIACO—Val d'Anio	W. Brockedon	J. Cousen	118
ASSISI—Convent of San Francisco	W. Brockedon	T. Higham	119
LORETTO, the Adriatic in the distance	W. Brockedon	J. B. Allen	121
ANCONA, the Arch of Trajan and the Port	W. Brockedon	J. Cousen	123
BOLOGNA, general view from the Heights	W. Brockedon	T. A. Prior	125
FERRARA—The Ducal Palace	S. Prout	J. Godfrey	129
PADUA—The Municipal Palace and Market-place	S. Prout	J. Carter	131
VENICE—The Rialto and Ponte di Rialto	W. Brockedon	T. Higham	133
VENICE—Baptistery in the Church of Saint Mark	D. Roberts, R.A.	J. Carter	144
BASSANO, on the Brenta Trentine Alps	W. Brockedon	J. T. Willmore	145
VICENZA, the Piazza dei Signori and Ragioni Palace	J. D. Harding	J. Cousen	145
BRESCIA	W. Brockedon	J. Carter	147
ROCCA D'ANFO, on the Lake of Isso	G. Barnard	H. Adlard	148
BERGAMO	W. Cowen	R. Wallis	149
LOUVERE, on the Lake of Iseo	W. Brockedon	J. Cousen	150
COMO, from the South-west	G. Barnard	A. Willmore	151
VARESE, from the Sacro Monte	W. Brockedon	J. T. Willmore	153
MILAN	W. L. Leitch	T. Higham	154
PAVIA, and Bridge of the Ticino	C. Stanfield, R.A.	J. Carter	156
LA TORRE—The Waldensian College, Val Luserna	W. Brockedon	J. W. Appleton	158
FORT BARD, Val d'Aosta	W. Brockedon	J. B. Allen	160
MURANO—Lagoons of Venice	W. L. Leitch	J. Templeton	161
POZZUOLI—The Ancient Puteoli, Bay of Baiæ	W. L. Leitch	W. Richardson	163

THE POLITICAL, RELIGIOUS, AND MORAL STATE OF ITALY.

BY DR. CAMILLO MAPEI.

PREFACE.

ITALY, the object of romantic regard to all civilised nations, is continually receiving a crowd of curious travellers who resort thither for the purpose of contemplating the beauty and magnificence of the country. Hence it would appear that almost all nations ought to cherish a right idea of its religious, political, and moral condition. And yet we find no other nation so badly judged of, if not with the few of superior intellect who can reason fairly from causes to their effects, at least with the many who are wont to allow their judgments to be guided by the outward appearance of things. It were an arduous task to enter into a minute examination of the causes that in spite of the frequent communications of foreigners with the inhabitants of the Italian peninsula, have led to no just estimate having yet been formed of their character and customs, and of the influence exerted upon these by religious and political systems. It is necessary, however, that I should briefly present the principal reasons why this has been the case. Without going farther it is enough that we reflect that of the four classes of travellers that visit Italy, that is to say, merchants, the rich, artists, and men of science, the first three are not in a state to form a correct idea of a whole people, since their attention is directed to one special object which attracts their whole regards. Mercantile men travel with an eye to business, the rich for the sake of amusement, artists in order to study the beauties of nature and the monuments of art. It is very clear that the first, intent as they naturally are on the success of their speculations, look almost exclusively to the general system of civil administration and of justice, and much less to the religious machinery of the country. Intoxicated with the delightfulness of the climate, amid the perfumes of the roses of Pesto and the fragrant orange groves of Pausilippo and Mergellina, the rich, passing successively from the public promenades to the theatre and from these to joyous meetings, instead of casting their eyes on the misfortunes and sufferings of the people, and contemplating the wounds of a racked and tortured nation, are careful rather to avert their regards from these, so as not to mingle a most bitter drop in the cup of their enjoyments.

Judging of others by themselves, and by the pleasurable sensations that fashion their lips to a smile, they readily take up the false idea that the Italians are contented with their present condition, because they see them smile, without reflecting that their smile is a ray of the Italian sun. Artists, continually wandering among the ruins and the museums, contemplate Italy as she was in the days of her grandeur, and hence when they set themselves to consider what she is in her state of decline and despondency, they do not sufficiently moderate their judgments, but go beyond the bounds of truth. Just as to a person coming from the glare of noon, a chamber seems dark and obscure, so that the eye finds it difficult to distinguish particular objects, although others not thus dazzled with the sun, can see them clearly and distinctly. Men of learning alone, then, who travel with the view of practically studying society, could give a correct account of the present state of Italy, were the theoretical study of legislation under despotic governments enough; were it enough for a man but to know the articles of faith and the disciplinary canons of the Roman church in order to judge properly of the influence it exercises on the national manners. But while legislation in the greater part of Italy is such as accords with a civilized people, on the other hand the arbitrary spirit of absolute governments destroys its beneficial influence, by means of the secret ordinances with which it supersedes the laws in their application to particular cases, without such infamous proceedings meeting the eyes of foreigners. Many as are the corruptions of doctrine in what concerns faith and discipline in the Church of Rome, yet were its doctrines inculcated on the people as presented in the polemics of the defenders of the faith, the state of society would not in the end prove so unhappy; but the doctrines of the Church of Rome are one thing in principle, another thing in practice; one thing in books, another thing in the mouths of the priests from whom they are received by the people. After having made a monstrous amalgam of truths revealed in Holy Scripture and of human follies depending on *pharisaical tradition*, methods have been sought out likewise, for choking that portion of the good seed which still remains amid the thorns of error, the instruction of the people being intrusted to a body of clergymen generally ignorant and immoral. The eye of a foreigner finds it difficult to succeed in penetrating the darkness in which superstition and vice, clothed in sacred habiliments, nestle and conceal themselves. Hence it follows that it would be an arduous, not to say an impossible endeavour, to obtain, even by means of the most enlightened travellers, a complete acquaintance with the present condition of the Italian people, particularly if we reflect that under the moral torture of the police and the Inquisition, they are constrained to lie to all who interrogate them. Words dictated by fear to a nation suffering under tyranny, are often taken for genuine expressions by those who know not how frightful a thing tyranny is when propped by religion. To these sources we ought so far to attribute the errors into which those are apt to fall who write their *impressions received in the course of a journey*, after having run through the Italian peninsula in two or three months, accusing it *in general* of vices and bad tendencies which are really *special*, and more or less vigorous in one or other province according as the Empire and the Church weigh down its neck with a twofold yoke of iron. Another reason that leads well-informed travellers to give forth false judgments on the character and manners of the Italians, may flow from habits acquired in judging of other countries, that is, of ascending from *particulars* to *universals*. Now Italy may be pronounced that country of all Europe in which generalization ought least to be attempted. Being detached from diverse races, Greek and Asiatic, to which were afterwards added others from the North and West, the frequent invasions by various peoples that have in later times desolated, sometimes one, sometimes another part of the garden of Europe, which has allured all to it with its charms, have so far influenced the character, the manners, and the morals of the inhabitants. Spaniards, French, and Germans by turns have remained for long periods, now in one province, now in another, as its lords, and have left behind them profound traces of their sway. Lombardy, which now groans under the chains of Austria, was in other epochs subject to French and Spanish influences, a companion in misfortune of the kingdom of the two Sicilies. The military occupation of the country under the directory of the French republic and afterwards under the imperial government of Napoleon, has recently contributed to fix foreign habits among those classes which feasted these strangers with the view of gaining favour with them. Hence one would make a false conjecture who should judge of the manners of the provinces by those of the cities, where chiefly the troops were quartered, and where the nobility, in their eagerness to obtain distinction, did their utmost to flatter them. But what traveller pushes his inquiries into the shepherd's hut or the cottage of the ploughman and the woodcutter under the shoulders of the Appennines? Who is there that ever sets himself to investigate the peaceful and simple manners of the villages and small towns where there are still preserved untouched, or at least uncorrupted, the patriarchal traditions of a people which has twice been the mistress of civilization to other nations? Alas, a judgment is passed upon Italy amid the din of its capital cities, Rome, Florence, Naples, Milan, and Venice, where the great affluence of foreigners has had an immense share in the corruption of the inhabitants. What strangers then ever enter Italy without having already conceived a prejudiced idea of it? Under the influence of this idea, they are easily struck with every, the slightest evil that confirms them in their preconceived opinions. Fully persuaded that the papacy has profoundly rooted itself in the minds of the Italians, when they see the churches crowded and observe the punctuality with which the outward practices of the Roman catholic religion are performed, they are convinced that all Italy willingly bows its neck beneath the feet of the pope and that it kisses the chains that bind it so harshly to the throne and to the altar, so as to make it the laughing-stock of other nations. They see the papacy display all the pomp of its full-blown ceremonies in Italy, and imagine that this parasitical plant grows there vigorously on a propitious soil, without perceiving that its roots are tainted and rotten, and that it is in a dying state. The ancient oak may continue to preserve the beauty of its youth to the eye of the casual passenger, but the shepherd who looks down upon it from the hill top marks the scarness of its crown, betokening the approach of death.

Born in the kingdom of Naples, educated in Rome, and having resided afterwards in my native country, in the various epochs of my life and the various positions in which I have been placed, I have had leisure to observe the tendencies at once of the church, the governments, and the people. A member not of the lowest rank of the clergy, I have scanned all that is ambitious, astute, and perilous in the court of Rome, and the last remedies which it has adopted, the fusion of the political and religious principle, and a servile alliance with tyranny. Warmly attached to social amelioration, I stooped from my position to question the griefs and the desires of the people. Hence the judgment which I come to present on the present state of Italy, will be most exact in what relates to facts and to the religious and moral state of the country. Love for my native land may prompt me perhaps to something like exaggeration when I come to speak of its political condition, but be it my defence to write in a country blessed with liberty and independence, prosperous owing to the wealth produced by commerce and industry, and great from the impulses of national love. It will not be ascribed to me as a fault that misfortune loses none of its wretchedness in my eyes when confronted with the spectacle of another's felicity; my judgment, however, shall be sincere. The slight knowledge I have found existing in England respecting the affairs of Italy, and the little disposition I perceive there to give credit to the representations of my country's miseries, have stimulated me to speak without reserve. The hope that the British nation, which has the deposit of the Gospel, and which has abolished the slave trade, is now turning its regards, though tardily, to the slavery of Italy, and will no longer participate in the unjust policy that oppresses her, is strengthened by the thought that Britain is alive to the conviction that the papacy stands ready to invade herself.

LIVERPOOL, 1847.*

---

* This Essay, extending in all to 108 pages, gives a very vivid picture of Italy at the period at which it was written. It is still of interest from its excellent accounts of the various provinces out of which the new kingdom has been formed, and from its lucid description of the geography, climate, and products of the country, and the habits and condition of the people. Its anticipations of the future progress of Italy have been realised with remarkable accuracy, thus proving the depth of view of the writer, and adding to the value of his testimony. It was written by an Italian gentleman of high education, who enjoyed ample opportunities of being fully informed on the subjects treated of. A Sequel to this Essay will be given, written by a competent person, which will follow up the narrative to the present period, and give a sketch of the remarkable events that have occurred in the Italian peninsula within the last few years.

GENERAL REFLECTIONS ON ITALY.

ITALY presents a totally different aspect to the man who descends from the Alps from that which strikes the eye on reaching the delicious shores of Naples, or the lone rude coasts of Ostia or Civita Vecchia. Although the natural disposition of the Italian people is the same, whether on the plains of Lombardy, on the shoulders of the Appennines, in Tuscany, or the Sabines and the kingdom of Naples, yet some differences may be recognised in the moral lineaments of those different populations, more or less considerable according to the different aspects of their respective territories. Let us cast a glance over the whole peninsula and the difference is manifest. From the sides of the Alps, Italy, as far as the Appennines, stretches in a great measure like one vast plain, fertile, luxuriant; full of life yet regular as the course of the rivers that water it. The Po, the Adige, the Oglio, the Dora, slowly and majestically traverse its fields, which are cultivated with so much minute attention as to have the appearance of delicious gardens.

Wherever the eye reposes one sees towering in the distance those considerable cities, Turin, Milan, Padua, Mantua, Verona, Parma, Placentia, Bergamo, Brescia, Crema, Cremona, Pavia, Lucca, Modena, with numerous villages interspersed, glowing with the bustle of an industrious people. Magnificent to one who contemplates it for the first time, is the view of such beautifully disposed fields, vineyards so well kept, such vigorous olive groves and orchards, succeeding each other on all sides; wide highways bordered with trees that run off in straight lines and lose themselves in the horizon; but the eye at last becomes used to the monotony of the landscape, to beauties that are repeated at every step. To vary the prospect, the traveller must look up towards the distant horizon, to the white cloudwrapt summits of the Alps, and to the gloomy ridges of the Appennines. If then we proceed towards the south, hardly shall we pass over the first mountains when Italy assumes new forms, and becomes invested with charms that multiply as we contemplate them. Every twenty miles the traveller finds himself with a new perspective before him. Here are torrents that thunder over the rocks with the impetuosity of a tempest, trees moaning in accord with the roaring sound, torrents which yet a little after may be crossed dryshod. Rapid and gurgling rivers precipitate themselves from rock to rock, forming magnificent and picturesque cascades. Here are silent valleys hemmed in with precipices; there vast uncultivated plains, having the appearance of deserts, the range of the wild buffalo. Here, on the one hand lie fertile plains covered with yellow harvests; there, on the other, rises a hill-side, clothed with shrubs that gradually thicken into a wood. Turn your eye to the shoulders of the mountains, and you will see majestic forests of oak and chestnut, and amid these, cresting the cliffs, the ruins of towers and castles that look like eagles' nests. And then, like the sun-beam after a storm, the smile of nature shows more beautifully by contrast as seen on the flowery banks of the Garigliano, where the extraordinary fecundity and suavity of the climate have well entitled the country to be called *felix* (happy). Farther on, the bay of Naples discloses the rich profusion of its charms, surrounded with a rugged garniture of mountains, like a glittering gem enchased in an iron ring. On advancing beyond this, the Appennines becoming more savage and alpine, stretch their arms across the entire breadth of the peninsula from sea to sea as far as Cape Spartivento.

From this description it will be seen that Italy may be considered as forming two grand divisions, northern and southern, having the Appennine range for their natural boundary. The principal chain of these mountains stretches in an irregular line from west to east. It starts from Cuneo and Tende, branching off from the maritime Alps, and skirting along the coast of Genoa, it traverses the duchies of Parma and Modena, which it separates from Tuscany. Then inclining towards the south, it enters the Papal states, skirting Umbria, Sabina, and the Mark of Ancona, as far as the frontiers of the Abruzzo on the coast of the gulf of Venice. From the Abruzzo it proceeds across the whole kingdom of Naples. Northern Italy, accordingly, comprehends all that part of the peninsula lying to the north of the Appennines, that is to say, between these and the Alps and the gulf of Venice. Hence this division contains Piedmont, the Lombardo-Venetian state, Parma, Placentia, Modena, and the four legations of the Papal states, that is to say, Ferrara, Bologna, Forli, and Ravenna. Southern Italy is comprehended between the Appennines, the Mediterranean, a part of the gulf of Venice and the Ionian sea. The duchy of Genoa, that of Lucca, Tuscany, the Papal states, and the kingdom of Naples belong to this division. Nor is the difference between these two divisions confined to appearance only. The nature of the soil and climate is not the same in both, and hence the character of the inhabitants presents the variety necessarily resulting from diversity of climate, although at the same time the same elements are found in both. The character of the Italians may be said to be made up of all the different qualities that distinguish other nations. The fire and energy of the south is tempered there with the reflective disposition of the north; while, on the one hand, the exuberant imagination of the eastern nations produces a disposition to indolence, and to indulge the flowery dreams of poesy and love, on the other hand the activity characteristic of the western tribes, incites them to engage in trade, and to cultivate the arts and sciences. Hence it is not difficult to discover in the Italian character a combination of the gravity of the English, the sprightliness of the French, the ardour and perseverance of the Spaniards, the reflectiveness of the Germans, and the fiery passions of the Arab and the Syrian. Diversity of circumstances will bring out the versatility of a nature comprising various elements and will develope the germs of new virtues, or new vices, which though at first sight they may appear contradictory, must be fundamentally referred to the temperature of the climate. The geographical position of Italy will justify this opinion though it may seem to have been dictated by predilection for my native land.

On the north, Italy marches with Switzerland and Germany, on the west it adjoins France. Hence it may justly claim a portion of the advantages which a rigorous climate gives to nations, by cooling down in them the ardour of the passions, and thereby rendering them better fitted for intellectual and moral development. The everlasting snows of the Alps temper the heat of the African sun which scorches Italy. The Appennines which emulate the Alps in height and in savage scenery, by traversing the entire peninsula lengthwise, secure a continuation of the advantages resulting from a temperate climate. In other respects, in proportion as Italy extends towards Africa, the action of the solar rays predominates, and the character of the inhabitants gradually becomes more lively and ardent. In fine, as we proceed farther towards Calabria and Sicily, opposite to which lie the immense scorching deserts of Africa, the Appennines which as far as the confines of Puglia, retain their primitive form of a chain of mountains leaving extensive plains on the right and left along the Mediterranean and the gulf of Venice, all at once divide into branches and occupy the whole extent of the provinces at the extremity of the kingdom of Naples, these from sea to sea being bristled and notched with mountains. While the provident hand of God has in the southern confines of Italy multiplied the highest mountains on which the north wind's breath copiously deposits the snows that tend to moderate the excessive heat of the sun, on the other hand, on the northern confines of that country, it has placed the vast plains of Piedmont and Lombardy, by which the kindly heat of the sun is kept from being overpowered by the frosts from the north. Hence it is that in Italy as a whole, the climate may justly be pronounced temperate, notwithstanding that some variety of temperature is observable on comparing one division with another; hence it is that the character of the Italians may be considered the same, notwithstanding that in the inhabitants of the north reflection controls energy of sentiment, and in those of the south, energy of sentiment is increased by reflection. The Calabrian and the Lombard may at a first glance present few traces of resemblance, but on a closer examination it will be found that fundamentally they possess the same natural peculiarities, the same independence, energy and perseverance; the apparent dissimilarity is the result of the oppression under which Italy has been groaning for ages, not at all of nature which is not in them a thing that varies. The brigandage of Calabria in 1700, was the expression of the very same sentiments that originated the Lombard League. Italy therefore cannot be considered to be a country exclusively oriental or meridional, but as one that participates in the advantages which nature has liberally bestowed on all the four quarters. To one who has passed a whole year in Italy the truth of these observations will seem very clear, if he but recall the impressions made on him by the variation of the seasons. An inhabitant of Lebanon arrives in Italy at the beginning of April, at the time when the vernal zephyr caresses with voluptuous wing the flowers that enamel the meadows, and when the air is loaded with sweet odours, from that of the violet that lies hid in the hedges to that of the rose which vaunts its charms in the gardens; at the time when amid the verdure of the fields, the fruit trees raise their blossomed heads and the orange trees seem to wait with impatience for the warming rays that revive them; at the time when beneath a limpid and azure sky the copious dews glisten to the silver radiance of the moon, at the time when the dawn empurples the mountain tops and gradually brings out the colours of a landscape where all is harmony and smiles, until the sun, emerging from the Adriatic, pours over Italy a baptism of light, and he might fancy himself still in Palestine. Spring gives to Italy quite the physiognomy of an Eastern country. It is then the land of pleasure, poesy and love. But let an Arab behold it in the heat of July, when the sun darts his fiery rays with all his force, when the scorched earth is cleft and gapes like the thirsty and panting bird in the track of a fountain; when the fields are whitening with corn and the meadows look like the sands of the desert; when of a sudden the atmosphere, whitened at first with mists, grows thick with clouds; when the whirlwind harbingers the tempest with volumes of dust, and the lightning flashes and the thunder roars incessantly like the lion's voice repeated by the echoes, when rain and hail and thunderbolts all come down together, and when, shortly after, the purified and re-invigorated earth presents itself like a charmed oasis, he might believe that he was still on the sides of his native hills, looking out on one of those grand commotions of nature which announce themselves so terribly and magnificently within the tropics.

Italy in summer presents quite the physiognomy of the regions of the south. It is then the land of strong and violent passions. Seen at the commencement of Autumn when the pulse and corn are collected in the modest dwellings of the peasantry, or in the vast storehouses of the rich, in sufficient abundance for the support of ten such countries, when hill and vale resound with the joyous songs of the villagers while employed in the bustle of the vintage, or of the rustics collecting the fruits or crushing the grapes in the wine-presses, when the fields are preparing for the seed, and when it is sown for the following year, when the shepherds and neatherds hasten to the plains with their flocks and herds from the mountain sides where winter is beginning to show itself; when showers are frequent, and the sun looks pale, and the clouds rise from the streams and valleys, it then looks like a part of western Europe, and Frenchmen and Englishmen will think they find in Italy some resemblance to the lands they have left. It is then a land of plenty and of laborious habits, and would be a land of industry and commerce, were commerce and industry to find instead of obstacles and threatened calamities, protection and encouragement. But what if winter in Italy is roughened with frost and whitened with snow! It is certainly not such a winter as is seen among the rocks of Siberia or beneath the cliffs of Mont Blanc, but the German or English tourist, provided he does not remain at the bay of Naples, will find the breath of the north wind very cold, and will be amazed at seeing snow and ice so common in a country which he may have pictured to himself as always covered with flowers. Snow falls frequently, particularly in the lands adjacent to the Appennines, and, towards the Adriatic, besides what is discharged by the northern blast, there is added from time to time the snows accumulated and driven over by the wind from the Levant, from the coasts of Dalmatia and from Greece. Alas, whoever shall travel during winter in Italy, would never suppose it to be one of the regions of the

South. Italy during the cold season is the country of reflection, of serious studies and of unimpassioned politics. In no other country of Europe are the limits of the seasons so distinctly marked as in that peninsula. Hence we find united in the people the four principal qualities that distinguish nations placed under the influence of particular climates, such as the sensibility of the East and the energy of the South, the activity of the West and the reflective habits of the North. To these, if we add frankness, sobriety, perseverance and hospitality, you will have the main features of the Italian character. The defects with which it is chargeable, are to be traced to the good original peculiarities of heart and mind with which the Italians are naturally endowed. Effeminacy of manners proceeds in Italy from excessive sensibility, fostered by the empire of a religion which speaks softly to the senses while it clouds and obscures the reason. The readiness with which the people shed one another's blood, must be ascribed to the violence of their passions, and the energy of their characters, provoked and exasperated by the injustice of the law courts in which an arbitrary spirit greatly prevails, and by the partiality with which the laws are administered under despotic governments. The religious and civil systems tend with one accord to turn to what is bad the best qualities of the Italian character. Rome, on the one hand, with the pompous apparatus of its ceremonies, lays hold of the imaginations and susceptibility of a people full of the poetical temperament, not in order to guide them to the morality of the gospel, to the love of God and of mankind, but to superstitious practices and to intolerance. The governments, on the other hand, dread the energy and activity of a people who find in the past a mighty stimulus to come out from that state of degradation in which the vicissitudes of time and the policy of the powerful have reduced them, and a most sufficient warranty of success. Hence science is openly, or at least covertly, persecuted by them, and education thwarted or controlled. Hence restraints are laid on commerce in order that the civilization of other nations may not be communicated by contact. Hence idleness and indolence are fostered. In the unnatural constraint under which Italy is groaning, not only are many good qualities of the Italian character kept down, but many defects altogether foreign to the disposition of a passionate and energetic people, have germinated, and have then been attributed to the Italians as vices essentially rooted in their very nature. The Italians are reproached with being reserved and insincere, without its being remembered that, compelled to conceal their sentiments in the presence of the lynx-eyed Inquisition and police, and that crushed beneath the oppression of a brute force which chains up the use of words and the free expression of thoughts however holy and becoming, they have been taught to dissemble and to lie by the advice of other nations which have charged Italy with imprudence every time it has dared to manifest its true sentiments of independence and liberty. While the common charge of imprudence is raised by all the nations against the sincere expressions of a people oppressed by tyranny, the accusation of insincerity thrown upon the Italian character ought to appear unjust to every reasonable mind. The history of free and independent Italy does credit to the sincerity of the national character of the Italians. Attilius Regulus presents an eternal monument of the good faith of ancient Italy. A glorious monument of the good faith and sincerity of the Italian character in recent history, is seen in the vote passed by the

Neapolitan parliament, on the 7th of December, 1820, on the departure of King Ferdinand I. for the congress of the allied powers at Troppau. The king promised to charge himself there with the defence of the interests of the people and of the rights of the constitution that had been granted; faith was given to the promise although it came from lips habituated to lying and to breaking the faith of treaties. This presents one of the most evident characteristics of candour and good faith. The national parliament then revealed to the nations of Europe what a treasure of sincerity lay in the hearts of a people usually charged with want of sincerity. That was the expression of a people free, independent, in the first moments of their recovered liberty. Now what idea ought not to be conceived of that same people, after enjoying for years the light of such a civilization as should draw forth all the good qualities that God has implanted in their hearts. We all know that slavery makes men wily and cunning. A man, simple and sincere as he may imagine himself, will at length grow sly and crafty within the walls of a prison. The irresistible desire for liberty will not be repressed by the sight of barriers and hindrances, and in default of force will call in the aids of ingenuity. Such is the nature of the human heart that when one of its strings is powerfully struck, the others respond to the blow. Hence it is that moral corruptions are never confined to one class of actions only, nor to one end. Dissimulation and hypocrisy are the necessary results of the Inquisition and the police, and then are apt to spread from religion and politics into the social relations, mutual distrust being fomented by the iniquitous proceedings of the governments. To this there is added the influence of pernicious theological doctrines. In the confessional, the sentence of absolution is openly said to be founded on *probable opinions* and on *mental reservations*. Let us calculate, in fine, what must be the force of the melancholy example set by a swarm of priests, monks, and friars who lie before God and man, and it will be found that the Italian people, instead of being a butt for taunts and accusations, ought rather to excite admiration for having resisted so long and combated successfully the combined efforts of politicians, divines, and armed foreigners to repress within them every generous idea. Granting that the defects referred to are not charged against them altogether without grounds, it would seem at least that the evil plant is not a daughter of the soil of Italy, and does not find full sustenance there. A comparison between Italy and France will suffice clearly to prove the preponderance of sincerity and independence in the Italian character over that of one of the greatest nations of Europe. Universal plaudits greeted the Russians, Prussians, and Austrians in Paris, on their entering that city as the restorers of the throne of the Bourbons, and the very same persons who shortly before were exclaimed against as enemies and oppressors, after the battle of Waterloo, when circumstances were altered, were saluted as deliverers and friends. But the German is always regarded as an oppressor in Italy, not only when he stands concealed within his mountains whence with his dark intrigues he strikes and crushes the rights of Italian nationality and independence, but also when from time to time he advances in arms to rivet its chain. No shout of applause has ever greeted the banners of Austria. The cities are mute when it enters them, and that silence amounts to a dignified protest; it does not give the lie to the sincerity of their aversion to foreign tyranny; it does not basely retract the threat uttered under an impulse of generous indignation, when a ray of hope promised freedom and victory. The genius of Italy dictated to Alfieri in the following lines, the expression of the independant and candid character of that country in contrast with France.

> Schiavi or siam sul, ma schiavi almen frementi
> Non quali, O Galli, il foste e il siete voi
> Schiavi al poter, qual'ch'ei pur sia, plaudenti.
>
> Now we are slaves, but slaves that with a frown
> Confront our tyrants, not such slaves as ye.
> Gauls! have been and still are—slaves lost to shame.
> Who with your plaudits greet whatever power
> Plants its proud foot upon your abject neck.

The same candour and independence of character is to be seen in Italy in the profession of religious sentiments. The enlightened class which laughs at the superstitions and the falsehood of the system of Rome, does not, in order to purchase favour with the powerful, stoop to practise superstitious customs and rites, unless such as are commanded under the bayonet of gens d'armes, with the anxiety with which people run in crowds at the sound of the bell to mumble prayers that come not from the heart, after the example of Louis XVIII., a bigot king ruled over by priests. On the other hand, when the French occupied Italy in the character of its lords, when irreligion was reckoned a just claim to favour, and blasphemy against Christ was considered to be a sort of charm for changing for the better a man's condition in life, the lower people did not relinquish their religious practices and made no show of holding their faith in small esteem. Hence the charge of insincerity is calumnious in general, and strangely exaggerated in so far as it may be partially true.

Let us now speak of religion in Italy, first giving a general idea of it in order the better afterwards to treat it more in detail. The Roman catholic religion has its roots in the heart and its force in the imagination of the Italians. It presents to a people endued with the germs of ambition and which has a most inextinguishable thirst for love, an innumerable host of glorious and amiable saints; it flatters vanity by erecting altars to men; it establishes the relations of a selfish friendship between devotees and their guardian saints; it offers in heaven a sort of human parliament which shares in the councils of the Almighty, and watches over terrestrial destinies, thus caressing the democratical tendencies of a people who have ever aspired and still aspire to political emancipation; it promotes indolence by indulgences and jubilees; it establishes a continuation of the sensible affections between the living and the dead—a most agreeable idea to constancy of affection;—it proclaims, as the basis of its doctrine, *unity*, which seems to include the idea of equality under the same laws, and of force and social charity, objects of the most eager desire to a people oppressed, harassed, and weak because divided. The antiquity of which it vaunts itself so proudly, constitutes a most powerful charm for a people who look to past times as the epoch of their glories. Aversion to the Romish religion, on the other hand, has its root in the intellect.

The superstition with which the Italians are reproached, is not essential to them, since intellect abounds with them. *In this country people are not born fools,* said a learned foreigner residing at Naples. Superstition would vanish on the avenues of public instruction being opened up. The infidelity prevailing in the educated class has its source in the rash judgment which hatred of oppression, becoming more and more intense in proportion as the understanding becomes enlightened, leads people to put forth against Rome. Youths educated in colleges and monasteries where there is the pomp of an apparent piety and of an ecstatic mysticism which they are taught to believe to be the sincere expression of the gospel, become convinced with their advancing years that those practices and that hypocritical fervour are nothing but a mask for covering political ends—are persuaded that religion in the hands of Rome is a means of satisfying its own avarice and of alimenting its own ambition, and that the thirst of universal dominion burns under the appearance of zeal for the propagation of the faith.

> Roma caput mundi quicquid non possidet armis
> Religione tenet. . . . . . .
>
> Rome, the world's head, now to religion owes
> What once it owed to arms. . .

Accordingly, while they indignantly cast off the yoke of Rome, they likewise reject the holy book of revelation which has been announced to them as containing the formal expression of the principles of Rome. No doubt of the soundness of such a judgment ever enters their minds, so as to conceive the idea of taking into examination the doctrines contained in the gospel, to see how far they accord with those announced from the Vatican. Hence they neglect the reading of the sacred books which alone can undeceive them. The evil is enhanced by knowing that protestantism, neither in doctrines nor fact, favours the cause of a people suffering under tyranny. I speak in favour of the religion of Jesus Christ, as delivered to the apostles. I shall tell what part protestant doctrines have in the diffusion of infidelity in Italy. I may give offence by my reflections and by the frankness of my language to those who in their religious zeal propose to effect a political object, but I shall gratify true believers—those who before all things seek the kingdom of God and his righteousness, those who desire that the gospel of Jesus Christ should triumph, not for the sake of deriving advantages from it but for the glory of its divine author and the salvation of souls. Whenever I have entered into religious discussions with Italian infidels I have felt myself met by two main objections to the divinity of the Bible, besides the usually alleged contradictions of the sacred text, now antiquated. The first of those lies in the doctrine of passive submission to established governments, although unjust and tyrannical; the other consists in the spirit of discord in the interpretation of the sacred books. The doctrine of passive resistance patronised by the encyclical letter of Gregory XVI. to the bishops of Poland, and by that other directed against the doctrines contained in the books of Lamennais, excites the dread and horror of every one whose breast glows with love to his country, and who has had the misfortune to be born in a land subject to the powers of tyranny. Reason recoils from the idea of a God who condemns a people to slavery and denies the right of defence against the invasion of their own proper rights and franchises. On the other hand, these hear the same doctrine announced, it may be said with unanimity, by those who, having cast off the yoke of Rome, make a profession of believing and observing the law of God, as recorded in the books of the apostles and prophets. From this they conclude that Christianity is against the good of society and opposed to the advantage of the people, while it favours their oppressors. Hence with them, to be a patriot and to be likewise a Christian, seems absurd. As far then as concerns the spirit of dissension which seems to flow from the various interpretations of the text, they confound sectarian fanaticism with that variety of opinions which is the necessary consequence of freedom of conscience. Hence they are prepared to consider as fruits of the unrestricted interpretation of the sacred text, the intestine wars that soaked the earth with blood in the age of the Reformation, rather than those peaceful discussions which rendered the human intellect fruitful instead of barren; discussions which when conducted in the spirit of charity, without which one who should speak with the tongue of angels would be no better than sounding brass, aid to keep alive in the heart the holy ardour for improvement with respect to the search after truth. It appears to them that that book cannot have a divine origin which admits such a variety and discrepance of opinions, thus presenting an obstacle to the union of people with people, province with province, city with city, and family with family. And as among the evils that have afflicted Italy, the most deplorable has been the want of a spirit of concord among the various parts into which it is divided, they consider it as a risk, nay rather a certain loss, to propose the Bible as a religious code; the more so as from the people having been brought up in the intolerance of the papal domination, religious discussions will find in them a prolific soil for mutual hatreds and disgusts. Accordingly, they regard the free study of the Bible as irreconcilable with the social condition of Italy. Moreover the charge thrown out against Protestantism as leading to *individualism*, is readily admitted and rigorously judged in Italy from that country itself having been its victim. It has seen the representatives of nations, free, protestant, and jealous of their religious and civil liberties, sitting in council with its oppressors, and favouring or at least not opposing tyranny. These reflections have thrown into the ways of rationalism many clear intellects, to whom love of country is the guide towards a better future. It does not enter into the scope of this essay to enter into an examination of these objections. But I consider it indispensable to hint whether the sin of the Italian generations present and to come, rushing to their ruin towards infidelity, may not weigh not only on the deluded who are its victims, on Rome which with its iniquities and its sacrilege inspires them with doubts against the Gospel of which it proclaims itself the infallible depositary and sustainer, but also on the nations which mingle political ends with zeal for the laws of God, giving the apostolic doctrine a wider extension than really belongs to it. Let them reflect that their judgment concerning the sense of a book which is at all times in their hands, is of great weight with those who know nothing of it but the name. Let them consider, then, that the excessive keenness shown in religious discussions among Christians of different opinions, is a stumbling-block to those who are fondly looking forward to a new order of things, to the era of fraternal union among civilized nations. The *Christian Union* among different denominations on the common basis of the Gospel, promoted by the Christians of Scotland and carried into effect at Liverpool during the first days of October last (1845), will prove a source of blessings to the entire world. Intolerance alone will keep aloof from it, and very great will be the advantage to the church of Jesus Christ for it to know where that evil plant, the enemy of charity, which is the essence of Christianity and the bond of union, strikes its roots.*

Let us now return to our reflections on the religious spirit of Italy. It is of importance that we recognise in the Italians an irresistible tendency to religion; and we find a mark of it in that touch of melancholy which generally manifests itself in eastern nations. Indued with a vivid imagination, amid the charms of a country so rich and fertile, from which they acquire the idea of the beautiful and the sublime, they feel in themselves a secret sentiment which carries their thoughts to the supreme Being, who has bestowed upon them superior advantages above other tribes that inhabit burning sands or frozen rocks. They behold in the pure and kindly radiance of the sun an emblem of the tabernacle of the Most High. The two evils that now afflict Italy, that is to say, infidelity and superstition, although contradictory in appearance, proceed from the same tendency of the Italian mind towards the Deity. The educated Italian, full of the idea of the infinite justice of a Being who is love and the centre of harmony to created beings, rejects revealed religion, which presents itself to him as ready with one hand to enthral the nations and with the other to crown and defend the fortunate possessors of power, and who longs for a religion that will protect justice and social prosperity. Were the gospel presented to him in its purity, breathing love and justice, he would renounce the foolish attempt of opposing to the laws of God the littleness of reason intoxicated by the passions. The people that are deprived of instruction, convinced that everything that relates to the worship of God is an impenetrable mystery, respectfully surrender themselves to the teaching of Rome, kiss the chains that press upon them as if they were God's handiwork, and doting, from an excess of the religious sentiment, form to themselves new ones. But let the day of liberty arrive, and the people then instructed will discover in the gospel a remedy for their profound social disorders; the seed of the divine word will find a fruitful soil in the hearts of multitudes of Italians.

While the Italian character, in its principal elements, is such as we have described it, yet it does not manifest itself in the same aspect throughout the whole extent of the peninsula, in as much as the climate, temperate though it be in all Italy, presents considerable varieties according as we proceed towards the East and South. This diversity is evident above all between the two grand divisions which we have traced, of Northern and Southern Italy. In the former the

---

* The labours of the Evangelical alliance being in a sense only begun, and it not being possible to foresee the practical results which may yet flow therefrom, the above decided opinion given by the learned author may by some parties be considered premature. Dr. Mappei's attention having been drawn to this fact, he replied in a note addressed to the publishers, "As to the *Christian Union*, I beg of you to leave my opinion as expressed, as the opinion of a foreigner, an Italian, formerly a Roman Catholic, upon whose mind the manifestation of the union of the members of the body of Christ has had great weight."

rays of the sun shine reflected from the everlasting glaciers of the Alps, and the latter is lighted by the sun that melts the snows of the Appennines. The Italians of the North have been inoculated with large admixtures of the distinguishing qualities of their neighbours, the Swiss, the French, and Germans. The contact they have with them and similarity of climate, have led to the introduction of habits of greater luxury, and of the new ideas that are current among those nations. European civilization, by its reflux from the Alps, and by breaking down the dykes which the despotism of Austria and the intolerance of the Vatican have erected along the extreme frontiers of the country, finds a way for itself among the Italians of the North and makes them seem sufficiently different from their brethren of the South, who, while completely separated from all more civilized nations, and prevented by new barriers within Italy from coming into contact with their brethren of the North, remain in a great measure destitute of the advantage of such communications. The Italians of the South still preserve the habits of their forefathers, and while in Northern Italy the vehement passions bend beneath the continual influence of the intellectual progress favoured by the near neighbourhood of enlightened nations, in Southern Italy those passions retain in a great measure all their ardour and energy. Civilization otherwise advances rapidly in the South of Italy, but flowing from other sources it pursues a different course. Here it is the daughter of Jansenism and of the war which in the last century the governments of Tuscany and Naples carried on victoriously against the pride of Rome. That of Northern Italy is the daughter of the reasoning habits of the French revolution and of German rationalism. Hence the latter finds less support in the multitude, and the former is universally felt because identified with the laws. The one combats all the old forms; the other endeavours to reform abuses. I shall treat of this subject in detail afterwards. The South of Italy is the land of antiquity and of glorious memorials of the past, the land of the fine arts. To it belong the enchanting descriptions of the poets and the praises lavished by travellers on the romantic scenes, the mild nights, the delicious splendour of the moon, the mountains tinged with the hues of the violet. Savage nature here offered to the daring pencil of Salvator Rosa, landscapes of marvellous sublimity. Here Raffaello created his Madonnas, giving them the features and the complexion of the Fornarina, soft as the climate and bright as the sky. Here Pergolesi, Cimarosa, Paisiello, Rossini, Bellini, and Donizetti drew inspiration and cheered the world with their melodies, drinking in the harmony which rises on all sides, particularly on a spring morning, when from the hedges, in the warbling of the birds—from the gardens, in the colours and the odours of the flowers—from the trees, in the whisper of the breeze among the leaves—from the brooks, the rivers, and the sea, in the murmur of the billows, there rises to heaven a delicious harmony, as if it were the hymn which grateful Italy addresses to the Creator for having made her so beautiful as she is. There the Colosseum, the Pantheon, the wonders of Michael Angelo, St. Peter's church, raise their heads majestically, proclaiming to the foreigner who gazes upon them that the glories of Italy are perennial and lasting. Here Dante restored the gift of speech to Italy, which had remained mute on being deprived of the language wherewith it had dictated laws to the world, and re-erected a temple to the muses of Ausonia. There the Secretary to the Florentine republic discoursed on the destinies of peoples and laid bare the baseness of tyrants. There Tasso entwined for himself a crown of laurel and myrtle. There Scipio, Cæsar, Cicero, Horace, Ovid, Catullus, had their cradles. Hither Virgil came for inspiration. Not indeed that Northern Italy is not likewise the land of glorious deeds, fertile in minds of powerful genius and poetical imaginations. It abounds in these, but its glory is of a later date; its great men have had a less imposing aspect;—Doria, Montecuccoli, Dandolo, Titian, Correggio, Ariosto, Alfieri, Canova. The painters of Southern Italy are distinguished by genius in composition and boldness in design; those of Northern Italy by delicacy of colouring and softness of contour. Architecture in Rome is gigantic and majestic; in Venice, the Rome of Northern Italy, more finished and regular. During the epoch of its first glory, Italy had for the theatre of its enterprises the southern division; during that of its more recent, its energy and the treasures of its wisdom have chiefly manifested themselves in the northern. The geographical position of Italy suggests to me an idea which comprises the story of its past times and hope for the future. It resembles a giant who reposes his head on the snowy summits of the Alps and his feet on the sands of Africa. In the epoch of its first glories, in the force of youth, it obeyed the impulse of a heart boiling with ambition and traversed the earth with vigorous steps, subjecting the nations to its sway. At a later period it lay rather exhausted by the excess of its own passions than overcome by the barbarians. Then substituting for the impulse of ambition and courage the counsels of the understanding and the powers of genius, it rose from its recumbent position, discoursed of wisdom to the whole world and lorded it over its very conquerors with the force of its words and the industry of its arms. The same hand that had brandished the sword now pressed the pen and became greater in literature and the arts than it had been in point of power and arms. The secret and the hopes of Italy are to be found in these two epochs. History in these has pointed out a new career to be traversed and a new crown to be put on, when re-entering the rank of nations, and obeying the impulses of the heart and understanding, it will find it easy to combine the energy of the southern element with the reflective disposition of the northern, force with science, art with industry. The present state of Italy is a transition state. The thoughts that ferment particularly in upper Italy and from that quarter reach to the extremities of the Calabrias, have prepared the elements of a new social order, and the first symptoms of a vigorous vitality are to be perceived not only in the accomplished cities of Lombardy but also in the rude villages of the Basilicata, which, towards the close of the last century, might be considered the Timbuctoo of Italy. The mind of Italy finds its formal expression in the philosophical principles which distinguish the Italian school from the German and the French. Far removed from the transcendentalism of Kant and from materialism, it is the expression of its own mind and heart.

Notwithstanding that the cities do not faithfully reflect the moral state of the nation, yet it will be of use to direct a look to them in order to observe at least the tendencies of the people they contain. Considered in this point of view, the capital cities of the two divisions of Italy as above traced out, present sufficient arguments for confirming the opinion already given on the diversity of character between the Italians of the North and South. Milan, Turin, and Genoa are the cities that now take the lead in Northern Italy. Florence, Rome, and Naples in the South. Milan is the seat of study and of intellectual activity, and in the face of the jealous and tyrannical vigilance of a foreign government, which endeavours to foment corruption by clipping the wings of genius, the Italian mind does not stop its flight in the career of progress, but from time to time causes a new ray of light to flash on the pages of its men of science and learning. Turin is the city of industry and of military activity as far as its present political condition permits; the moral state of the capital of Piedmont presents more regularity, and fewer disorders of minor magnitude, in proportion as idleness finds less favour there. Genoa is the city of trade, and although it has sunk from the lofty commercial position it occupied when the flag of the Genoese republic floated in every port of Europe and Asia, yet it still retains much of its old spirit of activity and independence. From an attentive survey of these three cities one is led to judge favourably of the maturity, the reflective habits, and the activity of the Italians. On the other hand, Florence is the city of urbanity, of elegance, of pleasing and genteel mental occupations. Rome, seated on monuments, and clothed in religious pomp, is the city of ambition; its aspect is majestic and solemn, its voice haughty and imperious. Naples is the emporium of the tumultuous passions, the seat of pleasure, the dwelling-place of the Syren. The warmth of the atmosphere and the fertility of the soil, dispose to indolence and pleasure, while the volcano which mutters hard by, with its sloping sides covered with smiling vineyards and delicious fields, is the image of her people, with jocund brow and smiling lips, and fiery passions at heart. The roaring of the mountain during an eruption, resembles the voice of Masaniello. By observing these three cities we discover the leading features of the southern Italian character, that is to say, the more vehement passions and energy of soul outweighing the power of reflection. I shall close these general reflections on the Italian character with the following considerations. Indolence is the chief defect of the lower classes, and the sole cause of the continuance of the present state of things. In order to keep them as long as they possibly can inert and listless, no method has been found equal to that expressed in the philosophical saying, *Ignoti nulla cupido*. The ignorance of the people is the palladium of despotism. Woe to it, should desires on the part of the people arouse their passions! Woe to it, should the spur of ambition awaken them from their shameful lethargy! The judgment passed on the Italians by Madam de Staël is most just. "Propose to them an object and in a short time they will overtake it—without some spur they will remain doing nothing." The small account made of the public opinion of foreigners with respect to them, in Italy, is usually attributed to the indolence of the Italian character. The hearty hospitality which these strangers meet with in a nation, not only ill used by the European policy, but outraged and vilified by all who have occasion to speak of them, leads people to pronounce this erroneous judgment on them. Hospitality is one of the finest qualities of the Italian people, for it is the offspring of a susceptible and affectionate natural disposition. Besides this natural tendency, one strong reason leads them to exercise it towards those who vilify them, and it is the conviction that the degraded state to which their country has been reduced, so that the name of the *Niobe of nations* has been rightly enough given to it by Byron, ought not to be imputed to them, but to the melancholy changes which have taken place, and to the violence of the oppressors. The Italians give a gracious reception to tourists, from the certain conviction that after having visited their country, and after having witnessed the oppression to which it has been subjected by the quadruple alliance, they will be disposed to judge more fairly of the descendants of the Romans and of the republics of the middle ages. Let us now glance at the political and civil state of the peninsula.

VIEW OF THE POLITICAL AND CIVIL STATE OF ITALY.

It is certainly one of the greatest glories of Italy that she never suffered herself, upon the fall of the Roman empire, to be completely conquered by the barbarians. She has thus been the connecting link between the ancient and the modern world. But this glory was obtained at the cost of her national unity. She came out from the long and painful struggle divided into various parts. It has been her greatest misfortune to have within her own bosom that element which is inimical to all nationality, the popedom. Every time that vicissitudes, or a generous feeling, has suggested the ideas of independence and unity, a voice from the Vatican has called in the stranger to disperse the forces that were tending towards association. On comparing the present condition of Italy with that of the Italian republics of the middle ages, it were folly not to acknowledge that she has benefited in so far as respects the union of the various elements that then struggled within her, although at the expense of her freedom and independence. Instead therefore of raising impotent cries against the past which has swallowed up Italian discords in its vortices, instead of lamenting the fall of the republics of Florence, Genoa, Venice, Pisa, Siena, and many others in Italy, they ought to rejoice at seeing the causes of division gradually removed, and as it were dissipated for ever. The existence of seven states where once there swarmed a hundred small and discordant ones, is a gigantic step towards national unity, so much the more if we consider that of the seven states now to be found in Italy, one *embodies* the spirit, the absolute power —one, the activity, the oppression—one, the strength, the troops and fleets of Austria. In such circumstances the unity and independence of Italy are become not only possible but easy. The same lamentations are rung through all points of the peninsula; the same wants impel the people towards social improvement. Misfortune has brought the desires of all and the hopes of all to a common level. Everybody knows that the Austrian cabinet rules directly one portion of Italy and indirectly all the rest of it. Members of the Lorraine family are seated on the ducal thrones of Parma, Modena, and Tuscany. The pope and the king of Naples keep their places under the protection of the bayonets of Austria, and hence are subject to the conservative counsels and authority of their protector. The king of Sardinia alone now and then manifests in his internal policy some independence, favouring, though weakly, progress, encouraging and protecting education and commerce; all which has given room to hope on the part of moderate liberals, that there is the possibility of a national emancipation, through a *confederation among the Italian princes* for regaining their lost independence. Balbo's publication on the *Hopes of Italy*, encourages the belief that the court of Sardinia cherishes the idea of putting itself at the head of such a coalition.— The briefness of this essay not permitting a minute account of each of the governments of Italy, I shall confine myself to giving an exact picture of some of them, and supply such an amount of information with respect to the rest, as may suffice to establish what are the most material points of difference. Among the governments indirectly dependent on Austria, I shall treat at large of the kingdom of Naples. To this I am induced by many reasons; because it is the most extensive and populous of the Italian states, the least known to strangers, and, next to the dominions of the pope, the greatest sufferer from tyranny. I shall then speak of the pontifical states, now groaning under a bastard government which has no natural ties to society and to human nature; an infamous monument of the ages of ignorance, preserved to act as a bar to Italian civilization. Lastly, I shall speak of that foreign government which wastes and crushes the finest part of Italy. There will thus be presented a full view of the present state of the peninsula. Of Tuscany, Parma, and Sardinia, I shall say as much as will suffice for obtaining a knowledge of the degree of civilization permitted, and of the general defects of their administration and political organization. Besides that the present condition of these is better known to foreigners, as being less tyrannically governed, and that more frequent intercourse and commerce are maintained with them, I am led on another account not to speak of them at great length, and that is because it may prove more advantageous to poor forlorn Italy to disclose to the eyes of civilized nations the wounds that afflict her most.

The kingdom of the two Sicilies comprehends the whole of the extreme portion of Italy and Sicily. It was first called the kingdom of Naples and Sicily, distinguishing the continental part by the name of the dominions on this side of Faro, and Sicily by that of the dominions beyond Faro. They were two distinct kingdoms dependent on the same monarch; they had each its own laws, and Sicily preserved its constitution which had been bequeathed to it by the Norman kings, consisting of three representations called Bracci, Demaniale, Ecclesiastico, and Feudale, that is, of Commons, Clergy, and Nobility. This representative system was abolished in 1812, to give place to a new constitution, granted through English influence by king Ferdinand IV., and modelled in a great measure by Lord (William) Bentinck on that of Great Britain. But after the fall of Napoleon, when the dethroned kings resumed their seats on their ancient thrones, with the certainty of being able to exercise greater despotism than ever over their people, now exhausted with previous struggles, Ferdinand IV., by the decree of the year 1819, closed the Sicilian parliament, promising to open it again but with the idea of suppressing it. In point of fact the court of Naples has, step by step, abolished all the franchises of Sicily. Such was the reward bestowed by a grateful king on the Sicilian people, for the asylum accorded to him, and for the prodigious fidelity they had shown him amid the political vicissitudes which then agitated the whole of Italy and Europe. From that epoch the king assumed the title of king of the United kingdom of the two Sicilies. A very great advantage has accrued to Italy as respects the future, from this despotic step of the Neapolitan government, for it diverted the mind of the Sicilians from a path altogether opposite to that pursued by the whole of Italy, calling upon them to form part of the Italian people by making them share in the common slavery. Whatever affection had been manifested by the Sicilians for the Bourbon dynasty when they fraternized with the English in defending its rights against France, so much the more aversion do they now manifest towards it.

Sicily is governed at present in the same way as the kingdom of Naples; it pays the same taxes and suffers the same oppression. The code that by the royal decree of 1818, is now in operation, is that of France, modified in some points, and augmented in what relates to *leze-majesty* divine and human. Heresy, and sacrilege against the eucharist, are regarded in it as deserving the punishment of death, and blasphemy of seven years' imprisonment. To this last law there is usually given a monstrous latitude, by making disrespect exhibited towards the endless number of the saints of both sexes, and sometimes also towards images and the hierarchy, to be regarded as an offence against God. The French code, which proceeded from the most enlightened minds of France, acting at the instance of the vast genius of Napoleon, is one of the few benefits that many European nations have reaped from the warlike agitations of the monarchs of this century. Laws are the formulary of the morality of nations, and therefore the surest way to civilization. Under this point of view, the kingdom of Naples which, equally with that of Sardinia, has retained upon the whole the legislation of Napoleon, has seeds of moral progress in its bosom, which will sooner or later bear its fruits. According to the French civil code the bonds of matrimony were not made strong enough, there being an immense facility given to divorce, and a certain strictness was desiderated; but in the code of Ferdinand marriage was reduced to such strictness as to be indissoluble, except in the cases contemplated by the council of Trent, which perpetually reduced families to despair and introduced worse customs. Some reform was hoped for in the augmentation of the paternal authority which may be said to have been annihilated in the French code, but the reform was carried to such an excess as almost to make matters as bad as they were according to the laws of ancient Rome. There was added, as if in contempt of personal liberty, voluntary imprisonment in civil contracts. So much for the civil code. As for the penal, the severity of the punishments is excessive, and that of death frequent enough. The severity of the French code is unsuitable and unjust for the character of the Italians, particularly for those of the southern division of Italy. The basis of penal laws being to be found in the physical and moral nature of society, and feeling and suffering varying in different nations, the culpability involved in misdeeds, the power of enduring suffering, are not the same in all men; hence punishments adapted to some are for others either excessive or too light. The rigour of the punishments, and the too great readiness with which that of death is threatened in that code, might suit the circumstances of France when she had just emerged from the vortex of a bloody and unbridled revolution, but it was not adapted to Italy. It was hoped that in the new code of

Ferdinand the scale of crimes and punishments would at once undergo a certain modification, but they have been left as they were, for the severity of the penal code served the interests of absolute power, and the sanctioning of the penalty of death for crimes of leze-majesty divine and human, would without that severity have had too monstrous an aspect. The only changes are to be found in the abolition of the *pillory* and of *the confiscation of a criminal's goods*. The pillory, just and useful perhaps among nations which from education and civilization have an ordinary sense of shame, was most unjust in Italy where we find shame either nullified by corruption of morals or ignorance in the common people, or from natural disposition excessive. A young woman who had exposed her infant, the fruit of illicit love, in a winter's night, on the public road, where it died, on being convicted of the crime, was condemned to a long imprisonment, according to the French code, and to the pillory. Upon the first insults that were offered to her, she fell down dead, suffocated with shame. The punishment of confiscation, most unjust, in as much as it involves the punishment of innocent survivors and the enrichment of the public treasury, presented powerful inducements to an absolute monarch as Ferdinand IV. to preserve it for his own advantage; but public indignation and the general wish made him cautious, and the new code, in spite of the defects it retained, and notwithstanding the terror inspired by the law of leze-majesty, was received with much satisfaction. In the new code, we find altogether taken away in many cases, and restricted in very many others, the discretionary power given by the French code to the judges, within certain limits, of mitigating the penalty—a discretionary power tending to equalize differences of age, condition, sex, and capacity of feeling. In the reform of the two codes, the civil and the criminal, the former was made worse, the latter was improved, if we could but forget the inevitable laws of despotic governments dependant on Rome, as respects religious and political intolerance. The code of civil procedure has remained as it was. Regard is had in it to the competency of the judges being carefully ascertained; to judges being appointed according to the interests and the wants of the people; to property being secured by means of a public register of civil acts and hypothecs; to the uninterrupted order of the judges; to the independence of the judges; finally, which is a proof of the wisdom of the age, to the institution of a supreme tribunal, called the *court of cassation*, the prop and guarantee of the laws, one of the fruits of modern philosophical and legislative science. On the other hand the code of criminal procedure has been rendered worse. The old hope of having a jury, frustrated under the government of the French king, was once more doomed to disappointment; the power of imprisonment *per mandato d'accompagnamento*, which it was hoped would be abolished, was confirmed, the judging of an accusation which according to the French code was confided to four or six judges, is confided in the new one to three, or to five, revoking the benefit of an equality of voices; in the French code the judges of the accusation were not judges of the process, and in the new they are, thus involving the greatest peril to justice and obstacle to fairness of discussion, from the judges being already prepossessed against the accused; restrictions were imposed on cases of appeal to the supreme magistracy of the Cassation, and by limiting that tribunal, which is the grand support of the laws, and hence of liberty and of justice, it was intended that the wretched condition of the accused should be rendered still more wretched. Another most grievous defect of the French code has been preserved in the new one, that is, magistrates of exception, police courts, special courts, and military commissions. The false doctrine that the process is the arena on which the law combats the accused person, makes it seem advisable to the governments to deprive the law's enemy of arms and to give them to the law's defenders. It is sought accordingly in crimes that are most hateful to the government, to curtail the defences to the persons accused and to give greater scope for attack to the accusers. But if the process were considered as a *device for the detection of crime*, people would not fall into so very grievous an error as to pervert the true nature of the law by attributing to it a shameful partiality, and exposing it to the risk of rashly striking the innocent. One of the most valuable parts of the criminal procedure, preserved in the new code, is the public pleadings, a means of promoting justice more available as a security for the execution of the laws than the jury, which is a means of civilization. The publicity of trials, the moral conviction of the judges, public opinion acting as a check upon iniquitous sentences, are the fruits that proceed from it. The laws called correctional form another valuable part of the criminal code. Insults, slight assaults, violations of modesty, are severely punished; forming a most holy censureship which initiates the people to civilization, necessary for the Italian people, which, during past ages of feudalism and of the distinction of conditions, had lost the sense of their own dignity.

It now remains for us to speak of the military code, of that relating to commerce and the public administration. The military *code* or *statute*, which may be considered as preserving throughout the legislation of the ten years' domination of the French king, contains four most grievous blunders; these are, the absence of any distinction between a state of war and a state of peace; the excessive latitude given to the jurisdiction of military tribunals; the appointment of a prolongation of service and flogging as punishments; and the silence of the laws respecting the abuse of power. From the first there follows impunity or arbitrary punishments, in consequence of the rapidity of trials, and hence want of discipline and justice; the second separates the military from the civil state even in that which touches directly the social order, constituting it an exceptional body; the third blunder tends to tarnish that moral lustre of the military career, which forms the very nerve of armies, in as much as military service is given as a punishment, and stripes involve infamy. Finally, the fourth is contrary to all civilization and justice. Duties and rights are reciprocal, and the counterpart to the obedience of the soldiers is justice in commanding the troops. Every one sees that all these blunders tend to convert the army into a prop to despotism and a scourge to the people. The commercial code is made up of laws for the most part French as respects internal traffic, and of the old pragmatics of Charles III. as respects international trade, inasmuch as the French code, having been promulgated when the fury of war placed Europe under the oppression of the continental system, which aimed at the destruction of the commerce of England, made no provision for the external part of commercial legislation. The internal part is carefully drawn up; there may appear to be an excessive rigour in the trammels imposed on merchants with the view of preventing fraud, but it will appear most just to every one who sets himself to consider the corruption of past times and the growing avarice that accompanies the wants of a new civilization. The tribunals of commerce are formed of merchants chosen by merchants, and liable to be changed from time to time—commercial juries. The external or international part is regulated according to the treaties concluded with various other powers. The administrative code which, in the time of the French king, was faulty in the way of leaving too much to arbitrary power, tending to favour the persons and affairs of the administration, by establishing an exceptional magistracy, has become worse than before, inasmuch as it is no longer controlled by the council of state and is dependent on the ministry. The council of intendency in each of the provinces takes up in the first instance causes connected with the administration, and, in case of appeals being made, they are submitted to the royal court of Conti; but the whole is subject to the absolute will and pleasure of the minister for the Home department.

From the outline we have just traced of legislation in the kingdom of the two Sicilies, it follows that the germs of civilization, of equality, and of freedom, that are budding there so vigorously, exist in the legislation itself, and hence that the state of slavery and oppression in which people would have it to remain fixed, is absurd and contradictory. While the government with one hand presents to the people a law of progress, saying to it, *Go forward and advance towards your own improvement*, with the other it presents its weapons and enchains the people, so that they cannot move a step towards the generous object it proposes to their aim. The first to condemn arbitrary power and oppression are the codes, while the supreme absolutism of the king condemns the desires felt by the nation for a better condition, in the name of the codes. The law fructifies morality and ideas of justice to the people, while the government endeavours to demoralize society and destroys its rights. The equality of all in the eye of the law is indeed the fundamental principle of the code, but practically, on the other hand, the avenues to justice are closed against the poor, in consequence of the very heavy expense required in trials, much, as it has been already hinted, under the financial spirit of the code of civil procedure. That is so contrived as to impoverish private persons and to enrich the royal treasury. In this manner the advocates, a class which has in its hands the interests of the nation, have been brought to adopt the interests of the government. To paralyze the beneficial effects of the criminal code there is the secret code of police. In this manner the severity of the law that should properly be applied to crimes, is made to fall upon opinions. In this manner the *magistracy* is led to adopt the interests of a despotic government. Horrible to say, yet it is too true! Ignominious sentences are often pronounced, not based on conclusions from facts, but on grounds of mere probability, in order to stamp the seal of infamy upon the liberals. Secret ordinances of the ministry of justice acting in concert with the ministry of police, enjoin the judges to take account of the political and *turbulent* opinions (for this is the ministerial definition of liberal opinions) of the accused. In a trial for murder at the criminal court of Teramo, two persons were charged with the crime, Antonio Tomei, an artisan, and Signor Firmani, a young man of the best family connections. The former lay under two heavy proofs of guilt; a few hours after the commission of the been the public prosecutor (*il Giudice Regio*) had found in his house, while making the legal investigation, a *fresh-washed* dagger hidden beneath a bundle of twigs, and this dagger was found exactly to fit the wounds of the murdered person. Numerous testimonies established the fact of his having, on the day that the crime was committed, put on white pantaloons; in the search made at his house these were nowhere found, and he insisted that he had never put them on. The destruction of these pantaloons, when stained perhaps with blood, by himself or his relations, was a negative argument of the utmost importance when joined to that other of the dagger, for the moral conviction of the judges. The charge against Firmani was founded on his having, a year *before*, asked in marriage a rich young lady who had given her preference to the youth who had been slain. In Firmani's favour, in fine, there were honest testimonies to the fact of his having been, in the evening about the time that the crime was committed, engaged in light and cheerful talk with a family who were his friends. Tomei was acquitted, and was merely placed for two years under the surveillance of the police. Firmani was condemned to twenty-five years of imprisonment. Firmani was a *liberal*.

The decision of the courts is not based on the bare words of the text of the law, but on equity and the spirit of the law, which, under a liberal government, would be a source of immense advantages, and would prove a light of wisdom to the people, but under an absolute government leaves an open field for injury and injustice. Provided acts of injustice do not remain concealed from the conscience of a people enlightened by the eloquence of the bar in the course of public pleadings, they will only form and mature the people for better destinies. In order to comprehend the advantage to be found in the present state of legislation in the kingdom of the two Sicilies, in the face, too, of the contradictory tendency which it assumes under the impulse of an absolute government, it is well to know what it was before the French invasion. Down to the reign of Charles III. of Bourbon, the founder of the existing dynasty of Naples, eleven different legislations prevailed in the kingdom; these were the ancient Roman, the Lombard, the Norman, the Suabian, that of Anjou, the Aragonese, the Austrian-Spanish, the Austrian-German, the Feudal, the Ecclesiastical; in addition to which there were the customs required by the Greek empire of the east in the cities of Naples, Amalfi, Gaeta, and others governed at one time by officials sent from Constantinople. What has been an incalculable improvement is the unity of the codex and the law courts in which the law and the decisions are understood by the people. It would be desirable that the partial advantages that result from the comprehension of the laws to those who frequent criminal trials, might be rendered general, by introducing the system of teaching in public national schools the maxims of law, as those of religion, in the catechism, are taught by the parish priests, in order to instil into their minds the lessons of social morality which ought to be their guide.

In every commune there is to be found a *supplente giudiziario*, and a *conciliatory judge*. The attributions of the first (who is a substitute for the judge residing at the *capo circondario*, head office of the circuit, which comprehends four and more communes) are to watch over the peace of the commune and to take the first steps in inquests into crimes, giving immediate notice of them to the judge (*Giudice Regio*). The second decides pecuniary causes not exceeding six ducats in amount (about one pound sterling). Larger sums, up to twenty ducats, are decided by the royal judge; likewise without appeal. He, in fine, cannot decide in cases exceeding 200 ducats. It belongs to the judge royal, who has at his command one or more brigades of gens d'armes, to watch over the political opinions of the circuit; besides authority to condemn, in correctional cases, to the extent of a year's imprisonment. Crimes are tried at the criminal courts stationed at the chief towns of all the provinces. Besides the judge royal there were formerly in each of the provinces, two or more instructor judges, whose office it was to direct how the process should be conducted and trace out crimes, previous to the criminal courts taking cognizance of them; but they have now been abolished as involving a heavy charge on the finances without being of any evident utility. The civil courts established in every province of the kingdom, try causes involving sums above 200 ducats; from these there is an appeal to the grand civil court placed in each of the great divisions of the kingdom, that is, in Aquila for the Abruzzo, in Naples for Terra di Lavora, in Catanzaro for the Calabrias, in Lecce for Puglia; in Palermo, Messina, and Catania for Sicily. There is no appeal from the sentences that are pronounced by the criminal courts and by the grand civil courts; but they may be *revised* in the supreme court of cassation, an after recourse for the violation of the law. In confirmation of what has been said of the influence which the government exercises upon political opinions by means of the judiciary magistracy, it is well to reflect that the procurator general, or the public prosecutor in the criminal courts, is the centre into which are thrown all the affairs that concern politics and the public tranquillity of the province. He is in direct communication with the minister of the general police; all informations and charges come into his hands, so that the public spirit and the opinions of individuals through him come under the cognizance of the government. Hence his opinion in criminal trials, in what is called *requisitory*, has the utmost weight in the minds of the judges, who recognise in him one who possesses the confidence of the government. In fine, besides the courts in which law prevails over arbitrary power in consequence of the publicity of the pleadings, and which are the best part of the administration, there are two other courts, both of them atrocious and scandalous, namely, the *high police*, for opinions, and the *military commission*, for attempts at insurrection. The former, the heir of the holy office (of the Inquisition), is dark and impenetrable. Like the sword that hung suspended over the head of Damocles, it poisons all the joys that can embellish the citizen's domestic peace. Invisible, like the hand that wrote the sentence of Belshazzar, it strikes without the possibility of foreseeing the blow, or of escaping the consequences. The *intendant*, or political head of the province, invested with the powers of the ancient proconsuls, is its infallible judge, without appeal. It is true, indeed, that the sentences he pronounces do not exceed the limits of imprisonment, but they are not on that account the less atrocious and fatal. The arrests fulminated by *the measures of the police* are very frequent. Thrown into a prison, the wretch who is its victim sees those inexorable gates shut upon him, without knowing why they are shut, or when they will open to him again. There might at least be such a form of justice, as should admit of defence. From the insidious interrogatories to which he is subjected, the accused has hardly a gleam of light to help him to discover, amid the darkness, what the fault is that he is charged with. Meanwhile, torn from his family, his home, and his business, to the grievous damage of his interests, of his reputation, and of his health, amid the inconveniences, the hubbub, and the noxious vapours of an unhealthy prison, the gentleman (for it is always the better sort of people that are made the butts of insolent dunces) is compelled to wait there upon the clemency of his persecutors. Months, and sometimes years pass away, and hundreds of victims look forward in vain to being restored to their desolate families. Orders for *domiciliary visits* go forth also from the police tribunals, or are issued at the caprice of the intendants. In the silence of night, a band of gens d'armes knocks at the door of the honest proprietor, or man of letters, and enters in the king's name, for the purpose of impudently inspecting the secrets of families. The hand of the police inspector opens desks, rummages shelves, and unfolds family letters and bonds, perhaps of considerable value, visits the most secret recesses of the house, and carries off with him every thing that he thinks likely to supply proofs of a political crime, and often such objects of value as seals, rings with some suspected cipher, and so forth, which seldom find their way again to the owner's hands. The police is the Argus and the Briareus of fable, a monster with a hundred eyes and a hundred arms. The *supplente giudiciario* and the *sindaco* in the communes, watch the opinions of individuals. The judge royal, with his subalterns and gens d'armes, watches over the circuit. The sub-intendant watches over the district. Besides the satellites whom each of these puts in movement, and those who depend on the procurator general, others directly dependent on the intendant, on the provincial commandant, and on the police commissary resident in each capital city of a province, and on the police inspector resident at each head office of a district, swarm about every where. If the astuteness of such people, accustomed as they are minutely to watch whatever the citizens are about, does not succeed in detecting some blot that calls down misfortune on the head of the person who is watched, and the favour of the government on the person who watches him, there is often no want of officious informers, who, from motives of private rancour or mercenary advantage, carry accusations to the intendant's office, and these are always favourably received. Let it not be said that this is a defect in the morality of the people and not of the government, for if the latter were not to be content with anonymous delations, or, without abating from severity towards well-founded accusations, were to punish those that were calumnious, the social plague would not be so bad. But the accusations are received in secret, and although they are often found to be false, they are usually attributed to an excess of zeal for the public tranquillity, never to evil intentions. An ambiguous expression caught up, in times of political agitation in whatsoever part of Europe, from the mouth of a liberal, is often the first link in a chain of persecution by the police, directed against the friends of the imprudent person, particularly if among his letters some should be found not quite clear in point of meaning, and which might admit of a sinister interpretation. In this manner the social ties are relaxed; a spirit of misanthropy and isolation obtains the mastery in the better part of society, distrust consumes the germs of associations, and offers a plausible pretext for dissimulation. An arrest at the instance of the police, or a domiciliary visit, spreads terror throughout all the families that are connected with the person that has been arrested, all fearing lest the tempest should discharge itself upon them. Should it so happen that after a long and painful imprisonment he recovers his freedom, still the effects of the disgrace into which he has fallen with the government, make themselves felt most bitterly. The eye of the police pursues the unfortunate man who, as if he were infected with some contagious disease, perceives that his presence brings uneasiness with it. Although public opinion is in favour of all those who are subjected to such abuses of power, and in the secret hearts of men police persecutions excite esteem and respect, yet terror counsels them to conceal generous sentiments, for the manifestation of these would cost the incautious an infinite series of embarrassments and vexations. Still further to increase uncertainty, distrust, and despondency in the liberal party, care is taken to spread insulting doubts of the sincerity of the opinions professed by the warmest patriots. It is whispered in the ears of the pusillanimous that they are spies; and these whispers originate with the police. To it, too, may often be attributed partial attempts at revolution; it certainly takes care to provoke these for the purpose of discovering those warm partisans who have contrived to escape the crafty eye of spies, and to sound the leanings of the people, in order that, on knowing them, it may proceed to take violent measures and inflict chastisements. The revolution of the city of Aquila in 1841, if not originally excited, was marvellously seconded by the police. During the period immediately preceding such a crisis, to all appearance nothing is suspected, nothing is perceived, so that the liberal party may advance securely to its object. The authorities, ordinarily so active, so energetic, and sharp, seem to be sunk in a lethargic sleep, only to re-assume their energy in the bloody trials that follow the catastrophe. All this proceeds from the notion that an amount of force which is useless for the purpose of breaking the chain, may weaken the prisoner and make him relapse into a state of greater languor and exhaustion. Meanwhile, the condemnation of from two to three hundred persons to death, the galleys, or long imprisonment, rids society of the most impatient youths. This system of incitement to insurrection, well enough known to the Italians, deceives the foreigner, who is incapable of conceiving the perfidy of the agents of police in Italy. In the chief cities particularly, nothing is more common than to hear in the public places people talking freely against oppression, censuring the acts of the government, and sneering at persons in the employment of the police. Nothing is more natural to foreigners, who have been born in free countries, than to conceive the false idea that freedom of speech is no crime, and that the governments of Italy, although absolute, are mild and paternal. These are not aware that those who speak so keenly, and show themselves such fervid advocates of a better state of society, are agents of the police, who of set purpose scatter about inflammatory words, in order to excite the passions of the less prudent, and to obtain in reply some expressions of a wish for liberty, some sarcasm against the government, some glance at better times, so that they may run off to the ministry and carefully lodge accusations there. The central police has a register of all names of the subjects, with running remarks on their respective characters, on the opinions that they cherish, and the influence that they exercise. The informations on the educated classes of each commane are transmitted from the *supplente giudiziario* to the judges royal, and from them to the procurator general; from the *sindachi* to the intendants; and from the military chiefs to the commandant of the province; and each of these supreme inquisitors communicates with the central police, through the medium of the ministry of justice, that for home affairs, and that for war. The common people are considered as dependent on the parish priests, and hence remarks bearing on the lower classes, are transmitted from them to the respective bishops, and from them to the ministry for religious worship, which communicates them to that of police. In this manner the ministry of police has placed before its eyes an exact picture of the individual opinions of the whole kingdom. The excessive rigour that is adopted, and the state of violence which is made to press more and more upon the people, proves irrefragably that the police, in calculating its hopes and its fears, finds the latter better founded than the former. Besides the secret tribunal of police, there is also that for state offences, called the *military commission*. It has the commandant of the province for its president, and is composed of military officers who are appointed to try persons charged with attempts at insurrection, according to the military statute. The accused are allowed to choose an advocate for the defence, but great love of justice and generosity of feeling are required in an advocate who would take in hand so perilous a task. The odium of government is the ordinary consequence of such defences. For the most part the accused have an official defender assigned to them.

The penalty of death by shooting is the ordinary sentence, which is executed on the expiration of twenty-four hours, without giving room for appeal. Such facility for the shedding of human blood, which makes all civilized Europe shudder, ought to kindle the greater indignation; but how much the greater is the inconsistency of the government which seems to have adopted principles of philosophical moderation with respect to the punishment of death. Although in this code it is made common to a fearful excess, yet already it seems abolished, not having been applied for some time, except in the case of some very rare offence fitted to produce unusual horror. But for despotic governments it is a worse crime to desire the diminution of their power than the dissolution of society, to which crimes have a natural tendency. The provincial commandant is the military authority appointed to put down all popular movements, and to maintain things as they are. The intendant is the administrative authority, and the procurator general the supreme authority, in the judicial branch. These are independent of each other in the exercise of their respective powers, but come into contact in the sole point of keeping an eye upon the public mind and the security of the throne. Each of them watches over the other two, so that the government has a threefold warranty for the execution of its will; although, indeed, as each of them enjoys a share of absolute power, none can require any spur to redoubled zeal in defence of a system of which they all form a part. The intendant acts as a spy on the thoughts, the procurator general dissects the heart, and the provincial commandant chains down the arms of society as it moves onward. Therefore there are a tribunal for opinions, special courts for conspiracies, and courts martial for insurrections.

The municipal administration is directed by a syndic and the *decurionato* or communal council, varying in number, from ten to thirty, according to the population of the commune. In this council the affairs of the commune are discussed, and the resolutions adopted are transmitted by the syndic to the central administration of the province. A collector of the public revenues who corresponds directly with the receiver of the district; a cashier of the municipal revenues; two assistants to the syndic, with the names of First and Second Elect, are, besides the *conciliatore* and *supplente giudiziario*, the charges renewed in each commune every three years. The *decurionato* presents the candidates for each charge, and new members to supply the place of those of the municipal council who may happen to die within the three years. For each charge *three* individuals, taken from the list of the eligible inhabitants, are usually proposed. The proposed *three*, however, may be sent back by the intendant when the candidates do not enjoy the confidence of the government, and so a second, a third, and so on, until at length the person desired by the government is presented. It belongs also to the municipal council to propose the members for the district and provincial councils. These institutions have at first sight all the appearance of national representations, but if we consider them more closely, we find that they offer no, or very few advantages to the people. The persons who are called to form part of the provincial and district councils, besides that they must be proprietors with an income of not less than 300 and 200 ducats, respectively, must be such as enjoy the favour of the government, on which their election entirely depends; hence there is little probability of their being zealous for the public advantage. The district council meets every year at the head quarters of the sub-intendant. The provincial council meets in the capital of the province at the beginning of May, and continues its sittings during the course of the month. The president is directly chosen by the ministry from among the richest and most distinguished proprietors of the province. The attributions of the provincial council consist in setting forth the grievances of the provinces, in giving a formal expression to the demands suggested by the wants of society, in examining the state of the communal administrations, in discussing plans of public works, in bringing before the *sindacato* the conduct of public functionaries and censuring them when necessary, and, which most concerns the government, in partitioning the taxes and imposts among the communes. It is very clear that the idea that was to be embodied in this institution has been that of presenting a legal method of reforming abuses, promoting the weal and stimulating the progress of society towards a better state of things. The provincial council (the same may be said of the district council) is nothing but the right accorded to society of petitioning *once* a year. Now under a government sincerely desirous of promoting the good of the people this means might effect its object, but under a government at once despotic and hostile to all progress, it is not only rendered nugatory but is in many respects hurtful. The government, besides having made itself master of the election of the members, has given them no guarantee. The sittings are secret, and the results of the discussions remain concealed to the entire province. The way is closed on all sides upon the expression of public opinion, which is the sole defence of those magnanimous persons who would fain perform the duties incumbent on them in their difficult mission. Which of them would dare under such circumstances to open his mouth in complaining of the innumerable grievances by which the people are oppressed? Who would dare to censure the conduct of the public functionaries at the risk of being ever after the object of their implacable hatred? The only liberty left them is that of discussing plans of public works. But even this advantage, if we take a scarer view of it, will not appear so great. The provincial council cannot propose any public work without suggesting at the same time the funds by which it may be executed. Hence the whole authority of the council is directed to the looking about in all quarters for some forgotten source of revenue, or the creation of new ones. Of late years the zeal of the councillors has been laboriously employed in tracking out the traces of the *monti frumentarii*, corn lending institutions, which existed, for the benefit of the poor, in almost every commune previous to the wars raised by the French revolution, as they want the revenues to be applied to the use of public works. When all endeavours to trace out old funds have failed, the council makes an addition to the *fondaria*, or land-tax, of some *grani*, two and a half of which make a penny, hence called *addizionali*; and imposes on each family, according to the extent of its possession, one or two days' labour in the year or an equivalent in money. On being submitted to the royal approbation, the plan, together with a statement of the funds annexed to it, is either rejected, or after being accepted, is allowed to drop, in both which cases the government takes to itself the funds that had been proposed, or it is carried into effect, and the additional taxes still remain after the work has been completed. It rarely happens that plans of public works directed to the increase of foreign trade, are favourably looked upon. How often has it not been proposed that a port should be constructed at the mouth of the river Pescara, on the coast of the Adriatic, in order that there might be an outlet for the productions of the three provinces of the Abruzzi, where the trade of the interior is so inactive owing to the mountainous nature of the country, and where the produce far exceeds the consumption? The call has been constantly rejected. Catania, in Sicily, has at last obtained the construction of a port. It might seem at first sight that this concession was the fruit of the provincial council's perseverance, for it had during the course of five and twenty years repeated the most urgent efforts to obtain it; but it will appear otherwise to one who sets himself to consider the impatient spirit of that city, which, in 1837, made the warlike Ferdinand II. tremble upon his throne. It was thought desirable that a naval station should be formed there for facilitating the disembarkation of troops, in the event of new troubles which seemed not far distant. The advantages to accrue to the people, when placed alone in the balance, would not have sufficed to procure such a concession from the ministry and the king. On the other hand, projects for the erection of sumptuous buildings for the residence of public functionaries, and for the ornamenting of the capital cities of the provinces, are never rejected. The residences of the intendants boast such magnificence that they might be considered little royal palaces. What wonder, then, if the people, judging by the effects, should consider the provincial councils as rather opposed to their welfare than favourable and advantageous? From the provincial councils there ever come new burdens upon them, never any abatement of the old. It has been the astute idea of tyrannical sapience to divert the course of this beneficial institution towards what is evil, in order to instil into the minds of ignorant populations a dislike to national representative bodies.

Having thus cast a rapid glance at the legislation and administration of the kingdom, having touched on the chief disorders that prevail, it will be well that we point to their source; that is, to the governmental system. By the royal decree of 1821, after the fall of the constitutional government, it was established that the imperial power of the king should be independent, no doubt, of any national representation, yet tempered by two assemblies on which the king conferred the *voto consultativo*, a consultative voice, in the affairs of the nation, namely, on the *consiglio di stato* and the *consulta di stato*. The former is composed of twelve members at least, six councillors and six ministers. The latter counts thirty councillors for the state of Naples, and eighteen for that of Sicily, these residing in Palermo and those in Naples. The king treats of the affairs of the kingdom in the *consiglio di stato*, in which the drafts of future decrees and governmental measures are deliberated upon before being submitted for examination to the *consulta di stato*. The latter body directs its attention to the examination of the new decrees and newly projected measures that have been discussed in the *consiglio di stato*, under such a point of view as is pleasing to the king, so that the attributions left to it are extremely limited, in the matter of offering its counsels too. Although, however, it be a very narrow field that is left to these consultative assemblies, they might be of some advantage to the kingdom were they independent in the exercise of their attributions, and were persons called to take their places there who should enjoy a reputation for zeal for the public welfare; but matters are otherwise managed; for the choice of the members composing these two bodies depends on the king, who knows how to distinguish from among the many that are warm in their country's cause the few who make it their grand object to please him. Not only does the choice of the members belong to the king, but he can dismiss them at his pleasure whenever they show any unwillingness to second his absolute wishes. From all this it is clear that the above institutions, although they seem at first sight most useful supports, and to serve to temper the absolute power of the sovereign, may rather be considered as masks of a beautiful appearance, fitted to conceal the disgusting features of despotism. The ministers are considered as responsible, but only to the king. While the ministers, created by the king, and liable to be changed when he thinks fit, are the mere organs of the royal good pleasure, can it ever be supposed that they can be punished for any fault but that of opposition to the sovereign's will? In the year 1840, when the question of the Sicilian sulphurs was hotly agitated between Ferdinand II. and the English cabinet, the minister for foreign affairs, the Prince of Cassero, was conscientious enough to dare to manifest an opinion opposed to that of the king, and ceased to be minister. Can it be expected that the few honest men, influenced by the desire of enjoying the royal favour, or by unwillingness to become objects of the royal indignation, will not often cease to pursue the straight course on which they have entered attended by the public esteem, to commence a new career, dishonourable and infamous? The chevalier Lewis di Medici, a man of profound genius, and who had been twice a prisoner, as a partisan of liberty in the kingdom of Ferdinand (previous to the French invasion) and as a friend of the monarchy under the Partenopean republic, a man therefore of high reputation, was called to the ministry of the finances in 1821, under the auspices of Rothschild the Jew, and amid the applause of good people who augured a mild government from seeing him ask for the exile of the execrated Canosa. His good intentions were seconded by public opinion; but the hatred of the king, who (compelled by want of money) had unwillingly complied with the wishes of the banking protector, and yet retained the most intense rancour against him, had sufficient influence to make him depart from those maxims of moderation which had guided him up to that time. Feeling it intolerable to be so often in the company of his master without his ever even deigning to look him in the face, he saw that to please him it was necessary that he should forfeit the eulogies of public fame. Following in the footsteps of Canosa, so cruel to the unfortunate, he filled the prisons, he peopled the penal islands with convicts, he urged on the trial and punishment of those who had promoted the revolution of 1820. Restored to favour with the king, the whole kingdom was amazed to see the mind of Medici so much changed as to seem rather emulous of, than hostile to the ferocious minister whose banishment he had called for. Yet Medici, as he owed his appointment to Rothschild, was quite independent of the king in the exercise of the ministry! But what is to be said of those who doubly depend on the king, being influenced at once by gratitude and fear? The government of the kingdom of Sicily may, on good grounds, be considered as *despotic*, if not *de jure*, at least *de facto*. In so far as respects the promulgation of new laws this is manifest from what has been said; and even as respects the observance of the code now in force, this will equally appear, if we reflect that the choice of those who have to administer justice and to apply the laws in cases where the person and the interests of the king conflict with those of society, appertains to the king, and that he has it in his power to dismiss from office whomsoever shall dare to incur his displeasure. While the process of those who were tried for high treason for the proclaimed constitution in Monteforte, was still in discussion, it happened that the supreme court of Naples pronounced a sentence favourable to some of the accused; from that sentence it was augured publicly that the accused of Monteforte might be acquitted. The king, in spite of such rumours, *annulled* that sentence by a decree, and severely reprimanded the supreme court. The minister of justice, the chevalier de Giorgio, in support of the laws, dared to oppose this unjust and arbitrary rigour on the part of the king—he was *deposed*. Not content with this, the king, dreading lest the procurator general Calenda, a man of the greatest integrity, might favour the accused even in the face of the universal dread inspired by the annulling of the sentence of the supreme court, and by the deposition of the minister, was not ashamed to surrogate in the place of an honest man one of the worst reputation, the procurator general Brandusini. Thus, as matters stand, good institutions are rendered null, and the king can destroy with a breath the admirable edifice of the codes, by confiding the interpretation and execution of them to persons who, in the name of the law, favour absolute power. Meanwhile civilized Europe considers governments of this sort as not at all *absolute* but of a *temperate* nature, because based on the *suffrage* of councillors chosen from among the people! Meanwhile these governments are considered just and legitimate, at least by the conservative party!

Until 1838 the law admitted no distinction of conditions; it alone towered above all classes of society and saw nothing above itself but the will of the king. Dominated by one alone and

POLITICAL AND CIVIL STATE OF ITALY.   xxxiii

dominating over all beside, it seemed to preserve its own dignity even in its humiliation; the slave of policy it lorded it over public morals and made its severity fall upon all delinquents without distinction; but the decree of 6th April 1838, deprived it of the right of judging the clergy without appeal. Rome, which for a long time had cherished the idea of restoring the ecclesiastical immunities in the kingdom, has at length in a great measure obtained its end. Under the reign of Ferdinand I. its endeavours to this effect came to nothing; for, notwithstanding his superstitious fears, this king still retained in his mind the good seed which the Marquis of Tanucci sought to implant in him while a youth, that is, opposition to the ambition of Rome. Nor did the court of Rome, under his successor Francis I., obtain any advantage beyond an unlimited favour to the *Jesuit* party whose pupil he had been; his short reign did not permit him to complete the project of restoring the immunities of the clergy, and perhaps also the court of the Inquisition. He at least interested himself in it so far that his son Ferdinand II. perfected what he had been constrained to leave incomplete. Committed to the care of the Jesuits, the present sovereign was subject to the domination of Monsignors Olivieri, Scotti, and della Porta, not only through the influence given them by the will of the father, but much more through the ascendency they possessed over the mind of the queen Maria Christina. Her entreaties with her husband that he would comply with the demands of Rome were on the point of being favourably heard, when she ceased to live. Far from being discouraged by this untoward event, Rome knew as usual how to make the most of it for her own advantage. Availing herself of the good opinion which the deceased queen universally enjoyed for piety and a generous charity (qualities so rare on the throne of Naples), she thought that as soon as her ambitious views should be announced to the people, as a *voice* from heaven, by the mouth of the defunct queen, they would meet with no obstacle either on the part of the people or on that of the king, whom she knew to be tormented with remorse for having caused her death by ill treatment. A miracle was fabricated in which Maria Christina threatened from the tomb disgraces to the king and kingdom unless the dignity of the church were restored to its ancient lustre; unless the clergy should re-obtain their lost immunities. I defer relating the crafty machinations practised in such circumstances, until I come to speak of the religious state of Italy. Meanwhile the miracle obtained the object in view, and threw society in the kingdom of Naples many ages back. In virtue of the decree of 6th April, 1838, the bishops are authorized and obliged to have in their episcopal palaces a prison in which to confine priests at their pleasure, and to prolong their confinement as they may think fit. Then, if priests make themselves guilty of common offences, the trying of them belongs, indeed, to the ordinary judges, and these pronounce sentence, but it is reserved to the bishop to revise the proceedings, and, with the assistance of two adjoining bishops, to annul the sentence. At first sight the privilege accorded to the bishops in this decree, seems dictated by the spirit of respect which the Roman church has ever aimed at instilling into men's minds towards the clergy in general, and specially towards the hierarchy; if, however, it be examined more closely, it will appear manifest that under this religious veil there lurks a purely political purpose. What terrifies Rome and the monarchs of Italy is the progress of liberal ideas among the clergy throughout the whole peninsula, with the exception of the papal states where the priests form part of the government, and have the administration of public affairs in their hands. Generally speaking, old ideas are shaken, and the light of more humane ideas penetrates into the very darkest recesses of monasteries. Youth, after the first rush of an artificial fervour produced by the febrile state in which the mind is kept in colleges and monasteries, by presenting to it ideas of superstitious terror, returns to a natural state on returning to society. Social progress, like a rapid river, sweeps along with it all the objects it meets in its course. The clergy, both secular and regular, of the kingdom of Naples, with the exception of the bishops and the superiors of the religious orders, are generally partisans of a new order of things, and cherish the hope of seeing a brighter day shed its light on their country and them. I have already hinted at the source of such a tendency, when I attributed to Jansenist opinions the advance of civilization which is taking place in southern Italy. The clergy, so long educated by the government in the doctrines of Jansenius in opposition to the despotical principles of Rome, have learned to think liberally and to detest tyranny under whatever form. To direct political persecutions against the priests and friars, would be a most dangerous proceeding, in as much as opinions touch upon doctrines, and to proclaim their opinions to be false and criminal, would amount to awakening doubts in men's minds as to the rectitude of their doctrines. It is a fatal dilemma in which the Italian princes find themselves placed as regards the clergy. Either they must allow that body to pursue the course on which it has entered without endeavouring to throw obstacles in its way, and then, following the example of the clergy, the people will in a short time shake off the yoke. Or they will unsheath the sword of persecution against the clergy, and then the people, long habituated to recognise in that body the infallible guide to heaven, will consider its persecutors as tyrants. Again, were they to persuade their subjects that the clergy is leading them wrong, they would sap the foundation of Romanism, which reposes on the credulity of the multitude with respect to the sound creed and the infallibility of the ministers of the church; and Romanism is the main prop of absolutism. What then is to be done in such circumstances? Rome has come to the help of the policy of the Italian princes, and has contrived a dark labyrinth in the windings of which that portion which takes the side of Italian liberty, is lost. The prisons set apart for the priests in the episcopal palaces, give to the persecution that is directed against the liberal clergy, a character altogether canonical, and shield the government from popular odium. The priests are made to enter the episcopal prisons with the stain of immorality on their characters, and the public, instead of being scandalized at their persecution, applauds it; it loses all esteem for the patrons of the new order of things from seeing them always accused and condemned as guilty of immoralities, by a tribunal which they never suspect to be at all influenced by political aims. But how succeed in making public opinion give credit to such accusations? Why, where the freedom of the press does not guarantee public opinion, it may with all truth be asserted that public opinion is the slave of government. It will here be of use to give an idea how public opinion depends on the cunning tricks of the police. Anonymous accusations are showered by the servile tools of the government in the bishop's court against those priests who are considered most dangerous, whether from the influence they exercise by the social position they occupy, or from their talents. On the other hand it begins to be whispered by the bishop or his satellites that complaints are continually arriving from all quarters against such an one. Instead of showing any severity towards the accused the bishop abounds in courtesies and acts of kindness, avoiding in fine any examination of the charges preferred, even although the accused should call for a judicial inquiry. On the contrary, distinctions are often accumulated on those priests who it is intended should be ruined in public opinion; yet perilous distinctions, such as a parochial charge and the power of hearing confessions, which while, on the one hand, they give a vast scope for accusations, on the other hand persuade the people that no envy of the accused broods in the bishop's heart. From the mouth of the superior there never comes the mention of a fault attributed to them without ample praises being mingled with the accusation; the snake lies hidden among flowers. " He is a youth of high talent and good intentions. . . A sin ! which often belies the duties of his vocation ! . ." Such insinuations are repeated everywhere, are amplified, and the report *crescit eundo*. When calumny has for some time been whetted against them it is very easy to give a body to the shadow, or to find some blot in their conduct requiring that their actions should be sharply watched by every body: and they are led off to the prisons of the episcopal palace without a single sigh of commiseration for their fate being breathed by the people. But if an inquiry into their conduct should take place, it would be found that it was nowise worse than that of their colleagues, or that of the bishop himself, and often even better. Immorality, in the more extensive application of the word, that is, in the violation of the laws of the celibate, is a stain which attaches almost without distinction to all the Roman catholic clergy. Hence it is very clear that young men cannot escape confinement in the episcopal prisons when the bishop thinks fit to subject them to the scrutinising eye of society.

But it sufficed not to have punishments prepared for liberal opinions. There behoved to be advantages and protection held out to such as professed *absolutist* opinions, to the priests who sided as partizans with the government. All the springs of the human heart behoved to be put in motion in order to allure the clergy to follow the old path of servile attachment to the throne. This object was obtained by the monstrous right being accorded to the bishops, of annulling and correcting the decisions of the tribunals, when pronounced against priests guilty of ordinary delinquencies. If the sword of public justice ever threaten to strike the head of a priest who is a faithful partizan of the present state of things, the hand of the bishop can turn it aside. But that hand is never put forth when it happens to be a liberal priest that is doomed to punishment. These reflections will guide one to a favourable opinion with respect to the direction of public feeling in the kingdom of Naples in particular, and in the interior of Italy. The bishops, too, have, at their disposition, the *gendarmerie*, as in Rome the parochial clergy have the carabineers at theirs. And now we come to enumerate the grievances of the administration.

Since I have had occasion to mention it, I shall begin with the *gendarmerie*. This is a military body dependent on the minister of police, and intended to watch over the public tranquillity.

The gendarme is invested with an arbitrary power, and is protected with an inviolable character, so that he may well be considered an *armed magistrate*. It may be readily understood what use they make of the privileges accorded to them. Under the safeguard of the unlimited protection they enjoy with the government, and in the face of the terror they inspire, they can, with impunity, give vent to their passions, insult honest people, and throw desolation into families. The *processi verbali* (minutes of inquest) of a gendarme, has the validity of a juridical deposition, and cannot be arraigned *de falso* (as contrary to evidence). Particularly when the vengeance of the government weighs upon a province, or on a city, after some attempt at a revolt, the hateful character of this military and political body manifests itself in all its brutality. They demean themselves like conquerors; and their insolence is such as to disgust even those who are least squeamish about oppression. They often make an abatement of their bad treatment depend on sacrifices of money or honour, and answer the tears of mothers, sisters and wives, with the most outrageous and iniquitous proposals. How often does the threat of aggravating the horrible position of the beloved persons that are in their hands, fail to triumph over the severity of virtue! History will one day paint in black colours among the bloody scenes that have taken place in Bosco, Catania, Syracuse, Penne, Aquila and Cosenza, the lewd revelries and shameless proceedings of the satellites of power. Resistance to a gendarme in the exercise of his proper functions, is inexorably punished with seven years' imprisonment in chains. Now, a gendarme has a right to be presumed to be always in the exercise of his proper functions, since the police is considered to be always vigilant and active. There is now languishing in the prisons of San Francesco in Naples, a young man of good family, Signor Tito Garofoli, condemned to be in chains for seven years, for the crime of resistance to the public force. He happened to be betrothed to a young woman whom an official of the armed police was endeavouring to please. The latter, thinking that by getting rid of his more favoured rival he might succeed in making her forget him, met the young man when leaving the house of his bride at a late hour, insulted him, and then reported that he had received an insult. The scheme succeeded admirably, notwithstanding that the prudent youth, aware of what was sure to follow from the slightest resistance to a gendarme, instead of allowing himself to be transported with resentment, had conducted himself with discretion, for the gendarme had bitten his own hand so as to make it bleed, in order that he might have something to show by way of evidence that Garofoli had wounded him. But, although his rival had become the victim of superior power, he himself did not for all that succeed in gaining the girl's affections; for, throughout the whole civilized class of society, there prevails a deep-rooted and invincible dislike to the armed police. The prisons abound with such victims. The injuries inflicted by that body, which is numerously scattered over the whole surface of the kingdom, and its insolence and brutality, act powerfully on public opinion among the people, and instil and keep alive in them an abhorrence of the oppression of the government. As the persecutions by the police for matters of opinion, the bad administration of justice, the chaining down of men's minds with the view of preventing their progressive improvement, and the state of moral degradation presented to the eyes of other nations, crush the hearts of the educated class, as the excesses committed by the agents of the government, speak effectually to the people who, being incapable of thinking deeply, judge from the impressions made on them. The countryman who is unable to pay his taxes when they fall due, receives an unwelcome guest into his house, whom he is not only obliged to admit there with a good grace, but must likewise provide with two carlini a-day, as long as any part of his taxes remains unpaid. This guest is the gendarme. In proportion to the want of feeling that marks these men, does the pressure of the impositions gall the hearts of the people, and rouse feelings of indignation which, were they sufficiently nourished by a full knowledge of the degraded state in which they live and of their own rights, would lead to their making great advances in the ways of liberty and independence. The taxes, moreover, are exorbitant, and they are ill distributed, so that some of them press more heavily on the poor than on the rich. The *fondiaria*, which is a tax on landed property, amounts to more than twenty per cent. on the yearly returns. In order justly to appreciate the enormity of this tax, it must be borne in mind that the returns are calculated according to an estimate made by persons in the employment of the government. Lands are considered always to bear the same description of crops without any regard being had to the rules of agriculture. The different articles are estimated at the maximum, which is rarely reached. Wheat is valued at 54 carlini the salma (weighing 25lbs.), whereas, generally, it does not exceed 40. To this there is added the vicissitudes of the climate which often desolates the country with hail, severe drought, or floods; but while the crops are diminished, the impost is inexorable. From a calculation made by political economists it appears that, on an average of ten years, the half of the produce of the ground is absorbed by this land-tax. But it is the impost which presses least on the people who have but a few bits of ground in their hand, although, indirectly, they suffer very much from it, as the proprietors endeavour to indemnify themselves for the exorbitancy of the tax by getting higher terms for the lands in bargaining with the farmers. The taxes that gall the people are the multure tax on flour and that on salt. The former is felt in proportion to the flour consumed by a family. Now who does not see that the poor man and the artisan whose food mainly consists of bread, pay much more of it than the rich, whose table is loaded with exquisite viands, and who uses little bread? Salt, as well as tobacco and gunpowder, is a government monopoly. It sells at four grani the pound of twelve ounces, that is about twopence. But, if we consider the scarcity of money and the abundance of productions, it will appear manifest that the price is enormous. In the provinces the price of a chicken is five grani—twopence half-penny. Then the rigour of the government is excessive, for it makes it a crime to get salt by evaporating sea-water in the case of a poor man who endeavours to rid himself of the enormous pressure of this tax. The coast guard is ever on the watch—and a long imprisonment would be inflicted on any one who should take sea-water into his house. Invalids who require that article for bathing, are obliged to provide themselves with a special permission, obtained on presenting a medical certificate. As for the multure tax, some of the municipal administrations, compassionating the sad condition of the poor who suffer so severely from such an impost, have endeavoured to exempt them from it by classifying the citizens into rich, proprietors, and industrious, in such wise that a man's poverty should modify the proportion he pays of the tax. Who could believe it?—this magnanimous measure, instead of compelling applause, has often been vituperated by the provincial Intendants, for this reason, that any such condescension, besides involving a tacit reproach on the harshness of the impost, spoils the people by making them restive and refractory subjects. The *inscription* and *registration* tax that is on contracts, testaments, &c., is likewise very heavy, amounting often to five per cent. on the capital, and in some cases to ten per cent. The stamp duties form another exorbitant impost alike for the rich and the poor, especially when we consider the means taken in the code that regulates the law proceedings, to multiply the sale of stamps. The quantity of deeds required in every trifling civil cause, frightens honest people who recognise under the cloak of justice, the insatiable rapacity and greed of the royal treasury. It is enough to reflect that by law, in using stamped paper no page must contain more than 25 lines—that in case of exceeding this limit the notary, or attorney, or whoever may have been guilty, is subjected to a fine of *thirty carlini*—above ten shillings. The same fine is inflicted on those who, having made agreements on unstamped paper, wish to use these as legal documents in a court of law. The obligation to renew game licences every year, might also be looked upon as an expedient for enriching the treasury, if the government did not prefer being excessively chary in granting them—not choosing that, under pretext of killing game, the liberals should have fire arms in their houses. In order to obtain a game licence one must submit to a minute examination by the police. The customs form one of the most intolerable grievances, the duty being often more than the price of the goods on which it is levied. The tax for keeping the highways in repair and making new ones, is particularly burdensome to the industrious class. Those who have horses and mules, asses and carts for the transport of commodities, pay in much larger proportion than landed proprietors who are taxed in proportion to the rent. No regard is paid to the distinction between objects of luxury and those of necessity. The wealthy man who keeps his carriage is placed, in point of taxation, on the same footing with the farmer who keeps horses for the carriage of his corn. Hence the financial system bears more heavily on the people than on the easy class; but the latter suffers more from the moral oppression exercised by the police—a state of intellectual martyrdom, of which the simple rustic, thanks to the ignorance in which he is immersed, knows nothing. Another kind of impost, a voluntary one, consists in the drawing of public lotteries, which the Italian governments, to the scandal of civilized Europe, do not blush to maintain for their own advantage, by availing themselves of the excitableness of an imaginative people, and taking advantage of their passions for the purpose of sucking their blood. It would be difficult to find in the easy classes one who enriches himself by a farthing in this game. But it is truly deplorable to see the ignorant multitude blindly abandoning themselves to the remotest hope, to the improbable possibility of gain, and of their own free will throwing into the hands of the king all that remains over from the fruits of the ground, and from their hard day labour, after payment of the taxes, thereby depriving themselves and their families of their needful sustenance. It is a most painful spectacle for those who know better, to see, on the drawing day, the silly crowd undeceived, after hearing the numbers drawn from the urn, and after seeing hope vanish, to see it disperse in sullen sadness, despair on every brow and blasphemy on every lip, yet with the idea nevertheless of not letting fortune go, and pondering how to raise money for the next drawing. It is a harrowing scene to observe on the days that precede this *public theft*, exercised in the name of the law which warrants it, the poor man hunting out the usurer, that he may sell or pawn his remaining utensils, and perhaps post himself also in ambush at night in order to obtain by force from the passing traveller the *carlino* (four pence) required for the gratification of his passion for gambling. Whoever should seek to throw discredit on lottery gambling, would be made to feel by the police what it is to be denounced as a man of a *seditious and turbulent spirit*. While there are so many noble souls in Italy that deplore a scourge that proves so destructive not only to the wealth, but, which is worse, to the morality of the people, none dares to raise a cry of indignation against it, owing to the dread of prosecution. The mischief is still further aggravated by the friars, who fail not to avail themselves of all these immoral tendencies among the people, in order to promote their own interests, fomenting this social plague by pretending to a knowledge of the cabalistic art, so as to be able to foretell lucky numbers. The begging friars, and among these the Capuchins in particular, an order composed of persons from the very dregs of society, who by their ignorance and superstition find all the more favour among the people, make a trade of such fooleries, and are fed and provided for by their dupes all the more liberally the more grossly these are deceived; as it sometimes happens that among the thousands whom they have led to ruin, some one has the good fortune to gain for once, their credit receives new force and the people are confirmed in their folly.

Among the worst grievances that crush the poor country people, ought to be reckoned the protection and favour accorded by the government to the friars, and particularly to the mendicant orders. These may well be likened to the lazy wasps which devour the honey collected by the industrious bees. One would need to have been present at each of the various scenes that succeed one another in the course of the year, when the cunning and the superstition of the priests come into conflict with the simplicity of the people, in order to have a full idea of the horrible situation of the rural inhabitants of Italy. After the fatiguing labours of the year are over, between wretchedness and want, beneath the icy cold of winter and the intense heat of the dog-days, what remains to the husbandman of the produce of his little field? Let us approach the barn about sun-set, when the flail is laid aside, and the corn lies ready to be taken into the cottage. In spite of the exorbitance of the taxes there will yet remain to the poor man wherewithal to support his little family from the gifts which nature has lavished on Italy; but see all at once, approaching from afar, friars of various colours, white, black, and gray, each leading an ass or a mule, for the transportation of booty to the monastery. The poor creature feels a cold shivering run through his veins, while in the name of St. Francis, of St. Anthony, of St. Pasqual, &c. all that remains of the collected store is asked from him. Good sense would certainly suggest that he ought to shut his ears to their importunate beggary, but on the other hand, the superstitious feelings by which he is chained down under the name of *religion*, urge him to pour into their sacks the greater part of the little that remains to him. Some artful tales are always ready to be told for the purpose of convincing the refractory, and stimulating the generosity of the most prudent. According to what they say, their saints are at that moment, it seems, at the windows of heaven, looking out with far-sighted spectacles, to take note of the succours supplied to their faithful servants (the friars!), and to bless or curse according as matters turn out favourably or otherwise for their sumptuous table. An exact idea of such impositions, which are quite common through all Italy, has been given by Alexander Manzoni in his celebrated romance, *I promessi Sposi* (the Betrothed Spouses), when the foraging Capuchin goes to look for the nuptials in the house of the peasant Mondella. It will not be superfluous to relate here the miracle which he palmed off on that occasion, as a sample of others of a like sort, coined according to the various circumstances of the parties, by the *cercatori* (foragers) at the time of harvest.

"Now, you must know," said friar Galdino, "that in that monastery there was a father of ours who was a saint, and he was called father Macario. One winter's day, passing by a pathway in a field belonging to a benefactor of ours, a good man too, father Macario saw this kind friend beside a large walnut tree that he had, and four peasants shouldering their spades, who forthwith began to bare its roots. 'What are you doing to the poor tree?' asked father Macario. 'Why, father,' was the reply, 'it is years and years since it has given me any walnuts, and I am going to use it for timber.' 'Let it alone,' said the father, 'know that this year it will have more nuts than leaves.' The kind friend well knowing who it was that spoke thus, told the labourers to replace the earth about the roots of the tree, and, calling to the father, who continued his walk, he said, whatever the produce may be, one half shall belong to the monastery. The report of this prediction spread abroad, and every body ran to look at the tree. In fact, spring brought flowers and the fruit season nuts in abundance. The kind friend had not the consolation of beating them down himself, for when harvest came he had gone to receive the reward of his charity in heaven. But the miracle was just so much the greater, as you shall hear. The good man had left a son of a very different character. Now then at harvest the foraging friar went to demand the half that was owing to the monastery; but the son affected to know nothing about the matter, and had even the temerity to reply that he had never heard of Capuchin friars knowing how to make walnuts. Now, know you what happened? One day, mark this, the scapegrace had invited some friends like himself, and while making merry with them, told them the story of the walnuts, and laughed at the friars. These youths wished to see this immense heap of nuts, so he took them up to the granary. But mark now, on opening the door he went to the corner where the great heap had been laid, and just as he was saying—*look*, he looked himself and saw—what think you? why, a fine heap of dry walnut leaves! That was an example for you. And the monastery instead of losing, gained; for after so remarkable an occurrence, there was such a return from the begging for walnuts that a kind friend, out of compassion for the friar who conducted it *(cercatore)*, made a present of an ass to the monastery which helped to carry them home. And such a quantity of oil was extracted from them that all the poor came to take according to his wants; for we are like the sea which receives water from all quarters and makes a return by distributing it among all the rivers."

Such anecdotes are repeated under new forms every successive season, at the time of the gathering in of the various kinds of pulse. The begging for new wine, oil, vegetables, and fruits, is felt by the poor peasant to be as heavy a scourge as locusts or hail. Nor is the peasant subject only to the importunity of the begging friars who exist in vast numbers under various names, the Passionisti, the Minorite observantists, the Riformati, the Minimi, &c. &c., but further, to the urgent demands of those who are chosen every year for the task of collecting the means required for the public festivals of the patron saints, which are solemnised with great pomp and at great expense.

If the government had at heart the instruction of its subjects and the laying of some restraint on such exactions, the people would be rid of such voluntary impositions, which are all the more ruinous from having no limit but that of conscience, acting under the absolute sway of superstition. The upper classes, too, are certainly beset by such beggars; but these furnish few supplies to the monasteries, owing to their having for ever shaken off, to a greater or less degree, the yoke of superstition. But though their revenues are not eaten up by these parasitical plants, and in this respect they escape a voluntary imposition, they cannot obtain exemption from a new kind of enormous tax which has been recently invented. The *Guards of Honour*, a military body established after the example of Austria, are composed of young men belonging to wealthy and distinguished families. It began at first with a gracious invitation, hoping that all would willingly have presented themselves to participate in the honour of serving his majesty. But perceiving that the idea of guards of honour was a dream, and that very few accepted the invitation, the king changed his smiles into a frown, and it was established by a decree that all who kept riding horses should belong to it. As nobody obeyed this order, and the demands of the government met only with complaints, another decree settled that those who resisted should be subject to the payment of four carlini the day (one and five pence), and a gendarme lodged in their houses as long as they refused compliance; that if they should persist in refusal they should be led away as prisoners to a fortress; that if, further, this measure should prove of no avail, they should be obliged to form a part of an active corps of the line. The guards of honour are obliged to accompany the king when he happens to be on a journey, and to give their attendance at grand court solemnities, whether in the capital or in the chief town of the province; hence they are subjected to serious expenses, seeing they have no pay assigned them beyond a few carlini in the sole case of their having to come from the provinces into the capital, a sum hardly sufficient for the maintenance of a horse. Besides the enormous expense of a rich uniform, they have that also of providing themselves with a horse, from that which they possess not being ordinarily fit for military manœuvres. This atrocious act of despotism has been dictated by two equally odious ideas. The one is that of attaching families of high rank to the governmental system, with the fascination of an aristocratical distinction, or by the idea of honour, or of religion, as respects the duties rendered imperative by the oath taken by those who belong to the corps. The other is that of justifying in the eyes of the civilized nations of Europe the excessive rigour of the punishment inflicted whenever a member of the corps is found guilty of political opinions, seeing that the inexorable military code strikes him with every appearance of justice. Over and above this, it seems not improbable that it further aims at the impoverishment of those families of distinction among whom there is more education and progress than elsewhere, so as to induce them to seek for employment at the hands of the government, and thus to neutralise the influence which wealth always gives to the rich over the lower classes.

From all this it evidently appears, that while on the one hand the government chains down thought, on the other it endeavours with all its might to enfeeble and enervate the nation. Industry languishes not only from being deprived of every stimulus, but from being beset on all sides with obstacles. With the exception of some individual efforts, which may be likened to those shrubs that germinate spontaneously in an uncultivated country, the great mass of the people remain in much about the same stationary condition as their forefathers. Agriculture, the pasturing of cattle, and the mechanical arts, although far from the state of improvement in which they are to be found elsewhere, supply the means of living to the people and enrich the treasury, and that is thought enough. Instead of encouraging whatever forms the life of a nation, the force and the grandeur of a people, every means is employed to check it. Associations, those powerful means of realizing the hopes of such as have not sufficient money, or adequate talents, or energy, to undertake great things, are prohibited; or, at least, when not so imposing as to inspire the government with fear—for in every association it dreads a conspiracy—they are looked upon with an evil eye. These, from their very nature, are opposed to a despotic government, which is founded on the principle that in order to lord it over a people, it is necessary to sow divisions among them. How could it encourage the fusion of many wills, weak, wavering, and obscured by ignorance, into one which might prove powerful, resolute, and enlightened? The only existing associations in the kingdom of Naples are to be found in the capital, and are composed for the most part of strangers, with the permission of the police, which watches over all their movements.

Large manufactories do not flourish in the kingdom of Naples, if we except those of woollen cloths in Palena and in Arpino, those of silk in St. Leucio, of earthenware in Castelli, of paper in the island of Sora, of arms in Campobasso, and a few other branches of industry, of no great importance, or at least capable of great ameliorations. Hence the export trade is confined to the productions of the soil, of which the government has already engulfed a large proportion, while waiting for the opportunity of devouring a still larger on the entrance of foreign manufactures into the ports of the kingdom in return for raw materials and cereal fruits. Trade with the other Italian states by land, is rendered impossible by the multiplicity of the lines of custom-houses. Maritime trade, restricted as it is, is the sole kind of commerce by which the wants of the nation are so far supplied. The latest commercial treaties with the great commercial nations of Europe, and particularly with Great Britain, seem to have given a favourable impulse to the national activity. In 1830, the number of trading vessels belonging to the kingdom of the two Sicilies amounted to 6943, and the greater part of these were coasters and fishing craft. In 1833, they rose to 7600, and of these 2400 were above sixteen palms in depth of hold. The tonnage of Sicily alone amounted, in 1835, to 41,797, whereas in 1823, it was only 25,844; proving how far a little favour shown to commerce has gone to raise the people's energies; and what hopes might be entertained of the industry and commercial activity of Italy, were obstacles removed, and were freedom to vivify the benumbed energies of the Italians.

But of the commerce of Italy I shall have to speak hereafter. At present let us not lose sight of the political state of the two Sicilies. Despotic governments may with all justice be likened to a cankered tree which at times may possibly produce some not bad fruit, as free governments may be likened to a tree that is vigorous and productive of the best fruits, although it may at times produce some that is bad. All depends on the sovereign, and hence, should he happen to be indued with a good disposition and sound judgment, so as to own that a reign of terror and force is neither stable nor virtuous, the people may draw from it more advantages, though not better advantages, because they are not felt. Such was the first king of the present dynasty, Charles III., who prepared and cherished into fruitfulness the good seed of civilization, which, in spite of the efforts made to choke it, is now flourishing, and will give abundant returns. But his successors, degenerating from him, lend to the belief that the plant of despotism very rarely produces good fruits. Ferdinand and Francis have left such traces of themselves in history, that posterity will be amazed at Europe having not only tolerated the cruelty and the wickedness of those abhorred tyrants, but having in a certain measure even sanctioned them by sustaining them in the struggle which they have maintained against the progressive improvement of the people. It was hoped that the present king would pursue quite a different path from that rendered slippery with blood, which was trodden by his father and grandfather. But whether from the ascendancy Rome exercised over his heart when a youth, by means of the two prelates who had the charge of his literary and moral education, or from hereditary inclination, from the very commencement of his reign he adopted a system not less shamelessly oppressive and ferocious than that of his superstitious father. The political prosecutions commenced in the dawning of his reign in 1831, pursued with constancy and ardour in 1833, ceased not with the horrors and the executions in Sicily and in Penne in 1837; on the contrary, they showed fresh vigour in the proscriptions exercised in Aquila in 1841, and in the tragical end of the brothers Bandiera and their generous companions in Cosenza in 1844. The premier at Naples is the minister of police, as in England the premier is the first lord of the treasury, intimating that as commerce and the national prosperity form the chief aim of the English government, so in Naples the grand object of the government is the oppression of the people and the persecution of ideas of progressive improvement. Most lamentable condition of my native country!

In order to give a just idea of a state of things altogether strange to, and of a different kind from, the order of ideas prevailing among the English, it is necessary that I should clear away, with some facts, the common prejudice, that however much tyranny is to be condemned in Italy, so much the more imprudent and culpable is the spirit of insurrection fermenting there. Arguing from the discreet and rational way in which the people's remonstrances are brought before the members of the government in a country where the king is the executor of laws, of which the initiative and the sanction pertain to the representatives of the nation, persons under the influence of this prejudice cannot persuade themselves that the people should conspire and rise in tumults, instead of having recourse to the legal method of *petition*. But why, I hear continually repeated on all sides, why, instead of having recourse to threats and even to arms, do they not present petitions to the government? Who does not know that *collective petitions* are formally prohibited in Italy, and in *Tuscany* too, which is usually considered as the mildest of all the Italian governments? Who does not know that liberty of speech is a crime in Italy when applied to calls for social ameliorations? Who does not know that not only are public meetings and gatherings of the people not allowed, but private meetings likewise, whether literary, such as of the academies and educational institutions, or for amusement, that is, *balls, festive parties*, and such like, without a special permission from the police? Who does not know that where students are numerous, that is, at the universities and in the provincial cities where there are lyceums, they are prohibited from walking together by threes and fours? Hence how can it be supposed that public opinion has any scope for manifesting itself *pacifically* and *loyally*, seeing the governments declare it in set terms to be *turbulent* and *illegal*, on the sole ground that the royal will *(stat pro ratione voluntas)* ought not to be opposed even *by prayers*?

Let us illustrate with some facts the unfortunate position of the people of Italy, who are not even permitted the liberty of presenting *prayers* to the sovereign, who are sometimes blamed even for obeying the very orders of the king, and in whom petitioning collectively is reckoned as a crime. In July, 1837, an insurrection broke out in the city of Penne, having for its object the obtaining of a constitutional government. This rising being put down by the arrival of troops, many persons were condemned to death, a vast number to the hulks, to chains, to temporary imprisonment, or to banishment; still the royal vengeance seemed unappeased. A decree was issued, depriving the city of its privilege of being head of the district; that privilege was given to St. Angelo, to which accordingly were transferred all the offices and officers connected with the various branches of district administration. The choice of a city, situate on the sea-shore, far from the centre, and at a distance from the greater number of the communes, gave universal dissatisfaction to the whole district, not only because it affected the interests of all who had or who might have business connected with administration, but because it exposed them to damages and dangers, owing to the necessity of having to cross the numerous mountain torrents and rivers, without bridges, when swoln by the winter rains, the melting of the snow in spring, and the storms of summer. Hence a petition, drawn up in the humblest terms, began to be subscribed by common accord for the purpose of obtaining the re-establishment, as before, of the district offices in Penne, the central city, or, at least, the selection of some other place, better adapted to meet the wants of the communes which had had no share in the blame incurred by the city which had rebelled. The petition was signed by all those employed in the municipal offices, by the priests, by the landowners, by all persons, in short, who could write their names. The king was indignant at the temerity of the supplicants, and replied through the ministry of the interior, in a threatening tone, that he considered the request insolent and seditious, and that those should be severely punished in future who should dare to make any further resistance. The sole motive that had induced the king to make choice of the city of St. Angelo, was the pleasing impression that he had received at the time of his passing through it, from the wide extent of the horizon there, owing to its position on a delightful hill! Such is the way in which the petitions presented to the king of Naples are received!! But it will be said, perhaps, that in the particular circumstances of this case, the petitions in behalf of a city which had provoked the royal indignation, were mistaken for sympathy with it, and were considered accordingly as amounting to a participation in its offence.

The incident I am about to relate will show what account is made of the prayers of the people when altogether unconnected with political culprits, and when, moreover, they express feelings of affection and loyalty towards the person of the king. In 1838, the king, on his return from Vienna with his lately married queen Maria Theresa, had publicly intimated that he would pass a night in the city of Chieti. Sumptuous preparations were made, and a magnificent reception was about to be given to the royal guests. But as Leopold, prince of Salerno, the king's uncle, who had preceded him in his journey, had stopped at that city, and had made a liberal use of his wealth in distributions among the poor, the king, who is universally known to be very miserly, dreaded the disadvantageous contrast he would have had to encounter by remaining in the same city, changed his intention, and sent word by the telegraph that he was to pass on without stopping. On this notice being circulated, the municipal authorities, followed by a great affluence of people, went out to meet the royal train, and amid cheers and other marks of respect and gladness, they surrounded the carriage and took off the horses, intending to drag it along with their arms into the city, a distance of about two miles. On this the king, turning to the carriage window with a frown and pale with rage, cried out: *Servile wretches!!! Kings give orders to the people, not the people to kings! Gendarmes, drive away this rabble.* The people, silenced and confounded, anticipated the order given to the gendarmes, who hesitated to obey it, and retired, repenting of having virtually lied by manifesting sentiments which did not spring from heartfelt conviction. I was present on that occasion, and it was one that gave fresh force to my liberal opinions. But it may possibly be said that here, as the king had intimated what was his pleasure, it was imprudent to oppose him. One last fact, then, will clearly show that even when the people's desires perfectly accord with the royal will, the latter sometimes is offended at prompt obedience, considering it criminal. Strange indeed, yet not the less true! By the treaty concluded between king Otho of Greece and Ferdinand II. of Naples, a decree was published, in which permission was given not only to the Greek colonies established within the kingdom, but also to persons belonging to the Neapolitan nation, should they so desire, to pass into Greece, there to settle and enjoy the advantages which presented themselves to colonists from foreign parts, in consequence of Greece having been left to a certain extent dispeopled by the long and bloody war of emancipation. Many joyfully welcomed this spontaneous invitation on the king's part, and hastened to consolidate their property by selling houses and fields and flocks, even though at a heavy loss, under the presumed certainty of realising the advantageous circumstances in which they would find themselves in the hospitable land which they had chosen for their country. On the day fixed for the embarkation it was found that the passports promised to all that had showed a disposition to expatriate themselves, were refused by the ministry in virtue of orders from the king, who, seeing that the number of the emigrants was very considerable, dreaded lest it should strike foreigners as a symptom of discontent, and prove an example to others to pursue the same course. The Greek colonists alone embarked, while those who belonged to the country, with despair on their brows and amid the wailings of their desolate families, were compelled to return whence they had set out, not only with all their hopes dashed to the ground, but with a rancorous feeling of the losses they had suffered. I was a witness of the consternation of some of these wretched families.

These facts ought to convince Englishmen how difficult it is for a free people to pass a judgment on the social condition of other people subject to a despotic regimen. Some imagine that mere good sense suffices for judging of such things, without reflecting that good sense, in order to its passing sound judgments, would need to be fully informed about the laws, about all the habits, and all the various circumstances special to the people of which they desire to judge; and that good sense put forth in examining things under one particular point of view, under the influence of prejudices imbibed from infancy, is incapable of escaping from the circle of ideas that are habitual to it, or of disengaging itself from the trammels by which it is unconsciously held bound. The patronisers of the political and religious state of Italy who write in England, always make an impenetrable shield for themselves by appealing to the good sense of the English, knowing that English good sense will judge according to English notions; whereas Italy ought to be judged as things fall out in Italy, and not at all as they fall out in England. Deplorable error in logic, which induces people to believe to be false what are really true accounts of the religious persecutions and monstrous acts of injustice that are practised in my fatherland, and which leads very many to believe that Rome is now no longer what she once was! An Italian has no want of good sense, yet if an Italian, imperfectly acquainted with the political condition of Great Britain, should be told that the sovereign of England on offending a subject, would be constrained by the voice of the people and by the censures of the daily press, to retract the offence and to apologize for the insult given, he would declare, and with justice, that such a piece of information was contrary to good sense, and this declaration of his would be received there with applause, because the good sense of the Italians is accustomed to see acts of tyranny, and public opinion coerced by the bayonets of the gendarmes. Upon this ground there does not exist the man who will believe that the Pacha respectfully received the bowstring sent him by the Sultan, and strangled himself with his own hands. It is good sense that has taught the nations a proverb that attests the difficulty of judging rightly of others placed in different circumstances from our own—'The full belly does not believe in hunger:' [*Il satollo non crede al digiuno.*]

Hence the only possible mode of protesting under a government which makes no account of reasons, is that of efforts to break the chains. In the case of free governments, what is desired of the people is a rational obedience to the laws, and it is right accordingly that when they feel them-

selves aggrieved, they should give their remonstrances all the moral force that reason can supply;
to employ force would be a monstrous crime. Under tyrants again, who carry caprice and arbitrary power through a whole region, making the employment of reason criminal whenever it is opposed to their mere will, the right of defence becomes sacred. To accuse Italy of criminal efforts to break the yoke under which she groans, were atrocious injustice in an individual, but would be most atrocious and scandalous in nations to which Providence has committed the management of the destinies of Europe and of civilization. The very frequent insurrections that have followed, one after another, in the Pontifical states and in the kingdom of Naples, if not by the success, at least by the heroism of those generous souls who became their victims, have from time to time demanded the attention of all Europe, and have been the loudest protests against oppression. Which among civilized nations has ever raised its voice in favour of the oppressed? Not indeed that Italy expects to have her deliverance brought about by the arms of other nations intervening in the struggles which she has maintained, is now maintaining, and will ever maintain against tyranny; she is conscious of possessing sufficient force of her own to break the yoke of her oppressors. What in the name of equity she demands is, that she should certainly be left alone in the struggle, but that no foreign arms shall come to support her oppressors. She demands that faith be kept with those principles of non-intervention which are trampled upon when Italy is in question, and jealously observed with respect to other peoples. She calls on all free nations not to blaspheme the sacred name of liberty by binding themselves in alliance with despots, and to bear in mind that there is no neutrality betwixt good and evil,—that when the cause of truth is at stake, they who abstain from taking part in its defence, favour and become the partisans of error. These may be unpleasant truths, but it has been my duty to mention them, and it would not be right to prove wanting to what is duty, because of the displeasure that may be felt by those who are in fault. To those then who would make use of religious opinions for political ends, and who will not fail to accuse me of being a revolutionist, I will say that if they desire it, I will willingly engage to discuss their opinions with them through the medium of the periodicals, not being allowed in these pages to enter into such a discussion, and now content myself with repeating to them:—*how shall the Italians believe in the Gospel if it is not to be preached to them? how shall it be preached to them without there being liberty to preach it?*

From the political and administrative condition of the kingdom of the two Sicilies, I now proceed to examine that of the Pontifical states.

It is with no small gratification that I find myself called upon to write these pages on the political and administrative condition of the papal states, at the present time, when a ray of hope seems shining once more on their population, till now the most wretched in Europe. All appearances concur towards the belief that the accession of Pius IX. to the pontifical throne, may be viewed as the commencement of a new era, the dawn of a fine day, not only to the people that are subject to his temporal jurisdiction, but also to all Italy, and even to the world at large, by reconcilling those ideas of progress which are boiling in the breasts of the nations, 'with the religious opinions of which Rome is the centre. It is impossible for me to enter at any length on the smiling prospect which the new pontiff is hastening to present to the earth. Many are the reasons that divert me from doing so, but not the last is the obscurity which hangs over *the aim* of the proposed changes. The sincerity of a man's promises rests on the pureness of his intentions; as long therefore as it is not very clear whether it be the good of the people, or nothing more than the perpetuity of the temporal dominion, that the new Pope sets before him as his objects, it is idle to discuss the reality of the advantages that will redound to the inhabitants from the promised reforms. May not all this pomp of clemency and of a liberal spirit, turn out perhaps to be a stratagem to gain the people's affections, to be made available afterwards in securing their patient acquiescence when a foreign force, secretly invited by the pontiff himself, shall render the promises that have been made, and the hopes that have been conceived, alike nugatory? May not this swift transition from a pope replete with the spirit of the middle ages and with anathemas on his lips, such as Gregory XVI. showed himself to his dying moments, to a pope animated with the spirit of the nineteenth century, and talking of liberty, toleration, and progress, such as Pius IX. shows himself, be possibly one of those profound Jesuit contrivances conceived with the view of dazzling civilized nations, and more especially England, whose conversion, or to speak more correctly, whose riches Rome has for a long while been panting for. She too well knows that an insurmountable obstacle to England's return to Roman Catholicism, is to be found in the despotic principles and the intolerance on which the see of Rome is based, not only as respects religion, but politics also; she too well knows that notwithstanding the mild and flattering appearances which the abettors of Romish polemics would fain attribute to her, facts give the lie to their words, as long as the lamentations of oppressed subjects lead to the belief that the political is no less atrociously cruel than the religious inquisition. It was of consequence that this obstacle should be removed, that people should be induced to believe that with the change of times there would be a modification of the church's discipline, and that the monstrous idea of the past should thus be effaced from their minds. Hence, in order to give greater prominence to the present and a greater stimulus to hopes of the future, it has been thought well to reproduce the idea of the past in the predecessor Gregory, just as a skilful painter deepens the shading of a picture in order to give stronger relief to the figures which he wishes should chiefly catch the eye. Some years of a mild pontificate, it is thought, will suffice for completing the work that began with the Romanizing movement at Oxford, that itself having been a Jesuit machination. Nor need there be any fear that the proselytes gained by such a stratagem will escape from her hands, when Rome is pleased to take advantage of a favourable opportunity for removing the mask, seeing she knows how difficult it is, especially amid the ferment of controversy, for those who have become the advocates of the opposite principle, after having identified themselves with the system, to turn back from it, and expose themselves to the contempt, if not to the hatred of both parties. This scheme will not seem improbable to whoever knows that the now prevailing party in the Roman Church, has inscribed on its vesture: *The end justifies the means.* This scheme will seem most probable to whoever may have read Eugene Sue's Wandering Jew. Nor let the fierce and obstinate opposition which Pius IX. meets with in the cardinals and in the retrograde party, detract at all from the weight of these reflections. As for the last, the opposition may be sincere, those who make it being ignorant of the thread of the plot. And as regards the first, their opposition may be part of the farce, got up for the purpose of making the stratagem accredited; this suggests, also, one of the strongest arguments in favour of the probability of such an insidious machination. How can we suppose it possible, that so many men, consummate adepts in the arts of courts, profound scrutinizers of the human heart, wary and astute, at least from long experience of the cunning devices of others, should have deceived themselves with respect to the mode of thinking, and the tendencies of mind and heart, in Giovanni Mastai Ferretti, who had been educated and had grown up under the watchful eye of a policy which scrutinizes the thoughts, who had long lived in Rome and been employed in discharging public functions, who had sat in consistory with them in times rendered difficult by political vicissitudes? This will seem a paradox, an absurdity! And this paradox must be admitted as a fact if the opposition of the cardinals be sincere; otherwise we must admit the still greater absurdity that the Sacred college had unanimously chosen Mastai, knowing him to be disposed to favour liberal opinions!! Be this as it may, it is not my intention to pronounce judgment on the fact; the event will throw light upon it. I confine myself to declaring that while on the one hand love for my country would induce me to believe the new Pope's protestations sincere, on the other hand a secret presentiment, confirmed by the circumstances I have mentioned, makes me repeat the hemistich:

. . . . . . Timeo Danaos et dona ferentes.

Would that these reflections of mine would awaken in the minds of the English wary thoughts, and restrain that excessive confidence with which they abandon themselves to their favourite notion that civilisation may find patronage from the Romish system and modify it. Let men be cautious how they trust implicitly to all that is announced about the new Pope, when they reflect that endeavours have been made, I know not whether by a mistake or by a wicked purpose, to accumulate upon him the private virtues of another Ferretti, he too a cardinal, who at the deplorable time of the cholera's raging in Naples, furnished an example of heroical charity by not only distributing all his silver plate for behoof of the unfortunate persons in the hospitals, but also by exposing his own life in offering aid to the dying.

But how on such a principle, with my mind full of such doubts, can I permit myself to indulge in so much gratification and hope? Just because even should the Pope's promises come to nothing, whether from being insincere or from adverse circumstances, the highest advantage will accrue to the pontifical states, to Italy, and to the whole world, from the favourable demonstrations made in his seconding the desires of the people, in his making himself the advocate of toleration, in his awakening hopes of a better futurity. It has hitherto been taught from St. Peter's chair, both in bulls and by deeds, that the wishes of the people were sinful in so far as they should be opposed to the will of those in power; political intolerance had been sanctified with the name of justice; civil liberty, of whatever kind, was reprobated as opposed to religion. The people, although intolerant of the grievances they suffered from the governments, and desirous though they were of ameliorations, showed themselves backward, particularly in the pontifical states, in uniting with the educated classes in the frequent efforts that have been made to shake off the yoke, or at least to constrain the oppressors to be less unnaturally severe. This obstacle is now removed. The report, be it true or exaggerated,—that I know not,—has been bruited in all quarters, in Italy as well as elsewhere, that the Pope not only condescends to, but shows himself propitious to the seconding of the wishes of those very persons whom his predecessors condemned and excommunicated. The people who had been quite prevented from making any progress by superstition, have again been made to move onwards; their hopes have been excited; that which was but a streamlet has become a river. Who can stop its course? It is in this sense that I am delighted, and regard the pontificate of Pius IX. as the dawn of a fine day. The people of Italy are now convinced that the predecessors of the present Pope endeavoured to divert them from a good way by calling it a bad one, and made it their object to promote their own advantage, not that of the people. They now know that the construction of railways, which the last pope rejected as an invention of the devil, is a most useful measure for the prosperity of commerce, the facilitating of social relations, and the spread of civilization. Should another pope come and teach the reverse, or should the present Pope even choose to contradict himself, Italian good sense will be convinced from this, of which history has never convinced it owing to the ignorance in which it has been kept, namely, that the popes are not infallible, and that they do not *speak seven times a day with the Holy Ghost*, as the Capuchins and the Franciscans have made men believe till now. Let me be forgiven for this preamble before entering upon an examination of the political and administrative machinery of the papal government; present circumstances have impelled me to it.

By usurping the temporal dominion over a part of Italy, the pontiffs have evidently set themselves in contradiction with the Gospel. Jesus Christ, in eulogizing his precursor John, contrasted the hardships of his solitary and sober life, with the voluptuous luxury of courts. In speaking to the apostles he renewed the contrast, making Christian humility a counterpart to the pride of kings. Speaking of himself, he said that his kingdom was not of this world. This last declaration of the Saviour, on the other hand, instead of persuading the bishops of Rome to confine themselves to spiritual, without intermeddling with temporal matters, has become on the contrary, by jesuitical interpretation, a most powerful weapon for the defence of their temporal dominion. It is usually said that Jesus Christ intended it in the sense that the right to reign on the earth did not come to him from this world, but from the Father, not at all that his kingdom was not in this world. Accordingly, the popes attribute this very right to themselves, extending it over all other monarchs; since, notwithstanding that the universal empire imagined by Gregory VII. must ever be held a dream and a delirium, this monstrous theory is upheld in the schools in Rome. Upon this principle, it may easily be comprehended, that the government of the popes must be absolute and despotic, all reluctancy on the part of their subjects to comply with their wills being considered as sinful, and the pretension to impose limits on their divine authority thought absurd. On this same principle, likewise, they must naturally commit the subaltern exercise of that authority almost exclusively to members of the clergy, so that no layman shall be called to participate in the apostolic rights. Accordingly, one main defect of the pontifical government is ignorance of the way to manage public affairs. As the heads of the public offices all belong to the clergy, and are all educated in the monasteries or colleges, in sacred learning, and without any knowledge of public right, of political economy, of statistics, &c., they are compelled to have recourse to others to assist them in the discharge of their functions in the judiciary or administrative departments. Hence knaves and hypocrites are wont to prevail with their counsels on the cardinals and the prelates, converting to their own advantage the influence these possess, and giving vent to their private passions. A second defect appears in the government being wanting in centralization and unity, there being no fixed rule for determining the respective attributions of the ministers. Hence it is that one minister, whenever he pleases, may step into the department of another; a thing that must often take place, if it be considered that such an irregularity, being a perennial source of gain to sycophants, there is no want of persons to urge and stimulate to these invasions.

A third defect lies in the ministers being independent of the pope, if not *de jure*, at least *de facto*; inasmuch as there never occurs a case of their being called to give an account of their doings, and far less of their being punished for them. But if we reflect on what has already been intimated, that the ministers are generally under the control for the most part of vicious persons, it will appear manifest that the people are the sport not only of the absolute pleasure of the sovereign, but of as many despots also as there are ministers and unprincipled persons by whom they are surrounded. A fourth defect, the most pernicious of all, lies in the maintenance of public order and the administration of justice being placed on no solid foundations. The administration of the police and that of justice, are confided to two prelates—the consequence of which is that offenders, when they contrive to obtain for themselves the protection of a cardinal, escape the punishment due to their offences, and can elude the laws to the detriment of others in civil causes. Is it likely that cardinals who would think themselves degraded by submitting to the orders of other cardinals, will be humble enough to respect the injunctions of the *Uditore santissimo* (most holy auditor) or of the Governor of Rome, who are simple prelates? The mere enumeration of these defects may lead one to see that the pontifical government is a chaos, a labyrinth, in which law and justice cannot fail to be lost. Let us come now to the examination of the administrative boards in detail.

The government is composed, 1st, of a cardinal secretary of state; 2d, of a cardinal cammerlingo; 3d, of a prelate treasurer-general; 4th, of a congregation (or board) of cardinals for waters and highways; 6th, of an *uditore santissimo*; 7th, of a congregation for schools and colleges, composed of cardinals; 8th, of a military congregation; 9th, of the governor of Rome. The Secretary of state is always the head of the faction that chooses the pope. This circumstance is enough of itself to give the true idea of what a Secretary of state generally is. Ambition has already been to him the spur to his activity; intrigue has been the means of his success. Gratitude in the pontiff who has been elected, or the ascendancy acquired over his mind by the display of abilities, real or ephemeral, in defeating the opposite faction, gives him such power, that instead of being minister, he may be said to have a virtual share in the sovereignty. He publishes the laws in the pope's name, stating that he has received orders delivered vivâ voce to that effect. He has by right the disposal of all branches of the administration, without acquainting the respective ministers beforehand, in special cases; hence it happens that his arrangements are very often quite opposed to those that have emanated from other ministries. He has the monstrous right of derogating the laws with a simple note, called that of the Secretaryship of state, whether in the case of his being consulted by a tribunal, or even owing to his engagements to some private person who may have an interest in it. It frequently happens that civil causes, after being decided in courts of first and second resort, are definitively lost in the last court of appeal, the judges declaring that by virtue of a note of the Secretaryship, those articles on which the party at the bar rested his right, no longer existed for that particular case. Besides the monstrosity of the arbitrary act implied in derogating a law, to the loss of families for the most part poor, and in favour of the rich, who are the persons that have it in their power to draw to themselves the favours of the cardinal Secretary, he has in this infamous prerogative the injustice to attribute a retro-active force to the law! The Secretary of state has a similar prerogative also in regard to the sentences of death pronounced by the tribunals. Should he want to liberate a condemned person, it suffices that he pass near the place of punishment in his carriage, in diplomatic pomp, which is usually called in *fiocchetto*, in full puff, and the condemned person becomes *ipso facto* absolved from the sentence of death. I was in Rome at a time when the nephew of a cardinal was to be executed for a horrible crime. The report spread that the Secretary of state would come out *in fiocchetto* for the purpose of remitting his sentence, and the people tumultuously collected in a crowd on the street along which the culprit had to pass. The Cardinal Vicar happened accidentally to pass through that quarter in returning from the Vatican, and the people, mistaking his carriage for that of the Secretary of state, compelled it to fly by attacking it with stones, thrown with such force as to damage it. This occurrence proved a warning to the Secretary of state, who was already preparing to leave the palace, and the cardinal's nephew, as I have already related, even with his head on the block, turned his eyes full of hope, to see the desired *Fiocchetti*, underwent his fate, and public justice was satisfied. It happens not unfrequently that the Secretary of state opposes even the execution of the pope's rescripts; sometimes, it must be confessed, doing thereby an act of justice, from those rescripts being calculated to injure the rights of other persons, the pope being accustomed for the most part to grant them on the mere asseveration of the petitioner, without any investigation of the case. The confusion in the Secretary of state's office is increased by those who are employed in it, instead of having the affairs connected with the various branches of the service distributed under their proper heads, having the provinces parcelled out among them. Hence it happens that as they are not circumscribed within any precise limits, each acting independently of another, disposes of the same affairs that another may have already disposed of, seeing that various *minutanti* (the title given to the head functionaries) have charge of the affairs of one province. Sometimes there arrive in one province orders from the Secretary of State contradicting each other.

The Cardinal Camerlingo may well be called the Proteus of fable. Looking at some of the functions allotted to him, it will appear that he may be considered as the minister of finance, for he is supreme head of the treasury, and has the supreme direction of the customs and of the mint. Seen from another point of view, one would take him to be minister for the home department, for he presides over the annona, the provision board, fine arts, industry, agriculture, and commerce. Under another point of view he seems director-general of the post-office, for he has the administration of that department. Viewed under another aspect, he appears as director-general of the waters, highways, and bridges, being supreme magistrate with respect to these. But none of those characters is exclusively his. There is a lord-treasurer placed over the treasury and the customs; and there is a president of the mint. These act independently of him. There is a lord-prefect of the annona and of the provision board, and a board for the museums, a board for the post-office, a congregation of cardinals for the waters and highways, and all these are independent of the Camerlingoship. From this it may be seen what contradictory regulations must emanate from the mutual conflict of these various powers! The cardinal Camerlingo assumes the supreme authority over the state on the death of the pontiff, and retains it until the election of a new one. He proceeds to verify the death of the sovereign, generally striking his forehead with a small silver hammer, and directing the notary to draw up the official report of his death. On leaving the palace the Swiss guard is declared to be loosed from its engagement with the defunct; he makes a new contract with it, and proceeds attended by it to his place of residence. The office is held for life.

The Treasurer may really be called the minister of finance. He has the right of administering all the property that belongs to the state, and of disposing of it as he pleases; he creates debts; makes acquisitions; sells without rendering any account of his doings. The apostolical constitutions prohibit under the heaviest penalty the criminal attempt *(l'attentato)* of calling on the Treasurer to give an account of his transactions. Could he not be obliged at least to draw up an antecedent scheme of income and expenditure? No, he is under no restraint, as if it seemed to be the absolute pleasure of the sovereign that the public treasure should be dilapidated. Large contracts are entered into on a simple proposal, without any competition, with the sole view of benefitting some noble family. The collection of the public taxes is also secured by contract, and the *amministratori camerali* (as the provincial collectors are called) have a premium which is ordinarily three or four-fifths more than like employments were farmed out at under Napoleon; with this sole difference, that the provincial collections were then the only ones contracted for, and that to these are now added the communal collections, which the *amministratore* afterwards sub-farms to great advantage. The chief scourge of the financial system is unquestionably the arbitrary power of the Treasurer, but it suffers no less loss from a want of unity which renders it in the highest degree expensive. Could not the separate administrations of salt and tobacco, of the customs, of the tax on consumption, of registers and stamps, of the lottery, of mortgages, and of the public debt, be united in one single board, and then divided into sections? The Treasurer cannot be removed but upon his being made a cardinal. On receiving his cardinal's hat, he lies under no obligation to do anything beyond going through the formality of leaving on his table the keys of the treasury, which, as may be readily conceived, is always found empty. There is a proverb in Italy in which the shrewd sense of the people has summed up the moral disorder of the men in power, namely, "*Chi piu ne fa e' Priore*," i. e. he who is the worst is Superior. This proverb, coined originally with the view of being applied to the monkish brotherhoods, in which the least deserving and the intriguing have the foremost place, if now applicable in all its truth to governments, may be emphatically applied to the pontifical, in which the crimes of malversation and peculation are rewarded with the dignity of cardinal. What wonder that the public debt has risen to such an extent that the interests alone amount to £558,333 sterling! Besides the yearly pension to each of the cardinals, who withal enjoy the richest benefices, there are endless pensions granted to ladies under the specious names of widows in peril *(vedove periclitanti)*, to spies, and to all those that have sufficient astuteness to gain favour with a prelate or cardinal; intolerable burthens to a state, small in extent, badly administered, and on the brink of ruin from debt.

Among all the branches of the administration the most expensive to the state is that of the waters and highways. This congregation (or board), which is composed of cardinals, has a council under it composed of its engineers. There is a separate central board of directors for works connected with the national highways, which has its council of art and engineers of the first and second class, besides those for extraordinary service. There is an administrative council for the operations required by the streets of cities, with an engineer at head quarters, as well as engineers of the first and second class. There is withal a presidency of waters and banks, and an administrative council for the aqueducts in Rome, with engineers, a council of art, and other functionaries such as those above mentioned. Finally, there is a general board for the hydraulic operations of the government, with a council of art, engineers of the first and second class, inspectors, &c. Then in the provinces there are engineers, inspectors, and others of the first and second class, who attend to the execution of hydraulic operations and to the national highways. In Bologna there is a commission called *del Reno*, which exercises jurisdiction over the rivers and torrents of the four legations, to which there are attached many engineers, inspectors, and engineers of the first and second class. Hence it is evident that this branch of the administration absorbs an immense part of the public treasure, not only from the superabundant number of the persons employed, but unquestionably too from their being much over paid. The inspectors have ninety scudi a month, engineers of the first class sixty-five, those of the second class forty-five. The head engineers and the members of councils have much higher pay. The total cost of this branch of the administration is more than double what it was under the kingdom of Italy, which was so much more extensive than the present pontifical state. The more manifest will the oppression that it brings with it to the people appear, when we consider that the streets and highways in the Roman state are in the worst condition, as travellers can testify. But in multiplying the number of the persons, the object aimed at is not the public good, but the giving of situations, at once lucrative and easy, to persons who in any way, whether from natural ties, or from those of party, or even from less honourable motives, are favourites with those in power. The same object has been aimed at in the establishment of the congregation of good government. This, too, is composed of cardinals, and presides in a special manner over the affairs of the marches and comarches. The limited sphere assigned to it, affords no room for serious abuses. Its most serious defect is its being totally useless, inasmuch as the few functions assigned to it might have been concentrated in another department of the ministry, but the saving of expense is no object with a government in search of partizans for its support.

The *Uditore sentissimo* has a good right to be called the minister of justice, his department being the general superintendence of all the judges and courts. According to the established laws of the country this does not belong to him of right, for directly the only jurisdiction that belongs to him is that over the causes of widows, persons under age, and the poor. It is on this account that he receives the title of *sentissimo*, most holy, because it is a most holy office to protect the weak against the strong, and the poor against the extortions and preponderance of power possessed by the rich. But since his going beyond the bounds marked out for him by the laws, the opposite title would suit him best. Recourse is had to him in causes which in the ordinary course of justice ought to be held as finally determined, and he arrogates to himself an immense power, for on him depends the annulling of rights acquired through the medium of the courts of law. While, on the one hand, he exercises a direct and most hurtful power over the causes of citizens, and hence over the interests of the public, on the other hand no advantage accrues to the public from the right of oversight he possesses with respect to the rectitude and integrity of the judges. Viewed in this light his attributions are rather nominal than real, seeing that the heads of the provinces, who have withal a right to exercise such a superintendence, do as they see fit, without making any account of the ordinances of the minister; all which falls true much oftener in the four legations administered by cardinals. The *Uditor sentissimo* being a *Prelato di fiocchetto*, the same as the Treasurer, is entitled to the cardinalship, and cannot be removed from office without being raised to that dignity.

The congregation for schools and colleges (*degli studii*), the members of which are all cardinals, has been established apparently to promote, but in reality does all in its power to strangle, public instruction. It is to be noted that, generally speaking, those who compose it are under the spiritual direction of the Jesuits. Hence it is not strange that the method of instruction tends to darken the lights of intelligence, and to make progress go back. Efforts are made in every way to impede the prosperity of the philosophical sciences, and to have the slight philosophical knowledge that is indispensable for the liberal professions mixed and adulterated with the ideas of Roman theology. The courses of instruction in the pontifical states, are regulated with the index of prohibited books in hand; hence the best works are excluded from them. Endeavours are made, if not directly, indirectly at least, to suppress the reading of Dante, so very precious and dear to the Italians, who recognise in it the germs of the future liberty of Italy. To prohibit it, would be imprudent, but it is encouraged in none of the schools of the pontifical states. It is thought desirable that Italian literature in general should languish, and the utmost efforts are made to have it superseded by the Latin. The natural and physical sciences are kept under as much as possible, seeing that they train the mind to research and analysis, those two irreconcilable foes of the Roman theology. Hence it is the whole aim of this congregation to give prominence to the ecclesiastical sciences, and to enhance the influence of the Jesuits, who, accordingly, are the instructors of youth throughout the whole of the Roman state.

The military congregation is composed in great part of prelates and a few officers; the Secretary of state presides and acts as minister for the war department. Its chief defect is its having become for many years past altogether useless, and hence a mere burthen to the state, seeing that the pontifical government is now convinced that from the universal prevalence of discontent among its subjects, the troops of the line, though increased in number, would not make face, I do not say against all the provinces in case of insurrection, but against the Romagna alone. Had it not been for the protection given to the Vatican by the bayonets of Austria, what advantage would Gregory XVI. have derived from the hundreds of thousands of scudi be lavishly expended in augmenting the number of his troops, and from elevating to the dignity of *defenders of the throne and the altar*, ruffians stained with atrocious crimes and taken out of the prisons. Seeing that Austria and the Allied Powers are always ready to fly to the spot for the preservation of the established *order*, would it not prove a most serviceable measure to lessen this useless expense by disbanding the troops? Would it not be proper to send back the cardinals that compose the military congregation to the study of theology, and especially to discuss the proper interpretation of that passage of the New Testament, addressed by Jesus Christ to St. Peter, *qui gladio ferit gladio peribit*; they that take the sword shall perish with the sword?

The Governor of Rome is the minister of police; he has the special direction of public order in the capital, and the general charge of it within the state; besides this, he has the command of the *gend'armerie*, called in Rome the carabineers. In the provinces the police is specially intrusted to the Legates and Delegates, and these appoint at their choice a co-official for the discharge of the necessary functions. These, particularly if they be cardinals, act independently of the Governor. But this does not suffice; the bishops *ex officio*, keep an eye over manners and opinions, and act independently of the Governor and of the heads of the provinces. The inquisitors themselves further enter into this department, and act independently of the bishops and of the police functionaries. The absence of unity alone would suffice in the organisation of this branch, to make it evidently most vexatious to the subjects and a source of injustice and disorder. Many other defects besides concur to render the police a scourge that proves the utter destruction of public morals. Our most essential defect lies in the partial or total unfitness of the persons employed, who certainly are not chosen from the better part of the community. These revolt from entering a branch of the administration that is held in odium, inasmuch as it is directed against opinions rather than against vice. Moral and social qualities which ought to be eminently good in those who are charged with the oversight of public morals and with the maintenance of social order, are generally found wanting in the satellites of absolute power, and especially where hypocrisy gives the first and highest title to favour with the government. Another most grievous defect lies in the pitiful emoluments granted to the persons employed, so that vexatious measures and extortions are of frequent occurrence. A third defect, common, however, to many too of the civilized governments of Europe, lies in the police being principally employed in the discovery of crimes rather than framed for their prevention. Instead of directing attention and provident measures to the causes that give rise to disorders, with the view of removing them, all attention is directed to effects, in order to have the ferocious gratification of indulging public revenge, to which the name of *justice* is hypocritically given; it is not considered that this justice comes to be exercised by those who are accomplices in crimes, seeing that, although they have it in their power and although it be their duty, they do not remove stumbling-blocks. Hence it may be inferred what the police is in Rome, where by the union of the two powers, religions and civil, there is attributed to the governmental system the same immobility that has been declared essential to the religious system, because *infallibly* constituted. To correct the abuses of the government, to which, for the most part, the crimes and immoralities of the people may be traced, is considered in Rome as an incurable wound inflicted on the authority of the Popedom. The police accordingly may be likened to one of those *Bravi* (bullies) of the middle ages, who waited in the lobby to assassinate one of their accomplices that might have incurred the baron's dislike. As has already been noticed, the Governor, however desirous to do so, finds it often altogether out of his power to punish crimes, should a cardinal be pleased to undertake the protection of the culprit. A recent example will suffice to convince those who are slow to believe that persons of the most eminent merit make themselves shameless defenders of crime. A priest in 1843,* had been guilty of an aggravated rape in Rome, nor could the strictest searches on the part of the carabineers and the agents of the police, avail for the discovery of his place of concealment. The Pope, shaken by the clamours of the public, which threatened to turn into a tumult, ordered the Governor to be called, and bitterly reprimanded him for making no efforts for the satisfaction of public justice in so urgent a case. The Governor replied that as long as there were palaces having the privileges of sanctuary, into which the police had no right to enter, it was impossible for him to discharge his proper duties; but let him have special authority, derogating all such privileges, and in the course of a few hours the guilty person would be in the hands of the police. The Pope, rendered courageous by necessity, gave the Governor full powers, and the culprit was found in one of the

---

* This case was noticed in the *Times* at the period at which it occurred.

REFLECTIONS ON ITALY.

private apartments of *his Eminence* the Cardinal Secretary of State! The Governor cannot be put out of office unless by being promoted to the cardinalship.

Having thus enumerated the branches of the administration, let us now take a hasty view of the civil and criminal legislation. As for the civil law, the pontifical state is ruled in appearance by the common or Roman law, modified by the canon law, and by the Apostolical constitutions, not by the various *motu-proprii* of Leo XII. The Roman law, known by very few, besides its not being adapted to present times and present habits, has been monstrously disfigured by an infinitude of theories, interpretations by doctors, and ancient and modern decisions of the Rota, in such a manner that even the most shameless wrong may appeal to it in its own defence. In it the judges always find a pretext for veiling the partiality of their decisions. The canon law and the Apostolical constitutions, a vast sea of matter, are still less known than the Roman law, and from their very nature participate in the spirit of intolerance and of privilege which dictated them in ages in which reason, silenced by the Episcopate, had lost the consciousness of her own proper rights. The *motu-proprii* of Leo XII. give full power to establish testamentary trusts, authorize parish priests and confessors to receive wills without any solemnity and in the presence of only two witnesses; deprive women of the inheritance of their kinsfolk when competing with males, and make their rights of dowry so uncertain and perplexed that they easily fall victims to the avarice of their husband's relations. The testamentary wills received and dictated by the confessors, on the one hand, enrich the churches, while lawful heirs, on the other, despoiled and under the pressure of want, people the monasteries, and young women, defrauded of their prospects and relinquishing all hope of being married, go to bury themselves in a convent. The spirit of civil legislation in Rome, is that of making a mystery of the law, that of protecting the despotism of the men in power, and keeping the people in ignorance of their rights.

What shall I say of the criminal legislation? The whole body of the criminal statutes consists in things called *Bandi*. In these ancient laws the punishments are very severe, and not proportionate to the nature and gravity of the crimes to which they apply. The honour, liberty, and life of the citizens are placed at the arbitrary disposal of the judges, but though this code be indeed worthy of the times in which it was written, yet it is at least *written*, and the subjects have it in their power to know what is claimed from them and what they are threatened with in case of transgression. But what is incredible is, that there is still a people in Europe, in the nineteenth century, without any law of penal process. In the Roman state the liberty and the life of accused persons depend on the opinions of the prosecutors, and who for the most part form their opinions from those books which at one time authenticated torture, and have laid the foundation of criminal sentences in confessions extorted by torments. It horrifies one to think that in the papal states, the criminal courts have the right of forming for themselves a particular method of regulating processes, and that the prosecutors of one same court, may act according to their discretion without any dread of being called to account for their capricious doings by any person whatsoever. The prosecutors can imprison the accused and prolong their imprisonment although innocent, pretexts being never wanting with which to vail such acts of injustice. Let not these notices be thought exaggerated, being taken from the memorials which the insurgents in the four Legations presented to the allied powers in 1831, and being quite accordant with the notions I could collect, during my long stay at Rome, from honest men of the law who deplored the state of things. The spirit of the code of civil process, is that of multiplying lawsuits, of spinning them out interminably, and of dragging every thing to Rome. Hence it throws the poor into despair, it augments the preponderance of the rich, it tempts the ill-disposed to try their fortune by hazarding capricious lawsuits, and it corrupts men's morals. Two supreme courts are established at Rome, the Rota and the Segnatura. The attributions of the Rota are: 1st, To take cognisance, as a court of appeal, of all causes where the interest at stake exceeds 825 scudi: 2d, To take cognisance of the same causes, as a court of revision. The chief defect of this court lies in the serious amount of expenses incurred and in the tedious length of the suits. A single suit before the Rota ruins both gainer and loser. The practitioners, who by way of reproach get the name of *masse-orecchie* (crop-ears), foment rancorous feelings and protract litigation, in which one is never sure of success, whatever the number of favourable decisions; hence, when any one has lost a cause in the provinces, it is usual for him to dishearten the gainer with the sarcastic saying: "We shall have it reviewed at Rome."—The attributions of the Segnatura are most important, or, to speak more correctly, are most frightful. It rests with that court to grant or to refuse leave to appeal, and to circumscribe or to annul the judicial acts and sentences of all the courts belonging to the state, nay, even to concede the entire restitutions in causes that have been decided, in order to their being submitted to a second revision. Not indeed that this court can refuse appeals, for it is a maxim sanctioned by all legislations, that the right of appeal cannot be refused, and much more is this the case with the canon law and the Apostolical constitutions, which consider the right of appeal as one of the essential prerogatives of the popedom. The Segnatura only judges whether the appeal ought to be received in *suspensivo*, or in *devolutivo*. It is a most crying grievance in the code regulating processes at law, that the Prefects of the Segnatura are empowered to suspend the course of lawsuits by means of citations subscribed in *denso*, in virtue of which an appeal from any sentence is interposed, although not subject to contestation, as are, for example, the interlocutors in decrees for execution of sentences past. Another defect is, that the judges who vote are for the most part chosen from among young prelates having neither experience nor learning, and that ordinarily the most important offices of Auditor and Subauditor are intrusted to practitioners (*curiali*) who, in consequence of the monstrous viciosity of the legislative system, are not the most honest class in Rome. These are cunning enough in the exercise of their functions, to get the courts to adopt equivocal maxims, and even contradictory maxims, in order that they may afterwards cite them in their own causes. These defects have made the public hold the court of Segnatura in abomination, and have subjected it to most just complaints. To the code for regulating processes at law, ought to be added the civil and criminal judiciary Faculties of the Legates and Delegates of the provinces. The *motu-proprio* of Leo XII. excludes from the attributions of the Legates and Delegates, any intermeddling with civil suits.

But that regulation is derogated by Brieves of nomination with which the Legates and Delegates are furnished. Hence they become judges, or commit to assessors the cognisance of various most delicate causes, among which we meet most frequently with those of *concorso* (competition of claims) and interdiction. These causes are usually treated in *via economica*, that is, with a parsimony of justice and of reason, by substituting caprice for law. In the trials of competitions of claims, the creditors may be constrained to submit to the judgment called *di concordia*, which is grounded on the consent of a majority of creditors. But creditors are not obliged to show cause for their claim, and debtors are dispensed from the obligation of rendering an exact state of their affairs. Creditors, accordingly, are forced to be content with whatever is offered by their debtors. It is useless to consider that the majority is formed of supposititious creditors. Often the caprice of the heads of the provinces manifests itself most shamefully. Orders are directed to the executive officers, called *cursori*, that they must not dare to lay hands on the person, or to attach the property of a debtor, from whatever judge the requisition may have come, and whoever may have been the creditor, or the title on which the debt was claimed. As for judicial interdicts, the assessor takes secret information on the prodigality or the fatuousness of the person who it is intended shall be deprived of his civil rights; on this inquest (*contenziosa notizia*) is formed the edict by which the unhappy person, who has not undergone either interrogatories or judicial examinations, and who is not allowed the right of defence, is deprived of the administration of property. But there is something even worse. These arbitrary decisions affect substance; others of them strike at liberty and honour. The legates who are cardinals, and whose attributions are not confined within any limits, seeing that the pope, in the bulls that he grants them on sending them to govern the provinces, says of them, that it is to God alone and not to him that they have to render an account of what they do: *Deo, et non nobis rationem reddituri*, judge, without appeal, crimes deserving punishments reaching to ten years of the galleys, without the solemnity of a trial and without defence. A thing incredible, but most true! Who will find it possible to believe that the heads of the provinces are empowered to grant safe conducts to public robbers after having already fallen into the hands of justice, who naturally make use of them by never returning to prison again? What wonder then if the people are indignant, and from time to time fly to arms in order to shake off an intolerable yoke!

The state is divided into Legations and Delegations, and these again into Communes. The Legates and Delegates settle what shall be the provincial expenditure, independent of all control. If the treasury refuse to pay a part of it, the provinces are compelled to payment. The communes in the Legations depend entirely on the legate; in the Delegations, they depend indeed on the delegate, but these are bound to present a budget of the municipal expenses for approval to the congregation of good government. The inexperience in the affairs of government of the heads of the provinces, who are often bishops, very often exposes them to the ascendancy of the secretary-general, of the first accomptant, of the steward, and even of the chamberlain, which cannot seem strange after the luminous example given by Gregory XVI., who disposed of the temporal treasures of the state, and the spiritual ones of the church, according to the caprice of the chamberlain. The provinces that have a monsignor (bishop) for delegate, and a cardinal for bishop, know not any distinction of head.

Besides the prisons and the forts, which, down to the death of Gregory XVI., were gorged with persons imprisoned for their political opinions, there is a vast building in Rome called the *Holy Office*, the mere name of which suffices to make it understood that it is not empty at the present day. Notwithstanding all the efforts of the defenders of the Roman system, to obliterate the stain of intolerance and of a spirit of persecution, which history and the profound convictions *(coscienza)* of the people, attribute to it, it is an undeniable fact that in the pontifical state, the Inquisition is always in full vigour. This is evidenced not only by the gloomy building which bears the name but likewise by the existence of persons bearing the name and exercising the functions of inquisitors, both in Rome and in the provinces. But, it will be said, may not the congregation of the Holy Office have been established possibly for appearance only? May not the cardinals who compose it possibly attend the council merely for their amusement? A profound mystery veils from all eyes the terrible doings of that secret tribunal, the members of which are bound to the strictest secrecy by an oath and by the penalty of excommunication, which, in case of transgression, would subject them to the rigour of that tribunal. Hence no one knows what victims are buried in those vaults, or what tortures are put in practice there. The pope presides at that congregation alone, while others meet under the presidency of a cardinal!!! Is it wished in this way that people should understand that the sole business deserving the special attention of Christ's pretended vicar, is the punishment of heresy? When Roman catholics are reproached with bloody persecutions against heretics, their divines are wont to reply craftily, that the Church has no part in the condemnation and punishment of heretics, except the indispensable one of declaring them to be such when the civil power asks this at their hands, but without having any thing to do with the punishment which is sanctioned by the penal laws in catholic countries. But how will they defend the Inquisition in Rome, where the pope promulgates the code, sanctions the penalty for heresy, and declares who are heretics? Should they reply with another artifice, that one must make a distinction betwixt the two powers, that is, that he declares, as pope, what is heresy, and punishes it, as king, I then ask of them whether the pope presides at the congregation of the Holy Office as pope or king? Not as king, for there affairs of conscience are judged, and there even the *intention* is subjected to scrutiny. There accordingly he presides as pope, he makes laws as pope, he applies them as pope; that is, he condemns heresy and heretics in the exercise of his spiritual power.

There is another edifice in Rome called "St. Michael of the bad," where it is usual to incarcerate persons guilty of impudent manners. Over the gate of that building, as over that of the Holy Office, might be inscribed, "Mystery." It is a common saying in Rome, that honest people are often imprisoned there among persons of ill fame, for having resisted the unbridled desires of men in power, and among dissolute youths there groan the brothers and kinsmen of some unhappy maiden, whose ruin is meditated, for having wished to show themselves jealous of their family's honour. Let not the mournful picture of the disorder in the papal government be thought exaggerated. In confirmation of the things I have stated, and of the nefarious caprice that lords it over all things in the place of law, let it suffice to relate a very recent fact respecting the Dominican friar Ahbo, parish priest of Minerva in Rome, a man enjoying the protection of the cardinals, esteemed and revered by the chief families, thought to be a model of virtue, and on the eve of being raised to the prelatureship, who on being discovered to be guilty of the most unutterable turpitudes, and of atrocious murders in the persons of his nephews for the purpose of concealing them, was condemned to death. Through the intercession of the Cardinal Secretary of state, the sentence of death was commuted for an imprisonment, long indeed, yet only for a time, which it was afterwards meant to shorten by the frequency of the indults, of which the popes have always been lavish in favour of persons found guilty of ordinary crime. The people rose in a tumult, and the Pope was constrained to recall the unjust reprieve, desiring, however, that by a special privilege, the execution should not be public, but that it should take place in the castle of St. Angelo. The people again rose in a threatening manner, dreading with good reason lest, under the pretext of such a privilege, it might be intended to save the criminal, and desired that the city guard, composed of burghers, should witness the execution. The newspapers of France and England relate this scandalous event, which in itself presents a summary of the miseries of about three millions of Italians, subjects of St. Peter's successor.

As for political persecutions, I need say nothing about them, for it is easy to infer what is likely to be the reaction among the enlightened class in the papal states, while at once spectators and victims of the violent and irregular acts of the government; and, hence, what has been hitherto the rigour exercised against opinions. But more than from any reasoning, may be inferred from the frequent insurrections and from the ill-suppressed indignation of the provinces. As an irrefragable proof, however, I will relate a fact which makes one horrified when we consider that the unhappy person who was the victim, was not by birth a subject of the Pope, nor had ever plotted against his throne, and, which is more, was taking measures for leaving Italy as a voluntary exile. Baron Luigi Falconj, my friend, who had taken part in the insurrection that broke out in Aquila in the Abruzzi in September, 1841, had been fortunate enough to escape from the vengeance of the king of Naples, and traversing secretly the pontifical states, was proceeding in a fishing boat at Civita Vecchia to seek an asylum on board the French steamer. He was followed by the Pope's carabineers, and overtaken just as he was reaching it; he was then conducted to Rome and sent back by the Pope to Naples, attended by an escort of sixty dragoons!!! This fact needs no comment.

Nevertheless, Dr. Wiseman, author of the critical article which has for its title *Italian Apostates*, inserted in the 23d No. of the *Dublin Review*, blushes not to compare Rome with London, to eulogize the justice that is administered in Rome with the view of making people believe that the narrative of Raffaelo Ciocci, under the title "*Iniquities and Barbarities of the Roman Church in the Nineteenth Century*," is a tissue of fables. And that article has been believed by many, because the astute reviewer makes frequent appeals in it to *English good sense*.

But if the English shall go on judging of things in Italy with English good sense, without endeavouring to put themselves in a capacity for judging of them with Italian good sense, I fear England may be fascinated by the charmer who charms wisely.

I shall conclude these reflections on the political state of Rome with some considerations on the acts of the new Pope's government, and on the hopes that have been conceived of him. Much is said of the amnesty granted to those imprisoned for political offences, without attending to the political clause where it is said that those to whom the amnesty applies are to subscribe a declaration binding themselves not to disturb the public peace. This condition would have been useless, had there been any sincere intention of reforming abuses, secularising the government, and granting a constitution. On the cause of the public clamour and discontent being removed, there would have followed the removal of the effect, and in case of some turbulent persons making seditious manifestations, even after the reforms were granted, the law, with the applause of public opinion, would be sure to strike them. The solemnity of that clause, as long as the reforms are not granted, deprives the amnesty of all value by tending to demoralise those good people with a pretence of renouncing their generous convictions. Hitherto no *essential reform* has been effected, such as would secure to the people a stable and permanent amelioration. Nor can such an amelioration be hoped for as long as the people's rights are not acknowledged and guaranteed by laws, which would be directly contrary to the doctrine announced dogmatically *ex cathedra* by the last Pope, and accepted unconditionally by all the bishops of the Roman catholic church. Hence it follows that the new Pope, even should he desire it, could not without incurring the stain of heresy, sanction the contrary doctrine, by acknowledging in the people *rights that should limit absolute power*. One most interesting circumstance, notwithstanding all that is said, accompanies the enthusiasm that has been called forth in the people of Rome by the hope of a better futurity, which may serve to confirm what has been said respecting the dissoluteness and the violence that characterize the Roman clergy. The unanimous cry of the people which recommended the Pope not to take any food when he went to visit the *Jesuits* or *other Fraternities*, furnishes a clear testimony that the people of Rome have solid ground for suspecting *these holy Fathers* to be capable of the blackest crimes, whatever Dr. Wiseman may think to the contrary. But if this argument, taken from the public opinion of the people of Rome, does not suit him, I hope he will admit as good and authoritative that drawn from the very conduct itself of the existing Pope, who, according to the notices that appear in the newspapers, uses all possible precautions in order to avoid the risk of poison, ordering his victuals to be brought to him some hours before meals, allowing them to cool, and then having them examined by a chemist, who heats them over again in a small stove brought for the purpose into his presence, and partakes of them.

It is now time to pass from the Pontifical, and to give an idea of the political organization of the Lombardo-Venetian state.

Before entering on this examination, it will be useful to call attention to the fact, that the Austrian government in Italy is subject to all those evils which are inseparable from a foreign government placed over a reluctant people which aspires after independence. Although there may be the best intentions in the cabinet of Vienna towards the Lombard and Venetian provinces, although the utmost endeavours may be put forth for promoting the prosperity of their inhabitants, never will it be possible for the tribes of Italy to prosper in such a manner as they would prosper, even in less favourable circumstances, under the impulse of a national government. The idea of being subject to force and not to right, deprives even that which is good of all charms, and causes it to be received with distrust and peevishness. All the national elements converge towards a secret resistance against the invaders of the most sacred right, such as is that of *nationality*, which may be defined as the *conscience* of peoples. This resistance then is interpreted by the government in the worst sense of turbulence and rebellion, so that in order to its repression, recourse is had to force. This provokes fresh reaction, and thus, reciprocally, reactions augment in energy until the moment of a crisis arrives. Exactly the same thing happens to England with respect to Ireland as that which happens to Austria with respect to Lombardy. The most serious difference in the two positions consists solely in the different political circumstances of the two governments, Austrian and English. Fundamentally, however, the position is the same. All the efforts put forth by England for the advantage of Ireland, are ill received, and the reaction which is inevitable wherever force decides right, has the effect of making the English attribute the evils of Ireland to the mere indolence of a people demoralized by superstition, while Ireland attributes all her miseries to English selfishness. I have mentioned Ireland to give an idea of the dislike felt by the Italians to the Austrian domination; not at all that I would compare Lombardy, which is a most flourishing and civilized part of Italy, with Ireland; although the latter is free, and the former not only without independence, but destitute of all enjoyment of freedom. But besides this difference we find another, and most essential one, in the *conservative* element in the English government being tempered by the *progressive* element, whereas Austria represents in Europe the principle of Chinese immobility. This *ultra-conservative* principle of Austria admirably explains what must be the violent state of the Italian provinces that are subject to her, whilst every where throughout Italy, and especially in Lombardy, the progressive element is in a state of ebullition and advancement, absorbing old ideas from day to day. Although, then, Austria might have the best intentions in the world, these can only be directed to the conservation of the old system and to impeding progress, that is, to the opposing of all that the people desire. But Austria has no good intentions towards Italy, for she knows that the usurped dominion which she directly exercises over the Lombardo-Venetian states, and indirectly over the Italian princes, whose arbiter she has rendered herself by taking them under her protection, will not be of long duration; hence she has no other object but that of prolonging it to the utmost possible length, and nevertheless extracting from them those greater advantages than the mere act of extracting from them will prove. The maxim that supplies her with a rule is that *of resisting all progress*. But if, in spite of all her efforts, any kind of progress shows itself victorious, and advancing to perfection, she has another convenient maxim at hand, that is, the *patronising* of it, for the purpose of *neutralising the*

POLITICAL AND CIVIL STATE OF ITALY.

consequences, by giving it the sanction of her name. Thus Europe remains deluded, for Europe attributes to her what proceeds from Lombard energy, and Europe knows not that this plant which has grown up in spite of the northern winds and blasts, is condemned not only to barrenness, but to bear noxious fruits in consequence of having poisonous grafts inserted into it.

The Lombardo-Venetian government has for its head the viceroy, a member of the imperial family, who exercises the supreme executive authority. He has a royal Chancery. The legislative power, the selection of the leading functionaries, and the administration, belong to the cabinet of Vienna. In Vienna the direct and indirect taxes are settled; also the post-office regulations, a most important branch under absolute governments for *tracking out the designs of secret correspondences*. Vienna has the selection of persons for all the first charges in the government, the Podestas, the Delegates, the Deputies of the central congregation, the counsellors of the tribunals, the government, the court of exchequer *(magistrato camerale)*, the administrators of the finances, the Prefect of the Monte-di-Pieta, all persons employed in any *new institution*, the professors, &c. Vienna settles the salaries of public functionaries, pensions, and the budget of the annual expenditure. All enterprises, and all speculations that exceed the amount of 3000 florins, must be submitted to revision and approval at Vienna. Thence, besides, people must wait for the dispositions for sales of crown property *(beni Demaniale)*, without auction, and for extraordinary expenses. Public instruction, the regulations of the high police, military levies, &c. likewise depend entirely on the Aulic council and on the Emperor. Hence, behold! in reality the Lombardo-Venetian provinces deprived of the advantage of a *local government*, and reduced to the miserable condition of provinces subject to a foreign and distant government. Nevertheless, an ostentatious display is made of the concession of a local government! Persons in the employment of the state, are chosen in a great measure from Austrians and Tyrolese. Now of what consequence is it that about an equal number of Italians (were this indeed true) are employed at Vienna? The Austrians command in Italy and the Italians serve in Austria. The Police especially is, one may say, entirely organized by Austrians, and the same may be said of the Direction of the Posts, of the presidents of the tribunals, and of the heads of almost all the other branches. Hence it follows that the local government still comes to be powerfully influenced, in the *executive*, by the Austrian system. After the fall of Napoleon, Austria, on having restored to her a more extensive dominion in Italy, wished to make herself appear generous, and on the 24th of April, 1815, gave to the Lombardo-Venetian state a phantasm of a constitution, modelled upon the Germanic Diet, or perhaps more provincial states, without any legislative power whatever, and altogether dependent on the absolute will of the Emperor, being nothing more than *consultative* meetings. In the proclamation sent forth in those circumstances by the Emperor Francis, he expresses himself thus: "It is the desire of the Emperor that colleges should be formed of persons taken from the various classes of the state, in order that his Imperial and Royal Majesty may be made acquainted, in a regular form, with the wants and the wishes of the nation." The institution of these Provincial and Central congregations accordingly, being solely intended to bring the desires of the people to the knowledge of the sovereign, in order to their being of some practical utility, ought to have been guaranteed in such a manner that the people should have in them true organs of their wishes. On the contrary, as has already been remarked of the provincial councils in the kingdom of Naples—an imitation of the provincial states in the Austrian dominions—no guarantee has been accorded to the members that compose it; not only so, but the government has rendered them servile to it, by reserving to itself the choice of members and by settling lucrative salaries on those who compose the central congregation. Each of them receives from the public treasury 2000 florins (£200).

Let us now see how these congregations are organised. The provincial congregation consists of four, six, or eight proprietors, according to the population of the province; one half of these are nobles. Every royal burgh has a representative in it. The choice of the deputies of the whole province is made by the communes through the medium of the municipal council, which sends up two names of persons resident in the province, and of whom one must be a noble. Every royal burgh transmits three names of its citizens. The provincial congregation receives these lists, and from them selects three candidates for any vacant post. The central congregation examines the choice of the candidates made by the provincial congregation, and has the right of excluding those individuals whom it does not deem fit, and then transmits the lists to the government, either at Milan or Venice. Further, the government has the right of excluding any one, under the obligation, however, of giving a reason for doing so at Vienna; but if there be no objections found, the individuals named first in any lists are confirmed deputies for entering into the place of those who, having exercised their functions for six years, go out of office. Meanwhile half of the number is renewed every three years; and the same organization is observed in the central congregation. The Delegate of the province is the president of the provincial council. The necessary qualities for being elected are citizenship of the kingdom and residence in the province or in the burgh for which the candidate is proposed; he must have property to the amount of 2000 crowns, and he at least thirty years of age. For nobles the patent of nobility granted by the emperor, is required. Persons employed in the public service are excluded from them, besides common criminals, or even persons only subject to criminal trial, or bankruptcy. The same grounds carry exclusion from the central congregation. The provincial deputies are not paid, and hold only an honorary rank, but their services, which are so useful to the government, form a step to their admission into the central congregations, or even for other lucrative employments. Their attributions are limited to the administration of the taxes in the province, to the revision of the accounts of the communal revenues, to attending to the construction and upholding of the bridges and roads, excepting those with which the government charges itself; and the superintendancy of charitable institutions. The central congregations are two in number, one having its seat at Milan, the other at Venice. Each province has two deputies there, one of whom is a noble, and there each royal burgh has a representative. The choice of the deputies is regulated as follows. The municipal council of each of the communes proposes two candidates, a noble and a proprietor, to the provincial congregation, which selects from the various lists, three nobles and three proprietors. The central congregation, through the medium of which the candidates are presented to the government, recommends one of them according to its own judgment. On the other hand the royal burghs present three candidates to the central congregation, and that again transmits these to the government with a recommendation of one of them in preference to the rest. In order to one's being elected, besides the three other requisites already mentioned, it is necessary to be in possession of four thousand crowns. Two remarks will suffice to make it clear that certainly the desires of the people are rather the excuse for establishing a new species of aristocracy than the true aim of this organization, which tends to a violent separation from the interests of the nation, of the families of most distinction, in order to bind them insensibly to the governmental system. The first of these remarks is, that for the members of the central congregation, in order to their election as such, it is not necessary that they should reside in the Lombardo-Venetian kingdom, all that is required being residence in any part of the Austrian dominions; clearly showing that it is the intention of Austria to have the election made to fall on her nobility or her rich residents at Vienna, with the view of disposing of the favours of government to the best advantage. The second is, that the emperor reserves to himself an unlimited right to exclude any person whomsoever, although *elected* by the communes, *chosen in preference* by the provincial congregations, *recommended* by the central congregations, and *approved* by the local government, showing that the high police of Vienna is that which regulates the elections, and consequently, that these instead of being favourable to the people's interests, cannot but be servilely compliant with the desires of the foreign dominator. The provincial congregations exercise the following functions: First, The repartition of all the extraordinary taxes. Secondly, The complement of the repartition of the tax on real estates *(fondi)*. Thirdly, The inspection of the communal revenues, and the division of the public imposts among the several provinces, cities, and communes individually. Fourthly, The distribution of military services. Fifthly, The superintendency of the bridges, canals, highways, and railroads. Sixthly, The superintendency of charitable institutions. But it is not sufficient for the absolute power of Austria to make sure of the personal attachment of the members that compose these assemblies, in order to commit to them the definitive management of affairs, although circumscribed in extent and of the smallest prominence, it has wished to limit besides the exercise of these attributions, by restraining the force of their deliberations to the *consultative vote*. Moreover, this consultative vote can be emitted by them solely respecting those matters that form part of the above-mentioned sections, but on which the government has not yet sent forth any regulation. Affairs are discussed at general meetings, but the president has the right of appointing particular commissions for the treatment of special matters. The governors of Milan and Venice preside respectively over the central congregations.

Pass we now to the civil and criminal judiciary administration. Besides the lower courts, called *Preturas*, for civil causes involving minor sums, and for correctional causes, which are 133 in number, there is in each province a tribunal of the first instance which decides not only civil but also criminal causes, and mercantile ones. But for the two provinces of Milan and Venice, the tribunal of the first instance for civil causes is distinct from that for the criminal; and, besides these, has a *chamber of commerce*. Causes are tried in appeal by the two tribunals called the *General court of appeal* and the *Higher tribunal of criminal justice*, the one of which has its seat at Milan, the other at Venice. The Senate of Verona is the supreme tribunal of the whole kingdom, that is, the *Grand Court of Cassation*. It is impossible to give even a remote idea of the Austrian legislation, it being exceedingly voluminous, consisting of above eighty volumes. Where shall we find a judge capable of acquiring a perfect knowledge of so vast a collection? Where shall we find a subject who can say that he knows his duties and his rights? Besides this defect, there is another most grievous vice in the selection of the judiciary functionaries, and it is the system of the Austrian government to pay those whom it employs at the lowest possible rate. To this we must add their frequent removal from one place to another, a circumstance which exerts a fatal influence on the administration of justice, by burdening the functionaries with useless and heavy expenses, retarding the expedition of business, and augmenting the difficulty of judging with a full knowledge of the cause in hand. In conclusion, as the acmé of evil, the first posts in the judiciary hierarchy are filled with Germans, who, accordingly, hardly knowing even a few Italian phrases, are not capable of trying causes in which not only a perfect knowledge of the language but that of the dialects also is indispensable. Hence it will appear manifest that the administration of justice must be at once most costly and most tedious for the litigants. As for civil causes, which certainly are not within the possibility of the poor, even the rich, taught by fatal experience, seek to escape from them. But how escape the mischievous effects of such an order of things, in criminal causes? The accused are confined in prison for months before they are examined and tried, and frequently for years. The system of *secresy* in the procedure, authorises one to apply the term *inquisitions* rather than *administration* of justice, to the criminal tribunals. The destiny of the accused is placed in the hands of a counsellor, who is at one and the same time judge and defender; for in the formation of the process, which is secret and devolved on him alone, it rests with him to put together the circumstances that are favourable, or the reverse, to the innocence of the accused. In fine, over against the other tribunals stands the Police, a tremendous court, which throughout all Italy wages a fierce hostility against opinions, and, further, is all the more intolerable in the Lombardo-Venetian state, seeing that those portions of the population are more powerfully incited towards ideas of a better futurity, not only from the mere desire for liberty, but also from having a still keener longing for national independence. There are in Lombardy alone 300 agents of police, 672 gendarmes, 1233 police guards, an infinity of keepers, under-keepers, prison-guards, assistants, and guards of fortified places. There are guards for the frontiers, communal guards, guards for the woods and forests, urban guards, all subject to the orders of the police. Various names are given them with the view of palliating to the eyes of the public, and especially of foreigners, the turpitude of this inquisitorial system. There are spies in the service of the Viceroy, of the Governor, of the Director of Police, of the district Commissaries, of the Bishops and of the parish priests, although these have no need of them, having both the right and facilities for acting as spies themselves. A gentleman who had once the charge of a parish in Venice, now a Protestant, assured me that in the exercise of his parochial functions, he received frequent letters from the Venice police board, inclosing special notices respecting the private conduct of some and about the domestic occupations of others. Therefore it is that in order to their being parish priests, besides the approval of the bishop, they must have that of the government too. And all these, by their making a show of having the interests of the government at heart, are authorized to do any thing, even to the giving vent to their passions, from that of thirsting for money to the gratification of private revenge. The persecutions of the police are in no other part of Italy so fierce, though very fierce, as in the Lombardo-Venetian states. In the kingdom of Naples, in the Papal states, in Sardinia, the punishment of death is denounced on those only who take up arms against the government, while conspiracies are punished by the longest imprisonment and forced labour *(l'ergastolo)*; but in Austrian Italy the penalty of death is extended to conspirators also, although they may not have made any attempt implicating them in the guilt of leze-majesty. Silvio Pellico, Gonfalonieri, and those other generous souls who, in 1821, *thought* about the emancipation of their fatherland, were condemned to death. Imprisonment of the harshest kind, or harsh in the Spielborg, was in their case a respite. That accordingly which for other kingdoms of Italy is justice, for Austria is a favour.

As for Finance, for the reader to perceive how heavily the hand of Austria lies upon the Italian states, it is enough to point to the fact that while their population forms only the eighth part of that of the empire, it contributes to the imperial treasury above a fourth part of the entire revenues. The Lombardo-Venetian state, with 4,660,000 inhabitants, pays 34,240,000 florins; the remainder of the empire counts 30,869,000 inhabitants, and pays 101,212,000 florins. On making a calculation we find that each individual of the Italian states pays 7 florins, 40 kreutzers, while in the other Austrian dominions each individual pays 3 florins, 10 kreutzers, that is, less than the half. The hand of the Austrian government is perceived in enormous import duties on colonial produce, on wines, spirits, &c., creating a contraband trade which is the ruin of Milan, the grand depot of the wares of the country; it is seen in the prohibitory system with respect to foreign silk, cotton, and woollen manufactures, which also fosters smuggling, owing to the insufficiency and the dearness of the manufactures of the state. The Austrian system may be seen in the vexatious customs regulations, which impede the free circulation of manufactures and of colonial productions, even in the interior of the state, which impose a fine should a few pounds weight of manufactures be passed from one city to another without a previous license, which subject merchants, especially in the districts placed along the frontiers, to having their warehouses inspected and their houses searched, by day or by night, by the custom-house officers, often too several times a week. The Austrian system makes itself keenly felt in a most obscure code of finance, which gives scope for arbitrary judgments and caprices, imposing taxes on the various branches of art and industry at random. The man of trade feels the hand of Austria not only in the mercantile tax, but much more in the heavy expense which he is bound to pay in the protests of bills of exchange even for sums below a hundred livres Austrian money; the lowest cost in such cases being 8 livres and 64 cents. Austrian despotism reveals itself overwhelmingly in the augmentation of the public debt of the Lombardo-Venetian kingdom to about 25,000,000, without any just reason, in 1840. The despotism of Austria reveals itself in the enormous postage taxes, so that a letter from Milan to Placentia, at the distance of 14 leagues, pays 40 cents.; 60 from Milan to Modena; 80 from Milan to Bologna or to Florence. The despotism of Austria manifests itself finally in the hinderances opposed to the construction of the many railways now in progress, not having it in its power to prevent them amid the universal enthusiasm of Europe; in imposing a new postal tax on the line from Milan to Monza, and in declaring that at the completion of the whole enterprise, it will take it into its own hands on its own account. It is impossible to recapitulate all the grievances of the Italian states under the Austrian government. Not the least of these, and that perhaps which bears most sensibly on the Lombard energy and activity, is found in the hinderances by which, in one mode or other, the government thwarts the aspirations of the people towards any amelioration. This kind of moral oppression does not strike the eye of a superficial observer, but it is not therefore the less serious. In Lombardy, thanks to the vigorous vitality that glows in the descendants of the heroes who routed the Germans at Legnano, the sluggishness of Austria is triumphantly overcome. But in Venice, under less favourable circumstances, the moral oppression of the Austrian system presents the saddest results. In Venice, which counts hardly 110,000 inhabitants, 52,000, under various titles, receive charitable assistance.

Let us now make a few remarks on public instruction. This comprises three kinds of study; the Gymnasia, the Lyceums, and the Universities. The course of studies at the Gymnasium lasts six years. No one is admitted there under the age of ten, so that a complete course of study extends to a man's being twenty-five years of age. Here one sole master teaches history, geography, arithmetic, the elements of algebra, religion, poetry, and rhetoric. Among other things Latin is taught. In the Lyceums the course is one of two years. Here there are taught algebra, physics, mechanics, philology, philosophy, natural history, and universal history. Italian literature is excluded. Philosophy is taught according to the German method. What wonder then if Italian philosophers are excluded? Afterwards, in the Universities the Austrian system unblushingly reveals itself. Vienna directs the examinations of the professors, and Vienna judges of their merit. Their merit consists in nothing but boundless submission to the government. Vienna proposes subjects for instruction. Woe to that professor who would desire to change a maxim, a theory in the doctrine prescribed; the loss of his chair and imprisonment would be the consequence. German authors are preferred in the schools of medicine, of the faculties of law, of statistics. Disorder reigns in all the faculties, but particularly in those of medicine and mathematics. That, indeed, which most interests the government is the watching of youth from the commencement of their studies, being aware that in proportion as the intellect becomes enlightened, generous sentiments of honour and patriotism revive in Italian breasts. The masters are obliged to inform the government minutely with respect to the conduct of the students, both in the Gymnasiums and the Lyceums. Afterwards, in the universities, the surveillance becomes so intolerable and vexatious, that it might well be deemed a prohibition of study; students are laid under the obligation of permanent residence in the cities that are university seats. Hunting and the exercise of fencing are forbidden. Orders are issued under severe threats not to allow moustaches to grow, or should youthful wantonness tempt a student to have them, to cut them off. Then comes the necessity of a hypocritical submission to the external forms of religion, to which not only the police but even the university professors constrain them to submit. Then, as in every association despotism dreads a conspiracy, the student must avoid every appearance of association, and keep himself isolated. On every the slightest pretence he finds himself the butt of insults from the soldiery and the guards of the police. The student, if he belong to the class of the people, must suffer the inequality sanctioned by the regulations in favour of the sons of persons in public employment, of proprietors, and the nobility. A heavy expense attends the various examinations for degrees. But over and above the eventual expenses, most oppressive by themselves are those necessary for obtaining the degree of doctor, a young man being obliged to live sixteen, and often nineteen years, far from his family, to enable him to frequent the gymnasia, the lyceums, and the universities. And after all these expenses, other difficulties remain to be overcome before they can attain to a capacity for being of use to themselves and their families, as they are obliged for many years to work as alunni, that is to say, without remuneration, and all those avenues to employments that are granted through the medium of the police being shut against them. The number of advocates and notaries is limited: engineers must have four years more of practice, and about 12,000 Austrian livres of caution. Nobody can teach, not even as an elementary master, without the sanction of the government; and studies pursued under an unauthorized master, are declared to be null. There is a severe prohibition against studying at foreign universities. The elementary schools, the establishment of which is due for the most part to the paternal charity of generous individuals, have been rendered almost useless by the government, since it usurps the direction of them for the purpose of making them subserve its own ends. Ignorant and careless masters, few in number and ill paid, are chosen by the government, and may be displaced by the commission that presides over the schools. The masters are obliged, not only as spies, to watch the conduct of the boys, but also to teach them to act as spies upon one another. The same may be said of the Charity Boys' Schools, (*asili pei ragazzi*,) founded and endowed by private benevolence, but directed by the government. Moral instruction is directed to the forming of the tender minds of infants to servility, by teaching them that *the power of the Emperor extends over their property equally as over their persons*. In spite of these obstacles it may happen, however, that the genius of Italy freely soars aloft, but Austria fails not to clip its wings. There is a censorship for literary journals, for to speak of politics is a crime, and in the whole kingdom there is no other political journal but the *Privileged Gazette* of Milan, written under the direction of the Police. Foreign journals are not permitted, if we except those that patronize absolute power, and further, for these there is a tax of ten cents for each number. There is a censorship for books both in Milan and in Venice, and as many other censorships as there are provinces, for publications not exceeding one printed folio. There is a censorship, moreover, for engravings and for theatrical representations. Finally, there are special censors for theological works, for medical, and for mathematical works. In all this, nothing is contemplated but the imposition of chains upon thought. But should one succeed at times in satisfying the censor, it is found that the police never loses its right to suspend the printing after it has commenced, and to lay its hands on the portions already published, to the severest hurt of the authors, and to the loss of individuals and printers. Such are the doings of Austria in Italy. All its endeavours tend, as has been said, to the prolongation of its dominion, and hence its efforts to suppress thought. Its whole object is to extract the utmost advantage possible from the fairest and most fertile of its provinces, and hence it does not lose a single favourable opportunity of devouring its revenues. In proof of this, suffice it to remark that availing itself of the completed fact, *(fatto compito)*, that the Lombards paid an excessively high land-tax under the French, it has always chosen to draw it without the diminution of a cent, although under the French the state of continual war formed its justification, and from 1815 till now, the very long continued peace ought to have proportionably reduced it. In such a state of things the sum of 60,277,000 Austrian livres, over and above the expenditure, goes to enrich the treasury of Vienna every year!

After having considered the governmental system of Austria with respect to the Lombardo-Venetian States, it will not be beside the purpose to cast a rapid glance at the policy she adopts with respect to the chief Italian princes. Notwithstanding that according to the treaty of Vienna, after the fall of Napoleon, all the Italian princes were independent, and had full and absolute authority over their own respective dominions, yet Austria has never thought that they ought to be so with respect to her. She considers herself empowered to exercise a protective authority, not only in the perils that threaten them, but also in the measures they should adopt for securing the tranquillity of the people. The Austrian ambassadors in the Italian courts, exercise an influence, and an ascendancy, which neutralise whatever may be the good intentions the governments may have had. We have noticed the similarity that exists between the provincial councils of the kingdom of Naples and those of Austria, and every one can perceive the likeness between the Austrian system of police and the picture already given of the Neapolitan. As for Tuscany, the dukedom of Modena, and that of Parma, no one has any right to wonder at it, seeing the reigning families in these are branches of the house of Austria, and naturally feel a deference for the throne from which they derive their origin. As for the kingdom of Naples, besides the facts already mentioned, others are supplied by recent history. Ferdinand I., after having conceded the constitution to the kingdom which unanimously called for the *fulfilment of the promise* made by him when he was in Sicily, for the purpose of detaching the people from their affection for Joachim Murat, left Naples with the consent of the Parliament to go and defend his own rights, and those of his people, in Vienna, before the Allied powers. It cannot be doubted that such was his good intention, seeing that in writing from Vienna to his son, and in other *spontaneous* demonstrations before his setting out, he emphatically attested that it was his desire to observe the oath that had been sworn. The Allied powers, and Austria more than any other, induced him to change his language and to declare his people rebels. When on being afterwards restored in Naples by force of the Austrian's arms, he grew fierce in shedding blood in torrents, it was whispered to the king's exculpation, that *such was the will of Austria*, although the Austrian cabinet seemed to inculcate clemency and moderation. Then, as for the Pontifical states, in the insurrection of the Legations in 1831, the impudence of Austria reached its climax. Contrary to the treaty of non-intervention, she lorded it over a house not her own. But if she would excuse herself on the ground of having been invited by the Pope for the re-establishment of *disorder*, who can ever excuse the overbearing act exercised by her in arresting on the high sea the Brigantine Isotta, making *her prisoners* ninety-nine liberals who had got out of prison by the capitulation of the fortress of Ancona? How will it justify the severe imprisonment to which they were subjected in Venice, and from which they were delivered only by the intervention of France? The diplomatic note which prince Metternich directed to the English Ambassador at Vienna in July 1832, respecting the reforms projected in the Pontifical State, and rejected by the Pope, is a most curious document. Two most important ideas may be learnt from it. The first is the hypocrisy of Austria, who therein declares certainly her *readiness* to give advices, but makes a show of having a dread of usurping the right of command to the prejudice of an independent prince such as the Pope!! What delicacy of conscience!!! The second is, that with all this conscientious repugnancy, the Austrian cabinet made an offer of its readiness to place at the disposition of the Roman government, *experienced Austrian functionaries, who knew Italy well*, (from the long habit of oppression), *in order to assist it in introducing all practicable ameliorations in the difficult circumstances in which it was placed.* That is to say, after the specious pretence of its unwillingness to infringe the pope's rights of independence, it made an offer of its readiness to act as lord and master in his state, as if, forsooth, reforms were impossible in Italy, unless they came from German hands!

The only Italian state that shows any restiveness under the influence of Austria, and that begins to display a firm determination to act as master in its own house, is that of Sardinia. As has been already hinted, the book published by Balbo, intituled *Speranze d'Italia*, (Hopes of Italy), gives ground to believe that the Court of Turin nourishes the idea of emancipation from the preponderance of Austria. In other respects Italy shows herself backward to believe the insinuations of Charles Albert, remembering the cowardly or treacherous flight from the liberal standards, to which he had spontaneously run in 1821. Besides this, if indeed it be true that he proposes to make amends for that passage in his life, why does he not begin to condescend to the desires of his people, who have long been panting for a national representation? This step would make all Italy believe in the sincerity of his projects, would secure for him again the love and esteem of all Italians, and would deprive Austria for ever of all hope of aggrandizing herself in the peninsula. Whatever otherwise may be the opposition of the Court of Turin to the pretensions of Vienna, it will be gratifying in a two-fold sense, not only by its keeping alive and further enkindling in Italy the glowing desire felt for independence, but also by its covering with shame the other Italian courts while exhibiting them as *voluntarily enslaved to* the foreigner; and this exhibition will school the people into the forming of right judgments on such governments.

We shall now devote a few words to giving an idea of the states of the king of Sardinia and then of Tuscany. However the Sardinian government may at present appear in some measure progressive, it is indubitable that it has followed hitherto the same violent course trodden by the other Italian princes. Scenes of blood have been witnessed from time to time in the Genoese territory and in Piemont. The wish for freedom has deep roots in the inhabitants of those districts, and it is all the more formidable as the idea of national honour has been less obscured in them. Piemont has never been equally with the kingdom of Naples and with Lombardy, degraded so far as to be a foreign province, and has always seen in the house of Savoy, which it has obeyed, an ardent and jealous zeal for the national honour. On the other hand Genoa does not belie the glories of her republic. Hence the seed of liberty which the civilization of our day has scattered everywhere, has found in them a soil admirably adapted for its growth. In other parts of Italy ideas of liberty have found an hinderance in the indolence and in the degradation bequeathed by foreign dominations; in the Sardinian continental states they have found none but favourable elements. Hence no wonder that in them the progress should appear greater. Not, indeed, that it is so really, seeing that taking difference of circumstances into account, the whole of Italy may boast of having produced equal fruit in the cause of its regeneration. Hence from the tendency towards liberty being most lively in the Sardinian states, and the government being absolute, it will readily be understood that their political condition cannot be supposed to be different from the other Italian peoples. But if one would conclude from their not being seen to rise in arms against the government, that they are quite satisfied with their lot, he would judge amiss. It has been said in the *general observations* on the character of the Italians, that in northern Italy reflection predominates over the energy of the passions, while in the southern part, the energy of the passions is increased by the imaginative vivacity of reflection. One ought to make allowance then, for the Piemontese and Lombard temperament, in explaining the political phenomenon presented by the Sardinian and the Lombardo-Venetian states, compared with other Italian peoples. Besides difference of temperament, the situation of these two States has a great share in this, in as much as they lie contiguous to other liberal states, whence it happens that they not only participate in the habits of their neighbours, but in other respects find themselves within reach of information with regard to the present state of Europe, so as calmly to wait for the not distant crisis, the final struggle betwixt the old aristocratical forms and the new democratical spirit. To this we must add that the court of Turin has adopted, as has already been observed of Austria, the system of taking under its own management, such instances of progress as the nation has matured, for the purpose of subjecting them to its sway and of neutralizing their effects; the result of which is, that the nation loses its exasperation and silently pursues its work of civilization, while in the kingdom of Naples, in the Pontifical states, and in the duchy of Modena, all that the people have desired has down to this day been rejected with violence, so that re-action has become inevitable. The form of the Sardinian government and the general administration of the kingdom being similar to that of the kingdom of Naples, I abstain from speaking of them. The system of municipal administration varies in the capital cities and in the provinces. Turin and Genoa have by special privilege oligarchical municipal assemblies. In Turin there is a body of sixty *Decurioni*, half of whom must be nobles. These elect every year two syndics and ten counsellors, together with other subaltern officers, and these compose the so-called Congregation or magistracy. Upon the demise of any of the sixty, the charge of Decurions being one for life, the vacant place is filled up by the votes of the entire body and of the congregation, so that the king has nothing to claim in the election. In Genoa there is a grand council and a little council. The grand council is composed of forty Decurioni, half nobles, who in 1815, when it was first instituted, were chosen by the king, but now are elected by the votes of the grand council. This assembly meets thrice in the year. It elects ten counsellors and other functionaries, having at their head two Syndics and a royal commissioner, and it is denominated *the little council*. The administration of the city, the police, public institutions, and the municipal revenues are under the direction of the little council. The two Syndics, one of whom is a noble, are chosen directly by the king from a list presented to him by the great council. These remain in office for three years, but of the other members of the little council, one half is renewed every year. There are two or three cities besides that have much about the same form of municipal assembly, but the provinces in general are constrained to receive the choice of the municipal functionaries, from the *intendants*, or governors of the provinces, and hence to have their internal affairs regulated according to the wishes of the government, not at all according to their true wants. Thus far as regards the continental provinces. The island of Sardinia still preserves its ancient national assembly called *Stamenti*. These parliaments consist of three sections: an ecclesiastical chamber composed of prelates, a military chamber composed of nobles, and the royal chamber consisting of the sworn heads of the seven *demanial* cities and of the syndics of the communes. These chambers meet separately and communicate their deliberations by messages. It rests absolutely with the king to convoke or to dissolve them. In so far as their power extends, the preponderance is on the part of the nobility, and hence oppression remains on that of the people; because the prelates themselves, too, are for the most part nobles, as likewise are the sworn heads. Then as feudalism still retains its vigour in Sardinia, it will be easily understood that the syndics of the communes must bow to their preponderance. It may be said, no doubt, in praise of the Sardinian government (if indeed praise is due to a levelling tendency common to all absolute powers) that various laws have been promulgated for uprooting feudalism in that island. In virtue of these laws the feudal jurisdictions have been abolished, and hence also the baronial courts; the feudal rights consisting in personal services have been commuted for money payments. But the complication of interests, the customary usages, and above all the weakness of the progressive element in this island, have led to these laws having been followed with little or no effect, and feudalism still exists there. Sad consequence of Sardinia not having been enveloped in the political whirlwind of the French revolution and Napoleonic empire, and of its not having participated in the beneficial effects which resulted from these to the cause of the people. Albeit that political tempests are to be dreaded and deplored, as the scourge sent forth by God's hand to punish the sins of nations and rulers, they may be likened to the hurricanes, which while on the one hand they cause devastation and ruin, on the other hand purify the atmosphere, renew the face of nature, and prepare the soil for a more vigorous vegetation. Sicily, too, like Sardinia, found itself deprived of those very advantages, but more favourable circumstances of genius, of greater nearness to the continent, and of a more energetic will in the governors, have promoted the extirpation of feudalism. It must be remembered, however, that the Sardinian government has exerted a certain measure of influence in preserving prejudices in favour of the nobility, by choosing noblemen in preference to others, for public charges and as officers in the fleet.

The legislation of the Sardinian government may be said on good grounds, to be modelled, or at least reformed, as has already been mentioned elsewhere, after the French code, seeing that in the duchy of Genoa, the civil and commercial codes are substantially the same with the code Napoleon, with the sole restrictions noticed in speaking of the Neapolitan code. In Piemont the ancient code was subjected to essential modifications in 1813, and from that time gradually revised, corrected, and ameliorated, so that it may now be considered as renewed and placed on a level with the progress made by the people. It is not thus as to the criminal code. The principle of equality is apparently recognized, indeed, in the law, but the publicity of trials, which affords a mighty guarantee of justice, is not conceded. Endless procrastination in the judges is another essential defect in the criminal procedure. It is true, indeed, that to obviate these defects, severe laws for the regulation of the civil and criminal administration were published along with the code. Severe penalties have been established for every abuse of power on the part of the judges. But when all might be efficaciously remedied by establishing better foundations, whose interest is it to give an impulse to a provision for particular cases, all the more inefficaciously as there is there no liberty of the press or of mutual association for the purpose of giving effect to one's own rights? May not the application of those laws possibly be confided to judges who are themselves obnoxious to like accusations? Of what avail can these laws be in case of abuses, or in causes originating in political motives? From 1821 downwards, there has been a cessation of the despotic measures which gave a stimulus to insurrection in Piemont, namely, the *safe-conducts*, and the *royal billets*. The former of these were privileges of protection granted by the king to noble debtors, in virtue of which the rights of creditors remained for some time in suspense. The royal billets authorized those nobles whose lands had been sold during the French invasion, to recover possession on paying the original sum disbursed by those who then acquired them. All this was done for the purpose of indemnifying or remunerating those of the nobility who had remained faithful to the person of the king. These arbitrary acts, although they have ceased now, will show what are the spontaneous fruits of the evil plant of absolute power.

Public instruction, although the government makes a show of favouring it, although, in fine, for the middle classes, it is placed within easier reach than in any other part of Italy, yet meets with the most serious obstacles. The regulations issued in 1834 gave the preference to clergy men in the matter of instruction, when the qualifications of competing candidates are in other respects equal. And as the state swarms with Jesuits protected and caressed by the government, it may readily be inferred that instruction is entirely engrossed by them. The *magistrato della riforma*, residing at Turin for the public instruction of Piemont, of Savoy, and of the county of Nizza, and the *Deputazione degli studj* in Genoa, are composed of laymen, and whilst the former enters most warmly into the instruction of the classes that are in easy circumstances, the latter is most favourable to elementary instruction, although its good intentions are frustrated by the regulations above mentioned. As there may be clearly seen in the former the remains of the aristocratical spirit, so in the latter the germs of the old republican spirit are budding afresh. In the island of Sardinia elementary instruction is making such progress, that out of three hundred and ninety-two villages, more than three hundred have at present free schools for children. Unfortunately the great number of monasteries prevents people from feeling the necessity for having establishments for boys belonging to the middle classes, from whom it would more easily spread afterwards to the lower classes.

About Tuscany I shall say all that is necessary to explain the tranquillity which it enjoys amid universal agitation. When with the republic in Florence there fell the last hope of liberty in Italy, the Medici family exercised a harsh absolute government, which was all the more unpleasant, the more fresh were the recollections of a prosperous democracy, and the more advanced the enlightened intelligence, the civilization, and the literature there, as contrasted with the other Italian peoples. It is true that in other parts of Italy at that time, the inhabitants were groaning under a foreign sway, but the sense of suffering was not so keenly felt on account of the moral and intellectual degradation in which they had been plunged by foreign domination. The age of Leo X., protecting the arts and literature, and crushing freedom, was an epoch of the most atrocious oppression for the Tuscan mind, however history may pourtray that epoch with a forehead crowned with light. Then, when after the lapse of two centuries, the house of Lorraine ascended the Ducal throne of Tuscany, that people, in whom the hope of a better state of being had begun to wane, yet in whom the generous sentiments of republics were not extinct, found themselves vivified at once by the provident cares of the new governors, who from opposition to the court of Rome, undertook the amelioration of the people's destinies. Leopold's administrative and religious reforms, although combatted and maligned at first at the instigation of the friars, proved afterwards sources of well-being and of civilization. Justly appreciated by the present generation, these have captivated universal affection to the reigning family, which has never belied itself, and after having given the first impulse to these reforms, has maintained and improved them. This gratitude and affection on the people's part, while they foment, on the one hand, the hope that during the future, reforms will go on to the extent of the concession of a national representation, that supreme desire of all Italians, on the other hand, induce men to excuse the tardiness and reluctancy of the government in condescending to the people's wishes. There is a general persuasion in Tuscany that the Grand Duke would do prodigies, were it not for insurmountable obstacles, and were he not tied down by the political system of Austria. Meanwhile, in spite of the reforms, Tuscany is not only on a level with other Italian states as respects its governmental system, but is in some measure beneath that of the Lombardo-Venetian states. It is enough to notice that according to the statistics, the number of children that receive elementary instruction in Tuscany, is in proportion to the population as 1 to 68, while in the Lombard provinces it is as 1 to 12, and in the entire Lombardo-Venetian kingdom as 1 to 10. It is very true, however, that instruction is not laid under bonds in Tuscany as it is in Austrian Italy, and no mention is made in the statistics, of private instruction which prevails most extensively in Tuscany, and not at all in Lombardy. The Tuscan government is absolute; there are no provincial councils there, and the municipalities have very narrow powers, their decisions, in matters of importance, being dependant on the government. The police there is severe, perhaps rather more so than elsewhere in Italy when we consider the pacific disposition of men's minds in Tuscany; which sufficiently shows to those who know how to argue from effects to causes that the sacred flame of liberty and independence glows likewise in Tuscan breasts, so as to require strict vigilance on the part of the government. It will be enough to mention here the order issued by the high police of Florence, to take away the inscription placed over the house of Alfieri. Tuscany has one advantage above the other Italian states, and it is this, that the Jesuits have no standing there. Not long since an attempt was made to open a Jesuit establishment; the people rose in a tumult, and the citizens and the clergy sent supplications to the government *individually*, because collective petitions, even under that *most mild* of all the Italian governments, are prohibited. And the Jesuits missed their blow. One of the purest glories of Tuscany is its having demonstrated to nations that boast of greater civilization than Italy, that the punishment of death is not in their case necessary as a bugbear to deter men from committing crimes. The abolition of capital punishments sanctioned by the grand duke Leopold, has produced the marvellous result of the diminution of crime. The reigning family of Tuscany being a branch of the imperial family, it may easily be understood that it acts according to the impulse that proceeds from the Austrian cabinet. This leads people to think that the mild appearances of despotism in Tuscany are directed to advance the interests of Austria, having for their object that of exciting the desire for a mild government. Still, dislike for the German remains profoundly rooted in Italian minds, founded on the desire for independence. But if love of fatherland and of national independence were not enough to make foreign oppression detested, Italy, besides the desolating spectacle of the Lombardo-Venetian states, has recently had before her eyes a still more nauseous spectacle of the influence of the mischievous Austrian spirit, in the fierce duke of Modena, who declared *that a king's prime minister ought to be the hangman*. The reigning family in Modena is itself, too, a branch of the house of Austria. The dukedom of Parma, under the government of the widow of Napoleon, may justly be considered as subject to the immediate dominion of Austria, seeing that German troops garrison Placentia. Although the French code has been retained there, its good effects have been nullified by the many modifications of it, dictated by Austria, and by the system of law procedure. The dukedom of Lucca, reserved to form part of Tuscany at the death of the duchess of Parma, when the present duke will succeed in that state, presents the beautiful spectacle of a people owning the lands they cultivate, a stimulus of the utmost consequence to activity and industry. Few poor people are seen going about begging, seeing that if they fail to obtain land the labourers emigrate for Corsica or the low shores *(maremme)* of Tuscany and the Pontifical states. Were the system of breaking down estates into fractions to be adopted generally, what advantages might not society derive from it? How would it elevate the tiller of the ground in point of dignity, and augment his activity and industry, to feel that he was not a slave compelled to sell the labour of his arms for the benefit of the rich! This system made the Tuscan republics of the middle age so powerful, and was abolished when the aristocratical spirit smothered the good institutions of the communes. It has survived in Lucca, owing to that having been the last to fall of the republican institutions of that epoch, although now for a long while deprived of independence and of the democratical spirit. Public instruction in Lucca, although not in a prosperous state, is more extensive than it is in Tuscany, the number of boys receiving elementary instruction being to the population as 1 to 54. Private schools, however, are much in use.

In order to fill up the picture of the political state of Italy, I ought not to omit these two diminutive states, the principality of Monaco, and the republic of S. Marino. The former of these, situate within the territory of the Sardinian states, with a population of about 12,000 inhabitants, is governed by a prince formerly a peer of France, who had it bestowed upon him as a fief under the empire. He obtained from the congress of Vienna, nominally if not in fact, the independent sovereignty of that corner. The king of Sardinia has the right of protecting him, and it is well known what is meant, at the present day, under the name of protection; a veil fitted to hide political thefts. The republic of S. Marino, in like manner, is under the protection of the pope, in whose dominions it is situate. It reckons only about 7000 inhabitants. May it not be the seed of the future destinies of Italy? It is impossible to read the future; but arguing from the great teacher of affairs, history, it may be easily inferred that, according to the ordinary course, the people will always pant to escape from despotism to complete liberty, and that tyranny begets popular regiments. Let it not be said that despotism, as it exists at the present day in Italy, cannot be called tyranny. Without entering into the confutation of this idea, which the reader has it in his power besides to find in the facts already related, I will only say that for the less fierce aspect of absolute power in our days, we are indebted to the obstacles which the advanced civilisation of the nations places, or threatens to place, in the way of potentates, not at all to any modification of the selfish tendency of despotism. I will say in plainer terms, that absolute kings are constrained to assume the mask of moderation. But if modern tyrants are in some measure unlike the Neros and Caligulas, the people, also, are no longer such as they were when easily contented with bread and with public amusements, *panem et circenses*. The Italians aspire after emancipation and the free exercise of thought, and these are precisely what their rulers fiercely refuse. Hence the tyranny exercised by these, is so much greater than that of the ancients, in proportion as the present civilisation excels the ancient rudeness and ignorance. Let me now be permitted to repel with indignation the excuse, constantly on the lips of the enemies of Italy (and the enemies of Italy are all the partisans of the *status quo*), namely, that it is not yet ripe for liberty. Those who repeat this mendacious insult, are the very same who have given liberty to Greece! What comparison is there between the civilization of Italy and of Greece? If it be true that civilization consists in the social virtues, in the love of letters, in the splendour of the liberal arts, and in industrious habits, Italy has a right not only to despise being compared with Greece, but to be placed on a level with the most civilized nations, taking into account the obstacles which it has encountered and still encounters, and the facilities that other people have had for their own improvement. Who knows not that liberty begets generous sentiments and strengthens good tendencies, while oppression disseminates corruption and tends to enervate all energy of mind and heart? What nation is there which, like Italy, after the total loss of its liberty and independence, has preserved the Muse's laurel crown in all its freshness? The genius of Italy has outrun that of other nations, in casting itself loose from the chains of tyranny; Galileo, Volta, Vico, Beccaria, Filangieri have opened up new paths in the sciences. But if even then, one would give the precedence to Greece over civilized Italy, because the former vigorously battled with its own oppressors, he falls into a most grievous error in confounding not only circumstances and facts, but further Italian civilization with the desperation of the Greeks. In Italy the desire for liberty is the offspring of thought and reason; in Greece it was produced by the brutality of the outrages which that country received. In the latter it was a fierce feeling of revenge; in the former there are manifestations worthy of a refined state of feeling. One of the fairest pages of Italian history is presented by the revolution of 1820, in the kingdom of Naples, and that in 1821 in Piemont, in neither of which was there a drop of blood spilt in the name of liberty; and moderation presided in all the proceedings of the new government. The same glory belongs to the insurrection in central Italy, in 1831. Let these pages be contrasted with the emancipation of Greece and with the first French revolution, and it will be seen how ripe Italy is for liberty. Then, as respects the difference of circumstances, I cannot refrain from taxing with impudence the enemies of Italy who dare, with manifest self-contradiction, to blame that country at one and the same time for being too *impatient* under the yoke of its legitimate rulers, and for not being sufficiently energetic in its impatience, in maintaining the war against its oppressors! But with those who defend erroneous principles contradiction is inevitable. Nor is it borne in mind that the Austrian, English, and French fleets fought in behalf of the Greeks at Navarino, while all Europe beholds with folded arms the efforts of Italy, and the European powers have armies ready to cross the Alps and to crush Italian liberty at the moment of its appearance. Nor is it remembered that brave sons of Italy fought under the Greek and Spanish banners, while nobody comes forward to make common cause with Italy; and while it was publicly declared from the French tribunes in 1831, in announcing the refusal of all sympathy with the insurrection of central Italy, "that French blood ought not to be shed for foreigners," forgetting that Italy had lavished hers in torrents in behalf of France. It is not recollected, in fine, that Greece fought under the flag of *religion* against the Mahometan oppressor, and that catholic Italy was taught to regard the flag of her oppressors as religious, and that of liberty as infidel. When the European nations direct their thoughts to the recent insurrections in Italy conducted by the educated class, and coldly seconded by the multitudes, without the enthusiasm that accompanies popular movements, they definitively pronounce as their judgment that the people have no relish for the word liberty. If they would but be at the trouble of taking the circumstances that have been mentioned into account, they would form a different conclusion, and confess that the people, taught by fresh experience of foreign intervention, and not aware, owing to the many barriers placed by despotism betwixt province and province, that the selfsame desire for liberty glows throughout all Italy, believe themselves exposed to certain loss without any probable hope in their favour. This idea paralyzes all their powers, and admirably explains the want of energy displayed in the partial Italian insurrections. The first element necessary for the success of an enterprize, is a belief in its feasibility, that is, full confidence being reposed in the force that is to be devoted to it. This made Alfieri say:

> . . . . . . *L'opinione del volgo*
> *Che il nostro petto invulnerabil crede*
> *Il nostro petto invulnerabil rende.*
>
> . . . . . . The popular opinion
> That holds our breast to be invulnerable,
> Itself our breast renders invulnerable.

Nor have the excommunications fulminated by the pope against the liberals, any great weight with the masses in Italy, since the clergy have begun to take a part in the onward progress and cause of the nation; were it not for this, should we not perhaps see the masses rise in arms against the educated class, as they were some half a century ago, even to wage a fanatical warfare on the mountains of Calabria, the Abruzzo, Tuscany, and Piemont, against the republicans and the French armies? On the contrary they second, or at least do not oppose, the movements in behalf of liberty. In order that no one may suppose that my patriotic feelings have led me to form exaggerated opinions, it will be of some use for me to quote the words of a French writer who has studied the political and religious position of Italy. La Mennais, in his small work intituled: "The Ills of the Church" *(Les maux de l'Eglise)*, thus expresses himself: "If Italy, for a single day, were left to herself (that is, without foreign intervention), if the existing order of things had no other support but the exhortations, the prohibitions, and the commands of the head of the church, the day following would see revolution extend from Turin to the extremities of Calabria." What idea, accordingly, ought we not to conceive of the progress made by Italy, if it has advanced so far as to combat religious prejudice with success? Some will suppose that the progress made by Italy, may have sprung from the political agitations that prevailed during the occupation of the country by the French. But this would be a very false idea as far as respects the masses, although it may so far hold true as respects that part of the population which is in easy circumstances. The French invasion has contributed rather to retard the progress of the masses by having given them an odious idea of liberty, by vilifying and trampling on every thing held sacred, and making open profession of irreligion. The pope's excommunications launched against the ideas of liberty, found a solid foundation in the public opinion of the people, who had seen the fruits of the tyrannical liberty of the French republic. In this sense, too, the progress left by the French invasion in the easy classes, has hitherto contributed not a little to retard the progress of the people. The people now, however, are convinced from facts, that whatever be the opinion of the liberals with respect to religion, in all the attempts that have been crowned with success, and in which these have assumed the reins of government, no violence, no offence has ever been done to men's consciences, and the clergy and the church have been respected. Let the praise of this fall on those good men who have removed the most serious stumblingblock in the way of the people's progress. But to what, then, are we to trace the progress of the population in the various parts of Italy? This is what we shall see in speaking of the religious state of the peninsula.

RELIGIOUS STATE OF ITALY.

It has been intimated elsewhere already, that the progress made by Northern Italy, differs from that of Southern Italy, inasmuch as the former may be considered as a participation in the progress of the neighbouring nations, while the latter, owing to the remoteness of the other European states, has felt but faintly the impulses they could communicate, and these indeed have sometimes exerted an adverse influence. The progress of Southern Italy has been one fruit of the struggle betwixt the civil power and the court of Rome, whereas the progress from abroad communicated to Upper Italy, is the fruit of reason disdaining subjection to the authority of revelation. Both these progressive movements lift the standard against Rome, but on the one flag is inscribed *Christianity*, on the other *Philosophy*. Hence the progress of Northern Italy, confined from the first to the educated classes, has not found any warm reception among the common people. There has on this account been a mighty impulse given to the activity of the educated class, in propagating instruction among the lower classes, to which we may trace the spread of elementary schools by means of the united efforts of the wealthy and the learned. On the other hand the progress of Southern Italy has found a solid foundation in the people, in so far as it has rested upon the Gospel, and has patronized their cause without doing offence to the essence of religion, by at once removing them from intellectual oppression, and teaching them a better way of being Christians. Hence the progress that distinguishes Southern Italy points out to the wise and prudent men who have undertaken to direct it, that the easiest method of persuading the multitudes is the amelioration of the codes, and the publication of laws directly adverse to papal ambition. Jansenism and Deism, both in the past and present century, have modified the religious ideas of the people of Italy. Not indeed that the people know any thing about Jansenius and his opinions, for their ignorance is most profound, and neither governments nor clergy have thought it for their advantage to enlighten the masses. But the constant opposition of the governments, and of one part of the clergy to the pretended claims of jurisdiction on the part of the pontiff, have taught the people that one may be catholic without any slavish and total dependence on the pope, and that their ancestors had been victims of the most enormous abuses, all germinating from the Vatican, and regarded with veneration as religion; and that hence the pretensions of Rome, always announced as the voice of God, might and ought to be conscientiously rejected.

Let us now examine minutely the origin of the Jansenist progress in the different parts of Italy, and the various circumstances which have had an influence in promoting or in stifling it. The kingdom of Naples, the grand-dukedom of Tuscany, the dukedom of Parma, and Lombardy, had almost contemporaneously the same impulse when their respective sovereigns undertook to engage in a tilt against Rome. The emperor Joseph II., as long as his mother Maria Theresa lived, attempted nothing in the way of reforming the abuses of the Roman court in his states, for he was restrained from doing so by that mother, she being a most superstitious person, and scrupulous in regard to the forms of religion. At her death, however, in 1780, he eagerly rushed forward to the aim that he had proposed to himself. He cut off the free and secret communication of the bishops with Rome, prohibiting their executing the pope's rescripts and bulls, except in those cases in which they were approved by the government; he abolished the ecclesiastical immunities; he subjected the regular clergy to the bishops of the dioceses in which they resided, in such a manner that Rome ceased to have any direct influence over either the secular or the regular clergy; he abolished the monasteries, with the exception of those which undertook the education of boys. And he effected many other reforms which I do not mention, reserving them to be spoken of in detail, or when describing such as were carried into execution in the kingdom of Naples under the ministry of the Marquis Tanucci; seeing that all the reforms introduced at that time, were animated with the same spirit. Leopold, grand-duke of Tuscany, brother of the emperor Joseph, went still farther, having proposed to himself the suppression of monachism. He placed it not only under the bishops, as his brother had done in Lombardy, but even under the parish priests. He suppressed the Inquisition; he subjected the profession of monastic vows to the severest restrictions. He improved the condition of the parish priests, by bestowing on them the revenues of simple benefices and of rich convents, and by abolishing tithes. In the dukedom of Parma, under the ministry of the French De Tillot, who governed the state during the duke's minority, similar though less important reforms took place; the immunities enjoyed by the ecclesiastical courts were abolished; restrictions were laid upon the Church in regard to the acquisition of property, and ecclesiastical goods were subjected to the common rule of taxation. In no part of Italy, however, were the reforms so great and so important as in the kingdom of Naples under the reigns of Charles Bourbon and his son Ferdinand. The Church had reached the utmost summit of preponderance throughout all Italy after the council of Trent, through the increase of regular (conventual) communities, and the number of bishops and of priests, who were cordially bent on keeping the people in ignorance, and on multiplying superstitions. But this was the case more than elsewhere, in the kingdom of

Naples, owing to its servile subjection to the dominion of the Spaniards, who were of all men most fervid in their zeal for the Roman church, and owing to the remoteness of the states in which religious liberty was endeavouring to diffuse the light of the Gospel among those who were in want of it. The clergy were immensely rich, and exerted the most ample influence over men's consciences. In the kingdom of Naples there were about 112,000 ecclesiastics, while the entire population did not exceed four millions of inhabitants, that is, they stood in the proportion of twenty-eight to a thousand. There were twenty-two archbishops and a hundred and sixteen bishops, a superfluity arising from the Roman court having adopted the system of multiplying to excess the bishops in Italy for the purpose of securing a majority in favour of the popedom at the council of Trent. The property of the Church, exclusive of the royal domain, amounted, according to some exact and circumspect authors, to two-thirds of that of the whole kingdom; according to others who, indeed, seem better informed, to four-fifths.

Such was the state of the kingdom of Naples when Charles of Bourbon, son of Philip V., king of Spain, reconquered the kingdom for himself and for his descendants from the hands of the Germans. Tanucci, professor of laws in Pisa, was Charles's right arm in the reforms of the kingdom. When peace between the government of Naples and that of Rome was broken, in consequence of the insults given by the Roman populace to some Neapolitan soldiers, although Clement XII. made honourable concessions to pacify the government of Naples (after having called in vain on Austria and France for assistance against it) Charles, urged by the finest Neapolitan geniuses and by the favourable nature of circumstances, to revive reasons of state against the unjust usurpations of Rome, succeeded in wresting from the greedy clutch of the Vatican the abatement of many of its pretended claims to jurisdiction, in virtue of a *concordat*. From that moment, Church property, which until then had enjoyed an immunity from taxation, was subjected to payment of half the common tribute, and all future acquisitions to the whole; precise limits were drawn betwixt the property of the clergy and that of the laity, which had till then been confounded among the estates of the Church, to the advantage of the clergy; privileges were reduced, customary favours recalled. The right of asylum, which until then extended to almost all crimes, was restricted to a few of the lighter offences. Formerly guilty persons found an inviolable asylum not only in the churches, but likewise in the chapels, the monasteries, the gardens attached to them, and in every building that had a common wall with the churches, or that stood in contact with them. It was now laid down as law that personal immunities are granted to the clergy alone, whereas they had previously been extended to the attendants of the bishops and to the lowest persons employed in the ecclesiastical courts, to the tithe collectors, to the servants and those who lived with the priests, and hence also to their concubines; the immunities were likewise restricted. The jurisdiction of the bishops was restricted and that of the common courts enlarged. Strict disciplinary regulations were established, and in order to keep down the number of priests, difficulties were interposed in the way of ordinations. This concordat was the first step to civilization and to the modification of religious ideas among the Neapolitans, although the hopes of the learned might extend farther. Nor among the well informed men of that epoch were there wanting ecclesiastics of high reputation, to give their support to wise reforms and to become their boldest patrons. Among these I will name only the philosophic Abbot Genovesi, and Monsignor Galliani, both Jesuits. But the concordat cleared the way for greater reforms, for the government interpreting, extending, and even going beyond its stipulations, enjoined lay jurisdiction, restricted the ordination of priests to ten for every thousand inhabitants, denied the validity of papal bulls not accepted by the king, impeded the acquisition of new property by the Church, and pronounced the censures of the bishops to be null when directed against subjects for having obeyed the laws. If contests arose about the proprietary rights of laymen and the clergy, they were always decided in favour of the former. All the licentious acts of the clergy were inexorably punished. Two friars of high degree in their orders, opposed the royal judge in a case of asylum; Charles ordered the criminals to be dragged by main force out of the church, and banished the two friars for ever from the province. A church was pulled down in Abruzzo, because erected without permission from the government, which had forbidden the erection of new churches, because they were already so numerous as to exceed the wants of the population. It refused licences to the Jesuits for founding new conventual houses; it withstood the haughty pretensions of that order, by prohibiting it from making new acquisitions. Although Naples may not have been the first to drive the Jesuits from her bosom, but the fourth after Portugal, France, and Spain, it has the glory nevertheless of being the first to pass laws tending to bridle their pride, as it was also the first among the Roman catholic states to make opposition to the Church, a rule of good government.

When, in 1759, Charles passed to the throne of Spain, and his son Ferdinand, a minor who had not yet completed his eighth year, succeeded him under a numerous regency, the Marquis Tanucci prosecuted the reforms that had been commenced. It was established that the king's ministers should see to the disposal of the goods and chattels of deceased bishops, abbots, and beneficed clergymen, and that the revenues of vacant sees should be laid out on works of public utility. Divers monasteries and convents were suppressed, and the property belonging to those establishments was vested in the commune. Tithes were first restricted and then abolished; it was declared by law that monasteries and convents, churches, pious places, confraternities, and episcopal seminaries, comprised under the title of mortmain, should be incapable of making new acquisitions; and by acquisitions were understood any new property, the enlargement of houses and conventual institutions, the dotation of churches and chapels, the endowments of monks and the patrimonies of the priests; and the eleemosynary gifts for festivals, processions, and masses beyond the prescribed limits. The same law prohibited notaries from writing testaments that should convey new acquisitions to them; it prohibited exchanges to prevent evasions of the law. In order to diminish the immense property of the Church, the same law declared that the rent of mortmain lands granted to husbandmen for a limited time under a long lease, or released to the same tenants, shall be equivalent to a fee-duty, and hence, according to the nature of this contract, the Church should have right to the canon alone, the proprietorship belonging to the husbandmen. By other laws, blows were struck at the pretended rights of the pope. Lay jurisdiction was still farther enlarged, while the ecclesiastical was to the same extent diminished. The number of priests was reduced from ten to five for every thousand inhabitants. It was enjoined that only sons should be neither priests nor friars, and that a family having one son a priest, should have no more such. If under Charles it was declared that no bull of the pope should be received without the royal assent, by a new decree it was further established that the old bulls, although they had already and from time immemorial passed into ecclesiastical laws, should be null and void, obtaining all their validity from the king's placets, and being revocable at the discretion of the king and his successors. Recourse to Rome without the royal consent, was prohibited; hence grants of benefices executed by the Roman chancery were annulled by the king: hence a check was put on the pensions granted by the pope upon the revenues of the bishops: the pope was hindered from uniting, separating, or changing the boundaries of dioceses; and, finally, the regulations of the Roman chancery were abolished. Matrimony was defined to be a civil contract by nature and a sacrament by accession, and consequently matrimonial causes to be of lay competency. While by these laws the powers of the bishops were increased to the loss of Rome, on the other hand episcopal authority was restricted and lowered. Bishops were prohibited from interfering with public instruction, and while by one law they were deprived of the powers of censorship with regard to the writings of others, they were themselves subjected to the common censorship in the case of their wishing to publish any work of their own. From very ancient times the bishops had the monstrous right of instituting legal proceedings against laymen for leading a dissolute life, and this became a pretext for indulging revenge and an instrument of greater oppressions, by condemning those who had the misfortune to oppose the ambition and greed of the priests to pine in episcopal prisons. Trials for wantonness were forbidden, and the episcopal prisons were shut. Personal immunities, which had been restricted by Charles, were now altogether abolished; the ecclesiastical sportulas were subjected to a tariff; and pious places were released from payments to bishops; various exactions that had been made by the bishops from a very remote period, were revoked for ever, and when they wanted to allege in their favour the right of proscription, the law expressed itself in this most wise maxim: *il vescovo come prepotente non prescriv*, i. e. proscription cannot be pleaded in favour of a bishop exceeding his powers, a maxim which triumphantly explodes all the sophisms of those who patronize the state of things established by force and not by the people's choice.

Ferdinand, on his arriving at majority, began the acts of his reign with the expulsion of the Jesuits, a bold and energetic measure which nobody lamented. He replied to the threats of Rome by retaking the temporal dominion of Benevento and Ponte-corvo, by disapproving and prohibiting in his states the brief issued by Clement XIII. against the duke of Parma, in which an excommunication was fulminated against all the kings that had banished the Jesuits. Accordingly, under the pontificate of Pius VI., he filled up the vacant archiepiscopal see of Naples against the pope's will, and laughed at his remonstrances. Shortly afterwards he made Francis Serrao, the learned author of many writings against the papal usurpations, and a most judicious Jansenist, bishop of Potenza, and when the pope refused to consecrate him, Ferdinand declared that he would have him consecrated according to the ancient discipline of the Church, and that he would do the same with respect to all the bishops whom he might choose in future. He refused to submit any longer to the custom that had prevailed in the court of Naples, of presenting every year to the pope a white horse, richly caparisoned, together with seven thousand ducats of gold; a gift dictated by devotion, and which papal pride openly called a tribute due to him as lord paramount of the kingdom. Ferdinand had by this time married Caroline of Austria, sister of Joseph and of Leopold, who gloried in the good laws of her brothers, a powerful incentive in making him follow in his father's footsteps and emulate his connections. The kingdom overflowed with Jansenists, and these gave support by means of their influence on the consciences of the masses, to the efforts of the learned, the ministers, and the magistrates, in diffusing by their authority and by their example the good doctrines of the reforms, while the writings of Filangieri, of Pagano, of Galanti, of Conforti, of Genovesi, formed a good preparation for the minds of those who governed the country.

In expelling the Jesuits the king had promised to introduce better order into the system of public instruction, and he applied himself with ardour to the task. He appointed salaries for teachers of reading and writing in every commune. Schools were erected in every province. The instructions were given publicly, and the professors were elected by public trial. The episcopal seminaries, of which the bishops were only directors, were declared to depend immediately upon the king. The bishops were deprived of all right of interference in public instruction. To a bishop who had raised a complaint against some professors for not observing the rules of the Roman catholic faith, the king caused this reply to be sent, that the sole duty of the masters of the schools was to profess and observe the rules of the Christian faith. Other bishops who claimed it as their right to interfere in instruction, or to cite the pontifical bulls against it, were censured and repulsed.

Thus were reforms carried out until the French revolution came and changed the mind of Ferdinand for the worse, by making it fierce and austere. For a course of about sixty years the kingdom of Naples had been taught to separate from the idea of religion what Rome set up for religion, that is to say, the ambitious designs and the avarice of the clergy. Old ideas came gradually to be buried along with those who had imbibed a prejudice in their favour from infancy when such abuses seemed sacred rights, and two new generations had entered upon a path altogether new. The laws were transfused into the conscience of the people. Besides the longer duration of the reforms in the kingdom of Naples than in Tuscany, where they commenced only in 1775, there are other reasons that explain how the progress of religious ideas is in a certain measure greater in the kingdom of Naples than elsewhere in Italy. The first of these is, that the reforms in the kingdom of Naples were developed step by step, while Joseph II. in Lombardy and Leopold in Tuscany ran too fast. Thus men's consciences received no shock. No condemnatory sentence from Rome reached the ears of the people in Naples; whereas in Tuscany first the sentence fulminated from Rome against the council of Pistoja, and afterwards the retractation of bishop Ricci, who was chiefly instrumental in carrying through the religious reforms under Leopold, first excited the people to tumult, and afterwards disheartened those who took part in favour of the reforms. In Lombardy aversion to the foreign hand that wanted to plant the good seed there by main force, caused it to be disowned and rejected. In the kingdom of Naples, on the contrary, the love felt by the nation for Charles was extreme, and such as enabled him to do prodigies of valour for a people dispirited by long servitude, when the Germans advancing to the reconquest of the kingdom, were defeated at Velletri. Not less was the affection which they entertained for Ferdinand up to the time that he became a tyrant, so that the French republican army under General Championet, after being everywhere triumphant, found a grave in the Calabrias and the Abruzzi chiefly, and in the other provinces, at the hands of the inhabitants who had armed in defence of the reforming king. The love of the Neapolitan people towards Charles before commencing the reforms, was a sure pledge of success; the love of the people to Ferdinand, after having accomplished the boldest reforms, was a testimony of gratitude to him, and an historical monument attesting to other nations that make a jest of Italian superstition, that Italy, far from disdaining reforms, welcomes them as the greatest benefits, when they come as the gifts of love and wisdom, and when no insurmountable obstacles are placed in their way.

From the French invasion till now every thing has been done to bring back the people to the old superstition but in vain, although progress has been in a great measure prevented. The suppression of the wealthy monastic orders which took place under the French government, immensely contributed to enlighten the people with respect to the true character of the monks and friars. Considered till then as persons withdrawn from the world, of an austere nature, and not subject to like passions with other men, they were held in esteem by the common people, notwithstanding that the educated class did not lose occasions of bringing their vices and immoralities to light. The mystery that involved conventual institutions and the spirit of corporation, threw a veil over all the irregularities of the religious orders. When at their suppression the hooded crowd spread themselves about, each returning to live in the world and in contact with society, that veil was removed, and the people could detect the true features of monkery, the spirit of intrigue, selfishness, and hypocrisy, combined with turpitude. This holds with respect to all Italy. Then for the kingdom of Naples in particular, the epoch of the constitutional government was one of immense progress. The clergy, both secular and regular, shared from the first in the general movement, and afterwards seconded it with ardour; so that when, more lately, the excommunication of Pius VII. struck all who had participated in the new order of things, the clergy found themselves involved in the catastrophe. But as the clergy had not only suffered nothing in that political revolution, but had been respected and favoured even so far as to be admitted to form a part of the national representation, seeing that of seventy-two members, of which the parliament is composed, ten were ecclesiastics, the most lively regret and affection for the constitution remained in that enlightened portion of the latter body which could appreciate the advantages of liberty. The excommunication from the pope was of no farther avail than to divert from the good path that part of the clergy which had submitted to the change of government as a duty of obedience to the powers that be, and as a matter of necessity, that is, the indifferent in the matter of politics, and the few partisans of Rome. The greater part of the clergy, accordingly, remained liberal in mind and desire. Meanwhile the people had a new and most useful lesson as regards religion. As under the constitutional government the clergy had pronounced eulogies from the pulpit and the altar on the new order of things, inflaming their hearers to the defence of the rights of independence against the Austrian arms which were moving towards the frontier, the people became habituated to the idea that liberty as already constituted by wise laws, by universal consent, and by the oath of the king, instead of being opposed to religion, was something holy and inviolable. What effect, then, ought it not to produce on this same people to hear it condemned from the same pulpit and the same altar, as a sin against religion? How were the people confounded at hearing benedictions invoked on the Austrian arms, and at beholding the ferociousness of the king in shedding the blood of citizens, announcing that his oath, most solemn and free, had been annulled by the pope? What was not the people's horror on hearing eulogies from the mouth of the clergy in favour of the king's tyranny and breach of faith involved in the violation of his oath, and the publication of the pope's excommunication as a rule of the catholic faith? Italian good sense could not avoid the conclusion that either the clergy had deceived them at first, or were deceiving them then. The whole force of catholicism, as understood at Rome, consists in unbounded credit being given to the teaching of the clergy as the organ of the church's infallibility, and consequently in removing all circumstances that might suggest a doubt as to the purity of ecclesiastical instruction. Rome knows that doubt is naturally followed by a desire for knowledge, and knowledge by the fall of superstition. While therefore, on the one hand, the church excited doubts in men's consciences, on the other the church itself, that is, the liberal portion of the clergy, did interest itself, and still interests itself, in resolving these in favour of liberty, and hence against Rome, because Rome has condemned liberty, and ever does so.

The matters that have been discoursed upon thus far, will enable the reader to perceive that in Italy it is now a century since people began to distinguish in what religion really consists, and to separate the idea of the popedom from that of catholicism; and that from the expulsion of the French downwards, they have begun to separate the political from the religious idea. Previous to the Jansenistic reforms, Rome tyrannised over the governments and the peoples of Italy; subsequently to those reforms, the governments shook off the yoke of Rome and prepared the people's consciences for a like result; since the formation of the holy alliance betwixt the king and the pope, fusing the two systems, religious and political, into one, the people, placed in the dilemma of renouncing every idea of social amelioration if they obeyed the dogmatic bulls of the popes, or of renouncing all religious conviction if they wished to follow the impulse of philosophy and of good sense, have taken the third way opened up for them by Jansenism, that is, of distinguishing the right from the abuse; and having been taught how to distinguish the church from the popedom, protest every day, submitting to Rome in spiritual things, but recalcitrant to its instructions as respects politics. On traversing Italy from point to point, this idea will be found clearly fixed in every mind; an evident proof of this is found in the late history of the various insurrections that have been seconded by the people, in spite of the excommunications previously fulminated against rebellions. What a prospect for the future to Italy when it shall obtain its civil liberty, inseparable from religious freedom!

But is it not true perhaps that superstition reigns in Italy? And how can superstition be reconciled with such religious progress as has been described? This seeming paradox is easily explained if regard be had to the populations of the South and East, to the interests of the priests and still more of the friars, and as respects the kingdom of Naples in particular, to the example of the court from which the reforms emanated. Liveliness of imagination, accompanied with a love of the marvellous, and with indolence, is, as has been observed in speaking of the Italian character, a quality that counterbalances the contrary element, which, indeed, is powerful there, namely, reflection and activity. Hence, in proportion as imagination is more lively and indolence greater, superstition exerts a greater influence over the people. It has been already observed that instruction, and hence reflection and activity, prevail more in Upper Italy and in Tuscany than in the kingdom of Naples, while the imagination is more ardent on the volcanic soil of the two Sicilies; the consequence of which is that, in the latter, superstition is much more prevalent. On the other hand, enthusiasm is the child of imagination, and this explains how the idea of liberty, and hence energetic resistance to the obstacles opposed to it by the Vatican, is so much more fervent in the kingdom of Naples, and in the Pontifical states, than in other parts of Italy among the lower orders. It is clear that one may be most superstitious, and at the same time most attached to the cause of social well-being. Now the religious progress in Italy, that is to say, opposition to the ambitious arts of Rome, has originated in the desire for independence in the reigning princes, and has increased with the desire for freedom in the people. Add to this, that Jansenism, which began the reforms and abetted them, was unalloyed in those wise persons who dictated the laws, but in the greater number of the clergy, not being sufficiently enlightened to comprehend all the importance of the principle which it had adopted, remained infected with the errors to which these were habituated. The essence of the Jansenist doctrine is to attribute the efficacy of grace to God and to deprive man, that is, the priests, of the power, which the catholicism of the popes has usurped, of opening the gates of heaven to believers. The ignorant and corrupt clergy could not attain to the elevation of this doctrine. They easily persuaded themselves that the external practices of religion, attributing their efficacy to God, either directly or through the medium of his saints, would tend to the same end; and so the popular superstitions were left almost in the same state as before the reforms. And it was their interest too that it should be so, since they derived advantages from the superstition of the people without being wanting to the observance of the laws established by the governments, these tending only to emancipate themselves from the yoke of Rome, and not at all to disabuse the people of the errors of Romanism. In this, too, the kingdom of Naples was more unfortunate than the other kingdoms of Italy, since the two reforming kings, Charles and Ferdinand, were of themselves very superstitious, to which we may ascribe there being no care taken to give a better direction to public opinion so far as relates to the superstitious tendency. Divine providence, indeed, has ordered things thus for the greater advantage of my country in its future, and now not remote destinies, for had reforms been precociously accumulated against both the abuses of the popedom and the abuses of Christianity, a risk would have been incurred, owing to the extreme ignorance of those times, of exciting religious fanaticism and interposing obstacles in the way of other possible reforms. Italy now waits for only a ray of freedom, and her superstitions will gradually disappear.

For the conviction of those who, notwithstanding these reflections, are inclined to regard as a paradox the religious progress of Italy in the face of the existing superstitions, I will adduce an incontrovertible historical fact. It is known how gross the superstition of the populace in the city of Naples is, and it is well known in history how the Neapolitans have ever abominated, even during times of the deepest ignorance, the name of the Inquisition, waging war upon it, sending embassies to distant kings and rising in tumults, on the mere suspicion of there being any intention to establish among them that abhorred tribunal. The latest example of this generous indignation on the part of a people so credulous and so superstitious, was given in the year 1746, under the popedom of Benedict XIV., when the archbishop cardinal Spinelli was bold enough to renew the attempt that had so often misgiven. On reading, cut in stone, over the gate of the edifice destined for the infamous tribunal, *Sant' Ufizio* (Holy Office), the city rose in a tumult, disowned and threatened the authority of the king, who indeed was tenderly loved; neither the lowest of the populace, nor that class alone which was superior in point of wisdom and liberty, but men of all classes and all conditions, even to simple country clowns, unanimously and eagerly united together, as if by one common instinct, in one sole desire, threatened with death two cardinals, and did not allow their excitement to subside, until the king signified by an edict his disapproval of the archbishop's proceedings, caused the inscription to be erased, and abolished the tribunal. The archbishop was constrained by public odium to renounce that rich archiepiscopal see, and to leave the city. Cardinal Landi, who was sent by the pope to obtain from the king some remission of the rigour of the edict, had enough to do to save himself by flight, as he would otherwise have fallen a victim to the popular fury.

What has been said of religious progress in Italy cannot be strictly applied to the Pontifical states, where the temporal government is in the hands of the pope. It is matter for wonder, however, that whether owing to what they hear from the inhabitants of other parts of Italy, or to their own good sense, the people of the Pontifical states participate in the same public opinion which attributes to the pope jurisdiction over spiritual matters, and denies to him any right of interference in political affairs. Superstitious and credulous though they be as respects religion, they have ever champed with impatience the bit of the papal administration, and been ready to fly to arms in order to overthrow the papal throne. In the educated class, indeed, and in that of the artizans, so profound is the hatred entertained for the priests, as to spur them to reject with abhorrence all that comes from that quarter, even to the Gospel itself. In other parts of Italy the Guelphs have recovered their footing for the purpose of maintaining the national independence, and the clergy, at least a great part of them, seconds their generous efforts, whereas in the Roman states modern Guelphs have found a Ghibelline clergy.

As regards Piemont, religious progress is less than elsewhere in Italy, and the reaction against Rome participates in what prevails in Lombardy, that is, it is founded on philosophy and rationalism; it is confined accordingly, to the educated class, thanks to the efforts of the Jesuits who have public instruction in their hands. The king of Sardinia has favoured and caressed that order for a long while, although it is now announced that he shows a progressive tendency. The king of Naples has himself too re-established them by committing education into their hands. In the city of Aquila in the Abruzzi, the Jesuit house was declared by a royal decree to be re-established in 1839, and the teaching in the Lyceum confided to them. The municipal body presented a petition to the king, praying that he would remove this public calamity. The petition was blamed and the Jesuits were sent, but they were received with a shower of stones amid the hootings and cat-calls of the people, so that the public force had to come to protect them. Austria, too, shows a disposition to re-establish them.

All the governments are in close league with the popedom in Rome, in the hope of their mutually supporting each other. The possessors of real power flatter themselves that the voice of the pope has power to persuade the peoples to renounce the idea of independence and of liberty; and the pope, on the other hand, thinks that by dint of arms Italy may renounce the ever-increasing opposition to the abuses that prevail in religious matters. Nor do they reflect that in this way they labour to accelerate their own fall, for the people of Italy will always shun the altar more, the greater the number of bayonets they see sent forth by Austria and from Switzerland, and will always have the greater detestation for tyranny, the more furious they see it to be in forbidding thought and doing violence to conscience.

It has been a great benefit to Italy that the monasteries and convents were suppressed in the time of the French, for their houses and estates having been sold, or applied to other objects, it was found impossible at the restoration to replace the conventual brotherhoods on their old footing. In every city, particularly in the kingdom of Naples, there are public buildings, lyceums, town-halls, prisons, hospitals, military barracks, and magnificent private residences, which were inhabited forty years ago, by friars and monks. Further, those conventual institutions that have been restored, no longer contain the same number as formerly. It calls for special remark that those orders, that possess property, such as the Camaldoli, the Cistertians, the Dominicans, the Carmelites, and others of a like kind, that require certain qualifications of fortune and birth in those who want to belong to them, have few novices, which shows how civilisation is advancing among the classes that are in easy circumstances. On the other hand, the mendicant orders, composed of the lower class, are numerous. As for the friarhoods, it is certainly to be remarked that liberal ideas are much more widely diffused, particularly among the young, that is, after the first movements of Italian liberty which were not accompanied with any violence against the clergy. This is far from implying, however, that the begging orders are not grievously hurtful to the people in whom they nourish superstition. From them there are distributed among the people hundreds and hundreds of religious toys, such as false relics, marvellous armlets, thaumaturgic prayers, cabalistic arts, remedies against witchcraft and witches, and other fooleries, employed for the purpose of extracting money from poor dupes.

One of the orders which is most distinguished by its retrograde tendency, is that of the friars of the Most Holy Redeemer, founded by Alphonso Liguori, lately canonised, and consequently called that of the Liguorinians. This order was instituted as a substitute for that of the Company of Jesus towards the close of the last century, and from its intriguing spirit, its intolerance, and the support it offers to despotic power, may be said to be a worthy scion of the Jesuitic tree. The government of Naples protects them in preference, even to the Jesuits, and sends them from one quarter to another, under pretext *of missions*, to spy out and sound public feeling, while acting as confessors. Many of the bishops have for some time been chosen from among them. Woe to the poor diocese that is visited with such a scourge. In the diocese of Chieti in the Abruzzo, the archbishop is a Liguorinian, who has ruined the diocese under the idea of reviving the middle age. Among other machinations that have been employed for this purpose, he succeeded in making heard during the night, by means of an old woman who had been suborned for the purpose with the promise of eternal glory, strange sounds, howlings, and other devilries, in the house of a very rich old man who had shown himself, and continued to show himself refractory in not executing legacies for masses to the church. He thought he should excite the terror of the diocese on account of such a want of compliance in executing such deeds, but instead of that only raised general laughter and mockery.

It would be too long to relate all the tricks that are put in practice for the purpose of increasing, or, say rather, of preventing the daily manifest decline of superstition. I stop for a little only to mention the many miracles that are wont to be fabricated for this purpose. The fable of St. Philomena has had marvellous success, and has found credit not only in Italy but wherever Roman Catholics are met with. A large book has been made up of it, which increases in bulk every year, containing the miracles God has wrought through her intercession. To give an idea of these, I will relate one of them which has fixed itself deeply in my memory, as apparently the most singular in the whole collection. A little girl, between six and seven years of age, having got for breakfast from her mother a good piece of bread, fancied that she would like to have a bit of cheese, more because she was fond of good things than because there was any hardship in eating the bread by itself. On the mother refusing she made a noise and lamentation, so that as a punishment she was shut into a garret. Half an hour after, her mother not hearing any noise, opened the door of the room and found her child smiling with a fine piece of cheese, and on being asked how she had come by it, the little innocent replied that a very beautiful lady had come to console her, and had given it to her, and on the mother pressing her to say if she knew the lady, the girl pointed to a print of St. Philomena that hung on the wall, saying that she perfectly resembled that. From this pretended miracle it follows that the saints of modern invention are most sympathetically disposed to gratify a nice tooth in others, and accordingly are at variance with the Roman church which enjoins abstinence. For my part, in this affair I conceive that the engraver of the print must have wrought the greater miracle of the two in divining so precisely the physiognomy of St. Philomena without ever having seen her.

Nor does the falsehood of the miracles that are registered in that book reveal itself only in the absurdity of the motives on account of which they are said to have happened, but I have had occasion to investigate the truth of a fact mentioned there, and have found it of false coinage. The most important miracle related by it, is that of a still-born child, declared to be so by the physician in attendance, after employing various and exact tests to ascertain whether there was a spark of life in the cold little body. It is said that after prayer to St. Philomena, the baby cried. Now, happening myself to have come into that part of the country where the miracle is said to have occurred, to preach a sermon there, I wished to inform myself about it, when I found I was the only person there that knew anything of the matter! As Francis di Lucia, the person who composed the book, resides in Mugnano del Cardinale, where the sanctuary of St. Philomena stands, at a short distance from Naples, where it is commonly believed that the Abruzzi form a half savage because a mountainous country, he thought that that miracle could never be questioned on account of the distance and the inhospitable position of the place, situated among the mountains and called *Novelli*. It is one of the ordinary tricks employed to accredit miracles, to say that they took place in remote regions; the want of newspapers, and of a free communication betwixt place and place, making it almost impossible to detect the lie. Besides, should any one succeed in discovering any of these sacred lies, he is compelled to shut his mouth as to the result of his investigations, if he would avoid incurring the censure of the government, which would charge the denunciation of a false miracle with the spirit of irreligion and impiety; and even admitting that some bold person were to despise that risk, his discovery would discredit the miracle only with a few, while the millions of the credulous would continue to hold it authentic, and the Roman church is in any case sure to gain by it. How many things are there not related in Italy of the miraculous medal of the Virgin in France! A Jesuit preaching on the efficacy of carrying this incomparable talisman about one, related that the present king of France, Louis Philip, having been induced by his wife, though with reluctance, to suspend one of them from his neck, has by virtue of this escaped death in the various attempts that have been made to kill him.

But the miracles trumped up by Rome are mainly directed to the inculcating of the maxims that are of most service to her, so that after having drawn the superstitious faith of the masses towards some male or female saint, they may be willing to receive from their mouths such instructions as are now-a-days disseminated in the encyclical letters and bulls of the popes. The doctrine which Rome has most at heart is that of submission to royal despotism, and, accordingly, she contrives that the saints always speak in favour of absolute governments against liberty. The apparition is well known of the archangel Raphael to a French rustic of the name of Martin, predicting the restoration of Henry V., now Duke of Bordeaux, to the throne, as settled in heaven in 1840. Heaven was made to speak in order that the thing might happen. But the calculations came to nothing. Saint Philomena in like manner in Italy, in her pretended apparitions, speaks of politics exactly in the style of the pontifical bulls.

The defunct queen of Naples, Maria Christina, whom Rome intends to canonize, has marvellously promoted, as has been already intimated elsewhere, the ends of the popedom, in persuading the king by a pretended miracle so far to re-establish the abolished immunities of the clergy and the jurisdiction of the bishops. One morning the poor widow of a soldier presented herself at the royal palace with a petition to lay before the king, wanting to be admitted to a conference, as having to communicate a matter of the utmost importance to the king. On being repulsed by the guards she insisted, made a clamour, and on being threatened unless she would be quiet, she broke out into such lamentations that the officers of the guard and others ran to see what was the matter; and passing from mouth to mouth, the news of this strange pertinacity reached at length the apartments of the king, who was told of it by persons belonging to the court. He then gave orders that the woman should be brought before him, being curious to know what this most important secret might be, of which she announced herself the messenger. The widow, after presenting the petition in which she asked for a pension, told the king that the glorious Maria Christina, sainted and beatified in heaven, had several times appeared to her in vision, encouraging her to present herself in her name to the king her husband, and to say to him on the part of God, that most heavy chastisements and grievous scourges threatened the kingdom and the throne, and that God's wrath would not be appeased until the church should be re-established in its former splendour, and God's ministers have restored to them the power usurped from them by his ancestors. The king, in consternation, or pretending to be so, replied that if the mission entrusted to her were really such as she affirmed it to be, his blessed spouse would not have failed to authenticate it with some miraculous sign; otherwise any one might have it in his power to boast of visions that were the mere creatures of his own imagination. Well then, rejoined the woman, "Santa Maria Christina told me that if your majesty refused credit to my words, it would be enough that I presented you with this ring, which she in the vision placed on my little table, and which on awaking in the morning I actually found there;" and so she presented the king with a ring. The king broke out into an ecstacy of astonishment, on recognising in it the very rich marriage ring with which the deceased queen had been buried. He called together the courtiers who had been present at the obsequies, at the sealing of the three coffins, and at the closing of the mausoleum, and they unanimously confirmed the fact that the ring had been left on the finger of the corpse. The mortuary instrument, indeed, left no doubt as to this. All that remained was to ascertain whether it was the same or another the likest thing possible to it. The report of what had happened spread like wild-fire through the city. The king with the court, the archbishop with the clergy, and the nobles of the city, with the most scrupulous formalities, attended at the examination of the seals, and they were found not to have been touched. The wonder and religious joy of the bystanders were raised to the highest pitch when it was seen that there was no ring on the finger of the queen. Thus the miracle was sanctioned, and care was taken to propagate an account of it by means of the press. The people readily believed it, on account of the very high opinion they had had of the deceased queen. Rome exulted in the fortunate result of her fraud. Intelligent persons groaned in secret at the new obstacle interposed in the way of progress. Woe to the man who should have exposed the trick, and reasoned on the fraud that had been practised; on the facility, in these times, of obtaining seals perfectly resembling any that one would wish to break; on the opportuneness, the convenience, and advantage derived from mystery in the stillness of night, which afforded facilities to the cardinal archbishop and his accomplices in the Imposture, to consummate it within the walls of a church impenetrable to every prying eye; on the facility possessed by the archbishop, by means of the directors of consciences, of finding in some petty soul of a female devotee, a fit instrument for acting the part of visionary, particularly with the smiling perspective of attracting universal wonder and veneration in consequence of having been found worthy of having celestial messages addressed to her, and at the same time of a life rendered easy by the enjoyment of a rich pension which she would receive immediately from the royal munificence. Still more luckless would be the man who should have reasoned about the political object of this sacred imposture, namely, leading the people greedily to drink in the idea that in heaven the absolute power of the king and the privileges of the clergy were made matters of special care; and hence that the king himself, too, might have had a share in that sacrilegious falsehood. But in spite of the miracle and of the superstitious veneration entertained towards the deceased queen, the king is held in constant detestation, and the bishops dare not avail themselves of the privilege they have wrested, from dread of the public opinion which had been already formed against the abuses of the ecclesiastical dignities.

I proceed to say somewhat of religious practices in Italy. From the things that have already been said, it comes out that the educated class in that country, particularly wherever they owe any progress they may have made to the philosophy of France and to German rationalism, are inclined, one may say generally, to deism, and sneer not only at the doctrines taught by Rome, but even at the idea of a divine revelation. I have discoursed elsewhere about the origin of such mental blindness. The middle classes, consisting of such as are neither wholly ignorant nor sufficiently educated to form a proper judgment and a religious conviction, either follow the religious impulse given by the legislation of the country, and by the Jansenistic religious progress, if conscientious, or if depraved in point of morals, they adopt the cynic sneer of the unbelieving, in order that they may show themselves off as men of spirit, or to smother remorse for an ill life. This, which is the most numerous class, composed of persons of all descriptions, proprietors, artizans, soldiers, and, further, of part of the lower people inhabiting the towns, has for its limit the earlier period of life; in as much as afterwards, when old age comes on, they go to the contrary excess of superstitious terror; for just as the voice of the passions becomes weak, conscience resumes her proper rights, and these too become all the more burdensome the more impure a man's previous life has been. This class, then, in old age, re-enters among the common people whose faith is sincere. The villager, although superstitious, is generally animated with a sincere religious sentiment: and it is a spectacle at once soothing and melancholy to see him conscientiously, and in the simplicity of his heart, exactly observing practices that have been inculcated on him as duties; to observe how absorbed he is in church with a modest thoughtfulness, during the recital of prayers of which he does not understand the meaning, and remaining for hours on his knees before the altars of the Virgin or the Saints. What would not be the energy of his faith, were it solely directed to the Author of the faith? All however, the enlightened, the moderately enlightened, the superstitious and the simple, all run in crowds to the churches on festival days, but it is easy to distinguish the former from the latter, not only from the indifference of their behaviour, their babbling, and from their having the air of beaux and gallants, but also from their never being seen at church during novenas and in other religious exercises of pure devotion, not of precept; a very clear proof that nothing but the bayonet of the Swiss and the gendarmes urges them to the outward observance of the religion of the state. To the classes which have been already mentioned there should be added another, which in truth is not very numerous, and consists of the hypocrites by necessity, that is, those who eat the bread of the government without any real merit; while those among them who are indebted for their employments to their talents and to their merits, certainly practise religion without ostentation, either because they think it their duty, or on the principle of submission to command.

And now as to the clergy. The greater part of them, owing to the goadings of their conscience, belong to the class of Deists; and consist of those who in the factitious fervour of the crafty education adopted by Rome for candidates for the priesthood, and for monachism, have been taught to consider the Roman Catholic religion as the sole ark of safety, and to regard Protestantism as an inconsistent system, conducing to religious indifference and to individualism. These finding themselves afterwards in contradiction with their own conscience, finding it beyond their power to obey the law of celibacy, contrary as it is to human nature, in all climates, but specially in the Southern races, and finding it impossible to escape from a state that does violence to their natures, and withal a state of sin, in as much as the marriage of priests is declared null by the church, and is forbidden by law, rush into Deism. What distinguishes the deistic priests from the same class among the laity is, their having no cynic sneer on their lips, and their not rendering themselves scandalous to the believing part of the people; although, on the other hand, they render themselves guilty of hypocrisy by affecting zeal for the external practices of religion. Another part of the clergy belongs itself, too, to the class of the half-informed, that is, to those who are not instructed enough to form for themselves a conviction, who live carelessly in the gratification of their passions, with the idea of afterwards repenting when the passions are calmed. These form afterwards in their old age the most powerful support of catholicism as understood at Rome. There is not wanting a last class, although very restricted in point of numbers, who, reasoning from the very principles of the Roman church, have succeeded in emancipating themselves from the law of celibacy. Thoroughly persuaded as they are, from their knowledge of church history, and of the times of the apostles, that celibacy is enjoined, not by the law of God, but by the command of the church, and knowing, on the other hand, that the church's precepts do not bind a man with much serious inconvenience, according to the adage most universally received in the Roman church and forming an axiom in canon law, have come to the conclusion that the same thing holds with respect to celibacy. Apropos to this, an educated priest belonging to this class has said, in the phraseology of Scripture, that celibacy is that yoke which our fathers could not bear, seeing that otherwise we should never have been born. Nor must it be supposed that the men of this class abandon themselves to a life of immorality; they seek out a companion whom they usually indoctrinate with the same principles, with whom they interchange mutual promises of conjugal fidelity; seeing that according to the Roman doctrine the two contracting parties are the true ministers of the sacrament of marriage, and the parish priest no more than the legitimate witness, whose will does not affect the validity of the sacrament. This class, accordingly, is the only moral one among the clergy, if indeed we except a very few in whom either fanaticism, or ambition, or a temperament cooled down by infirmity or old age, renders obedience to the law a matter of less difficulty. What has been said of the clergy in general, further applies to the regular clergy, or monks and friars.

Among the abuses of the Church of Rome, the two that have most influence with the populace, and that make them murmur against the clergy and Rome, are immorality and avarice. People universally lament the betrayal of the honour of families, and one rarely finds an Italian that is not convinced of the general corruption of the clergy; small accordingly is the esteem entertained for the ministers of religion, though there may be the very utmost respect for its observances and its doctrines. Public opinion, in this respect, has been formed by the clergy themselves, who have launched among the people the saying of Jesus Christ, in speaking of the Pharisees, by applying it to themselves, namely, "Do what the priest says, not what he does." Now if we bear in mind that the Gospel is not read by the people, it will appear manifest that the priests themselves must have taught it to the people; and in fact these words are very often heard from their mouths when they happen to be reproved for their libertinage. What shameless confessions are there in that excuse!

Avarice, one of the many features of selfishness, is one of the inseparable consequences of the state of isolation from family ties, and from society in which the Roman Church has placed the priest. The defenders of celibacy usually allege in its support, that matrimony, by making it necessary for people to occupy themselves, and to care about temporal property, and that the desire to accumulate money for children, would distract the ministry and call off their attention from the church. They do not consider that the state of isolation resulting from celibacy, brings along with it the melancholy reflection that in ill health and old age, there will be none engaged by ties of blood, gratitude, or duty, to render them those services of affection which the married usually enjoy, and that being obliged accordingly to have recourse to hirelings, or to nephews gloating upon wealth, they stand much in need of gold; that if it be considered how easily a man flatters himself with the prospect of living to extreme old age, one may infer how insatiable in general is the thirst for amassing wealth among the priests. One of the most evident proofs of the tendency to avarice in the Romish clergy, is to be found in the theory that the Roman Church has recently sanctioned, in canonizing its author St. Alphonso dei Liguori, whose moral theology carries weight as an authority among Roman Catholics. In Book II., sec. 3, 5, 31, and 32, he expresses himself thus: "The obligation of almsgiving in a rich person does not at all arise from the superfluity of wealth in his possession, but solely from the urgent necessity of his neighbour.

. . . . Simple individuals are not bound to show any eagerness in finding out the poor for the purpose of giving them relief. All they have to do is to make sure of not being deceived when they suspect the extreme indigence of any one. . . . . In the common necessities of the poor there is an obligation to give alms from time to time, when after satisfying the needs of nature and the exigencies of rank any thing remains over; but it is unnecessary to say, that there is no obligation to despoil one's self of every thing superfluous for the benefit of this sort of poor people. . . . . In a case of serious necessity, it is probable that there is an obligation to take from what is superfluous for the relief of a neighbour, when at least there is probable ground for believing that there is nobody else to relieve him," (this being what a priest will never believe, from a spirit of charity, and that he may not think evil of other people). "When our neighbour is found in extreme necessity," Liguori goes on to say, "one is ordinarily bound to relieve him on his property in some way necessary to the dignity of his rank. I have said ordinarily, for if the injury done to your rank shall appear to be more serious than the death of the poor man, there will be no obligation." This revolting doctrine, so opposed to the Gospel, tends only to foster the avarice of the rich, among whom the priests do not rank last; and it is the doctrine forsooth of a saint! The avarice of the priests in Italy is proverbial.

On the other hand it is a subject of murmuring that dispensations for marriages among relations, by blood and marriage, are got at Rome for money, where the rich have rights to the most extensive privileges denied to the poor. In the kingdom of Naples there is the bull called *della crociata*, which is distributed every year to such as want to be relieved from the severity of the abstinence imposed by the Roman church on fast days from eggs and milk food, at the cost of thirteen *grani* for the common people, double that for those in easy circumstances, and of five *carlini* for a whole family. This bull, which is in vigour, indeed, in some other province of Italy, was granted for the benefit of the court of Naples by Clement XII. on king Charles becoming again reconciled to him after the rupture that has already been spoken of. It is presumed that the money exacted for this piece of stamped paper, goes to maintain the fleet that is employed in the suppression of the Barbary corsairs, and to redeem Christian slaves out of their hands. Now, however praiseworthy this object might so far have been at the time of the bull being granted, it has no longer any existence now, seeing that piracy has been abolished; notwithstanding which this religious tax still subsists, and the pope and the king tell a lie every year. The people meanwhile become confirmed in the idea that the church is greedy of money.

Confession, too, of late years, has become a subject of peevish complaint, not only among intelligent Roman catholics, but also among the more public-spirited of the people, from its being manifestly prostituted to political purposes, by spying out opinions while dealing with consciences, and then by subjecting people to persecutions, or at least taking advantage of this espionage for the purpose of sifting the efforts of the liberal party. The revolution was about to break out in Rome during the carnival of 1831, but was prevented by the measures adopted, after notice of it had been received in confession from the wife of a tailor who had sewed the tricolor cockades. We are told, it is true, that the confessor had got the penitent's permission to give the information, but every body knows in Italy that such a permission is extorted by refusing absolution to whoever will not give it. In the kingdom of Naples, after the revolution of 1820, it was publicly reported that the priests would make up the lists of those persons who had taken a warm interest in the cause of independence and liberty, on the coming round again of the Easter that immediately followed the fall of the constitutional government. When an insurrection of any kind is dreaded, the government usually sends missions into the provinces that are supposed to be most zealous and resolute. These missions are ordinarily entrusted to the Liguorinians. The common rumour that the confessional has become an instrument in the hands of the police, is no groundless suspicion then, but has a plausible and clear foundation in the concordat of 1818, betwixt Rome and Naples. There we find the oath which has to be sworn by the bishops prescribed in the following terms: "I swear and promise on the Holy Gospels, obedience and fidelity to the royal Majesty. In like manner I promise that I will not have any communication, or take part in any meeting, or keep up within or out of the kingdom any suspected union which may prove hurtful to the public tranquillity. *And if either in my own diocess or elsewhere I shall come to know of anything bring on foot to the prejudice of the state, I will reveal it to his Majesty.*" These last general words afford good ground for the belief that even information obtained by means of the confessional, comes within range of the obligation contracted by the oath. This will appear still more evident if we consider, on the other hand, that the popes in their bulls against secret societies, fulminate the sentence of excommunication against those who belong to them; and, on the other, that *absolution from that sentence is reserved to the bishop.* People know of themselves that the bishops make every effort to show their zeal in behalf of the government, and fail not to pry into the secrets of men's consciences, being themselves chosen by the government, and looking to it for favour for themselves and their families. Nor does what has been said hold true with respect to the kingdom of Naples and the Papal states only; the same method is employed with all the governments in Italy. It will suffice as a proof to mention a fact that happened at Leghorn in 1841, at the time of the insurrection of central Italy. The wife of a house-agent having gone to confession, was so perplexed with the questions put to her by the confessor that, poor woman, she could not help telling him something about her husband's secrets. Hardly had two hours elapsed after her leaving the church, when the police inspector and gendarmes presented themselves at the man's house for the purpose of making a perquisition. The result was that the poor husband was thrown into the dungeon of a prison, there to do penance for the confession made by his wife. Yet Tuscany was in those times mildly governed, and of all the governments of Italy was that which ought to have been supposed exempt from such abominations, that is to say, from the prostitution of religion to the espionage of the police. What then might be expected from the other governments? It is worthy of observation, indeed, that such revelations are generally made by women, showing how just are the reflections of M. Michelet in the book he has published under the title of *Le Pretre, la femme, et la famille* (The Priest, the Wife, and the Family.)

From what has been said we may clearly infer that the foundation of the Roman catholic religion in the Italian populations, is already so much shaken, that its whole fabric is now in a tottering state. Doubts as to the holiness and good intentions of the priests, are creeping over the country and extending among all classes of society. The Romish Church has now absolute submission for its foundation. Yet there is no catholic country in which the principle of absolute submission is less received, and meets with more contradiction than it finds in Italy. This spirit of opposition to the tyranny which Rome exercises over men's consciences, increases more and more, and acquires force and energy in proportion as the progress of improvement spreads from cities into the country. But what will it be when new ideas traverse the peninsula with the speed of railways?

It remains for me to give a general idea of the influence which religion exercises on the people's morals. From what has been said of the slight observance, or the no observance at all of celibacy, it may be inferred that the Roman catholic religion, instead of laying any restraint on the fervid passions in Italy, rather contributes to the relaxation of morals. What is most deplorable in this respect, is that the scandalous example presented by the clergy has acted most directly on that part of society for which the moral duties are most sacred, namely, married persons. The marriage bed is the object chiefly aimed at by the priests and friars, in order to avoid the risk of having the depravity of their lives brought to light, by the fruits of their illicit amours. Could accurate statistics be framed of the transgressions of the celibate, I venture to say that the cases of seduction would be to those of adultery as one to a *hundred*. Delicacy forbids my going into a minute examination of the clergy's share in the demoralization of the people. This, however, is beyond doubt, that were the clergy to lie under the burthen of no other sin but that of plotting against the faithful observance of the marriage vow, that would be found enough to bring them in as guilty of the greater part of the disorders of society. By this the peace of families is destroyed, the education of children is corrupted and vitiated, interests are divided, the passions are let loose; hence infinite crimes and miseries. The picture becomes so much the sadder when we consider that Rome declares matrimony indissoluble. It would seem that in not admitting divorce, its object had been to favour the turpitude of the clergy. But however Italian civilization may now have laid some restraint on so great an evil, nevertheless, with the utmost grief, I find it necessary to bewail the misery of the lower orders, who still remain exposed to the insidious seductions of the priests and friars. It is not out of place to mention here an opinion recorded in all the Romish church's books on morals, respecting children born in adultery, namely, that should a mother feel remorse of conscience at the thought of such a child sharing in the family inheritance, she ought to do her utmost to induce the wretched victim of its mother's sin to enter some monastery or convent, and thus not to receive any part of her husband's patrimony. Thus the divines have not only found a remedy for their own remorse and that of their accomplices, but have opened up besides a most spacious way for bringing new friars in crowds into the monasteries. Apart, however, from these considerations, and judging from statistics, I cannot omit stating that however owing to the fault of the clergy, vicious tendencies have increased in the course of the last bygone centuries among the Italian masses, yet the morality of young unmarried women seems to be greater in Italy than in other civilized countries. It will suffice to give a proof. In the kingdom of Naples, which is considered as the least civilized part of Italy, in the statistics for the year 1832, bastards were to legitimate children as one to twenty-two, and in the Lombardo-Venetian kingdom as one to twenty-seven, while in the statistics of England for 1830 they were as one to nineteen. But if, in addition to these facts, we take into account the difference of climates, political oppression, the ignorance in which the masses are kept, the difference indicated by these cyphers will seem still greater.

As for theft, Italy has been severely judged by other nations; people founding their opinions on the old stories of banditti or on recent assertions of travellers, who, from having been victims of the cupidity of the vetturini, (men who lend carriages and horses for hire), inn-keepers, shop-keepers, and porters, with whom they may have had to do in travelling, speak in condemnation of the national character. The character of a nation cannot be justly estimated if we judge by places that are much frequented by travellers. It is in the provinces that the national character reveals itself in its true light. On this point I shall confine myself to addressing an invitation to English tourists to frequent in the tours they make the provinces rather than the capitals, if they would really wish to form a correct estimate of what is national in Italy. An Edinburgh Journalist has been pleased to charge me with making myself the partial eulogist of Italy without considering that the exaggeration of evil, supposed or real, into which all have fallen who have written about Italy, has made it incumbent on me to put in strong relief whatever good there is in my country. Had but justice been done to Italy, it would have been my duty to have modestly refrained from eulogising it.

To return to the subject, I find it necessary to call attention to the influence which confession exerts upon the people in respect of theft, not being such as the defenders of Roman catholicism boast that it is. However it may be that in some particular cases of certain precise sums being taken from known individuals, confessors cannot avoid inculcating the duty of restitution, generally speaking, in cases of petty thefts accumulated without its being possible to distinguish them, at the expense of various unknown persons, as happens in the case of dishonest tradesmen and shop-keepers, from the impossibility of general restitution, the confessors cut the *Gordian knot* to their own advantage by imposing on penitents the obligation of *having masses said*. But be that as it may, however, the inculcation of the duty of restitution is not confined exclusively to the confession of the Roman catholics. What Christian reading the Gospel, does not perceive the restitution of what is taken improperly from others, inculcated by Jesus Christ in the house of Zacchens. But by how many evils, and by what a pest of bad morals, is this vaunted importance of the Confession countervailed! We find an irrefragable proof of the iniquities to which confession serves as a veil in the papal bulls against solicitations, that is, seductions, in confession. But what avail the pretended rigours of the Romish church when set against the astuteness of its ministers in seeking the gratification of their boiling passions? May it not perhaps be enough, in order to their being eluded, for the confessor, on being made conscious of another's frailty, to wait for circumstances that may be favourable to his depraved aims? Further, although this

cases be included in the condemnations, it is clearly almost impossible to prove the charge. Nor is the confessional a source of immoralities only; it is also a most pernicious forge of intrigues that prove most fatal to domestic peace. Without entering into minute details, I will only mention the great part that confessors usurp in the making of testamentary dispositions, in which the least that can be looked for from the most conscientious is, their advising people to leave rich bequests to the church, or legacies for perpetual masses, to the prejudice of the heirs.

One of the most deplorable consequences of the celibacy of the clergy is the roughness and austerity of manners necessarily consequent upon a law which interdicts and dries up the fountains of the most tender affections. The harsh, dry, or, to say least, serious character of the Roman Catholic priest, is an argument besides in favour of their sanctity; hence it proves a safeguard, in the opinion of the people, against any imputations whatever of blamable frailty, and insures their being respected. From this harshness and austerity in the clergy, the greatest mischiefs result to society. Besides what is notorious, that it opens to men of the most unbridled passions the way to acts of excessive turpitude by their abuse of an ill-acquired confidence, there is another evil likewise which is still more universal and not less pernicious, and that is the immoderate rigour shown in the bringing up of children. Besides that education in general is confided to the clergy, families are regulated according to the maxims that are inculcated by confessors. That text of the Bible, *He that spareth the rod hateth his own son*, is repeated unceasingly in the ears of fathers and mothers, without ever calling to mind that other passage from St. Paul, *Provoke not your children to anger*. It would present a most melancholy picture were I to describe the life of a child during the course of its education until its majority. Threats, castigations, and reproofs on the one hand, on the other a timid and mute submission, all attempts at exculpation prohibited, diversions rarely occurring, and even then embittered with the dread of the rod. It is useless for me to pause for the purpose of developing the mischievous fruits of such a system. It will not be out of place, however, to note that it is intended by its means to dispose the new generations to absolute submission to the Church and the State. In fine, I shall give an idea of this system by relating a saying that used frequently to be in my father's mouth: *I desire*, he would say, *that you, for ten years after my death, may tremble at my name on reading it on my tombstone.* And yet he was a man who most fondly loved his children, although he always showed himself severe to them, and rarely gladdened them with a smile.

Let us now take a final survey of the whole of the religious practices, rites, and instructions of the Romish church, that we may see what are those ties that chiefly bind the masses of Italy to its communion. Among the doctrines that exercise the most powerful sway over the people's hearts, and that attach them most to the clergy, we must give the first place to that of prayers for the dead. I have noticed elsewhere that for a nation remarkable for tenderness and warmth of affection, the idea of keeping up a communication of love and friendship with objects that are dear to us, even when separated from them by death, is most consolatory and genial. It is said of some nations that they have the custom, when they take their meals, of leaving a place at the common table for the deceased members of the family, and considering them as present. No wonder, therefore, that prayers for the dead form one of the strongest ties for attaching the nations of the South to the Roman communion. The practice of burying the dead in churches, so prejudicial and unwholesome, has its origin in this doctrine, and in the misdirected fondness of the masses for their relatives. Hence the greatest difficulties have been encountered in Italy in endeavouring to introduce the general use of burial grounds; all the more since the clergy, with the abolition of sepulture in churches, must submit to lose part of the revenue arising from the belief in purgatory, that practice being a most powerful incentive with those who attend church, to open their purses when hearing discourses on the torments of souls suffering the purgatorial fire.

To show how strongly the hearts of the Italians are influenced by thoughts about the dead, we have only to attend to the form in common use among the poor, both when they ask alms and when they thank the donor on receiving them. " *Charity for the love of God,*" are the first words that the beggar addresses to the passer by, and if the latter seems not to heed, he usually adds, " *for the sake of the soul of your father and that of your mother . . . . ;*" after having got something, he expresses his gratitude thus: "*May the souls of your dead (friends) be blessed !*" Woe to any one who should imprecate maledictions on the deceased relatives of a country villager; he would become mad with rage and might run into dreadful excesses. Hence the Christian who should propose to himself the preaching of the gospel to Italians, or to Roman Catholics in general, ought to make it his first concern not to make too rude an assault on a prejudice which is so dear to them. In order to accomplish this, two methods may be adopted, both very gentle and not likely to give offence. The first is, to show them in what the *communion of the saints* consists, and the communication of the living members with the mystical body of Jesus Christ, making them to understand that if their deceased relatives have died in the vivifying faith of the Saviour, and if they themselves be regenerated in the blood of the Lamb, death, instead of severing the bonds of affection, has strengthened them, and glorified believers love them with the same love of Christ. The second is, to invite them to pray, and in their prayers to begin with thanking God for the innumerable benefits bestowed on all the saints, on the blessed Virgin Mary, the Apostles, the Martyrs, and especially on our deceased kindred and on ourselves, &c. In this manner they will be convinced that there is no intention entertained of depriving them of the consolatory belief in the certainty of the bonds of affection between the living and the dead. They will be convinced that in announcing the gospel to them, it is nowise meant to inspire them with sentiments of little respect or of disrespect towards Mary and the Saints, but only to keep this respect and this affection within their proper limits.

Love for the beautiful, which abounds so much in the Italian races, and which has made them as a nation so passionately fond of the fine arts, painting, sculpture, and music, finds aliment also in the Roman Church, which bestows its benediction on the fine arts by converting them into an element of religious worship. The pomp of her sacred ceremonies, the splendour of her worship, and of the furniture and habiliments that are employed in it, hold likewise a large share in the charm that fascinates the southern populations and allures them to Roman catholicism. However strange it may appear to many, I cannot refrain from expressing my conviction that *images* and the *splendour* of the *churches* may perfectly harmonise with pure Christianity, when those images are only used as outward means of fixing the attention on the things they represent, and when the splendour of the worship is directed to pure ends, not to the indulgence of pride and superstition. I do not think that that harshness in judging of others, which the re-action in religious discussions is apt to induce, and which may, without impropriety, be called Protestant intolerance, can be reconciled with the spirit of the gospel. These reflections will, with some people, bear the aspect of *a residue of Romanism;* sensible persons, however, will clearly see from the spirit that has dictated this essay how far removed I am from Romanism. But if any doubt remain, it ought to vanish on reading a last observation on the doctrine which most recommends itself to the passions of the people of Italy, and which forms the strongest of the ties that bind them to the Church of Rome.

The Church of Rome teaches that the good works of a Christian, in a state of grace, merit the glory of paradise. On the other hand, it teaches that if the Christian falls into sin, he loses, no doubt, all *the good works* previously accumulated, yet by no means for ever, but only as long as he fails to repent of the sin he has committed. Hence the sinner in the Church of Rome returns into the possession of all his good works at the very instant of his repentance. In the language of theology, the good works of the sinner, performed during his sinful state, are called *dead works*, and avail nothing—good works, anterior to sin, are called *works made dead*, which *come to life again (reviviscunt)* by means of repentance. This doctrine suits well with the character of the South, so passionate and so ready, under the impulse of circumstances, to abandon itself to virtuous or vicious transports with equal ardour. The carnival is preceded by the fastings and the prayers of Advent, and precedes the haggard looks and the repentance of Lent. The games, balls, theatres, revels, and mad outrageous mirth of the carnival, are immediately followed by the devout practices, the manifold mortifications, the fasting and penitential tears of Lent. This alternation of good works and of sins, this facility of accumulating a treasure of good works for everlasting glory, without relinquishing one's diversions or making war upon the passions upon earth; this little difficulty found in obtaining absolution from sins which people mean to commit again as soon as the season for repentance is past, are very strong enticements to the masses, and powerfully serve to endear to them the Roman Catholic religion. I do not say, indeed, that the doctrine of the Roman Catholic church is such as encourages sin, and promises absolution from sin to those who mean to return to it again; but I certainly do say, that the people view the matter in that light, and cannot but do so, owing to the profound ignorance to which the masses are condemned by the Church of Rome. How can they attach any other meaning to it? The church herself *tacitly* encourages this erroneous interpretation of her doctrine, an interpretation most fatal to morality and to the salvation of souls. The church has never proscribed, or at least reprobated, the custom of representing the archangel Michael with scales in one hand, a sword in the other, and the devil beneath his feet. The usual interpretation given by the common people (and in this term we must include the greater number of the friars and monks) to this image is, that when one is at the point of death, the archangel Michael sets himself *to weigh the dying person's good works against his bad*, and according as the former or the latter preponderate, conducts his soul to heaven, or hands it over to the devil, to be dragged to eternal punishment; but if neither of the scales weighs up the other, that is, if the good works are in equilibrium with the bad, he will open to the soul the gates of purgatory, in order that its fires may consume the bad and purify the good—as with gold in the crucible. Such representations of St. Michael are to be seen in the churches—so that, how can the people fail to be led into error?

Here we see the grand charm that attaches the masses with so firm a hold to Romanism, that is to say, the persuasion that it is possible to conciliate a sinful indulgence of the passions with Christian virtue—Christ with Belial. That rigid virtue which springs from faith in Jesus Christ, which is the death of the old man that we may live of the life of the Saviour, acts as a bugbear on the Roman Catholic, all the while he remains ignorant that the doctrine of the Church of Rome condemns that very thing which he fancies it approves. The grand force of the Church of Rome consists in the ignorance of the masses. While in controversy she furbishes up and burnishes the arms of her doctrine, so that they dazzle those that look at them, she leaves them to grow rusty in the hands of her own followers, so that they can scarcely be recognized. The Roman Catholic doctrine, as it is recorded in books, is infinitely remote from that which she sanctions in practice and in discipline. The whole secret of Romanism lies in this *illusion* of making people believe that it teaches the doctrine that it defends in controversy with so much noise and as with the sound of a trumpet, while it really teaches a different and a *corrupting* doctrine. The *clergy who teach*, and the people who receive instruction without being authorized to investigate its soundness, are the springs of that insidious machine. Let the masses but instruct themselves, and Rome will behold her empire over men's consciences escape from her grasp.

And now I come to the close of this essay, in order to complete which, I would need to say something on the commerce, the industry, and the arts in Italy; but the limits prescribed to me will only admit of my summing up the subjects that have been discoursed upon, with the view of deducing from them such lessons as may be of use to the reader.

Italy has, at two different epochs, been the nursing-mother of civilization to other nations—she has in herself then the elements of life and energy. But how has she fallen into that state of debasement and impotency in which she has now been languishing for three centuries? The investigation that this question would require, would necessarily occupy many a long page, were I to think of treating it in detail and to follow out the various ideas that present themselves to my mind; but, concentrating these in one, I would point to the cause of all the woes of Italy, in the new aspect assumed by Romanism in the sixteenth century, synthetically represented by Jesuitism. It will strike every one who sets himself to examine the history of the church, that society has always followed the development of the religious idea, and the political form of society has been nothing more than a copy and image of the form of the church. When the bishop was nominated by the acclamation of the people, the head of the people was elected in the same manner. When the bishops formed a sort of feudal league, the pope, in attempting to raise himself to an absolute supremacy, found the same resistance in them that at that epoch the kings of Europe found in their barons. When the bishops re-asserted their rights, and when at Basel, and at Constance, the pride of the popedom was humbled, the *communes* of France, the *cortes* of Spain, and the parliaments of England, followed the example in the political order of things. A council deposed the pope—the state deposed the emperor and two kings. Now, as at the council of Trent, the church of Italy, and along with it catholicism, allowed itself to be entirely absorbed by the Vatican—in such a manner that, from that epoch down to the present time, the pope has represented the church—so, in the political order, kings have represented the state. "*France, that is, myself,*" said Louis XIV. The absolutism of kings followed the absolutism of the pretended head of the church. Hence the nationality of Italy disappeared, and it is nationality that forms the force of nations. Italy was the first to lose her nationality, and hence with it all weight in political Europe. Spain gradually lost her splendour from the time that Philip II. gave his kingdom the form that had been assumed by the Roman Church, that is, *absolutism*. France, Austria, Portugal, and all the rest of Europe that remained subject to Rome, came to be regulated according to the sacred model *of absolute government*. The French revolution broke the charm, and all nations in which the spirit of democracy is boiling, have felt again the throbbings of renovated life, and of these Italy is not the last. Woe to the nations to which Romanism gives absolute law! Woe especially to those nations which, from being embued with aristocratical maxims and prejudices, allow themselves to be seduced by Rome; once seduced, they will find it a hard task to withdraw themselves from servitude. May Italy serve as an example to England, to which Rome's gloating eyes are now directed, as to an exceedingly rich and desirable prey. The English aristocracy cannot fail to favour the efforts of the church of Rome, when called to make head against the ever-waxing efforts of a democracy that threatens their privileges. Oxford cannot hesitate in the choice between Rome with its despotism, and Protestantism with its evangelical maxims tending to *equality*. Never let England forget that Italy owes her degradation to the popedom, and, accordingly, that she too will cease to be great, prosperous, and free, when Rome shall regain her ancient ascendancy in this kingdom. The celebrated Vincenzo Gioberti, in his work on the Primacy of the Italians, endeavours to separate Jesuitism from the popedom, and while he attributes the ills of Italy to Jesuitism, he makes himself the warm defender of the Roman pontificate. But how often do even men of great genius allow themselves to be the dupes of an illusion! To condemn Jesuitism and laud the popedom, while the popedom lauds Jesuitism and identifies itself with it!!! and condemns those that make war upon it!!! To conclude, therefore, and in warmly recommending my readers not to allow themselves to be seduced by the bland appearances that Romanism assumes, I cease not to repeat that they should not lose sight of the political and moral state of Italy, as being that from which they may gather what Romanism essentially is. *A tree must be judged by its fruits.* But if they would ascribe bad fruits to the Jesuitical tree, is not that a bud of Romanism? May the Lord deliver the earth from both.

SKETCH

OF

THE HISTORY AND PROGRESS OF ITALY,

DURING THE LAST FIFTEEN YEARS (1847-1862).

IN CONTINUATION OF DR. MAPEI'S ESSAY.

BY THE

REV. GAVIN CARLYLE, M.A.

SINCE the former Essay was written, the fortunes of Italy have materially changed. Groaning under Austrian oppression, the people of that country were, for many years after 1815, among the most miserable and down-trodden in the world. With high aspirations after liberty—with much native genius, which would have fitted them to use it with moderation—they were under various pretexts ground to the dust, and made the slaves of a despotism which ruled at Vienna, but found its strongest support in Rome. The people of Italy could not patiently submit to such a yoke; while their princes, having no security in the hearty devotion of their subjects, leaned upon this foreign power for support, and called for its aid in every time of emergency. All men of true political insight felt that this could not last long. Even Metternich himself, the ruling mind of the system, feared that it would fall to pieces so soon as his ingenious contrivances for its support gave way—and he himself lived to see the first symptoms of its destruction.

From 1815 to 1848, Italy was never at rest. The volcanic fires moved beneath the soil, and tremblings of the earth were often felt, which showed that the eruption was approaching. In 1820 the constitutional movement took place in Naples, referred to in the previous Essay, which gave evidence of the wisdom and moderation of the liberal party, and which was crushed only by the unwarranted and illegal interference of Austria, and the foulest treachery on the part of the king. Austrian troops were permitted by the European powers to take possession of the city in 1821, to aid the king in treading out the last embers of the constitution which he had sworn to maintain. The treaty of Laybach, to which our own country consented, not greatly to the credit of the government of the day, supported this interference. In 1823 Prince Metternich, then in the height of his power, uttered the dictum, "The representative system, with the institutions which necessarily result from it, cannot, and ought not to, be established in any state of the Peninsula." Thus Austria, without any just right to such authority, dictated a policy to the entire Peninsula.

In 1822, Austria attempted to decide the fate of Sardinia by setting aside Charles Albert, Prince of Carignano, then heir to the throne, because, when acting as regent in the absence of Charles Felix, he had appeared to be favourably disposed to the constitutional cause. She first sought to have the Salic law set aside, that the Duke of Modena, one of the most abject of her tools, son-in-law of the reigning king, might succeed to the throne. Defeated in this manœuvre by France and Britain, she attempted next to get the infant Victor Emmanuel nominated immediate successor, on the understanding that he should be early removed to Vienna, and educated there, under the auspices of the family of his mother, who was an Austrian princess. This plan was also defeated by other powers; but its attempted accomplishment showed her resolution to hold all parts of Italy in her power, and to prevent the least opportunity of the establishment of constitutional liberty. Such treachery, however, often over-reaches its own ends. These plots were probably never forgotten by Charles Albert, and fixed his determination, deeper than before, to stand by his country, and to regard Austria as her inveterate foe.

A general insurrection, which was stimulated by the success of constitutionalism in Paris in the previous summer, took place in the year 1831, in Central Italy. Though it was overcome, and though numerous victims were cruelly imprisoned, tortured, and killed, the country was never again effectually at rest. Here and there the flame unexpectedly burst forth, and even where no signs appeared, it was well known that the people were burning for vengeance, and were waiting impatiently for the first opportunity to break their chains. To Mazzini, though he promoted many foolish schemes, the credit must be given of having kept alive the desire of the Italians for liberty and unity, at a time when everything seemed to be against them. He often may have appeared to do mischief by urging men to expose their lives in fruitless attempts; but these attempts were noised abroad, and the very cruelty of the measures taken to repress them made the iron burn into the soul of the people, and prevented them from sinking down into sluggish or despairing indifference. This credit must undoubtedly be given by all impartial persons to Joseph Mazzini, however much his policy in the war of 1848, and his frequent attempts to force republicanism upon his unwilling countrymen, may be censured.

Charles Albert appears to have formed a resolution, from the beginning of his reign, to resist the encroachments of Austria, and to promote the independence, and perhaps the liberty also, of his fellow-countrymen. His reign indeed began inauspiciously enough. He belied the hopes of the liberal party by surrendering the power into the hands of the clergy, so that Piedmont was for some years one of the most priest-ridden of the Italian kingdoms. This policy may have resulted partly from his naturally superstitious temperament, but appears to have been dictated chiefly by motives of policy. He knew how insignificant was the power of Piedmont in comparison with that of Austria, and felt that it was necessary to put Austria off her guard, and to proceed wilily in the preparation of his schemes. He had experienced once the imminent danger of expressing liberal opinions in the presence of so determined a foe, and knew not but that, if he were to do so again, he might lose his throne, without benefiting his country. There are many indications that the acts of the latter part of his reign resulted from no sudden change of policy, but were only the development of a scheme which he had contemplated from its commencement. It seems now to be placed beyond doubt that his remark, at an early period of his reign, in reference to the strict economy that he had introduced into his finances, "It is to enable us to do great things," bore reference to the ultimate object he had in view. His disregard of Austrian interference with his military arrangements in 1838, may be regarded as of equal significance, and also a phrase which he is said at the time to have frequently repeated, "The time is not yet come." Gualterio remarks that the ruling purpose of his mind was most forcibly disclosed in some of his retrospections and observations in 1840. In these, the following passage was transcribed from Deuteronomy:—"Thou mayest not set a stranger over thee that is not thy brother." When these different facts are put together, and associated with the determination of the latter acts of his reign, when he refused to separate himself from the cause of Italy after all other Italian princes had deserted it, there are strong reasons for believing that he had in view the emancipation of Italy from the intolerable Austrian yoke during his entire reign.

Strangely enough, the revolution which convulsed Italy, and extended its influence over Europe, began within the walls of the Vatican. The election of the liberal Cardinal Mastai Ferretti to the popedom, in June, 1846, gave new hopes to the liberal party, which were stimulated by the first act of his reign. On the 16th of July, 1846, one month after his election, he granted an amnesty to all Roman subjects imprisoned or exiled for political offences. This event caused a jubilee of transport, which vibrated through all parts of Italy. The pope was hailed everywhere with gratitude and affection, and great hopes were entertained that the Papacy would head the liberal movement. Such hopes were seen to be utterly baseless by those who understood the genius of the popedom; but they filled the minds of the people, and caused a general rejoicing. The pope made himself easy of access; listened to the complaints of his subjects; examined into the state of the convents by personal inspection; removed the most irksome restraints of the Jewish population; supported projects for the making of railroads, and otherwise promoting the material interests of the States; dismissed dishonest officials; contemplated measures for the extension of solid education; sanctioned the establishment at Rome of a political journal; formed a council of state, composed of deputies from the provinces, to assist him in deliberating on the requirements of the country; secularised many of the official appointments; conceded the formation of a national guard; and, as the crowning act, granted a constitution.

The pope, when he had begun his reforms, was undoubtedly led on to greater lengths, and at a more rapid pace, than he had expected. It would, however, be unjust to represent him as intentionally wishing to deceive the people. He had for many years been among the most liberal of the cardinals; he had seen with pain the abuses tolerated under his predecessor; and he wished to ameliorate the state of the people, and perhaps to deliver them from the foreign yoke. If he violated all his promises at a later period, it was rather because he had attempted an impossibility, and found himself in a position where he had lost all control; and because he felt that his duties to the church were supreme over all others, and that her interests were committed to his charge, than from any premeditated design to betray the cause which he at first supported. We rather see, in his failure, the utter impossibility of reconciling the papal system with the liberal tendencies of the present age, than anything crafty or treacherous in the man. He weakly attempted to reconcile what, to all far-sighted men, whether friends or foes of the Papacy, was, from the first, seen to be irreconcilable.

The pope had no sooner begun to excite the hopes of Italy, than the other princes were compelled, willingly or unwillingly, to follow his lead. Charles Albert alone among them rejoiced in the opportunity, beginning that career of reform from which he never receded. On the 30th of October, 1847, there appeared a royal decree, which granted not only the desired liberty of the press, but embodied extensive and important changes in the criminal courts and the action of the legislature, and regulated the powers of the police. On the 8th of February, 1848, the constitution of Sardinia was proclaimed amidst the enthusiasm of the people. This constitution embraced religious as well as civil liberty, and broke down the barriers which for centuries had shut up the ancient church of the Vaudois within the fastnesses of the Alps.

From this period, Charles Albert went forward in the cause which he had undertaken with unflinching energy. He not only disregarded the counsels of Austria, which were delivered in a threatening tone, but was stimulated by them to proceed with greater determination. The critical period had arrived for which he had long prepared; the wrongs of the past to himself and his country were treasured up in his memory, and were now to be avenged; the hour of deliverance had come from that intolerable yoke of the Jesuits, to which he had submitted in order the better to cover his ultimate designs; now or never, the battle of Italian independence was to be fought, and nothing would tempt him to surrender the sacred cause. The people of Lombardy, excited by the general revolution which, successful in Paris, had everywhere become popular, drove out the Austrians from Milan, and invited the Sardinian king to its defence and aid. Staking his crown upon the result, Charles Albert entered the Lombard territory, and was received triumphantly at Milan. He then advanced, almost single-handed, to the formidable line of the Mincio and Adige, fought the famous battle of Goito with 18,000 men, and took the fortress of Peschiera.

Had Charles Albert been properly supported at this juncture, it is not improbable that Austria might for ever have been expelled from Italy. Weakened by revolutionary war in Hungary, and threatened with revolution even in Vienna, she could scarcely have stood the shock of an attack of the united forces of Italy. But Mazzini and the republicans, suspicious of Charles Albert's motives, and fanatically attached to the republican idea, stood in the way, refusing to give their co-operation. Their suspicions of the king were perhaps justifiable, after the long reactionary course which he had pursued; but their determination to bind their countrymen to the republican cause, before the enemy had been expelled—to force republican principles upon them, whether they would or not—was imprudent and arbitrary. The Italians have not forgotten this wrong, and it has for ever destroyed the cause of Mazzinianism in Italy. The king, however, was scarcely entitled to expect, all at once, the full confidence of his countrymen. It was necessary that he should be sacrificed, and that Italy's brighter day should dawn under the influence of his son.

The tide began soon to turn. The reaction commencing in Paris with the dreadful days of June, when many thousands fell in civil conflict in the streets, excited anew the hopes of Austria and her allies. Italy was scarcely prepared for the good fortune which seemed so suddenly to have arisen for her. Torn asunder by internal conflicts, there was no unity of plan for opposing the common foe. Anarchy prevailed in the councils of the new governments. At Florence and at Rome, affairs soon fell into a state of confusion through the rivalship of various factions. Charles Albert, deserted of all, could not single-handed retain the provinces he had won. In the month of July, Radetzky had congregated a hundred thousand troops around Verona, in a perfect state of discipline. The Piedmontese army did not number above sixty thousand. A portion of it was engaged in carrying on the blockade of Mantua. The rest were exposed to separate attacks in various parts of the famous Quadrilateral. Charles Albert, who felt that his army was thus exposed to destruction in detail by the management of Radetzky, who was in position to fall upon various portions of it in succession, determined to risk a pitched battle, or was rather forced to this alternative. The battle of Custoza was fought. The forces of the Austrians nearly trebled those of the Sardinians. The latter, after a valiant defence, were put to flight, and driven in confusion to Milan. Lombardy speedily fell again under Austrian rule, and Parma and Modena were also restored to their fugitive princes. As the year advanced the confusion in Rome and other cities increased, and the strife of the different parties gave sure indication of the failure of the national cause. In the month of November all Europe was startled by the daring murder of Count Rossi, the pope's constitutional minister, upon the steps of the Capitol, as he was proceeding to the chamber of deputies. Soon afterwards the pope fled from Rome, and the capital of the Papacy was left under the rule of the republican party.

The year 1849 opened under strangely confused aspects, as regarded the Italian people. The Austrians had, as we have seen, reasserted their power in Lombardy; though Venice, the Queen of the Adriatic, still proudly maintained her independence. The pope was in exile at Gaeta, while a liberal ministry, whom he denounced, continued to rule in his name at Rome. His policy destroyed the influence of the constitutional party, and assisted the cause of the republicans, whose triumphs were hailed by the reactionists. At length, upon the 8th of February, 1849, the pope's deposition from the temporal power was pronounced, the populace saluting the announcement with frantic applause; and the Roman republic, a name which recalls so many sacred associations, was proclaimed.

This formal deposition of the pope roused the antagonism of the Catholic nations, who began to vie with each other for the honour of restoring the "holy father" to the sacred city. France was then in the full tide of reaction. The republic of 1848 had come upon the nation unawares. The Paris socialistic mob who recalled, by their threats, all the horrors of the former revolution, had been conquered in June. The nation, appealed to in December, had returned by an overwhelming majority, the avowed aspirant to the empire—the legal successor of Napoleon Bonaparte. The priests were again plotting, as in the old legitimate times, to guide public affairs. General Cavaignac, in order probably to gain their influence in the election, organised an expedition to Rome. After his election to the presidency, Louis Napoleon hastened to carry out this expedition. In this determination he was guided as much by a desire to obtain for France a footing in Italy, and thus to check the Austrian domination in the Italian States, as by the fear of the republican party. He hurried the expedition, that France might alone have the glory in the eyes of churchmen of restoring the pope, and that the French might have Rome in possession and might obtain a strong footing in Italy, before Austria recovered from the shock of revolution. Thus the French undertook the siege of Rome, a much more difficult task than had been imagined, which brought to them but little glory.

This siege of Rome will long be memorable in the annals of Italy. The Romans could not at first believe that the French had hostile intentions towards them. Scarcely a year had passed since this volatile people had startled all Europe, by the overthrow of a monarchy, and by the proclamation of a republic, with "liberty, equality, fraternity," inscribed on its banners. France had itself been the chief instigator of republicanism in Italy—and could it be that France, with its new government, its republican assembly and president, even though that president was a Bonaparte, was already prepared to overthrow its own allies? Thus thrown off their guard, the Romans were at first prepared to receive the French soldiers with open arms as protectors.

When, however, the purpose of the French became apparent, the Roman people, indignant at the treachery, and inveterate in their hatred of the papal government, rose, with a courage worthy of ancient times, to defend their city from the attack of the invaders. On the 30th of April, they vigorously repelled the first assault, and proved to General Oudinot, who was in command of the French forces, that he would have no easy task in attempting to capture the city. The old Roman blood showed itself in the spirit of their defence. The French were convinced of their error, and by treacherous negotiations put off further assaults till the arrival of an overwhelming force. General Garibaldi, in the meantime, cleared the country of its Neapolitan invaders, driving them back with a greatly inferior force, after two pitched battles, in which they were miserably defeated. On the 3d of June, Oudinot, treacherously violating the truce, attempted to take the city by a coup-de-main. But he had not even the fortune to see his treachery successful. Several important positions were surprised; but the inhabitants, by a vigorous sortie, checked further progress, while they failed, however, after a long combat, to regain the lost positions.

Now began the twenty-seven days' combat, which has seldom been surpassed, both for the spirit of the people and the bravery of individual acts, in the history of the many sieges of the world. The population kept together as one man. No discordant voices were heard. If some priests wished good fortune to the besieger, they were compelled to disguise their sentiments, and to cheer on their fellow-citizens. The most perfect order prevailed. Never was the city so secure. Every avenue might be traversed in safety at midnight. It seemed as if the virtue of patriotism had subdued, for the time, all the instinctive vices of the people. Men of the highest families gave their services as soldiers. Ladies of noble origin were incessant in their attentions upon the wounded. There were to be found among the strong, iron-framed women of the left bank of the Tiber, who have a tradition that they are the true descendants of the ancient Romans, many who acted as soldiers, directing and firing the cannon, or drawing the waggons with the cannon-balls. An inspiration appeared to have seized upon the whole city. Rome, dead for ages, was mixed with its old warlike spirit, and was prepared again to combat the world. The French were astonished. They expected to find a weak, vacillating people, led by a few petty tyrants, whom they would gladly be rid of; they found the city burning with hatred at its papal oppressors and with indignation against those who should attempt to restore the former government. Against such overwhelming odds, the battle could not but be lost; but it was hardly fought, inch by inch, and at length an honourable surrender was made.

Nor was this resistance of Rome, though desperate, to be regarded as useless. No country has ever lost in the end by the splendid acts of any of its cities and provinces. Spain, though it did not gain at the moment, owed much eventually to the bravery of the defence of Saragossa. The sympathy of other nations, and the admiration of the world, were attracted by its heroism, and such moral supports of a cause are often in the end worth armies. The heroic defence of Rome first convinced the free nations of Europe that Italy had within her the elements of true power, and it gave strength afterwards to the Piedmontese government, in pursuing alone for many years its liberal Italian policy. The Romans deserve liberty; and we hope that, after having set so noble an example of readiness to suffer in its defence, they will not long be left under the present hated government, but will soon see the new kingdom of Italy proclaimed from the Capitol.

The defence of another of the Italian cities, Venice, Queen of the Adriatic in the old days of mercantile splendour, was going on at the same time, and was much more prolonged. Under the direction of Manin, one of the most honest and prudent of the republican party, the citizens underwent every privation in defence of their city. They trusted to the successes in Hungary effecting a diversion in their favour, and therefore held out longer than they would have done under other circumstances. Nowhere was such liberality shown in supplying from private resources the wants of the public treasury. Eighteen families bound themselves to give eight millions of livres. Two gave up all their possessions to the last farthing. Upon forty others the subsidy of three millions having been imposed, payable in two instalments, the greater number cheerfully paid their whole quota at once—the others the second portion of theirs long before the appointed time. All who had specie at command hastened to place it at the disposal of the government, receiving back paper currency, which they knew would entail eventually a considerable, if not a total, loss.

While famine and cholera roamed through the devoted city, the bombardment was commenced in the beginning of August. The streets now presented a most mournful aspect. The sickly and famine-struck population crowded into those parts which were still out of the range of fire, or sought refuge in cellars, where the pestilence carried them away by thousands. The shops were closed, except here and there, where scant supplies of black bread were doled out to famished claimants. There was for twenty-four days no talk of surrender, till almost the last loaf had been consumed, and the last supply of ammunition spent. They then gave in sullenly, stipulating for the departure of those who had, by recent events, been most compromised.

Tuscany and the Romagna were also reduced in the course of the summer of 1849, and all Italy except Sardinia thus fell again for a time under the power of its Austrian rulers. The dungeons were speedily filled; the scaffolds reeked with the blood of patriots, who had not had the good fortune or the foresight to flee. Every promise of former times was ruthlessly broken; and Italy was again bound in captivity, and compelled to grind for her masters.

It would be a mistake, however, to suppose that the struggle of these years was useless, or that its effects were lost. The Italians had acquired a new confidence in themselves. The love of liberty, which had been all but extinguished, had been awakened anew. The people were taught the lesson that unity is power, and felt that, through their divisions, they had lost a noble opportunity. A martial spirit had been aroused, and a sense of their own power in battle awakened. They had learned also that the Papacy could never be the true supporter of liberalism, since the attempt had been made under a well-intentioned pope, but had miserably failed. Austria was now, more than ever, seen to be the recognized enemy, the more powerful oppressor, whose interests were in no respect associated with those of the country, and who held it by force of arms alone. Hope gleamed where there had been only despair, and athwart the sky there shone the brightness of a dawn—speedily to break forth into day.

Thus the sieges and defeats of 1848-49 were not thrown away, but remained, though buried for a time as seed in the soil, to burst forth into a new life. Victor Emmanuel stood by his country, and could not be moved, either by fear or tempting offers, to change the policy for which his father sacrificed his crown. He took the oath firmly to the constitution, summoned the chambers, and shared with them the government of his people. Massimo d'Azeglio, one of the most noble-minded and disinterested of Italians, was called to the head of the government. When fifteen years of age, he had accompanied his father, the Marquis d'Azeglio, then Sardinian ambassador to the Holy See, to Rome; and there he cultivated painting, poetry, and music with much success. He studied at Rome afterwards as an artist, living on a very small allowance granted to him by his dissatisfied father. In a few years he acquired the reputation of the first landscape painter in Italy. At this period of his history he became acquainted with the celebrated author, Alessandro Manzoni, whose daughter he married; and began to devote his attention to literature. His romances were full of national spirit, and reflected bitterly upon the evils of a foreign yoke. In the beginning of 1846 he issued a pamphlet, which produced much effect on the popular mind, called the *Casi di Romagna*, in which he described vividly the corruption of the papal government, with which he was familiar by personal inspection. Cardinal Mastai had read this pamphlet, it was said, with interest, and it had much influence in directing him towards that course of reforms which he adopted on his election to the papal chair. Another pamphlet, descriptive of Austrian cruelty, designated *Lutti di Lombardia*, was written by him in January, 1848, and aided much the national cause. He fought afterwards at the siege of Vicenza, where he received a severe wound. He was chosen a deputy to the Turin parliament in 1849, and was soon afterwards made president of the cabinet.

Such was the man whom Providence selected, in the midst of disasters, to direct the Italian movement, by preserving and solidifying the liberties of Piedmont. A lofty idealist, with purity of motive and singleness of aim impressed upon every feature of his countenance, he combined with the richness and gentleness, so to speak, of Italian genius, the iron determination of the old Roman. A man not fitted to steer the vessel through the shoals and the quicksands of minute diplomacy, yet well able to start her upon the career of progress. His loftiness of aim, and purity of motive, could not but rouse all the best feelings of the assemblies which he directed, and of the people which he ruled. Thus, in a short time, he gained the confidence of all, and an attempted move of the democrats retorted upon themselves, and proved that he was master of the situation.

Piedmont now went on, despite the rage and threats of Austria and her satellites, in the career of progress. The abuses of the church, which had reached an almost unparalleled height, were first assailed. A bill was prepared by Count Siccardi, but before its presentation to the chambers, the Count was despatched to Rome to remove, if possible, the opposition of the pope. The pope, now in the hands of the Ultramontanes, whom he regarded as his deliverers from his past follies, and the saviours of the church from shipwreck, took high ground, and would listen to no proposal to modify the authority of the bishops or the immunities of the clergy, "*even should the authority of the laws, or the security of the States, be endangered thereby.*" Such negotiations were seen to be useless. An act of civility had been done, and Siccardi returned boldly to pursue his course.

The wretched state of slavery in which Piedmont had been held by the Jesuits may be understood from the character of the first of the measures now proposed. The following were the chief points of the famous Siccardi laws:—The clergy for offences against the civil law to be rendered amenable to the ordinary tribunals; religious corporations to lose the right of receiving donations or bequests; the number of church festivals to be abridged; and marriages to come under civil regulations—as in France and Belgium. Thus those clerical tribunals which had been long overthrown in all Romish countries of advanced civilisation, even in Austria, had continued to flourish in this Subalpine region. Every effort was put forth by the clerical party to inflame king, lords, and commons against the proposed laws. The pope addressed a strong remonstrance to Victor Emmanuel personally. The machinery of the church was set at work. But all in vain. The laws were passed. The papal nuncio was recalled from Turin. The clergy were commanded to refuse the last sacrament and the rites of sepulture to those who had supported the measure, whether minister, senator, or deputy. The Archbishop of Turin openly forbade his clergy to observe the new laws. For this act he was sentenced to a month's imprisonment. The invectives of the Papacy now knew no bounds. D'Azeglio, in reply, gave a home-thrust to the papal court, which had appealed to the spirit of religion formerly displayed by the house of Savoy, by stating, "that his Sardinian Majesty above all things was an observer of the religion of an oath, well knowing that, in the actual perturbation of kingdoms, there was but one way to restore order, namely, to act with faith, justice, and loyalty, and to this did he attach himself."

Popular feeling was soon greatly excited against the violent proceedings of the church, by the refusal of the last sacrament to Santa Rosa, one of the members of the cabinet, who died in August of this year. This was done by express command of the archbishop. The dying minister was required to retract the part he had taken in the passing of these laws, but steadily refused, and died invoking eternal Justice to witness that it was demanded of him to do violence to his conscience. Popular indignation knew no bounds. The archbishop was compelled to authorize the funeral obsequies. The procession to the grave was of great extent, and flowers were showered from the windows on the hearse as it passed. The archbishop was first confined in a fortress, and then banished the kingdom. The government gained the victory. Their acts were ratified by the people.

On the death of Santa Rosa, Count Cavour succeeded to his place in the cabinet, the king showing his discernment in the remark, "Do you not perceive that this man will finish by supplanting you all?" Cavour belonged to one of the most ancient and wealthy families of Piedmont, but early began to struggle against the many narrowing influences of the political system which prevailed. It is related of him that when a mere boy he was enrolled among the royal pages, and provoked his dismissal by a witticism on the absurd formalities of the court. He was placed at a military academy afterwards, where he distinguished himself much. Scarcely, however, had the young officer been introduced into the circles of the capital, before his independence and sarcastic power gave such offence to courtiers, that his family received the hint to send him into honourable exile.

This led Cavour to live many years abroad, and thus gave him that general knowledge of politics which he afterwards turned to so good account. He spent much time in Britain, and studied with care the constitutional principles of the government, as well as the science of political economy. Returning to Piedmont as soon as the government of Charles Albert began to give indications of a more liberal tendency, he took an active part in forming the Associazione Agraria, the avowed object of which was the improvement of agriculture in its various branches. It had, however, much larger designs. It was intended to be the centre of a national intelligent awakening from the deadness of the past, to be the promoter of life and improvement in every direction, political and material. As events proceeded, and Charles Albert granted his liberal constitution, in November, 1847, Cavour and his friends established a new journal, the *Risorgimento*. This journal took up, from the first, a position of strong antagonism to the Mazzinians, whom it regarded as wild and dangerous dreamers, and defended the cause of constitutional liberty. It urged the king forward to the war against the Austrians in 1848. It soon obtained a great influence, and became the leading representative of the new constitutional party. Cavour, the mainstay of this journal, was elected a deputy in the first parliament in the end of 1847, and during that trying period, when the stormy contest between absolutism and democracy raged at its height, he kept the balance in his hands, and firmly opposed the democrats as well as the absolutists. To his clear, vigorous intellect is it in great part due that Piedmont did not go to the same extremes as Rome and Tuscany, and thus fall back with the reaction to the same miserable condition. Heartily hated by the democrats, he lost his seat upon a re-election in 1849, but regained it after the battle of Novara, on the beginning of Victor Emmanuel's reign. In parliament he at once took his place as one of the best debaters, skilled above all others in the clear, practical judgment which he displayed, and the rapid skill of his argument. When others soared in the regions of theory, Cavour struggled, breast to breast, with the difficult facts around him, watched every movement, and skilfully seized his advantage. He never rose to great eloquence, except that eloquence of force and clearness which in the end masters all other. His power was felt at once, and he was a chief instrument in carrying through triumphantly the Siccardi laws, his wide knowledge of men and countries, and especially of the history of Britain, enabling him to expose with withering scorn the bondage from which Piedmont now sought deliverance, and the intrigues and devices of the clergy to retain, at the expense of the liberty and intelligence of the people, the privileges of their order.

It is impossible to look upon the head and countenance of Cavour, without feeling that he had in his character more of Northern, and especially of English, than of pure Italian elements, many of the Lombard and Piedmontese families still bearing the impress of their Germanic origin. These express active energetic thought rather than high idealism, while sagacity and determination are written upon every feature. He was a man of business habits, and of clear knowledge of men, and would have taken the highest position amongst merchant princes. It is known as a fact that he actually did, by his mercantile skill, retrieve the sunk fortunes of his family, before he was able, by reason of the changes of the time, to enter upon the field of politics. With this mercantile skill, which is necessary to every successful politician, and the existence of which in so unusual a measure in Britain, is one cause of the success of its constitutional system, he combined a warm, single-eyed love of country, which made him keep always in view the one object—the resuscitation of Italy—the creation of the unity and liberty of the Italian states. When others were confused in the detailed, perplexing questions of the moment, Cavour kept before him a single design, and guided all the details of his policy towards one end. Knowing Austria to be the soul of the system of despotism, which had been revived with more than its former horrors, he kept his eye steadily fixed upon this power, resolved to court any alliance which would enable him to contend against her, held with her no terms, and quietly prepared for the coming struggle.

Such was the man—clear-sighted, sagacious, with great mercantile capacity, politic, ready always to subordinate the most varied details to his leading idea, and withal a true, simple-hearted, honest patriot, who would have borne imprisonment or death for the good of his country, and who died eventually in her service, knowingly wearing out his constitution by unceasing toils—whom Victor Emmanuel called to his counsels on the death of Santa Rosa; who was from that period the ruling spirit of Italy till his death; and who has left his impress deeply stamped upon the future of his country. A member of one of the highest and most ancient families, he devoted himself with ardour to the cause of constitutional liberty, never swerving from his purpose, and giving thus a new example to the world of the benefit of noble birth, when associated with patriotic principle. The name of the unpretentious, clear-sighted Camillo di Cavour will shine conspicuous for centuries in the annals of Italy, and his policy will, we hope, regulate her destinies in generations yet unborn.

As soon as Cavour entered the ministry, the effect of his vigorous mind began to be perceived. He became more and more the ruling spirit of the cabinet. D'Azeglio, a statesman rather of lofty idealism than of practical sagacity, felt that Cavour was his master in the direction of practical affairs, and with a noble disinterestedness, which does honour to his country, prepared to lay down the dignity which he had assumed under the most difficult circumstances, and to return to the unpretentious work of a landscape painter. In November, 1852, Count Cavour was installed as prime minister, and ruled the destinies of Italy to the time of his death, except for a period after the conclusion of the war of 1859, and other very brief intervals.

Under his guidance the cause of ecclesiastical reform continued to be pursued with a steady and vigorous hand. He had that power which is possessed only by men of large comprehensive views, of rising above temporary clamour, and the difficulties even of friends. He struck out boldly new courses for himself, convinced that he would gain the confidence of the public in the end. One of the boldest measures ever devised by a statesman was proposed and carried by him in 1855. England and France were then at war with Russia for the defence of Turkey. The campaign of the winter 1854-55, on the dreary heights of the southern point of the Crimea, had been disastrous to all concerned. If Russia also had suffered, she still held her fortress, while all Europe resounded with the sad narrative of the bitter sufferings of the British and French troops. In these circumstances, when a narrow-minded statesman would have been terrified to move, even if he had had a special obligation, Count Cavour resolved to take the initiative, by proposing that Piedmont send out a force to assist the allies. Had the plan been suggested by any one else, it would not have obtained even serious consideration. Russia had always been friendly to Sardinia. The increase of her influence in the Mediterranean would tend to strengthen second-class powers, by preventing the supremacy of France. The war had been one of disaster hitherto, though not of defeat. It was in fact no business of Sardinia's. Why should she put herself forward to meddle in matters which did not concern her? Such were the arguments of opponents—arguments which appeared to superficial onlookers to be entirely satisfactory. Cavour however, with quick eagle eye, saw an opportunity such as rarely offered for the advancement of the Italian cause. He dare not avow the full motives of his act, and thus had to defend it under much difficulty. Austria, influenced as she has almost always been by narrow selfish motives, was in great perplexity as to the course she should adopt in the circumstances. Bound to Russia by the events of 1849, and alarmed lest the great curtailment of Russian power should act at liberty the revolutionary element in Hungary and the east, Austria dared not take part against her; while on the other hand, she was too glad to see a power weakened which had treated her recently as a vassal, to wish to unite with her; and besides, she feared a war with the western powers which might kindle a conflagration in Italy. She therefore occupied the position of a weak neutrality which exposed her to the bitter hatred of the emperor Nicholas, and to the contempt of England and France, who understood her motives sufficiently well to give her no credit for disinterestedness. Cavour perceived this false position of the great enemy of his country. He perceived also, in the newly-formed western alliance, the centre of hope for Italy's future. Taking advantage of the opportunity when the Sardinian aid would be accepted as valuable, he proposed his measure for sending an army to the Crimea. We may state that he had been invited in the previous year to take part in the war by the Earl of Clarendon, who assured him of the warm admiration of the British people for the course pursued in recent years by Sardinia. After a fierce discussion in parliament, which lasted for several days, the proposal was at length carried, and a Sardinian army of 15,000 was soon after despatched in English vessels to the Crimea, under the generalship of General della Marmora, and amidst the enthusiasm of the soldiers. The valour and victory of the Sardinian army in the battle of the Tchernaya, roused a spirit of admiration in all Italy, and the results of this expedition thus aided much in giving to Sardinia the undisputed leadership among the Italian states. Count Cavour in the meanwhile had many obstacles to contend with. The queen and the only brother of the king died within a few weeks of each other, and the priests used all their influence to impress the mind of Victor Emmanuel with the idea that these calamities in his family were judgments on account of his rupture with the pope. For a time they appeared to have succeeded, when D'Azeglio stepped in, and, after being denied two audiences, wrote a most wise and noble expostulatory letter which completely brought back the king to his former counsels. The war now became more and more popular. Sardinia began to feel proud of her position among the nations, and the power of Cavour rose in undisputed ascendency. Towards the end of the year, Victor Emmanuel visited the courts of London and Paris, in company with his minister. He was everywhere, especially in England, received with enthusiasm, and the opportunity was taken advantage of by the wise premier, to mature further plans for the opening of the discussion of the Italian question.

In the peace congress of 1856, Cavour, who was appointed to represent Sardinia after D'Azeglio had been nominated and declined, found no opportunity formally to bring forward the Italian question, against the introduction of which Austria protested. After the terms of peace between Russia and the allied powers was concluded, Count Walewski, as premier, called the attention of the congress to the position of Italy. A proposition was made that the powers represented in the congress should address a representation to the petty Italian potentates, calling upon them to avert the danger of revolution in Italy by more equitable and liberal systems of government. Though the proposal fell to the ground through the attitude of the Austrian plenipotentiaries, Count Cavour was requested to indicate the reforms necessary to insure tranquillity in the Papal States. To this request he replied, according to his brief statement in the Sardinian parliament shortly before his death, by refusing to indicate any programme of the kind proposed. He declared his conviction that it was impossible for the pope to follow the advice given him, and stated that the only means in his opinion of restoring the Romagna and Marches to a healthy condition, and of rendering it possible to govern them without foreign occupation, was to separate the government entirely from that of Rome, and to make them judicially and administratively independent. When it became clear that the congress would separate without doing anything for Italy beyond giving her a sterile expression of sympathy, Cavour seized his opportunity to record a solemn protest in the face of Europe. In the famous memorandum addressed to France and England, at the close of the congress, he assumed to represent *all* Italy. He showed that its hopes had been disappointed by the conclusion of the war; that the revolutionary party would acquire fresh strength, now that the prospect of a diplomatic solution was postponed; that Austria was rapidly extending her dominion over Italy, and threatening the existence of all independent states; and that, in fine, "the government of Sardinia, disturbed within by the action of revolutionary passions, excited without by a system of violent repression and foreign occupations, and threatened by the extension of Austrian power, might at any moment be forced, by an inevitable necessity, to adopt extreme measures, of which it was impossible to foresee the consequences." The great fact was thus proclaimed to the European powers that the existence of constitutional Sardinia, and the maintenance of the Austrian system, were incompatible. The time had come when Austria must be openly met, and must be challenged at an early date, to prove her right to dominate over the greater part of the nominally independent states. On his return, Count Cavour declared openly in the Sardinian parliament:—"The result of the Paris negotiations has not been to improve our relations with Austria. I must say that the Sardinian and Austrian plenipotentiaries, after sitting side by side for two months, and co-operating in one of the greatest political works accomplished during the last forty years, separated with the intimate conviction that the political systems of these two countries are more opposed than ever. These differences may give rise to difficulties and create dangers, but that is the inevitable and fatal consequence of the system of liberty which Victor Emmanuel inaugurated on ascending the throne, and which you have ever since upheld. I do not think that the prospect of these perils ought to induce the king to alter his policy. The cause of Italy has been brought before that tribunal of public opinion whose verdict is without appeal. The trial may be long, but I am confident that its ultimate issue will be conformable to the justice of the cause."

The great statesman had chosen the proper opportunity to take a position in Europe, and to enlist sympathy against the Austrian system. From this period he began more directly to prepare for the contest which he saw, must, for life or death, be waged in behalf of the liberties of his country. He laughed to scorn the puerilities of Mazzini and the ultra-democrats, who encouraged the idea that

Italy unaided might venture an assault upon her great antagonist; and his efforts were consequently directed, after having stimulated moral sympathy, towards obtaining allies willing and able to support him. He sounded England as to active support; but England, perhaps wisely, has latterly refused to intermingle with the internal politics of the Continent, and no material support could be expected at her hands. He was thus thrown entirely upon France, which had entered Italy chiefly for the purpose of forming a counterpoise to Austria, and which had addressed various remonstrances, from time to time, to the pope, against his Austrian system. The French emperor willingly listened to the proposal, and kept it under consideration from the time of the breaking up of the Paris congress. Various communications passed between Sardinia and France, touching the condition of the Italian states during these years.

It was, however, after the attempt upon the life of the emperor by Felici Orsini, the most fanatical, though devoted and disinterested, of the Mazzinian party, that events began to be hurried forward to the consummation of a great Italian war. Up to this period the French emperor had been regarded as the conservative deliverer of Europe by the absolutists, and as the key-stone of the European system by the democrats. Could he only be assassinated, the republicans of Paris would again raise their heads; the revolutionary movement would spread like wildfire over Italy, Germany, Hungary, and Poland; the thrones would crumble before it, and all Europe would be republican and free. So hoped Felici Orsini. With the spirit of a martyr he devoted himself to the work. He had suffered in Austrian prisons; had made many miraculous escapes; and was just the man to dare or die for his country. We well remember, on meeting him a year before his name rang through Europe in connection with this plot, to have heard him declare that plots would never cease till his country was delivered. His eye flashed as he spoke of her wrongs, and the whole energy of his massive intellect was engrossed with this one subject. On asking him of what advantage plots could be, while the French emperor held the destinies of France under his control, a look of dark suspicion spread over his noble countenance, as if we had penetrated to some deep secret of his heart,—and he changed speedily the subject. In January, 1858, the tidings flashed from Paris of this daring attempt. Orsini had ventured his all in what he conceived to be a good cause, and nothing was now left to him but to die. Let none, however they may censure such fanaticism, cast reproaches upon the character of this heroic man. He knew what he risked, when he risked everything for the supposed good of his country. His method of action was mistaken; but his purpose was good, and he exposed his life in its accomplishment. The plot of Orsini produced excellent results for Italy, though in a very different manner from that which he had anticipated. Had he succeeded, revolution might have ensued, royalty might have been restored in France, and in the end the despotic powers would have been probably the gainers. As it was, he roused Napoleon to a sense of the danger of allowing Italy to remain in its position of degradation, and hurried him on in the maturing of those plans for its liberation which, in conjunction with Cavour, he had previously conceived. Active preparations were made during the whole of this summer, and, in autumn, Count Cavour paid his afterwards famed visit to Plombières, to arrange the details. On the 1st of January, 1859, the French emperor gave those significant hints to the Austrian ambassador which augured the approaching storm. Austria, which had been long watching her opportunity to crush Sardinia, now maddened by the dread of foreign interference, sent forward her armies with great despatch into Lombardy, and in a short period she had overwhelming forces on the Piedmontese frontier. Her plan was to crush Sardinia before France could interfere, and thus to destroy the Italian prestige, even should she herself be compelled afterwards to recede before the advance of the French armies.

We have regarded the history of Sardinia, during the ten eventful years from 1849 to 1859, as the history of Italy, since, during that period, all the other states were mere nonentities, their life being crushed out by the iron power of Austria. Before, however, considering the campaign of this memorable year, and its great results in the establishment of an Italian nation, we would cast a glance at the system pursued by Austria and her dependants in those provinces which they had won back by force of arms. Tyranny now became much more oppressive than it had been before. The Austrians and the priests, so far from having learned moderation from their misfortunes of 1848, determined to treat the people as slaves, and to crush for ever their national aspirations, by the exercise of cruelty the most atrocious. Even Tuscany, which before had been prominent as one of the best and most moderately governed of the Italian states, was subjected to this wretched system. The Austrian soldiers and the native police took delight in showing offensively to the people their absolute subjection. They refused to pay the recognised rates in places of public refreshment. They hustled the Italians out of the way in the public thoroughfares. They drew their swords and struck respectable citizens under the shallowest pretexts. We remember witnessing, in 1853, in the great square of Florence, a crowd collected to see the absurd chariot-races, on the day of the patron saint of the city, San Giovanni or St. John. The square was crowded with people—men, women, and children. As room had to be made for the so-called chariots, cavalry rode into the square with drawn swords, and in barbarous fashion drove the crowd back, striking right and left with the flats and backs of the swords, and inflicting, even on women, serious blows, if not wounds. The people were enraged, but what could they do? Florence sat like a city in mourning. No smile was to be seen on the countenances of any, except the malignant smile of hate and scorn. Spies were introduced as servants into private families, and the masters of families were often dragged forth to prison on their secret testimony, without any reason assigned. Under martial law, which continued to be exercised for years in many of the Italian cities, numbers were hastily tried and ignominiously shot and buried in a ditch, for no crime, but that of having been good patriots in the revolutionary times. Thus did Austria, and those petty princes, her dependants who have since been most righteously driven from their thrones, hope to crush out the spirit of the nation, and to destroy all desire for liberty.

Mr. Gladstone, in his letters of 1851, addressed to the Earl of Aberdeen, has depicted in dark colours the cruelties practised, and the entire absence of even the forms and decencies of justice, under the government of Ferdinand II. of Naples. He states, in the first of these letters, that "the general belief is, that the prisoners for political offences, in the kingdom of the Two Sicilies, are between fifteen, or twenty, and thirty thousand." He says, that from accurate inquiry, he believes that "twenty thousand is no unreasonable estimate for the whole country." "The Neapolitan government appears to have something of the art which Mr. Burke declared to be beyond him—he did not know how to frame an indictment against a people." "Confiscation or sequestration upon arrest is frequent, so that generally each case of a prisoner or refugee becomes the centre of a circle of human misery." An actual majority of the chamber of representatives, elected under the constitution by the people, had been imprisoned. Prisoners were confined for years without trial. Witnesses of no character were bribed to trump up charges against them. Chained together in damp noisome dungeons, with no protection against the cold or pollution of the atmosphere, they endured intense misery. "The prisoners had a heavy limping movement, much as if one leg had been shorter than the other. But the refinement of suffering, in this case, arises from the circumstance that here we have men of education and high feeling chained incessantly together. For no purpose are these chains undone; and the meaning of these last words must be well considered—they are to be taken strictly." He thus describes the state of Poerio, formerly prime minister, condemned on the evidence of a manifest perjurer in the government employ:—"I had seen Poerio in December, during his trial; but I should not have known him at Nisida. He did not expect his own health to stand, although God, he said, had given him strength to endure. It was suggested to him from an authoritative quarter, that his mother, of whom he was the only prop, might be sent to the king to implore his pardon, or he might himself apply for it. He steadily refused. That mother, when I was at Naples, was losing her mental powers under the pressure of her afflictions. It seemed as if God, more compassionate than her fellow-creatures, were taking them away in mercy, for she had, amidst her sorrow, trances and visions of repose. She told a young physician, known to me, that she had been seeing her son, and with him another person. The two were in different jails, and she had seen neither. Since I have left Naples, Poerio has sunk to a lower depth of calamity. . . . Never before have I conversed, and never probably shall I converse again, with a cultivated and accomplished gentleman, of whose innocence, obedience to law, and love of his country, I was as firmly and so rationally assured as of your lordship's, or that of any other man of the very highest character, whilst he stood before me amidst surrounding felons, and clad in the vile uniform of guilt and shame." Such was the condition of Naples when the late king pursued his victims, both from motives of policy and of personal vengeance. Nor was Naples alone. The system in that kingdom was perhaps worse than in other parts of Italy. The proceedings of the courts were more shameless; the dungeons were more loathsome and deadly; but in all the states, including the States of the Church, Modena, Parma, Tuscany, and the Austrian possessions in Lombardy and Venice, a system of lawless and cruel oppression was in full operation. The descriptions given by Silvio Pellico, Felici Orsini, and many others, show a depth of horror beneath the foundations of Austrian rule in Italy, which made it to be a constant danger to the peaceable states of Europe.

It was thus no cause of wonder that Italy hailed the advent of war in 1859; that the Romagna, Tuscany, and the neighbouring states rose, as one man, to sweep out the governments which had so miserably oppressed them. All Italy was on the qui vive for the first move forwards; and when the emperor of the French showed that he was in earnest in his support of the Italian cause, by his speech on the 1st of January, a chord of enthusiasm was struck which roused the whole people to arms. The ten weary years were over. Italy had learned moderation and wisdom from her sad experience. She had also had the opportunity of testing the truly national and liberal policy of Victor Emmanuel; and the Sardinian flag was to be accepted as that under which the nation was to unite, in concert with its French allies, for the overthrow of its oppressors and the establishment of its unity.

Count Cavour, feeling that he had behind him the immense army of France, proceeded now with a boldness which he dared not to have displayed in former times. The measure which gave chief offence to Austria was the rapid enrolment of volunteers from the Austro-Italian states, and the other territories under Austrian influence. Austria was enraged by this new manifestation of the purposes of Sardinia to head the Italian movement. The government of the Earl of Derby, which was then in office in England, anxious to avoid the dangerous collision which threatened, biased in favour of Austria, and alarmed above all at the threatened interference of Napoleon, proposed a general disarmament of the forces on both sides in Italy. This arrangement Count Cavour firmly declined, as it was seen that Austria could easily withdraw her troops to other territory, wait to see the disarmament of Sardinia, and then at some favourable juncture, it might be years after, pounce down upon her unexpectedly, and force her into a position of vassalage. Count Cavour could not afford to risk such a danger; and besides, he had his eye fixed upon the broad interests of Italy, and was patriotically determined no longer to leave the greater part of the country in a wretched state of vassalage. The Austrian troops continued to pour in during March and the early part of April, and to take the best positions for a speedy and overwhelming attack on the Piedmontese territory. Napoleon, however, easily kept pace with their aggressive movements. Numerous regiments continued to advance to the south and south-east of France, to be ready to embark at a moment's notice at Marseilles, or to cross the Alps by the Mont Cenis pass to Turin. For the last few weeks war was certain. There was only a race of preparations. In such a race, the French, with their rapidity of thought and movement, were sure to outrun the more sluggish Germans.

At length, upon the 19th of April, Count Buol addressed an ultimatum to the court of Sardinia.

This document did not reach Turin till the 23d of April, but its contents having been telegraphed to Paris from Vienna, the French troops were at once set in motion towards the frontier, so as to be able at the first moment to aid in the resistance. The ultimatum reached Turin upon the 23d of April, and gave the government three days to determine upon its course. The Sardinian government was required to place its army without delay upon a peace footing, and to dismiss the Italian volunteers. To this Count Cavour replied upon the 26th, declining the proposed terms at all hazards, and throwing the responsibility of the war upon Austria. On the same day the government of France announced to the senate and corps législatif, that if Sardinia were invaded, France must interfere for the protection of her ally, every means having been exhausted to prevent the outbreak of war. The French troops which had been concentrated at Marseilles and Toulon, and on the borders of Savoy, were at once set in motion, and already, before the expiry of the period of ultimatum, a large French army had penetrated into the Piedmontese territory. On the 26th, the day when the period fixed by the ultimatum had expired, the French soldiers were seen pouring into Susa, and a number of steam transports landed 10,000 men at Genoa. This landing is very graphically described in a letter to the *Siècle* by M. Edmond Texier:—"I arrived at Genoa on the first day of the disembarkation, and I need not tell you that the city wore the appearance of a *fête*. This long-expected disembarkation had attracted an enormous crowd, drawn from all parts of Piedmont, and even from the neighbouring states. . . . . The quay of this vast city of Genoa, which spreads in the form of a horse-shoe from the centre of the bay, its houses and palaces, arranged in tiers one above the other, presented a noble spectacle. The terraces near the sea were crowded by women, who, with their heads covered by those long white veils called *pezzotto*, waved handkerchiefs, and scattered flowers below. Hundreds of boats were skimming out of the port to meet our ships, and each as it passed alongside discharged a volley of flowers upon our soldiers. It was enthusiasm approaching delirium. To every shout raised from the quays or the boats, the soldiers replied by cries of '*Vive l'Italie!*' and women, children, men, old and young, wildly clapped their upraised hands—like people shipwrecked, who, having given up all hope of deliverance, see the lifeboats coming to their rescue."

The Austrian armies now advanced. They were taken by surprise at the rapidity of the French movements, which lessened the hope entertained of crushing the Sardinian army, if not also of obtaining possession of the capital, before assistance could be procured. They could not, however, without the entire loss of prestige, recede from their threat of invading the Piedmontese territory, and they possibly hoped that General della Marmora would venture a battle upon the open plain against a greatly superior force. Accordingly they began to cross the Ticino, upon the 29th of April, at Pavia and at Bereguardo. Troops continued to cross at these points for several days, and to advance into the country. On the 1st of May the Austrian right already held Novara, the centre Mortara, and the left Sannazzaro, a distance of twenty-five to thirty miles on the river Agogna, the second transverse river along the Po to Pavia.

The Piedmontese had long prepared a defensive position for their army. It is almost impossible to imagine a worse frontier-line for defence than that of Piedmont towards Lombardy. It forms a concave line, giving the advantage of a central position to the aggressor. With a powerful army, such as that of Austria, entrenched behind the Ticino, Piedmont could have had no security except in the strength of the fortresses to which she might retire. Alessandria, built at the confluence of the Tanaro and Bormida, had been selected as the best centre of defence, and large sums had been spent for many years in the strengthening of this fortress. It commands also the roads to the Apennines, and consequently to Genoa. The larger division of the Sardinian army retired in the direction of this fortress, leaving the Austrians to advance—securing by this means the double object of keeping the enemy in dread of an offensive movement for the division of his forces, and of protecting the advance by railway of the French troops from Genoa. The Austrians dared not to march upon Turin, not so much from fear of the force in front of them, which, even with the French auxiliaries, was greatly inferior in numbers, as from a well-founded opinion that if they went forward, they would be hemmed in between two armies, and thus destroyed.

The corps législatif of France having on the 2d of May voted the augmentation of the contingent for 1859 from 100,000 to 140,000, and sanctioned a loan of 500,000,000 francs by national subscription, the emperor next day conferred on the empress the dignity of regent during his absence, and published a proclamation to the French people, in which he announced this revolution, and recommended her and his son to the care of the army remaining in France, and of the whole people. On the 10th, at five P.M., he left the Tuileries in an open carriage, accompanied by the empress, and proceeded through a dense and enthusiastic crowd to the station of the Lyons railway. He embarked the next day at Marseilles, on board the yacht *Reine Hortense*, for Genoa, where he arrived on the afternoon of the 12th. The following extract from the *Times* correspondence gives a view of the enthusiasm manifested as he set foot on Italian soil. "As the smoke" (of the royal salutes from the town batteries) "blew away, or lifted here or there, it opened vistas of manned yards and vessels, draped in flags from truck to hull, and waving specks of every colour in the rainbow—hats, shawls, and handkerchiefs—while the deep roar of many thousand voices welcomed Napoleon to the land he comes to free. . . . . The arsenal presented a brilliant sight. The imperial guard, with their tall fur caps, were in full possession, lining the edge of the water as well as the battlements, except at the landing-place, which, as the post of honour, was held by the Genoese militia. A long line of chairs on the eastern side was occupied by ladies, apparently vying with each other in the splendour of their parasols; while a large vessel opposite heeled over, as I have seen Thames steamers do, with its freight of beauty, many a toilette fit for the most exclusive *salon* being mercilessly exposed to the chances of tarred rope and struggling crowd . . . . At ten minutes past two, the barge passed on towards the landing-place, now crowded with uniforms and decorated officers. The emperor sat where the steersman would do in an ordinary boat, between M. de Cavour and the Prince Carignon, and bowed repeatedly in acknowledgment of the enthusiastic shouts which greeted his appearance, and broke out again at the instant that his foot touched Italian soil. . . . . For the first time since the landing of their allies, the Genoese seemed thoroughly excited. . . . . They cheered and jumped up and down to see, and clapped their hands, and pushed for places, with an eagerness instructive enough to one who observed, that among the most enthusiastic were men of that party which but a few months ago sought the present hero's life." He thus describes also the reception in the theatre, the great centre of public life on the Continent:—"Soon after nine, and just before the ballet began, a general 'hush' running through the pit warned us of his majesty's approach. . . . The huzzas at the arsenal fade out of my mind when I think of the tremendous electrical shout that ran through the theatre, not given in regular time and for a definite object, as is our way in England, but each voice giving out its separate cry of 'Vive l'Empereur!' 'Viva l'Italia!' or 'Viva l'Alleanza!' and then cheering its own sentiment with 'Evviva!' repeated indefinitely. Every person in the theatre stood up, the ladies waving their handkerchiefs. . . . . The town was glorious indeed. . . . . The streets, one blaze of flags and light, with golden garlands surrounding the favourite watchwords of Italian liberty, were thronged with Genoese citizens and French soldiers, a well-behaved, intelligent, admiring crowd; while the churches seemed pinnacles of fire, raised in honour of their deity by worshippers of the sun; but there are those who will never forget Genoa, always beautiful—never more so than as it was seen from the sea last night. They will remember the amphitheatre of star-like houses rising silently from the sea—the strangely impressive sense of quiet and repose after the noisy streets and theatre—the Carignano church and the Lanterna on the extreme right and left, landmarks of the domain of light—the cathedral in the centre, raising its bright front above its neighbours—the sea, smooth as glass, hardly breaking the lines of bright sparks and many-coloured lamps which it reflected—the clouds above, a grand foil to the shining city, all the darker for a gathering thunderstorm, which, every now and then, by a single flash of lightning, seemed to show man that his utmost efforts were but a poor imitation of nature." Such was the nature of the reception given to the French emperor, as he came to rekindle the torch of Italian victories.

We would now briefly describe the plan of the campaign, which seemed to have originated in the mind of the emperor, and the secrets of which were at first confined within his own breast. The Austrians had for years been threatening the Piedmontese frontier, by fortifying Piacenza, which belonged to the state of Parma. This was intended to be the base of their operations, either for attack or defence. Though they had crossed the Ticino, and taken up a threatening position along the banks of the Agogna, as we have already described, a large force was detained in front of Piacenza, advancing into the province of Voghera. Napoleon, in order to conceal his plans, used every means, after his arrival at Alessandria, on the 14th of May, to convince the Austrians that the principal advance of his army would be in this direction. This induced them to weaken their force to the north, and to concentrate the main body of their army in the neighbourhood of Piacenza. Even when this northern force was thus weakened, it was impossible to attack it directly by crossing the Po at Valenza. The country to the north of the river is intersected with rice-fields and canals, and is quite unfitted for the manoeuvring of an attacking army. The emperor therefore determined to turn the right wing of the Austrians, which extended to Novara. To conceal this purpose, he kept a body of troops active in the neighbourhood of Voghera, and spread rumours of his intention to advance his head-quarters to that city. In the meantime, one division after another was quietly advancing to the north, until the centre of the allied army rested upon Casale, instead of Alessandria, as before. The Piedmontese were the first to cross the Sesia, and attack the frontiers of the enemy at Palestro. They were followed by the Zouaves, who put the Austrians to flight, and took many prisoners. This engagement decided the success of the flank movement by which the emperor had misguided his opponents, and the allies now at once advanced upon Novara, and made it their head-quarters. The Austrians, throughout the period occupied by this flanking movement, had remained inert, expecting the advance of the French on the ground they had chosen for defence, between the Sesia and Ticino. They were awakened from their dream by the capture of Novara, and its occupation by the French force, when it was now too late to defeat the manoeuvre. Nothing was left but that they should beat a hasty retreat across the Ticino. The rapidity and ingenuity of the French again came to their aid. There are two passages over the Ticino, one by the bridge of Buffalora, in front of which the Austrians had raised defences, the other near Turbigo, some leagues higher up, where there is no bridge, but a ferry. The river is here shallow and fordable, and full of islands, so that it is easy to throw pontoons across. The allies, seeing the probability that they would be stopped at Buffalora by the destruction of the bridge, attempted still to carry out their flank movement and to cross by the upper passage. A feint of attack was, however, made near Buffalora, when the Austrians hastily retreated, and attempted to blow up the bridge, an attempt in which they succeeded only partially, so that the damage was easily repaired so far as to admit the crossing of troops and even of artillery. The French emperor had thus a double means of attack. He had moved over a force at Turbigo on the north, and he was now able to pass also at Buffalora. The position on the opposite bank once forced—the grand road to Milan would be opened.

The attempt to accomplish this led to the battle of Magenta, in which, for a time, the force of the allies was exposed to greater danger than had been anticipated. The French emperor had calculated too much upon the blundering inertness of the Austrians, from which he had derived such advantages. They had at length understood his tactics, and began to march their army with much speed towards Magenta. The French had expected easily to occupy this position with the two sections proceeding from the north, and over the bridge of Buffalora, and, at first, only a small force was sent, under General Mpcmahon, quite unequal to the task of meeting and repulsing the

Austrian army. For a time it appeared as if the Austrians were about to gain the day. The emperor, seeing the mistake, despatched with speed large reinforcements across the bridge, behind which he had established his own head-quarters, at San Martino; and after a long, and by no means certain or easy contest, the day was gained. The Austrians fled in confusion, and the plains of Lombardy lay open to the advance of the troops of France and of Italy. The French loss was about 7000 or 8000, the Austrians about 18,000, including 7000 prisoners. It was remarked that the Austrian soldiers had little heart in the battle, and that a very unusual proportion of those killed were officers, advancing before their men to urge them forward. The Italians had not much part in this engagement. They themselves complained of being kept in the back-ground, while the French soldiers blamed their tardiness. There can be no doubt that they would have wished to be foremost in the fight, and would have fought as bravely as their allies. Their absence arose from no want of courage on their part, and from no intended slight of the French emperor; but from the same cause which prevented a large portion of the French force from being engaged, viz. the expectation that these positions would be gained before the Austrians would arrive in force to defend them, and in consequence without a general battle.

An eye-witness thus describes the scene which presented itself at Magenta on the morning of the 5th of June:—"Several square miles of carnage, well nigh 2000 dead and dying lying about, in some places in heaps, in others dotted all over the ground in every attitude; some with that placid countenance which indicates a well-aimed bullet in the heart or in the head, stiffened in the very position in which they were when the fatal lead struck them; here one with his right arm close to the hip, and with his fist clenched, as if he was still holding the musket ready for the charge; there another, with his hand to his mouth and showing his white teeth, as if still ready to bite off the end of the cartridge; the next man as calm as though he were reposing; another near him with his features distorted, and his limbs cramped, exhibiting all the horrors of the death-struggle from a bayonet-wound; further on, one with his head off; another with his limbs shattered; a third reduced by a cannon-ball to a formless heap, in a pool of blood; and so on, in all the endless varieties and forms of death. It was a study for an anatomist, or a gloomy painter of horrors. And all around, mixed up with the dead, were the wounded, some only just breathing, and too helpless to crawl under the shade of the next vine, or to chase away the flies feasting on the sweat of death; others covering down in a ball, shivering under the scorching sun; others looking up imploringly, and craving a mouthful of water. . . . All the front, where the battle had raged most furiously, resembled the remains of a great rag fair; shakoes, knapsacks, muskets, shoes, cloaks, tunics, linen, all stained with blood, lying about in every direction; the soil trampled down, and ploughed up by cannon-balls; trees shattered; leaves with bullets through them; every inch of ground the scene of some drama of heroism and ferocity, or of some tragedy of war and misery. And on this stage were moving about numbers of soldiers of all arms, many of them actors in the scenes which had passed, others attracted by curiosity, and listening to the stories of most disastrous chances, of moving accidents; or examining dead and wounded with that morbid interest which on such occasions seems to benumb all feelings of humanity, and cover each heart with a triple armour of insensibility. Among the crowd, the fatigue-parties worked cheerfully at their nauseous task of removing the wounded and burying the dead. Although scarcely twelve hours had passed since the battle, most of the dead were already half naked, which would have been inexplicable, had we not seen mysterious figures prowling about under the trees on the outskirts, and others in the distance, making off with large bundles; they were the peasantry in the neighbourhood, the human vultures who had done this sacrilegious deed. The dead were collected in heaps near the places where they fell, a long trench dug beside them, and twenty or thirty laid in each. Whoever makes a pilgrimage to the battle-field of Magenta, may trace by these little tumuli where the battle was fiercest. Little wooden crosses are erected over these tumuli, on some of which may be seen even now the withered flower-wreaths hung up as pious memorials by their departing comrades."

HISTORY AND PROGRESS OF ITALY.

Amidst universal jubilation in Italy, which thrilled the Peninsula from one extremity to the other, the Austrians were fleeing vanquished, and Milan, the magnificent capital of Lombardy, was open to Victor Emmanuel and his powerful ally. It is surprising that the panic-struck, retreating army of the Austrians was not hotly pursued by the large body of French troops and the whole of the Sardinian army, who were still fresh and prepared for attack, having been excluded by the circumstances already explained from all part in the battle of Magenta. Such a fresh army following up the recent victory, might, it was thought by many, have annihilated the Austrian force in Italy, and might then have swept with ease even through the famous Quadrilateral, and carried their victorious standards to Venice. The supineness of the victorious army for some days after this battle seems explicable only upon the supposition of deep politic designs of the French emperor, which made him not desirous of too speedily crushing the Austrian power, or too rapidly procuring the entire liberation of Italy, especially through the active agency of Italian troops. However this was, the Austrians were permitted a quiet and orderly retreat.

On the 8th of June the emperor and the king made their entry into Milan without any display, but at the head of their troops, hot and dusty with the march. This was befitting the position of affairs at the time. The shortest route was chosen to the palace. The news of their arrival spread, however, with the quickness of lightning, and was made patent by one frantic shout of joy, in which the whole city seemed to give vent to its feelings. "The scene itself," writes one upon the day of entry, "while the two sovereigns actually passed, it is impossible to describe. Imagine the madness of enthusiasm, the whole heart of a people poured out before those who had delivered them from long thraldom. Not an eye remained tearless. All the outward decorations disappeared before the greeting of the people; the flowers so long prepared for the occasion were almost forgotten in the emotion of the moment, and fell often long before those had passed for whom they were intended. For the first time, I saw emotion pierce through that mysterious and impenetrable countenance of the emperor—he would have been more than a man had it been otherwise." The deepest manifestation of enthusiasm was, however, reserved for the Piedmontese troops, who marched in the train of the king. Among these were many of the sons of Lombard families, who had long been exiled from their own country and its beautiful capital. The sight of the feathers of the Bersaglieri, and of the modest gray dress of the Piedmontese, proved that the cause of Italian liberty was again triumphant. The sad ten years had come to an end, and Milan hailed the restoration of her children.

While the allies were preparing to drive back the Austrians, and were fighting the battle of Magenta, they had a very powerful auxiliary in the force of Garibaldi, the renowned Italian hero. This remarkable man, who was born in the year 1807, has had one of the most strange and adventurous careers on record. His achievements have been extraordinary, both by sea and land. With a fiery, impetuous character—a stern, chivalrous sense of honour—a courage which never fails him in circumstances the most desperate—a marvellous readiness of resource—and withal a gentleness and kindness, almost feminine in the minuteness of its attentions—a hatred of all policy, and the simplicity of heart of a child—he is the very man to be the idol of the brave, and to lead them unfalteringly through combats the most unequal and battles the most hopeless. Garibaldi has spent the most of his life at sea, and his virtues as well as his weaknesses are those specially of the sailor. His father was a fisher, and he was trained himself to the same calling. His mother was a woman of great superiority and nobility of character. Various stories, more or less authentic, are told of his youth; as, that he wept for hours because he had hurt a cricket—that he saved, when only thirteen, the lives of some companions who were sailing between Nice and Villafranca, and who could not manage their boat overtaken by a squall, when Joseph swam out to the rescue—that he was the recognized leader of a youthful band, and excelled them all in singing, swimming, boating, and athletic exercises. He early became a sailor, and spent some years in mercantile voyages between the Levant and the Black Sea. On one of his voyages, when his ship was lying at Civita Vecchia, he obtained leave of absence to visit Rome, and from that time his interest in the political affairs of his country, the ancient glory of which its capital so vividly recalled to mind, began to developa. In 1831, when the hopes of Italians were excited by the accession of Charles Albert, he became introduced to Mazzini, and took part in a republican conspiracy formed at that time, under this leader's guidance. After having returned to his sea occupations for some years, he joined, in February, 1834, a party of republicans, who, under the guidance of Mazzini, made a descent from Vaud and Geneva upon Savoy. He escaped to France on the failure of this enterprise, and again returned for a time to sea. His desire for a public life, in which he might ultimately aid in delivering his country, induced him now to offer his services to the Bey of Tunis, who gladly accepted them. He was disappointed, however, with the discovered aimlessness of such a career; and in 1836, gave up his command of a ship, and proceeded to South America to engage in the wars of that region. His career in South America, into which we have not space here to enter, was one of the most extraordinary adventure. He was engaged in many of the republican wars, and had often hair-breadth escapes from dangers, which he overcame only by a valour almost superhuman. Here he married also the renowned Annetta—heroic as himself. In 1849 he took a most conspicuous part in the wars of Italy, specially in the famous defence of Rome, in which he was indeed the chief actor. Had his advice been taken at the earlier stage of the conflict, Italy might probably at that time have achieved her liberty.

Garibaldi is not adapted nor designed for a statesman, nor fitted to guide the great current of a nation's policy; but for striking the key-note of high patriotic spirit, for reviving the memories of the past, for giving to Italian youth a heroic devotion to the national cause, for inspiring military ardour, no man can approach him; and it is not too much to say that he has been the chief means of raising the degraded name of his nation, and giving a new impetus to the Italian people. The name of Garibaldi will, for centuries to come, strike the noblest chords of the Italian heart, and prevent Italy, when in danger, from sinking again into slavery.

Garibaldi no sooner heard the sound of approaching war in 1859, than he prepared again to gather round him his brave comrades of the former war, and to raise a force of volunteers, to be used in such a manner as the Piedmontese government should recommend. The National Society of Turin, of which Garibaldi was vice-president, printed instructions in the beginning of March, in preparation for the coming struggle. The Sardinian government now authorized the formation of a corps of volunteers, the commander of whom was to be Garibaldi. Numbers of young men, of the best families, flocked in daily from Lombardy, Tuscany, Parma, Modena, &c., to enrol themselves under the flag of their chief. The concourse of volunteers was soon so considerable, that a second division had to be formed. A project was started to attach a hundred mounted guides to the first division—the chasseurs of the Alps—when immediately a hundred young men, belonging to the richest families, offered their services, proposing to find their equipment at their own charges. On May 20th Garibaldi left Turin with 3700 men, and arrived the same evening at Gattinara. On the 23d he reached Castilotto at the foot of the Lago Maggiore, and crossed the Ticino upon that night, that is, several days before the advance of the allies began. He was most anxious to be the first to enter Lombardy and raise the flag of independence. To avoid surprise, he gave out that he was about to proceed to Arona, on the left bank of the lake, when after night-fall he crossed at Sesto-Calende, and was at Varese, half-way to Como, in the morning. Here he traversed again the same ground which he had occupied eleven years before, under so much less favourable auspices. The people of Lombardy had long been prepared for his arrival, thanks to the exertions of the *Società Nazionale Italiana*, which had its branches all over Italy. Garibaldi at once addressed a proclamation to the Lombardese, calling them to arms. The alarm-bells were sounded in the villages, and numbers of youths flocked to his standard. A small Austrian detachment at Gallatari advanced to Sesto-Calende to cut off the retreat, but they were repulsed by a force left in charge of that place. On the 30th of May Garibaldi himself was attacked in Varese by a strong column coming from Como. This attack was unsuccessful. He took the Austrian position at San Fermo, between Como and Varese, and entered the town of Como itself, when the whole Alpine country declared for Sardinia, and volunteers flocked in from all parts of the mountains. On General Urban advancing, however, with his flying corps of Austrians to attack the volunteers, Garibaldi was compelled to retreat to Laveno on Lago Maggiore, which he attempted vainly to take, having with him no cannon. Urban in the meantime seized Varese, and, as a punishment to the inhabitants, delivered over the town to brutality and pillage, and left it a ruin. On the 2d of June the Cacciatori were again at Varese, and on the night of the following day at Como. This was the day of the battle of Magenta, and, from the period of that victory, they continued to advance steadily, always in advance of the left flank of the allies, rousing and organising the country on the southern slopes of the Alps, recruiting and following on the heels of the Austrians. Before the allies entered Milan, Garibaldi was in Lecco, on the eastern branch of Lake Como. Before the allies had crossed the Adda, he was at Bergamo; and while they were crossing the Adda, he was already in Brescia. These movements exceedingly annoyed the Austrians, and helped materially to hasten their retreat. They were hemmed in by means of them, and never knew where they might meet the general and his light troops. When the peace of Villafranca was signed, Garibaldi was at Terano with 5000 men, and was about to attempt to cut off the communication between the Tyrol and Verona.

Meanwhile the main armies advanced towards the Mincio and the Quadrilateral, and there was fought, on the 24th June, one of the greatest and most furious battles that has ever been recorded—the famous battle of Solferino. During the night all the Austrian forces recrossed the Mincio without the allies having perceived them. By this great movement they obtained an essential advantage, in being enabled to choose their own place and time, and to draw up a plan for the engagement, which they met with no difficulty in realizing, and by means of which they ought to have won the battle of June 24. They had fortified their position with much care at San Martino and Solferino. Early in the morning, the Piedmontese patrols of scouts that had been sent to explore the field, were encountered by bodies of Austrian troops, and an unequal but furious struggle commenced. Only two of the Italian divisions, those of Chucchiari and Mollard, made head against the hostile force, so formidable from its numbers and momentum; but these divisions held their ground intrepidly. Two other Piedmontese divisions, the Durando and the Fonti, rushed furiously to their rescue, to enable them to sustain the shock of the superior Austrian force; and then Victor Emmanuel—a patriot king and warrior—marched forwards with his staff into the engagement.

Disastrous indeed would have been the result of that great day, if the first onslaught of the sixty thousand Austrians had not encountered such a heroic resistance from the twenty-five thousand soldiers of the Mollard and Chucchiari divisions. The Piedmontese, driven back to the Brescia, and perhaps routed, would have been cut off from the main body of the allied army, and the Austrians would have been able to attack the French in the rear with their entire force. The Piedmontese held their ground; and Napoleon, with the intuition of a veteran general, or of a condottiero of the Bonaparte lineage, discerned the importance of San Martino and Solferino as the two keys of the position. Solferino was intrusted to the French, San Martino to the Piedmontese; the tasks were equally important, equally affording scope for the acquisition of glory; and they were both performed. We will not describe the process of this great battle. The eight regiments of the French cavalry, the Zouaves, the imperial guard, and the artillery, attacked in turn the compact files of the Austrians bearing down towards Solferino. The German batteries were taken by the few soldiers who succeeded in reaching them alive, when the bulk of their comrades had fallen in the same attempt; the terrified artillerymen gave place, and then re-occupied their position by the aid of reinforcements, and were anew driven back. The strongest point in the field was the cemetery, where these movements took place.

The combat lasted ten hours; the soldiers had taken no food, the heat was intense, and the fatigue of the struggle almost insupportable; but neither hunger, heat, nor fatigue overcame them. The soil was cumbered with many thousands of the dead and wounded of both armies, and the forcing of the position appeared impossible. Napoleon came forward, and in the midst of the volleys of cannon-balls, sprang into one of the places most exposed to the fire of the artillery, and cried, "Soldiers, I will not withdraw hence till you have taken Solferino." An instantaneous acclamation resounded throughout the legions; the assault was renewed with incredible impetuosity on three sides; and the Austrians had no time given them to make out the meaning of that shout, that threefold attack, and that fresh impetuosity, before they were overpowered, thrown into confusion, and thundered at from their own cannons, now turned upon the fugitive squadrons, which were leaving behind them heaps of corpses. In this manner Solferino was taken, and the Germans there defeated.

At San Martino, during the same time, the Piedmontese were performing prodigies of valour, resisting the repeated furious attacks of very superior numbers, and making a memorable display of the power of the few pieces they had of artillery—not, however, without being terribly harassed by the hostile cannons, which were taking deadly effect on their flank from San Martino. For many hours they fought unrefreshed under the burning heat of the sun; several times did they appear to be giving way to the overpowering force of the foes, and as many times they renewed the attack with incredible ardour—but in vain. The Austrians several times retired or wavered, but always succeeded ultimately in rallying under the protection of the formidable artillery of San Martino. At last the riflemen push forwards, and the whole force of the infantry behind them; they clear a road for themselves with their bayonets; they win the platform, and San Martino is taken, while a long shout of "Viva la Savoja! viva l'Italia!" echoes through the lines. But the enemy had powerful reserves of fresh troops; they rallied, charged, and compelled the Piedmontese to retire in good order. The skies, however, were lowering, and a storm now burst forth of wind, hail, and lightnings; this elemental turmoil gave the Italians an opportunity of rallying; and when the sun came out, the conflict was renewed more fiercely than ever. It was now six in the evening, and most of the troops had been fighting from five in the morning; they were furious at perceiving that, after so many efforts in the unequal struggle, they might be at last compelled to return to their positions, leaving the results of the battle undecided. But what was to be done? All on a sudden the question is solved by the appearance of the warlike king, who advances fearlessly; his countenance, his example revives the courage of the soldiers, who make a last and desperate effort. "Children," he cries, "San Martino must be taken;" and he plunges into the thickest of the fray. And San Martino is taken. From that moment the defeat of the Austrians was complete and irrecoverable.

The allies were in want of a reserve; not from any lack of foresight on the part of the generals, but because all their forces had been absolutely required in the great combat, in which the enemy had had every advantage from his numbers, from his preconceived plan, and from the accidents of warfare, and to which his legions had consequently come up fresh and under cover. It became, therefore, impossible to pursue the fleeing and routed army; if it had been otherwise, very few of them would ever have recrossed the Mincio. It was therefore a great triumph to have occupied all its positions by the evening, and to see it retiring defeated, if not overthrown; although the soldiers, who had already fought from five in the morning to nine in the evening, were unable to follow up and complete the victory. This would have been beyond any human power. In this manner the Austrians sustained another defeat, in a battle to which few can be compared, either in ancient or modern times, for the magnitude of the forces employed on both sides, the fury of the combatants, the alternations of success, the extent of the carnage, and the importance of the result. The battle of Solferino and San Martino destroyed the prestige of the immense military power of Austria, and inflicted a wound upon that empire from which it can never again recover.

After this engagement, no other course remained open to Austria than that which she adopted, of withdrawing her dispirited and reduced battalions within the fortifications of the Quadrilateral. She even employed a portion of them in occupying the Stelvio Pass, evidently under the impression that she would have had to defend her German frontiers. Ten thousand of the French had now disembarked in Lesini, one of the islands of the Dalmatian Archipelago, near Istria, with the intention, it was supposed, of proceeding to vigorous operations in Hungary; the Piedmontese were investing and bombarding Peschiera; Prince Napoleon was advancing from Tuscany with 35,000 men in the direction of Verona; the emperor crossed the Mincio and established his head-quarters at Valeggio, with the intention of investing Verona by the assistance of the troops conducted by Prince Napoleon.

Peace! Under what conditions? Are the Austrians to depart from Italy? No! they will remain; but they will no longer have Milan with its fruitful provinces. These are ceded by the Emperor of Austria to the Emperor of the French, and made over by the latter to King Victor Emmanuel. And what about the famous Quadrilateral? It remains in the possession of Austria. And Venetia? It remains here also!

Words of indignation circulate like wildfire through all Italy at the news of the treaty of Villafranca. The bitterest epithets are applied to the unfaithful ally. Yet more; Cavour, the great statesman, renounces the direction of affairs, and retires into private life. But the faith of the people in their king is not weakened; they know him, trust him, and continue to hope in him.

When the first impression of consternation has passed over, hope revives in the hearts of the Italians. It was thought by many that an imperious necessity had urged the emperor to the fatal compact. Prussia was threatening him; all Germany was jealous of the progress of the French army, suspicious of Louis Napoleon, and indignant at seeing the dominion of her children expire in Italy. Only one part of the treaty of Villafranca afforded a ray of hope to the Italians. It was agreed that the dispossessed princes were not to be restored by force, but with the consent of their subjects; and by this stipulation the more profound imperial diplomatist overreached his young antagonist, and reduced the treaty to a dead letter.

Naples for some time gave no signs of life; not that there was not abundant patriotic spirit in her, but the presence of a numerous police force, of a formidable army devoted to the king, and of the Swiss mercenaries, made a rising of the liberals an impossibility. But the means of her future salvation were supplied from the quarter from which they could least have been expected—from the Swiss mercenaries. Among these were mutinies, riots, homicides; and it became necessary to dismiss the whole body from the service of the Bourbon king. This was a great misfortune for him, inasmuch as he was thus deprived of his most unscrupulous defenders. As may be readily believed, the Swiss mutiny was in no respect a political movement; but originated in the irritated professional feelings of the officers, on whom new restrictions had been imposed by the short-sighted policy of the government. Such acts of imprudence would never have been committed under King Ferdinand, who knew how to estimate the value of his Swiss troops.

Rome meantime was arming and collecting within her gates a scum of adventurers from all parts of Europe. Thus were all requisites being prepared for an attack upon Piedmont, in the interest of the reactionary cause. Here was the King of Naples, ready to furnish a contingent of 35,000 men to recover the Legations; there stood some thousands of Papal troops; yonder stood Austria, ever in readiness; there again stood the reactionists from every part of Italy, among whom many of the clerical body, and nearly all the higher prelates of the country, appeared in the foremost ranks. But Central Italy was going on bravely with the work of her own reconstitution. The people, after having decreed the exclusion of the dynasties that had lately ruled them, and having declared that they themselves would adhere to Piedmont, began to request that the Prince of Carignano, the king's cousin, might be their regent. It was a noble action—their renouncing their glorious municipal traditions in order to become members of a united Italy; and above all, the Tuscans deserve commendation for having sacrificed their artistic and literary recollections, and the martial histories of their great cities. The Prince of Carignano did not accept the regency, but he sent them Buoncompagni as his commissioner. This he did for fear of crossing the purposes of the emperor, who remained, or affected to continue, constant to his original project, as conceived after the peace of Villafranca. A congress was again proposed, and almost arranged, from which the now sufficiently humbled pride of Austria no longer attempted to exclude Piedmont. But to this project of a congress England pointed out obstacles; she refused to take any part in it except on condition that the Italians should decide, as they had a right to do, on their own destinies. Much was said, argued, objected to, and arranged, in order to bring about this congress; week after week, and month after month, its convocation was spoken of as a certainty, but yet never realised; and at last the congress came to nothing, and the Italians proceeded to act for themselves towards their own reconstitution. And in fact they had done great things in this interim. Their proceedings were slow and quiet, but not the less efficacious. All parts of the work were advancing towards their completion. Piedmont, towards the end of the year, had succeeded virtually, if not formally, in uniting nearly a moiety of Italy, including several most noble cities, under one government, to the entire satisfaction of the people and their authorities, who desired nothing better than to see the system completed and established, so that they might regard it as a normal condition of their existence.

We have now reached the commencement of the year 1860. The affairs of Europe are apparently in a more settled state. The great effervescence has subsided of suspicions, jealousies, and animosities, diplomatic as well as national. Germany is no longer incensed against the Italian cause; for she has not yet seen the development of those portentous changes, of which the beginnings render the year 1859 one of the most remarkable in the records of history. Austria, still groaning under the effects of the almost mortal blow that she has received, knows not what to do or to say, how to remedy her position, to repair her finances, or to reorganise her army; she stands hesitating and uncertain, self-engrossed, and only showing signs of life by exciting strife in Italy—clandestinely rather than openly. England displays in the most marked manner her sympathies—sympathies deeply cherished by the people, and supported by a wise and liberal government. And Italy meantime is labouring more and more prudently and energetically at the great work of nullifying the disastrous effects of the peace of Villafranca. She is proving herself equal to the occasion, by the prudence of her people, and the ability and firmness of her leaders, in such a manner that the idea of a European congress has to be brought forward to quiet her. But Austria discerns the peril, and manoeuvres to interpose obstacles, while she professes to give her adhesion to the project. And so the negotiations are spun out indefinitely.

Meantime Italy is arming, her regular troops are augmented, not with much alacrity, it is true, after the discouragement produced by the peace of Villafranca, but yet to a sufficient extent, thanks to the precautions of the government, and the concourse of exiles from the oppressed Italian provinces. The organization of the National Guard goes on very effectively. Garibaldi warmly commends the Milan division of it. "I have confidence in the patriotism, good-will, and energy of the National Guard of Milan, which in the day of the conflict will act worthily of itself. I recommend you all, my friends, to co-operate in this liberal institution, the safeguard of the laws, rights, and freedoms of the people. The peace of Villafranca has left a vast career open to Italian bravery." In this he was speaking the truth. The National Guard throughout Italy proved itself an element of safety to the country, and an effective institution for fostering the Italian army.

The Jesuits were expelled in a quiet, legal manner, without uproar or futile demonstrations, from

Parma, Modena, and the two Romagnas. This was also a great step forward. But how many Jesuits still remained, not in jesuitical but in priestly habits; how many without the insignia of any peculiar order! But now the tide of events surrounds them, and however many Jesuits in heart may remain, they keep themselves quiet, awaiting the time to show themselves, and hoping that their hour will yet come.

And now, the impossibility of gaining anything by the congress having become apparent, we again see Austria, the pope, and Naples, in a more cautious manner, but with very decided views, planning an interruption of the course of affairs by endeavouring to unite all their resources, their strength, and their cunning, to jeopardize the over-advancing cause of Italian unity. By rousing the fanatical animosities of the bigots and of the legitimists, the pope, or we should rather say Cardinal Antonelli and the grandees of Rome, churchmen as well as laymen, undertake to collect from all parts of the world, and from all nations, an army of 50,000 soldiers, and money enough to maintain them. The French legitimist nobility, and the Austrian government with its numerous and well-organised officers, are to supply a sufficiency of instructors, captains, and even generals.

And now Austria must combine with the pope. Austria too will do her best, if an opportunity arrives, for throwing her hundred thousand armed men into Italy, or if she can escape the danger of utter subversion that besets her. But at all events she will clandestinely send thousands of troops under other names, other insignia, not to count all the officers she sends out. In short, the pope is to reckon upon her; she will do her best, and more than her best, for the holy father—for the cause of religion.

Naples, moreover, has a fleet, and has a hundred thousand disciplined troops, with brave and skilful officers. The army of Naples is devoted to its king and to the pope. Surely, therefore, Naples can send some fifty thousand men and more to co-operate with the Austrian and Papal forces. Undoubtedly the three arch-despots had begun to calculate upon having an army of 150,000 or 200,000, without Austria's ever engaging in open war. Consider with all this the co-operation of the clergy, and the immense influence which they might exercise on the minds of the simple country-people, and of all the ignorant in general: and what formidable elements of mischief were here in the hands of the anti-national governments. The combination was indeed an alarming one. Only a general was wanting to the league; and a general was soon found of European reputation—a reputation, however, that was destined to be shattered in the present enterprise.

Emboldened by his confidence in the new league, the pope publishes an encyclic letter, defying the power of his enemies: he spares not even the Emperor of the French. This letter the *Univers*, that gigantic organ of the Ultramontane party, republishes with studied contumely. It prints in capitals all the vaunts of the Papal party, and the name of the emperor always in small type. A sentence of interdict, that civil interdict which is alone valid in the times in which we now live, is launched against the *Univers*, and it issues no longer to diffuse darkness throughout the world.

The man who had in his character all the astuteness of a diplomatist, combined with all the boldness of an agitator or tribune—the man who in his versatile nature so wonderfully combined grandeur of conception with heroic aspiration, and with dexterity in execution—the man who was determined at any price to save his country, regenerate it, and make it great—saw that this was the moment to lay aside subtlety and to come to the most daring decision. He accordingly threw down the nocturnal and mysterious pen of the diplomatist, and assumed that of the father of the people, the awakener of the millions. He wrote a letter to Thouvenel, which was a masterpiece of prudence mingled with daring, such daring as in another man might have appeared rashness and worse; but was not that in Cavour. He affirmed that in justice, in prudence, in reason, he could not accept the programme of the French government; that it was not possible, it was not right, for the king to attempt to refuse a second time the offers of the people of Central Italy, if they willingly gave themselves up to him; that a refusal would cost him the confidence of the nations who were freely submitting to him for the love they bare him, forasmuch as he was to them the personification of their common country, the well-beloved champion of the regeneration of Italy. What could France reply to this intimation? Could she oppose it by main force, or must she submit to the result of universal suffrage? The latter plan was the safer. Certainly, however, France would not have submitted to it without secret conditions. And thus the condition of the cession of Nice and Savoy was probably agreed upon. It is impossible to express the excitement to which the letter of Cavour gave rise among the people of Central Italy; it was praised, it was extolled; the programme was accepted with rapturous enthusiasm. Never was the boldness of a man more fortunate, for never had it been more seasonable. This boldness was the quintessence of prudence.

No sooner was all said than it was done; there was no time wasted. The decree for calling the people to vote was promulgated by the governors of the three provinces. The enthusiasm of the people was incredible, their joy universal—boundless; it was a fever, an ecstasy which communicated itself to all—and everywhere. There is no more discussion, no more of party feeling among those who read it; their hearts only speak to one another. The Italians are for the first time called upon to make Italy a kingdom, and they are astounded, affected, overcome by the greatness of the conjuncture. Their Italian hearts throb in their bosoms with a new life of love and of patriotism. The question proposed is simple and peremptory: "Annexation to Sardinia, or a separate kingdom." Annexation was voted for almost unanimously. In Romagna itself there were 202,659 affirmative votes for it, and only 254 for a separate kingdom: thus were the thunders of the Papal excommunication defied.

From the southernmost extremity of Italy a cloud now arose, portending future changes of great magnitude; a cloud fatal to Bourbon despotism, but fruitful in good fortune for Italy. In Sicily there was open insurrection. Whether in the whole island or in part, whether with victory inclining to the insurgents or otherwise, is as yet unknown; all channels of communication are under the control of the Bourbon government. The few private letters that get abroad are either incomplete, in consequence of the well-founded fears of the writers, or else pervert the truth for party purposes of one kind or another. At any rate, the insurrection is a fact; it is a fact that the insurgents are divided into bands, which are everywhere favoured and aided by the people; the land will support them in carrying on a guerrilla warfare; for the mountains will afford an inviolable asylum to the patriot bands. It is a fact that the 30,000 soldiers whom the Bourbon king maintains in the island are not sufficient to hold it in subjection, and that large and speedy reinforcements are solicited from Naples. Thus king Francis becomes unable to send troops to the assistance of Lamoricière, the general of the Papal forces, and thus the proposed conjunction of the Neapolitan, Papal, and Austrian forces becomes a less plausible project.

Such was the position of affairs in Italy at the end of April. France was standing idle, because the bait had been thrown into the mouth of the lion, by the cession of Savoy and Nice, otherwise she would most probably have given some trouble, not to the pope, but to king Victor Emmanuel. Nevertheless all danger was not removed, for the enemies of Italy were not inactive, and Lamoricière was collecting and organising his Babylonish army, holding his head-quarters principally at Ancona.

Where is Garibaldi? It is not known. It is hoped that he may be moving, that he may have moved to strike a great blow. But where? some say in the Romagnas, some in the Neapolitan territory, some say in Sicily. But with what means? with what forces? About all this, little or nothing can be said; but it is certain that his means must be very scanty, his forces very small; two, or at most three merchant vessels, and a handful of men. Wherever he may bend his course he will find ships belonging to the Neapolitan fleet—and troops, if he can elude the vigilance of that fleet, to hinder his landing, or, if he lands, to scatter his followers like clouds before the wind. His friends dread the consequences of his imprudence; his enemies anticipate them with exultation. Still the former have some grains of hope mingled with their fear, and the latter of fear with their exultation. Garibaldi is a known man; although he has not triumphed in his remonstrances against the cession of Nice and Savoy to France, yet this was a political defeat, and of military defeats Garibaldi has no experience; and his friends still hope that he will maintain his reputation and achieve great successes.

On the 11th of May, two steamers, the *Piemonte* and the *Lombardo*, pass between two Neapolitan ships of war, two English ships being present. If the men on board the latter did not cheer the patriots with their voices, their hearts no doubt were not the less beating high with hope and sympathy for them. The steamers passed the Neapolitan men-of-war without receiving any molestation, and landed a few troops at Marsala, about one thousand men, and no more. They were not in military uniform, their bearing was not eminently military, but this because it was not a time for parade evolutions. However, the thousand men were soldiers, and more than that, they were heroes. The Neapolitan ships fired on the city after the landing had been effected; they fired even on the empty vessels, and took the precaution of capturing them in due form, when their defenders had left. They might very well have taken the patriots at first, but they did not; was it out of fear or owing to a secret complicity that they abstained? No! there was assuredly no connivance, for the documents that were then brought forward do not afford the slightest evidence of any. After the landing at Marsala, and throughout the subsequent advances of Garibaldi, up to the victory of Calatafimi, he kept on issuing high-spirited addresses to the Sicilians.

Soon began a succession of victories, which wore almost a fabulous appearance, and of which the records will be almost incredible to a future age. At Calatafimi, on the 15th, was performed one of the most heroic feats of arms recorded in modern history. The combatants were as one to six, and the position of the royalists was very strong. The contest was an obstinate one, nor was the victory easy, because, as Garibaldi himself states, "though the enemy gave way to the bayonet charge of the Alpine Chasseurs, who were opposed to them in the garb of civilians, yet they fought valiantly, and only relinquished their positions after a furious hand-to-hand struggle." So he has elsewhere said in a letter to the "Committee for the Million of Rifles:" "I must confess that the Neapolitans fought like lions, and I have certainly never met with a more obstinate resistance in Italy, nor encountered such valiant combatants. Such soldiers, if well generalled, would make the first troops in the world."

In this manner 1000 Garibaldians had put to flight 6000 opponents, who had offered a resistance deserving of a better fortune, though the cause for which they fought had not been worthy of it. Landi, the marshal who had been defeated at Calatafimi, began to retire upon Palermo, and was terribly harassed in his march by the guerrilla bands of the mountaineers, who had been aroused by the news of the success of the patriots, and who hung upon his flanks incessantly. Garibaldi now formed a plan of attack upon Palermo of almost unparalleled boldness. He proceeded towards the city, but without his march being discerned by the enemy, because he advanced across steep and rugged places, over the sides of the mountains or through hidden glens, by paths that were almost impracticable; he was not discerned, because he sent detachments in a conspicuous manner towards other places, to make it believed that he had given up the idea of attacking Palermo, under the impression that it was impregnable. These detachments were composed of native insurgents, who were flocking together by thousands from all the surrounding country, commanded by officers chosen from their own body, or from the brave men who had come over with Garibaldi. The enemy was deceived. Garibaldi pretended to keep aloof from Palermo, though he was steadily approaching it. General Lanza, who commanded at Palermo, was misled; he expected to have to encounter the enemy elsewhere, and sent a considerable force to Parco. Hereupon Colonel Orsini feigned to retire still further with a portion of the insurgents and Garibaldians, and a few thousand of the royal troops took courage to pursue him down to Corleone. It was at this moment that Garibaldi struck the great blow at Palermo; he came at dawn, and would have come unexpectedly, but the shouts of the Sicilians gave notice of his arrival to the enemy, who sounded an alarm, and fired upon the approaching patriots. Garibaldi, at the head of only 1000 men, assaulted the position defended by Lanza, which contained full 14,000. The struggle was furious, but nothing could resist the patriotic forces and their general. Garibaldi quickly entered Palermo, and the inhabitants then rose upon the garrison. The royalists retired to their strongholds, and a furious bombardment began to desolate the city; one half of which, however, was in the possession of Garibaldi by mid-day. The bombardment continued till the next day, spreading ruin through the city, and causing the sacrifice of countless lives. The troops of Lanza were discomfited and chased from one place to another, till many began to desert to the enemy; their provisions were failing them, and their friends outside the city were receiving continual checks. In this position Lanza knew not what to do, he was surrounded on all sides, and had no hope of relief; he had nothing left for it but to surrender or to die. He asks for an armistice, and obtains it; and the armistice is followed by a capitulation, a disastrous one for the royal cause, but lenient to the troops engaged, who were left free to depart for Naples with all military honours. All Europe was astonished at the event; and the rage and terror of the King of Naples were indescribable. Garibaldi assumed the dictatorship of Palermo and Sicily, which he began to govern in the name of Victor Emmanuel.

We will not dwell on Garibaldi's administration in Sicily, his salutary precautions, his errors (caused only by the magnanimity of his nature), on his generous actions, on the enthusiasm of the people, on the consternation of the reactionists throughout Europe, on the astonishment and delight of the liberals, or on the number of converts in Italy and abroad that were drawn over to the cause of the nation by the enthusiasm which the hero's prowess had excited.

The "too late," which is so often answered to fallen tyrants by their ill-treated subjects, was now heard, as it will not have been heard for the last time, by the King of Naples. He who had so long persisted in his suicidal obstinacy, now at last overcome with consternation, and despairing of the preservation of his power by any other means, granted his people a constitution. But while he seemingly obtained the approbation of the great powers, and even of France, for this unwilling concession, his subjects in great numbers found occasion to intimate to him this "too late" by their behaviour and their countenance.

Garibaldi organized his Sicilian troops, among which the old Italian soldiers served as a cement to keep together a brave and splendid army. And now General Medici reaches Palermo with 3000 veterans, and here comes Cosenz with 2000 troops; and if among these there are some young men who have never before fought, it is otherwise with those who come from Northern and Central Italy; having sustained two years of continual trials, excitements, and military experience, these are all veterans. And now the Bourbon sends messengers to Turin, in hope of charming down the tempest, by making propositions to the Italian government. Cavour is a man that will not allow himself to be blinded. It is required that an offensive and defensive league should be concluded against Austria, and that sufficient guarantees should be given, such as an exchange of garrisons; there must be Piedmontese troops in Naples, and Neapolitan troops in Piedmont, and then negotiations may be instituted. Such conditions are inadmissible for a Bourbon; who might feign an inclination to conciliatory measures, but who inwardly was thirsting for vengeance. But though these negotiations were continued without any prospect of being effectual, they hindered not for an instant the great work of Garibaldi. He left Palermo in an English vessel, called the *City of Aberdeen*, and took the direction of Messina, where he wanted to place himself at the head of some troops of his which had been sent forward previously. Some other companies, commanded by Medici, had already gained a slight advantage at Meri, over the Bourbonists that had sallied from Milazzo.

But the engagement at Meri was only a prelude to the much more remarkable and decisive one which, three days after, that is, on the 20th of July, took place at Milazzo, between the patriotic troops commanded by Garibaldi, and the royalists commanded by Colonel Bosco. The latter enjoyed the reputation of being a brave man, and one of the most able leaders of the Neapolitan army, besides which he had a good name for the rectitude, and in some respects the nobleness, of his character.

On the morning of the 20th, the first volleys were heard at about six o'clock, and the armies soon stood face to face, their front ranks extending over a line of nearly two miles, at an average distance of a mile and a half from Milazzo.

The Sicilians, without artillery, engaged against a far superior number, which occupied a most advantageous position, fought like brave men under the conduct of their invincible general, Garibaldi, and were victorious, after a fierce struggle, which had lasted from six in the morning to three in the afternoon, and that in the month of July and under the sun of Sicily. It ought to be said that the enemy never expected Garibaldi would have had a part in the engagement; they imagined him still at Palermo, surrounded by all the difficulties and annoyances of a civil administration. But Garibaldi came upon them by surprise, at the head of his soldiers, and under his powerful sword the troops were driven back, little by little, towards the castle.

Here the turmoil became terrible, and the city was invaded on all sides; Garibaldians and Neapolitans together rushing pell-mell into it. The latter were pursued and overthrown in every corner, and compelled at last to flee headlong towards the fort, leaving the city and some important outworks in the hands of the victors. The number of the killed and wounded in Garibaldi's army amounted to about 1200, and on the other side to nearly 3000. The fortress soon capitulated, and Bosco retreated with his troops towards Naples, having received all the honours of war.

From this moment the heroic Garibaldi lost no time in sending the flower of his troops to invest Messina. The Bourbonists shut themselves up within the citadel, and left the city in the hands of the conquerors, that is, first of Medici, and the day after of Garibaldi, who was received by the Messinians with enthusiasm. An agreement was entered into, by the mediation of Medici, between Garibaldi and the troops in the citadel, the two parties having to remain in their positions, and promising not to molest one another, and the convention being signed by Marshal Del Cary on the side of the Bourbon king, and by Medici on the part of Garibaldi.

And now the conquest of Sicily could be termed complete, as the royalists retained only the citadel of Messina, and the cities and fortresses of Agosta and Syracuse. Garibaldi therefore thought it better to leave behind him these remnants of the Bourbonists, to be overcome by regular sieges, in order that he might push on to the mainland of Naples. He therefore urged on his preparations with the greatest activity, and collected at the Faro a small fleet, chiefly composed of boats, well provided with all the requisites for easily effecting a landing on the opposite shores of Calabria.

Here it must not be dissembled that it was precisely the prodigious successes of Garibaldi that put the Italian government in a difficult position, and imperilled the regeneration of the Italian peninsula. In this way diplomacy now came in with counsels—but counsels that savoured of a disposition to threaten—in order to arrest the triumphant career of Garibaldi. The king, choosing the smallest evil, wrote to Garibaldi to desist, to be content with that which he had already done, and not to push on towards the mainland. This was perhaps the first time that a king had ever commanded a subject with a hearty desire to be disobeyed. But Garibaldi, though personally a loyal subject of the king, here feels the duty of obeying him a less powerful motive than his desire of liberating his country, and while he protests his loyalty, he avows at the same time that he cannot withhold him from the performance of that task, and from raising his sovereign to the sublime dignity of sole king of a united Italy. And with this view, while the world are awaiting his next step with suspense and anxiety, he makes preparations, in part open and in part secret, for a landing in Calabria. Garibaldi had in readiness near the straits a hundred barks and 8000 men, to cast over at any moment upon the mainland. He only awaited an opportunity to do it securely and unexpectedly. And the opportunity soon arrived.

The first Garibaldians landed in Calabria on the 8th and 9th of August, under the command of Missori. They were few in number, and found it impossible to make themselves masters of the positions occupied by the Bourbonists, but they were able to scatter over the mountains of Calabria, to form nuclei for the organization of the insurrection, and to prepare the way for the great captain. And in fact the province of Basilicata very soon rose in arms to the cry of *Long live Italy and Victor Emmanuel!* the Bourbon garrison in Potenza had been routed and dispersed, and a provisional prodictatorial government was there established. Meantime, on the 19th, Garibaldi set sail from the Sicilian shore, and landed at Capo d'Armi, at the extremity of the Calabrian shore, and thence advanced in the direction of the mountains. Missori and his troops were soon enabled to effect a junction with him. The army of liberators, henceforth to be called the Army of the South, reached Reggio, where it had to endure another encounter with the Bourbon troops, who were routed as usual. After several engagements, in which the bayonet had been used with the effect it seldom fails to produce in the hands of patriots, the royalists were driven to capitulate. In these circumstances the citadel of Reggio was deserted by its defenders, and fell into the hands of the patriots, with a quantity of military stores, which was highly valuable to them. At San Giovanni some resistance was offered by the royalists, but they were defeated and dispersed as usual.

From this time no further obstacle awaited the progress of the victor. His forces were increased from one moment to another by volunteers flocking to him from Sicily, and by the spread of the insurrectionary movement in Calabria; cannons, weapons, and stores of every kind, were also more accessible.

On the 25th August, after other feats of arms, Garibaldi began to invest and occupy Palmi; from whence he wrote to the commandant of Messina: "Our march is a triumph; the people are in ecstasy; the royal troops are disbanding themselves." From hence he proceeded to Monteleone, then to Cosenza, where the royalist general soon capitulated.

On the 31st he wrote from Agrifoglio to the prodictator of Sala, which had risen: "Stand firm, and organize your revolution: there is no need of your coming to meet me; on the contrary, I shall come as early as possible to you. Tell the world that with my brave Calabrians I yesterday made ten thousand soldiers, under General Gbio, lay down their arms: the trophy of the surrender was composed of twelve field-pieces, ten thousand rifles, three hundred horses, nearly as many mules, and immense military stores. Adieu: I am setting out for Rogliono." And so he pushed forwards, while the brave General Türr was landing with four thousand soldiers at Sapri.

Francis II. now began ordering his army (for he had yet a numerous one) to muster on the line of the Volturno. He himself ignominiously quitted Naples on the 6th of September, and directed his course towards Gaeta; and Garibaldi bade the Neapolitans expect him shortly. And the Neapolitans immediately invited him, in a letter written by the minister of the interior, Liborio Romano.

From the morning of the 6th the city was all in a commotion. Tricolor banners, with the cross of Savoy in the middle, were streaming in all the streets to welcome the entrance of the illustrious warrior. At half-past eleven the general arrives with a few officers, and is there met by the authorities and by the national guard. In spite of the broiling heat, the throngs of people were immense: at his appearance it is impossible to describe the joy, the enthusiasm that prevailed, or the acclamations, which were swollen by the voices of thousands in every rank, from the lowest to the highest. They could not satisfy their eyes with the sight of their heroic liberator, whom they conducted in triumph to his palace.

The following were among the words which he addressed to the Neapolitans in his programme. " As a child of the people, it is with genuine reverence and affection that I present myself in this noble and brilliant centre of so many Italian populations, which many ages of despotism have not been capable of humbling, or of reducing to bow the knee in the presence of tyranny."

By his entrance into Naples, Garibaldi had become the master of the Neapolitan fleet, the commanders of which willingly submitted themselves to him. He gave it up to Admiral Persano, to hold till the king should have been consulted about accepting it. Perhaps there were some men with him who had dissuaded him from this surrender; perhaps, if he had left time to evil counsellors to act upon him, he might have been led to keep this fleet for his own martial operations, and in this manner have rendered it useless to the royal government. But all this was prevented, to the immense gain of Italy. The navy became Victor Emmanuel's, and it was this fact chiefly that prevented the Mazzinians, in their unhappy political machinations, from doing much harm subsequently.

Meantime the Piedmontese government was not inactive. An occasion for progress had offered itself. Garibaldi, with his victorious legions and the ultra-liberals of Naples, and indeed of all Italy, were crying: "We must go on while the enthusiasm lasts; we must push into the Papal dominions; we must liberate these unfortunate provinces;" some even said, "We must go to Rome, whether the French like or do not like." If they oppose us, we must come to blows with them. Let that be done by arms which diplomacy cannot accomplish, or else will not." These were perilous cries, which would perhaps have involved Europe in war, as well as imperilled the existence of Italy.

There were here certainly good grounds for Piedmont's coming forward, and if she encountered any opposition from France it must have been a very faint one. Decided military movements were accordingly seen in Piedmont, Tuscany, and Romagna, and troops were pressing towards the Papal frontiers, where large bodies of men, commanded by able generals, were soon concentrated in perfect readiness for action. It soon became fully ascertained that the French in Rome had orders to defend only the patrimony of St. Peter, that is to say, Civitá Vecchia, Viterbo, and Rome, as well as the person of the pope, and that with this view additional reinforcements had been sent out by Napoleon; but that he would go no further. But Lamoricière endeavoured to diffuse terror by atrocious manifestoes, in which he threatened with pillage and destruction whatever city might revolt, and adopted similar measures to defend himself from his enemies in Naples and Piedmont. But these last he feared less, because he relied on the policy of Napoleon to protect the pope. But in all probability Napoleon was very well disposed to see this home-bred enemy of his own receive a lesson from the Piedmontese—and he did receive one, perhaps a better lesson than either France or the world expected. Cialdini now came forward with a considerable force as far as Fano on the Adriatic, and Fanti to Perugia in the valley of the Tiber. Hence advancing they defeated the enemy in various engagements, till they had driven him back upon the lines of Ancona.

Fanti achieved a brilliant victory at Perugia and every city upon his line of march received him with acclamations as a deliverer. Having quitted Fano he occupied Sinigaglia, driving before him General Klanger, who took refuge in Ancona. This city Cialdini soon invested, occupying all the military positions in the neighbourhood, namely, Jesi on the left, Castel Fidardo on the right, and Osimo in the centre. Lamoricière resolved to move against Cialdini, and advanced in two columns, having his rear protected by considerable reserves. The foremost column he commanded in person, and General Pimodan the second. Cialdini divined the nature of his tactics, and having brought together a sufficient force at Castel Fidardo, essayed there to cut off the communication of the enemy with Ancona. He succeeded, and did not neglect to station bodies of troops in the necessary positions, in order to prevent a sally from that fortress. Thus the plan which Lamoricière had formed of taking the Piedmontese by surprise was frustrated by the firmness of their general; and Lamoricière suddenly found himself, with about eleven thousand men, in front of Cialdini, who was ready to receive him. The French general would not retire; he was perhaps confident of victory. The engagement was a severe one, and the Papal leader was defeated with the loss of six cannons and a quantity of weapons, leaving about six hundred prisoners behind him, among whom was Pimodan. The foresight of Cialdini frustrated an attempt at a sortie on the part of the garrison of Ancona, which was driven back within the walls. With some difficulty Lamoricière himself, with a few attendants on horseback, escaped at full speed through the gorges of Monte Conero, by which he reached Ancona; and Cialdini completed his victory by compelling all these mercenaries to capitulate, on condition of being sent to their respective countries.

In this manner Lamoricière was shut up in Ancona, without a chance of escaping, because in good time Admiral Persano arrived with his fleet to command every outlet by sea.

Ancona was forced to capitulate after a furious assault of a few days, during which the tedious process of regular approaches had been superseded by the heroic impetuosity of Cialdini's troops, who were supported with equal skill and courage by the naval forces under Admiral Persano. Lamoricière returned to France, having learned all too late the difference between commanding French troops and commanding mercenaries, and having earned in the service of the pope a disgraceful termination to a long career of military glory.

While these important events were taking place in Central Italy, the Bourbonists succeeded, though with a loss of 2000 men, in mastering the important position of Cajazzo, in which they intrenched themselves. But the advance of Victor Emmanuel's troops through the Marches and Umbria towards Naples, excited hopes that this partial disaster might soon be retrieved for the Garibaldians. And this movement Garibaldi announced in the most generous terms as follows:— "The brave soldiers of the army of the North have crossed the frontier, and are already in the Neapolitan territory. We shall soon have the pleasure of pressing those victorious hands."

And presently, on the 1st and 2d of October, there was a well-contested engagement near Santa Maria and Caserta, between the Garibaldians and the royalists. The former obtained a complete victory after an incessant fire of nine hours' duration. The royalist generals had hoped, in the event of their being themselves victorious, that they might have fallen upon Naples, and devastated with fire and sword both that metropolis and the whole kingdom. The troops of Garibaldi derived here great advantages from the presence in the mêlée of so many regular troops, and so many officers from the Italian army, and to this fact the brave dictator alluded in the order of the day as follows: "The brave and highly disciplined soldiers of the North, commanded by the valiant Major Luigi Saldo, have to-day displayed what Italian valour can do when combined with discipline; and have shown whether this ancient queen of the world can be again trodden down, so long as her children shall be of one mind, and shall all act in concert for the redemption of their native country."

The victory of the Volturno may be considered as one of the most splendid military achievements in the war for the independence of Italy.

Meantime the parliament was hastily convoked. Cavour spoke with the usual magic effect. He urged with the most cogent arguments the immediate annexation of the Two Sicilies, of the Marches, which had so recently been subjugated, and of Umbria. The annexation was voted for almost unanimously, that is to say by 290 against 6.

After the battle of Volturno, by which the royalists were driven back, partly upon Capua, and partly upon Gaeta, Garibaldi found it more than ever advisable to stand still and await the aid of the regular troops in order to complete his work. The taking of Capua was difficult in itself, but did not require any extraordinary means of attack; it was otherwise, however, with Gaeta, which was considered one of the strongest places in Europe, and for which many great captains, and the first Napoleon himself, had had to endure great sacrifices of time and lives. Besides, the garrison of Gaeta was very numerous, and fit to be termed an army in itself.

The pope, filled with terror by the exploits of the royal liberator and his champion, both of whom he denounced as impious and sacrilegious, appealed loudly to the Catholic powers for succour.

King Francis from his lair at Gaeta addressed loud complaints to all the European powers. Spain proved herself hereat wonderfully tender of the interests of the pope, and the dear kinsman of her queen, and demanded a congress of the Catholic powers. Even Napoleon reinforced the garrison of Rome, and formed, it was supposed, the intention of doubling it. And Victor Emmanuel sent his army into the territory of Naples, and himself started to complete his grand task in person. The English nation displayed a sincere enthusiasm for the Italian cause, and was destined by its moral support to confer an inestimable benefit upon the new kingdom by the alacrity with which it acknowledged its creation.

The 21st day of October saw enacted, in good order, and by an immense concourse of voters, the *plebiscitum* in the provinces of Southern Italy. Meantime the royalists evacuated Cajazzo, which was forthwith occupied by the Garibaldians; and Victor Emmanuel inflicted a defeat on them at Teano. At the same place, on the 25th of October, occurred the meeting between Victor Emmanuel and Garibaldi, which produced a profound sensation among the Italians.

But now Prussia, Russia, and France herself are protesting. Prussia expresses her disapprobation with much circumlocution, but her ambassador remains at his post. France protests, or feigns to protest, and recalls her ambassador from Turin. Russia protests loudly and haughtily, and recalls her ambassador likewise. And Italy goes onward.

Presently the garrison of Capua capitulates (2d Nov.), having been unable to resist the united force and courage of the armies of Northern and Southern Italy, which have been assiduously pressing her on all sides. Gaeta alone remains in the power of king Francis.

On the 3d of November, General Sonnaz, commanding the advanced guard, effected the passage of the Garigliano, after having driven back and routed the Neapolitans, while the fleet at Gaeta was harrassing them in the flanks. Sonnaz very adroitly seized this opportunity, and made himself master of the mole of Gaeta and the surrounding positions. King Francis was now shut up in Gaeta, while a body of 13,000 men, with two cannons, was cut off from the fortress and reduced to crossing the Roman frontier, as their best alternative, at Terracina, where they were disarmed by the French troops.

Nevertheless the French admiral, Lebarbier de Tinan, presents himself now with the French fleet in front of Gaeta, where for many weeks he played, on behalf of France, a game very odious to the Italians, in defending Francis Bourbon, by preventing Persano from co-operating by sea in the attack upon Gaeta.

Garibaldi now fulfils his mission. After having accompanied the king, on the 17th of November, to Naples, where the popular transport was indescribable, and having seen him legally invested with the sovereignty of the new provinces, in virtue of the *plebiscitum*, this man, so great in his victories, and equally great in his moderation and simplicity, having refused the title of prince which had been offered him in acknowledgment of his brilliant achievements, retired to the lonely isle of Caprera, where he thenceforth lived a simple and rural life, while he awaited another occasion of offering the service of his arm to Italy, as soon as it could be valuable to her.

Gaeta, which continued to be besieged by General Cialdini, was, if not an impregnable fortress, at least one of which the capture might well occupy many months. Not on one side alone, but all sides, arises a natural barrier of formidable cliffs, which makes the place almost inaccessible. The soil is rocky throughout, which increases materially the difficulties of constructing the approaches. All the heights are occupied with castles, towers, or fortifications. Towards the sea, again, Gaeta is protected by formidable batteries; but still more by the French fleet, which will not permit any approaches by the ships under the command of the gallant Admiral Persano.

Under all these circumstances, the approaches to Gaeta are constructed with incredible alacrity, skill, and perseverance. Cialdini is a great general, but he has here many obstacles to encounter. But now Napoleon is forced to decide upon a step, which has become necessary in order to still the exclamations of all the liberal part of Europe, and to obviate the loss of all the advantages which he may derive from the title he has acquired to the gratitude of Italy. The French fleet is now withdrawn from the waters of Gaeta, under the pretext that a demonstration of sympathy for the misfortunes of Francis II. has been perverted into an act of political intervention. And this proceeding was the more necessary for the emperor's honour, because under the ægis of French protection, the Bourbonist reactionaries had proceeded to the most atrocious extremities in many parts of the Neapolitan territory, and especially in the Abruzzi, under the guidance of the Count of Trapani, and by the infamous co-operation of the Papal government. The French fleet having been withdrawn on the 19th of January, 1861, General Cialdini by land, and Admiral Persano by sea, commence a devastating bombardment. Victor Emmanuel is not present at the scene, because he has already quitted Naples, having left the Prince of Carignano as his substitute, with Nigra and Liborio Romano as his ministers; a combination highly gratifying to the Neapolitans. Gaeta, in spite of the bombardment, holds out through the 19th and several of the following days. The Italians are encouraged by the speech of Napoleon at the opening of the French chambers, in which he clearly affirms his determination to maintain the principle of non-intervention. And this is all that the Italians desire of him.

Cialdini and his brave troops repeat at Gaeta the prodigies of valour and endurance which have been displayed at Ancona. Their skill and energy are irresistible. The garrison is decimated by their projectiles, in spite of ramparts and casemates. At last a bomb, discharged from a ship, falls upon and explodes a powder-magazine within the fortifications, producing a terrible destruction of lives and works; and on the 13th of February the Bourbon, having been compelled to capitulate, embarks in a French vessel to take refuge in Rome. And so ended the Bourbon rule in Naples, the most atrocious and the most hypocritical tyranny which the world has ever witnessed.

The first Italian parliament is convoked at Turin on the 18th of February. It afforded a spectacle perfectly novel in modern history; and assuredly the hearts of the Italians must have beaten high with a just pride at the thought that their noble nation was here represented by its own delegates, not in consequence of any mere accidents of political history, but by the effect of their own valour and judgment, of which they had given so many proofs in civil and military difficulties, which might have appeared insurmountable. It was a noble spectacle to behold that king, who had never swerved from the good faith he owed to his country, with a radiant and martial countenance, opening his mouth for the first time in the new national assembly. And it was a noble thing (and such it was discerned to be), when, with the calmness of a pure conscience and of a fearless heart, he began to say, "At one time my words sounded bold; it being as wise to dare in season as to wait in season. Devoted as I am to Italy, I have never hesitated to expose my life and crown for her sake, but no one has a right to risk the life and destinies of a nation." Other words followed which it must be satisfactory to Englishmen to recollect: "The government and people of England, of old the native country of freedom, have loudly declared for our right to be the arbiters of our own destinies, and have lavishly bestowed on us their good offices, the grateful remembrance of which will be imperishable."

The senate was in the first place invited to acknowledge Victor Emmanuel as King of Italy. The validity of the election in this manner received a more imposing sanction, because it was seen to commence with the grandees of the country. Thus the King of Piedmont was almost unanimously voted King of Italy, without the phrase by the grace of God, under the name of "Vittorio Emmanuelle Secondo." A few days afterwards the parliament adopted the same decision, and almost unanimously likewise. Thus the Italian nation, for the first time in its history, had elected its own king.

Austria sees that she is in a bad case, and grants a kind of constitution to the peoples under her

away. Messina falls also, at last, under the irresistible bombardment of Cialdini. And thus the Bourbon rule is at an end in every part of the kingdom of the Two Sicilies.

At Rome the Bourbon, with all his family, begins to conspire, to coin money, and to recruit thousands upon thousands of disbanded Bourbon soldiers, escaped convicts from the galleys and houses of correction, and a scum of desperate adventurers from all parts of Europe, together with a few simple-minded people, who are tempted for their own destruction to attach themselves to this horde of murderers. To these are joined a portion of the clergy, and especially of the prelates of all Italy, with their countless satellites, who will henceforth plot in darkness to destroy her king, and raise up enemies against him by unscrupulous artifices, abusing the character of their profession and the imposing rite of confession, to intimidate devotees, and to bring them into relations with the partisans of the Bourbon and the pope, in order to produce all kinds of disorders in the Neapolitan territory, and to foster there a sanguinary and atrocious system of brigandage.

Garibaldi, a man of burning heart and of strong passions—though only strong where he believes that duty sanctions them—makes in parliament a violent attack upon the ministers, or rather upon Cavour personally, characterising as fratricidal the opposition which the latter has instituted to the claims of the army of the South. A surprising commotion is produced in the house; shouts are raised on both sides, and the meeting at last has to be adjourned. When quiet had been restored, many accusations and excuses were uttered on both sides, and not without considerable bitterness. What a triumph for the retrograde party in Italy and throughout the world! To crown all misfortunes, the papers were full of a letter from Cialdini to Garibaldi, in which the former, with the most acrimonious expressions, renounced the friendship of the latter. But who would have believed it? The two men who like and dislike, not from personal impressions, but according to the dictates of a boundless affection for their common country, after one immoderate outburst of feeling, recollect themselves, become aware how much evil might accrue to Italy from a quarrel between its two champions, draw near to one another, speak to one another in private through the mediation of their king, come to a mutual understanding, are pacified, and make a solemn agreement that they will rather seek to build up by their friendly co-operation than to pull down by their enmity; and Cialdini is a third in that reconciliation. Garibaldi retires again to his solitude.

Garibaldi had now obtained some not inconsiderable concessions in favour of the army of the South, the demands of the officers of that body being mostly satisfied, except in the case of the least worthy, through the agency of a mixed commission, composed in great part of generals from the volunteer army, in whom both Garibaldi and the public had implicit confidence. Hereupon a decree was passed that the army should be organized as quickly as possible by a general levy throughout the kingdom, to the number of 300,000 men—a measure proposed with great warmth by Garibaldi, seconded by the ministry, and approved by the house. Nor was this sufficient. A loan of twenty millions of pounds sterling to support the great expenditure required for the civil reforms, the army, and the construction of the railways, is passed in the parliament by an immense majority. The National Guard is next organized on a more effective footing; by which means Italy was provided with some hundreds of thousands of able defenders without any burden being imposed on the government; and a few weeks later was passed the law for the mobilisation of 143,000 men of this National Guard, a law which would have been perilous in any other country, but which proved salutary for Italy, because of the populations being animated by the true spirit of patriotism. This law was passed towards the middle of June.

A great proof of patriotism was given by parliament in the law for the unification of the national debt, a great part of the voters for which law had to suffer personally through it, by reason of the previous immense inequality of the public debt in Piedmont and in the other provinces. But this was a just and patriotic law, and was readily sanctioned by men of all parties.

In the month of July the law was passed for the appropriation of the convents to civil uses, by which stop the anger of the pope was again braved without pusillanimity. A comprehensive and compendious law for the construction of a network of railways throughout Italy, was further voted by a great majority; and immediate operations were decided upon, in order that this source of public prosperity might as soon as possible be rendered available. Some of these laws only had been voted, though the rest followed shortly afterwards, when the world was struck by an event which occasioned general sorrow, and in Italy a profound emotion. Cavour finished his glorious career on the evening of June 3, being still in the prime of life and apparently in the enjoyment of very good health. With Cavour sank the most active promoter of Italian regeneration, and the very life of the cause; one of the greatest diplomatists whose names appear in history, and still greater because the liberation of his country had been the only end on which he had concentrated the great powers of his mind, by thinking of nothing, living for nothing but the noble design of seeing Italy united, free, and independent. Never did a man die with more glory, nor having better merited it than Cavour; the admiration excited by his vast and comprehensive intelligence, and all the subtlety, address, and versatility of his conduct, was unalloyed by any doubt as to the continued purity of his motives. Italy at this catastrophe was for a time struck with ineffable grief and consternation. But she soon recovered, and began to trust that the work so happily inaugurated by this great man might be completed without his help.

In appointing a successor to Cavour, king Victor Emmanuel had no difficulty: the opinion of the public had already elected one. This was Baron Ricasoli, a man of rare, or rather of unique uprightness, of great firmness, and of a patriotism that was proof against all trials; and the man who had been the principal promoter of the annexation of Tuscany to Piedmont.

Besides all this, and besides his iron will and antique austerity, Ricasoli was known as one of the most decided antagonists of the Papacy, in regard to its temporal authority: it was moreover proclaimed that he was not averse to a large measure of religious reform being introduced, if occasion favoured.

Napoleon at last decided on recognizing the new kingdom, reviving diplomatic communications with it, and establishing an ambassador at Turin. These points he tardily conceded, to gratify his old ally England, which had already, during many months, recognized the kingdom of Italy. The example was soon followed by other powers. From the very beginning of his career Ricasoli had made repeated solemn declarations in the parliament, which were regarded as imprudent by timid minds, but which produced an excellent effect at home and abroad. He declared that his programme would be Rome, the capital of Italy, and the expulsion of the Austrians from Venice; which programme, however, would submit to the laws of necessity, and would not be carried out without caution, or proper consideration of the policy of friendly nations, and above all of the principal ally of Italy. Another of his solemn declarations gave great satisfaction to Italy, and to all liberal minds in Europe. It had been asseverated that the recognition of Italy had been made conditional upon the cession of the island of Sardinia. This rumour—whether consistent or not—had deeply agitated the whole of Europe, and especially England, to such a degree as to elicit from the mouth of Lord Russell, in full parliament, a formal declaration, that nothing would be more likely to break up the alliance between France and England, and perhaps to pave the way for a coalition against Napoleon, than this cession. But Ricasoli removed all occasion of misunderstanding, by loudly declaring that neither promises, nor threats, nor benefits, should ever induce him to give up an inch of Italian ground to any foreign power. And such an assurance from Ricasoli was sufficient to convince every one, because it was well known that he was not a man of artifice and equivocation, and that the promise he had given would never be recalled.

Meantime Italy was suffering more and more deeply from the hordes of brigands, which were supported in the Neapolitan territory by the intrigues of the pope, the Jesuits, and the infatuated Bourbon. Thousands and thousands of assassins were infesting this beautiful country, never assuredly meant by nature to be a receptacle for such atrocious criminals—and making it a scene of spoliation, arson, and cruel massacres of women, children, and aged men, of which no tongue could give account. But even for these evils the Italian government began soon to find a remedy. Cialdini was the man it found capable of putting down these scandalous proceedings, and punishing the offenders. He had a numerous body of regular troops under his command, and reinforcements were speedily forthcoming. Cialdini accordingly set out for the place of his destination; and San Martino resigned his functions of lieutenant-governor, in the performance of which he had shown a superfluous lenity and urbanity, prompted by a too solicitous desire of making personal friends, which had had the effect of increasing the number of the disturbers of the public peace, till they amounted well-nigh to an army. Moreover, Cialdini had the skill to avail himself of an immediate and very effective resource in the National Guard of Naples and the provinces; which had always been well disposed, but was now, through the deference with which the general treated it, confirmed in its good-will, alacrity, and desire to serve Italy by clearing her soil of the brigands. And in this way, whereas more than thirty thousand men had previously been required to repress this evil, a far smaller number was now found sufficient; because from unwarlike citizens they had been transformed into gallant soldiers.

Cialdini furthermore called to the service of his endangered country the dispersed Garibaldian troops; and with these, and with his regular soldiers, as well as the National Guard, was soon able to press closer upon the malefactors, whose bands, though incessantly recruited by Bourbon and papal machinations, were now rapidly driven from place to place, surrounded, taken prisoners, shot, and almost extirpated.

Since the Neapolitan brigands were thus repressed, if not conquered, Italy has been proceeding gradually to regulate her internal affairs, and prudently to assimilate her local institutions. But in this sphere enormous difficulties still remain to be surmounted by her—political difficulties from abroad, religious difficulties, legal difficulties, arising from the recent amalgamation of so many different states, which, though all alike Italian, have been separated from one another by the annals of so many centuries. Then again, Austria remains to be attacked and overcome by force of arms, since she will not yield to persuasion. Rome remains to be annexed, and declared the capital of the kingdom, for important political, historical, strategical, and statistical reasons. It remains to bring the pope by moral compulsion, inasmuch as all persuasion is useless, to divest himself of his temporal power, and to live contented with a spiritual supremacy—this perhaps being the greatest difficulty of all. It remains to appease thousands of hungry applicants for place, dignity, and power;,many of whom are totally undeserving, and ought therefore to be silenced with a simple refusal, while many, however, among them have been meritorious officers under the former rulers of the country, and are now in absolute want of the means of subsistence. It remains to repress the increasing fury of the clerical party, which leaves not even the most flagitious means untried to weaken and endanger the reviving welfare of the Peninsula. It remains for Italy, in short, to overcome the most fearful obstacles from within and from without, to do which, her patience, endurance, and moderation must yet be taxed for a long time. But her children have hitherto given continual proofs that they are equal to the great task, for never yet has a revolution been initiated with so much moderation as the Italian has been. And though the opposition to its consummation is formidable, yet it is gradually being overcome by the will of a great people, and by the favour of Providence, which has encouraged by so many visible tokens the process of Italian regeneration. And accordingly—although the re-action is making great efforts—though the so-called legitimists are plotting in darkness under the papal ægis to abolish the novel phenomenon of a united and powerful Italy—though endless intrigues are being carried on between the two great despots at Rome and at Vienna—though even the friends of Italy may be becoming her enemies—she will triumph in spite of all.

That this is the case is proved by the whole series of events, of which we have given a rapid outline; and the very obstacles which the process apparently encounters will but confirm the final result. If there had been no difficulties in the raising of the great edifice of Italian regeneration, it could never have been so solid, and so calculated for permanence. The great point is, that Italy should still go forward for a while with the same firmness, the same good-will and prudence, as heretofore; that she should be discouraged by no temporary impediments; that her efforts should continue to prove the same temper and self-reliance; that she should pursue the grand work of national armament without being intimidated by the threats of the pope, his adherents, or the clergy generally; and that she should seize the right moment to contend with Austria, without anticipating it by an infelicitous impatience. And so will she soon attain all her desires, and become united and independent: so will she attain that rank among the nations of the world which is due to her on historical grounds, and on account of her geographical position and her population; and so will a new epoch of glory and greatness be in store for her, to which she will certainly be welcomed by the unenvying and enthusiastic sympathy of Great Britain.

The great work of religious reformation is that alone, however, which can secure to her permanent liberty and security; and it is to be earnestly hoped that the many active means now employed may lead to the adoption of a pure faith, and to an entire deliverance from the ecclesiastical system which has crushed Italy for more than twelve hundred years.

ITALY

ILLUSTRATED & DESCRIBED

ITALY,

ILLUSTRATED AND DESCRIBED.

NICE.

NICE is said to have been founded by the Massilii, about 600 B.C. Its original name of *Nicæa* (*victory*), given to it to commemorate the conquest of the Ligurians by the Massilii, has been converted by the French into Nice, and by the Italians into Nizza. The ancient city, of which all traces have disappeared, occupied the site of the present citadel: its fortifications were sufficiently strong to repress the incursions of the Ligurians and the mountain tribes, and to protect the navigation in its vicinity. Nice became, at length, subject to Rome; and, on the decline and ultimate dismemberment of the empire, it passed through all the vicissitudes to which the Roman provinces were then exposed. It was afterwards ceded to the Counts of Provence, and formed part of the ducal territory of Savoy, along with which it was ceded by Sardinia to France in 1860.

In 1543, Nice sustained an attack from the combined forces of Francis I. and the Turks, on which occasion the city was saved by an act of female gallantry, worthy to stand on record beside the more recent heroism of the Maid of Saragossa. In one of the assaults, the Janissaries had actually planted the crescent on the ramparts, when a woman, named Catherine Segurana, the wife of a poor citizen, rallied the retreating garrison, and struck down the Turkish standard-bearer with a hatchet. This instance of bravery inspired her countrymen with new energy; they returned with enthusiasm to their defences, and drove the assailants from the walls. The citizens of Nice raised a statue in honour of the heroine; but the descent of her fame has suffered from the fidelity of the sculptor, who, by a too faithful portraiture of the "amazon," has conveyed to posterity "a fearful record of her ugliness."

The present aspect of Nice is described as being that of a pretty, small city, not fortified, stretching round the back of a steep, rocky mount, whereon, till recently, stood the ruins of the once formidable castle. These ruins are now removed, and the ground is converted into a delightful promenade, whence is obtained a magnificent view of the coast and inland scenery. The architectural character of the city is not uniform: in the older portions, the avenues are narrow, and deficient in point of cleanliness; but the streets, squares, and terraces, which have sprung up in consequence of the great influx of visitants, are spacious and elegant, and impress the stranger, whether ennuyée or invalid, very strongly in their favour. The names of the streets are written up both in French and Italian; but the dialect of the Nizzari differs considerably from either of these languages, and possesses much interest on account of its alleged antiquity, and also as being the dialect of the Troubadours, whose minstrelsy gave the first impulse to poetry in modern Italy. The King of Sardinia was anxious to restore its Italian nationality to Nice; but owing to its position with respect to France, and even more, perhaps, to its mixed population, there is a strange jumble of language, appearance, and manners.

Nice does not contain any public buildings worthy of particular regard. The cathedral of Santa Reparata, built in 1650, is in the ordinary Italian style of architecture, and presents little to attract attention. The pictorial decorations, which form so prominent a feature in the churches generally, render no aid to this edifice, the few which it contains being equally mediocre with the structure itself. In one respect, this cathedral stands on equality with all the churches of Italy—in the number of lazzaroni who carry on their mendicant profession within its sanctuary. "The Sunday after we arrived," observes a recent writer, "we were driven from the cathedral by the importunity and disgusting appearance of the beggars, who, at Nice, as in all Italian cities, pursue their occupation with the same industry and pertinacity in the church as on the street."

The Croce di Marmo, or Marble Cross, commemorates the conference between Francis I. and Charles V., in which Pope Paul III. endeavoured to adjust the differences between those rival monarchs, and effect a reconciliation. In this the pontiff only partially succeeded; the sovereigns regarded each other with such deep animosity, that at this conference, so named, they could never be persuaded to meet together; and Paul, with much difficulty, procured their joint agreement to a ten years' truce, during which period each was to confine himself within the territory presently in his possession. The Croce di Marmo gives name to the faubourg in its vicinity, which is also called the Citta degli Inglesi, from its being that part of the city in which the English principally reside. It stands apart from the rest of the town, and contains some good houses, with pleasant gardens attached. In the neighbourhood is a chapel of the English Church, erected in 1821, by permission of Vittorio Emanuel. It stands in the midst of an English burial-ground, which has become a place of deep interest from the numerous records scattered over it of the young and beautiful who came hither—to die.

In the city of Nice itself, there is as little to interest the antiquary as the lover of art; but in the environs some remarkable remains are still existing. A pleasant drive leads to the modern village of Cimella, occupying the site of the ancient Civitas Cemellensis, once a place of considerable importance. In this neighbourhood are the remains of a Roman amphitheatre, named by the peasants the Bath of the Fairies. Other remains are discovered in the contiguous farms and vineyards, presenting less obvious traces of Roman structure. In the church of the Franciscan Monastery, which occupies a delightful position in this vicinity, is a very good painting by Ludovico Brea, the only artist of eminence whose name is associated with Nice. Other excursions, presenting great variety of scenery, may be made through the environs of Nice. Amongst the objects of interest may be mentioned the Convent of San Bartolomeo, in which is an altar piece of considerable merit; the Il Vallone Oscuro, a fine mountain gorge, worthy the pencil of Salvator Rosa; and the La Fontana del Tempio, a valley not less remarkable for its beautiful repose than is the Vallone Oscuro for its wild and savage grandeur.

The picturesque features of Nice and the surrounding country, and the salubrity of the climate, were too highly rated by early visitants, and there is now a tendency to undervalue the natural features and qualities of this locality. When it first became a place of resort, it

was recommended as a suitable residence for persons suffering from pulmonary complaints; for this class of invalids, however, experience has shown that it is not well adapted. The cloudless sky common to Italy is almost always visible, but the air is very piercing and highly unfavourable to disease of the lungs. The invalid is, moreover, much exposed to the two winds named the *bise* and the *marin*, the former bringing cold, and the latter damp. The comforts so amply found in the houses and hôtels, counteract, to a great extent, the inconveniences resulting from climate; but the medical testimony of the present day does not recommend a lengthened stay at Nice to those who exhibit consumptive tendencies, or in whom, at least, these tendencies have made any decided advance. To other classes of invalids, this locality offers renovation of health, resulting, perhaps, less from peculiarity of climate than from the exciting and sublime scenery by which it is environed. To the tourist, Nice is an interesting and pleasant place of sojourn before crossing the Alpine barrier of Italy.

VINTIMIGLIA.

ABOUT six miles from Mentone, in the route from Nice to Vintimiglia, and in the immediate neighbourhood of the latter place, stands the Bridge of St. Louis, built across a ravine, on rocks whose height is from three hundred to four hundred feet. An aqueduct is also thrown over the ravine, which adds considerably to the beautiful effect of the bridge, beneath which the water falls in a succession of cascades. Both the bridge and the aqueduct were constructed by the command of Napoleon, and they serve alike as monuments of his enterprise, and grateful recollections of a man more remembered for his unrelenting ambition than for beneficence to his species.

The little town of Vintimiglia, seated on a high rock above the Mediterranean, and commanded by its still more lofty castle, is situated on the right bank of the Roya, close to its junction with the sea, and presents a most picturesque appearance from every point of approach. From the side towards Nice, where the road is level with the town, and elevated far above the sea, the wild masses of overhanging cliffs are speckled with the aloe, the prickly pear, and even the palm tree, which last vegetates thus far from the north in some deep recesses of the coast, and gives it almost an Eastern character. Beyond this grand foreground, the eye gathers up the white and shingled line of coast to Bordighera, and the headlands which mingle in the haze with the horizon. The approach from the Genoese side is strikingly different. Vintimiglia, surmounted by its castle, is seen perched on a precipice, the access to which is by a bridge, crossing the broad winter's bed of the Roya, whence by a steep, abrupt, and winding ascent, we approach the town. The view chosen for this work shows the junction of the Roya with the Mediterranean, and presents in picturesque combination the bridge and castle already mentioned.

Vintimiglia is a place of great antiquity, the Albium Intemelium of the Romans, and the capital of the Ligures Intemelii: it is mentioned by several classical historians, and more particularly by Tacitus, who calls it a municipium, and relates, concerning it, the anecdote of the

VINTIMIGLIA.

Ligurian mother, who, when the town was taken by Otho, died by torture rather than divulge the place of her son's concealment. In the middle ages, Vintimiglia repeatedly changed masters, the possession of it being obstinately contested by the Genoese, the Dukes of Savoy, and the Counts of Provence. Previous to the invasion by the French, it was the frontier town between the States of Sardinia and Genoa. It is now an episcopal see, founded, according to tradition, by St. Barnabas, the apostle, who is stated to have first preached the gospel here.

The Duomo, or cathedral, an ancient structure, now considerably modernized, is supposed to have been a temple of Juno. Some portions still exhibit a rude and singular Gothic style of architecture, peculiar to the Riviera, and at present unnoticed by writers on this subject. Various inscriptions, attesting the antiquity of the town, are inserted in this building, and are also to be found in other parts of the city. The church of St. Michael, another ecclesiastical structure, was anciently a heathen temple, dedicated to Castor and Pollux. It is the custom, throughout the Continent, to leave the churches open during the day and evening. This privilege of free access to a place of worship takes its value from the estimation in which the building is held, not merely as a gathering place for worshippers, but as a spot holy and apart, a hallowed retreat from all that is secular and profane. On entering a church in the gloom of evening, the mind can scarcely resist the touching sentiments of the scene, as the eye wanders round the aged structure, dimly revealed by the light of a single lamp, and discovers a groupe of women kneeling in deep abstraction, and making silence more impressive by the low and whispered murmurs of sighs and prayers. It is, however, only the poetry of religion that the spectator feels.

Vintimiglia has been strongly fortified, as being the spot where the defence of the Sardinian territory against any aggression on the part of the French must necessarily begin. This city divides with San Remo, a wealthy town, about sixteen miles to the eastward, the advantage of supplying palm leaves to Rome for the ceremonies of Palm Sunday. A vessel, with a cargo of these sacred branches, has regularly sailed every year since 1587; and the privilege of sending them is still retained in the Bresca family, by whom it was obtained in a remarkable way from Pope Sixtus V. Thousands had assembled to witness the raising of the obelisk in the centre of the colonnade of St. Peter's. The multitude were enjoined to observe strict silence, that the orders of Fontana, the engineer, might be heard by the workmen employed in the operation; and a violation of this order was to be punished with immediate death by hanging, a gallows for that purpose having been erected on the spot. The obelisk had nearly reached its destined position, when Fontana noticed, with deep anxiety, that the ropes had stretched to the utmost, and that there was danger of their breaking from extreme tension. At this moment, a shout was heard from the crowd, "*Bagnate le corde*" (wet the rope). This was instantly done: the wetted cords contracted, and the obelisk was raised to and rested in its place. A man now stepped forward, and surrendered himself to the punishment he had incurred by breaking silence: it was the Capitano Bresca, the master of a merchant vessel of San Remo. Fontana embraced him amidst the cheers of the multitude, introduced him to Sixtus, and obtained his immediate pardon; and the Pope, besides rewarding him with a considerable pension, gave him the hereditary privilege of supplying the holy see with palm branches for the service of the Church of Rome.

In the neighbourhood of Vintimiglia is Monte Appio, a shoulder of the Alps, or perhaps of the Apennines, it being difficult to decide with certainty where the one ends and the other begins. A castle, consisting of two stone towers, and said to be of Roman structure, is still existing on this mountain, together with other fortifications, supposed to be of Genoese origin.

GENOA.

Near to the main road between Vintimiglia and Bordighera, and by the side of the river Nervia, stands the ancient castle of Dolce Acqua, an interesting relic of the feudal age. This structure occupies a site of remarkable beauty, and is thus rendered not more attractive to the historian and antiquary than to the lover of the picturesque.

GENOA.

GENOA, the superb! Such is the designation accorded to this queenly city by the host of admiring visitants who yearly throng thither to gaze upon its magnificent structures, and to examine the treasures of art which they enshrine. Tourists contend with each other to do honour to Genoa, and well nigh exhaust the language of eulogy in its praise. In the words of one writer, "It looks like a fairy city of white marble rising out of the sea, the blue waters of which are only one shade deeper than the cerulean sky with which, at a distance, they seem to mingle." By another, we are told, that not to her churches, though many in number, large in size, and rich in decoration, does "Genoa owe her splendid *individuality* among the cities of the earth. It is to her palaces, with their marble terraces, their hanging gardens, and their stately halls; it is to the unspeakable brightness of the sea that bathes her shores, and of the sky that is her canopy; of the bold hills that are her buckler to the north, with the innumerable villas which seem to smile upon her from among them; and, though last not least, it is the overflowing fertility of the golden garden in which she lies, with its orange groves, its lemon trellises, its myrtles, oleanders, and pomegranates, which, altogether, give it an aspect and a charm that would be sought in vain elsewhere." Lastly, and best of all, we have a poet's testimony to the magnificent spectacle presented in the seaward approach to Genoa :—

"At length the day departed, and the moon
Rose like another sun, illumining
Waters and woods, and cloud-capt promontories,
Glades for a hermit's cell, a lady's bower,
Scenes of Elysium, such as night alone
Reveals below, nor often—scenes that fled
As at the waving of a wizard's wand,
And left behind them, as their parting gift,
A thousand nameless odours. All was still;
And now the nightingale her song poured forth
In such a torrent of heart-felt delight,
So fast it flowed, her tongue so voluble,
As if she thought her hearers would be gone
Ere half was told. 'Twas where in the north-west,
Still unassail'd and unassailable,
Thy pharos, GENOA, first displayed itself,
Burning in stillness on its craggy seat;

GENOA.

> That guiding star, so oft the only one,
> When those now glowing in the azure vault,
> Are dark and silent. 'Twas where o'er the sea—
> For we were now within a cable's length,
> Delicious gardens hung; green galleries,
> And marble terraces in many a flight,
> And fairy arches flung from cliff to cliff,
> Wildering, enchanting, and, above them all,
> A palace, such as somewhere in the East,
> In Zenastan, or Araby the blest,
> Among its golden groves, and fruits of gold,
> And fountains scattering rainbows in the sun,
> Rose, when Aladdin rubb'd the wond'rous lamp;
> Rose, if not fairer; and, when we shot by,
> A scene of revelry, in long array,
> The windows blazing. But we now approach'd
> A city far renown'd; and wonder ceas'd."

This exquisite description rivals the scene which it pourtrays: that it is not a mere poetical rapture, we have the assurance of one, who says, in reference to the same view,—" I know of no words expressing beauty, splendour, and majesty, that are strong enough to do it justice."

Tourists unite in the opinion that Genoa is most impressive in its general exterior, and is best seen from the sea. Some indeed have spoken disparagingly of the streets and buildings, as losing, on a near approach, much of the beauty which they assume at a distance; others again, give to this city the superiority over Naples and Constantinople, inasmuch as it fulfils the expectations which are raised by the first and general view. The streets of Genoa are narrow, and more so as compared with the height of the palazzi which form them; but in an Italian city, that gloom which pervades the confined avenues of a town in northern Europe, is unknown. The truth appears to be, that the magnificent coup d'œil obtained from the Gulf of Genoa presents an assemblage of beauty that is by no means favourable to the after survey of the city in detail;—that, in short, the one is *necessarily* far more impressive than the other.

Tradition has given to Genoa an existence prior to that of Rome, and the Genoese trace the foundation of their city, and its name, to Janus. It took part with Rome in the war against Carthage, and afterwards remained in alliance with her. On the decline of the Western Empire, it fell into the possession of the Lombards, from whom it was taken by Charlemagne, who united it to the Ligurian coast, and gave the command of the territory to a count. During the struggles for the crown of Italy, between the German emperors and the Berengarians and other claimants, the Genoese asserted their independence, and established an elective government by consuls, whose names are recorded from the eleventh century. Genoa acquired an early naval and military reputation in her contest with the Saracens, against whom she united with the Pisans, and ultimately succeeded in defeating the invaders on their own coast. The Genoese next distinguished themselves in the great crusade, under Godfrey de Bouillon, and, not long after, in their struggle with the Moors. But these victories excited the jealousy of the Pisans, between whom and the Genoese a protracted warfare was carried on, which ended in the total destruction of Pisa as a maritime power.

Some time before the final defeat of the Pisans, Genoa found another and a more powerful rival in Venice. The Genoese having assisted Palæologus in recovering Constantinople from the Franks, obtained, as the reward of their services, the suburbs of Pera and Galata, and

Smyrna. This acquisition of territory raised the jealousy of the Venetians, and led to a war between them and the Genoese, which, though occasionally interrupted by intervals of peace, and conducted with various success, resulted in the ultimate triumph of Venice. Along with this discomfiture, Genoa had to sustain herself against the internal discord arising from the intrigues and struggles of her nobles for power. The election of Captains of Liberty, and subsequently of the Council of Twelve, and the Council of Twenty-four, attended with all the dissensions of the Guelph and Ghibelline factions, led to scenes of tumult and disorder that threatened utter desolation to the city and territories of Genoa. Wearied with these outrages, the citizens at length elected a chief magistrate for life, under the title of Doge, and the government continued in this form for nearly two centuries, not unaccompanied, however, by much popular violence, arising from factious opposition to the supreme power.

Advantage was taken of the feuds of the Genoese, by the visconti of Milan and the kings of France, who alternately possessed the city. But at this period, rose up one of the greatest men of the middle ages, one singularly adapted for the time in which he lived, and for the circumstances into which he was thrown. This was Andrea Doria, a native of Oneglia, in the States of Genoa, who after serving many Italian princes, attached himself to Francis I., from whom he received the command of a fleet in the Mediterranean. The factions of Genoa had led to the possession of the city by the French, who placed a garrison there that oppressed the citizens. Doria remonstrated, and was ordered into arrest, when he immediately passed over with his whole fleet, to Charles V., and acted in concert with him for the expulsion of the French, which being effected, the Emperor offered Doria the sovereignty of Genoa. This he declined, but immediately proceeded to re-organize the republic, and to extinguish the factions. A council of sixteen was appointed, presided over by a Doge, whose election was for two years only; five censors were also elected for five years, to act as guardians of the laws, and Doria himself, with the title of "Father and Liberator of his Country," was appointed censor for life. To the great council, in which all the nobles sat, were added every year, seven plebeians, from the respectable classes of society, four from the city, and three from the territory of Genoa. These were intended to serve as a clock upon the aristocracy, and as a salutary watch over the interests and liberties of the people. Under this government, Genoa flourished; and the death of Andrea, at the advanced age of ninety-four, after a life of arduous enterprise, and of eminent usefulness to his country, was lamented as a national calamity,—possibly the greatest that the republic had hitherto sustained.*

The government established by Andrea Doria, continued from the commencement of the sixteenth century, till the invasion of Italy by Bonaparte, when a democratic party fraternising with the French, rose upon the government for the destruction of the aristocrats of Genoa, who for the time defended themselves against the outrages of the confederates; but ultimately the French Directory obtained possession of the city, and established a garrison within its defences. In 1790, Massena was besieged in Genoa by the united powers of England and Austria, and was at length compelled to capitulate, though not until he had achieved a high military character by his gallant defence of the place. After the battle of Marengo, Genoa

---

* Columbus, the discoverer of America, was contemporary with Andrea Doria. Genoa long claimed the honour of having given birth to the great navigator; but the recent discovery of a will, made by Dominic, the father of Columbus, has transferred that honour to the little town of Cogoleto, situated about eighteen miles west of Genoa.

was again in the possession of Napoleon, who at first gave it a nominal independence as a republic, but afterwards annexed it to France, forming out of it the three departments named Genoa, Monte-notte, and the Apennines. In 1814, the city surrendered to the English forces commanded by Lord William Bentinck, and the following year it was united to the government of Sardinia, by the Congress of Vienna. Since that time much has been done for the strengthening of its garrison, the improvement of its port and harbour, and the advancement of its commercial interests. The approaches to the city also have been widened, new streets formed, and public institutions founded for the benefit of the community.

Genoa has been repeatedly increased in size, and its walls as frequently extended. Traces of the Roman walls are said to be still discernible; and some of the gates of the circuit raised by the Genoese, in 1155, are yet standing. Another circumvallation was completed in 1537, which included many of the previous suburbs of the city. This line is in the semi-modern style of fortification, but very strong; and the ramparts, which afford delightful promenades, are connected with a public garden of great beauty, named the Acqua Sola. An additional circuit extends all around the neighbouring hills, forming a vast semicircle, supported by forts, redoubts, and outworks, and constituting a line of fortification second only to the defences of Paris.

Passing from this brief glance at the historical records and general features of Genoa, we proceed to a brief description of the palaces and public buildings of the city. But where to begin, and where to end, are difficult points to determine: to describe whole streets of palaces, each palace a rich repository of art, would require volumes in place of pages.

The Strada Nuova consists entirely of palaces, all, with the exception of two, constructed by Alessio. The colossal magnitude of the doors and windows in the fronts of these edifices, gives them an air of magnificence, of which no description could convey an adequate idea. On entering their portals, the spectator cannot repress his admiration of the grand and imposing spectacle which opens upon him. "Gallery rises above gallery around the whole quadrangle, pierced by arcades and sustained by marble columns. The vaults and walls are painted in fresco, and adorned with rich moulding, gilding, and bas-reliefs. You ascend by spacious stair-cases, composed entirely of marble, each broad step being generally a single slab, and sometimes a solid block. The apartments are almost universally painted in fresco, and adorned with rich furniture and the finest productions of the arts." This brief description may serve generally for the buildings themselves; but in the decorations of the saloons and apartments, and in the value of the works of art which they contain, some of these palaces enjoy a celebrity far beyond the rest. The Palazzo Brignole contains the most valuable private collection of pictures in Genoa, amongst which are found, a St. Sebastian by Guido, an Annunciation by Ludovico Caracci, a Flight into Egypt by Carlo Marattl, and a number of portraits by Vandyke, admitted to be the finest specimens of this master existing in Italy. The architecture of this structure has been much admired, but the façade is less imposing than that of some others; the cortile is very fine, and from the marble terrace of the upper story, a beautiful view is obtained over the contiguous gardens and palaces. The Palazzo Serra is chiefly remarkable for the gorgeous magnificence of its saloon, which has obtained the appellation of Palazzo del Sole, the Palace of the Sun. "The decorations of this apartment, exclusive of the pictures and porcelain, which are of great value, are said to have cost forty-four thousand pounds. This ill-judged magnificence in one room throws the rest of the apartments into the shade, and gives the impression that the palace is not sufficiently grand for it. Each side of this saloon is supported by marble columns, richly gilt, and between them are placed mirrors which extend from the frieze to the floor. There is a fire-place at each end, with mantle-pieces of great beauty, and exactly similar, and on them stand vases of ancient Sevres china that excite the admiration, if not the envy, of every connoisseur. The doors are frosted with powdered lapis lazuli, which produces a very rich effect, and the architraves and pannels are finely carved and gilt. The furniture of this saloon is of the most splendid description, and the *ensemble* has more solid grandeur than is to be found in any other apartment throughout Italy." The saloon of the Palazzo Cataneo contains several pictures of great merit: amongst others, a Philosopher in his Study, by Domenichino; the Stoning of Stephen, by Ludovico Caracci; and St. Joseph and St. John adoring our Lord, by Raphael.

The old ducal palace, Palazzo Ducale, though now no longer a regal residence, being used only for government offices, is one of the most magnificent erections in Genoa, and carries the fancy back to the middle ages more powerfully than any other; although the edifice, as it now stands, is almost, if not entirely, a *rifacimento*, the original building having been destroyed by fire. The marble statues of all the heroes of the Genoese republic, which once adorned the hall of the grand council, were pulled down and broken to atoms by the French, and the niches which they occupied have been filled by statues of straw, with plaster heads, and white calico draperies. There is something exceedingly ludicrous in the idea of the substitution, but the general effect, on entering the room, is astonishingly delusive.

In the Strada Carlo Felice, stands the Palazzo Pallavicino, justly celebrated for its saloons of paintings. A mere catalogue of these works of art would be uninteresting. It may suffice to mention that they include fine specimens of the following masters:—The two Caracci, Rubens, Spagnoletto, Guercino, Vandyke, Raphael, Albano, and Franceschini. The Palazzo Reale, in the Strada Balbi, formerly in the possession of the Durazzo family, but now a royal residence, contains a choice collection of pictures, some good antique statues, and a number of excellent frescoes. The Palazzo della Università, a noble building, is distinguished by its extensive library, and museum of natural history. To attempt a detail of all the palaces in Genoa, would far exceed the limits of the present work; one, however, remains to be mentioned which is in several respects more interesting than any of those to which we have adverted, namely, the Palazzo Doria. This building, originally the Palazzo Fregoso, was almost entirely rebuilt, under the direction of Montorsoli, a Florentine architect, and the celebrated Perino del Vaga, to whose pencil the palace is indebted for its richest decorations. The frescoes of Perino are beyond all praise; and it is subject of regret that the hand of decay has already touched several of his finest works. In the gallery of the palace, leading to the terraced garden, are portraits of Andrea Doria and his family. The garden itself is decorated with fountains, statues, and vases; and the walks of cypress and orange, unite in magnificent picturesque, with the arches and columns of the structure. The descendants of the Dorian family reside in Rome, and leave the palace of their great ancestor to its fate. The beauty of the edifice, the exceeding value of its works of art, and, beyond all, the historical associations inseparably connected with it, deserve more generous treatment.

Next to her palaces, the churches of Genoa deserve high regard; the most splendid of these structures were erected by private individuals and families; and though they, in common with all the buildings and institutions of Italy, suffered severely during the occupation of this country by Bonaparte, they retain enough of grandeur to attest their former greatness.

The metropolitan church of San Lorenzo was built in the eleventh century. The archi-texture exhibits a combination of Gothic and Saracenic ornament; and the exterior of the building is cased with black and white marble, disposed in alternate stripes, producing an effect more startling than tasteful. The interior is chiefly remarkable for an altar, adorned with four columns of porphyry, and for an iron urn, which is said to inclose the remains of the saint to whom the church is dedicated. A remarkable relic, named the Sacro Catino, is yearly exhibited to hundreds of prostrate and admiring devotees. According to *tradition*, it is a plate, composed of a single emerald, presented by the Queen of Sheba to Solomon, and subsequently placed before the Saviour at the Last Supper. "The Sacro Catino was taken by the crusaders when they conquered Palestine in the twelfth century; and when the plunder was divided, this supposed valuable prize fell to the lot of the Genoese." The French afterwards took possession of this treasure, and sent it to Paris with the intention of converting the gem into specie; a scientific examination, however, proved the matchless emerald to be nothing more than a plate of coloured glass. It was eventually restored to the church of Lorenzo, through the intercession of the king of Sardinia, on which occasion his Majesty assured its adorers "that it was the real, true, genuine, and inestimable emerald, sinking the history of its mineralogical examination at Paris, any hint of which would incur the penalty of excommunication at Genoa." This relic is preserved in the Sacristy, the keys of which are entrusted to the Clavigeri, who are solemnly bound to retain them in safe custody.

The Church of San Stefano contains a fine painting of the martyrdom of St. Stephen, by Raphael and Giulio Romano. This work of art is deservedly esteemed, and gives celebrity to a building not otherwise remarkable. During the Napoleon era, it formed a principal ornament of the Louvre, at that time enriched with the choicest spoils of Italy. The Church of Saint Ambrogio is a magnificent structure, displaying rich marbles and paintings in great profusion; and it contains, amongst other works of great merit, two pictures by Rubens, and the celebrated Assumption by Guido Reni. Over one of the altars, there was recently a figure of the Virgin most extravagantly attired: her robes formed of flowered brocade and tissue, and her neck graced with a coral necklace. To blend the horrible with the ridiculous, eight swords were thrust into her breast. On the same altar, was laid an effigy of the infant Saviour, dressed in a costly robe, and fine lace cap! The Church of San Matteo, erected by the Dorian Family, is remarkable for its statues of the Evangelists, and more so as being the last resting place of Andrew Doria, whose tomb, enriched with the sculptures of Montorsoli, attracts universal regard, both as a work of art, and as the reminiscence of a man justly renowned. The Piazza di San Matteo is the spot whence Doria proclaimed liberty to the Genoese, and on one side of it stands the house presented to him by his countrymen.[*]

> —'Tis less in length and breadth,
> Than many a cabin in a ship of war;
> But 'tis of marble, and at once inspires
> The reverence due to ancient dignity.
> He left it for a better; and 'tis now
> A house of trade, the meanest merchandise

---

[*] There is a discrepancy amongst writers regarding this public gift to Doria: some state that the Palazzo Doria was presented to him; others affirm that the small house in the Piazza San Matteo was the only gift of the citizens, and that Andrew removed thence, as his wealth increased, to the Palazzo Freguso, and after nearly reconstructing it, gave it the name of his family.

GENOA.

> Unshaving its floors. Yet, fallen as it is,
> 'Tis still the noblest dwelling—even in Genoa!
> And hadst thou, Andrew, lived there to the last,
> Thou hadst done well; for there is that without,
> That in the wall, which monarchs could not give,
> Nor thou take with thee, "that which says aloud,
> It was thy Country's gift to her Deliverer."

One of the objects of interest in Genoa, and not the least, is that singular and bold arch called the Bridge of Carignano; interesting in the first place, from its construction, hanging, as it does, over a huge ravine between two hills, and having houses of six or seven stories high underneath it; and in the second place, from the motive assigned to the proud patrician by whom it was erected, who, not bearing to see the commonalty of the city, fagging from one part of it to another, by the steep ascent of the hills, caused this imperial accommodation to be provided for them.

Amongst the public buildings of Genoa, none can be regarded with greater interest than the edifices connected with the noble charities of the city. The Albergo de' Poveri gives shelter to a multitude of poor within its walls, and dispenses extensive charities beyond them. In the centre of this Institution, stands the church of Santa Maria, containing a celebrated basso-rellevo by Michael Angelo, representing the Virgin bending over the dead Christ. The Ospedale del Pammatone unites the splendour of a palace to all the necessary details of an extensive hospital. And the Sordi Mutti, founded in 1801, by a poor monk, named Ottavio Assarotti, for the reception of the deaf and dumb, is much celebrated. There are no fewer than fifteen conservatories in Genoa, devoted to the protection and assistance of the female sex. Some are houses of refuge, some penitentiaries, others schools and asylums; in all, the great design is to rescue the weaker sex from poverty and vice, to raise up the fallen, to shelter the oppressed, to teach the ignorant, and to comfort and cherish the forlorn outcast and helpless orphan for whom no other home is open. The French, to their lasting disgrace, ruined some of the charitable institutions of Genoa, and greatly injured others; but the Sardinian government contributed munificently to those which remained and required assistance, and it continues to uphold all that have survived the rapacity of Napoleon.

The character of the Genoese people and territory is not very favourably pourtrayed in the Italian proverb: "Land without trees, sea without fish, men without faith, and women without virtue." These censures have been discountenanced in part by intelligent travellers; and we apprehend that the entire proverb has gained currency rather by its point than its verity. It cannot be denied, however, that this traditional aspersion has been cast upon the Genoese, and perpetuated upon them, from the time of Virgil down to that of Dante. The latter poet denounces them as a race of men who ought to be swept from the earth by some signal destruction. Nevertheless, it must be remembered, that poets are not the best authorities for historical truth; and we may indulge an occasional doubt of their veracity, knowing, as we do, that *fiction* is their peculiar province.

LERICI.

THE town of Lerici is situated between Cape Corvo and Spezzia, in the concave of a valley which terminates in a bay offering one of the most secure harbours on the coast. It is supposed to owe its designation to a hill in the neighbourhood which was formerly clothed with the Quercus Ilex, and which for many ages bore the name of Mons Illicis. The etymology is not, however, determined with much precision either from the shrub or the mountain. A mythological origin is likewise assigned to this place; but, so far as the derivation of the name is concerned, with no happier results. Hercules is reported to have erected a temple here to deprecate the wrath of Venus, after he had slain her son *Eryx*—whence, as the etymologists say, comes *Lerici*.

Lerici was anciently held by the Pisans, to whom the emperors of Germany delegated an authority to prevent the erection of any fortress on the Mediterranean shore, between Monte Corvo and the mouth of the Arno. From the Pisans, the possession of the place passed to the Genoese, who, in 1250, became masters of Lerici, and surrounded its castle with walls and towers. Thenceforward the town remained under the sovereignty of Genoa, which successfully resisted the efforts of the neighbouring powers, at distant intervals, to regain possession. It was here, as history records, that Andrea Doria renounced his allegiance to Francis I., and entered into the service of Charles V.; an event which is commemorated by a stone still existing in a garden at Lerici. Charles V. afterwards set sail from this port with a powerful naval armament for the conquest of Algiers.

The harbour, formed by the Gulf of Spezzia, constituting the port of Lerici, is enclosed by semicircular hills, terminated on the left by a rock, upon which rises, amidst the batteries, the solid tower, seen in our view. The battery of Maralonga stands towards the mouth of the gulf, whilst on the headland, which shuts in the harbour on the north, lies the rock of *Cera pelata*, and the battery of St. Theresa. The Gulf of Spezzia particularly attracted the regard of Napoleon, who considered it so much finer, as a harbour, than that of Genoa, that he projected converting it into a vast naval establishment; but for this, among the rest, he was *not* ordained. This gulf is rendered interesting to the classical reader, by the assertion of the Ligurian commentators, that it is *the* gulf, described by Virgil, into which Æneas was driven by the storm. The general features harmonize sufficiently with the description, to render the opinion plausible; though they may not suffice to vouch its accuracy, and establish it as a fact. A cavern situated about a mile to the north-east of the town of Spezzia, and a ruined edifice, bearing over the door, the Inscription *Nympharum domus*, seem to offer "confirmation strong" in favour of the assumed identity. The description referred to is in the Æneid, book I. and lines 158—160.

The death of Shelley, the poet, is associated with Lerici. On the 7th July 1821, he went to Leghorn to have an interview with Mr. Leigh Hunt, and returning thence to Lerici, his boat was lost in a violent storm, off Via Reggia.

CARRARA.

THE town of Carrara derives all its importance from the marble quarries in its neighbourhood, which have been wrought from time immemorial. The immense revenue produced by them, has rendered the history of Carrara more eventful than it would otherwise have been. These treasures, apparently inexhaustible, excited the cupidity of all ages, and led to successive contests for possession of a locality so enriched by nature. These quarries occupy three or four descending ridges which unite in a lofty mountain, named Monte Sagro. Ascending the little stream that flows through the town, the tourist arrives at the beds of dove-coloured marble called *bardiglio*. Higher up the valley, are the beds of white marble; only a few of which produce a material of such fine grain and transparency as to suit the highest purposes of sculpture. At a greater elevation, the marble becomes less pure in colour, but larger in the block. The Lunigian or Carrara marbles have been quarried, with little interruption, for upwards of two thousand years, and judging from appearances, another and as long an interval may elapse before their stores are exhausted. A vast number of men are constantly employed in the quarries; and the duty on the exports exceeds two thousand pounds annually.

The excursion to the quarries is a work of toil, the road being inaccessible by carriages; but the natural beauty of the scenery, and the interesting associations connected with this cradle of the arts, are sufficient to compensate for all the difficulties of the approach. The quarries of Crestola and Cavetta are usually first visited: from these is obtained the white wax-colour marble; and from the hill of Silvestro, on the opposite side, is taken the blue-veined, or dove-coloured, variety. Near to this, in the hill of Carpevola, are found the white marbles called *mossa*, the flexible marbles of Bctogla, and the great masses of the quarries of Polvaccio. The Fantiscritti, situated about three miles from Carrara, possess a peculiar interest for the historian and antiquarian. In these quarries are three small figures of Jove, Bacchus, and Hercules, sculptured high on the side of a vertical mass of rock; and the ground is covered with large masses of marble columns and architraves, left unfinished by the sculptors of ancient Rome, when the power of the empire declined. The statues of the deities, from their small size, have obtained amongst the peasantry the title of *fanti*; and the name of the quarries is compounded of this appellation, and *scritti*, the latter term having referred to the scribbling propensities of tourists, many of whom have deemed it necessary to inscribe their names upon the rocks.

After contemplating the beautiful material which nature has provided in these quarries for the sculptor's ideal of the form divine, and suffering the imagination to revel amidst recollections of human genius, it is mortifying to witness the reckless mode in which the blocks of marble are conveyed down the descent leading to the town of Carrara. There is an utter ignorance, or an entire neglect, of all mechanical aids, either with a view to lighten the toil of the labourer, or preserve the marble from injury. The very approach to the quarry is choked with masses of rock, which a little well-directed labour might speedily clear away; over these obstructions, the marble must pass, at the very outset of its removal; and when these impediments are overcome, it is rattled down the descent in a manner which perpetually causes the blocks to be broken. The whole process is attended with so much difficulty and danger, that it can scarcely be witnessed without a feeling of terror. The blocks are placed upon a rudely constructed carriage, drawn sometimes by six oxen, at others by only two; the number varying according to the nature of the path to be traversed. At the points of sudden descent, the exertions of the men who have charge of the convoy are truly frightful, and not unfrequently attended with dreadful accidents. To break the fall of the vehicle from one mass of rock to another, the conductors bound from side to side of the rude machine, at the imminent hazard of life and limb; at this moment, endeavouring to preserve the balance of the weighty mass, and in the next, goading the oxen into the most painful movements and positions. If an engineer of Britain, or of any country where the simplest rudiments of engineering science are known, had charge of the transit, he would at once clear the approach to the quarries, and lay a rail along the descent; and this done, the removal would be effected with a degree of ease and safety, not less admirable than the present method is laborious, dangerous, and uncouth. As it is, the destruction of the marble, and the injuries sustained by the workmen, are a constant theme of lamentation; and these evils are visited upon the sculptor, who has to pay a price proportionate to the risk of transit. Sir Francis Chantrey on one occasion paid eight hundred pounds for a block of marble; a sum which few can afford, save they who have princes for patrons.

The city of Carrara itself is beautifully situated near a junction of small valleys, all in a high state of cultivation, the scenery of which is enclosed in every direction, except towards the sea, by lofty mountains that give form, richness, and celebrity to a territory not exceeding thirty square miles in extent. It is annexed to the neighbouring duchy of Massa, hence called Massa-Carrara, and till recently was possessed by the Duke of Modena. The name of Carrara is supposed to be derived from *Carrariæ*, caves or quarries; and the origin of the town may be traced back to a remote period, when the excavations of the marble were first begun by the Romans, this origin being none other than the huts of the workmen, and subsequently the more permanent dwellings of the superintendents and officers who directed their labours.

The history of Carrara has almost exclusive reference to the marbles; either in regard to the working of the quarries, or to the erection of structures for which they furnished material. Augustan Rome was indebted for its magnificence to the marbles of Carrara and its neighbourhood; and the ancient sculptors gave preference to them, to the neglect of the quarries of Paros and Pentelicus. Laws were instituted by the Roman emperors to regulate the working of the mines, and to protect them from any infringement by individual or private enterprise. These restrictions operated unfavourably in a commercial point of view, and prevented mercantile traffic in the marbles; but it is questionable whether the splendour of the Imperial City would not have suffered, if extensive exports had been permitted; the patriotism of private speculators would not, probably, have withstood the temptation of a foreign contract; and the chisel might have wrought too industriously for the market, and too indolently for the embellishment of Rome.

During the long and dark period which followed the decline and extinction of the Empire.

the marble quarries lay neglected; the barbarian hosts who swept like the locust over Italy, had no sympathy with art; and so far from aiding its advance, they sought rather to annihilate all traces of its past achievements. The quarries passed from one possessor to another, simply as so much territorial surface; and in the petty wars which subsequently arose between the Genoese, the Pisans, and the Lucchese, they fell successively under these several republics. It is to the Pisans that the revival of art is chiefly to be attributed: they resumed the working of the quarries; and the marble works of the neighbourhood again resounded with the labours of the sculptors, employed by Nicholas Pisano and his pupils. Then it was that a thousand Christian temples arose, the materials for which were drawn from the quarries of Carrara; and in this city itself was raised a cathedral, inferior to none of the Gothic Italian structures of that period. The succeeding history of the quarries, traces them into the possession of various noble families of Italy. Early in the sixteenth century, the government of this territory devolved upon Alberico, son of Count Lorenzo Cybo, who assumed the title of Prince of Massa and Marquis of Carrara. To this prince, Carrara owes the construction and extension of its walls; the formation of its fine piazza, which still bears the name of Alberico; several of the public fountains which adorn the city; the erection of a palace for the sovereign; establishments for the fine arts; municipal statutes, which are deemed models of jurisprudence; and a most liberal convention to furnish sculptors and artificers in marble with the productions of his quarries. A female descendant of the same family founded the Academy of the Fine Arts. She assigned to it, in 1779, a new edifice, from which it was transferred, in 1818, to the palace of the sovereign, and enriched with excellent copies of the most celebrated statues.

Amongst the most remarkable buildings of Carrara, besides the Academy, may be seen its collegiate church, slowly built in the thirteenth, and adorned with sculptures in the fifteenth century: this splendid college has a Chapter of fourteen canons, and other dignitaries. Other sacred edifices exist in Carrara, all of them, as might be expected, rich in marbles. One may be remarked for the beauty of its foreign materials—the Temple of the Madonna della Grazia. The two piazzi, various streets, and some private habitations, are adorned with fountains, yielding an abundant supply of fine water. In the Piazza Alberico is a colossal statue, raised by the Carrarese to the memory of their last sovereign. There are many good dwellings and marble palaces in Carrara, but structures are wanting which unite richness of ornament with chasteness of style, such as might satisfy the eye of the stranger, who knows that he is entering into a country of artists, and into the immediate vicinity of the richest and most celebrated emporium of marble in the world. Its chief attraction, however, is found in the contemplation of its vast and celebrated quarries, in the Academy, and in the numerous galleries and work-shops of its statuaries.

Carrara may be regarded as one entire *studio*; the majority of its residents being artists, who have come hither to pursue their studies in a locality where material for their work can be readily and cheaply obtained. You see them in all costumes, of all ages, and of various capabilities; the young tyro and the confirmed sculptor, both alike working industriously, either for fame, or for the wherewithal to live,—or for both of these together. The joint productions of so many artists, render Carrara a vast museum of sculpture, where may be obtained specimens of the art in all its stages, from the mere chimney-piece ornament, to a relievo or statue of exquisite beauty and finish. It is not unusual for the eminent sculptors of Rome, to prepare their works from the blocks, at Carrara; this lessens the size and weight for transport, and affords means of ascertaining the purity of the marble. Excellent copies of the most admired statues can be bought at Carrara at a much cheaper rate than in any other place. Statues of Napoleon, and busts of Wellington, are executed in great numbers by the Carrarese sculptors, and of the latter, hundreds have been sent from this work-shop of art, to different quarters of the globe.

PISA.

BEAUTIFULLY situated on the banks of the Arno, sheltered from the north by a range of hills, and open to rich plains on the south, stands the celebrated city of Pisa, once the rival of Genoa. The origin of this city is referred to a period even more remote than the destruction of Troy; but the first mention that is made of it in Roman history, is by Polybius, who states that the harbour was much frequented by the Roman ships in their voyages to Sardinia, Gaul, and Spain. Livy relates that it was colonized by the Romans, 180 years before Christ. And Strabo speaks of its early importance, and of the extent of its commerce; it being the depôt for timber for the Roman fleets, and also for the splendid marbles of the neighbouring quarries, destined for the structure and decoration of the public buildings of Rome.

After the fall of the empire, Pisa was subjected to many vicissitudes. It was subsequently erected into an independent republic, under a nominal allegiance to the emperors of the Carlovingian dynasty. In 874, the Pisans successfully opposed the Saracens, who had made a piratical descent upon the city. Nearly a century after this, Otho I., on his return from Rome, received the homage of the Pisans, and extended towards them a regard, which permanently attached them to the interests of the empire. The republic directed its naval strength, on several occasions, against the Moors and Saracens, and ultimately succeeded in establishing its maritime power and commercial importance. The Genoese now began to take alarm at its growing prosperity; and towards the end of the eleventh century, those wars commenced between the two republics, which at length ended in the total ruin of Pisa. These hostilities were, at first, occasionally interrupted by a union of forces, against their common enemies, the Moors and Saracens; but ambition on the one hand, and jealousy on the other, forbade any permanent peace; and in 1282, the final struggle took place, by which Genoa was left with no rival, save Venice, to dispute its power in the Mediterranean.

The subsequent history of Pisa is little more than a detail of its struggles with Florence, Lucca, and the Milanese; intermingled with domestic feuds, which form part of the romance of Europe in the middle ages. Amongst the latter, the story of Ugolino is an incident of fearful interest. Possessed of great power, he had exercised his tyranny and cruelty in proscribing all who were impediments to his ambition. At length, in 1288, he was accused of

betraying his country into the hands of the Florentines; and in an insurrection, headed by the archbishop Ruggiero, he, with two of his sons, and two grandsons, were seized, and confined in a tower on the banks of the Arno. The key of the dungeon was thrown into the river, and the captives were left to die of hunger. The unhappy fate of Ugolino and his sons has been immortalized by Dante, who vents his indignation against their tormentors:

> "Thou modern Thebes! what, though, as fame hath said,
> Count Ugolino did thy forts betray,
> His sons deserv'd not punishment so dread."

And our own Rogers, in a beautiful description of the Arno, numbers amongst the pollutions of its waves, the casting therein, the key of the "Tower of Famine:"

> "Sullen was the splash,
> Heavy and swift the plunge, when they received
> The key that just had grated on the ear
> Of Ugolino—closing up for ever
> That dismal dungeon, henceforth to be nam'd
> The Tower of Famine."

Pisa, shorn of her greatness by Genoa, and distracted by internal tumults and treachery, struggled on for upwards of another century; till, at length, to fill the measure of her indignities, she was sold to the Florentines. Gabriello Maria, her then master, who had been secured in his government by Charles VI. of France, agreed to the proposal of Marshal Bouricault, the king's representative, to yield her up to Florence for 400,000 florins, to be equally divided between Bouricault and himself. The Pisans rose up to resist this infamous transfer; when Bouricault concluded his bargain with the Florentines by accepting 206,000 florins; and on Gabriello demanding an equal share of the money, he caused him to be beheaded on a charge of treason against the French king. The Pisans did not, however, yield up their city without a struggle; they endured all the horrors of a siege for twelve months, before they surrendered to their purchasers. They made subsequent attempts to regain their independence, but with no permanent success. In 1509, being again besieged by the Florentines, they were starved into a final surrender. The wealthy and noble families went forth from their city into voluntary exile; and the young men sought employment and distinction as mercenaries in the then factious states of Europe.

Pisa is now but the sepulchre of what it was; its inhabitants are reduced from one hundred and twenty thousand, to one-sixth of that number; and it is visited for those remains of its former greatness which, as evidence of middle-age splendour, are unrivalled in any city of Italy. The four edifices, on which the unfading celebrity of Pisa rests, are the Cathedral, or Duomo, commenced in 1063; the Baptistery, begun in 1152; the Campanile, or Leaning Tower, built in 1174; and the Campo Santo, which was completed in 1283. These buildings are so situated as to form a striking coup d'œil, at once magnificent and sublime; and words are unequal to describe the effect produced on the mind by a survey of these venerable and majestic structures, "fortunate," as Forsyth happily remarks, "both in their society, and their solitude."

The Cathedral, or Duomo, is a noble edifice, of which the prevailing characteristic is massive dignity. The beautiful marble of which it is built, is of itself a wonder to eyes unused to see this precious material in such great abundance. This church must certainly rank amongst the finest in the world, whether we regard the vastness of the entire design, or the elaborate richness of its separate details. It is the work of two Italian architects, Buschetto and Rainaldo; and is dedicated to the Virgin, in pious commemoration of the victory gained by the Pisan consul, Orlandi, over the Saracens.

The bronze gates of the Duomo attract universal regard for their exquisite beauty: they were modelled in 1602, from the designs of Giovanni di Bologna, to supply the place of the ancient doors, which were destroyed by fire, on the night of 15th October, 1590; on which occasion also, the entire building suffered considerable damage. The general restoration of the structure, has been conducted with such judicious reference to its original character, that no discrepancy obtrudes upon the eye of the connoisseur: every thing is in such perfect correspondence, that it is only from historical record we ascertain the fact of a partial destruction having once taken place. The bronze gates are divided into compartments, each containing an historical event, and sometimes a device or emblem allusive to that event. The centre gates have eight compartments, which contain the history of the Virgin, from her birth to her glorification. The doors on the right and left have six compartments each, the whole embracing the history of our Lord. In the transept, called the Crociera di San Itainieri, is the single bronze door which escaped injury from the fire; this is an interesting relic of ancient art, and at the same time an evidence of the taste and skill displayed in the renewal of the doors which were destroyed.

The whole building stands upon a terrace ascended by steps. Passing into the interior, the spectator contemplates with awe and admiration, the impressive and magnificent scene presented to him. Five aisles are supported by a forest of Corinthian columns, with shafts of granite, or marbles of different colours. The roof is flat, with compartments and rosettes richly carved and gilt. The windows are filled with stained glass of wonderful brilliancy; and in place of an eastern window, as in our cathedrals, the building is terminated in this direction, by exquisite mosaics of colossal size, representing our Lord, with the Virgin on one side and St. John on the other. These works of art are universally esteemed for their grandeur and beauty. The high altar, erected in 1774, but partially rebuilt in 1825, is a rich and elaborate pile of marbles and lapis lazuli; and connected with it are decorations exhibiting the most exquisite taste and felicitous execution. Many of the ancient works of art, which formerly adorned this edifice, were either partially or totally destroyed by the fire; and some of the monuments have been removed to the cemetery of Campo Santo: the building is, notwithstanding, still rich in relics of its olden grandeur. It contains many paintings of great value; including the celebrated *St. Agnes* by Andrea del Sarto, a picture of inestimable worth. A bronze lamp of fine workmanship is suspended from the nave, of which it is said, that it suggested the theory of the pendulum, to Galileo,—a tradition sufficient, of itself, to render this lamp an object of great interest to the beholder.

The Baptistery, the work of Diotisalvi, is a remarkable building, exhibiting in its general character a strong resemblance to the Duomo. "Of its profuse collection of ornamental treasures of all descriptions," says an elegant writer, "I can only say, that it struck me as being a sort of museum into which the piety of the Pisans sent every thing they happened to find of rich and curious, that they knew not how to dispose of elsewhere." The interior is a noble circular church, supported by eight columns of granite, with rich Corinthian capitals. The pavement in front of the altar, is wrought in mosaic work, the combined effect of which is gorgeous; other portions are enriched with monumental figures and relievi. In the centre of the building stands a magnificent font, fourteen feet in diameter, marvellous both for material and workmanship. It is adapted for baptism by immersion, and would contain six or eight adults. Four smaller fonts, or basins, are disposed around it; but their use does not appear to be known. If the conjecture of some writers be correct, that they were originally designed for the administration of the baptismal rite to infants, and by sprinkling, whilst the large font was to be specially reserved for immersion,—it forcibly reminds one of the ludicrous anecdote related of Sir Isaac Newton, that he caused a large hole to be cut in the door of his stable for the cat, and a smaller one for her kittens. The carvings and other ornaments of the fonts are rich and profuse, though some few of them are not worthy of the artists to whom they are attributed.

The great ornament of the Baptistery, is the pulpit, or reading desk, by Nicolo Pisano, the founder of the Pisan school of sculpture. "This pulpit well deserves all the celebrity attached to it, the degree of which celebrity in its own city may be judged of by the fact, that, in former years, when the denser population sent more crowded congregations to the church, on the fête days, it was the custom for the authorities of the town to send an armed civic guard to watch over its safety, by preventing the pressure of the multitude upon it." It is a hexagon of oriental alabaster, or, according to some, of Parian or Carrara marble, resting upon nine pillars of different kinds of marble. The alternate columns are supported by lions, and the centre one rests, rather oddly, on St. John and his eagle. The relievi which adorn this chef d'œuvre of art are of great beauty both in design and workmanship: they are five in number; and represent the Nativity, the Adoration of the Magi, the Presentation in the Temple, the Crucifixion, and the Last Judgment. The general appearance of this pulpit, is that of a small temple or shrine, happily conceived and elaborately wrought.

The Campanile, or Leaning Tower, has been so often described, that there is scarcely an object of interest in the world with which people generally are better acquainted. The peculiarity on which its fame principally rests, is its fearful inclination from the perpendicular, which seems to threaten the instant fall of the structure. It ought, however, rather to be called the *contorted*, than the *leaning* tower; for neither pen nor pencil can convey an adequate idea of its irregularities. An opinion was long entertained, and is still held by some, that the inclination of the building was a contrivance of the architect; but there is abundant evidence to be seen, in the immediate neighbourhood, that the leaning has resulted altogether from the foundations having sunk more on the one side than on the other. This sinking, it would appear, began to be observable long before the structure was completed; and the architect endeavoured to remedy the evil, by an irregular curvature, which no perspective can represent, and which could not, without much difficulty, be truly shown even in a model. The Campanile is a seven-storied circular tower, each story supported by an open Corinthian portico. The basement arches are solid, and exhibit some mosaics and sculptures. The ascent to the summit of the building, is by two hundred and ninety winding steps, which lean variously, following the irregularities of the tower. The prospect from the top is extensive and interesting, embracing the Mediterranean, and reaching, in fine weather, even to the island of Corsica.

There is something inexpressibly grotesque in the appearance of the Campanile, a quaintness which throws it entirely out of harmony with the sacred and magnificent buildings in its vicinity. "As you pass from one part of the Campo Santo to another, you open to your eye the top of the edifice, while the lower part still remains concealed; or, if you take your contemplative walk in the other direction, a contrary phenomenon appears, and the lower part of the tower presents itself, while the currently straight line of the building from behind which you are passing, cuts it strangely in half the other way. The very shade that it casts upon the ground is monstrous, and, in short, it is absolutely impossible to get your mind into the harmonious state of religious sublimity, unless you fairly turn your back upon the leaning tower." One fact remains to be mentioned, which confers interest upon the Campanile, and in some measure reconciles us to its singular deformity: Galileo from this tower made his first experiments upon gravity and the descent of falling bodies.

The last of the four great objects of interest in Pisa, is the celebrated cemetery named the Campo Santo. It is related that the archbishop Ubaldo returning from Palestine, brought thence fifty-three vessels laden with the earth of the Holy Land, which he deposited in this spot. It has also been gravely stated, that "independently of the high value which religion gave to this sacred soil, it had a physical virtue which approached the wonderful, namely, the property of consuming bodies in twenty-four hours." Looking, however, to the extent of the cemetery, we may be allowed to doubt this efficacy, seeing that fifty-three galleys of earth could not cover this vast enclosure to any great depth. The Campo Santo was not inclosed by walls till the completion of the cloister in 1278. This structure, the work of Giovanni di Pisa, is beyond compare the most magnificent cloister in existence. It consists of four sides of long and light arcades, above a hundred and five thousand yards in circumference, and of a most noble width. A fine area of turf occupies the centre; and along the sides of the cloister are ranged monuments, sarcophagi, and vases, of every *artistique* age and country; while the walls are covered with innumerable frescoes, which, as remains of art, are invaluable. To attempt particular description of this celebrated spot in a brief and general sketch, is impossible; we could at most give little more than a dry catalogue of its sculptures and paintings, which would utterly fail to convey any distinct idea of its marvellous beauties. Let it suffice to say, that none visit this city of the dead without feeling that there are hallowed spots of earth;—that there are localities whose awful magnificence invests them with sanctity, and within whose pale are gathered mighty sympathies and associations which the outer world is too narrow to contain.

We must pass rapidly over the remaining features of Pisa. The Lungo l'Arno, a continued quay on both sides of the river Arno, contains some interesting buildings. Amongst these the Palazzo Laufreducci* is remarkable for the links of a chain over a majestic portal, and the enigmatical motto—*alla giornata*, signifying "day by day." This inscription has greatly puzzled the antiquaries, and to this day it remains unexplained. Why the chain and inscription should be placed over the portal of this palace, it may be difficult to determine; but the expressive adaptation of the motto to the device is surely obvious enough. "Day by day;" why it contains the whole history of a pining, monotonous captivity. In the Piazza de Cavalieri, formerly stood the Torre della Fame, or Tower of Famine. With a singular disregard for a locality, so remarkable for the tragedy connected with it, the Pisans have permitted all traces of this structure to disappear. It was ruined so early as the sixteenth century, but a portion of the walls remained till a very recent period. All vestiges of the tower are now, however, lost; and a smart modern house occupies its site. Shade of Dante! the Smiths and the Browns locating in the Torre della Fame!

* Lord Byron resided for a time in this palace.

Amongst the ecclesiastical structures of Pisa, may be named the monastery of Santa Caterina, a stately building, adorned with rich marbles and sculptures, and containing some interesting tombs. The abbey of San Nicolo is a fine structure, containing some mosaics of an early age, and a number of paintings of inferior character. The church of San Matteo is in the Gothic style. Connected with it is a convent, remarkable for the beauty of its cloister, and for a painting by Aurelio Lomi, representing the glorified Redeemer surrounded by saints and angels.

The character of Pisa, as a place of temporary sojourn for the tourist and invalid, is variously stated by different writers. Some complain of its unendurable *tristesse*; others speak favourably of its quiet, as compared with the gayer cities of Italy, and find ample compensation for the absence of bustle and excitement, in the grandeur of its principal buildings, and the beauty of the scenery in its neighbourhood. The climate of Pisa is remarkably mild during the winter, and appears on the whole to be suited to invalids suffering under pulmonary complaints. It is said that twice as much rain falls here, within the year, as in London; but Pisa has this advantage, that the rains fall there in torrents, and hence the Pisans enjoy longer intervals of sun-shine than the inhabitants of Britain. It is undoubtedly a pleasant thing ".to see the sun shine every day," yet rain in *torrents* is a fine antithesis; but that everlasting drizzle of water comminuted into vapour, so characteristic of our own climate, is most decidedly unpoetical and uncomfortable.

LEGHORN.

HISTORIANS have laboured industriously to establish the antiquity of Leghorn; and its name and situation appear to identify it with the ancient *Herculis Liburni Portus*, or Port of the Liburnian Hercules. To trace the derivation of its name, we must discard the French appellation of Ligorne, or Leghorn, and adopt the more euphonious Italian term, Livorno; the latter word being easily deduced from the classic *Liburni*. Livorno is indebted to antiquity for nothing beyond a name. It seems never to have attained any consideration in ancient times; and, indeed, it remained a petty village, almost immersed in swamps and sea-weeds, till the Medicæan princes turned their attention to its port, and by a series of regulations equally favourable to the interests and the feelings of the mercantile body, made it the mart of Mediterranean commerce.

In the thirteenth century, Livorno was a wretched village, undefended by walls; but in the fourteenth century it rose to some importance under the government of Florence. The Florentines, who had been for ages bankers to sovereign powers, and merchants to the subjects of those powers, were then without a port, the want of which had long operated against the extension of their commerce. At length, in 1421, they obtained Livorno, by purchase, from the Genoese, who, for present gain, most unwisely sold it, and thus raised a powerful rival. The Florentines having now obtained access to the sea, their opulence rapidly advanced, and under the powerful influence of the Medici, their newly acquired port rose to distinction. It was fortified by Alexander de' Medici; and Cosmo I. constituted it a free port, and induced many Greeks to establish themselves within its walls. The city, for it became one, rapidly increased; a canal was cut, and the port enlarged. To Ferdinand I., the immediate successor of Cosmo I., is Livorno chiefly indebted for its improvement: and to his wise and prudent policy, the permanent foundation of the city, as a great mart of commerce, is entirely attributable. He built the Molo Ferdinando; added a new fort; and constructed many public works, at once useful and ornamental. But the prosperity of Livorno was mainly secured by the judicious conduct of this sovereign in granting liberty of conscience to all strangers,—a gift which rivalled, and far exceeded, Cosmo's liberty of commerce. There is no act which marks more distinctly the enlightened policy of Ferdinand, than his grant of universal toleration, by which he placed upon record this great truth: that large social and commercial relations are utterly incompatible with sectarian jealousies. The population of Livorno was inconsiderable, until Ferdinand's invitation to the inhabitants of every nation to make settlement there, brought a vast influx of strangers, and more especially of Jews, which latter had been driven from Spain by the tyranny and cruelty of the Inquisition.

Ferdinand II. built the Arsenal, the Custom House, and that part of the city named, from its numerous intersections by canals, *Venezia Nuova*. The subsequent history of Livorno affords little of interest to the historian beyond the statistics of its commerce. It suffered in the common fate of Italy, during the Napoleon visitation. It fell under the power of the French in 1796; and was retaken by the English in 1799; but returned again to the French in 1800, and remained under their protection till the memorable events of 1814 destroyed their power in all the countries they had subdued. Within late years, the suburbs of the city have been surrounded with a wall; and the entire population is now estimated at about 60,000 inhabitants, of whom upwards of 8000 are Jews. These last have not increased in proportion to the rest of this mixed population; but no small portion of the wealth and trade of the city is in their hands.

Livorno possesses few structures, or works of art, to arrest the attention of the connoisseur and artist. Its features are, for the most part, those of a bustling maritime town. By the mercantile traveller it must ever be regarded with interest, as the gathering place of nations, in which men of every creed and clime unite for the cultivation and extension of commerce. And to all who take interest in the social relations of mankind, Livorno presents the gratifying spectacle of a community composed of many distinct bodies, mingling in good faith and amity; each body being protected in the enjoyment of its own religious opinions, alike secured from obloquy and restrained from intolerance. There are places of worship for every distinct people and creed. Amongst these may be named, the Greek Church; the Melchiti, or Greek Church in the Arabic language; the Eastern or Schismatic Greeks, and the Russian Greek Church; the Catholic Armenians; the Arabian Maronites; the English Episcopalian Church, and the various forms of English Dissent; the Scottish Presbyterian Church; a Lutheran and a Calvinist Church for the Germans and the Dutch; a Mosque for Mahomedans; and the finest Synagogue in Europe for the Jews. Thus the residents from all nations have established churches, chapels, and cemeteries, in conformity with their own modes of worship. The burial ground attached to the English chapel, contains several beautiful marble tombs, one of which, distinguished from all the rest by a cameo, the work of Chantrey,—covers the remains of Smollett. This cemetery, named the *Campo Inglese*, was formerly a general place of sepulture for our countrymen; there being no other English burial ground in Italy, before the present century.

The only monument that can be referred to the age of the republic, is the Torre del Marzocco, or Torre Rossa; the first name derived from the lion, placed upon it as a weather-cock, and the second from the colour of the marble of which the building is constructed. The Duomo, or Cathedral, is remarkable for its façade, designed by Inigo Jones; and for the paintings on the entablature by Ligozzi. The statue of Ferdinand I., a noble work of art by Pietro Tacca, stands upon the quay adjoining the harbour. The pedestal is supported by four kneeling figures, of colossal size, said to represent some Turkish slaves who had attempted to steal a Tuscan galley, and who were executed by order of Ferdinand. There is some difference of opinion regarding the prototypes of these figures; but if we even admit the mildest interpretation, that these kneeling slaves are merely allegorical personages, we can but regret that they should form the support of a monument erected to the memory of a prince, whose distinguishing fame is identified with free commerce and liberty of conscience. The fettered limbs, and the despairing, grief-worn countenances of these slaves, are either utterly out of place, or they offer inevitable evidence of vindictive spirit on the part of the prince whose statue they sustain.

Although there is little in Livorno, compared with other cities of Italy, to interest the antiquarian or the lover of art, the general features present an interesting and picturesque appearance from the neighbouring elevations. From the Monte Nero, whence our view is taken, the city is seen at a distance of five miles, and beyond it are the mountains of Carrara; but between these, a great extent intervenes in the Maremma of Pisa, where alone, in Europe, camels are bred for beasts of burden. Immediately above the Church of the Madonna of Monte Nero, which forms a prominent object on the right, is seen the distant city of Pisa, lying at the foot of the mountains. The Monte Nero is covered with the suburban residences of the merchants and rich citizens of Livorno; the beauty of which is pleasingly indicated in the foreground of our view.

The Monte Nero, or Black Mountain, is said to have derived its name from the dark colour of the woods which formerly covered the hill. It was in this wood that the portrait of the Virgin, which makes the region so sacred, was finally deposited. This picture, according to *veritable* tradition, after an unrecorded sojourn in Negropont, suddenly took a flying fit, and at length dropped upon the shore of the Ardenza; and its locomotive powers being then exhausted, the Virgin ordered a shepherd to transport it to the neighbouring Monte Nero,— the spot where for five centuries she has received the devotion of the faithful Livornese. It is one of the numerous portraits for which, it is said, the Virgin granted sittings, and is remarkable for *not* being attributed to St. Luke, who, according to the traditions of the Romish Church, was painter and sculptor to the Holy Family. This picture, so celebrated for its miracle-working powers, is said to be "*da manso ignoto*" (by an unknown hand); it represents the Virgin sitting on a cushion ornamented with gold flowers, bearing on her left arm the infant Christ, who holds a bird tied to a thread. After the picture had been placed in an oratory, and worshipped there for above a century, the Archbishop Giuliano of Pisa consigned it, as a precious charge, to a small religious community of the Gesuati; but when this cloistered institution was suppressed in 1688, by order of Clement IX., the sacred picture was, in the following year, confided to the guardianship of another order of monks, called the Teatini. Under these fathers, not only was the convent of Monte Nero built, but, in 1720, was commenced the present superb church, which was completed in fifty years at a great expense, and dedicated to the Virgin. When the establishments of the regular clergy were generally suppressed in Tuscany in 1783, the charge of the picture was given to the seculars of this Church of the Madonna, which became parochial; but in 1792, the Grand Duke, Ferdinand III., having restored some of the convents, intrusted the treasury of this miraculous picture, and all that belonged to it, to the monks of Vallombrosa; and, the following year, a sufficient number of them came hither, and assumed the guardianship of this greatly celebrated shrine, which they have ever since retained.

The Church of the Madonna of Monte Nero, is remarkable for its rich display of marbles and costly decorations, the gifts and contributions of grateful benefactors. Forsyth, in his wonted irreverent and sarcastic manner, gives the following amusing description of the shrine: "On Monte Nero is a most magnificent church, raised by the piety of sailors to an old picture of the Virgin, which had flown from Judæa through the air, and perched on this hill for their especial protection. To this miraculous daub they ascribe all their escapes; and as proofs of its saving power, they have covered the walls with cable-ends and crutches, the barrels of guns which had innocently burst, the chains of delivered slaves, and a thousand ex-voto pictures bordering on caricature. No Italian ship sails past the hill without saluting our Lady of Monte Nero. A thousand sterns in the Mediterranean bear her name and effigy. Under her invocation I had embarked in two different feluccas; but, finding me out to be a heretic, she would never let me finish my voyage."

To the south of Livorno, the whole coast between the rocky headlands of Monte Nero and Piombino, is a long sweep of low, sandy beach, with three or four lonely, diminutive castles, intended as a check upon the piratical incursions of the Barbary corsairs. Opposite the port rises the island of Menaria, and some miles beyond it, that of Gorgone:

<blockquote>
Adsurgit ponti medio circumflua Gorgon,
Inter Pisaeum Cyrnaicumque latus.*
</blockquote>

Rutilius.

Farther to the south, but within sight of the coast, is the island of Elba, for whose petty sovereignty Napoleon was compelled to exchange the throne of France:

<blockquote>
"There sunk the greatest, nor the worst of men,
Whose spirit antithetically mixed,
One moment of the mightiest, and again
On little objects with like firmness fixed,
Extremes in all things :"—
</blockquote>

Childe Harold.

---

* Between the Pisan and Cyrnean lands,
'Mid the white waves the sea-girt Gorgon stands.

FLORENCE

Of all the fairest cities of the earth,
None are so fair as Florence.
    Rogers.

ITALIAN History presents nothing more interesting and exciting than the annals of Florence. Tracing this city downwards from her first appearance on the page of legitimate history, as a Roman colony, till also became the very temple of literature and art,—we gather in our progress such instances of indomitable courage in the dark ages which succeeded the fall of the empire; such union of the highest chivalry of romance with the sanguinary scenes which marked the struggle between rival parties; such displays of pure patriotism and unbounded munificence on the part of the first merchant princes of the Medicean family; such thrilling tragedies connected with the subsequent history of this distinguished house, when its descendants, forgetting their virtuous and patriot origin, sunk into oppressors of their country, and riotous slaves of profligacy and prodigality;—and, interwoven with these, the glorious imaginings of Dante; Petrarch's impassioned strains; the "Hundred Tales of Love," of the elegant, but impure, Boccaccio; the dramatic triumphs of Alfieri; the heaven-ward contemplations of Galileo, who walked amidst the brightness of the firmament, whilst the thunders of the Vatican were directed against him, and the terrors of the Inquisition were arrayed before him;—and, blended with these again, the triumphs of Painting, the triumphs of Sculpture, the triumphs of Architecture:—we gather from the annals of Florence such salient points as these, to distinguish above all common records an historical drama, played upon Roman ground, and represented in its various acts by a dramatis personæ of princes, and of men greater and more ennobled than princes.

The antiquity of Florence cannot be traced back, with certainty, farther than sixty years previous to the Christian era. Then it was, that a division of Roman soldiers were sent thither, after the battle of Perusia, by Octavianus. Little remains to distinguish its history as a Roman colony, either in recorded achievements, or in architectural remains of former greatness. Beyond a few traces of an amphitheatre, and some inscriptions, nothing is presented to the eye to identify Florence with the empire. Ecclesiastical history has preserved an account of persecutions and martyrdoms in this city, under Decius, in the third century; and in 313, Felix, one of its bishops, attended a council in Rome. When the Goths made irruption into Italy, the Florentines distinguished themselves by a bold defence of their city; from whose walls they triumphantly repulsed the barbarian host, first in 405, and subsequently in 542. We afterwards find the city in the possession of the Longobards, who made the district one of their dukedoms; but in their hands, Florence itself became little better than a deserted mass of ruins. On the defeat of the Longobards by Charlemagne, Florence was raised from its forlorn condition; but it never shone forth in all its lustre, till governed by its own magistrates, and under laws enacted by its own authority, it acquired the name and the energies of a republic.

In the latter part of the eleventh, and the beginning of the twelfth century, when the disputes between the Church and the Empire were violent, and when every Italian town became involved in their contests, Florence was under the jurisdiction of the Countess Matilda, who, dying in 1115, left her inheritance to the See of Rome. Florence had then a very limited territory, but already the commercial character of its people had shown itself, in their transactions with the Levant and with France. Before the death of Matilda, the Florentines had made a grand struggle for liberty, by opposing the appointment of a new vicar nominated by the emperor; on which occasion an obstinate battle was fought at Monte Cascioli, about six miles from Florence, wherein the imperial vicar was slain, and the troops of the empire discomfited. Notwithstanding the bequest of Matilda, successive popes, from motives of policy, acted with great moderation towards the Florentines, and laid their authority lightly upon them; by which means they effectually won them to the side of the Church, and arrayed them in permanent hostility against the empire. Thus was Florence established as an independent commonwealth, attached to the Guelphic, or Church party, in opposition to the Ghibelline faction, which gave its support to the emperor. As the community of Florence increased, many partisans of the emperor became citizens, and the seeds of dissension were sown within the city itself. Thenceforward, till the time of the Medici, the history of Florence is a fearful record of party strife.

The dissensions of the Florentines may be altogether referred to the dispute for supremacy between the Church and the Emperor; but out of this original ground of quarrel, not unfrequently arose private bickerings, in which the party epithets of Guelph and Ghibelline were made subservient to the fierce passions of powerful and rival families thirsting for each other's blood. In 1215, the whole city was divided into two great factions, in consequence of a domestic tragedy, the subject of many a drama and picture. A young man of the Buondelmonti family had been betrothed to a young lady of the family Uberti. He broke faith with her, and married a Donati, for which he was stabbed in the streets by the Uberti. The citizens took part, some with the one family and some with the other; and as the Uberti were for the Emperor, Frederick II., and the Buondelmonti and Donati were partisans of the Church, these domestic quarrels were combined with the public and political struggle which so long hung like a curse upon Italy.

> O Buondelmonti! what ill counseling
> Prevailed on thee to break the plighted bond!
> Many, who now are weeping, would rejoice,
> Had God to Ema given thee, the first time
> Thou near our city camest.
>
> *Paradiso*, XVII. 139–143.

We cannot enter minutely into all the vicissitudes which attended the strife of parties in Florence. Ages passed in a frightful monotony of tumult and massacre, relieved occasionally by an act of devoted courage and patriotism, or by an incident destined in after-times " to point a moral and adorn a tale." Governed sometimes by its bishop, sometimes by its nobles, and not unfrequently by its people, Florence experienced all the varieties and all the agitations of republican administration. Sometimes convulsed by the rival pretensions of the former, or by the licentious claims of the latter, it was converted into a field of battle, a theatre of guilt and assassination; at intervals, under the sway of a wise and virtuous magistracy, it exhibited tokens of peace, industry, and prosperity; and in its frequent wars with the neighbouring states of Siena, Pisa, and Lucca, it obtained a fame that placed it upon a level with the other commonwealths of Italy. But ever and anon, the volcano of intestine division, which never ceased to give indication of its presence, broke forth into terrible eruption, that swept before it the peace and order, and happy presages, to which a brief interval of quiet had given birth. About the middle of the thirteenth century, the Guelphic party had utterly expelled the Ghibellines from Florence. They recorded their successes in the annals of the city, as "the year of victories;" and on this occasion, they first coined their fine gold florins, bearing the municipal emblems, St. John the Baptist, and the Lily. Within a few years, almost before the acclamations of triumph had ceased, the proscribed Ghibellines returned to take vengeance upon their enemies. The Guelphs were now, in turn, expelled from the city, which was only saved from utter destruction by the patriotism of Farinati, himself a Ghibelline. When his party proposed to raze Florence to its foundations, and scatter its population over the surrounding country, he indignantly declared that he would rather unite with the Guelphs than consent to the proposal. Florence was saved; and her defender still lives in the poetry of Dante.

> To that affray
> I stood not singly, nor, without just cause,
> Assuredly, should with the rest have stirred;
> But singly there I stood, when, by consent
> Of all, Florence had to the ground been razed,
> The one who openly forbade the deed.
>
> *Inferno,* X. 87—92.

The tide of circumstances again rolled in favour of the Guelphs, who in 1025 returned in triumph to Florence, whence they drove the garrison of their opponents. Thenceforward the strength of the Ghibellines declined; and their triumphs were confined to partial and temporary advantages, which failed to re-establish their supremacy, but sufficed to perpetuate the horrors of intestine strife and tumult. An attempt on the part of Pope Nicholas III. to mediate between these factions, utterly failed; and centuries passed away leaving only records of enmity and bloodshed. Other parties also arose; and the contests of the Bianchi and the Neri, are as distinguished in the history of hatred, as those of the Guelphs and Ghibellines. Amidst all these disasters, Florence prosecuted her commercial enterprises with great success, and also entered into fierce contest with the other republics of Italy, some of which she reduced to entire subjection.* The wealth of the Florentines must in these ages have been immense: the physical force of the city and neighbourhood could not furnish strength for their warlike expeditions; and their armies were therefore composed of mercenaries, commanded by a foreign leader, and maintained at great cost. With the growth of her commer-

---

* Florence exult! for thou so mightily
Hast thriven, that o'er land and sea thy wings
Thou beatest.

Inferno, XXV. 1—3.

cial importance, there sprung up in Florence contentions for supremacy between the nobles and wealthy citizens; and ultimately the *grandi* were overborne, and excluded from all the offices of the republic. In a few years, jealousies arose between the citizens themselves, when proscription and exile fell upon the weaker party; and out of these strifes, the Medici and the Ricci sought monopoly of power by pandering to the prejudices of the lower trades. The Albizzi afterwards obtained ascendancy at the head of the wealthy citizens, and founded a new aristocracy, which held the government, in spite of tumults and conspiracies, for fifty-two years; and from 1400 to 1433, Florence enjoyed a period of quiet, the longest, says Macchiavelli, in her history. At length, the Albizzi were overthrown by Cosmo de' Medici, with whose family the subsequent history of Florence is identified.

The first merchant princes of the Medicean family, wisely content with the ascendancy which the affection and the gratitude of their country gave them, blended the policy of the statesman, the disinterestedness of the patriot, and the munificence of the sovereign, with the economy of traders, and the affability, the ease, and the simplicity of citizens. Such was the effect of these virtues, set off by learning and discernment, that history presents few great men to our observation more worthy of esteem and admiration than Cosmo, the "Father of his Country," and Lorenzo, "the Magnificent." To these founders of the Medicean family Florence is indebted for the world's interest in her fortunes.

Cosmo de' Medici, by a course of prudent policy, increased his wealth and popularity, and became a great patron of art and literature; but the restless disposition of the Florentines interrupted for a time his patriotic and munificent designs for the benefit of his country. Through the intrigues of the Albizzi, a sentence of banishment for ten years was recorded against him; but within a year from his departure, he was restored to the seat of government by the unanimous voice of the people, and received with every demonstration of joy. He now rallied around him the wise and the learned of all countries, established libraries and institutions, and endowed hospitals; yet he so carefully avoided ostentation that his munificence and benevolence excited neither jealousy nor envy. He died in 1464, leaving behind him a name to which history presents few parallels. This citizen prince was succeeded by his second son Piero; Giovanni, the elder son, having died before Cosmo. Piero survived his father only five years, and then left the government to his son, Lorenzo, "the Magnificent."

Lorenzo distinguished himself above all his predecessors by his princely foundations for the encouragement of the arts and literature; his gardens in Florence, furnished with the finest statues and works of art, became an academy for study; and by the influence of his example, the higher classes of the Florentines were invited to follow his pursuits, and the lower order of citizens were encouraged to adopt them by his liberality. The age of Lorenzo de' Medici stands out as one of the brightest eras in art, science, and literature. Many of the extraordinary men of that time had been preceded, in the same country, by minds worthy of contemporaneous fame. Giotto and Brunelleschi, Dante and Orcagna, had preceded Michael Angelo, Galileo, Da Vinci, Cellini, and Politiano; but few have followed who would, in that age, have been distinguished. The powers of the painters, sculptors, and architects, of that day, were not confined to one, or all of those pursuits together; they were the engineers, civil and military, the mathematicians, mechanics, chemists and anatomists of their time; they were poets, artists, and philosophers. Since their day, none have appeared to compete with them in excellence, in any one of their pursuits; and none have succeeded, as they did, in combining these pursuits, and in embracing, both in theory and practice, all the human knowledge of their time. There were, indeed, giants in those days; and at the mention of their names, we recall their contemporaries, their works, their munificent patron, and their country, which they rendered illustrious.

The zealous efforts of Lorenzo for the happiness and prosperity of his country, were insufficient to extinguish that spirit of faction which had for so many ages disturbed the tranquillity of Florence. The Pazzi, who had been admitted into family alliance with the Medici, jealous of the popularity and consequent power of Lorenzo, conspired for his overthrow; but their design failed in its principal object, and accomplished only the assassination of his brother Giuliano. The "Conspiracy of the Pazzi" forms the subject of a tragedy by Alfieri. The poet has not pourtrayed the character of Lorenzo very faithfully; he was too stern a republican to acquiesce in the supremacy of the Medici, how great soever their private virtues might have been, or their public benefits to the commonwealth. It, moreover, better suited dramatic purposes, that his conspirators should appear in the character of men bold and resolute for the right, than in that of moody malcontents and ruthless assassins. The following passage, in which Lorenzo taunts the father of Julian for his son's contumacy, breathes more of tyranny than of patriotism:

> "Go; if thou carest for thy son pursue him;
> To adapt his conduct better to the times
> Instruct him; and to this do thou thyself,
> By thy example, aid him. Equally
> With him indeed thou hatest me, yet thou
> Hast yielded to me, and dost yield. Engraft
> Thy own discretion on his headstrong will.
> I do not e'en pretend regard for you;
> Ill have ye feigned; and nothing it annoys me.
> Haste, but obey; and yet obeying, tremble.
> Go then, and tell to this thy mountebank,
> And pigmy Brutus, that his prototype,
> The real Brutus, fell in vain with Rome."

On the death of Lorenzo, at the early age of forty-four, his son Piero rose to his place; but the latter wanted the capacity and the virtues of his father; and after offering vain concessions to Charles VIII. of France, he was driven from Florence. The French troops entered the city, and, aided by the citizens, destroyed the palace of the Medici, and dispersed in a single day the wonders of art, and the rare manuscripts, which had been collected by Cosmo and Lorenzo. Subsequently, the Medicean family were restored to Florence; but though the liberty of the city and the glory of the Medici survived Lorenzo, they began from the fatal period of his death to decline; till Cosmo, a descendant from the first Lorenzo, decorated with the empty title of Duke, resigned the nobler appellation of the first citizen and the father of his country, and usurped by force that government which the gratitude and veneration of his countrymen had deposited with generous confidence in the hands of his ancestors. Cosmo had no sooner risen to the coveted distinction of the ducal coronet, than he removed to the Palazzo Pitti, there to exhibit the vanity and ostentation which formed such striking features in his character. Here it was that his Duchess, Eleonore de Toledo, gave birth to offspring whose crimes entailed no less misery on themselves than on others; and from this palace went forth that gorgeous procession, the first exhibition of his ambition to play the sovereign, on the occasion of the baptism of his first-born, Mary. But the pride of Cosmo was soon to be humbled. His second son, Giovanni, fell by the hand of his brother Garzia; and the latter was stabbed by Cosmo in the presence of the unhappy mother, Eleonore, who in a few days after died of a broken heart, and followed her children to the grave.* Cosmo afterwards resigned his authority into the hands of his eldest son Francisco, whom he nominated regent. Thenceforward he surrendered himself to sensual indulgences; and his subsequent marriage with a lady, formerly his mistress, gave umbrage to his son, to whom he was compelled to make concessions fatal to his peace. To conciliate the regent, he promised that his new wife should never have the title, or be treated with the honours of grand duchess; and she, disappointed in her ambitious hopes, treated him in turn with indifference and neglect. Forsaken by his wife, and reduced to a state of helplessness, by repeated attacks of gout and apoplexy, he was at length removed by order of the regent to the ducal palace. Here, having lost not only the use of his limbs, but his speech also, he lingered for a few months, making the walls echo with the sighs and groans wrung from him by recollections of the past, and dread of the future. Let ambition derive a lesson from Cosmo, grand duke of Florence, surrounded with the "pride, pomp, and circumstance" of sovereign authority, and

> That very Cosmo shaking o'er his fire,
> Drowsy and deaf and inarticulate,
> Wrapt in his night-gown, o'er a sick man's mess,
> In the last stage—death-struck and deadly pale.
>
> *Rogers.*

The annals of the Medici, from the time of Cosmo till the extinction of the family, are one dark list of cruelty and crime. Florence ultimately became an appanage of Austria, and so remained till engulfed by Napoleon. On his overthrow it passed to a branch of the Austrian line, which was dethroned in 1850, and the sovereignty transferred to the King of Sardinia.

Florence is pleasantly situated in a vale intersected by the Arno, graced by numberless hills, and bordered at no great distance by mountains of various forms rising gradually towards the Appenines. The whole vale is one continued grove and garden, where the beauty of the country is enlivened by the animation of the town, and the fertility of the soil is redoubled by the industry of its cultivators. White villas gleam through the orchards on every side, and large populous hamlets border the roads, and almost line the banks of the river. The city itself spreads along the side of the river, which forms one of its greatest ornaments, and contributes not a little to its fame. Florence presents in its interior neither the splendour of Genoa, the cheerfulness of Milan, nor the grandeur of Venice; the character of its architectural aspect is that of thoughtful and sober dignity. It is impossible however to imagine anything finer than the view which this city presents from the neighbouring elevations. Our limited space will not permit us to enter into a minute detail of the palaces and public buildings of Florence, and the noble works of art which they contain: indeed a mere catalogue of the latter, would of itself extend to a volume. It must suffice, that we glance rapidly at the leading structures, cursorily noticing as we pass along the peculiar points of interest in each.

Commencing with the churches, the Duomo, or Cathedral, claims our first regard. In

---

* This domestic tragedy has been dramatised by Alfieri, but with a total want of regard to historical truth.

strength and magnificence this building ranks amongst the first of the kind in Europe. Its walls are encrusted with black and white marble; and its pavement, the work, in part, of Michael Angelo, is composed of variegated marble wrought in devices of great beauty. It is adorned both within and without by marble statues, the works of the most eminent sculptors; and its paintings are master-pieces of art. This structure is principally remarkable for its octangular dome, erected by Brunelleschi in the fourteenth century, and which suggested to Michael Angelo and Bramante, a model for the dome of St. Peter's. The last, however, is of a circular form, and hence is more pleasing to the eye; but in point of skilful construction the dome at Florence is in no degree inferior, whilst it has the superior merit of being a first conception.

The Cathedral of Florence is not altogether dependent on its architectural beauty for the interest it excites. In it was assembled the celebrated council, where a Greek Emperor, surrounded by the patriarchs of the Greek Church, sat enthroned next to the Roman Pontiff and his prelates; when the two most ancient ecclesiastical communions were united for the last time in the bonds of faith and charity. Here also the Emperor, Frederic III., environed by his vassal kings and dukes, sat in imperial state, and distributed the honours of knighthood among his attendants. And the pavement of this church received the blood of Giuliano de' Medici, when he fell beneath the daggers of the Pazzi. This structure is also hallowed by the dust which it enshrines. Here repose Giotto and Brunelleschi, side by side; Marsilino Ficino, the restorer of Platonic philosophy; and many others, whose names are linked to fame. At some distance from the choir, and on the northern wall of the church, is a very ancient picture of Dante. This painting, of which the authenticity is doubted, is the only monument which Florence has raised to the memory of her most illustrious poet. The republic once endeavoured, through the mediation of Michael Angelo, to obtain the bard's remains; but the citizens of Ravenna, faithful to their trust, and to the indignation of Dante against his ungrateful country, steadily refused to resign them.*

Close to the front of the Duomo, but totally detached from it, rises the Campanile, or belfry, adorned with allegorical tablets and many highly finished statues. This building was erected by Giotto, who was commanded to construct an edifice which, both in dimensions and in elaborate workmanship, should excel the finest works of Greece and Rome. It is a square tower in the pure Italian Gothic style, rising in the same dimensions to the very top, the diminution of proportions being left to the natural effect of perspective. The beauty of the building re-

---

* When Dante had been driven into exile by the Guelphic party, the people of Ravenna afforded him an asylum; and after his death, they raised a magnificent tomb to his memory. The epitaph says,—" An exile from Florence, he was received at Ravenna, which enjoyed his presence during his life-time, and honours him after his death . . his tomb, dear to the muses, the senate and people of Ravenna secured, repaired, and adorned, as a treasure of their own, by their own authority, and at their own cost." Dante makes a touching allusion to his banishment in the " Vision:"

Thou shalt leave each thing
Belov'd most dearly: this is the first shaft
Shot from the bow of exile. Thou shalt prove
How salt the savour is of other's bread;
How hard the passage to descend and climb
By other's stairs.

sults in no small degree from this circumstance; for had the sides been inclined from strict parallelism, the eye would have reduced the proportions too rapidly.

> By the gates
> Wondrously wrought, so beautiful, so glorious,
> That they might serve to be the gates of Heaven,
> Enter the Baptistery.
> *Rogers.*

The Battisterio di San Giovanni is an octangular building of great beauty, surmounted by a cupola and lantern. The exterior is coated with black and white marble. The interior is adorned with the sculptures of Donatello; and the cupola, supported by pillars of granite, is covered with mosaics wrought by a succession of Florentine artists. This church is the Baptistery, not of St. John's parish only, but of the whole city of Florence; and the annual number of baptisms is said to average three thousand five hundred. The high reputation of this structure is principally derived from its three brazen portals, or doors; one of which was executed by Andrea Pisano, in 1330; and the other two by Ghiberti, in the early part of the fifteenth century. They are celebrated for the exquisite beauty of the basso-rilievos with which they are adorned; these have reference to the leading events in Sacred History, including the life of St. John, and the ministry of our Lord. Michael Angelo is reported to have said of these doors, that they were worthy to be the gates of paradise.

The Church of San Lorenzo is less remarkable for its own internal beauties than for the edifices united or connected with it; these are the Sacristy, the Medicean Chapel, and the Laurentian Library. Externally, the Church of St. Lorenzo is mean and unsightly; but the interior presents all the graces of architecture. Two pulpits of singular beauty, the work of Bertoldo, stand in the nave; and in the pavement near the high altar, a slab of porphyry, exquisitely inlaid with verd antique and precious marbles, marks the resting place of Cosmo de' Medici, "the father of his country." There are two Sacristies; the Sagrestia Vecchia, designed by Brunelleschi, and the Sagrestia Nuova, built by Michael Angelo. The first is remarkable for a singular allegorical painting over the altar, and for the sarcophagus of Giovanni de' Medici, by Donatello. But the Sacristy of Michael Angelo exhibits the most felicitous union of architecture and sculpture; the buildings and monuments having been planned with mutual reference to each other. Here are several statues commemorative of the Medici; and the famed allegorical statues of Morning, Noon, Evening, and Night. Some of these are highly finished, whilst the rest, by their very imperfections, attest the power of Michael Angelo. The highest praise has been bestowed on these works, both in prose and verse, by native and foreign writers, whose descriptions and allusions have directed the traveller's attention towards their repository:

> That Chamber of the Dead,
> Where the gigantic forms of Night and Day,
> Turn'd into stone, rest everlastingly,
> Yet still are breathing.
> *Rogers.*

The Medicean Chapel, which is still unfinished, was begun in 1604, and was originally intended for the reception of the Holy Sepulchre, the acquisition of which had been promised to

Ferdinand I. by an Emir of the Druses, who offered his aid to steal this relic from the Holy Land. The *pious* intention failed; and the structure was thenceforward destined to be the mausoleum of the Medicean family. The building is still in an unfinished state, and some parts contrast violently with others; there is notwithstanding a gorgeous yet solemn magnificence about this chapel, which strikes the beholder with awe and amazement; and enough has been accomplished to show that if the structure were finished in accordance with the original design, it would be the most sumptuous mausoleum in the world. Its form is octangular, its diameter ninety-four feet, and its elevation to the vault two hundred feet. It is lined with lapis lazuli, agate, jasper, onyx, and other precious stones; furnished with sarcophagi of porphyry; and supported by granito pilasters with capitals of bronze. The niches between these pilasters are of touchstone. Underneath is a subterranean chapel, where repose the bodies, whose names are inscribed on the sarcophagi above. The crucifixion of our Saviour, a group in white marble by Giovanni di Bologna, and a Virgin by Michael Angelo, grace this dormitory of the dead. Description is utterly inadequate to convey any idea of this magnificent building, wherein the skill of the artist is rivalled by the preciousness of the materials with which he wrought. The mosaics are exquisite; the cenotaphs of the Medici exhibit a costly display of chalcedony, jasper, mother of pearl, turquoises, and topazes; and the statues of Ferdinand I. and Cosmo II. are marvellous works of art. It is highly improbable that this structure will ever be completed; at least, in accordance with what is already done. Eustace says, indeed, that the materials of the inlaid pavement are still in store; but if so, what labour of art must be bestowed to work these materials, before the pavement could worthily hold companionship with the mosaics on the walls. And if the pavement were finished, there would be yet more to do, to render the kingly mausoleum of the Medici a perfect work.

The cloister of San Lorenzo opens into the Laurentian Library, which originally consisted of manuscripts collected by the first princes of the Medicean family. After their dispersion, in the time of Piero, some were recovered, and many were subsequently added by Leo X. and Clement VII. These are of rare value, and give to the collection a celebrity equal to that of the Vatican. The library now contains upwards of nine thousand manuscripts, including the richest treasures of literature that the world can boast.

The Church of Santa Croce, a noble and richly decorated building, having much of the character of the Duomo, holds pre-eminence over the other churches, on account of its being the Westminster Abbey of Florence. Here repose the remains of men, whose names have gone forth into every civilized land, in connection with all that is illustrious in literature, science, and art. The mausoleum of Michael Angelo is a marble sarcophagus, raised upon an oblong platform of the same material, and surmounted by a bust of the deceased. Seated on the platform are three fine emblematic figures of Painting, Sculpture, and Architecture, in various attitudes alike expressive of grief. The tomb of Alfieri, the work of Canova, is also a sarcophagus, bearing a bust of the poet in bas-relief, and elevated upon two huge elliptic bases of marble. A colossal statue of Italy, clad in flowing drapery, leans upon the tomb, and bows her castellated head in sorrow. The monument to Macchiavelli supports a statue of Justice, holding in one hand a medallion bearing a bust of the historian, and leaning with the other on the balance and the sword. Galileo's tomb is appropriately adorned with statues of Geometry and Astronomy. Besides these, there are also monuments to the poet Filicaja, to Lanzi the connoisseur, to the theologian Lami, the historian Bruni, the statesman Signorini, and a host of others whose genius and fame render sacred the earth which covers them, and give a lustre beyond the reach of art to the tombs which commemorate them.

> In Santa Croce's holy precincts lie
> Ashes which make it holier, dust which is
> Even in itself an immortality,
> Though there were nothing save the past and this,
> The particles of those sublimities
> Which have relaps'd to chaos:—here repose
> Angelo's, Alfieri's bones, and his,
> The starry Galileo, with his woes :
> Here Machiavelli's earth return'd to whence it rose.
>
> But where repose the all Etruscan three—
> Dante, and Petrarch, and scarce less than they,
> The Bard of Prose, creative spirit ! he
> Of the Hundred Tales of love ?
>
> Childe Harold.

"The all Etruscan three," Dante, Petrarch, and Boccaccio, sleep in exile ; Dante at Ravenna, Petrarch at Arqua, and Boccaccio at Certaldo.

> "And Santa Croce wants their mighty dust."

We pass on to a brief mention of the palazzi of Florence; of which, space permits us to notice only a few of the most striking features. The Palazzo Vecchio, in the Piazza del Granduca, is a noble structure. Here passed the most stirring events of a period pregnant with all the virtues and crimes that usually mark the struggle between the defenders and assailants of liberty. In front of the entrance to this massive edifice, are placed the colossal statues of David and Hercules ; the first by Michael Angelo, and the second by Bandinelli. The Palazzo del Podesta was formerly the residence of the chief criminal magistrate of the Florentine republic. It is now used as a prison. The palazzo Ricardi is worthy of remark as the palatial residence of the first Cosmo de' Medici. The Palazzo Pitti presents the greatest attractions to tourists and visitors ; being the residence of the sovereign, and also the building most intimately connected with the fate and fortunes of Florence. The erection of this edifice was begun, early in the fifteenth century, by Lucca Pitti, an opponent of the Medici. After the disgrace of Pitti, the structure came into the hands of the Medicean family. This building is in the true Florentine style, and its prevailing character is that of massive dignity. Some of Salvator Rosa's finest works exist here ; amongst which is a battle piece, full of force, life, and energy. Rubens' picture of the Four Philosophers is esteemed one of the most perfect works of this master. Andrea del Sarto's St. John in the Wilderness, and the St. Mark by Fra Bartolomeo, are greatly admired. And Vandyke is here shown in some of his most perfect performances. Canova's Venus forms one of the grand ornaments of the Pitti palace. And amongst the paintings, the celebrated Madonna della Seggiola, of Raphael d'Urbino, stands distinguished for majesty of conception, and artistic excellence in all its details.[*] We regret

---

[*] This magnificent painting has recently been made patent to the public of Britain, through the medium of a beautiful engraving, included in the series of Illustrations prepared for the Imperial Family Bible. Before that plate was engraved, the only transcripts from this picture, accessible to the community at large, were worthless caricatures, utterly inadequate to convey the faintest idea of the original.

FLORENCE.

that we are compelled to pass these treasures of art with such brief notice; but our rapid sketch does not admit of more extensive description.

The glory of Florence is the Uffizj, or Gallery, erected by Cosmo I. to be the seat of magistracy, and which is now a repository of art, second only to the unrivalled collection of the Vatican. The first vestibule contains busts of the Medici family. The second vestibule exhibits a fine specimen of ancient sculpture, the Florentine Boar; and a remarkable example of *restoration* in the Apollo Cœlispex, of which scarcely any thing beyond the trunk, the right thigh, and a portion of the right arm, belongs to the original sculptor. The corridors are adorned with paintings and arabesques; busts of the Roman emperors; the Bacchus and Faun of Michael Angelo; and the David of Donatello. The Hall of Niobe presents a group of noble figures, illustrating the fate of the unhappy mother who, proud of her offspring, claimed superiority over Latona. In the Tribune " stands the statue that enchants the world," the far-famed Venus de' Medici. This unrivalled work of art, was discovered in a broken state, and some portions were wanting; but the fragments have been united with wonderful skill, and the necessary restoration made. That this statue possesses excellence of the very highest order, is sufficiently evident from the unqualified commendations bestowed upon it by the best judges. It is, however, amusing to read the thousand and one critiques on the Venus, by tourists male and female; the whole, with very few exceptions, characterized by an amusing absurdity. We have been invited to mark the purity of the Venus, and then desired to note her sensuality; one tells us that she is a nymph rather than the Paphian Queen, and another sees in her something perfectly transmundane, celestial, and madonna-like! Some few have sense and candour enough to decide, that the statue is an exquisite portraiture of woman placed in very peculiar circumstances. Amongst the sculptures of the Tribune, should be particularized, the Wrestlers or Lottatori; the Arrotino; the Apollino; and the Dancing Faun. Passing over the paintings and other works of art, which are too numerous for us even to catalogue, we may name the Egyptian Antiquities, the Vases and Terra-cottas, the Medals, the Cabinet of Gems, and the Collection of Drawings and Engravings, as so many sources of refined amusement presented to the connoisseur in the Gallery of Florence.

" There be more things to greet the heart and eyes," in Florence, than we have glanced at, " there be more marvels yet ;" but we have already exceeded our limits, and we must rest content with having indicated a few leading characteristics of this famous city. It remains only to notice very briefly two localities in its neighbourhood, to which Milton has given a classic interest. The one is the beautiful village of Fiesole, placed on the summit of a lofty and broken eminence, overlooking the Arno and the city of Florence. To this spot, the scene of his converse with Galileo, Milton refers in that well-known passage:

> The moon, whose orb
> Through optic glass the Tuscan artist views
> At evening from the top of Fesole.
>
> *Paradise Lost.*

The other locality is Vallombrosa, celebrated for its abbey and beautiful scenery.

> Autumnal leaves that strew the brooks
> In Vallombrosa, where the Etrurian shades
> High over-arch'd embower.
>
> *Paradise Lost.*

CERTALDO.

THE little township of Certaldo, in the Val d'Elsa, is principally remarkable for its being the disputed birth-place, and the undisputed resting-place of Boccaccio. It was formerly the seat of an extensive *Vicariat*; and the remains of the old town, occupying the summit of a hill which rises abruptly from the plain, present a striking and picturesque appearance. The modern town, built at the foot of this eminence, is divided into two portions, between which passes the road, named the Traversa, leading from Poggibonsi to Siena. History has recorded little of importance concerning Certaldo. In 1164 it was conveyed by a diploma of the emperor Frederick I. to Count Alberto of Prato, a descendant of whom yielded up the place to Florence. The rebellion of the Alberti, at Simifonte, led to the destruction of the castle of Certaldo, and the town was thenceforward declared to be a district of the Florentine Republic.

Dante ascribes the degeneracy of the Florentines, in his day, to the admission of families from the neighbouring villages, into Florence, and to their mixture with the primitive citizens. Before the acquisition of contiguous territories had extended the citizenship, he tells us,—

> ——the citizen's blood that now is mix'd
> From Campi, and *Certaldo*, and Fighine,
> Ran purely through the last mechanic's veins.
>
> *Paradiso, XVI. 47—49.*

And he applies the defeat at Simifonte as a taunt against the descendants of these intruders into civic privileges:

> Such a one as hath become a Florentine,
> And trades and traffics, had been turn'd adrift
> To *Simifonte*, where his grandsire plied
> The beggar's craft.
>
> *Paradiso, XVI. 59—62.*

The French and the Italians are at issue regarding the birth-place of Boccaccio. The former contend that he was born in Paris, in 1313; the latter admit the correctness of date, but denying the locality, stoutly assert that he was born at Certaldo. There is no evidence to settle these rival claims. It is, however, certain that he was educated in Florence; and with the exception of six years of mercantile drudgery in Paris, he spent nearly the whole of his life in Italy. The Decameron, on which the fame of Boccaccio rests, was written at the court of Naples, by desire of queen Joanna, a sovereign equally celebrated for her beauty and licentiousness. It consists of a series of one hundred tales supposed to be related by a society of young people of rank, who had fled from Florence during the dreadful pestilence which, in 1348, devastated

that city. These tales are elegantly written, and are full of sprightliness and wit; but some of them are very offensive to moral purity.

In the year 1361, a Carthusian monk, named Father Ciani, wrought upon the fears of Boccaccio, by declaring to him that he was commissioned to warn him of his approaching end, unless he repented his irregular life and licentious writings.* The impression produced upon Boccaccio, lasted only till his health was restored. Whether the monk's commission was genuine, may be questioned; but surely the attempt to arrest a voluptuous writer in his course of impurity, deserved not the sneer which a modern poet has cast upon it:

> "The Friar pour'd out his catalogue of treasures:
> A ray, imprimis, of the star that shone
> To the wise men; a phial full of sounds,
> The musical chimes of the great bell that hung
> In Solomon's Temple; and though last not least,
> A feather from the angel Gabriel's wing,
> Dropt in the Virgin's chamber."

The literary reputation of Boccaccio, led to his being employed in various missions and offices, by the republic of Florence. The latter part of his life appears to have been occupied in the collection of classical manuscripts. Returning, at length, to his paternal home at Certaldo,†

> Boccaccio to his parent earth bequeath'd
> His dust.
> *Childe Harold.*

He died on the 21st December 1375, at the age of sixty-two; and was buried in the church of San Jacopo e San Filippo, at Certaldo. In 1503, a cenotaph was raised to his memory, and a marble bust, the latter sculptured by Giovanni Francisco Rustico. Boccaccio's monument is frequently visited, both by foreigners and natives, as well as the house he inhabited, consisting of two or three small chambers, and a low tower, upon which Cosmo II. placed an inscription. The house is preserved with great care by the Marchioness Lenzoni Medici, who has become its possessor.

---

* Boccaccio, relating this transaction to his friend Petrarch, says:—" A Carthusian of Siena, whom I knew not, came to me at Florence, and asked to speak with me in private. 'I came hither,' says he, 'from the desire of the blessed father Petrosi, a Carthusian of Siena; he charged me to represent to you your extreme danger, unless you reform your manners and your writings, which are the instruments the devil uses to draw men into his snares, to tempt them to sinful lusts, and to promote the depravity of their conduct. Ought you not to blush for such an abuse of the talents God has given you for his glory? What a reward might you have obtained had you made a good use of that wit and eloquence with which He has endowed you! On the contrary, what ought you not to fear, for devoting yourself to love, and waging war with modesty, by giving lessons of libertinism both in your life and writings!'"

† It may be noticed that Florence, as well as Paris, disputes with Certaldo the honour of having given birth to Boccaccio.

SIENA.

PRESERVING its ancient name of Siena, or Sena Julia, almost without change, Siena can with certainty be referred to the time of the empire; and indubitable traces of Etruscan origin, give this city a still higher claim to antiquity, although no mention is made of it amongst the towns of Etruria. The Sienese have ever been vain of their remote descent; to this, and to their love of distinction and frivolous display, they are indebted for the moral anathema which Dante has recorded against them:*

> Was ever race
> Light as Siena's? Nay not France herself
> Can show a tribe so frivolous and vain.
>
> *Inferno*, XXIX. 117—119.

Siena appears to have escaped the ravages of the northern hordes, who held their course generally along the shore of the Adriatic; and until the eleventh century, it is probable that it remained in a state of peaceful obscurity. Ecclesiastical history mentions a bishop of Siena, as early as the sixth century; † and a council was held there in 1058, at which Nicho-

---

* The descent of the Sienese from a Roman colony is forced upon the attention of the traveller, by the oft repeated figure of the she-wolf. Their vanity is attested by the eagerness with which the artisans sought a patent of nobility in connection with the purchase of an estate. And their frivolity and vanity are seen in combination, in Agostino's banquet to Leo X., on which occasion the whole papal court were served with a succession of silver plate, which, as the removes went from the table, was cast into the river. Another instance, and the one to which Dante more expressly alludes, refers to a club of young prodigals named La Brigata Godereccia. There were men who could club a purse of 200,000 ducats, and spend it in a few months. They roasted pheasants with burning cloves, shod their horses with silver, and played other pranks equally absurd.

† Albero, a bishop of Siena, caused Grifolino of Arezzo to be burned as a necromancer; the latter having promised to teach the son of Albero the art of flying, and failed to fulfil his promise.

> In sport I told him
> That I had learn'd to wing my flight in air;
> And he, admiring much, as he was void
> Of wisdom, will'd me to declare to him
> The secret of mine art: and only hence,
> Because I made him not a Daedalus,
> Prevailed on one, supposed his sire, to burn me.
>
> *Inferno*, XXIX. 107—113.

There is a cutting satire in the last line of the quotation, referring to the domestic relationships of the papal priesthood.

SIENA. 39

las II. was elected pope. When the contest afterwards arose between Gregory VII. and Henry IV. of Germany, the Sienese declared for the emperor; and the refusal of the Florentines to receive him, was the commencement of a hatred between the two republics which led to frequent wars.

The plebeian orders in Siena devoted themselves assiduously and successfully to manufactures and commerce, and for a time the executive government was left in the hands of the nobles; but these last becoming intolerant, the people demanded a share in the legislature, when the *grandi* retired in dignified disgust to their castles in the country. Flushed with success, the democracy attempted to intermeddle in the affairs of the empire, and through motives of vanity left the Ghibelline interest, to support their townsman, Alexander III., on the papal throne. Their presumptuous interference was punished by the emperor Frederic Barbarossa, who divested them of all their franchises, which they afterwards, on their abject submission, obtained again by purchase. In 1258, we find the Sienese giving shelter to the proscribed Ghibellines of Florence, and subsequently acting in concert with them against the Florentines at Montaperto, where the Guelphic party were utterly routed.* The nobility of Siena, returning from their estates, came humbly back to the city, where most of them renounced the insignia of rank, and entering into mercantile speculations, rose to the distinction of rich merchants. Soon, however, a mushroom nobility sprang up in their place, from the ranks of the democracy; and the disorders which arose, in consequence, in the government, led to internal discords which rendered the city an arena of perpetual contest, till at length it fell into the hands of the Medici. From that time Siena dates her decay. This city which, in the days of her prosperity, could send forth one hundred thousand armed men from her thirty-nine gates, is now reduced in population to little more than eighteen thousand; and her present aspect offers nothing to indicate her former importance,—her inhabitants are lost in torpor, and the grass is growing on the very pavement of her streets.

> —Empty lodgings and unfurnished walls,
> Unpeopled offices, untrodden stones,†—

are now the characteristic features of Siena.

The city stands on the summit of a bleak hill, and is celebrated for the purity of its air, and the absence of mosquitoes. English visitants who pass the summer in Italy, usually fix their residence at Siena. Of its thirty-nine gates, eight only remain open. Entering by the Florentine gate, into a long irregular street, "you see men," says Forsyth, "you see groupes proportioned to the extent of Siena. Leave this line, and you pass into a desert." The principal objects of interest to the traveller, are the Lizza, the Citadel, the Cathedral, and the Piazza del Campo; all of which are to be found in the less frequented avenues of the city. As for the palazzi, they are, for the most part, palaces only in name, possessing few works of art, and exhibiting nothing particularly striking in their architecture.

---

* When destruction caught
The maddening rage of Florence, in that day
Proud—
Purgatorio, XI. 112—114.

† Shakspeare.

The Lizza, which occupies the site of a fortress erected by Charles V. in 1551, is decorated with statues, and is the favourite walk of the Sienese. The Citadel, built by Cosmo I., at the northwest extremity of the town, is in the form of a pentagon, with five bastions. The Piazza del Campo is sloped like an amphitheatre for public games; like that, it forms the segment of a circle, in the chord of which stands the Palazzo Pubblico, a building of different dates and designs, parcelled out to different and incongruous uses. One portion is assigned to the theatre, another to the courts of law, and a third to a prison.

The Cathedral exhibits the piebald architecture so common to the ecclesiastical structures of Italy: "we find marble walls polished on both sides, and built in alternate courses of black and white; a front overcharged on the outside, and plain within; a belfry annexed, but not incorporated with the pile; a cupola bearing plumb on its four supports; circular arches resting on round pillars; doors in double architraves; and columns based upon lions tearing lambs." The edifice groans beneath the load of its ornaments, which, however meretricious, strike the eye forcibly, and extort admiration in defiance of the judgment. The pavement is a kind of engraved inlay, called *pietra commessa*, wrought by a succession of artists from Duccio down to Mecherino. Scriptural subjects, and emblematic devices referring to the cities once in alliance with Siena, together with no fewer than ten different sibyls, are displayed on this pavement, which is now, after a century of exposure to the general tread, protected by a covering of boards. The vault of the nave is of a deep azure colour, and is studded with stars, to represent the firmament. The cornice is surmounted with busts of the Popes, down to Alexander III.; amongst these, the bust of Pope Joan is said to have formerly held place, with the inscription, "*Johannes VIII., Femina de Anglia*." The catholics repel with indignation the assertion that the papal seat was once held by a female; and they prove by historical evidence that such could not have been the case. It must be admitted that the zealous opponents of the papacy have, on some occasions, by departure from truth, unwittingly adopted the papal dogma, that the end justifies the means.

The Baptistery under the choir of the cathedral is worthy of observation, both for its architecture and for the works of art which adorn it. The Chigi Chapel "glares with rich marble, silver, gold, bronze, and lapis lazuli," and contains a statue of St. Jerome, and another of a Magdalen by Bernini, the latter said to be merely a statue of Andromeda transformed. The Sacristy, or Library, may now be called a library without books, for it contains only a few illuminated volumes of church music. The walls are decorated with frescos, said to be from the designs of Raphael when very young; they have little to recommend them beyond this traditional association. The roof is covered with mythological pictures. In the centre of the library stands a mutilated group, representing the Graces, and considered by some authorities to be one of the finest examples of Grecian sculpture. Amongst the other ecclesiastical structures of Siena, the church of Fonte Giusta claims distinction, chiefly as the depository of Peruzzi's celebrated sibyl, in the act of foretelling the birth of Christ to Augustus. "This figure," observes Lanzi, "Peruzzi has contrived to invest with such an air of inspiration, that even Raphael himself, when treating similar subjects, can, perhaps, hardly be said to have surpassed him; and yet less can Guido or Guercino."

The School of Siena, which the Sienese assert was the earliest in modern art, has gone to decay. Of its greatest masters, few are known or held in esteem at the present day. The most eminent was Beccafumi, by whom the pavement of the cathedral was partly wrought.

The citizens of Siena are annually awakened from their torpor, on the festival of Santa Caterina, the tutelary saint of the city. "On this occasion, the senators, who, though divested of all their ancient privileges, still retain their red mantles and the title of Eccelsi, aid in the solemn procession, which exhibits the waggon that was conquered from Florence, and a votive wax-work which is conveyed with solemn pomp to the cathedral. At this festival, the horse-races of the piazza revive, among the different wards of the city, the same rivalry that prevailed in the four factions of ancient Rome; and scores of new sonnets are recited, in solemn academy, on the same holy theme that has employed the Sienese rhymesters for three hundred years."* Boxing, which ranks amongst the holiday pleasures of Siena, is said to have been introduced, in the year 1200, by St. Bernardine, as a comparatively innocent vent to the hot blood that prevailed in his day. The pugilistic encounters of the Sienese frequently assume a ludicrous character. If a man finds himself overmatched, he usually shouts "*in soccorso!*" (help!) and by the aid of the first comer, turns the tables upon his antagonist. The latter also finds his abettors, and the combat thickens, till in the end, the street wears the appearance of the stage at the conclusion of Tom Thumb.

To the south and south-west of Siena is the Maremma, which, in its largest extent, stretches along the shore of the Mediterranean from Leghorn to Terracina, and reaches inland as far as the first chain of the Apennines. This insalubrious tract of country, which takes its name from its contiguity to the sea, includes the Campagna of Rome, and is terminated by the Pontine Marshes. Whether the whole plain of the Maremma was anciently as unwholesome as it now is, cannot be ascertained: the probability is that it was formerly more healthy, for we have evidence of its having been both fertile and well-peopled in earlier ages. It is a plausible conjecture, that when Italy fell under the power of the barbarians, the drains, no less than other works of the empire, were either destroyed, or suffered to go to ruin; and that the natural moisture of the soil, added to the deposits of a tideless sea, acted upon by the summer heats, have ever since impregnated the atmosphere of this district with mephitic and deleterious qualities. Some of the modern towns of the Maremma are at all times thinly peopled, whilst others are much frequented during the winter months, but nearly deserted in the summer: it is however in the country parts, that the depopulation is most observable. As family after family became extinct, their possessions devolved upon the community, until at length an entire district was left *owner-less*, when it was annexed, under the name of a *bandita* (or privileged place), to the nearest villages. There are villages possessing seven or eight of these *bandite*, which have not inhabitants enough to cultivate a fourth part of their domains. Hence, the people of the higher and more healthy tracts, migrate to the Maremma to feed their cattle, to sow corn, make charcoal, saw wood, cut hoops, and peel cork. "The most usual season of descent is the winter; but a portion of the mountain peasantry also assist in getting in the harvest. Most of the summer workmen imbibe the diseases of the place, and some even of those who are employed in winter operations, decamp too late, and leave their corpses on the road, or crawl away 'like poisoned rats to die at home.'"

---

* Forsyth witnessed, at this festival, the beatification of Piero Pettinagno, a Sienese comb-maker, whose piety had been celebrated five hundred years before, by Dante.

The hermit Piero, touched with charity,
In his devout orations thought on me.
Purgatorio, XIII. 119, 120.

AREZZO.

HISTORY refers to Arezzo, under its classical name of Arretium, as one of the twelve principal cities of Etruria. It is celebrated for its resistance of the Roman power; and for a middle-age history of turbulent vicissitude. It claims to be the birth-place of Porsenna, Mecenas, Petrarch, Vasari, and of a lengthened host of *dii minores*;—the latter indeed are so numerous as to have originated the taunt, that the Arretini reckon their *illustrissimi* by quantity rather than quality. If we may credit Dante, the Arretini were, in his day, a quarrelsome race. The poet anathematizes all the cities of the Val d'Arno; and whilst tracing the course of the Arno, he says with reference to Arezzo, that the river

> sloping onward, finds
> Curs, snarlers more in spite than power, from whom
> He turns with scorn aside.*
>
> *Purgatorio*, XIV. 48—50.

Prior to its subjugation by the Romans, Arezzo was governed, like Rome itself, by a senata. About three hundred years before Christ, it had so far fallen under the power of the empire, as to be compelled to sue for peace; and though a nominal truce was granted, and afterwards renewed, the city was thenceforward virtually in subjection to the Romans. In the second Punic war, Arretium furnished Scipio with arms and money, and it continued for a long time faithful in its relations to Rome; but in the Social war it took part with the enemies of the empire, and drew upon itself the exterminating vengeance of Sylla.

Arretium suffered severely from the Goths under Totila. It afterwards passed from the Longobards to Charlemagne; and subsequently, when a hundred petty princes and powers sprung up in Italy, it was governed by its bishops, who, having become feudal counts, held the city and territory in the name of the emperor. In the eleventh century, the Arretini erected themselves into an independent republic; but they unavoidably fell into the Guelph and Ghibelline factions, and became divided amongst themselves, until at length the Ghibelline party ejected their opponents from the city. The Ghibellines then made war against Florence, but were defeated with great loss at the battle of Campaldino, in 1289.† A century later, we find the Arretini achieving conquests, under the guidance of their general, Tarlati. On the

---

* The Arno, in its passage, leaves Arezzo about four miles to the south.

† Dante was present in this engagement; where he served in the foremost troop of cavalry, and was exposed to imminent danger. Leonardo Aretino refers to a letter of Dante, in which he described the order of the battle, and mentioned his having been engaged in it. The poet was then in his twenty-fourth year.

death of the latter, Arezzo renewed the contest with Florence; till, in 1384, it was taken by a famous Condottière, Ingelram de Couci, who sold the city to the Florentines for 40,000 gold florins. In 1531 it became part of the territory of the Medici, and it has ever since formed part of Tuscany.

Arezzo is pleasantly situated on the declivity of a mountain range, and is in general a well built city, retaining the honours of an episcopal see, and still exhibiting some remains of its Etrurian origin, and fine examples of the ecclesiastical architecture of the middle ages. The Cathedral, built in the Italian gothic style, was begun in 1250, and completed by Marchione, at the end of the same century. The interior of this structure is characterized by a gloomy magnificence. The painted windows executed by Guillaume de Marseilles, early in the sixteenth century, are greatly admired, especially those of the tribune, one of which represents the Calling of Matthew. In 1286, Giovanni di Pisa erected the marble screen at the high altar. It is covered with bas-reliefs referring to the history of San Donato, the tutelary saint of the city, and is said to have cost 30,000 gold florins. The tomb of the Aretine bishop and general, Guido Tarlati, is one of the grand ornaments of the cathedral. It was executed by Agostino and Angelo da Siena, in the early part of the fourteenth century. In sixteen compartments of beautiful sculptures, are pourtrayed all the important events in the life of Tarlati. Amongst other objects of interest, the tomb of pope Gregory X., by Margaritone, is worthy of observation. A large chapel, the most recent addition to the Cathedral, is consecrated to the Madonna of Arezzo, "a little ugly figure of chalk found in the rubbish of a cellar," yet deemed, nevertheless, more potent than the palladium of old which fell down from Jupiter.

The church of Santa Maria della Pieve is supposed to occupy the site of a temple of Bacchus. It underwent extensive repairs, indeed was nearly reconstructed, by Marchione in the beginning of the thirteenth century. The front has four stories of ornaments, and the tower, which rises from it at one angle, has five stories more, full of little columns with fancy capitals, and exhibiting the wildest irregularity in all the details. Behind the high altar is Vasari's picture of St. George.

Amongst other public buildings of interest, may be enumerated the Loggie of the Piazza Maggiore, constructed by Vasari; the church of Santa Flora, remarkable for the painting on its cupola by Padre Pozzi; that of San Francesco, containing the frescoes of Pietro della Francesca; the church of Sant'Angelo, in which is the celebrated fresco of the Fall of the Angels, by Spinello Aretino; and the Fraternità, a superb gothic structure, originally founded for the relief of the poor, and as an asylum for widows and orphans, and now including an extensive library and museum. We must not, however, omit adding to these, the house in which Petrarch was born, and that wherein Vasari resided. The first is close to the cathedral; it has been repaired in late years, and bears an inscription testifying that here Petrarch first drew breath, on Monday, July 20, 1304.* The latter is in the Strada San Vito, and remains nearly in the same state as when occupied by Vasari.

---

* A well, still existing in the immediate neighbourhood of this house, is the scene of Boccaccio's comic tale of Tofano and Ghita. See the Decameron, Day 7, Novel 4.

CORTONA.

FEW cities present such incontestible evidence of remote antiquity as Cortona. Carrying back its mythological origin beyond the foundation of Troy, and taking undoubted place, by consent of authentic history, as the most ancient city of Etruria, it remains to this day a remarkable example of unchanged locality, presenting within the same area, and circumscribed by the same walls, a town whose existence can be traced back with certainty for nearly three thousand years.*

Cortona stands amidst its vineyards, on the acclivity of a steep hill, and appears to hang like a panoramic picture upon a back-ground of dark mountains. From the church and convent of Santa Margherita, occupying the summit of the eminence on which the city is placed, a magnificent prospect is obtained of the Thrasimene and Clusian lakes, the mountains of Radicofani and Santa Fiora, and of the wide variegated Val di Chiana, skirted with vine-covered hills, and beautifully strewed with white cottages, *fattorie*, and villas, and with convents of sober gray. The original walls of Cortona form the foundations of the modern walls built in the thirteenth century. Two thirds of the former are still existing; and for a quarter of a mile the magnificent Etruscan masonry is uninterrupted; then comes a portion which is Roman, then a modern repair, then Etruscan again. From her walls, and other coeval remains, Cortona takes all her celebrity; and as these are objects of interest to none but the classical scholar, the historian, and the antiquarian, this city is rarely visited by the butterfly swarms of tourists who yearly throng into Italy. By them, however, who can summon up the associations which give value and interest to the remains of elder time,

---

* Hetruria, or Etruria, the country of the Tusci, (whence the modern name, Tuscany) was anciently divided into two parts,—Etruria beyond the Arno, and Etruria on this side the Arno, which distinction has reference to the situation of Rome. The first division included the country about Genoa, the Val di Magra, the Duchy of Carrara, the State of Lucca, and part of the Pisan territory. The second division was much more extensive, and comprised the whole of modern Tuscany; and it was this portion that was divided into the twelve cities or communities of Etruria, of which mention is so frequently made. Cortona was the seat of the Cortonensis, one of those twelve Etrurian tribes. Poetical tradition attempts to identify Cortona with an ancient town named Corytus, after its founder, the then king of the country. This Corytus had two sons, Jasius and Dardanus, the latter of whom slew Jasius in order to obtain undivided sovereignty, after his father's decease. To this Dardanus the foundation of Troy is attributed; and hence the assumption that Cortona is of more remote origin than the Trojan city. Passing by these unworthy fables, we have the testimony of Dionysius of Halicarnassus, that several centuries prior to the ordinarily assigned era of the Trojan war, tribes of the Pelasgi came over into Etruria, and founded Cortona and other colonies. And in connection with this testimony, we have existing remains to fix beyond question the high antiquity of this Etruscan city. The classical reader will be aware, that although Dionysius flourished in the Augustine age, his geographical writings are founded upon those of Eratosthenes, who lived two centuries and a half before Christ. We have therefore clear evidence that Cortona was esteemed an ancient city upwards of two thousand years ago.

Cortona will not be reckoned the least remarkable amongst the cities of Italy. Troy itself, though shrined in ancient song, is little more than "the unsubstantial pageant of a dream;" but here is the palpable reality of a city, at least cotemporary with the towers of Ilium, and, if poetic tradition may be trusted, of a date and origin even more remote.

Little is known of the history of Cortona under the Romans. That it must have been in alliance with that people at an early period, is evident from the record of its fidelity to Rome throughout the second Punic war. History is silent during the empire. About the twelfth century it assumed an independent government; and it ultimately became involved in the quarrel between the temporal and spiritual powers. After several centuries of distraction and disorder, Cortona was, in 1409, sold to the Florentines, for 60,000 gold florins, by the Neapolitan mercenaries which she had summoned to her aid for the expulsion of the Casalli family. From that period the city remained subject to Florence.

Amongst the public buildings of Cortona, the most remarkable are the church and convent of Santa Margherita, containing the tomb of the patron saint, and several paintings of considerable merit; and the cathedral, said to be as old as the tenth century, in which are paintings by Pietro da Cortona and Luca Signorelli, both native artists, and a magnificent sarcophagus, named the tomb of Flaminius, adorned with a bas-relief representation of the combat between the Centaurs and Lapithæ. The Museum of the Academy, the Museo Corazzi, and the Museo Venuti, present interesting collections of Etruscan antiquities.

PERUGIA.

> Between Topino, and the wave that falls
> From blest Ubaldo's chosen hill, there hangs
> Rich slope of mountain high, whence heat and cold
> Are wafted through Perugia's eastern gate.
>
> *Paradiso*, X. 40—43.

PERUGIA claims historical celebrity as one of the most ancient and distinguished cities of Etruria. Its foundation long preceded that of Rome, and like the origin of Cortona is almost lost in the distance of time. As a seat of antiquity, Perugia must, however, yield in point of interest to Cortona, which exhibits more palpable and extensive evidence of Etruscan origin.

Perugia, or Perusia, in conjunction with the other Etrurian states, obstinately resisted the power of Rome; but when, at length, it became subject to the Romans, it remained in faithful alliance with them. In the war between Antony and Octavius, this city unfortunately took part with the former, and shut its gates against the master of the world. Compelled by famine to surrender, it experienced all the calamities attendant upon the seizure of a hostile city. On this occasion more than three hundred distinguished citizens were sacrificed to the vengeance of Octavius. One of the principal inhabitants devoted his own house as a funeral pyre for himself and family, and thus kindled a conflagration which spread throughout the city and reduced it to ashes. Perugia rose, however, immediately from its ruins, and under the name of Perusia Augusta, became once more a place of importance. It afterwards, in the reign of Justinian, sustained a seven years' siege by the Goths; but it was ultimately reduced by Totila. The subsequent history of Perugia differs little from that of other Italian cities. Possessing for a time a political independence and a free municipality, it next became subject to tyrants who rose above its laws and controlled its privileges. It endured the horrors of the Guelphic and Ghibelline factions; opposed the efforts of the popes to unite it to the Papal States; and at length came under the government of Braccio Fortebraccio da Montone, one of those remarkable persons which extraordinary times produce, and who, happily for Perugia, was one of the wisest and best men that rose to power in the middle ages. The valour and wisdom of this eminent warrior at once overthrew the enemies of his country and effected reconciliation between the factions which disturbed its peace. After his death, his family retained the sovereignty, under a nominal obedience to the church. At length the government passed into the hands of the Baglioni family, whose ambition aroused the anger both of the Pope and the people; and ultimately, after several struggles for supremacy, Perugia was reduced to subjection by Paul III., who annexed it to the Papal territories.* During the French Empire this district formed part of the Tiberine republic; but in 1814 it returned to the government of the church. In 1859 Perugia took part with the revolted Italian states in asserting their right to freedom. In consequence of this the town was attacked in June of that year by the Papal troops, who, after all resistance had ceased, inflicted an atrocious and indiscriminating massacre on the hapless inhabitants. In 1860 it was conquered, along with the legation of Umbria, by the army of Victor Emmanuel.†

---

* This imperious prelate built the citadel, between the years 1540 and 1544. Having excited the people to revolt by his obnoxious salt-tax, he raised this formidable structure to overawe them. The court of the citadel bore exhibited this haughty inscription:—Ad coercendam Perusinorum audaciam, Paulus III. edificavit. *Built by Paul III. to restrain the audacity of the Perusians.*

† The Lake of Perugia, the celebrated Thrasymenus of the ancients, is a noble expanse of water, about ten miles in length, by seven in breadth. It has three islands, the Polvese near the southern extremity, and the Minore and Maggiore about a mile from the northern shore. The banks ascend gradually, and in some places rapidly, from its margin; and as they are clad with wood, and speckled with villages, they form an outline of singular beauty. Such also was the ancient appearance, according to the testimony of Silius Italicus, through whose muse the spirit of the lake makes utterance:

Lo! I am Thrasymene, the wonted lake
Upon whose banks, to lofty hills that swell,
Still dwell the tribes that erst from Tmolus came.

A plain in the immediate neighbourhood of the Thrasymenus is celebrated for a great battle fought there between the Carthaginians under Hannibal, and the Romans under C. Flaminius, B. C. 217. The result of the engagement was most disastrous; the consul in command, and no fewer than 15,000 Roman soldiers, were left dead upon the field.

—such the storm of battle on this day,
And such the frenzy, whose convulsion blinds
To all save carnage, that, beneath the fray,
An earthquake reel'd unheededly away!

Childe Harold.

PERUGIA.

Perugia is an episcopal see, said to have been founded A. D. 57, and to have had for its first bishop, Ercolano di Siria, one of the followers of St. Peter. Seated on the summit of a mountain, this city commands from its ramparts, and particularly from its citadel, an extensive view over a vast range of fertile country, varied with hill and dale, and enlivened with villages and towns. It contains many churches, convents, and palaces, which do not, however, require particular description, since they differ little or nothing from other Italian edifices of the same character, except in their pictorial decorations.* Perugia is the centre of the Umbrian school of painting, and the works of her most distinguished master, Pietro Perugino the instructor of Raphael, are to be found in the churches, palazzi, and public institutions of the city. The Sala del Cambio (the Exchange) is enriched with the frescoes of Perugino, representing the prophets and sibyls, the philosophers and warriors of antiquity. The paintings of this master are scattered over Italy, but his merits can be most justly estimated in Perugia, his adopted city and the chief treasure-house of his genius.†

Livy relates, that "such was the mutual animosity of the combatants, so intent were they upon the battle, that the earthquake which overthrew in great part many of the cities of Italy, which turned the course of rapid streams, poured back the sea upon the rivers and tore down the very mountains, was not felt by one of the combatants!"

> Far other scene is Thrasimene now;
> Her lake a sheet of silver, and her plain
> Rent by no ravage save the gentle plough;
> Her aged trees rise thick as once the slain
> Lay where their roots are; but a brook hath ta'en—
> A little rill of scanty stream and bed—
> A name of blood from that day's sanguine rain;
> And Sanguinetto tells ye where the dead
> Made the earth wet, and turn'd the unwilling waters red.
>   *Childe Harold.*

* The Cathedral, or Duomo, is a fine gothic edifice of the fifteenth century, containing, amongst other works of art, the Deposition from the Cross, by Baroccio. The church of the convent of San Francesco, is the depository of the bones of Braccio Fortebraccio, which are here kept in a side chapel, enclosed in a miserable box; they are subjected to the indignity of being handed to visitors for inspection, on payment of a small gratuity. The church of Santa Maria Nuova contains the Adoration of the Magi, by Perugino; and the St. Sebastian and St. Roch, by Sebastiano del Piombo. The Benedictine monastery of San Pietro de' Casinensi is rich in paintings, including the Infant Saviour embracing St. John, the earliest known work of Raphael,—an Ecce Homo, said to be by Titian, and the two fine pictures of Christ Bound and the Flagellation, by Guercino. There are, in all, upwards of one hundred churches, and about fifty monasteries in Perugia; some of these structures possess few works of art, whilst others contain many fine examples of the best masters of the Perugian school.

† Perugia has, on several occasions, been nearly depopulated by the plague. In the visitation of 1348, 100,000 persons are said to have perished; and in that of 1524, Pietro Perugino was among its victims.

CHIUSI.

JANUS-LIKE in its aspect, the city of Chiusi looks back upon remote times which veritable history cannot reach, and forward through a succession of ages embracing the origin, progress, triumphs, decline, ruin, and ultimate dismemberment of the Roman empire. Of all the cities of Etruria, this one is the most remarkable and the most interesting for its classical associations. Anciently known as Clusium, the seat of Etrurian royalty, it is identified with a people whose history is a mystery; whose advanced civilization and extensive acquaintance with the elegant arts are attested by existing remains; and whose distant original reduces the foundation of Rome to a thing of yesterday. Romulus, partly by conquest, but more, perhaps, by courteous treatment, united to his interest several of the Etrurian towns, and thus consolidated the power of his infant kingdom. At a later period, an Etruscan exile, named Lucomo Damaratus, established himself as king of Rome, under the title of Lucius Tarquinius. Every reader is acquainted with the circumstances which led to the expulsion of the Tarquins; the pathetic history of Lucretia, the assumed idiotcy of Junius Brutus, and the united voice of a people impatient of tyranny and wrong. At this juncture, the assistance of the Etrurian league was sought for the re-establishment of the Tarquins; and Porsenna, king of Clusium, despatched an embassy to Rome, demanding the recall of the exiled family, or the restoration of their estates. Neither demand was complied with; Porsenna therefore led a numerous army against Rome, and invested the city. The incidents of this siege are familiar to us; they exhibit a degree of bravery, magnanimity, and generosity to which history presents few parallels. When the city had well nigh been reduced to extremity, Mutius Scævola, "to his own hand remorseless," daringly attempted the life of Porsenna, and having failed in his purpose, he held his hand over a pan of burning coals until it was consumed, to intimate to Porsenna his contempt for any tortures that awaited him. The king struck with admiration of his bravery, concluded a truce with the Romans on honourable terms; and subsequently perceiving the baseness of the Tarquins, he drew his army from the city, and thus by an act of lofty generosity spared Rome to fulfil her proud destinies. The name of Porsenna was thenceforward hallowed amongst the Romans; and in their after wars with the Etrurians, the city of Clusium was regarded with veneration, as a locality too sacred to be wasted with fire and sword.

The city of Clusium itself had afterwards to sustain a siege by the Gauls, on which occasion Rome came forward in its defence, but only succeeded in turning hostilities against herself. Brennus, the general of the Gauls, raised the siege of Clusium, and sat down with his army before Rome. The Romans were compelled to seek a truce; when, amongst other things, it was stipulated that the Gauls should receive a thousand pounds' weight of gold, the payment of which, however, was suspended, on the arrival of Camillus from exile, at the very moment

that the gold had been brought forth, and Brennus had insultingly cast his sword into the scale to increase the weight, alleging that it was the part of the vanquished to suffer. When the whole of Etruria fell under the power of Rome, and became part of her territories, Clusium was regarded as an ally rather than as a subjected city. It shared the fortunes of Rome, and fell with the empire. From being the metropolis of Etruria, it sunk into a petty principality of Italy, and ultimately became the seat of a bishopric.

Chiusi has suffered many vicissitudes, and offers in the present day little evidence of its former greatness, beyond a few remains interesting to the scholar and the antiquary. In picturesque beauty, however, it claims general regard. Seated on an eminence, in the midst of a fertile neighbourhood, it overlooks the lake to which it gives name, and commands extensive and varied prospects of singular beauty. The cathedral has evidently been constructed from the remains of more ancient structures; a fact which accounts for the disappearance of the monuments of Clusium. This building presents, in other points of view, nothing that claims extended notice. Chiusi is principally interesting in our day, for its museums of Etruscan antiquities, and, more especially, as being the *City of Sepulchres*. The museum of Signor Casuccini is esteemed one of the finest collections of Etruscan remains now existing. It includes every known variety of vase, with a large assemblage of sarcophagi and sepulchral monuments; and it is receiving daily accessions. The tombs in the ancient necropolis of the city are numerous, and have "an awe about them placed," created by historical associations. The tomb of Porsenna cannot be determined with precision; of four large tumuli which yet remain, each claims to be the mausoleum of the great Etrurian king.

RADICOFANI.

FOLLOWING the direct route from Siena to Rome, the traveller crosses the volcanic mountain of Radicofani, where all is utter sterility and nakedness. The road does not ascend so high as the village of Radicofani, which is situated at the base of the cone, whereon are still seen the extensive ruins of a fortress, once a place of strength and importance. The village itself contains nothing to attract attention, except the wild dress and appearance of its inhabitants. The shepherds are clad in goat-skins to protect them from the inclemency of the atmosphere, which has, in this district, little in common with the general climate of Italy. This rude costume may plead classic antiquity in its defence; for we learn from Juvenal that such was the dress of the shepherds in his day:—

> The poor, who with inverted skins defy
> The lowering tempest, and the freezing sky.

RADICOFANI.

The fortress, erected by Desiderius, king of the Lombards, was often conspicuous in the history of Italy. In the course of events, however, it lost its importance; and the Tuscan government hesitated whether to maintain or dismantle it, until, at length, the powder magazine exploded, and so consigned it to ruin. This castle was once held by Ghino di Tacco, a daring leader of banditti, whose seizure and treatment of the abbot of Cligni, are related with great humour by Boccaccio.* The abbot, it appears by the story, had deranged his digestive organs by high living, and was, at the time of the rencontre, on his way to the baths of Siena, to regain his health. Ghino, shrewdly judging that a low diet would be as efficacious as the bath, placed the abbot, for some days, on a very restricted regimen. The result proved the sagacity of Ghino: the abbot quickly recovered his appetite, and "desired nothing so much as to eat." Having succeeded so happily, the bandit changed his treatment, and extended all courtesy to the patient, offering at the same time to restore the whole or any portion of his booty. The abbot, impressed with a truly aldermanic gratitude for the restoration of his appetite, took back only a small part of the spoil, and departed from the castle with a very high opinion of Ghino's honour, if not of his honesty. On his return to Rome, the abbot mediated between the Pope and his mountain physician, and prevailed upon his Holiness to pardon Ghino, and receive him into favour at the papal court. The Pope was soon convinced of Ghino's worth, (probably, as a renovator of decayed appetites), and in token of reconciliation, created him a knight, and made him prior of an hospital. Dante makes allusion to this knightly robber:—

> Here of Arezzo him I saw, who fell
> By Ghino's cruel arm.
> *Purgatorio, VI. 14, 15.*

The victim referred to by the poet, was Benincasa of Arezzo, eminent for his skill in jurisprudence, who having condemned to death Turrino da Turrita, brother of Ghino di Tacco, for his robberies in Maremma, was murdered by Ghino, in an apartment of his own house, in the presence of many witnesses. Ghino was not only suffered to depart in safety, after the commission of this fearful deed, but was ultimately, on account of his general liberality and courtesy to those whom he plundered, invited to Rome, and knighted by Boniface VIII.!

In the earlier periods of Italian history, when disorder and lawless outrage prevailed generally, the first bandits were probably men of noble nature, who assumed the mountain-robber's wild and fearful life, to avenge or to redress their real or imaginary wrongs. When pronouncing judgment upon them, we must keep constantly in view the condition of society and the popular sympathies linked with it. The emperors, the popes, and the factious nobles, were engaged in continual contest for supremacy; and in this contest, ferocious valour and skilful intrigue obtained the victory, whilst the timorous and undesigning were compelled to yield in the protracted struggle between might and right. Men soon begin to admire whatever extorts their fears; and hence the popular sympathies of Italy came to regard ferocity and cunning as the attributes of greatness. And these sympathies were legitimately exercised when they were extended to the first bandits of Italy,—men who having suffered wrong, went forth to their wild warfare to work retaliation upon the authors of their injuries, and to throw defiance in the teeth of tyrants before whom society bowed with trembling. That a

* Decameron, Day X., Novel 2.

romantic generosity mingled, in no small degree, with their deeds of violence and blood, is attested in several instances. It is related in the life of Tasso, that the poet, on one occasion, wandered into the very meshes of the brigands' snare; but no sooner had he made himself known to the outlaws, than their rude voices and threatening gestures were exchanged for expressions of reverence and respect, and he was suffered to pursue his way unmolested.* This little incident is beautifully imbodied in poetic language by Rogers:—

> Time was, the trade was nobler, if not honest;
> When they that robb'd, were men of better faith
> Than kings or pontiffs; when, such reverence
> The poet drew among the woods and wilds,
> A voice was heard, that never bade to spare,
> Crying aloud, "Hence to the distant hills!
> Tasso approaches; he, whose song beguiles
> The day of half its hours; whose sorcery
> Dazzles the sense, turning our forest-glades
> To lists that blaze with gorgeous armoury,
> Our mountain-caves to regal palaces.
> Hence, nor descend till he and his are gone.
> Let him fear nothing."

It must not, however, be denied, that the chivalry, so to speak, of bandit life has long ago departed. Unredeemed cruelty and villainy are the characteristic attributes of the banditti of recent times. Some of these outlaws are men whose atrocities have driven them forth to the mountains as their sole refuge against an outraged community; yet these are the least dangerous, for "the plague-spot visible" is impressed upon them, "the guilt that says, Beware:"—the traveller has more to dread from them who unite with the robber's deadly ferocity, the peaceful occupations of rural life:—

> "Such
> As sow and reap, and at the cottage door
> Sit to receive, return the traveller's greeting;
> Now in the garb of peace, now silently
> Arming and issuing forth, led on by men
> Whose names on innocent lips are words of fear,
> Whose lives have long been forfeit."

It is only within a comparatively few years that the road between Siena and Radicofani, and more especially across the frontier district of the latter place, could be traversed with any degree of safety. The unfortunate traveller was formerly betrayed in his inn, all requisite information concerning him was thence conveyed by spies to the mountains, and even the postillions who conducted him along the road, gave signal of his approach to the bandits with whom they were in league.

About four miles from Radicofani, is a hot transparent spring, which issues from the Monte Amiata. This water holds in solution a considerable portion of sulphur and carbonate of lime, of which advantage has been taken to form casts. The water is suffered to fall in a broken shower upon moulds, and the calcareous deposition hardens into cameos and intaglios of exquisite beauty.

---

* Ariosto, likewise, was once surprised by banditti, who treated him with similar respect.

BOLSENA.

Bolsena's eels and cups of muscadel.
Purgatorio, XXIV. 25.

BOLSENA is identified with Volsinium, or Vulsinium, one of the twelve chief cities of Etruria. The Volsinii so far maintained their independence, after the conquest of the rest of Etruria by the Romans, as to retain their own laws and form of government. They afterwards became an opulent and flourishing people. At length, enervated by dissipation and luxury, they confided the defence of their city, and all the active duties of citizens, to their manumitted slaves, who ultimately became tyrants over their former masters, and committed the most atrocious outrages against persons and property. In this extremity, the Volsinii besought the assistance of Rome; when the Consul, Q. Fabius Gurges, gave battle to the freedmen and routed them, but lost his life whilst pursuing them into the town. Decius Mus, the lieutenant of Fabius, then laid siege to Volsinium, which held out for twelve months, but, at length, surrendered (206 B. C.) to the Consul, Fulvius Flaccus, who caused all the freedmen to be put to death. This city, which had so long preserved its independence, was then razed to the ground; and so great were the spoils, that Pliny, upon the authority of Metrodorus Scepsius, states that two thousand bronze statues were removed thence to Rome. The inhabitants erected another city in the immediate neighbourhood, but it rose to no importance, and history mentions little more concerning it, than its having been the birth-place of Sejanus, the favourite of Tiberius.

The modern town of Bolsena does not occupy the exact site of the ancient city, but is situated farther down the hill, and nearer to the neighbouring lake. It contains few objects of interest, except a mass of ruins, part of which are the supposed remains of a temple in honour of the goddess Nortia;* and the church of Santa Christina, famous for the miracle of the *Bleeding Host*. This miracle, or, to speak more correctly, this juggling trick, is said to have taken place in 1263, when a Bohemian priest, who entertained doubts regarding the doctrine of transubstantiation, had his scepticism removed by the ocular proof of blood flowing from the consecrated wafer, or host, during the sacrifice of the mass. To commemorate this blasphemous mummery, Urban IV. instituted the festival of *Corpus Domini*. A dark and dirty vault is shown as the scene of the miracle; and the precise spot where the blood fell is protected by an iron grating!†

---

* The goddess Fortuna was worshipped by the Etrurians under this name. They marked the years by fixing nails in her temple.

† This fraud had not even originality to recommend it as an ingenious trick; it was the mere repetition of an imposition that had frequently before been practised upon the credulity of an ignorant people. So early as the year

The Lake of Bolsena is a magnificent sheet of water, nearly twenty-seven miles in circumference. It has two small but picturesque islands, named Bisentina and Martana. The latter, which is of less extent than the other, is the scene of the imprisonment and murder of Amalasontha, queen of the Goths, the only daughter of Theodoric, and the niece of Clovis. Distinguished for talents and virtue, this princess secured the friendship of the emperor Justinian, and the cotemporary sovereigns of Europe regarded her with admiration. Deprived of her son, who died from intemperance at the early age of sixteen, she gave to her cousin Theodatus a share in the regal dignity. This treacherous kinsman excited a revolt against her, and after imprisoning her in the island Martana, caused her to be strangled in her bath, A. D. 535. Some ruins are still pointed out as the remains of her prison. On the Bisentina, were villas of the Farnesi, where Leo X., returning from the pleasures of the chase at Viterbo, resided for a short time, to enjoy the amusement of fishing. The fish of the lake, more particularly the eels, are in great request; and Dante irreverently records of Martin IV., that he died by eating of them to excess. His holiness was accustomed to have his eels killed by being put into the wine called *vernaccia*, in order to heighten their flavour.* The church on the Bisentina, built by the Farnesi, and decorated by the Caracci, contains the relics of Santa Cristina, the patron saint of Bolsena.

The lake is bounded by volcanic rocks, and has the form of an extinct crater, but the extent of this sheet of water is opposed to the hypothesis of a volcanic origin. It is surrounded with beautiful scenery, and a luxuriant soil; but the prevalence of malaria on the lake, and along its borders, interrupts the labours of the husbandman, who dares not sleep in the vicinity of the land he cultivates. Nearly all within sight of Bolsena, is a vast solitude,—its expansive waters without a single sail, and the shores without inhabitants. Nothing can convey to the traveller a more fearful impression of the ravages of malaria in Italy, than the solitude and silence which here claim dominion absolute over a locality, adapted, so far as the eye can judge, to be an earthly paradise.

600, we find pope Gregory using similar means to convince a Roman lady of the actual presence. During the sacrifice of the mass, this lady, it is said, smiled at the idea of calling a morsel of bread the body of the Lord. The pontiff, therefore, prayed for a sensible manifestation of the presence, which done, the sacramental bread, it is added, "was changed into bloody flesh." Paschasius, who lived in the ninth century, and defended the doctrine of transubstantiation most strenuously, declares that the Lord's body and blood have often appeared visible on the altar. And Odo, in 960, performed a miracle, the very prototype of the one which gives celebrity to Bolsena. Some of the clergy having denied that the elements of the eucharist were substantially changed by consecration, Odo prayed during the solemnization of mass, and the host in the hands of the priest "began to drop blood."

* Dante, in fixing the purgatorial punishment of Martin IV., anticipated the retributive code recommended by Rageau San. His holiness wanders amongst the shadowless ones with all his papal voracity undiminished, but—powers of endurance!—there is nothing to eat, and as little to drink.

He purges by vain abstinence away
Bolsena's eels and cups of muscadel.

Purgatorio, XXIV. 24, 25.

VITERBO.

FOUNTAINS and beautiful women give fame to Viterbo, a city distinguished in ancient history as the Vanum Voltumnæ, where the Etrurian cities held their general assemblies; and in mediæval periods, as the arena of turbulence, outrage, and ecclesiastical insolence. It is now the seat of a bishopric; and the capital of one of the largest delegations of the Papal States, extending over two hundred and five square leagues, and embracing a population of more than one hundred and thirteen thousand souls. In this city numerous conclaves of the papal college were held, at which no fewer than six popes were elected between the years 1261 and 1281.

The cathedral, a gothic edifice dedicated to San Lorenzo, is supposed to occupy the site of a temple of Hercules. Several popes are interred here; and the edifice is adorned with paintings of various degrees of merit, by artists of questionable and unquestionable fame. One incident linked with the history of this church, relieves it from the wearying monotony of statue and picture celebrity. At the high altar of this cathedral, Guy de Montfort, son of the Earl of Leicester, slew prince Henry of England, during the celebration of mass. Simon de Montfort, the father of the assassin, fell at the battle of Evesham in 1265, fighting against Henry III. To retaliate for his death, and yet more to avenge the indignity offered to his body after the battle, his son Guy sought, by "patient search and vigil long," to fulfil his vow of hatred and vengeance against the family of Henry. Prince Henry, the brother of Henry III., was sojourning at Viterbo, on his return from Africa, when Guy de Montfort also arrived in the city. The latter, learning that the prince was attending mass at the cathedral, rushed upon him, and thrust him through with his sword; and afterwards dragged the lifeless body from the church into the public square. For this filial enormity Guy has been damned by Dante, who places him in a river of boiling blood, in the seventh circle of hell, and under the immediate guardianship of the Minotaur and Centaurs.*

The cathedral of Viterbo is rendered interesting to English travellers by another incident. In the piazza of this edifice, Adrian IV., the only Englishman who ever rose to the pontifical

---

* Giovanni Villani relates that "the heart of prince Henry was put into a golden cup, and placed on a pillar of London Bridge, over the river Thames, for a memorial to the English of the cruel outrage." Dante says of Guy de Montfort,—

He in God's bosom smote the heart
Which yet is honoured on the banks of Thames.

Inferno, XII. 119—120.

chair, caused the emperor Frederic Barbarossa to hold his stirrup whilst he dismounted from his mule. The haughty monarch appears to have grimaced on this occasion, but he *did* stoop to the indignity; and having thus acknowledged the supremacy of the church, he received, in payment of his obedience, the kiss of peace. One finds it difficult to reconcile with the lofty valour of chivalrous times, so abject a submission to the hateful tyranny of ecclesiastical despotism.

The episcopal palace, now greatly ruined, is remarkable as the seat of a conclave assembled by the command of Charles of Anjou for the election of a pope; when, after thirty-three months of deliberation, the cardinals elected Tibaldo Visconti to the papacy, under the title of Gregory X. It was here also that the cardinals elected Martin IV. to the pontifical seat, though not until Charles had raised the citizens of Viterbo into insurrection, and had removed the roof of the building, to hasten the decision of the holy fathers. Letters it is said are still preserved in the archives of the city, dated from "the roofless palace." In the church of the convent of Santa Rosa, is preserved the body of the saint to whom the structure is dedicated. This holy maid excited the people against the emperor Frederic II.; but on the triumph of the Ghibellines she retired into exile. On the death of the emperor she returned to Viterbo, and there dying at the age of eighteen, received from the Guelphic party the honours of canonization. Her reputed miracles are many, and the greatest reverence is paid to the gilt tomb which contains her blackened and disfeatured remains.

The gothic church of San Francesco is enriched with the celebrated Deposition from the Cross by Sebastian del Piombo; and in the church of the Osservanti del Paradiso, is the Flagellation, by the same master; and also a Madonna, attributed to Leonardo da Vinci. An Incredulity of St. Thomas, by Salvator Rosa, graces the church named della Morti; and a remarkable fresco by Lorenzo di Giacomo da Viterbo is preserved in the church of Santa Maria della Verità. The tomb of Galiana, the most beautiful woman of Italy, gives celebrity to the church of Sant' Angelo in Spata. The beauty of this lady, who appears to have been another Helen, led to a war between Rome and Viterbo; and when at length the Romans were reduced to capitulate, they stipulated to be allowed a last sight of Galiana, who was accordingly shown to them from a window still existing in the tower of the ancient gate of St. Antony.

The court of the Palazzo Pubblico contains two large Etruscan tombs; and an elegant fountain. In the hall of the Academy are preserved the frescoes of Baldassare Croce, the pupil of Annibale Caracci. And the Museum is richly stored with Etruscan antiquities.

The fame of Viterbo, for fountains and lovely women, has not departed: the first are numerous, and are highly worthy of regard for their antiquity and architectural beauty; the latter also are not few, and we may add that they likewise are deserving of the *tenderest* regard. not, however, on the score of antiquity. One little fact, a scandal to the fair fame of the maids of Viterbo, remains to be noticed. Olimpia, the beautiful and dissolute daughter of Innocent X., is said to have had many lovers. The palazzo San Martino, the scene of her intrigues, still exhibits her portrait; and with this structure are connected dark tales of trap-doors and mysterious disappearances, very intelligible hints, in their way, to those who "love not wisely, but too well."

ORVIETO.

NOTHING is known of the early history of Orvieto, beyond what is gathered from existing evidence of Etruscan origin. The city stands upon a rock of volcanic tufa, at the base of which flows the river Paglia. The position is well adapted for military defence; and the ruins of its walls and fortress are sufficient to attest to its strength and importance in the middle ages. This city was a stronghold of the Guelphic party; and no fewer than thirty-three popes retired hither, at different periods, to find a shelter from the violence to which the rage of contending factions exposed them. It is now the seat of a cardinal bishop, and numbers a population exceeding six thousand persons.

Orvieto is principally remarkable for its Duomo, or cathedral; and this structure itself has a two-fold interest,—first, as deriving its origin from the famous miracle of Bolsena; and, secondly, as being the joint production of a host of the most talented artists and artificers. We have already alluded to the miracle in our description of Bolsena, and if the reader have not in his memory what is there related, he must refer back to connect the story. The priest whose scepticism had been so wonderfully removed, departed from Bolsena with the bloody napkin, and other evidences of the miracle, and presented himself to Urban IV., then resident at Orvieto. The priest, it would appear, had sent an avant-courier to announce his coming, for his holiness, attended by several cardinals, repaired in solemn procession to the bridge of Rio Chiaro, to welcome the relics and their bearer. The successor of St. Peter beheld in the relics the infallible tokens of a miracle, and at once resolved that an edifice should be constructed for their especial reception. The design was furnished by Lorenzo Maltani, of Siena; but the first stone of the edifice was not laid till 1290, and then by Nicholas IV., the ninth pontiff in succession from Urban.* Thenceforward, however, till the end of the sixteenth century, this remarkable and costly structure was in constant progress; and in this long interval almost every artist of eminence in architecture, sculpture, and mosaic, was employed upon the work. History records thirty-three architects, one hundred and fifty-two sculptors, sixty-eight painters, ninety workers in mosaic, twenty-eight workers in *tarsia*,† and fifteen

---

* Urban IV. assumed the pontifical chair in 1261, and Nicholas IV. in 1288; in twenty-seven years, therefore, nine popes had fretted their hour upon the stage. The brief reigns of the popes is a remarkable feature in the annals of the papacy. From St. Linus the first Roman bishop in 66, down to Pius VII. in 1800, the reigns of the popes average little more than five years. Eustace mentions, as the last ceremony at the inauguration of a pontiff, that as the vicar apostolic "advances towards the high altar of St. Peter's, the master of the ceremonies kneeling before him, sets fire to a small quantity of tow placed on the top of a gilt staff, and as it blazes and vanishes in smoke, thus addresses the pope, *Sancte Peter, sic transit gloria mundi.*"—Holy Father, so passes the glory of the world. Truly, the ceremony is very pertinent and significant.

† In-lay work.

ORVIETO.

*capi maestri,** as having contributed to the erection or embellishment of this extraordinary building.

The Duomo is built of black and white marble, and the façade is exuberantly enriched with mosaics and sculptures;—of these alone it has been said, that it is worth a journey to Orvieto to examine and study them. The interior of the church is in the form of a Latin cross. Here the spectator's attention is riveted to the colossal statues of the Apostles, the works of various sculptors. At the high altar are the celebrated figures of the Virgin and the Announcing Angel. These sculptures are not, however, esteemed faultless: the angel is said to betray declining art and corrupt taste; and the attitude and expression of the Virgin are so little in consonance with the evangelical narrative, that the beholder grows irreverent in thought whilst contemplating the figure. There is too much of the tragic muse, and too little of the humble Mary. She starts from her seat at the salutation, grasps the chair with convulsive energy, and looks very unamiable. The chapel of the Santissima Corporale contains the miraculous relics. These are inclosed in a magnificent reliquary, executed in solid silver by Ugolino Veri of Siena. In form it represents the Duomo, and it is embellished with exquisite sculptures and enamels. The chapel of the Madonna di S. Brizio contains a miraculous image of the Virgin; but, to all, save good catholics, it is more remarkable for its frescoes by Signorelli, and the group of the Pietà by Scalza, together with other works of art. The paintings in this chapel exhibit a grotesque medley of sacred and profane subjects, too often observable in the churches of Italy.†

Next in interest to the Duomo, is the Pozzo di San Patrizio, or Well of St. Patrick. It was sunk for the purpose of relieving the garrison of Orvieto, when, after the sack of Rome in 1527, Clement VII. took refuge here with his whole court. It bears a great resemblance to Joseph's Well in the citadel of Grand Cairo. The depth is about 200 feet, and the width across the top 44 feet. The descent is by a double spiral stair-case which a mule can ascend and descend with ease. Orvieto having ceased to be a garrisoned city, this well is regarded only as a local curiosity.

Orvieto is celebrated for the wine to which it gives name. The traveller is met, at his entry into the city, by persons offering flasks of this beverage for sale, and making loud proclamation of its virtues.

---

* Designers.

† This church is the scene of a facetious novel by Franco Sacchetti, which is in substance as follows:—Cola, a blind man of Orvieto, having collected a hundred florins by "the beggar's craft," placed them, for security, under a tile in the church. He was observed by a certain Juccio Pessicheruola, who waited Cola's departure, and then took possession of the treasure, leaving no traces of his handy-work to betray the theft. Cola returning a few days after discovered his loss. By the assistance of a young boy, who acted as his guide, the blind-mendicant found out the thief. He then resorted to a cunning expedient for the recovery of his money. He visited Juccio, confided to him the concealment of the hundred florins, apprised him that he was about to add another hundred to the hoard, and intrusted his assistance to invest the two hundred florins profitably. Juccio promised his assistance, and departed, so soon as Cola left him, to replace the one hundred florins whence he took them. No long time after, came Cola to ascertain the success of his experiment, when to his great delight he found his lost treasure restored. It is needless to add, that he neither deposited a second hundred, nor suffered the original sum to remain longer in danger. Juccio subsequently returned for his prize, and was much chagrined to find that he had been out-witted.

NARNI.

ANCIENTLY known as the Narnia or Nequinum of the Romans, the modern city of Narni refers to the times of the empire, with which it is still further identified by the magnificent ruins of the Bridge of Augustus, still existing in its vicinity. The original intention of this structure was to continue the Flaminian Way, by connecting the lofty hills which overhang the river Nar.* It consisted of three arches, built of massive blocks of white marble, fitting into each other with such accuracy as to render cement, or any other means of uniting the masses, unnecessary. From its solidity, it is highly probable that this bridge would have remained entire to the present day, had not the foundations of the middle pier given way, and so caused the fall of the two arches on the right bank of the river. Addison regarded this bridge as "one of the stateliest ruins in Italy," and through a long course of ages it has been esteemed one of the noblest relics of imperial times,—a proud memorial of a people whose o'er-vaulting ambition built for eternity. The ruins are seen to great advantage from the modern bridge which crosses the river a short distance above them. This point offers many picturesque combinations for the sketch book, particularly when the position is so chosen, as to bring the convent of San Casciano into view, through the remaining arch of the bridge. No view, however, is more striking than the one obtained from above the ruins on the right bank; here, the utility and grandeur of the structure in its perfect state, are at once evident; whilst the valley of the Nar, and the city of Narni on the opposite hill, combine to make up a scene of singular beauty. The ruinous mass between the two nearest piers, is said to be the remains of a fortress erected there in the middle ages.

The city of Narni itself is remarkable for little beyond its antiquity, and picturesque appearance; it is badly built, with steep and narrow streets, and exhibits every mark of poverty and decay. At the foot of the rocky heights upon which it stands, the Nar rolls its turbid and impure waters through a deep and vast fissure in the limestone rock, wherein are caverns which are used as habitations. A broken path leads down to the river, to the point where the Augustan bridge bestrides the stream. As the birth-place of the emperor Nerva, and Pope John XVIII., Narni, despite of its dirt and poverty, enjoys a distinction which cities of more inviting and promising aspect cannot boast.

---

* To readers unacquainted with classical topography, it may be acceptable information to be told—that the Flaminian Way (so named from the consul Flaminius, who was defeated by Hannibal at the Lake Thrasymenus) was a road leading from Rome to Aquileia, a port still retaining its ancient name, and situated on the northern coast of the Gulf of Trieste. This town, built by a Roman colony to repress the incursions of the barbarians, was beautified by the emperors, who frequently made it their residence. The Flaminian Way led directly from Rome to Ariminum (now Rimini), and thence by passage across the Adriatic to Aquileia.

CASCATA DELLE MARMORE.

TERNI.

> Lo! where it comes like an eternity,
> As if to sweep down all things in its track,
> Charming the eye with dread,—a matchless cataract,
> Horribly beautiful!
>
> *Childe Harold.*

TERNI, the ancient Interamna of Umbria, is in the present day a thriving little town, in which the manufacture of silk and woollen fabrics is carried on to some extent. Beyond the fact of its being the birth-place of Tacitus the historian, and of the emperors Tacitus and Florian, it offers in itself scarcely anything to attract the attention of travellers. The interest of this locality centres altogether in the Cascata delle Marmore, or Marble Cascade, a magnificent waterfall celebrated throughout Europe, and more popularly known as the Falls of Terni.

Byron has remarked upon the extraordinary fact, that the two finest cascades in Europe—those of Terni and Tivoli—are both artificial. The formation of the Cascata delle Marmore originated in the necessity for providing an outlet for the waters of the Velino, which anciently, in consequence of calcareous deposits shallowing and contracting its bed, often overflowed and inundated the valley of the Nar. To counteract this evil, Marcus Curius Dentatus, in the year before Christ 271, caused a canal to be cut, to carry the Velino into the Nar. This work appears, however, to have been conducted with too exclusive a reference to the protection of Rieti, and with little or no regard to the safety of Terni; for the waters of the Velino being discharged over a precipice of great height in the vicinity of the latter place, the upper valley of the Velino was relieved from inundation, by the sacrifice of the lower valley of the Nar. In the frequent disputes which arose between the inhabitants of the two valleys, regarding this channel, the Reatines sought counsel from Cicero, to whom they subsequently erected a statue in acknowledgment of his services.

For nearly 1700 years from its first construction, this canal continued to carry off the superabundant waters of the Velino, till at length, about A.D. 1400, it became so much obstructed that the Reatines were compelled to clear it, and in doing this, they gave a direction to the waters which again threatened the lower valley with ruin. To terminate the serious disputes thence arising, an entirely new channel was cut, which preserved peace between the two valleys for nearly a century and a half, when this new outlet also failed to fulfil its purpose. Paul III. then gave orders for the construction of a canal sufficiently large to carry off all the waters of Rieti; and though Terni, and other cities situated below the falls, protested against the proceeding, the work went forward to completion. This channel,

CASCATA DELLE MARMORE.

however, like the former ones, did not long answer its purpose; and, at length, Fontana the celebrated engineer undertook to render the canal permanently effective. He commenced by re-opening a considerable portion of the old channel cut by Dentatus; but instead of following it to an obtuse junction with the Nar, he cut a new portion at right angles to the valley, and the consequence of this unfortunate blunder was, that vast quantities of fragments of rocks, brought down by the Velino, blocked up the course of the Nar, and produced below the Falls the floods so much dreaded. Fresh disputes arose out of this disaster, and continued without intermission till 1785, when the oblique angle of junction was restored, and other measures taken to secure the lower plains from injury, and since that time the two valleys have been at peace.

The Falls of Terni are distant between three and four miles from the town. They are approached by a road ascending from the valley of the Nar as far as Papigno, whence a branch road leads to the bottom of the Falls. From this point, the spectator sees the principal fall, and also two or three minor cascades, which, although of little importance in themselves, add considerably to the collective grandeur of the scene. Ascending the hill, the tourist arrives in full view of the waters of the Velino, and beholds them foaming and tumbling down the precipice. He is next led to a projecting eminence, whence the cataract is seen rolling on, "like an eternity," in one unbroken fall, bursting into foam which surrounds it like a mantle, and plunging into the deep abyss that rises to meet it at its coming in thick clouds of vapour. At this point, the spectator is admitted into a small building seated on the very edge of the projecting rock, and said to have been erected by order of Napoleon; here he looks forth, with a feeling of security, upon "the hell of waters" raging before him and beneath him. Descending from this building, and crossing the Nar, the tourist reaches the little summer-house, from which an uninterrupted view is obtained of the cataract in all its extent.

Of the character of the country above the Falls, but in connection with them, no engraving hitherto published has conveyed any idea. The view from the valley of the Nar, shows all the lower cataracts fore-shortened, and excludes the country above; and the prospect from the top of the Falls, is made indistinct by the mists. Our scene, representing the cataract in its relation to the surrounding country, is taken from the high ground above the right bank of the Nar, opposite its confluence with the Velino; it thus commands an extensive view above and beyond the crest of the cascade; the mountains where its waters take their rise, and the direction of the valleys through which they pass, are seen; whilst the eye embraces the entire cataract from the first great plunge of 300 or 400 feet, through all the continuous and lower falls, to the stream of the Nar,—a collective depth of nearly 1000 feet. *

---

* Wilson, the painter, visited these Falls in company with Sir Joshua Reynolds. Sir Joshua relates, that for a moment Wilson stood in mute astonishment at the sublimity of the spectacle, and at length unconsciously exclaimed —" Well done, water, by God!" Let the reader pardon the apparent irreverence of the exclamation, and then contrast it with the insipid remark by Addison, that "these Falls are superior to the water-works at Versailles."

CIVITA CASTELLANA.

ANTIQUARIANS were, until within the last few years, much divided in opinion regarding the sites of several ancient cities, each of which had been identified, by different authorities, with the modern town of Civita Castellana.[*] It is now, however, pretty clearly ascertained that this town marks the locality of the classic Falerium, the capital of the Falisci, and one of the cities of the Etrurian league. It is situated on the Flaminian Way, at the distance of thirty-seven miles from Rome, and though containing within its walls nothing of great interest to the traveller, the picturesque beauty of its site and neighbourhood, and the classical associations connected with them, render it worthy of regard by the antiquarian, the scholar, and the man of taste.

---

[*] Civita Castellana has been variously regarded as the site of Veii, Falerium or Falerii, and Fescennium, three famous cities of Etruria. The insulation of the town by deep ravines, running almost entirely round it, seemed to favour the hypothesis of its having been the ancient Veii, so celebrated in classical history for its resistance of the Roman power under Camillus. This city, which sustained a siege of ten years, was larger and far more magnificent than Rome itself. The Romans, whose city had recently been much injured by the Gauls, were anxious to migrate to Veii; and the authority and eloquence of Camillus were scarcely sufficient to change their resolution. At length, however, he prevailed, and Veii was destroyed. The recent discovery of inscriptions, marble columns, and fragments of temples, has determined the true situation of Veii to be at La Storta, about twelve miles from Rome.

The city of Fescennium is now ascertained to have had its site at Galese, a few miles north-east of Civita Castellana. The famous Fescennine Verses, invented by the Fescenni, are frequently mentioned by the Latin poets. They were a sort of rustic dialogue in which the failings and vices of mankind were exposed to ridicule. With a considerable share of satirical humour, they blended a too great licentiousness of language. They ultimately became a vehicle for gross and slanderous attacks upon patrician families; and Augustus was compelled to proscribe them, as being more offensive by their immorality than corrective by their satire. In his Epistle to Augustus, Horace thus alludes to them:

Fescennina per hunc inventa licentia morem Versibus alternis opprobria rustica fudit; Libertasque recurrentes accepta per annos Lusit amabiliter; donec jam saevus apertam In rabiem verti coepit jocus, et per honestas Ire domos impune minax. *Epist. II. 1. 145.*	Here, in alternate verse, with rustic jest, The clowns their awkward raillery express'd. And as the year brought round the jovial day, Freely they sported, innocently gay, Till cruel wit was turn'd to open rage, And dar'd the noblest families engage. *Francis.*

Falerium, or Falerii, whose site is now fixed, by the best authorities, at Civita Castellana, is rendered famous by the noble conduct of Camillus. The Falisci having rendered assistance to the Veientes during the siege of Veii, Camillus invested their city. Whilst the Roman army lay before the place, a schoolmaster went out of the gates with his pupils, and delivered them into the hands of Camillus, as the surest means of inducing the citizens to sur-

CIVITA CASTELLANA.

The principal approach to Civita Castellana is by a magnificent bridge of many arches, thrown across the deep ravine which separates the town from the neighbouring heights. This structure, which bears strong resemblance to the Pont du Gard near Nîmes, was constructed by Cardinal Imperiali in 1712, and is considered one of the finest works of papal times. Remains of the ancient Falerium are discoverable in the ravine; through which flows the river Triglia, a small affluent of the Tiber. The modern town stands upon an insulated rock; the walls rising on the edge of a perpendicular precipice, and formed in general of large blocks of stone, which are probably the remains of the ancient rampart. The Citadel, which forms a striking object in our illustrative view, occupies an isthmus that connects the town with the higher grounds. This building was begun by Alexander VI., in 1500, and completed by Julius II. and Leo X. It is now used as a state prison, but its defences are wholly inadequate to protect the town against an enemy.

The Cathedral ranks next in interest to the Citadel. This structure is of the thirteenth century. It has a portico of small columns of granite and marble, and a mosaic frieze. The middle door-way is of Lombard architecture, and is decorated with ancient mosaics. The interior is much modernized and contains nothing remarkable, if we except some sepulchral tablets with effigies, dating from the fifteenth century. This church is regarded with veneration by the religious, as being the depository of the bodies of S. Gracilian and Santa Felicissima who suffered martyrdom at Civita Castellana, in the third century. Besides the cathedral, there are no buildings of consequence except the convents, and these exhibit nothing in their architecture or interior decorations to claim extended notice.

The prospect which is obtained from the tower of the citadel is far more interesting than the structure itself. From this point the spectator commands an impressive view of the deep ravines which wind and twist in various directions, and almost entirely surround the town, whilst at a distance is seen the Mons Soracte,* or Sant' Oreste, famous for mythological and classical tradition; the plain of Nepi, anciently celebrated as the Ciminian forest, upon whose

---

reader. The Roman general, filled with indignation at the baseness of a man who could betray a trust so sacred, caused him to be bound, and in this condition to be whipped back into the town by his scholars. When the Romans destroyed Falerium, another city bearing the same name was built in the plain, about four miles distant. To distinguish between the two, the second city is named Faleri ; its site is identified with Santa Maria di Falleri.

* To the east of Civita Castellana, and at the distance of twenty-six miles from Rome, rises the Sant' Oreste, or sacred mountain of Soracte, which, according to mythology, was under the immediate guardianship of Apollo, who is thence styled by the poets, Apollo Soractis.

Summe deûm, sancti custos Soractis Apollo,	O Phœbus! guardian of Soracte's woods,
Quem primi colimus, cui pineus ardor acerva	And shady hills ; a god above the gods!
Pascitur.	To whom our nations pay the rite divine,
Eneis XI. 785.	And burn whole crackling groves of hallow'd pine.
	Pitt.

Here was a temple of the god ; and from this place went forth those oracular responses whose utter vagueness rendered the infallibility of the Pythoness unimpeachable, and gave to her pretended revelations one genuine characteristic of a voice divine—mystery. Some report that on Mount Soracte was a fountain whose waters boiled at sunrise, and instantly killed all such birds as drank of them. Other fables are not wanting, to invest with marvels a spot which a deity had chosen for his peculiar residence. Horace in his ninth Ode refers to this mountain :

impenetrable labyrinth the Romans once looked with awe and terror; and the neighbouring lake beneath which a city is said to lie submerged.* Leaving the town, the tourist makes excursions to the classic localities in the neighbourhood; and perhaps no where, within the same compass, can so many associations of ancient site and tradition be brought together.

CIVITA VECCHIA.

THIS town, the principal port of the Papal States, and usually designated the port of Rome, was an important maritime station in the latter times of the empire. Anciently known as Centumcellæ,† it afterwards took the name of Portus Trajani, or the port of Trajan, from the magnificent harbour constructed there by the emperor Trajan. The depth of the water within the haven varies from fourteen to twenty feet. Two immense inflected piers enclose the harbour, which is defended at its entrance by an artificial island, or breakwater, resembling, both in construction and appearance, the modern sea-barrier erected in Plymouth Sound. The younger Pliny, in a letter addressed to Cornelianus, and written from Centumcellæ, makes interesting reference to the imperial works then in progress.— " This delightful villa," he writes, " is surrounded by the most verdant meadows, and commands a fine view of the sea, which flows into a spacious harbour in the form of an amphitheatre. The left hand of this port is defended by exceeding strong works, and they are now actually employed in carrying on the same on the opposite side. An artificial island, which is rising in the midst of the haven, will break the force of the waves, and afford a safe channel to ships on each side. In the construction of this wonderful work of art, stones of a most enormous size are transported hither in a large sort of pontoons, and being piled one upon another, are fixed by their own weight, and gradually accumulating in the manner of a natural mound. It already lifts its rocky bank above the ocean, while the waves which beat upon it, being tossed to an immense height, foam with a prodigious noise, and whiten all the sea around.

Vides, ut alta stet nive candidum
Soracte.
Ode IX. 1.

Behold Soracte's airy height,
See how it stands a heap of snow !
Francis.

* The Lago di Vico, or Lacus Ciminus, presents the appearance of a crater, and the physical structure of the surrounding hills bears testimony to its volcanic origin. The city of Succinium, according to tradition, was swallowed up by the sudden sinking of the earth. It is mentioned by ancient writers, that when the water was clear, the ruins of the city might be seen at the bottom of the lake.

† Previous to Trajan's erecting a villa at Centumcellæ, and subsequently converting this town into a secure harbour for the ships of Rome, this place was mean in character and thinly inhabited. Indeed, the very name of Centum cellæ, or the Hundred Cellars, is indicative of the wretchedness of its dwellings.

To these stones are added larger blocks, which, when the whole shall be completed, will give it the appearance of an island just emerged from the ocean! This haven is to be called by the name of its great founder, and will prove of infinite benefit, by affording a very secure retreat to ships on that extensive and dangerous coast."

When this sea-port was destroyed by the Saracens, in 828, its expelled inhabitants retired inland, and built another town, which, however, they evacuated in 854, and returned to re-occupy their former site, which thence obtained the name of Civita *Vecchia*, or the *old* town. On the establishment of the papal power, the restoration of the harbour became an important object with the government. Julius II., in 1512, ordered the construction of the fortifications, which were completed by Paul III. And, in 1500, Urban VII. built the walls of the town.*
The massive architecture of the buildings around the basin, and the exterior appearance of the place towards the sea, raise an expectation that is not realized on entering the town.

Civita Vecchia is the capital of a small delegation, and numbers a population of nearly eight thousand inhabitants. It was erected by Leo XII., in 1826, into an episcopal see, to which was united the diocese of Porto and Santa Ruffina. The largest prisons of the Papal States exist here; these are capable of holding 1200 convicts, and it is seldom that the cells are unoccupied. In 1849, a French army landed at Civita Vecchia to replace Pius IX. on the pontifical throne, presenting the somewhat inconsistent spectacle of a nation, which had only a few months before shaken off regal authority, interfering to reimpose a similar yoke on another nation, whose grievances furnished them with a much more legitimate ground of revolution than the people of France.

This port was constituted by Clement XII. a free port—that is to say, a port into which produce may be imported, and either consumed or re-exported, free of duty. Quarantine regulations, however, are strictly enforced. Civita Vecchia enjoys a flourishing trade, and is a regular place of call for steamers between Marseilles, the Italian ports, and the Levant. It thus forms a central point, where travellers may assure themselves of rapid and certain conveyance to all parts of Italy and the Mediterranean.

---

* The re-construction of this harbour was committed to Michael Angelo. It is a grateful task to record of the papacy that it has wrought some good. True, it has enslaved the minds of men, and erected a spiritual despotism fearful in power, and terrible in activity; but it has also, and that not in a few instances, emulated the patriotic spirit of elder Rome, and disbursed its ample revenues—how obtained we stop not to inquire—in the erection of public works, not more eminent as examples of art, than useful to the community at large from their purpose and design.

ROME.

Thou art in Rome! the City that so long
Reign'd absolute, the mistress of the world;
The mighty vision that the prophets saw,
And trembled; that from nothing, from the least,
The lowliest village (what but here and there
A reed-roof'd cabin by a river side?)
Grew into every thing; and, year by year,
Patiently, fearlessly working her way
O'er brook and field, o'er continent and sea,
Not like the merchant with his merchandise,
Or traveller with staff and scrip exploring,
But hand to hand and foot to foot, through hosts,
Through nations numberless in battle-array,
Each behind each, each, when the other fell,
Up and in arms, at length subdued them all.

Thou art in Rome! the City, where the Gauls,
Entering at sun-rise through her open gates,
And, through her streets silent and desolate,
Marching to slay, thought they saw gods, not men;
The City that, by temperance, fortitude,
And love of glory, tower'd above the clouds,
Then fell—but falling, kept the highest seat,
And in her loneliness, her pomp of woe,
Where now she dwells, withdrawn into the wild,
Still o'er the mind maintains, from age to age,
Her empire undiminish'd.

Rogers.

GRANDEUR is the characteristic of Rome;—the associated grandeur of a long antiquity, of an unparalleled history, of a succession of magnificent architecture, and of a resplendent stream of art descending from imperial ages to the present time. Twenty-six centuries have passed since the foundations of the "Eternal City" were laid;—since Romulus gathered around him the restless spirits of ancient Italy, to form the germ of a community whose fame was afterwards to fill the earth. From their rude huts on the Tiber— lowly dwellings, yet dignified, for they were the nucleus of Augustan Rome,—the first Romans went forth conquering and to conquer. The nations submitted to them; one people after another sought alliance with them; and the gradual increase of power, and its concomitants, consolidated their infant kingdom, and gave to the throne of their adventurous chief a fixity not to be shaken. Taught by the nations they subdued, the early Romans spared from the work of conquest time enough to apply the lessons which a wise policy dictated to them. Adopting the religion, the laws, the useful arts, and, to a great extent, the manners and customs, of the vanquished, they at one and the same time conciliated the enemies they had overthrown, and collected within their own city the most estimable arts and institutions of neighbouring nations. The kingly authority under which Rome, for upwards of a century and a half, continued to grow in prosperity and extent, came suddenly to an end: tyranny which had dared to erect itself in the presence of a free people, was put down; and thenceforward it was declared, that no king should ever reign in Rome. Then commenced the consular government, which was interrupted when Julius Cæsar assumed imperial power, and finally extinguished when Cæsar Augustus was called to the supreme authority by the unanimous consent of the Roman senate and people. In the long interval between the last king and the last consul, the Romans fought and worked their way till they held undisputed mastery over the then known world. What reader of history needs to be told of their achievements, of the hundred-armed grasp with which they gathered the nations to themselves, of the territory they held, of the wealth they amassed, of the magnificence they created? So vast at last were the limits of the empire, that the much coveted and esteemed title of a Roman citizen became an unmeaning and empty name. But Rome had departed from her vow; she who had given sentence against kings, again confided her liberties to the guardianship of one man. The boast of Augustus may be allowed, that he found the city of brick and left it of marble; and of succeeding emperors, it may be granted that they embellished Rome, insomuch that no city might be likened unto her. Yet amidst the magnificence and luxury of imperial rule, the decay of the empire began to be visible. The national character was corrupted; the daring valour and the stern virtue of consular Rome, gave place to an effeminacy that enfeebled the arm, and a sensual luxury that debased the mind. With few exceptions, the emperors themselves were monsters of sensuality, demons of cruelty, exercising absolute sway over a people reduced to abject servility, and recommending by imperial example vices too hideous and disgusting even to be named. The Augustan age was, indeed, a brilliant epoch;—so brilliant that all succeeding times have referred to it as a standard of national greatness in literature and art. Yet amidst magnificence which might have begot undying love of country, and patriotic zeal in its defence; amidst all that art and literature gave forth to adorn and beautify, to elevate and refine;—there sprung up the antagonistic powers of luxury and indolence, whose deadening and corrupting influences converted the evidences and results of national greatness into presages and preparatives for national decay. And wherefore was it so? Rome bowed itself as one man before Augustus: his nod was law; the permanent principles of moral and social order were forgotten in implicit obedience to the will of Cæsar. Thus was Rome prepared for the times that awaited her; thus by abandonment of her independence, was she fitted to sink into degradation, and to wallow in the very depths of moral pollution, so soon as an emperor should appear to enforce the one by his tyranny, and to countenance the other by his example. Such an emperor was Tiberius, the immediate successor of Augustus; a wretch infamous for his vices, a tyrant detestable for his cruelties. From the time of Augustus till the reign of Jovian, a period embracing thirty-six emperors, only seven individuals can be named who exhibited virtues eminently worthy of a throne. Vespasian, Titus, Trajan, Adrian, Antoninus, Aurelius, and Constantine, stand forth as prodigies on the imperial list: in an age of polytheism they might have been regarded as gods who had descended upon earth for the preservation of Rome. Victorious in arms, prudent in policy, and severe in manly and kingly virtue, they at least retarded the downfall of the empire. But the evil was too deep for cure: a succession of just men might have reformed and reanimated the Roman people; their occasional appearance served only to rouse indolence to temporary exertion, to restrain but not to banish luxury, to disturb but not to eradicate vice. Though hastening to decline, Rome sent forth her imperial legions to conquest; and for a time also she successfully opposed the incursions of the barbarian hosts who hovered over the confines of the empire like vultures watching for the prey. But this does not falsify the view that has hitherto been taken of imperial Rome: "No man," says the satirist, "ever reached the heights of vice at first;" and no nation has ever thrown aside her greatness in a day. The long glories of republican Rome could not suffer instant eclipse: a gradual decay of ancestral virtue, a gradual advance in vicious refinement—operations as sure in effect as the dropping water that wears the marble underneath,—these were at work, and they finally issued in the extinction of the Roman name.

The Roman empire, almost immediately after the death of Aurelius, offered a melancholy illustration of a modern apothegm—that between the sublime and the ridiculous there is only one step. The imperial ensigns were held by the Prætorian guard, who openly exposed them for sale, and readily granted them to any purchaser who would meet their demands. Scarcely had one aspirant for sovereign sway taken his seat, before he was dragged thence to make room for a successor, another purchaser of imperial dignities. From Commodus to Diocletian, the period of a century, disorder reigned throughout the empire, and the lives and liberties of the people were at the mercy of an avaricious soldiery. Honour and virtue were extinct. Rome was deserted by her guardian genii. When Diocletian divided the imperial dominions into four separate governments, over which presided two emperors and two Cæsars,—and when immediately after, Constantine removed the seat of empire from Rome to Byzantium,—then, indeed, "the beginning of the end" was seen. For a century and a half longer, Rome wrestled with her destiny; she abandoned her conquests, and gathered her legions round her to repel the attacks of the barbarians, who now began to threaten the city itself. On the death of Theodosius, his sons made a permanent division of the empire into Eastern and Western. Of the first of these we lose sight; and of the latter little is left to record save its final catastrophe.

Whilst Rome was hastening to decay, barbarian kingdoms were rising up on every hand: the Vandals in Africa, the Huns in Scythia, the Visigoths in Gaul and Spain;—each originally a community of rude and daring spirits, the very counterpart of the first Romans. Temperate, frugal, and brave, these people possessed all the qualities requisite for success in arms. Long before the ruin of Rome had become inevitable, these warlike hordes prowled around the borders of the empire, and succeeded in permanently or temporarily detaching the fairest provinces. Watching with eagle glance the declining strength of the masters of the world,—profiting by the disasters which beset the Romans from without, and the pernicious influences that were working surely and silently within the city,—observing how the Romans retired from scenes of former conquest, and concentrated themselves for the final struggle that was impending,—these barbarian hosts disdained to continue longer a predatory warfare against the extremities of the empire: they made bold irruption into the Roman territory, swept like the avalanche across the pleasant fields of Italy, carrying terror in their front and leaving utter desolation behind them, nor paused on their march till they had reached the very gates of Rome. Attila of the Huns, with four hundred thousand followers, invaded Italy in the time of Valentinian. He entered with his army into Rome, and the work of spoliation had begun, when the timid emperor purchased an inglorious rescue. Attila retired laden with treasures, Alas! for the nation that redeems herself, save with the sword. Alas! for the people who can offer no better resistance to a hostile invader than to cast upon him the spoils of temples and palaces, and the gold of the treasury. Every talent in the hand of Attila was an argument for fresh invasion, an invitation to other kingdoms to come down and share the wreck of an empire. The last days of Rome were at hand. In the time of Honorius, the first of the Western Emperors, Alaric, king of the Visigoths, appeared in Italy, fresh from the conquest of Greece. The wrath of this Destroyer of Nations was for the instant appeased by unlimited concession. Subsequently, however, he strengthened himself by alliance with the Goths and Huns, and set forth towards Rome. The hour of accumulated vengeance had come: fire and sword devastated the city; and of all its magnificence, nothing remained of Imperial Rome, save the Christian churches, which, together with their treasures, the barbarian consented to spare. Rome had not, however, utterly fallen: she was to be destroyed, but her time was not yet fulfilled. Like her own soldiers, in the best days of the republic, who, staggering beneath the blows of their assailants, fought on, and at length yielded up life sullenly and by degrees,—she protracted her final overthrow by unavailing attempts to restore her greatness. She arose from her ruins, and preserved a name amongst the nations: it was too late to claim her former proud title of mistress of the world.

The barbarians returned to their prey: they poured down like the locust upon Italy: from the forests of Scandinavia, from the deserts of Africa, from the wilds of Scythia, they came forth in successive myriads to plunder and destroy. They came with their wives and their children, their slaves and their flocks, to make settlement upon Italian ground. The lands they deserted were instantly occupied by more remote tribes of barbarians, who in turn rushed forward to obtain a share in the spoils of Rome. Thus, like an impetuous and unbroken stream, or like a torrent continually increasing, they rolled on sweeping everything before them. These were adventurers, not warriors. They followed in the rear of the armies to render the work of devastation complete, and to secure permanent advantages from the triumphs of their countrymen. Genseric now led his Vandals to Rome: the threatened destruction was partially averted by the intercession of Leo I., emperor of the East. The city escaped the flames; but the sword did its work upon the wretched inhabitants, and the spoiler left little behind him that fire could consume. The interval of rest was brief. The cry was still, They come! Within twenty years after Genseric retired, carrying with him into Africa thousands of Roman prisoners to groan in bondage,—Odoacer, king of the Heruli, advanced upon the city, wrested the imperial ensigns from the hands of Augustulus, and put a final termination to the empire of the West (A.D. 476). Thus was Rome cast down, never to rise again. She was given over to the barbarian; a long and dark night was before her; and a far distant twilight was, after the lapse of ages, to break forth, not upon "the Roman's Rome," but upon a city oppressed and trodden down by rival claimants and foreign domination, and by a spiritual despotism from which escape should be hopeless.

In the history of the world, we cannot find a period so beset with calamities and afflictions to the human race, as that which transpired from the death of Theodosius till the establishment of the kingdom of the Lombards. Rome was, indeed, the centre of desolation; but that desolation radiated thence over all the civilized portions of the globe. Upon southern Europe more especially fell the withering influences of barbaric rule. The Great Northern Hive came down from the colder regions of our continent, in numbers numberless, to sweep away the old inhabitants of those fertile provinces which they sought to occupy. Slavery in its most hideous form; a mental darkness unpierced, save by a few feeble rays of intellectual light; art proscribed, and all her triumphs cast down, broken, destroyed; outrage, tumult, massacre;—such were the features of barbarian Europe, from the end of the fourth till nearly the end of the sixth century. The contemporaneous authors who successively witnessed the miseries of this long period, find language inadequate to portray the horrors that surrounded them. The Scourge of God, the Destroyer of Nations, are the fearful epithets by which they distinguish the leaders of the barbarian hosts. The names of Attila, Alaric, Genseric, and Odoacer, have descended to modern times with a terrible significance, each appellative alike expressive of lamentation, mourning, and woe.

The Dark Ages did not terminate with the expulsion of the Ostrogoths. It was not until the Lombards had given place to the Franks, and these in turn had been superseded by the Germans, that the twilight of the Middle Ages broke forth upon Italy. Indeed, subsequent centuries offer darker pages of Italian history, than present themselves in the reign of Theodoric, and his successors. At the commencement of this barbarian dynasty, which began A.D. 480 (on the expulsion of Odoacer), and continued for sixty-four years, there was a display of moderation, justice, and clemency, too remarkable to be overlooked. The comparatively liberal institutions of Theodoric, who pursued an enlightened policy, seldom exhibited by the Gothic kings, mitigated the evils to which Italy had been exposed under the Heruli. The latter princes of this line had to contend against the power of Justinian, who sent his celebrated general, Belisarius, to recover the western provinces, and restore the extinct division of the empire. Italy endured even more during this struggle, than whilst she lay beneath the undisturbed rule of the barbarians. Which party soever triumphed, the natives suffered; and the dreadful retaliation of Totila, when he recaptured Rome from Justinian, caused universal terror and dismay, and drove the Romans to despair. Ultimately the Eastern emperor prevailed; and the kingdom of the Ostrogoths ceased. Rome was thenceforward, for fifteen years, under the government of Narses, Justinian's general, who, at length, to escape impending censure and disgrace, invited the Lombards into Italy to aid in protecting him against the imperial arms.

The Lombards were a powerful German tribe from the banks of the Danube. They eagerly accepted the invitation to descend upon the rich valleys of the south; and shortly after their arrival, they founded the celebrated Lombard kingdom, which, commencing A.D. 568, continued for upwards of two centuries, or until A.D. 774. Their sovereignty never embraced the whole of Italy, of which a large portion, including Rome, continued to be held by the Greek, or Eastern emperors. For a length of time, the government of the country was divided between the emperors of the East, the Lombardic kings, and the Germanic chiefs, or dukes, who had succeeded in establishing independent principalities in the dominions of the Lombards. When pope Gregory II. denounced the emperor Leo as a heretic, and thereby instigated the imperial provinces to revolt, these last became subject to the Lombards, who sought also to annex the then independent republic of Rome to their territories. This act of aggression caused the bishops to seek the aid of Pepin, king of the Franks, who came over into Italy and expelled the Lombards from the imperial provinces. They were finally vanquished by Charlemagne, the son and successor of Pepin, and the founder of the Frankish empire.

The Franks were a German people who, under Clovis their king, established a monarchy in

Gaul, which during the reign of Charlemagne rose to be one of the great empires of the world. The sovereignty of the Franks in Italy extended as far south as Naples; but after the death of Charlemagne, and the partition of his dominions, his successors maintained little more than a nominal authority. When the Carlovingian dynasty was deposed, in the person of Charles Le Gros, in 888, Italy was ravaged by contending tyrants till 910, when the popes and the leading men of the country invited Otho the Great to their assistance. Since then, Italy has always remained subject to the German emperors, if we except that brief period, in modern times, when the successes of Napoleon gave him possession of this southern portion of the Austrian dominions. At this point in the political history of Italy we must stop: it would lead us too far, even to glance briefly at the many separate and rival governments established in the Middle Ages. The disputes of popes and emperors, and the constant feuds between republics and principalities, could not be detailed with any degree of perspicuity in this brief abstract.

Before proceeding to a slight review of the rise of the papacy, the growth of its power, and its ultimate supremacy, it may be well to notice a few of the predominant features in the history of the temporal sovereignties which, on the fall of the empire, held successive authority in Italy.

It is a remarkable fact,—a fact for which, at first view, we are little prepared,—that fallen Rome dictated to her barbarian conquerors both language and laws, and also much of the general economy of civil and social life. Imperial institutions were preserved, either entire, or with slight modifications; the Latin tongue was made the basis of a common language, to be spoken in after times by the amalgamated posterity of the Roman and the barbarian; and with regard to minor details of national distinction, it may be asserted that the leaders of the Germanic tribes were, for the most part, more anxious to Italianize their own people, than to convert the Italians to the rude and primitive manners which prevailed in northern Europe. With the fact before us, we can account for it in two ways; the barbarians, by pursuing a policy, formerly practised by the Romans, might seek to render their yoke more tolerable to the conquered, by preserving and respecting the national characteristics of their country; but, in another view, we cannot suppose the barbarians to have been insensible of the value of many institutions that had been preserved intact and uncorrupt amidst the rubbish of the empire. Probably in the first centuries of the dark ages, we are scarcely justified in assuming that the barbarians were actuated by any motives of sympathy towards the conquered; for with such a supposition, we could not reconcile the exterminating cruelty of the invaders, which for a long period made Italy a scene of utter desolation. The truth may be, that the barbarians sought only their own advancement in the institutes of civil and social life, in what they adopted of Roman origin; and that they warred ruthlessly against literature and art, as a necessary prelude to the permanent subjection of a refined people; and to clear away what they deemed useless encumbrances and seductive allurements, equally dangerous and valueless to a nation whose dependence was upon the sword. Darkly ignorant as were the barbarians, and unprovided with written laws, they had arrived at some of the great principles of civil polity; and not a few of the best institutions of modern times may find an origin in the usages of the rude tribes of the north. Monarchical authority was recognized by them, and when they came southward, they appear to have had an hereditary nobility. The privileges of these nobles were confined to eligibility for election to the throne and the subordinate offices of state, and to the right of gathering around them mercenary followers to assist them in their fierce quarrels with each other. The rights of citizenship were denied to the poor, and to foreigners; to the one, because his poverty prevented him from fulfilling the terms of franchise, in the service of arms; and to the other, because no dependence for war could be placed on a foreigner or conquered enemy. Lands were divided into districts, each district being under the jurisdiction of a chief, the original of the more recent Count. These chiefs were subject to the kingly authority; and in time of war each led the inhabitants of the district over which he presided, to aid the general cause. The supreme military command was given to the Herzog, or Duke, whose office resembled that of Dictator amongst the Romans, being conferred for the occasion, and lasting no longer than till the end of the campaign. Every reader knows somewhat of the institutions of ancient Rome; and we must leave him to infer the results that followed from engrafting upon them the native institutes and customs of the barbarians.

We have already alluded to the wise policy of Theodoric, by which he mitigated the evils that oppressed Italy, and succeeded to a great extent in reconciling the Italians to gothic rule. His concessions towards the emperor of the East, and the respect and protection which (though himself an Arian) he extended to the Western Church, produced peaceful results. He acted justly towards the community, without respect to Goth or Roman; and made strenuous exertions to improve the resources of the country. He brought the swampy lands into a state of cultivation, drained the Pontine Marshes, and rendered many districts habitable that before were too unwholesome for human residence. It is worthy of remark, that during his reign, Italy, which under the empire was indebted to foreign countries for its corn, was not only enabled to supply its own wants, but also to export a large surplus of grain to Gaul. Unhappily for the Italian people, the successors of Theodoric did not tread in his steps: in the true spirit of Goths, they sought to establish their power by unrelenting cruelty and rigorous exactions. Nor were the Italians benefited by exchange of masters, when the Lombards took possession of their country; for these new rulers claimed one-third of his yearly produce from every native proprietor. But the sufferings of Italy were much aggravated at this period by the operations of the feudal system, which now began to prevail throughout Europe. The laws both of the Lombards and of the Franks allowed creditors to reduce their debtors to villenage, and to sell them into hereditary slavery. During the sovereignty of these dynasties, the miseries of feudal tyranny reduced the Italians to a painful and degrading servitude. Italy did not, however, endure the severities of the feudal system to the same extent, or for so long a period, as other countries of Europe. The perpetual conflict between a number of independent principalities, the frequent quarrels between the temporal and spiritual powers, and the constitution of the free cities of the Middle Ages—these wrought successively in favour of liberty, and laid considerable restraint upon the tyranny of the feudal chiefs. The ascendancy of the papal power also gave a measure of freedom to the people; for the emperor who was the source of feudal authority, was likewise the enemy of the holy see. The institutions of the Middle Ages were utterly opposed to the principles of feudalism: they united, it is true, with other causes to render Italy an arena of perpetual disorder; but it is some atonement that they at first held in check, and subsequently overthrew, one of the most atrocious systems of tyranny that the world has ever known.

Having traced Rome from her origin, through all the vicissitudes of temporal rule, till the opening of the eleventh century, when the darkness of barbarism began to disappear in the returning light of literature and art,—it remains that we take a slight view—cursory and imperfect it must necessarily be—of the rise and progress of that spiritual domination which has trodden Italy into the very dust, and made her,—what neither Austria nor France, each with its manifold wrongs, *could* have made her—

> The Niobe of Nations!
> Childless and crownless in her voiceless woe.

Christianity was introduced into Rome in the early times of the empire. It was a remarkable spectacle to behold the first converts to the Christian faith, testifying to God and His Christ in the midst of heathen abominations, and in the face of a nation devoted to vicious indulgences. The purity of life and simplicity of doctrine which characterized the followers of Jesus, formed a beautiful contrast to the morality and the religion of the heathens. The infant church of Rome appears, at first, to have attracted little attention from the proud community in which it dwelt. Scorn and contempt were, for a time, the only weapons that assailed the Christian converts of Rome. But when the new sect had not only increased in numbers, but had also gathered adherents from the patrician ranks, it began to exert an influence not to be destroyed by scoff and jest. So long as it was a company of mean men, having no repute in the estimation of the world, its practical rebuke of heathen idolatry and wickedness was little regarded; but the case was far different (humanly speaking) when increasing numbers, and that kind of influence which the world recognizes, rendered it an object of imperial jealousy and hatred. It had ever been the custom with the Romans to give place in their temples to the gods of conquered nations; and before the introduction of Christianity, they were preeminently distinguished for toleration in matters of religion. This, however, is readily accounted for: the variations in heathen worship presented no startling contrast; they were merely so many separate features in *one* corrupt faith, which, as it sprung originally out of the pride and vanity of the human heart, so it commended itself in its ghastly unity to all the nations of heathendom. But Christianity was opposed to heathen worship at every point: the one was moral purity itself, the other a pander to all the vicious propensities natural to man; this inflated its worshippers and ministered to their pride, that enjoined humility to its followers, and proclaimed the empty nothingness of earthly grandeur. No wonder, then, that imperial Rome arose to vindicate her thousand gods, and to pour forth her exterminating wrath upon the votaries of a religion which threatened to silence her oracles for ever; and which, moreover, smote with withering rebuke the monstrous enormities of both emperor and people. The sufferings of the Christians commenced under Nero, A.D. 64; and continued till the time of Constantine, A.D. 328. Ten distinct periods of fiery persecution, separated by intervals of relaxed severity, fill up the lapse of time between these two emperors. Every cruelty that malice could devise and tyranny inflict, was employed for the extirpation of a faith that would make no compromise with the works of darkness. But the sword of the legionary, the agonizing fire, the sharp pangs of ingenious torture, all were unequal to overthrow a cause which was of God. The church of Christ exhibited during these trials a purity and faith never exceeded—perhaps never equalled—in all her succeeding history.

Constantine was a deadlier foe to Christianity than all the persecuting emperors taken together. His *political* adoption of Christianity as the religion of the empire, introduced a deadly element into the Christian system, whose pernicious evils are not exclusively confined to the Roman church, but lurk insidiously, to a greater or less extent, in the constitution of every church that has been *established* since his day. The truly apostolic church of the first ages exhibited every grace; she was in the world, but not of the world; her bishops and pastors were humble-minded men, who sought no earthly honours, who dreamed not of supremacy, who appealed to no sword, save that of the Spirit, to propagate and establish the faith. It was the unnatural union of temporal with spiritual power that transformed the Christian church of Rome into a temple of Satan,—that took from her, humility, long-suffering, gentleness, and kindness, and gave her in place of these, haughtiness, wrath, fierce anger, and devouring hate. It was the spirit of this world, let loose upon the subdued yet still corrupt heart of man, that drew aside a Roman bishop from his duties as a spiritual overseer, to indulge in the criminal excesses of a temporal supremacy. It was this spirit whose malignant broodings brought forth the monstrous contradiction of a *persecuting Christian* church. Up to the time of Constantine, the Roman church had suffered much, and proclaimed peace: after Constantine, she became a destroyer, and peace dwelt not with her. And to which of the churches that have arisen since the age of the first Christian emperor of Rome, can we point and say, that in it are discoverable no traces of the evil which Constantine inflicted upon Christianity when he made it the partner of an earthly throne?

Constantine adopted Christianity as the religion of the state; but he did not put down heathen idolatry. The truth appears to be that Christianity had assumed a *respectable* appearance, and the emperor was desirous to preserve quietude in his dominions; and *therefore* it was that he was tolerant towards the new faith, nay, indeed, gave it priority of position—and why? because heathenism was discountenanced and like folly showed when confronted with the Gospel. It is a notorious fact, that long before the coming of Christ, the utter worthlessness and the dreadful abominations of polytheistic worship were the scoff and scorn of the very heathen themselves. In the calm retreats of philosophy, a system of belief was inculcated, totally opposed to the doctrines and modes of worship enjoined by the national creed. The people, indeed, were for the most part satisfied with their deities. And why not? Every bad passion was protected by a god, and its indulgence was *enjoined* as the only acceptable worship in his temple! Thus, then, Constantine recognized Christianity because numbers had embraced it, and even its enemies were beginning to respect it; but he tolerated heathen worship lest the people should resent the dismissal of the gods in whose service they delighted. But what was the consequence of this imperial compromise? Look to the church of Rome, and in her rites and ceremonies, her festivals and solemnities, see the deplorable results of this temporizing policy. It is most important that we have a clear perception of the primary corruption of the Roman church; for out of that proceeded all the monstrous enormities which history chronicles against the papacy. Constantine restrained some of the more openly gross rites of heathenism, but when he had done this, he gave equal protection to the altar of Jove and the church of Christ. The heathen pontiff and the Christian bishop had nearly equal eminence: each was recognized and respected by the civil power. What was the result in regard to Christianity? Its followers began, under episcopal sanction, to adopt the worse than empty splendour of heathen rite and ceremony. Heathenism was *engrafted* upon Christianity, and that not in externals only, but also in the internals of doctrine and belief. And ultimately there were superadded to heathen corruptions, the vain rites and superstitions of pagan worship; until, at length, what was at first a pure Christian church, was transformed into a pantheon for the preservation of a multiform idolatry.

The supremacy of the bishop of Rome was never alluded to in the first ages of Christianity. The early fathers are altogether silent regarding St. Peter's primacy, upon which this supremacy was subsequently founded. It was not until nearly the end of the second century that "this hereditary lie of the popedom"* obtained currency. At that period it began to be asserted that St. Peter was the first bishop of Rome, and that he consecrated his successor. Waiving the arguments which render it matter of doubt, even to the present day, whether St. Peter ever visited Rome at all,—we put the Roman *hypothesis* to the test of one searching question: Supposing St. Peter to have held the bishopric of Rome and to have appointed a successor from whose hands all future bishops should receive consecration by hereditary transmission of episcopal authority,—how are we to account for two centuries of silence regarding this extraordinary circumstance? how reconcile our minds to the hesitation and want of confidence with which the assertion was at first sent forth? and how overcome the startling difficulty, that no sufficient testimony has been brought forward, to this day, to support the assertion? It will not do to tell us of *tradition*, and to say that what was at first tradition, afterwards became recorded fact. There was no tradition current regarding St. Peter's bishopric, at the period when he was first said to have been the primal bishop of Rome; the originators of the assertion refer to no such tradition; at least to none sufficiently recognized to warrant its becoming the foundation of a recorded event. But, in truth, such a circumstance never *could* have commended itself with due authority to the belief of mankind, after floating for two centuries through the falsifying and uncertain medium of tradition. It was a *great* event. It ought to have been on record within the canon of Holy Scripture. We mean, that if it had been fact in place of fiction, its consequences were of such magnitude and of such vast importance to the Christian church, that it ought not to have rested on any merely human testimony, and much less ought it to have been conveyed through the unsafe channel of oral transmission from father to son. We must estimate the greatness of this event from the overwhelming assumptions which have been based upon it by the papacy. Mark the links in the papal chain: St. Peter was invested with the keys, he was the chief of the Apostles, the delegated Head of the Church; he was the first bishop of Rome; he consecrated his successor in that see; from that successor consecration and ordination have been uninterruptedly conveyed to the clergy of the Roman church; the bishops of Rome, each for the term of his episcopate, have been Christ's vicegerents on earth, clothed with the supremacy of Peter, invested with universal authority over the church on earth, and consecrated as pure fountains whence alone the streams of Divine Truth could flow! Admit St. Peter's supremacy, to which, however, the New Testament offers abundant denial;—and grant the *little* fact of his primacy in the Roman church, which has nothing worthy the name of authority to support it;—then, perhaps, some feeble show of argument may be made in favour of the remaining assumptions. We have already seen what corruptions were introduced into Christianity in the time of Constantine; let us mark as we go along the new features of the papacy as successively developed: it may be profitable to recur to them as arguments affecting the claim of the Roman church to universal supremacy.

The defenders of Romanism refer with triumph to the ancient precedence of the bishop of Rome as confirmatory of his supremacy. This precedence was, however, simply one of order, not of power. Priority of position was accorded to the Roman prelate as bishop of the metropolis of the empire, in the same manner that precedence was granted to the bishops of Antioch,

---

* D'Aubigné's Preface to the English Translation of Ranke's "Popes of Rome," published by Blackie & Son

Alexandria, Constantinople, &c., solely on account of the importance attaching to those cities. But so far from the bishop of Rome deriving from this precedence unlimited control over all the Christian churches, he did not even hold supreme authority over the Roman clergy. The seat of honour was given to him, but his authority at first did not exceed that of a president in an assembly; he preserved order and assisted in council, but his voice could not outweigh the opinions of his brethren and unduly influence their decisions. It was long after the promulgation of the first fiction of Romanism—namely, the primacy of St. Peter—that advantage was taken of it to build up the supremacy of the Roman hierarch. About the beginning of the fifth century the pontiffs and their minions fabricated what may be termed the grand romance of pope Peter's Roman episcopacy and ecclesiastical supremacy. Improving upon the first simple and unvarnished assertion, they sought to establish it by substantial evidence. "Simon a magician is introduced, accompanied by Helen a goddess, who had been taken from the Tyrian brothels, and transformed from a courtezan into a divinity. Simon, by the arts of necromancy, had obtained an infamous notoriety; and the apostle, it would appear, was conducted to Rome for the purpose of withstanding the enchanter. The new pope was opposed to the old conjurer. Simon, in presence of Nero and the whole city, flew up into the air. But Peter kneeling invoked Jesus; and the devil who had aided the magician's flight, struck with terror at the sacred name, let his emissary fall and break his leg."* This was certainly *one* way of bringing Peter to Rome and installing him in his diocese. As a sample of Roman ingenuity in the manufacture of fictions, it is not amiss. We leave it without comment. The reader who desires more *evidence* in support of Roman supremacy, may refer to the writings of Cyril, whence, in substance, the above brief but edifying extract is taken.

The true foundation of the papal supremacy is to be found quite away from the fable of St. Peter's primacy. That fable served, indeed, and still serves, as a colourable pretence for the assumptions of the Roman church; but taken apart from the circumstances of the times when this church yearned for authority and temporal wealth, it is a foundation utterly inadequate in the first instance to establish a claim to supremacy, and afterwards to sustain it. The uses which were made of that supremacy so soon as it was conceded, are sufficient evidence of the spirit in which it was sought, and an equally clear testimony that for Christian and spiritual purposes it would never have been assumed. The church of Rome was never more supreme than when amidst persecution and poverty she testified to the Truth. She could neither claim nor hope for a loftier supremacy than might have been secured by holding fast her primitive integrity. He who declared His kingdom to be not of this world, never designed that His church should deck herself in the gauds of earthly vanity, and gather around her the pride, pomp, and circumstance of a temporal empire. Looking to the time when, and the circumstances under which, the church of Rome claimed supremacy, and eventually secured it,—that very supremacy becomes an argument powerful for her overthrow. It disrobes her of every Christian grace; and exposes her to all men as a mere pretender to holiness, a greedy claimant for the power and wealth of this world, a polluter of the sanctuary, who having first cast down the ark of God, raised up the throne of her supremacy to fill its place.

The power of Romanism grew insensibly. When the Roman church was first recognized by Constantine, and for some considerable time thereafter, she made no attempt to grasp at temporal

---

* Edgar's Variations of Popery.

sovereignty. She heathenised herself from motives of policy, and made of Christianity and Idolatry a miserable jumble of ill assorting things, but she carefully avoided overstepping the bounds of ecclesiastical authority. She had, however, an eye towards the future. She gradually and silently accumulated wealth, that fulcrum of power,—and she waited the favourable moment to use it with advantage. The heathens murmured little to see the temples of their gods despoiled to furnish adornments for the Christian churches; or even to behold these temples taken entire and applied to Christian uses. A harmony had been established between idolatry and the gospel, between light and darkness, between Christ and Belial: Christianity and Idolatry began to differ in little except the name. It was not, however, desirable that Christianity should be altogether identified with heathenism. A new power was to be established, and so to be established that no fear might remain of its being afterwards absorbed back into heathenism. It was not enough, therefore, to convert idolatrous temples into Christian churches. New edifices must be constructed on a model studiously different from the old temples of Rome. These were the Basilicas, or first cathedrals, seven of which, including St. Peter's and the Lateran, were erected by order of Constantine. These ancient structures have disappeared; but their architectural magnificence is attested by the awe and admiration with which they were regarded by *barbarian* Rome.

—— the grim brood, from Arctic shores that roam'd,
(Where Italics for ever, as she wheels,
Sparkles a mother's fondness on her son,)
Stood in mute wonder 'mid the works of Rome,
When to their view the Lateran arose,
In greatness more than earthly.

Paradise, XXXI. 76—31.

In the reign of Valentinian III., the pope purchased a title of supremacy as the last authority in matters ecclesiastical. This title was disputed, and the decrees of the Roman hierarch were long resisted; but perseverance and favouring circumstances gradually confirmed this supremacy. Once invested with unlimited power in his spiritual jurisdiction, the pontiff beheld the way to temporal sovereignty open before him. Rome had by this time fallen under barbarian rule; but even the ruin of the Roman empire, operated favourably to advance and realize the pretensions of the Roman church. The barbarians brought with them a rude Christianity—a Christianity not much worse than that which prevailed in Rome. It differed however from Roman Christianity in the character of its *alloy;* the latter was incorporated with imperial idolatry, and the former was obscured by barbarian superstitions. The papacy could not, however, have desired a people more blindly superstitious than the barbarian conquerors of Rome. They yielded themselves to the church and became its tools; and this they did the more readily when they beheld their holy trees and fountains favourably regarded and recognized by the spiritual pastors of Rome. Just as the heathens were converted by admixture of heathenism with Christianity, so were the barbarians conciliated when they beheld their cherished superstitions blended with the ceremonies and ordinances of the Roman church.

It was in the sixth century, during the reign of Gregory, that the papacy boldly asserted its supremacy. Mauricius, emperor of the East, had granted the title of universal bishop to the patriarch of Constantinople. This awakened Gregory's jealousy and hostility, and in the height of his resentment he denounced the assumption as impious and profane, and endeavoured to arouse all the powers of the earth to extinguish the title. When, shortly after, Mauricius was assassinated by Phocas a centurion, Gregory sought his own advancement by flattering the murderer, and hailing him as "the joy of heaven and earth." This timely adulation was successful: Phocas conferred the title of universal bishop on the Roman pontiff, who no longer beheld in it any thing antichristian or profane. The temporal power of the papacy, though exercised to a great extent, was not, however, formally recognised until the famous grant of Pepin the Great, by which the pope was invested with the secular authority of a sovereign prince, over an assigned territory, and confirmed in his previously obtained title of supreme head of the church. From this time forward, the Roman prelate boldly exerted himself for the accomplishment of his ambitious designs; until at length the secular authority bowed to the ecclesiastical, and the pope of Rome was acknowledged to be the temporal and spiritual head of the world.

Whilst the papal supremacy was gradually establishing itself, the machinery by which it was ultimately to effect the entire subjugation of christendom was as gradually evolved. When by the mere force of reiterated assertion, the primacy of St. Peter came to be admitted as a great fundamental fact, it was necessary to join with it another *fact*, namely the unbroken succession of the Roman hierarchs in the Apostle's seat. The Apostolical Succession is undoubtedly of vital importance to the papacy, for without legitimate descent from their primate, the Roman bishops could not possibly be received as true successors of St. Peter. Difficulties apparently insurmountable are, however, to be overcome before this vaunted succession can be admitted. At a very early period there were schisms in the papacy, and rival popes, each claiming to be the true vicegerent of heaven. Subsequently there was a great disruption arising out of the removal of the papal court from Rome to Avignon; when the Christian world was distracted by the rival pretensions of contending popes, the one thundering in Italy, and the other discharging his spiritual artillery from the seat of his retirement. Amidst popes and anti-popes, French hierarchs and Roman pontiffs, anathemas and counter-anathemas, how is our judgment to be guided in determining which claimant for universal supremacy was the true vicar apostolic, and by consequence the only pure channel through whom the church was to be supplied with duly-appointed ministers? Such difficulties meeting us in our attempt to trace out the veritable successors of the apostles, might of themselves settle the question of the apostolical succession as one that can never be decided on the data of the Roman church. What, however, shall we say regarding the *value* of this descent, if we admit for argument's sake that it has been perpetuated in the papacy? In course of time the papal court became so notoriously profligate and corrupt, that the abominations of the imperial palace, to which we have already alluded, were cast into the shade by the exceeding wickedness of *spiritual princes*. The Vatican became a brothel and a slaughter-house, in which the men who blasphemously assumed the title of Christ's vicegerents on earth, boldly denounced Christianity as a lie, and devoted themselves continually to Satan as his agents for the demoralization of Rome. Let the mind picture for itself the daily routine of pontifical occupations at this period. Days spent in gluttony and excess; nights employed in works darker than the darkness that shrouded them. But the reverse of the picture is more horrible and ghastly: behold these gross feeders and midnight debauchees standing in the holy place to dispense Christian ordinances, and to bid successors in the ministry go forth to their work!

With the primacy of Peter, and the apostolical descent of the Roman hierarchs, is necessarily connected the Infallibility claimed by the sovereign pontiff of the Roman church. It must be obvious that the claim to infallibility could not be dispensed with, without endangering the supremacy of the papacy. Peter was the chief of the apostles; the authority of Peter resides exclusively in the popes: admit these propositions, and it is ridiculous to think that a pope is fallible: what would be the weight of his authority, and the value of his headship, if he could err? No: the supremacy and the infallibility of the pope must stand or fall together. There are differences of opinion regarding the infallibility, but upon the Italian system it is given to the pope personally; or when it is annexed to the church, we are told that by the church we must understand the Roman pontiff. This doctrine is acknowledged by grand councils. We shudder to read of infallibility in connection with such men as John, Boniface, and Alexander; and yet we are called upon to acknowledge that these monsters of iniquity "were enlightened with divine illumination, and were as unerring as the Son of God." This is the language in which papal eulogists speak of these hierarchs. It is amusing, however, to turn from this admission of the pontiff's infallibility, and observe the opposition which has frequently been exerted against his decrees, and the state of perplexity in which this unerring man has oftentimes been placed,—a man of whom it was once blasphemously said, in the council of the Lateran, that he possessed "power above all powers, both in heaven and earth." Grand councils, it has already been said, acknowledged the infallibility; other grand councils rejected it: the papal decrees were treated by these last with little ceremony, and on several occasions they complimented the pontiff with an anathema and the imputation of heresy. In these dilemmas, the poor pontiff had frequently much ado to decide between his infallibility and the opposition it encountered: in some cases he preserved his title to unerring wisdom by rescinding or altering his decrees, and virtually acknowledging himself to be in error. If space permitted us to enter into a more minute inquiry, we should discover that this thing named infallibility was sometimes limited, at others enlarged; that it was defined, and re-defined; and occasionally so much qualified that it and fallibility became nearly convertible terms. In fact, we should find the vicegerent of heaven to be, even in his own communion, in the melancholy position of a man ever practically in the wrong, and always theoretically right.

Supremacy in power, and infallibility in wisdom, though built upon insufficient bases, were bold and politic assumptions, powerful for the subjugation of a barbarian people. With the extinction of the empire began that long era of mental gloom so expressively denominated the Dark Ages. And let it be remembered that this gloom was not a partial cloud overhanging the city of Rome, but a night-like pall that extended its murky folds over the whole of Europe. There was no benign influence to counteract barbarian ignorance and policy. All that constitutes intellectual power was placed under ban by those rude conquerors, who owed everything to mere physical prowess, and little or nothing to the arts and adornments of civilised life. Nothing could be more acceptable to the Roman church, or more conducive to the establishment of its despotism, than the general condition of Europe on the fall of the empire. The barbarian people who then became lords paramount, were the very men to acknowledge the supremacy and further the views of an arrogant and ambitious hierarchy. Steeped to the very lips in grovelling and debasing superstitions, and possessed only of imperfect notions of Christianity, utterly insufficient to initiate them into the wisdom and power of the Gospel, but well adapted, by a singular perversity of the human mind, to render them the slaves of bigotry, these men soon came to bow themselves deferentially to the Roman church. They owned her supremacy, poured barbarian wealth into her lap, and erected at her bidding those rudely magnificent structures with which the ecclesiastical history of Europe is so extensively connected. Ecclesiastical libraries were the only depositories of learning; and to these laymen had no desire to obtain access. Thus the church monopolized learning; and the advantages she thence derived, were not employed to lift an unintellectual people from darkness into light, but to overawe that people, and bow down their necks beneath the hopeless yoke of superstition and error. The ignorance which pervaded the ranks of the laity at length extended itself to the clergy. Learning began to be regarded as no necessary preparative for the clerical profession; and so long as a man could publicly utter the offices of the church from the book, or repeat them by rote, it was deemed quite unimportant whether or not he understood the language in which they were written. But even in this, the shrewd policy of the Roman church was manifest. The ignorance of the laity had enabled her to build up her dominating throne; and it was rightly judged that an ignorant priesthood, who would never call in question the commands of their superiors, were the fittest auxiliaries to aid in supporting and propagating a system of religion based on no better foundation than a cumulus of falsehood.

Long before the mental horizon brightened with the returning dawn of literature and intellectual art, the Roman church had established herself too firmly to yield her supremacy to the improved institutions of the Middle Ages. The popular mind had become so deeply imbued with her superstitions, and had been so long accustomed to lie in entire subjection to her will, that none dared to rise up and denounce her as the great deceiver of christendom. The secular power did indeed join battle with her; but the ultimate result was rather favourable than otherwise to her supremacy. She wielded a power neither of earth nor heaven: she terrified the hosts of her adversaries by excommunication and anathema, and by a fearful display of vengeance—impotent it is true, yet before which the daring soldier shrunk back pale and terror-stricken. Taught from earliest infancy to regard the pope as God, and the external rites of Roman worship as the only passport to heaven, he quailed before a sentence that cut him off from all participation in religious ordinances, and cast him forth as an impious and heretical wretch whose contact none might endure without incurring a like sentence, and surrendering himself to everlasting torments in the world to come. The ordinary weapons of warfare could not contend against a power like this: they secured a temporary victory on the battle-field, and seemed to threaten the authority of the church in secular matters; but, in truth, they achieved nothing; the discomfited pontiff ascended his spiritual tribunal, and christendom trembled at denunciations that made the conqueror pall in resolution whilst the wreath of victory was green upon his brow.

At an early period when gloom and austerity were accounted Christian graces, the monastic spirit began to prevail. Men were persuaded to yield up all their temporal wealth to the church. This wealth was devoted to the building and endowment of religious houses; and the pious donors retired from the world to become the Superiors of these institutions. Both men and women, of noble and even of regal rank, frequently devoted themselves and their riches to religious purposes, under the assurance that by such sacrifices they made effectual and sufficient atonement for the grossest enormities, and secured beyond all doubt their final admission to a future state of bliss. These monasteries became fruitful nurseries of superstition and crime. The inmates of these institutions, cut off from all human sympathies, and brooding in melancholy, mistook altogether the spirit and design of the Gospel. Painful penance was substituted for Christian endurance; Roman dogmas for Christian truth; and a wearying, lifeless round of monotonous rite and ceremony, for that reasonable service which God requires from his creatures. The celibacy of the Romish clergy rendered the monasteries a useful machinery in the hands of the church. No tie of husband, wife, child, was suffered to interfere with the utter subjection of the monk to the will of his Superior. Subsequently, indeed, these institutions became dens of infamous iniquity; but for a considerable period the religious vow appears to have been faithfully observed; and when it became no better than a shallow device, the church could afford to wink at depravity which, stealthily indulged, secured her votaries without endangering her power. The monks proved faithful emissaries of the church; they insinuated themselves into the bosom of families, and reigned like little popes in the sphere of their visitations. They taught the people that implicit obedience to the church, and a rigid performance of external ceremony, constituted the sum and substance of religion. It may easily be conceived that in course of time, religious error was not the only evil that monkish intercourse introduced into social life. We are compelled to believe that at an early period these visitations were used as a means of procuring a criminal solace for the unnatural restrictions imposed upon ecclesiastics by the laws of the church.

The primacy of Peter, the apostolical succession, the supremacy of the Roman church and its infallibility in the person of its pontiff, were not empty assumptions merely designed to gild a pageant and minister to ostentatious display. They were artfully contrived means for the attainment of a great end,—namely, the entire subjection of the temporal to the spiritual power, and the final deposit of all authority in the hands of the Roman pontiff. This end was attained when kings consented to hold their crowns and kingdoms as vassals of the pope, and ranged themselves under his banner as the creatures of his will. War and peace were then dependent upon the fiat of the Roman see; and compacts were formed or alliances dissolved in submissive obedience to papal command. If any rebellious "son of the church" dared to resist the mandate of Rome, his subjects were instantly released from their allegiance, and compelled to throw off his authority. If monarch and people united in obstinate resistance, the whole kingdom was laid under ecclesiastical censure. In this case all religious ordinances were suspended, the consolations of religion were refused to the sick and dying, and even the dead were left exposed on the highway to rot beneath the sun. The accumulated curse of a national interdict was too dreadful to be borne. Men could not at once shake off the superstitions that enthralled them. After a vain resistance they submitted unconditionally to the church, whose policy it well suited to receive back her rebellious children so soon as they gave signs of contrition and obedience. The power thus to wield mankind at will could not be maintained without blood. The spirit of liberty would occasionally arise and level her spear against the usurpations of Rome. Communities and nations of men rose up from time to time to resist even to the death the spiritual and temporal bondage of the papacy. What was to be done with men who laughed at anathemas, and mocked at the highest pains and penalties the church could inflict? The crusade was preached; and "the army of God" went forth to sweep from the earth, if it were possible, the very remembrance of a people who had dared to array themselves against the vicegerent of heaven. Neither sex nor age escaped in the universal slaughter. And happy, indeed, were they who fell in the fury of the conflict, before the oppressor had leisure to refine upon cruelty and devise ingenious torments. The heart bounds with indignation, yet sickens, at the hellish atrocities perpetrated by the "warriors of the cross." Their victims were destroyed by tortures too dreadful in agony and too disgusting in detail to be openly unveiled. Yet these filthy and inhuman deeds do stand on record, an imperishable testimony against the blood-stained church of Rome.

Whilst the papacy visited with its terrors all heretics and resisters of its will, it could not (or did not) silence the satirical tongues that were busy with its fame. Its assumed sanctity and the immoral lives of its priesthood were suffered to become the theme of sarcasm, and that too with something very like impunity. Shortly after the revival of letters in Italy, the most powerful and elegant writers employed their pens in exposing the charlatanism of the church and the sensual lives of the clergy. The Decameron of Boccaccio reflects the habits of the Italian priesthood too faithfully: the power of his satire and the elegance of his style scarcely compensate for the gross immoralities of his writings. The severe Dante, in the latter part of the thirteenth century, scourged Roman imposture and wickedness with a merciless lash. His strictures equal in severity anything that has been said of the church of Rome since the days of the Reformation:

> ———————the book of God
> Is forced to yield to man's authority,
> Or from its straightness warp'd: so reckoning made
> What blood the sowing of it in the world
> Has cost; what favour for himself he wins,
> Who meekly clings to it. The aim of all
> Is how to shine; e'en they, whose office is
> To preach the Gospel, let the Gospel sleep,
> And pass their own inventions off instead.
> One tells, how at Christ's suffering the wan moon
> Bent back her steps, and shadow'd o'er the sun
> With interrenient disk, as she withdrew:
> Another, how the light shrouded itself
> Within its tabernacle, and left dark
> The Spaniard, and the Indian, with the Jew.
> Such fables Florence in her pulpit hears,
> Bandied about more frequent, than the names
> Of Bindi and of Lapi in her streets.
> The sheep, meanwhile, poor witless ones, return
> From pasture, fed with wind; and what avails
> For their excuse, they do not see their harm?
> Christ said not to his first convent̃icle,
> 'Go forth and preach imposture to the world,'
> But gave them truth to build on; and the sound
> Was mighty on their lips: nor needed they
> Beside the Gospel, other spear or shield,
> To aid them in their warfare for the faith.
> The preacher now provides himself with store
> Of jests and gibes; and, so there be no lack
> Of laughter, while he vents them, his big cowl
> Distends, and he has won the meed he sought:
> Could but the vulgar catch a glimpse the while
> Of that dark bird which nestles in his hood,
> They scarce would wait to hear the blessing said.
> Which now the dotards hold in such esteem,
> That every counterfeit, who spreads abroad
> The hands of holy promise, finds a throng
> Of credulous fools beneath.

Intoxicated with her supremacy, the Roman church became singularly unmindful of the means by which that supremacy had been secured, and as singularly negligent in provision for the perpetuation of her power. She had bowed the minds of men by the austerities of ecclesiastical discipline, and the apparent sanctity of clerical life; she had chained kings to her footstool by a bold and haughty defiance of all secular authority. She ought not to have thrown aside the mask that awed the multitude; she ought not to have permitted jest, satire, sarcasm, and exposure to undermine that supremacy which she had extorted from the *fears* of mankind. Yet both of these she did: she unveiled herself, in the lives of her clergy, as a thing foul alike in morals and in faith; and she suffered her abominations to be chronicled against her, and to become the theme of ridicule and licensed mockery. This was a sad mistake. It was a shallow policy to exhaust ecclesiastical vengeance on impugners of her rites and doctrines, and to terrify with denunciations and anathemas all who lifted a strong arm against her supremacy; and then in a mere bravado of reliance upon the power she had accumulated, to adopt no sufficient means for intimidating the satirist and jester whose daily attacks were rendering her a by-word and a proverb, even in her immediate realm of Italy. The papacy began to be a fearful, hated thing: her abominations were loathsome in the eyes of mankind; but the antagonist power which was ultimately to free the nations from her chains, was yet in its infancy, and men continued to yield a submission which she had still sufficient authority to compel.

At the very time when austerity of discipline, assumed sanctity of life, and bold assertion of unlimited power, were essentially necessary for the safety of the papacy, at that time it was that she relaxed her wonted jealous guard over her supremacy—at the very moment when watch and ward were most necessary. The thick darkness, in the midst of which the corruptions and assumptions of the Roman church had their birth, and whose shadow was the only wall of defence around the papacy, began to disperse. Knowledge began to be diffused; literature and art revived; men began to *think*. Circumstances combined to threaten the permanency of Romanism.

Despotism, whether temporal or spiritual, can be established only in a *dark age*. The mass of the people must be blinded and *cowed* by ignorance to render them the unresisting slaves of a tyrant, whether his chains manacle the bodily limbs, or the diviner part, the mind. Ecclesiastical despotism, of all others, is the most offensive to an enlightened people. Men who can read and think, fail to discover in the Gospel any delegation of authority to human hands by which one man, or even a body of men, can hold communities and nations in a perpetual and oppressive thraldom. They perceive that Christianity is *persuasive*, not compulsive; and that true religion stands distinguished from false religion principally in this,—that she neither wounds with the sword nor galls with the fetter, but wins followers by gentleness and kindness, and expressions of love.

The revival of letters, the return of civilization throughout Europe, the advance of refinement, the march of the spirit of freedom,—these together formed a strong combination against the temporal and spiritual tyranny of a church, whose rites and ceremonies, dogmas and doctrines were, one and all, mere cunningly devised fables suited only to an age of ignorant credulity. From her first false assumption to the time when her supremacy was admitted, the Roman church had to maintain a continual struggle; but she had to sustain a fearful contest when her gross filthiness had rendered her a jest, when she had suffered her lewdness to become "the burden of a merry song," and when the light of literature and expanding knowledge made open discovery of the hollow and rotten basis upon which she stood. The unchristian doctrines and practices of Romanism were impugned at an early age; and the annals of martyrdom record the active zeal and the dying agonies of men who lifted up a testimony for the Truth, whilst the world around them was lying under Roman bondage. These were the bright and particular stars that shone forth from time to time in the long and dark night of superstition and error. The destruction of these *heretics* seemed for the time to confirm the power of the papacy; but these high examples of Christian heroism were not forgotten; in due time they came up as great precedents to urge on the argument of truth against falsehood. When the Reformation burst forth in resistless might through the instrumentality of Luther,

The solitary monk that shook the world,

then were the first martyrs appealed to as arbiters in the contest, as men who had skilfully set the battle in array, but fell before the victory was won.

Pitiful were the shifts, desperate were the expedients, to which Romanism resorted to ward off the attacks of Luther; at one time endeavouring to intimidate by anathema, at another trying all the arts of Jesuitical persuasion to turn the Reformer from his purpose. But the standard of Truth had been unfurled in God's appointed time: disaffection to the papacy spread; and the Roman pontiff, bewildered and perplexed, became almost a supplicant for his supremacy. The world beheld a great phenomenon. Papal supremacy was *triumphantly* resisted; and no mean section of christendom left the Roman communion for ever. From this shock the papacy has never recovered to the present hour. She continued thereafter to maintain a certain influence, but as we shall presently see this was maintained, and still continues to exist, only by sufferance of the temporal powers in alliance with her. In her extremity, the papacy again employed the cunning which she seems in part to have laid aside in her days of palmy prosperity. She began to affect great moderation; ceased to obtrude her secular authority; and retired within the privacy of her spiritual functions. Since the days of the Reformation, the position of the Roman church has been—to compare great things with small—that of a fettered malefactor armed with a lash to scourge his fellows in bondage. It was only by stooping both her temporal and spiritual sovereignty to the secular powers, that a sufferance was accorded her of vending her delusions throughout the civilized world. Kings and emperors were once reduced to hold the stirrup of the Roman pontiff; the latter came in turn to be an obsequious dependant upon secular rulers. Of late years the temporal power of the papacy has been shaken to its very foundations; and but for the support afforded by the presence of French troops, the miserable and effete ecclesiastical government would long ere now have been supplanted, either by an independent commonwealth, or a constitutional sovereignty like that now established over the greater part of the Italian peninsula. The year 1848 witnessed the humiliating spectacle for papal christendom of the successor of St. Peter obliged to flee in the disguise of a lacquey, to avoid the vengeance of his infuriated subjects, and take refuge in the adjoining kingdom of Naples. Though enabled by foreign intervention to return again and resume his apostolic sway, his subsequent occupancy of St. Peter's chair has been productive of anything but increased reliance on the stability and beneficial results of the pontifical government. Already have the fairest provinces of the Papal States succeeded in shaking off the yoke and incorporating themselves with the Italian kingdom, and nothing now remains of the Church's patrimony but the city of Rome and surrounding territory. Among many judicious Catholics the non-essentiality of temporal sovereignty to the dignity and spiritual power of the head of the church has come to be largely recognized. To this consummation the aspect of affairs at Rome is evidently inclining; and in the event of the death of Pius IX., it is not likely that the partizans of arbitrary government, whether civil or spiritual, will be able to force on the Roman people the renewal of a sway which has rested like a dead weight on their energies and progress for so many ages.

It is undoubtedly a fearful thing in a religious point of view to behold a nation clinging to the blasphemous idolatries of the Roman church as the refuge of their future hopes. But never let it be imagined that the faded power of the papacy can be recovered. Let none fret themselves with anxiety lest any untoward revolution of affairs restore the supremacy of the Roman hierarch, and re-introduce into Protestant countries those fearful engines of wrath and destruction over which the dust of ages has been accumulating. The cell of the Inquisition, and the chamber of torture, are obsolete enormities, never again to be tolerated in countries where wholesome government has long prevailed, and where the people have acquired a knowledge of Christianity sufficient, at least, to teach them that captivity and torture are not its recognized means of conversion. Before the crusade can be preached, and a papal army make irruption into Protestant countries to win men back to Romanism, by the persuasive arguments of fire and sword, and all manner of torments,—there must first come over all christendom a mental and a moral darkness, such as the world has never yet known; the human mind must stoop to a degradation too revolting to be contemplated; and even the pulse of freedom, which has hitherto beat, however faintly, in the veins of the veriest slave, must become motionless and extinct. The Dark Ages with all their barbarian ignorance, the feudal system with all its degrading oppressions,—could these return again, they would be unequal to the task of restoring Roman supremacy in Protestant lands. That supremacy, it is true, arose under their auspices; but men *knew* not the power they nursed and fostered. A superstitious and ignorant people regarded with awe and veneration the sanctity and austerity which veiled the ultimate designs of the Roman church; but could they have penetrated into her secret purposes, they would not have so laboured to build up a tyranny that was to crush their posterity. Whatever temporal changes, therefore, shall come in future times upon Protestant nations, even though they should extend to the return of barbarism and ignorance, they will offer no facilities for the restoration of papal supremacy. Men would have to *forget* the character of Romanism before they could be again deceived.

We hear, indeed, in the present day, somewhat too much of the conversion of individuals, both lay and clerical, to the communion of the Roman church. So far as these individuals themselves are concerned, we must deplore their secession from the Protestant faith; but it is little less than ridiculous to give these desertions the weight of a great national calamity. Many motives may be assigned for this falling away; *any* motive, save that of love for a system of religion so full of manifest error, and so debased by crime. The laic may be one whose heart has ever remained unimpressed by the simple ritual of a reformed church, and who has therefore sought in Roman worship for that false excitement which can alone render religion tolerable to him. The cleric may be one who has vacillated and wavered between the extreme limits of the outward and visible form of Christianity; changing his creed like his coat,—

"To one thing constant never."

Or, he may be one who made ill choice of a profession, when he took his vow of ordination as a minister of Christ, yet so little understood the nature of the service upon which he had entered as to deem it merely a patent for supremacy of place.

If there is a church professing to be reformed, that exhibits Romish tendencies, and evinces an anxiety to fraternize with the papacy, we cannot deny that this is a great national calamity: still we may over estimate the calamity of a relapsing church. The evil to be deplored rests mainly in this: that the people will be left churchless; no fear ought to be entertained lest they follow their pastors into Romanism. When the laity secede to Rome, it is for license or excitement; when the clergy move thither, it is to recover somewhat of that supremacy which the churches of the Reformation denied to Rome, and claimed not for themselves. Hence, the clergy and the laity will never be seen travelling to Rome in company with each other. The truth of this general proposition is not affected by the isolated exceptions which the present day affords.

Rome can be appreciated only by educated minds. To nine out of every ten tourists who toil their weary way thither, in obedience to the dictates of wealth and fashion, the city of the seven hills presents an exterior of some beauty, but of much less interest than is generally supposed. Without their classical and historical associations, the remains of ancient Rome, with few exceptions, are masses of ruin and desolation, upon which the tourist may cast a passing glance, and marvel that such heaps of rubbish are suffered to lie undisturbed. In the department of art, educational preparatives are not less necessary; for to what purpose is it, to look upon paintings and statues with an eye that can appreciate only colossal size or brilliancy of colour ! And with regard to the people of Italy, their manners and customs, their institutions, their church ceremonies,—in short, everything that distinguishes Italy and the Italians from any other country and people,—how little is to be rightly observed or understood by those whose minds are not imbued with liberal learning, and stored with a well-digested knowledge of Roman history from the building of the city to the extinction of the empire, and thence through countless vicissitudes to the present aspect and condition of modern Rome. That the majority of visitants to the eternal city are utterly incompetent to form any just estimate of what is there presented before them, is abundantly evident from the vapid dulness of their reports when they return home. And amongst those who favour the world with their Recollections of Rome, how few record anything beyond the merest common-place,—shreds and patches of information gathered from ignorant ciceroni, interwoven with a sickly sentimentalism, so ineffably ridiculous that it touches only the risible faculties. Byron has said, truly and beautifully—

> Rome is as the desert, where we stand
> Stumbling o'er recollections.

In one sense or other, all find the desert, but few comparatively stumble over a recollection worth recollecting.

The antiquities of Rome refer for the most part to the times of the empire. Of the kingly period a few remains may be traced by the industrious antiquary: viz. the Mamertine Prisons, begun by Ancus Martius, and enlarged by Servius Tullius; the Cloaca Maxima of Tarquinius Priscus; and a portion of the celebrated rampart of Servius Tullius. The monuments of the republican era are likewise few. This period was not favourable to the erection of great public edifices: the Romans were continually engaged in wars that allowed few intervals of rest; and moreover the nature of the consular government was too transient for the accomplishment of such works as were afterwards designed and consummated by the emperors. The boast of Augustus, to which we have before referred, that he found Rome of brick and left it of marble, is a strong testimony that the city, during the republican period, contained few erections remarkable for magnificence. Nearly at the close of this period several public works were constructed, whose remains form nearly all the relics that can certainly be identified with consular Rome. The most considerable of these were the military ways paved with large blocks of lava; and the magnificent Via Appia, constructed by Appius Claudius, which still remains perfect through a great portion of its course. Of the ancient republican temples, that of Fortuna Virilis, now the church of Santa Maria Egizziaca, is the only one existing; if we except some substructions below the walls of San Nicolo in Carcere, and four columns of the temple of Hercules Custos in the cloisters of the Sommaschi. The remains of the Marcian Aqueduct, of the Theatre of Pompey, and of several bridges, refer to the age of the Republic. But the most remarkable memorials of this period are the tombs on the Appian Way, many of which are commemorative of men whose names are identified with the glory of Rome.

Under Augustus Rome assumed a magnificence she had never known before. It was the aim of this emperor to extend the limits of the city, and to embellish it with works of splendour and luxury. The palace of the Cæsars on the Palatine; and the temples, arcades, theatres, and innumerable buildings of the Campus Martius, were amongst the works of Augustus. The existing relics of this reign are the remains of a Forum, in which are three columns of the Temple of Saturn; three beautiful columns at the angle of the Palatine, supposed to be ruins of a Temple of Minerva; the mausoleum of the emperor between the Corso and the Tiber; and a few others. Agrippa, the friend and favourite of Augustus, erected the Pantheon, which remains to this day the most perfect monument of ancient Rome:

Pantheon! Pride of Rome!
Relic of nobler days, and noblest arts!

Tiberius began the Prætorian Camp; built the Temple of Ceres and Proserpine, some remnants of which still exist in the church of Santa Maria in Cosmedin at the Bocca di Verita; and added considerably to the palace on Mount Palatine. Claudius constructed the magnificent aqueduct which continues to be an object of admiration to the world. When the palace of the Cæsars was destroyed in the general conflagration of Rome, Nero raised in its place his famous Golden House, whose extent was not less remarkable than its amazing splendour. This emperor rebuilt a large portion of the city; and completed the circus of Caligula, wherein the first Christians were "butchered to make a Roman holiday." The Flavian Amphitheatre, better known as the Coliseum, (so named from the colossal statue of Nero—placed in it) was begun by Vespasian and finished by Titus. It is said to have been erected by the compulsory labour of twelve thousand Jews and Christians. It contained, during the public shows, one hundred and ten thousand spectators, of whom above ninety thousand were seated. This vast building is supported by three rows of columns, of which the lowest is of the Doric, the second of the Ionic, and the highest of the Corinthian order. The inclosures for the wild animals are still standing. This structure is regarded as the noblest ruin in existence.

> A Ruin—yet what ruin! from its mass
> Walls, palaces, half-cities, have been rear'd;
> Yet oft the enormous skeleton ye pass,
> And marvel where the spoil could have appear'd.
> Hath it indeed been plunder'd, or but clear'd?
> Alas! developed, opens the decay,
> When the colossal fabric's form is near'd:
> It will not bear the brightness of the day,
> Which streams too much on all years, man, have reft away.
>
> But when the rising moon begins to climb
> Its topmost arch, and gently pauses there;
> When the stars twinkle through the loops of time,
> And the low night-breeze waves along the air
> The garland-forest, which the gray walls wear,
> Like laurels on the bald first Cæsar's head;
> When the light shines serene but doth not glare,
> Then in this magic circle raise the dead;
> Heroes have trod this spot—'t is on their dust ye tread.
>
> "While stands the Coliseum, Rome shall stand;
> When falls the Coliseum, Rome shall fall;
> And when Rome falls—the world." From our own land,
> Thus spake the pilgrims o'er this mighty wall
> In Saxon times, which we are wont to call
> Ancient; and these three mortal things are still
> On their foundations.
>
> *Childe Harold.*

Domitian constructed the beautiful arch commemorative of the destruction of Jerusalem by Titus. The Mausoleum of Hadrian is now the Castle of St. Angelo, and the Bridge of St. Angelo was formerly the Pons Ælius leading to the tomb of this emperor. The baths of Caracalla are remarkable from the extent of their existing ruins, and also as being the depository whence the Farnese Hercules, the Toro Farnese, the Torso of the Belvidere, and other celebrated statues of antiquity were taken. The preceding are a few of the most striking remains of antiquity in Rome. It is matter of wonder that so many remains exist to the present day. The barbarian conquerors of Rome sought to efface all memory of its magnificence; and the vestiges they spared were afterwards subjected to a more systematic spoliation by the ecclesiastical power which became dominant after the time of Constantine. Not only were the ruins seized upon as ready material for the construction of new edifices, but even the Coliseum and other noble structures were regarded as quarries for the use of the papal architects. Notwithstanding this wholesale pillage and destruction, enough remains to form the mausoleum of the Roman empire.

We shall confine our further notices of the city, to the descriptions of the scenes and objects which form the subjects of our illustrations.

THE PIAZZA DEL POPOLO,

FROM THE PINCIAN HILL.

The Piazza del Popolo, the first spot within the walls of Rome upon which the traveller from the north of Europe sets his foot, is a spacious but irregular piazza, entered by the Porta del Popolo, a modern substitute for the Flaminian gate. The present portal, built by Vignola in 1561, from the designs of Michael Angelo, is of the Doric order; and in the intercolumniations are statues of St. Peter and St. Paul. The inner front, completed under Alexander VII. from designs by Bernini, is ornamented with decorations intended to commemorate the visit to Rome in 1667 of Christina Queen of Sweden.

On entering the gate, the first object that strikes the observer is the fine Egyptian obelisk of red granite, erected by Fontana in 1589, during the pontificate of Sixtus V. This is one of the two obelisks said to have been placed by Rhamses I. in front of the Temple of the Sun at Heliopolis, the On of Scripture. The site of this ancient city is now marked by the remaining obelisk. The one under review is coeval with Moses. It was removed to Rome by Augustus after the conquest of Egypt, and erected in the Circus Maximus, where, in the time of Valentinian, it had fallen from its pedestal, broken into three pieces. It remained buried in the earth until 1587, when it was removed, and shortly after placed in its present position. The length of the shaft alone is seventy-eight feet; and the entire height from the ground to the cross with which it is surmounted, is one hundred and sixteen feet. It still bears an inscription testifying that its dedication to the Sun was renewed by Augustus.

Beyond the obelisk are two churches with domes and façades alike;—the one, Santa Maria in Monte Santo, and the other, Santa Maria de' Miracoli. The street in the centre between the churches is the Corso, the principal street in Rome, leading through the heart of the city to the capital. This street is celebrated for the horse-races held in it during the carnival. The avenue on the right of the Corso is the Via Ripetta, running parallel with the Tiber to its principal quay, the Porto di Ripetta; and the street on the left is the Via Babuino, leading to the Piazza di Spagna, and thence direct to the Quirinal Hill. On the left of this street lies the high ground of the Monte Pincio, whence our view is taken. During the occupation by the French, under General Miollis, this mount was beautifully laid out into public gardens, terraces, and walks, and led to the French Academy,—formerly the Villa Medici,—and to the church of the Trinità de' Monti. This last named edifice contains one of the finest Italian pictures,—the " Descent from the Cross," by Daniello di Volterra. This work of art having been greatly injured by time, the French attempted to remove it, with a view to its future preservation. They placed a flat frame-work against the picture, and sawed down the face of the wall with great labour; but when they had succeeded in detaching the painting, the wall fell before it could be removed and destroyed it. A few fragments only of the genuine production have been preserved. On the Pincian Hill, and near the Trinità de' Monti, were formerly the houses of Poussin and Claude. Many modern artists have established their studies in the same locality,—probably with the hope that the mantle of departed genius may there descend upon them.

Our illustrative view, taken from the public walk of the Monte Pincio, commands a great extent of modern Rome, and embraces amongst other features St. Peter's and the vast range

of the Vatican Palace, the Castle of St. Angelo, the distant Monte Mario, and the Janiculum Hill. The Tower, nearly in the fore-ground of the view, belongs to the church of Santa Maria del Popolo. This structure, founded in 1099, is reported to occupy the spot where the ashes of Nero were found and scattered to the winds. The victims of his cruelty were said to haunt the neighbourhood, and terrify the inhabitants, until the erection of a church appeased their manes and gave a sacred character to the locality. This church contains a statue of Jonah by Raphael. It is a work of great merit, and incontestably proves that this artist, like Michael Angelo, might have risen to the highest fame in sculpture, if he had chosen to withdraw his attention from painting. Raphael died at the early age of thirty-seven, and left behind him more pictures and designs of immortal excellence than were executed by the hand, or ever emanated from the mind, of any other painter.

SAINT PETER'S.

—lo! the dome—the vast and wondrous dome,
To which Diana's marvel was a cell!

. . . .

. . . .

Rome: its grandeur overwhelms thee not;
And why? It is not lessened; but thy mind,
Expanded by the genius of the spot,
Has grown colossal.
Childe Harold.

THE Basilica Vaticana, or church of St. Peter, at Rome, is the most stupendous and magnificent temple in the Christian world. It stands between the Janiculum and Vatican hills, and occupies the site of the Circus of Nero,—a spot memorable for the sufferings endured there by the Christian martyrs, whom Nero accused of having caused the conflagration of Rome.

So early as A. D. 90, Anacletus, bishop of Rome, built an oratory where St. Peter's now stands to commemorate the martyrs. In 306 Constantine the Great erected a basilica on the same spot, which continued from that time to be the great attraction of the Christian world. In the reign of Nicholas V., 1450, the building had fallen into ruin, and that prelate set about its reconstruction. It had then stood eleven centuries, and was tottering to its fall. To pope Julius, however, is due the honour of having commenced with vigour the present magnificent structure. Under the advice of Bramante, the walls of the old basilica were razed; and on the 18th of April, 1506, Julius laid the first stone of one of those enormous pillars that support the dome. This was done with all the ceremonies which the importance of the undertaking, and the grandeur of the occasion demanded. This stupendous work was carried on during the reigns of thirty-five popes, which extended to nearly three centuries. It was ultimately completed by the erection of the sacristy, at the end of the year 1794, and under the pontificate of Pius VI. The cost of this great work exceeded twelve millions sterling. The sums which its construction demanded impoverished the resources of the church, and led under Leo X. to the adoption of the sale of Indulgences as a means of providing funds for carrying on the undertaking. It must strike the mind as a most remarkable fact, that the erection of this vast temple gave a fatal blow to that very supremacy which it was intended to glorify and exalt. Had the progress of St. Peter's not required funds far beyond the ordinary means of the church, the sale of indulgences had perhaps never been devised, and the circumstances which led indirectly to the Reformation would not have taken place.

St. Peter's is approached by a wide street conducting in a straight line from the Bridge and Castle of St. Angelo. On entering the court, the spectator views two colonnades, each consisting of four rows of lofty pillars, sweeping off to the right and left in a bold semicircle. In the centre of the area which these colonnades inclose stands an Egyptian obelisk of granite, ascending to the height of one hundred and thirty feet, and on each side of it plays a fountain whose waters fall into a basin of porphyry. Two covered galleries, three hundred and sixty feet long, and twenty-three feet broad, connect the colonnades with the vestibule of the church, which is approached by three successive flights of marble steps. The front of St. Peter's is supported by a single row of Corinthian pillars and pilasters, and is adorned with an attic, a balustrade, and thirteen colossal statues. Above the façade rises the matchless dome which, whether viewed from the outside or the inside of the building, constitutes the chief feature in the edifice. Two smaller domes, or cupolas, complete the front view.

The interior of this magnificent temple is best described in the language of Eustace, which by a Procrustean process we adapt to our narrow limits.

Five lofty portals open into the portico or vestibule, a gallery equal in dimensions and decorations to the most spacious cathedrals. It is four hundred feet in length, seventy in height, and fifty in breadth, paved with variegated marble, covered with a gilt vault, adorned with pillars, pilasters, mosaics, and basso-relievos, and terminated by equestrian statues of Constantine and Charlemagne. A fountain at each extremity supplies a stream sufficient to keep a reservoir always full, in order to carry off every unseemly object, and perpetually refresh and purify the air and pavement. Opposite the five portals of the vestibule are the five doors of the church; three are adorned with pillars of the finest marble; the one in the middle has valves of bronze. Advancing up the nave, the spectator's attention is directed to the variegated marble pavement, and the golden vault that rises above his head. But how great is his astonishment when he reaches the altar, and standing in the centre of the church, contemplates the four superb vistas that open around him; and then raises his eyes to the dome resting on its four colossal piers, glowing with mosaics, and extending like a firmament, at the prodigious elevation of four hundred feet. Around the dome rise four cupolas, small when compared with the vast concave they neighbour, but of great boldness when considered separately. Three cupolas on each side of the nave cover the divisions of the aisles; and other six, of greater dimensions, canopy as many chapels. The whole of these inferior domes are lined with mosaics. The high altar stands under the great dome, beneath a canopy supported by four twisted pillars fifty feet in height. The entire height of the canopy, including the massive pedestal upon which the pillars rest, is one hundred and thirty-two feet. Behind the high altar stands the Cathedral, or *Chair*, of St. Peter, an enormous structure of bronze, consisting of a group of four gigantic figures of so many fathers of the Greek and Latin churches, supporting the throne of the apostolical primate. This edifice is seventy feet in height, and is occupied on gala days by the pope.

Beneath the high altar are the remains of the old Basilica of Constantine, in which is the tomb of St. Peter. The descent is by a double flight of steps into an area, whose walls, forming the approach to the tomb, are enriched with alabaster, lapis lazuli, verd antique, and beautiful marbles. The rails which surround this space are adorned with one hundred and twelve bronze cornucopiæ which serve as supporters to as many silver lamps that burn continually in honour of the apostle. The entrance to the tomb is by bronze folding doors; and by the same area the sacred grottoes may be visited, in which are deposited the remains of emperors, pontiffs, and princes. Amongst the tombs of St. Peter's, the most remarkable one to English visitants is the monument of the Stuarts, which commemorates those pseudo-monarchs, James III., Charles III., and Henry IX., kings of England! The smile with which the inflated inscription is usually read may not, however, conceal the fact, that these descendants of a long line of royal ancestry "had the crown" in hereditary prospective, and were denied the regal seat by the voice of the people only when their dynasty had manifested unfitness to govern. Kings may learn wisdom at the tomb of the Stuarts.

The ascent to the roof of St. Peter's is by a well-lighted staircase, winding round with an ascent so gentle that mules can ascend two abreast with the greatest ease. When the spectator reaches the platform of the roof, he is astonished at the number of cupolas, domes, and pinnacles that rise around him; and the galleries that spread on all sides, and the many apartments and staircases that appear in every quarter. Crowds of workmen are to be seen passing and repassing in every direction, and the whole has rather the form of a town than that of the roof of an edifice. It is here only that the dimensions of the dome can be felt in all their force. The vast platform of stone on which it reposes as on a solid rock; the lofty colonnade that rises on this platform, and by its resistance counteracts, as a continued buttress, the horizontal pressure of the dome, all of stone of such prodigious swell and circumference; the lantern which like a lofty temple sits on its towering summit; these are objects which must excite the astonishment of every spectator. The access to every part, and the ascent even to the inside of the ball upon which the terminal cross rests, is perfectly safe and commodious.

The illustrative view, taken from the gardens of the Janiculum Hill, by Eastlake, embraces a noble prospect not only of St. Peter's and its magnificent approaches, but also of the entire range of the Vatican Palace: it is proper, therefore, that we offer some brief notice of the latter structure.

The Vatican* was erected by different architects at different eras, and for very different

---

* The Vatican Hill is supposed to derive its name from the prophecies or oracles (*Vaticinia*) formerly delivered there by the seers, or soothsayers. We find allusions to this mount in the Latin poets:—

    Reddderet laudes tibi Vaticani
    Montis imago.   *Horace, Odes* I. 20. 7.

That the echo of the Vatican Mount may repeat thy praises.

    Aut quis
    Simpuvium ridere Numæ, nigrumque catinum,
    Et Vaticano fragiles de monte patellas
    Ausus erat?   *Juvenal, Sat.* vi. 341.

    Or who
    Dared to deride the wooden bowl of Numa, and the black dish,
    And the brittle ware from the Vatican Mount.   *Madan.*

Juvenal alludes to the sacrificial vessels, some of which were made from the clay of the Vatican Hill.

purposes; and it is rather an assemblage of palaces than one regular structure. A palace appears to have been attached to the basilica from a very early period, probably from the time of Constantine. In the eighth century Charlemagne resided in the palace of the Vatican during his coronation by Leo III. In the twelfth century, the building having gone to decay, it was reconstructed by Innocent III.; and a century later it was enlarged by Nicholas III. After the return of the popes from Avignon, in 1377, this palace became the papal residence, since which time successive pontiffs have laboured to make it "the largest and most beautiful palace of the Christian world." It is now the theatre of some of the most imposing ceremonies of the Romish church; the repository of the records of ancient science, and the temple of the arts of Greece and Rome.

All the great architects and artists whom Rome has produced were, each in his age, employed upon the Vatican. The extent of the structure is immense, and includes an area of twelve hundred feet in length, and a thousand feet in breadth. Its elevation is proportionate, and the number of apartments it contains almost incredible. Galleries and porticos sweep around it and through it in all directions, and open an easy access to every quarter. Its halls and saloons are all on a great scale, and by their multitude and loftiness alone give an idea of magnificence truly Roman. The walls are adorned or rather animated by the genius of Raphael and Michael Angelo. The furniture is plain, and ought to be so: finery would be misplaced in the Vatican, and would sink into insignificance in the midst of the great, the vast, the sublime, which are the predominating features or rather the very genii of the place. The grand entrance is from the portico of St. Peter's by the Scala Regia, the most superb staircase in the world, consisting of four flights of marble steps, adorned with a double row of marble Ionic pillars. This staircase springs from the equestrian statue of Constantine which terminates the portico on one side; and whether seen thence, or viewed from the gallery leading on the same side to the colonnades, forms a perspective of singular beauty.

It were vain to attempt a description of the Vatican throughout. It must suffice to refer very briefly to two or three leading points of attraction.

The library consists of a double gallery of two hundred and twenty feet long, opening into another of eight hundred feet, with various rooms, cabinets, and apartments annexed. These galleries and apartments are all vaulted, and adorned with paintings embracing a vast range of sacred and profane subjects. The books are kept in cases; and, in the Vatican, the student seeks in vain for that pompous display of volumes, which he may have seen and admired in other libraries. The number of volumes and manuscripts in this library has been so variously stated, that little reliance can be placed on any of the authorities. The most moderate computation fixes the number of the manuscripts, at the present time, at nearly twenty-four thousand, and that of the books at thirty thousand. The library is open daily, except during the recess, and every facility of reference is afforded to learned travellers by the keepers and interpreters. It could scarcely be thought that in modern times an institution like this, which ought to be respected and held inviolate by the whole civilized world, would suffer injury even from an invader; yet the organized banditti of Napoleon made it an arena of plunder and outrage. "The French invasion," says Eustace, "which brought with it so many evils, and like a blast from hell checked the prosperity of Italy in every branch and in every province, not only put a stop to the increase of the Vatican library, but by plundering it of some of its most valuable manuscripts, lowered its reputation, and undid at once the labour of ages."

The Sistine Chapel, so named from the pontiff Sixtus IV., by whom it was built in 1473, from the designs of Pintelli, is one of the wonders of the Vatican. It is chiefly celebrated for its paintings in fresco by Michael Angelo and his scholars. The roof was begun in 1508 and finished in 1512, in the pontificate of Julius II. The architectural decorations of this ceiling form the framework of a series of paintings, which remain to this day a wonderful testimony of the artist's powers. The subjects include sublime conceptions of the progressive work of Creation, and embodiments of the types by which the coming Redemption was foreshadowed to the Jewish people. From the colossal size of the figures, and their exquisite artistic execution, these paintings command the admiration of the world. On the end wall opposite the entrance to the chapel, is the great fresco of the Last Judgment, a work which strikes the merest novice in art with astonishment. This sublime work was designed by Michael Angelo in his sixtieth year, at the request of Clement VII. After a labour of eight years, it was completed in the pontificate of Paul III., the painter then being little short of seventy years of age! Paul IV. objected to the nudity of the figures in this matchless painting. "Tell him," said Michael Angelo, "to reform the world, and the pictures will reform themselves." The painter however so far yielded to the pope, as to allow Daniele da Volterra to drape the most prominent figures; but he revenged himself upon Biagio, who first suggested the indelicacy, by placing him in hell, in the character of Midas; and when this person complained to the pontiff, the intercession of the latter failed to move Michael Angelo, who told his holiness that though he might have effected Biagio's release from purgatory, he had no power over hell.

The Chamber of Raphael, which is in fact a series of rooms, is devoted to the works of this great master. Here, amongst many other noble productions, may be seen the Expulsion of Heliodorus from the Temple, the Miracle of Bolsena,* Leo arresting Attila at the gates of Rome, and the Deliverance of St. Peter. In an adjoining gallery are the Tapestries of Raphael, those wondrous works of art, of which the Cartoons are preserved (?) in Hampton Court. The French carried off the Tapestries and sold them to a Parisian Jew, who actually burned one for the sake of the gold and silver thread with which portions of the work were wrought. The Israelitish scoundrel failed in his experiment, and gladly accepted the offer of Pius VII. to purchase the remainder of his reset.

In the gallery of the Vatican are two paintings deserving especial notice, namely, the Transfiguration by Raphael, and the Communion of St. Jerome by Domenichino. The first of these was painted for the Cathedral of Narbonne, and was not completed when, at the early age of thirty-seven, the illustrious painter died. This masterpiece of his genius was suspended over the artist's corpse for public homage, whilst the last traces of his hand were yet visible upon the canvas. The Communion of St. Jerome was painted for the Church of Ara Cœli, but the ignorant monks quarrelled with the painter and threw his work aside. They subsequently commissioned Poussin to paint an altar-piece, and in place of new canvas gave him the Communion to be painted over. Poussin threw up his commission with indignation, and loudly proclaimed the excellence of Domenichino's performance.

The Museum contains an extensive collection of ancient sepulchral inscriptions and monuments; and its numerous apartments are stored with remains of classic sculpture. To catalogue works of art, that must be seen to be appreciated and understood, is a mere waste of

---

* See pages 52, 56.

words. We may, however, name a few of the sculptures, which are popularly known through the medium of engravings, or of plaster casts:—The Cupid of Praxiteles, the Statue of Demosthenes, Minerva Medica, the Fawn of Praxiteles, the Statue of Mercury, the Torso Belvidere, the Laocoön, the Apollo Belvidere, and the Genius of the Vatican.

THE BASILICA OF SAINT JOHN LATERAN.

The ancient Basilicæ (so named from Βασιλεύς, a king, whence Βασιλική, a royal house, a seat of authority, a court of justice) were the tribunals of the Roman magistracy during the latter times of the empire. These structures were simple in their character, and consisted of a nave, (*testudo*), and two side aisles (*porticus*), the latter separated from the nave by two rows of columns, from which sprang arches to support the wall that sustained the central roof. Transepts (*chalcidica*) were sometimes added to the extremity of the building, thereby giving it the form of the letter T. The nave terminated in a curve, which, as being the immediate seat of the judge, was named the tribunal. These few particulars are worthy of notice, inasmuch as *all* places of Christian worship to the present day, bear striking resemblance to the ancient basilicæ. On the fall of the empire, the Roman church, it would appear, was allowed to appropriate some of these structures as places of worship; and the bishop assumed the seat of the temporal judge in the tribunal.* When Constantine made Christianity the religion of the empire, he erected a number of costly structures on the plan of the basilicæ, and with especial reference to Christian uses. Thus the character of ecclesiastical architecture was fixed, first by the choice of the church, and afterwards by the recognition of that choice by Constantine. In course of time the original model was modified by the removal of the transepts from the extremity of the building, so as to form a cross, which, according as the transepts were nearer to or farther from the centre of the building, obtained the name of a Greek cross, or a Latin cross. From the time of Constantine to the present age these leading characteristics of church architecture have universally prevailed; and in the wide range between the Vatican temple and the meanest conventicle, the main features of the ancient basilicæ are still presented before us. In the Roman church the tribune is at once the seat of a temporal and a spiritual judge. In the cathedrals of the reformed episcopal church, the bishop occupies a different position, and the tribune terminates with the communion table, close behind which rises a screen, thus leaving no space for a throne similar to that of the Roman pontiff. Parish churches have, for the most part, more of the simplicity of the early basilicæ, and modern dissenting places

---

* We can scarcely regard the first usurpation of the ancient Basilicæ by the Roman church as an accidental circumstance. The choice of these edifices appears to have been dictated by the desire for supremacy. These structures were the immediate products of magisterial authority, and long association had connected with the Tribune the awful attributes of a judge. Here, then, it was, upon the exalted tribune, that a Christian bishop fixed his throne and dwelt apart from the people; having the elevated steps of the tribunal, and even the altar itself, interposed between him and his congregation. Is any so blind that he sees not here the high priest in the holiest place, and a temporal ruler in his judicial seat?

of worship almost uniformly exhibit the divisions of nave and aisles, with occasionally a circular end answering to the ancient tribune.

The Basilica of St. John Lateran* was one of the structures erected by Constantine. After its destruction by fire in the beginning of the fourteenth century, Clement V. began a new edifice on its site, preserving as far as possible what remained of the former building. Various pontiffs from Clement to Sixtus V. enlarged, remodelled, and embellished this structure. Sixtus added the portico to the Scala Santa, or Sacred Stair, which constitutes one of the most valuable relics of the church. In the time of Innocent X., Borromini was allowed to load the nave with cumbrous ornaments which disfigure the building in the estimation of architects and men of taste. In 1734, Clement XII. completed the renovations by the addition of the principal façade. After so many changes, it may be supposed that few traces of the ancient basilica of Constantine are now to be seen. If anything might atone for the atrocities of Borromini, it would be the fact that his meretricious ornaments serve as a foil to the beauties of the Corsini chapel which stands in the nave. This superb structure, built in the form of a Greek cross by Clement XII., is from the designs of Alessandro Galilei, and may be regarded as one of the most perfect buildings of the kind existing. Nothing can surpass the magnificence of this chapel: the pavement is the finest marble; the walls are incrusted with alabaster and jasper, and decorated with basso-relievos; six pillars adorn the recesses, and of these the two on each side of the altar are verd antique; the other four are porphyry, with bases and capitals of burnished bronze. Over the altar is a mosaic copy of Guido's painting, S. Andrea Corsini, now in the Barberini Palace. The tombs with their statues are much admired, especially that of Clement XII., whose body reposes in a large and finely proportioned antique sarcophagus of porphyry. The Corsini chapel, though it may not altogether escape criticism, must strike the spectator very forcibly by its beauty. The valuable materials that form its pavement, line its walls, and adorn its vaults, are so disposed as to mix together their varied hues into soft and delicate tints; while the size and symmetry of its form enable the eye to contain it with ease, and contemplate its unity, its proportions, and its ornaments without effort.

The Lateran was long regarded as the first of Christian churches, and an inscription over the door still sets forth its pompous claim to distinction: *Ecclesiarum Urbis et Orbis Mater et Caput*—The Mother and Head of all the churches of Rome and of the world. The Chapter of

---

* This celebrated Basilica occupies the site of the sumptuous palace of the senator and consul elect, Plautius Lateranus. Suspected by Nero of being a partaker in the conspiracy of Piso, Plautius was beset in his palace by the imperial guard, and after his seizure he was conducted so suddenly to execution, that no time was granted him to take leave of his wife and children. Juvenal is of opinion that the accusation of treason was a mere device on the part of Nero to obtain easy possession of the treasures of the most wealthy senators:

> Temporibus diris igitur, jussuque Neronis,
> Longinum, et magnos Senecæ prædivitis hortos
> Clausit, et egregias Lateranorum obsidet ædes
> Tota cohors.   *Juvenal, Sat.* x. 15.

> Therefore in direful times, and by the command of Nero,
> A whole troop Longinus, and the large gardens of the wealthy Seneca
> Surrounded, and besieged the stately buildings of the Laterani.
>   *Madan.*

the Lateran continues to hold precedence over that of St. Peter's. One of the first forms in the election of a pope, is the taking possession of the Lateran palace; and the coronation of the pontiff is always celebrated in this church. The Lateran has long ceased to be the seat of ecclesiastical Councils:* its fame is now confined to imposing ceremonies, and to the exhibition of relics of grossly ridiculous, yet blasphemous pretensions. Among these last are the heads of St. Peter and St. Paul, encased with silver busts set with jewels; a lock of the Virgin Mary's hair, and a piece of her petticoat; a robe of Christ sprinkled with blood; some drops of his blood in a phial; and some of the water that issued from his side. But the Scala Santa, before referred to, is perhaps the most remarkable of all the relics. It is composed of twenty-eight steps of marble, brought from Jerusalem by Santa Helena, and affirmed to be the identical stairs by which Christ ascended to the judgment seat of Pilate. Devotees ascend these stairs on their knees, and from the number of penitents who claimed to perform this meritorious labour, it became necessary, even in the time of Clement XII., to cover the steps with wood; and this protecting envelope is said to have been thrice renewed.

The Baptistery of the Lateran, according to the custom of the early ages still observed in Italy, though near, is yet detached from the church. It is named San Giovanni in Fonte, and is the most ancient baptistery of the kind in the Christian world. The episcopal palace of the Lateran, which from the time of Constantine until the return from Avignon was the papal residence, is now an hospital; a portion only being reserved for the temporary accommodation of the pope when he comes to perform service at St. John's church.

The illustrative view is taken from the top of the Claudian Aqueduct. In the foreground are the buildings which contain the Triclinium of Leo III., a name applied to some mosaic figures removed from the old Lateran palace. On the right is seen a famous obelisk of red granite, the largest now known, originally brought from Heliopolis by Constantine, and afterwards erected on this spot by Fontana, in the reign of Sixtus V. On the left are the walls of Rome, beyond which lies the wide-spread and now desolate Campagna—the expressive type of the physical, spiritual, intellectual, and moral condition of Italy under the sway of the papacy.

---

* The second, third, and fourth councils of the Lateran excommunicated and condemned all heretics, and gave them over to the civil power, which was commanded to extirpate them. By the fourth council it was decreed that "the suspected, unless they proved their innocence, were to be accounted guilty, and avoided by all until they afforded condign satisfaction. Kings were solicited, and, if necessary, compelled by ecclesiastical censures, to exterminate all heretics from their dominions. The sovereign who should refuse, was to be excommunicated by the metropolitan and suffragans; and if he should prove refractory for a year, the Roman pontiff, the vicar general of God, was empowered to transfer his kingdom to some champion of catholicism, and absolve his vassals from their fealty."

Many of our readers may desire to know something of the character of these awful councils. Nazianzen, a Roman saint, describes the Byzantine assembly, which was the second general council, as "a cabal of wretches fit for the House of Correction; fellows newly taken from the plough, the spade, the oar, and the army." The Council of Lyons demoralized the city in which it was convened. Matthew Paris, a contemporary historian, gives the farewell address of Cardinal Hugo to the people, after the dissolution of the assembly. "Friends," said the Cardinal, "we have effected a work of great utility and charity in this city. When we came to Lyons we found three or four brothels in it, and we have left at our departure only one; but this extends, without interruption, from the eastern to the western gate of the city!" More than seven hundred *public women*, according to Dachery, attended the Council of Constance, and another authority states the number at fifteen hundred. In Bruys, 4. 39, it is said, "*sept cens dix huit femmes publiques*," and in Lebhrem, 16. 1435, the number is increased to "*xvn. meretrices cognobandae*." One favourite courtezan is said to have gained *eight hundred florins* by her traffic with the holy fathers. And this was the council that consigned Huss to the flames!

PRATICA

PRATICA is a locality of no importance except to the antiquary, who finds in it the site of the ancient Lavinium, the city founded by Æneas in honour of his wife Lavinia. It is distant about eighteen miles from Rome, and three miles from the sea coast; and is so afflicted with malaria, that its meagre population of some sixty souls carry in their countenances the melancholy evidence of its fatal presence amongst them. A large baronial mansion of the Borghese family exists at Pratica; and from its lofty central tower, the spectator obtains an extensive panoramic view of the surrounding country.

Lavinium was the regal city of Latium during the reign of Æneas; but after his death, his son Ascanius built Alba Longa, and removed thither the seat of government. We learn from Virgil that during the wanderings of Æneas, the prophetic Helenus directed the Trojan fugitive where to find a large white sow, with thirty young ones white like their dam, and declared that in the place of her concealment he should make settlement and build a city. Dionysius relates that Æneas was led to the site of Lavinium by this white sow; but the fable appears to be a little confused. The god of the Tiber, according to Virgil, revealed to Æneas the prophetic sty, and informed him that it was to be the site of a city (Alba Longa), which after thrice ten years Ascanius should build as the metropolis of the empire. The only information we can extract from the fable seems to be this: that it was not always the path of ill luck to "go to the pigs;" at least in classic times, when little pigs were oracles.

CASTEL GANDOLFO.

THE village of Castel Gandolfo, principally remarkable as the summer residence of the popes, is situated about twelve miles from Rome, on a spot of singular beauty, in the immediate vicinity of the Lake of Albano. It derives its name from the Gandolfi family, by whom it was possessed in the twelfth century. The Savelli, who afterwards became the proprietors, held the castle nearly four hundred years against the popes and barons and the neighbouring towns. It was sacked in 1436, by Eugenius IV., in consequence of sanctuary having been given to an enemy of the pope; but the Savelli resumed possession in the reign of Nicholas V., and continued thenceforward to enjoy it until 1596, when the descendant of this house finding himself unable to maintain baronial dignity, sold the property to the Apostolic Chamber for 150,000 scudi. Clement VIII. annexed it to the temporalities of the papal see, and converted it into a pontifical summer residence. The palace was begun in 1630, from the designs of Carlo Maderno; it was afterwards enlarged by Alexander VII.; and subsequently, in the last century, restored by Clement XIII., who gave it the form which it retains to this day. It is a building of no great pretensions; but it commands fine views of the lake, and is surrounded by the ruins of towns which had existence before Rome itself, and the sites of ancient imperial villas. Since the restoration of the edifice by Clement, the Roman nobility have erected suburban residences in its vicinity.

Castel Gandolfo stands on a volcanic peak, nearly fifteen hundred feet above the level of the sea, and more than four hundred feet above the Lake of Albano. Adjoining the papal palace is a church dedicated to St. Thomas of Villanuova, containing an altar-piece by Pietro da Cortona, and an Assumption by Carlo Maratti. The lake, which is the great attraction of the locality, is between two and three miles long, and nearly three miles in width.*

OLEVANO.

IN the mountain road between Palestrina and Subiaco, on a rocky hill at the foot of Monte del Corso, stands the picturesque village of Olevano, a locality rich in materials for artistic study. Its history does not go back beyond the middle ages, and its name is derived from the appropriation of its revenues to provide incense (*olibanum*) for the churches in its neighbourhood. The approach to Olevano from the side of Subiaco is extremely fine. The old baronial castle of the thirteenth century, built by the Colonna family, stands on a massive rock of Apennine limestone. The town and castle now belong to the Borghese, to whom it gives the title of marquis. The views from the rocks in the neighbourhood of Olevano command the vale of Latium, bounded by the high range of the Volscian mountains. The town of Paliano, containing about three thousand inhabitants, is situated upon an insulated hill, and forms a striking object. During the middle ages the fortress of Paliano was the scene of many contests with the papal government.

---

* The most interesting circumstance connected with the Lake of Albano, apart from its natural beauties, is the history of its Emissary. This subterranean canal was constructed by the Romans, a. c. 394, whilst besieging Veii, for the purpose of lowering the waters which threatened to burst their banks and inundate the adjacent country. The Emissary is upwards of a mile in length, varies from seven to ten feet in height, and is not less than four feet wide in the narrowest part. In the Mont' Albano, which rises to the height of two thousand feet above the lake, may still be seen the spiracula, or air-holes, which served to ventilate this ancient tunnel. The construction of this canal was begun by command of the Delphic oracle, which directed that the waters of the lake should not be allowed to escape by their natural outlet. An Etruscan soothsayer had predicted that Veii should be entered by a path underground, and the Romans, who were previously unacquainted with mining, took advantage of the knowledge gained in the formation of the Emissary, to sink a mine by which Veii was eventually entered and taken.

The Alban Mount is the site of interesting classic traditions. On the ridge above Marino stood the city of Alba Longa. The theatre of the combat between the Horatii and Curiatii is in the same vicinity. The tombs of the heroes are probably some of the many mounds which still arrest the traveller's attention.

TERRACINA

A TWO-FOLD celebrity attaches to Terracina: It is the site of the ancient Anxur, a city of "shining stones," and it has been renowned since the days of Juvenal, as a nest of robbers and assassins.*

The modern town of Terracina consists of a few steep, narrow, and miserable streets, through which a path leads to the ruins of Anxur. In the cathedral are some remains of the ancient city; the most remarkable of these are the columns of the temple of Apollo. A portion of Terracina is as modern as the time of Pius VI. This pontiff gave celebrity to the town, and rendered his own name famous by his gigantic operations for draining the Pontine Marshes. The drainage of this swampy tract was first attempted by Appius Claudius, about three hundred years before the Christian era, when employed in carrying his celebrated road, the Appian Way, across the Marshes. Repeated attempts were afterwards made in consular, imperial, gothic, and papal times, but none of them were attended with more than partial success. In 1778, Pius commenced his labours, and continued to prosecute them with incredible ardour and vast expense for the period of ten years. To accomplish this one purpose of his mind, he sacrificed human life and apostolic treasures with equal indifference; and that his vigilant eye might be always near to scan the operations of his workmen, he fixed his residence at Terracina, and continually superintended the operations in person. Whilst the value of the undertaking cannot be questioned, the great vanity of the pontiff has detracted from the glory of the work. Pius set out with the determination of persevering in a straight line, despite of all obstacles that might threaten his progress. He designed to restore the Appian Way under the new appellation of the Line of Pius, and with this view he constructed his canal in a direct line from Cisterna to Terracina. The ambition of the pontiff militated against the utility of

---

* Anxur appears to have been founded by the Volscians, from whom it was taken by the Romans, in the year of the city 348. It occupied the summit of the eminence at the foot of which stands the modern town of Terracina. The ruins of the palace of Theodoric, king of the Ostrogoths, are still existing; and this edifice having probably been erected upon the substructions of the temple of Jupiter, the remains are regarded with great interest as relics *reperti Anxuris*—of proud Anxur. This city is frequently alluded to by ancient writers under one or other of its various names of Trachina, Tарpracina, Trachas, Tarracina, or Anxur; but it is by the latter appellation that we usually find mention of it in the poets. From the conspicuous and commanding site of his temple, Jupiter Anxurus was supposed to preside over all the circumjacent country, and to regulate the destiny of its inhabitants:

> quæis Jupiter Anxurus arvis   The fields o'er which Anxurian Jove presides.
> Præsidet.   *Æneid.* vii. 799.

The poets apply the epithets *superbus*, *splendidus* and *candidus*, to the city of Anxur; the first to denote the proud eminence of its site, and the latter two to express the glittering whiteness not only of the city itself, but also of the lofty rock on which it was built. Polybius places this city amongst those in alliance with Rome when the first treaty was concluded between the Romans and Carthaginians. After it was taken from the Volscians, it became a station for supplying the Roman navy with sailors and stores; and subsequently when the imperial seat was contested by rival claimants, the possession of this port was sought with great eagerness.

his work: his line was carried through the middle of the Marsh, without depth enough to sluice off the water from the lower parts, and yet at an expense that was ruinous to the papal treasury; and, moreover, this undeviating course carried the workmen into the most unhealthy districts of the fens, where they died in hundreds. Pius, however, completed his undertaking, and the tiara and keys, and the pontifical title, claim equal distinction in the Pomptinæ Paludes, with the milestones of Trajan and the tablets of Theodoric.* Where the Linea Pia terminates beneath the rock of Terracina, Pius erected the buildings which are seen in our view, consisting of a palace, public offices, wharfs, and granaries.

Nearly half-way up the rock which forms so remarkable an object in the view of Terracina, is seated a hermitage, stuck like a swallow's nest where it is apparently inaccessible. Below there is a deep excavation, near the gate towards Naples, which serves for the station of some persons employed by the government. The rock above, upon which rest the ruins of the palace of Theodoric, forms part of the range of mountains separated from the great chain of the Apennines, by the valley of Garigliano.

NAPLES.

NAPLES occupies the site of two ancient Greek cities, Palæpolis and Neapolis, though it inherits the name of the latter. Neapolis derived its appellation, which signifies *the new city*, from the Cumæans who settled in this locality, and probably rebuilt or enlarged the old city of Parthenope, so named from one of the Syrens who was said to have resided there. Livy relates, that Palæpolis and Neapolis joined the Samnites in a confederacy against Rome, and that after the space of two years the former city was taken by the Romans, at which time also the latter, which was then the more inconsiderable town of the two, probably shared the same fate. In little more than half a century from this period, Neapolis appears to have attached itself closely to the interests of Rome, and to have acquired under the protection of the republic no small degree of prosperity and importance. Its fidelity to Rome excited the resentment of Hannibal, who ravaged and laid waste the Neapolitan territory, but shrunk from the difficulties of an attack upon the city itself. For a long series of years after its gallant repulse of the Carthaginian, we find no mention of Neapolis; and it is probable that in the interval it enjoyed undisturbed tranquillity, and cultivated the advantages of its fertile soil and unrivalled situation. It was during this peaceful period, embracing the fall of the republic and the infancy of the empire, that its environs became the fashionable

---

* The Pontine Marshes, so infamous for robbery and murder in the days of Juvenal, had lost none of their ancient fame in the early part of the present century. The situation of Terracina as a frontier town between Rome and Naples, rendered it the stronghold of banditti, who escaped pursuit by flecing as circumstances required into either State. Scarcely twenty years have elapsed since organized bands of brigands pursued a fearful system of mutilation or murder to enforce ransom for those unfortunate people who fell into their hands. In 1826, so many forts and stations were established by the Austrians along the line of road near the frontier, that the brigands have since had no chance of successful attack or escape, and the scowling looks of the inhabitants upon the traveller, who now passes in safety, have, under such control, lost their terrors.

winter retreat of the Roman citizens, among whom there were few of any note who did not possess a villa in the romantic recesses of its shores. The presence of Horace, Virgil, and his imitator, Silius Italicus, and their fond attachment to its delightful scenery, were lasting and honourable distinctions; whilst the foul indulgences of Tiberius, and the wild and cruel freaks of Caligula, were its scandal and its scourge.*

The earliest interruption to the prosperity of Neapolis was the desolation caused by the first recorded eruption of Vesuvius, A.D. 79; in which the towns of Herculaneum, Pompeii, and Stabiæ, were destroyed and buried under showers of volcanic sand, stones, and scoriæ; in which also the elder Pliny, at that time commanding the Roman fleet on the coast of Campania, lost his life. In subsequent centuries, Neapolis shared the miseries incident to civil war, and foreign invasion; and on the fall of the empire it was plundered by the barbarian hordes that spread themselves over Italy. It afterwards fell a prey to the Germans, French, and Spaniards; until at length the latter became its undisputed masters, and after having carried on the government for many years by viceroys, at last gave it a king in the person of Charles IV.

No vestiges remain of the ancient beauty or magnificence of Neapolis. Its temples, its theatres, its basilicæ, have been levelled by earthquakes or destroyed by barbarians. The edifices of modern Naples, whether churches or palaces, are less remarkable for their taste than for their magnitude or riches. It is, however, probable that Naples is at present more populous, more opulent, and in every respect more flourishing than she has ever before been, even in the most brilliant periods of her ancient history.

Naples is seated at the head of a capacious bay, thirty miles in diameter, and which, from its resemblance to a bowl, has been named the Crater. The town is built in the form of a vast amphitheatre, sloping from the hills to the sea. It contains within its walls upwards of four hundred thousand inhabitants, and one hundred thousand more occupy the suburbs that stretch in a magnificent and most extensive sweep from Portici to the promontory of Misenum, a distance of sixteen miles along the shore. The internal appearance of Naples is in general pleasing; the edifices are lofty and solid; the streets as wide as in any continental city; the Strada Toledo is a mile in length, and with the quay, which is very extensive and well-built, forms the grand and distinguishing features of the city. Taken in detail, its architecture will not bear comparison with that of Rome; for the recollection of the Roman buildings makes everything at Naples look poor and paltry. Some of the churches, indeed, are striking to the eye; but only from their deformity. Within they are loaded with ornament to such a degree that the very excess of decoration injures the buildings it was intended to beautify. The altars, more especially, display an exuberance of riches: in these, jasper, lapis lazuli, porphyry, and all sorts of rare marbles, together with gilding, painting, and carving, are jumbled together without the smallest regard to simplicity or taste. Justly has it been observed, that in Naples every thing is gilded, from the cupolas of the churches to the pills of the apothecary.

It would be difficult to imagine the constant bustle and turmoil that pervade the Strada

---

* This delightful retreat of the ancients, like the fashionable marine localities of the present day, appears to have been the favourite resort of invalids, who went there for the recovery of their health. Martial, however, in one of his pointed epigrams, alleges that the luxuries of Neapolis, rather than their individual ailments, led invalids thither and prolonged their stay.

Toledo, the principal street of Naples; the people bawling and roaring at each other in all directions; beggars soliciting your charity with one hand, whilst they pick your pocket with the other; and the carriages cutting their way through the throng with fearful rapidity. The crowd of London moves rapidly in a double line; that of Naples is a general tide rolling up and down, and in the middle of this tide a hundred eddies of men. A diversity of trades disputes with you in the streets. You are stopped by a carpenter's bench; you are lost among shoemakers' stools; you dash among the pots of a macaroni stall. Every bargain sounds like a battle; for it is a custom with the Neapolitans to ask three times as much as is just.*

NAPLES FROM THE SANTA LUCIA.

THE Santa Lucia is a wide street, open towards the bay, whence a beautiful view is obtained, across the blue waters, of Vesuvius, the distant Appennines, the Mont Sant' Angelo, and the Cape of Sorrento. The houses on this quay are very substantial, and the prospect they command causes them to be much sought after by visitors as places of abode. Not a few persons, when engaging lodgings in this desirable quarter, are led in the ardour of expectation to imagine that they are *bespeaking* an eruption of Vesuvius. The Santa Lucia is a scene of Neapolitan bustle not much inferior to that of the Mole; around its fountain animated groups are gathered; and along the quay are stalls covered with land fruit and *sea fruit*, the latter consisting of oysters, mussels, &c. Our engraving brings into view the light-house of the Mole, a quarter of the city remarkable for exhibiting on gala days a motley train of humorous incidents. " Here stands a methodistical friar preaching to one row of lazzaroni; there, Punch, the representative of the nation, holds forth to a crowd; yonder, another orator recounts the

---

* The lazzaroni of Naples demand especial mention. The appellation of lazzari, or lazzaroni, is applied indiscriminately to all the mendicant thieves of Italy, but in its application to the fraternity of Neapolitan porters its meaning is less offensive. The term appears to be of Spanish origin, and to allude to the torn and tattered garments of the persons to whom it was contemptuously given. The lazzaroni of Naples are the poorer portion of the labouring class; and their distinctive character, as compared with the populace of other great cities, rests in two points; first, the cheapness of those articles of food which suffice for their wants; and secondly, the mildness of the climate, which renders them nearly independent of clothing and habitations. That the lazzaroni are an idle race cannot be denied; it is also said that they are not remarkable for honesty; yet many have borne testimony to their fidelity. Their daily occupation is little more than a continual lounge; selling of fruit, running of errands, and performing menial offices requiring little of either mental or bodily activity, constitute almost the entire round of their labours. When they have earned the small pittance necessary for daily support, they have no inclination to make further exertion; they then congregate around their favourite Punch, or recline in utter indolence to enjoy that inestimable luxury of Italian life—doing nothing. In earlier periods of their history, the lazzaroni were strong in their numbers, and in the bond of union which held them together; and they frequently played an important part on occasions of civil insurrection and foreign invasion. They were the only class in Italy whom the Spaniards feared. The viceroys of Spain named them with deference, and received deputations from their body with marked respect. Once a year they met tumultuously in the Piazza del Mercato, and named by acclamation their temporary chief, or capo-lazzaro. They have subsequently fallen in position; yet are they still sufficiently formidable to exercise great influence in seasons of popular or political commotion. This unique race offer in their persons the most faultless models for the sculptor; they gesticulate with the commanding energy of a savage; their language, though gaping and broad, when kindled into passion, bursts into oriental metaphor; and their ideas move in a circle, narrow indeed, but a circle in which they are invincible. Their exertion of soul, their humour, their fancy, their quickness of argument, their address or flattery, their rapidity of utterance, their pantomime and grimace, none can resist but a lazzarone himself.

miracles performed by a sacred wax-work, on which he rubs his *agnuses* and sells them, thus impregnated with grace, for a grain a-piece. Beyond him are quacks in huzzar uniform, exalting their drugs and brandishing their sabres, as if not content with one mode of killing. Opposite to these is a motley audience seated on planks, and listening to a tragi-comic *Aluofo*, who reads, sings, and gesticulates old gothic tales of Orlando and his Paladins."

NAPLES FROM VESUVIUS.

Visitors to Naples climb Vesuvius with the same devotion that pilgrims to Loretto prostrate themselves before the shrine of the Virgin; it must, however, be admitted that the Neapolitan devotees are the most rational class of the two. The view of Naples, and the magnificent bay with its islands and promontories, is worth a steep ascent over pumice stone and amidst ashes; and the phenomena of the mountain itself, even in its quietest mood, may well prompt and justify the undertaking.

We shall be pardoned for not adding another to the thousand and one descriptions of Vesuvius: in place of this, we offer a few particulars regarding the eruption of 1822, of which Mr. Brockedon was a spectator, and whose account, recorded at the time of its occurrence, we slightly compress:—

"The author's first visit to the mountain was on the 11th February, 1822. No unusual quantity of smoke or steam issued to excite expectation of immediate activity, and our party not only walked round the crater, but some descended into it as far as the suffocating vapours would allow; yet the guide, Salvatore, said the wells in the vicinity had become so dry as to leave no doubt of an approaching eruption. On the evening of the 21st, a few gleams of light appeared at long intervals on the summit; but on the following day we observed, on returning from an excursion to Portici, frequent and vivid flashes, accompanied with sounds like distant, heavy thunder; and the next morning smoke began to settle over the crater, and assume the form of a vast palm-tree. These indications of violent activity increased until the evening of the 23d, when, about nine o'clock, we saw streams of lava descend on the side of the cone towards Naples, dividing or uniting as channels in the old lava influenced their course, until they flowed together in a common channel that appeared to be the outlet of the Atrio del Cavalli: there the lava formed, in the darkness of the night, a red-hot net-work on the cone, and a lengthening line of fire as it pursued its course towards the base of Vesuvius. The explosions during the night were terrific; the house in which we resided in the Santa Lucia was violently shaken almost at the instant that the flash of the explosion was seen, although the sound reached us at an interval which marked a distance of about eight or nine miles between us and the mountain. On the following day, the 24th, the violence of the eruption having increased, we made preparation for a visit to Vesuvius. We left Naples about two o'clock, and drove to Resina, where we were furnished with mules for our ascent to the Hermitage. It is impossible to imagine the excitement of the scene as we rose on the mountain-side, and looked back upon the city and bay of Naples bathed in a flood of light, such as in Italy is displayed under a declining sun. A vast cloud of pure white vapour intervened between us and the cone of Vesuvius; but our proximity was evident from the awful and terrific explosions that burst upon our ears. As the sun declined, this cloud reflected all his bright and varying tints, from golden to roseate hues, till he plunged into the sea; when the last glowing colour faded rapidly in the transient twilight into an indescribable ashy hue. The cloud then became the screen to the fires of Vesuvius; and when greater darkness came on with night, even before we reached the Hermitage, a deep murky red began to pierce the vapour, which now became of a lurid and awful colour, arising from the molten lava that was not vivid enough to be perceived during the light of day; this colour, with each explosion, became for a moment more intense, and then subsided into its former deep and horrid glare.

On reaching the Hermitage, we found it a Babel of confusion; the poor host and his assistants were bewildered by the noisy application of hundreds of people for refreshments, made in nearly all the languages of Europe. The stenk of bread, wine, and other provisions, soon disappeared, and an empty larder was left for succeeding comers. From the hermitage we had yet nearly two miles to go. Our party started on foot, in the usual order, each two or three persons with attendants bearing torches; and it was an exciting scene to witness, amidst the awful thunderings and bursts of the volcano, the line of visitors braving its horrors. The march of each party, above and below us, was traced in the darkness by the tortuous course of these moving lights, as they marched single file by the zig-zag path of ascent made over the old lava. At length we reached the Atrio del Cavalli. Here the ladies of the party rested under the care of some of the guides, while the rest moved forward to ascend the mountain if possible, or to examine more closely the stream of lava. The sense of security experienced amidst throes of nature, which had frequently produced the destruction of surrounding cities, and of whose approaching issue no man could know the limit, was an unaccountable feeling; storms of thunder, which are appalling from their frequency, man, when he can, generally avoids; yet here, whilst the vivid lightnings played round the crater, and explosions louder than thunder made the earth tremble upon which we stood, no emotion of fear was excited: on the contrary, a fascination drew the visitors to the nearest point to examine the sublime phenomena thus offered to their contemplation. But a near approach was not unattended with danger. The explosions of the mountain were produced like the discharges of cannon, and whilst their fury lasted, were like successions of loading and firing. When an explosion took place, the contents of the enormous calibre of the crater were shot up to a height so great, that the projected masses of red-hot rock and lava emitted for a long time to be stationary in the sky, like dull stars; until at length the projectile force being spent, they returned, enlarging as they approached, and excited the horrid feeling that they might fall upon us: but of the millions of tons discharged, nearly all fell back, as perpendicularly as they had risen, into the fiery gulf, where they jammed each other in with a force of which the mind can form no just idea; and in proportion to the compactness with which they filled the crater, was the force required to burst this barrier at the next discharge. Occasionally, however, a piece fell outside, and rolling down the cone soon acquired a centrifugal force that burst it into a hundred pieces, which struck the points that checked their progress with the force of fragments of shell. The line of danger is therefore narrowly watched by those who approach it, and they shelter themselves behind the masses of old lava until the pieces have been stopped, or have passed over them. Yet this evening one gentleman had his arm broken by a fragment that struck him. On approaching the stream of lava, the heat was insufferable; but we climbed upon the scoriæ, which overlaid the flowing lava, without suffering inconvenience. These scoriæ on which we sat were restrained from advancing with the lava by the jagged sides of the old beds or craters, which checked their descent with the stream as a flood-gate restrains the passage of straw and wood. The sensation excited by sitting on the trembling masses, with the liquid lava passing beneath us, was indescribable; it was so near that we lit our cigars in its flows. Many of the visitors employed themselves in detaching small portions of the lava, and whilst it was in a viscid state, embedding coins in it by pressure, when the soft material collapsed over the edges and inextricably held them. We heard that some persons succeeded in reaching the summit of the crater by going round the mountain on the opposite side to the course of the lava; but we learned this too late to avail ourselves of it, not desiring to remain longer separate from our party.

On our return to the Hermitage we met hundreds ascending; and having found our mules with difficulty amidst the confusion, returned to Naples soon after midnight. We often looked back when very loud explosions recalled our attention to the wonders we had left, and to which crowds were still pouring out from Naples. We heard the next day that four thousand persons had ascended and visited the mountain on the previous night, and we afterwards learned that ten thousand ascended on the following evening. On the 26th, the explosions and eruptions of lava ceased, though the lava already discharged was still advancing. On the 27th, volumes of fine ashes were blown out of the crater, and hung over the bay like a heavy black cloud; these were so fine, and the air was so charged with them, that they grated in the teeth; and the author, when at Posilipo, found the paper on which he was sketching gradually darken with the layer of fine ashes ejected from the volcano. The following day, the 28th, he again went to Vesuvius to observe the progress of the lava. It had flowed from the crater about two miles and a half, and had crossed the road to the Hermitage, cutting off on that side the usual communication: in the latter part of its course it had destroyed some valuable vineyards, in which the celebrated Lachryma Christi is grown. At the farthest point of the yet advancing lava, the mass was about thirty or forty feet high, and two or three hundred feet wide, but it was now fast settling; its progress was so slow that it was chiefly marked by the falling over of the scoriæ, through the crevices of which the red-hot lava could be seen, thus seen, even by day.

CASTELLAMARE DI STABIA.

STABIÆ, whose site is in the immediate vicinity of Castell' à mare di Stabia, was a place of some importance before its destruction by Sylla; but in Pliny's time it had disappeared as a town, and was then occupied by villas and pleasure-grounds. The memory of Stabiæ is preserved to us principally by its participation in the ruin and overthrow of Herculaneum and Pompeii, during the eruption of Vesuvius, A.D. 79, in which so many towns and cities of Campania were overwhelmed.* It was in the neighbourhood of this place that the elder Pliny perished; and in the letters of his nephew to the historian Tacitus, the classical reader finds a graphic and interesting account of many incidents attendant upon the eruption, and a particular description of all the circumstances connected with the death of Pliny.

Castell' à mare di Stabia is situated at the foot of the table-land on which Stabiæ anciently stood. It has a handsome quay, erected during the occupation of Naples by the French; and it is altogether an agreeable locality, with much to recommend it to tourists as a place of temporary sojourn. The surrounding country is very beautiful. In the plain above the town

---

* The destruction of the cities of Herculaneum, Pompeii, and Stabiæ, took place, according to Pliny the younger, who was an eye-witness of that catastrophe, August 24th, in the second year of the reign of the emperor Titus, or A.D. 79. Frequent as have been the eruptions of Vesuvius since that which consigned those cities to oblivion, it appears to have shown no active indications of its volcanic nature for some centuries previously; for we find no memorial of any prior eruption of the mountain. Strabo, A.D. 25, describes Vesuvius as clothed with a most fertile soil, except at the top, which was totally sterile, being covered with stones which appeared to have sustained the action of fire. Martial, in an epigram written immediately after the eruption, deplores the desolated state of Vesuvius; and describes it before that event to have been overshaded by the most luxurious vines and vegetation, a retreat for which the gods of pleasure and gaiety forsook their most favoured abodes.

Herculaneum, Pompeii, and Stabiæ were three towns situated on the coast of Neapolis, and in the immediate neighbourhood of Vesuvius. The small town of Portici, distant about six miles from Naples, stands upon the entombed city of Herculaneum, whose partial excavation was begun in 1713. A peasant sinking a well in his garden found several fragments of marble; and this circumstance being reported to the prince D' Elbeuf, he purchased the spot, and continuing the excavations discovered various statues and pillars, and even an entire temple of the finest marble filled with statues. The Neapolitan government, after suspending the excavations for twenty years, bought the site; but in place of opening up the ground for further discovery, it stupidly erected a palace upon the ruins, and thereby sealed the sepulchre of Herculaneum. The excavations were indeed continued occasionally, and ultimately a basilica, two temples, and a theatre were discovered, and stripped of their numerous pillars and statues. The Museo Borbonico at Naples exhibits a large collection of bronze statues, pillars of marble and alabaster, paintings, and mosaics,—the spoils of this ancient city; together with a great variety of ornaments used in dress, weapons and armour, kitchen utensils and domestic furniture, agricultural and chirurgical instruments. These last-named relics are so numerous and complete that we are enabled, after the lapse of eighteen centuries, not only to see the inhabit-

is the royal villa of *Quisisana*, so named from the great salubrity of the climate. On the hill of Pozzana, noted like a thousand other places in Italy for a miraculous image of the Virgin, stands a wooden cross, remarkable for its having an altar of Diana for its pedestal. A temple of the goddess anciently occupied this locality; but it has given place to a church of the Madonna, and the pedestal of the cross is the only vestige that remains of the heathen structure. The views of Naples and its neighbourhood which may be seen from the sheltered and beautiful rides and walks in the vicinity of Stabiæ, are scarcely inferior to those that are presented from other points around the Neapolitan coast. The hills from Castell' à mare to Sorrento are covered with rich pasturages celebrated for the milk they produce, whence the entire range was anciently named the Mons Lactarius; but the fine form which towers above the rest takes its modern name of Sant' Angelo, from a miraculous grotto said to be haunted by the archangel Michael. It is the highest mountain in the neighbourhood of Naples.

---

ants of Herculaneum in their habits as they lived, but also to contemplate all the peculiarities of their domestic economy and every-day life. At Pompeii the traveller walks through a disinterred city, and surveys the remains of long departed ages in all their undisturbed relations, but he gathers his knowledge of Herculaneum from the details collected in the Neapolitan museum.

Pompeii was discovered about the middle of the last century. A labourer found, in ploughing, a statue of brass; and subsequently the temple of Isis was brought to view by some workmen who were employed in the construction of a subterraneous aqueduct. These discoveries naturally excited great expectations; and the work of excavation went forward until at length a large portion of the city was laid open. The volcanic deposit covering Pompeii was in some places scarcely three feet in depth; hence the excavations on this site were a work of small difficulty compared with the operations at Herculaneum.

Approaching Pompeii from Naples, both sides of the road, for nearly a furlong before entering the city, are occupied by tombs and public monuments, intermixed with shops. The carriage way still exhibits the tracks or ruts worn by the chariots, and the foot-ways are protected by curb-stones, in which frequently occur holes for fastening the halter. The principal entrance to the city is not striking for its beauty. The walls of brick and rubble-work are faced with stucco, which is covered with nearly illegible inscriptions. Within an arched recess at the gate of the city was found a skeleton, conjectured to be that of a sentinel, who in accordance with the strictness of Roman discipline died at his post. The street of the tombs, containing the monuments of distinguished men, lies to the east of Pompeii, and leads to the villa named Suburbana, at the entrance to which were found two skeletons; one held a purse containing many coins and medals, with the key of the door, and its hand bore a ring indicating equestrian rank; the other was probably an attendant occupied at the moment of death in the removal of some valuables which were found near them. In the subterraneous passage of this villa were many large earthen wine vases, ranged in order against the walls; and hither twenty-three of the family had retired for refuge. Ear-rings, bracelets, and other ornaments, were found with their skeletons; and the bones of the fingers of some still grasped small articles suddenly caught up for preservation.

It is truly a wondrous thing to be admitted to the temples, the theatres, and the domestic privacy of a people who lived nearly two thousand years ago. The inhabitants indeed are wanting; but a ramble through the silent streets of the city makes us acquainted with their domestic history as thoroughly as if we had been their contemporaries. It is interesting to observe their identity with ourselves in the ordinary routine of life. Sign-boards we discover are no new invention: at Pompeii rudely executed combats of gladiators mark the vintners' shops, the baker's trade is indicated by a mill and an oven, the druggist threatens under the device of a serpent, and the surgeon recommends his tender mercies by a painting illustrative of the raptures of tooth-drawing. In the passage to one house an inscription warns the intruder to "beware of the dog." On the walls of the city we see scrawled in red characters an advertisement that "a bath and nine hundred shops belonging to a certain lady named Julia Felix, are to be let for five years;" another, that "on the sixteenth of May there will be a show of gladiators in the theatre, which will be covered in on that occasion;" and a third, that "Municius Pomfidius Rufus will exhibit, on the 29th October, a combat of wild beasts." Alas! we are eighteen hundred years too late to take a lease, or to be present at the spectacles.

THE GATE OF SORRENTO.

> ———— once among
> The children gathering shells along the shore.
> One laughed and played, unconscious of his fate:
> His to drink deep of sorrow, and, through life,
> To be the scorn of them that knew him not,
> Trampling alike the giver and his gift.
> The gift a pearl precious, inestimable,
> A lay divine, a lay of love and war,
> To charm, ennoble, and, from age to age,
> Sweeten the labour, when the oar was plied
> Or on the Adrian or the Tuscan Sea.*
>
> *Rogers.*

THE fame of Sorrento is "antithetically mixed," a composition of sweet poetry and sour wine, Tasso's strains and the *vinum Surrentinum*. Regarding the first element of celebrity there is no difference of opinion amongst persons of taste; but the tastes of persons are not agreed upon the merits of the second. The poets, those revellers in fiction, have extolled the vintage of Surrentum in good set terms; but Tiberius, who was a lover of plain prose, and a matter-of-fact man, affirmed that it was only a shade better than diluted vinegar.

The town of Sorrento, anciently called Syrentum, from its local beauties, and afterwards Surrentum, is situated high above the sea, on the south-western promontory of the bay of Naples. It was probably built by the Phœnicians; although Strabo affirms that it was founded by Ulysses, and a certain priest of Sorrento, desirous to "out-Herod Herod," even attributes its origin to Shem the son of Noah. Frontinus says that it was colonized by Augustus, but mentions also that it was once occupied by the Greeks. After the fall

---

* Torquato Tasso, the son of Bernardo Tasso, a poor though noble native of Bergamo, was born at Sorrento, March the 11th, 1544, nine years after the death of Ariosto. The father of the poet was the author of many elegant lyrics, and of some volumes of letters. He possessed an ardent, restless temperament that descended to his son, whose misfortunes were mainly owing to this hereditary disposition, excited and acted upon by those brilliant powers of imagination which, whilst they won for their possessor a barren wreath from posterity, were destined to torment him through life like a consuming fire. Bernardo attached himself to the fortunes of Sansseverino, prince of Salerno, and when Spanish oppression had ruined his patron, and made himself an exile, he sought refuge in Rome. Thither his son Torquato followed him, and the young poet's parting embrace with his mother, who remained behind to look after a dowry which she had never received, forms a beautiful incident in one of his fragmentary pieces. After two years

of Rome, Sorrento appertained to the duchy of Naples and shared its political fortunes. Some of the defences of the middle ages are fast approaching the condition of the Roman ruins. The turretted fort in our view, presents within the walls a melancholy aspect of decay. It stands close beside the eastern gate, which is surmounted by a statue of San Antonino, regarding whose exaltation as the patron saint of Sorrento, an amusing story is told. When Sicardo, prince of Beneventum, besieged the citadel, in 830, the inhabitants, it is said, were reduced to great straits and perplexities, and were led, from despair of earthly succour, to intreat the assistance of San Antonino. They prudently accompanied their intreaties with substantial *bribes*, which last found their way to the treasury of the church, and by consequence to the favour of the saint. San Antonino appeared at the moment of need, armed with a cudgel that might have carried the prize at Donnybrook, and let fall upon the head and shoulders of the luckless Sicardo such a succession of convincing blows that the prince was brought to his knees, whence he arose with the prudent resolve to take to his heels. After this interposition in favour of the Sorrentines, San Antonino reigned paramount in Sorrento, and he has continued to do so to the present day.

---

study in Rome. Bernardo removed his son first to Bergamo, amongst his relations, and afterwards to Pesaro, in the duchy of Urbino, where he pursued his education in fellowship with the young prince, who subsequently became duke Francesco Maria the Second. In 1559, the boy repaired to Venice, where his father had been appointed secretary to the academy; and in the following year, parental solicitude devoted him to the study of the law. Arriving in Padua, between sixteen and seventeen years of age, he commenced his loyal studies by writing the poem of *Rinaldo*, which was published in less than two years at Venice. The poetic father, deeming it useless to thwart the bias of his son's disposition, kindly and wisely permitted him to devote himself to literature. He therefore entered the university of Bologna; and there, at the early age of nineteen, he began his *Jerusalem Delivered*. Leaving Bologna, he returned to Padua, where he continued his studies; and afterwards repaired to Mantua, to visit his father. During this brief leisure he fell in love, but not so desperately as to prevent his returning to Padua. About this time the cardinal d'Este, to whom he had dedicated his Rinaldo, invited him to the court of Alfonso the Second, duke of Ferrara. A dangerous illness detained him nearly a twelvemonth at Mantua; and it was not until the last day of October, 1565, that he arrived in the ducal city.

From the arrival of Tasso at Ferrara we must date that mingled career of glory and misery which constitutes the greater portion of the poet's life. He appeared at court at the very moment when preparations were making for the reception of the ducal bride. He was in raptures with the beauty and grandeur he saw around him; the duke and his two sisters, one of the latter the Leonora of his verse, regarded him courteously; and he worked enthusiastically upon his Jerusalem Delivered, loading it with praises of the house of Este. Forgetful of his Mantuan goddess, Tasso fell in love with the beautiful Lucrezia Bendidio; and Guarini, one of his rivals, accused him of courting two ladies at once. In 1569, the poet lost his father, and his filial grief produced a severe illness; from this, however, he recovered, and again joined the circle of courtly festivities. He shortly afterwards visited France; but before setting out made his will in due form, the articles of bequest being his poems, and certain properties pawned to two Jews. But the most interesting point in the document is the confidence with which he refers his prospective executor to the favour of the princess Leonora for any necessary assistance in carrying out the provisions of his testament. The strong expression which Tasso uses on this occasion, in referring to the princess—*per amor mio,* "for my sake"—is employed as an argument by those who connect his subsequent misfortunes with his presumptuous and too openly manifested passion for the princess. Tasso met with a favourable reception from the French king (Charles), and soon after returned to Ferrara. At this period the poet was approaching the zenith of his fame, and was in the enjoyment of a happiness destined to be brief. He occupied himself in perfecting the *Jerusalem*, and wrote his beautiful pastoral, the *Aminta*, which was performed before the court during the carnival, to the delight of a brilliant assembly. In 1574, he accompanied the duke of Ferrara to Venice, where he sought a printer for his *Jerusalem*, which after the delay of a year, occasioned by the illness of the poet, issued from the press to confirm the fame of its author. It

SORRENTO.

The promontory of Surrentum once bore a temple of Minerva, consecrated to that goddess by Ulysses. Pollius Felix, the friend of Statius, had a villa at Surrentum; and of the temple of Hercules which he enlarged, some ruins remain to this day. The ruined temples of Neptune and Diana are also still existing; and the reservoir, repaired by Antoninus Pius in gratitude for the benefits derived from a residence at Surrentum, continues to supply the modern town with water. The extraordinary ravines by which Sorrento is nearly surrounded are amongst the striking features of this singular and beautiful locality. The lofty arches that cross the gorge in our view, are of Roman construction, and over them lies the approach to the eastern gate of the town. Near the bottom of the ravine a steep and narrow path leads to the sea-shore.

Sorrento enjoys the most temperate climate in Italy, and during the summer months it is crowded with visitants, chiefly English, who make it their head-quarters for excursions to Pæstum, Salerno, Capri, and other interesting localities. To the gifted few who can appreciate genius, and who delight to trace its "whereabouts," the house of Tasso must be the chief attraction of Sorrento. This edifice is beautifully situated on the lofty rocks overlooking the bay of Naples. It was restored from a dilapidated condition by order of Joseph Bonaparte when king of Naples. This house, the tourists tell us exultingly, is now a palace. When Tasso dwelt there it was a temple!

might be thought that Tasso had now achieved all that ambition could desire, and would have reposed on his laurels; but at this time commenced those fits of depression which ultimately, through the malignity of hostile criticism, and unworthy neglect, overthrew a mind too sensitive to endure calmly the rude treatment to which it was exposed. Whilst much of his mental anguish may undoubtedly be referred to his own ardent temperament, there can be no doubt that the house of Este assumed a cold demeanour towards him, and that important malice decried his genius; and how fearfully these vexations must have wrought upon the mind of Tasso, let kindred genius—though less than the thousandth part of his—declare. Many inconsistencies of conduct marked the future career of the poet. Alternately impressing wrath upon his patron, and suing for re-admission to his presence, his position was truly humiliating. At length, a frenzied outbreak gave Alfonso the power, and with some show of justice, of consigning him to a lunatic hospital, where he remained, from 1579 till 1586, the companion of maniacs. Indeed, he had been driven mad, and frequently during his confinement he exhibited the hallucinations of a confirmed Bedlamite. Upon his liberation from the hospital, Tasso left Ferrara for ever, and repaired to the Mantuan court, where he was received with honour, and began to think himself once more happy. He corrected his prose works, finished his tragedy of Torrismond, and completed and published a narrative poem left unfinished by his father. But his peace of mind was soon interrupted; he felt that he was now subject to frenzy, and he confessed it. He left Mantua, and wandered from place to place, returning frequently to the same locality only again to leave it. A mortal illness was approaching; and at this moment, as if in mockery, the Pope granted to Tasso the honour of being crowned in Rome. The poet had three years before desired that honour, and now that it was conceded, he set forward to the capital; but before the ceremony could be arranged, he felt his end approaching, and desired permission to retire to the monastery of St. Onofrio, where he expired on the 25th April 1595, in the fifty-first year of his age. After his death, the ceremony of the coronation proceeded; his lifeless brow received the laurel wreath, and his body, wrapped in a magnificent toga, was carried by torch-light in solemn procession through the streets of Rome.

META.

AT the northern extremity of the Piano di Sorrento stands the small town of Meta, surrounded by objects of remarkable beauty and picturesque character, and containing within its precincts the traditional sites of two heathen temples; one of these, supposed to be that of a temple of Minerva, is now occupied by a fine church; and on the other, in the neighbourhood of the Capuchin convent, a temple of Venus is said formerly to have stood. This last is now appropriated to a sort of fortified farm, named a *masseria*. The situation of Meta above the sea renders the air fresh and pure, and causes the locality to be much esteemed as a place of residence. In the town are some remarkable ravines, not less striking in their appearance than the one at the Gate of Sorrento.

The illustrative view is taken from a point near the village of St. Agnello. Vesuvius is seen on the left, and on the right appears a bold head-land, the base of the Monte Chiaro. Meta is distant about three miles from Sorrento.

AMALFI.

<blockquote>
The time has been,
When on the quays along the Syrian coast,
'Twas ask'd, and eagerly, at break of dawn,
"What ships are from Amalfi!"
Rogers.
</blockquote>

THE city of Amalfi, a sea-port in the gulf of Salerno, is in the kingdom of Naples, from whose capital it is distant about thirty miles. The history of this place previous to the sixth century is uncertain and obscure. Tradition assigns the foundation of the city to Hercules and a nymph named Amalfi; and the principal inhabitants are anxious to trace back their descent to certain Roman patricians who, in the fifth and sixth centuries, sought refuge amidst the rocks and recesses of the neighbouring coast, from the inroads of Genseric and Totila. Amalfi ultimately became one of the great republics of Italy, but it has long since fallen from its high estate. After three hundred years of prosperity, it gradually sunk to its present position, that of a fishing-town; but the poverty of a thousand fishermen, as Gibbon remarks, is yet dignified by the remains of an arsenal, a cathedral, and the palaces of royal merchants.

The ecclesiastical history of Amalfi is recorded with more certainty than its early political annals, yet it is to these last that we shall hasten, for what can be more profitless than

to dwell at any length upon the thrice-told tale of monkish superstition and fraud. The bishops of Amalfi, we are told, have come down in uninterrupted succession from the time of Leone, who, in 967, was archbishop of this see. It is further related, that Cardinal Pietro Capuano, on his return from the East, whither he had accompanied the crusaders, brought with him and presented to his native city, the remains of the body of Saint Andrew. These precious relics, deposited in a silver coffin, were on the 8th of May, 1208, borne in solemn procession to the church of the Holy Apostle. Nearly a century after the deposition of the relics, a miraculous liquor was seen, by an old pilgrim, to ooze from the bones; and it has continued to flow ever since. This liquid, named the *manna of Amalfi*, has been a constant source of revenue to the church, and to this day it is sought as an unfailing preservative against shipwreck and sickness. The profits accruing from the sale of the manna were so considerable, that, in 1463, Pius II. ordered the head of the saint to be sent and deposited in the Basilica Vaticana in Rome, hoping thereby to become a sharer in the emoluments. The remains of St. Andrew were not, however, the only treasure that Capuano brought from the East; he appears to have been an indefatigable relic-hunter, and his success was commensurate with his zeal. He discovered and brought away the bodies of St. Macario, St. Viot, St. Cosmo, and St. Damiano, the first of whom was an Egyptian cœnobite, and the remaining three were martyrs. In addition to these, he obtained the heads of St. James the Less, St. Basil, and St. Diomed; the skull of St. Pancras; the hand of St. Philip the Apostle; and the arm of St. George the martyr; numerous bones in minute fragments of the Holy Innocents; three *great* bones of St. Zacharias, the father of St. John the Baptist; a thorn of the crown of our Saviour; and a *fine* piece of the wood of the cross; together with many other valuable and authentic relics, *quæ nunc persæriders longum est*—or, as the local historian says, "too numerous to mention."

The political history of Amalfi dawns in the sixth century, in connection with a ducal authority sanctioned by the exarchs of Ravenna. Subsequently, counts of Amalfi appear; and after these, we find an independent people under their Doges. At a later period the famous count Roger of Sicily either took the city under his protection, or appropriated it as a conquest. It was during his government that the Pisans, availing themselves of the absence of the Amalfians, who had accompanied the count to the siege of Averna, took and sacked Amalfi; and though the latter returned by forced marches to the rescue of their city, the Pisans succeeded in carrying off the celebrated Pandects of Justinian. Whence, or in what manner, the Amalfians obtained this treasure, history does not record; it is supposed, however, to have been purchased by some of the princely merchants trading with Constantinople. It was believed to be the original copy of the Pandects, in the hand-writing of the emperor himself. The Pisans were afterwards compelled to surrender their prize to Florence; but the date of its seizure by them is sufficient to identify with Amalfi those modern systems of jurisprudence which are based upon the Institutes of Justinian. After the sack of the city by the Pisans, Amalfi lost much of the importance it had gained by its commerce, shipping, riches, and acknowledged maritime authority. It was afterwards restored to an independent dukedom, under prince Orsini of Salerno; and the ducal authority was subsequently conferred on Antonio Piccolomini, the nephew of Pope Pius II. In 1650, this state was conveyed to Ottavio Piccolomini by a formal grant from the king of Spain. But the glory of Amalfi may be said to have terminated with the plunder of the city by the Pisans; for its subsequent partial restoration merely rendered its decline more gradual.

The character and the numerical strength of the population of Amalfi, in the present day, contrast strongly with the busy multitudes that crowded its streets and quays in the tenth and eleventh centuries, when the fleets of its Doges compassed the seas and traded to every known part of the world. The city now contains scarcely three thousand inhabitants, and these are poor fishermen, but in the days of its power and distinction it numbered a population of 50,000 inhabitants, composed of industrious artisans and princely merchants. It was one boast of the Amalfians that they coined their own money:—

>―――――――― " her coins,
> Silver and gold, circled from clime to clime;
> From Alexandria southward to Soumaar,
> And eastward, through Damascus and Cabul,
> And Samarcand, to thy great wall Cathay."

The commerce of the Amalfians naturally directed their attention to maritime jurisprudence, and their celebrated code, the *Tavole Amalfitane*, became the basis of those laws relating to navigation which continue to be acknowledged by commercial nations.

> " Then were the nations by her wisdom swayed ;
> And every crime on every sea was judged
> According to her judgments."

Amalfi shared the general enthusiasm, and joined the crusade for the recovery of the Holy Land from the infidels. Her merchants established an hospital in Jerusalem, which afterwards became the foundation of the famous order of the Knights Hospitallers of Jerusalem, and subsequently of Malta.

> ―――――― ―― " In Palestine,
> By the way-side, in sober grandeur stood
> An Hospital, that, night and day, received
> The pilgrims of the west ; and when 'twas ask'd,
> ' Who are the noble founders ?' every tongue
> At once replied, ' The Merchants of Amalfi.' "

The historian long claimed for an Amalfian the honour of having invented the Mariner's Compass, but this distinction recent researches have denied; although it is probable that the citizen Flavius Gioja (1301) improved the instrument and extended its use.

If the universal consent of history be worth anything, it declares the stability of commercial states to be as unsteady as the waters over which their vessels ride. Amalfi, the rival of Venice and Genoa, whose factories were established in every emporium of the commercial world, has become the habitation of a few fishermen, and its fame is now confined to reminiscences of past glory, and picturesque beauties of site and scenery over which time and conflicting temporal interests can work little of change.

> ―――――― " to him who sails
> Under the shore, a few white villages,
> Scattered above, below, some in the clouds,
> Some on the margin of the dark blue sea,
> And glittering through their lemon-groves, announce
> The region of Amalfi."

THE TEMPLES OF PÆSTUM.

> They stand between the mountains and the sea :
> Awful memorials, but of whom we know not !
>   *Rogers.*

ALL inquiry concerning Pæstum and its temples terminates in a few vague guesses; yet these, although historically valueless, add by their very obscurity to the interest which attaches to the memorials of a people utterly unknown. The silence of history contrasts with the ruined temples of Pæstum in a manner that powerfully affects the mind. Even the pyramids of Egypt yield in point of interest to these ruins : the former are immense structures of a character suited to withstand the combined action of time and the elements, and the mind readily admits that they belong to an age which authentic records cannot reach; the latter, on the contrary, are edifices of ordinary size, composed of architectural members whose details are liable to injury, and yet so singularly preserved that they might be the remains of a people not more than a century distant from ourselves.

> "Time was they stood along the crowded street,
> Temples of gods! and on their ample steps
> What various habits, various tongues beset
> The brazen gates for prayer and sacrifice !
> Time was perhaps the third was sought for justice;
> And here the judges sate, and heard, and judged.
> All silent now !"

Learned conjecture, taking the place of authentic history, attributes the origin of Pæstum to a Phœnician or Dorian colony. It was first named Posetan, or Postan, and was dedicated to Neptune. About five hundred years before the Christian era, the primitive inhabitants were expelled by the Sybarites, under whom the city assumed the Greek appellation of Posidonia. The Sybarites, in turn, gave place to the Lucanians, and these last to the Romans, who colonized the city and gave it the name of Pæstum. The poets, from Virgil to Claudian, allude to the blooming gardens of Pæstum, and celebrate "the Pæstan roses and their double spring." The final destruction of the city took place in the ninth century, when the Saracens drove out the inhabitants and compelled them to seek refuge in the neighbouring mountains. A Norman plunderer, Robert Guiscard, carried off a great portion of the ruins of Pæstum to construct and decorate the cathedral of Salerno. Owing probably to the unhealthiness of the district, the remaining memorials were not discovered till about the middle of the last century, when either a shepherd or a painter is said to have found them in the course of a morning's ramble from Capaccio.

The great antiquity of the Pæstan temples is determined by the style of their architecture, which is characterized by severe simplicity. The Romans seem never to have adopted the genuine Doric style, and since the Sybarites are said to have occupied the neighbouring plain at some distance from the temples, the inference is that these structures were the work of the primitive inhabitants. The temples are three in number. The one nearest to the foreground (referring to our view) is thought by some to have been a *curia*, or a *basilica*, and by others a market or exchange, since no vestiges of an altar have been discovered in it. The second building is named the temple of Neptune, and is the most majestic structure of the three. The distant ruin, designated the temple of Ceres, is much smaller than the other two. We shall not occupy space with an extended description of these buildings, since the engraving places them before the reader in a manner so satisfactory as to render textual comment unnecessary.

After their subjugation by the Romans, the Pæstans still retained a fond attachment to the institutions of Greece. Though forced to adopt a foreign dialect, and accommodate themselves to the manners of their conquerors, they were accustomed to assemble annually on one of the great festivals of Greece, to keep alive the memory of their origin, and to vent their lamentations in the ancient tongue of their country.

> "Parents and children mourn'd, and every year,
> ('Twas on the day of some old festival,)
> Met to give way to tears, and once again
> Talk in the ancient tongue of things gone by."

REGGIO.

SICILY is supposed at one time to have joined the Italian peninsula, from which it was afterwards rent by an earthquake; and in reference to this opinion the etymology of Reggio has been deduced from the Greek ῥήγνυμι, *to break*. Strabo, however, is of opinion that the ancient name, Rhegium or Regium, refers to the dignity and importance of the city at the time the appellation was given.

Reggio, the chief city of Calabria Ulterior, is situated on the Straits of Messina, opposite the Sicilian coast. The history of this place commences with certainty about seven hundred years before the Christian era, at which period it was founded by a party of Zanclæans from Sicily, together with some Chalcidians of Eubœa, and Messenians from Peloponnesus. The government of Rhegium was oligarchical for two hundred years, or until A.C. 490, when Anaxilaus II. usurped the sole authority. Under this prince the prosperity of the Rhegians reached its highest extent; but the latter succeeded in freeing themselves from the control of the sons of Anaxilaus, and ultimately secured a moderate and stable form of government. By preserving a strict neutrality in the hostilities between the Sicilians and their opponents, the Rhegians long maintained their independence; but they at length fell into the power of Dionysius the tyrant of Syracuse. During the war with Pyrrhus, this

city, at that time garrisoned by the Romans, was seized by a body of Campanians stationed there for its defence, and was exposed to all the licentiousness and rapacity of those mercenary troops. After they had held it for ten years, the place was besieged and taken by the Romans, who sent three hundred of its persecutors to Rome, where they were scourged and beheaded. On the fall of the empire, this city shared the common fate of the coast towns of Italy. It suffered severely from the Saracens; and in 1544 it was reduced to ashes by Barbarossa.

Reggio has often experienced fatal calamities from earthquakes. The walls of the city, rebuilt after their destruction by Dionysius, were totally overthrown during the great earthquake that preceded the Social war. In the last century it frequently suffered severely; and in February 1783, the same convulsions of the earth which were so fatal to Messina and a great part of Calabria, entirely destroyed Reggio. It was long before it arose again from its ruins; but its importance as the capital of the southern division of Calabria led the Neapolitan government to effect its restoration. The recent formation of a road from Naples to this extremity of the kingdom, must have a favourable influence over the prosperity of Reggio, whose neighbourhood is alike remarkable for its picturesque beauty and the fertility of its soil. The city is built on a gentle declivity. On the sea-side lies the *marina*, or esplanade, running parallel with the chief street; and the width of this avenue, and that of the transverse streets, renders Reggio one of the finest cities of the kingdom of Naples. The Straits of Messina, like a vast river, separate it from the shores of Sicily, where the snow-capped and towering Etna rises in all its majesty over the range of lower mountains.*

Julia, the daughter of Augustus, scandalized Rhegium by her presence, and here terminated her infamous life in exile. Names of worthier note, however, are associated with the ancient city,—those of Cicero, Titus, and St. Paul, the latter of whom records (Acts xxviii. 12, 13)— " And landing at Syracuse, we tarried there three days; and from thence we fetched a compass and came to *Rhegium*: and after one day the south wind blew, and we came the next day to Puteoli."

* It is in the Straits of Messina, and from Reggio, that the celebrated optical illusion named the Fata Morgana, is sometimes witnessed. "This singular exhibition has been frequently seen in the Straits of Messina, between Sicily and the coast of Italy, and whenever it takes place, the people, in a state of exultation, as if it were not only a pleasing but a lucky phenomenon, hurry down to the sea, exclaiming, 'Morgana! Morgana!' When the rays of the rising sun form an angle of 45° on the sea of Reggio, and when the surface of the water is perfectly unruffled either by the wind or the current, a spectator placed upon an eminence in the city, and having his back to the sun and his face to the sea, observes upon the surface of the water superb palaces, with their balconies and windows, lofty towers, herds and flocks grazing in wooded valleys and fertile plains, armies of men on horseback and on foot, with multiplied fragments of buildings, such as columns, pilasters, and arches. These objects pass rapidly in succession along the surface of the sea during the brief period of their appearance. The various objects thus enumerated are pictures of palaces and buildings actually existing on shore, and the living objects are of course only seen when they happen to form a part of the general landscape. If at the time that these phenomena are visible the atmosphere is charged with vapour or dense exhalations, the same objects which are depicted upon the sea will be seen also in the air, occupying a space which extends from the surface to the height of twenty-five feet. If the air is in a state to deposit dew, and is capable of forming the rainbow, the objects will be seen only on the surface of the sea, and will appear fringed with colours, as if seen through a prism."

BENEVENTO.

BENEVENTO, anciently *Beneventum* in the country of the Samnites, is a place of some interest to the classical historian. In this neighbourhood stood the town of Caudium, near which, in a place called *Caudinæ Furculæ*, a Roman army, under S. Veturius Calvinus and Spurius Posthumius, was compelled to surrender to the Samnites, and to pass beneath the yoke with every mark of degradation. Beneventum was a city of high antiquity, and claimed Diomedes for its founder. It long bore the inauspicious name of *Maleventum*, which was changed when it became a Roman colony into one of better omen. Its adherence to Rome during the second Punic War, obtained for it the thanks of the senate. After the fall of the empire, this city was possessed in succession by the Goths, the Greeks, and the Lombards. Under the latter people it became an independent principality, and ultimately rose to be a dukedom; and after having been governed by various princes, Lombard, Greek, and Norman, it at length fell under the dominion of the Roman pontiff. On the French invasion of Italy, and after the conquest of Naples, Bonaparte gave this city to Talleyrand; together with the title of Prince of Benevento; but on the termination of the Napoleon drama it was restored to the papal authority.

Benevento stands on a gentle elevation, at the foot of a bold ridge of hills. Its northern walls are bathed by the *Calore*, a river still enjoying its ancient name. A lofty bridge crosses the stream; and near this structure two heaps of stones are pointed out as the memorial of the burial place of Count Manfred of Suabia. This nobleman long maintained a struggle against Charles of Anjou and the pope; but at length, in January 1266, he suffered a signal defeat near Benevento, and rushing into the midst of his enemies, fell amongst a heap of slain. Charles, in a letter to the Roman pontiff, represented that the body of Manfred had received honourable sepulture; but this honourable interment consisted merely in throwing the corpse into a ditch, and permitting every soldier in the army to cast a stone upon it.

The citadel of Benevento, a structure of moderate but picturesque proportions, erected in 1323, is situated outside the city gates. The cathedral is a large fabric in the Saracenic style, but composed of ancient materials, the remains of imperial times. It is supported within by fifty columns of white marble, forming on each side a double aisle. Relics of Roman greatness may be traced at Benevento, in the remains of an amphitheatre and the ancient walls of the city, and in minor details of architectural decoration. The chief antiquity, however, is the triumphal arch of Trajan, forming one of the gates of the city. It consists of a single arch, and is of Parian marble, and entire, with the exception of a part of the cornice. Both sides are adorned with four Corinthian pillars raised on high pedestals. The frieze, panels, and indeed every part within and without the arch, are covered with rich sculptures, allusive to the achievements of the emperor. This triumphal arch is considered the most perfect thing of the kind existing; it appears, however, to be wanting in *simplicity*, the decorations being so crowded as to leave no repose for the eye, and no plane surface to give relief to the sculptures.

ISOLA DI SORA.

The climate of Benevento is humid and heavy, and strikingly in contrast with the pure air of Naples. The town has on the whole a good appearance; and it offers in the present day a better reception to travellers than it formerly afforded to Horace and his friends.

> Tendimus hinc recta Beneventum, ubi sedulus hospes,
> Pene macros, arsit, turdos dum versat in igne.
> Nam vaga per veteres dilapso flamma culinam,
> Vulcano, summum properabat lambere tectum.
> Convivas avidos coenam servosque timentes
> Tum rapere, atque omnes restinguere velle videres.
>
> *Hor. Sat.* I. v. 71—76.

> At our next Inn our host was almost burn'd,
> While some lean thrushes at the fire he turn'd.
> Through his old kitchen roll the god of fire,
> And to the roof the vagrant flames aspire;
> But hunger all our terrors overcame;
> We fly to save our meat, and quench the flame.
>
> *Francis.*

ISOLA DI SORA.

ISOLA DI SORA, a town of the tenth or eleventh century, is situated about two miles below the ancient Sora, which was successively held by the Samni, the Samnites, and the Romans. The neighbourhood of Sora is rendered classical by recollections of Cicero. The Arpine villa of the orator, the spot where the scene of his Dialogues with Atticus and Quintus on Legislation is laid, was situated in a valley watered by the Fibrenus. Everything in this locality is associated with the name of Cicero; an old ivy-mantled tower is still known as La Torre di Cicerone; and the foundation of an ancient bridge, some remains of which exist, is attributed to the father of Cicero.

The town of Isola is referred to in some records of the eleventh century under the title of *Insula filiorum Petri* (the island of the sons of Peter) which Petrus was a castaldus, or governor, of the district. The castle, to which the modern town owes its origin, is situated on a mass of rock that divides the stream of the Liris, which owing to this impediment in its course forms two cascades, the one a perpendicular fall of ninety-six feet, and the other a torrent rushing down an inclined plane of six hundred palms in extent. The divided waters insulate the castle and the town of Isola at its foot, and hence the latter has obtained its name. Isola once belonged to the Cantelmi family, until they, with other of the Italian nobles, conspired against Ferdinand, who in consequence reduced these feudal chiefs to submission, and bestowed their domains upon his adherents. The last possessor of this principality resigned it to the Neapolitan government in exchange for other estates, and from that period it was incorporated with Naples. The castle is still exteriorly an object of regard, but the "base uses" to which it is now applied, have destroyed the claims of the interior to any notice beyond that which is accorded by the Neapolitan cloth merchants, for whose fabrics it serves as a manufactory. Near the site of Cicero's villa, a Cartaria, or paper-mill has been established, which supplies the greater part of the paper consumed in the kingdom of Naples. This mill, seen in our view a little beyond the castle, on the right, is driven by the waters of the Fibrenus, which, after they have done their work at the factory, are led with considerable taste through the pleasure grounds of the proprietor.

Isola contains about three thousand inhabitants, all of whom are either directly or indirectly interested in the manufactures of cloth, paper, or iron-wire, to which the modern town owes its prosperity. Its connection with the Roman States has occasionally involved it in calamity. At some periods in the seventeenth and eighteenth centuries it was devastated by troops of brigands, one of which, under a celebrated commander named l'apone, used to levy taxes, and assume all the privileges of a feudal sovereign. On the first entrance of the French, in 1798, it underwent disasters of a similar nature, to which it was too often subjected at later periods, in consequence of the unsubmitting disposition of the natives.

SUBIACO.

SUBIACO is a beautiful little town, situated in the valley of the Anio, and surrounded by mountains which range as offsets from the Apennines. It is distant forty-four miles from Rome, and is much resorted to by artists for the picturesque scenery of its neighbourhood. The establishment of Monachism in Italy is intimately connected with this locality. It was here that the eremite, St. Benedict, in 515, composed those rules of monastic life which he afterwards imposed upon his community of monks, which thus became the leading order of regular monachism in Europe.

Subiaco derived its ancient name of *Sublaqueum* from the artificial lakes of the Villa of Nero, below which it was built. The ruins of this villa are still to be seen, about a mile from the town, and they take an interest from the record of Tacitus that it was here the cup of the tyrant was dashed from his lips by lightning, and the table at which he was reclining overthrown. In the vicinity of these ruins is the celebrated monastery of Santa Scholastica, founded in the fifth century. This building is remarkable for its three cloisters, the work of different ages, and it was once famous for its library; but the most interesting incident connected with its history is the introduction of the printing-press into Italy by the German printers Sweynheim and Pannarts. About a mile from Santa Scholastica stands the monastery of St. Benedict, environed by scenery of the grandest character. The building is

of different dates, and is built against the rocky hill on nine arches of considerable height, and consists of two stories. The cave in which St. Benedict lived in solitude, and where he wrote his rules of monastic life, is underneath the building. It is identified by some authorities with the oracle of Faunus, who according to tradition reigned in Italy 1300 years B. C., and was exalted into a deity after his death. If this conjecture is correct, the Holy Cave of Subiaco is the most venerable retreat of lying oracles extant. It contains a statue of its second oracle, St. Benedict, by Bernini.

The dark and narrow streets of Subiaco present a repulsive aspect. The church was built by Pius VI., who was abbot of the monastery for many years before his elevation to the papal chair. The abbatical palace, seated on the summit of the rock, was erected by the same pontiff. This edifice was anciently a residence of the popes, and was then accessible by a carriage road, but has long ceased to be so. The town of Subiaco seated on an eminence, crowned with this ancient castle, offers a scene of singular attraction and beauty.

ASSISI.

CONVENT OF SAN FRANCISCO.

———————— let none who speak
Of that place, say Assisi; for its name
Were lamely so delivered; but the East,*
To call things rightly be it henceforth styled.
Paradiso, xi. 49 – 50.

PROPERTIUS, Cimabue, Giotto, Dante, and Metastasio, names commanding homage, render Assisi deeply interesting to every lover of the sister arts of poetry and painting. Propertius, a native of the ancient Assisium, is regarded by classical scholars as the rival of Tibullus in elegiac verse. The paintings of Cimabue and Giotto gave a proud distinction to Assisi in the thirteenth and fourteenth centuries; and Dante, their contemporary, celebrates in immortal verse their artistic triumphs and the piety of St. Francis, whose religious fervour powerfully influenced their genius. Metastasio, the operatic poet of Italy, was born at Assisi at the close of the seventeenth century. He was the son of a common soldier.

Of the ancient Assisium we know nothing beyond its having been the birth-place of Propertius; but some remains of aqueducts and tombs, and of a theatre, together with a temple of Minerva, now converted into the church of Santa Maria della Minerva, bear testi-

———————————————————————

* Dante styles Assisi the "East," by way of eminence, in compliment to St. Francis.

mony to its importance in the days of elder Italy. The middle age history of Assisi refers almost exclusively to the foundation of a religious brotherhood, named the order of St. Francis. The founder of this community was a native of Assisi; and a little church, the Chiesa Nuova, occupies the spot where he was born. Here is shown the prison in which he was confined by his father, who was exceedingly provoked by his prodigal distribution of alms. From the brotherhood of St. Francis several reformed orders have sprung, and to one of these, the order of the Holy Apostles, belongs the Sagro Convento, or Holy Convent of St. Francis, a building to which, in every sense, a *catholic* interest is attached. For the catholic *particular* there is the body of St. Francis deposited in the subterranean conventual church; and for the catholic *universal* there are the frescoes of Cimabue and Giotto, adorning the roof and walls of the upper and middle churches.

The Sagro Convento was raised in the brief space of two years, in the interval between 1228 and 1230. It is an immense structure, and its walls in former times enclosed a greater number of monks than even the great monastery of Monte Casino. Including the subterranean church which forms the mausoleum of St. Francis, there are three churches rising one above another. The upper church is a fine specimen of Gothic, with lancet windows of painted glass. The roof and walls are decorated with frescoes by Cimabue, embracing a variety of subjects, amongst which are leading incidents in sacred history from the Creation to the Descent from the Cross, together with passages in the life of St. Francis, some of which last are attributed to Giotto. The seats in the choir were carved by one of the monks of the convent at the end of the fifteenth century. The campanile of this church is a massive pile, with stairs *à cordoni*, and commands from its summit an extensive and interesting prospect. The middle church has a gloomy and low appearance, but is rich in treasures of art. Giotto's three paintings of the Franciscan virtues, Poverty, Chastity, and Obedience, and a fourth named the glorification of St. Francis, occupy the four triangular compartments of the vault. In the cross-aisle is the celebrated Crucifixion by Pietro Cavallino, the pupil of Giotto, a fresco admired by Michael Angelo for its grandeur. In other divisions of the building, and in the adjoining chapels, are interesting works of art belonging to the school of Cimabue. The convent and its cloisters are not less interesting than the triple church. They contain a series of heads of eminent Franciscans by Adone Doni; and in the refectory is a fine painting of the Last Supper by Solimene.

Besides the Sagro Convento, Assisi contains other structures of great interest both as regards their architecture and internal decoration. Amongst these may be named the church of Santa Chiara enriched with the frescoes of Giotto; the cathedral dedicated to St. Rufinus the first bishop of Assisi; and the church of Santa Maria della Minerva, to which is attached the magnificent portico of the ancient temple of Minerva.

The city is surrounded with battlements and towers, and commanded by a lofty ruined citadel; and these features, combined with a long line of aqueducts, render Assisi one of the most picturesque scenes in Italy. A great fair is held here annually from the 21st July to the 1st August, during which period the grant of indulgences used to bring a multitude of visitors from all parts of Catholic Europe. Assisi is celebrated for the manufacture of needles and iron files; and of the former articles the yearly produce is four thousand pounds' weight.

LORETTO.

> A brace of sinners, for no good,
> Were ordered to the Virgin Mary's shrine,
> Who at Loretto dwelt in wax, stone, wood,
> And, in a curl'd white wig, look'd wond'rous fine.
>
> *W. Arnt.*

NO antique fame belongs to Loretto, which is, nevertheless, the most famous locality in the known world. But *what* a celebrity is that in which it rejoices! The distinction of having been, for five centuries and a half, the depository of a dilapidated cottage which the *catholic* wisdom of ages has decreed, and continues to decree, ought to be verily and indeed taken and received as the identical house of Joseph the carpenter, wherein he, together with the Virgin Mary, and the infant Christ, dwelt at Nazareth! And let no heretic throw discredit on the holy legend, for a pious hermit, accompanied by sixteen persons of reputation, made a journey to compare the walls of the house with the foundations remaining at Nazareth; and, moreover, the *bricks* are alive to this day at Loretto, to confirm the truth of old tradition.

When the crusaders abandoned Palestine, in 1291, the house of the Virgin, we are told, was borne through the air by angels and deposited in Dalmatia, where it appears to have met with little respect, for its divine carriers, three years afterwards, transported it thence to the opposite sea-shore of Italy, when two brothers quarrelled for the possession of it, and one slew the other. After this tragical event the angels resumed their labours, and carried the sacred habitation to the very spot where it is now fixed, which at that time was in the midst of a forest. Persons were found to bear testimony that they had seen the house hovering in the air, and many declared that they had found it in the morning on a spot which they knew to have been vacant the evening before. An old lady, named *Lauretta*, upon whose land it ultimately rested, had credulity or craft enough to assist in maintaining this monstrous tale, and thus gained the identification of her name with the miracle.

The miracle of Loretto gradually attracted the attention of the whole Christian world. Princes and prelates, rich and poor, hastened with pious alacrity to offer their devotions before the holy house. Gifts and votive offerings accumulated; a magnificent church was erected; gold, silver, and diamonds blazed around every altar, and heaps of treasures loaded the shelves of the sacristy; various edifices arose in the vicinity of the new temple, and Loretto became a populous city.

The Chiesa della Santa Casa, or Church of the Holy House, is a noble structure, planned by Bramante, and built in the form of a cross. Under the dome stands the Santa Casa, a building of brick, about thirty feet long, and fourteen feet high. The smoke of numberless lamps

LORETTO.

has so much discoloured the structure, that the material of which it is composed is not readily ascertained, except in some places where sceptical heretics have scraped the surface. The Romanists deny that it is brick, and affirm that it is a reddish grey stone unknown in Italy; but neither the denial nor the assertion can stand in the face of a fact. And why, after all, be so squeamish about the material? The miracle ought to be accounted so much the greater, if the angelic bearers not only conveyed the holy house beyond the reach of the infidel, but also converted the Syrian *stone* into veritable Italian *brick*. The interior of the Santa Casa is divided by a silver rail into two parts of unequal dimensions. In the largest division is an altar; and in the lesser one, which is considered peculiarly holy, is a cedar image of the Virgin, placed over the chimney-piece. This image is decked in glittering robes, wears a triple crown, and is adorned with precious stones. She holds an image of the Infant Jesus, and a globe. Her face is of an Ethiopian hue, and resembles that of an Eastern idol adorned with barbaric pomp, rather than that of the meek and lowly mother of Christ. The exterior of the house is cased with Carrara marble, enriched with *bassi rilievi* of subjects from the life of the Virgin, executed by the most distinguished sculptors of Italy. The church which enshrines the Santa Casa is profusely decorated, and contains not less than twenty chapels, many of which possess fine pictures, and admirable mosaic copies of the works of Barroccio, Luchero, and others. The wealth heaped upon "the Virgin Mary's shrine" *was* immense; it is still great, but the French laid sacrilegious hands not only upon the Queen of Heaven herself, but also upon her dowry; and when Napoleon afterwards, in 1801, restored our Lady of Loretto to the pope, he quite forgot to return the small matter of trinkets and bijouterie. Lassels, whose travels in Italy were published in 1670, describes some of the treasures of the Santa Casa, which for the edification of our readers we catalogue at the foot of the page.*

The city of Loretto is beautifully situated on the brow of a hill overlooking the Adriatic, and is distant from the sea little more than two miles. The approach from Foligno is striking.

---

* An altar of silver, the gift of Cosmo II., Grand Duke of Florence; a lamp of gold, as large as two men could carry, the votive offering of the Senate of Venice in a time of plague; two great candlesticks of pure gold, the gift of Magdalena d'Austria, grand Duchess of Florence; an old cupboard, with some little earthen dishes, the moveable estate of St. Joseph; a door of silver, provided for aforesaid cupboard by a Duke of Parma; a window of the holy house enriched with silver, said window having afforded ingress to the saluting angel; many silver lamps; the statue of the Virgin and her Son, done by St. Luke; the vault, or walls, of the Virgin, of divers colours and stuffs, whereof one, valued at forty thousand crowns, and presented by the Infanta Isabella of Flanders, is studded with diamonds to the number of three thousand, and over-wrought with twenty thousand pearls; crowns of diamonds for the Virgin and Child, given by a Queen of France; a bunch of rich jewels, presented by a Prince of Transylvania, and covering the breast of the Virgin's statue; a collar of rubies, pearls, and diamonds, with a rich cross attached, given by Cardinal Standrati; a glory of precious stones, adorning the niche in which the statue stands; a row of lamps of pure gold as big as a man's head, one whereof exceeds the rest, and was the gift of Sigismond, King of Polonia; to which add a profusion of rich vows and presents from great princes. But the treasury of the Santa Casa contained even greater riches than those enumerated. Here were entire services for the altar in amber, agate, lapis lazuli, and crystal; precious stones in prodigal excess; and piles of costly things of which even to write a catalogue would prove a laborious penance. Let us not, however, omit special mention of the richly enamelled silver-covered jewel, with the picture of the Blessed Virgin, the votive offering of two Bohemian Counts and a Gentleman, who were unceremoniously pitched from a high window in Prague, by the Calvinists, and yet, in consequence of the Virgin's intervention, received no damage from the fall!

From this point the dome of the Chiesa della Santa Casa forms a prominent object; on the left lies the fertile valley of the Musone, and around are the remains of the forest in which the holy house at length found an abiding rest.

ANCONA.

THE name of Ancona is derived from the Greek ἀγκών, and is supposed to refer to the form of the promontory upon which the city is built. This place is distant about fourteen miles from Loretto. Though situated so nearly together, these two localities differ in a very marked manner from each other. Loretto relies for its prosperity on the multitudes of pilgrims and devotees that visit the far-famed shrine, and supports its torpid inhabitants on the wages of imposture; whilst Ancona presents a scene of commercial bustle and activity, and finds employment for its citizens in the useful occupations of maritime trade.

We learn from Strabo that Ancona was built by a band of Syracusan patriots, who fled from the tyranny of Dionysius, and settled upon this coast. It is supposed by some to have had even an earlier existence, since it is mentioned, in the Periplus of Scylax, as having belonged to the Umbri; but this authority is by no means decisive, it being subject of dispute with the learned whether the Periplus is really the work of the author whose name it bears. Under the Romans, Ancona became a famous sea-port; and in the reign of Trajan those magnificent works were constructed which remain objects of admiration to the present day. Its situation on the coast, and its importance as a seat of maritime power, exposed it to the vicissitudes common to so many towns of Italy, after the fall of the empire. In 550 it was besieged by Totila, and in the same century it was seized and plundered by the Lombards, after whom came the Saracens, who surpassed their predecessors in outrage and oppression. It next became a free city, and in the twelfth century it was one of the most important towns of the league of Lombardy. In 1173, Ancona was besieged by Christian, Archbishop of Mayence, who had been sent into Italy by Frederick Barbarossa as his representative. This memorable siege furnishes many examples of patriotism and heroic self-devotion. The Venetians, the allies of the Archbishop, had built a vast ship, named Il Mondo. Wooden towers of great height and magnitude had been erected on the deck of this colossal ship, which was considered as the very centre of the power of the fleet. A priest of Ancona, observing the havoc which it occasioned, resolved to attempt its destruction. He swam out boldly towards the vessel, bearing an axe between his teeth, and succeeded in cutting the cables and turning the ship adrift amongst its allies, thereby rendering it a source of mischief to the besiegers themselves. After this daring performance he effected his escape from the Venetians who pursued him, and reached the shore uninjured. Another example of courage was given by a woman, who rushed with a lighted torch and set fire to a wooden tower erected by the besiegers. She stood calmly at the base of the tower, regardless of the missiles aimed at her, and there remained until the flames had spread over the entire battery of the enemy. It was during the famine occasioned by this siege, that the young mother, called "the heroine of Ancona," performed an act of exalted and noble charity, characteristic of her sex. This woman, who was young, handsome, and of high birth, observed a soldier too much exhausted to obey the summons which called him to battle. She withdrew her breast from the lips of her infant and offered it to the warrior, who thus refreshed went forth with his comrades to the defence of his country. Another example is given, in which fortitude and tenderness are equally conspicuous. A woman beheld her sons perishing for want of sustenance, and having no other means of satisfying their hunger, she yielded to the great necessity and opened a vein in her left arm, and *from her own blood* she formed by culinary preparation, a costly food that prolonged the lives of her children at the imminent risk of her own.

Ancona continued in the enjoyment of its privileges, as an independent territory, until 1532, when Gonzaga, general of Clement VII., under the specious pretext of defending it against the Turks, erected a fort and filled the city with papal troops. It thus became incorporated with the papal states; the aristocratic constitution which had existed for nearly two centuries was overthrown; the senators were expelled, and the principal nobles banished. It remained in connection with the holy see until 1798, when it was seized by the French, who in the following year surrendered it to the united forces of the Russians, Austrians, and the Turks. In 1808 it was again in the possession of the French, and formed part of the territory of Napoleon, as King of Italy; was restored in 1814 to the papal government; in 1860, was captured by the Sardinian army, and now belongs to the kingdom of Italy.

Few cities present a more imposing exterior than Ancona, but it is only externally that it is either striking or beautiful; the streets are dark and narrow; and, with the exception of the Marina, which was laid out by order of Pius VI., the whole interior has a miserable character common to the coast towns of Italy. The magnificent Mole of Trajan, and the triumphal arch erected in his honour, are the objects of chief interest. The greatest part of the Mole still remains, is a solid compact wall, formed of huge stones bound together by iron, and rising to a considerable height above the level of the sea; it serves now merely as a protection to the quays that are built within it. The New Mole, which is much lower, stands close to that of Trajan, and sustains a triumphal arch, of the Tuscan order, erected in honour of Clement XII., and raised in manifest rivalry of the one dedicated to the emperor, yet serving, at most, only as a foil to the beauties of the imperial monument. The arch of Trajan is still entire, though stripped of its metallic ornaments; the order is Corinthian; the materials Parian marble. It was formerly decorated with statues, busts, and probably inferior ornaments of bronze, but these were all destroyed by the gothic invaders of Italy, whose avarice and rapacity defaced every building and monument in which either bronze or iron was found.

The Cathedral, dedicated to San Ciriaco, the first bishop of Ancona, is built upon a com-

manding eminence overlooking the town and harbour. It occupies the site of an ancient temple of Venus, to which Juvenal makes allusion:—

<blockquote>
Ante domum Veneris, quam Dorica sustinet Ancon.

Juvenal, iv. 39

Where Venus' shrine does fair Ancona grace.

Dryden.
</blockquote>

The present structure is of different dates, ranging from the tenth to the fourteenth century. Many portions of the heathen temple are incorporated with the Christian edifice, a circumstance too often observable in the churches of Italy, where the idolatry of ancient Rome is frequently brought to mind not less by the buildings themselves, than by the ecclesiastical ceremonies enacted within them.

Ancona, with its suburbs, numbers a population of more than thirty-five thousand inhabitants. It is divided into two parts, the Old City and the New City; the former occupies the highest ground, and is the resort of the poorer classes; and the latter, situated on the slopes and along the shores of the sea, is inhabited by merchants and others, who form the wealthier portion of the community. This maritime city is the birth-place of Carlo Maratta. It enjoys, however, another distinction more generally appreciated, namely, the beauty of its women; to which let us add the more enduring distinction implied in the testimony of Eustace, who says that the morals of the people of Ancona are acknowledged to be pure, and the conduct of their females unimpeachable.

BOLOGNA.

HISTORY recognises in Bologna the Etruscan Felsina, the capital of the twelve cities of the Etrurian league. Its foundation is attributed to King Felsinus who reigned in Etruria 984 years before Christ. From his successor, Bona, the city obtained the new appellation of Bononia. Some antiquaries, however, refer the change of name to that period (B. C. 191) when the possession passed from the Gauls to the Romans. It attached itself to the fortunes of Antony, and the celebrated meeting between him and Octavius took place on a small island in the river Rhenus, between Modena and Bologna. In the reign of Claudius, Bononia sustained such extensive injury from fire, that a grant of ten million sestertii was made from the public treasury for its repair. The first Christian church (dedicated to St. Felix) was built here in the third century; but this edifice was destroyed in the persecution under Diocletian. Several distinguished persons endured the pains of martyrdom at Bononia in the first centuries of the Christian era.

Bononia appears to have suffered less from the barbarians than other places in the north of Italy; and in the middle ages it became independent of the German emperors, and at length obtained a charter from Henry V., (1112) granting to its citizens the right of choosing their own magistrates and municipal authorities. It subsequently became one of the foremost cities of the Guelphic league, and maintained a fierce contest with the Ghibelline party, which terminated with the signal defeat of the latter. Towards the end of the thirteenth century the city was divided into two rival factions named the Lambertazzi and the Gieremei, whose feuds arose out of a domestic tragedy. The Gieremei attached themselves to the Guelphs, and the Lambertazzi became the leaders of the Ghibellines.* The mediation of Nicholas III. was sought to appease this strife, but the tyranny of his legate interrupted the peace which his intervention had procured. A revolution took place in 1334, which ended in the sale of the city to the Visconti of Milan. After a period of anarchy, during which it frequently changed masters, Bologna was at length compelled to acknowledge the supremacy of the papal power, to which it has ever since been subject. Its position was temporarily changed by Napoleon, but when his star ceased to be in the ascendant, the former order of things returned, and the city was restored to the papal see. It is now incorporated in the kingdom of Italy.

The ecclesiastical annals of Bologna are inflated and of great pretensions, and give an odour of sanctity to the city, exceeded only by that of Rome itself. We shall pass these by. The University founded by the emperor Theodosius, A. D. 425, is celebrated for a succession of distinguished professors, amongst whom Mezzofanti, formerly professor of Greek and the Oriental languages, but now the Prefect of the Vatican and a Cardinal, claims especial notice. This extraordinary man is said to be master of forty languages; but the roundness of the number may excite suspicion that there is some exaggeration, and more particularly since Mezzofanti himself has disclaimed such extensive acquirements. It is, however, abundantly evident that

---

* We have already noticed (see *Florence*, page 26) that the protracted contest between the Guelphs and Ghibellines, the former the partisans of the church and the latter those of the emperor, was made subservient to the revengeful quarrels which occasionally arose between the noble families of Italy. We take the present opportunity of correcting a slight error into which an unfaithful authority led us, at page 26. We there stated that "a young man of the Buondelmonti family had been betrothed to a young lady of the family *Uberti*," whereas the lady was of the *Amidei* family. The Amidei took counsel of their kinsmen how they ought to resent the insult offered them by the Buondelmonti, upon which Mosca degli Uberti advised the assassination of the faithless lover.

The strife between the Guelphs and Ghibellines being so important a feature in the middle age history of Italy, a brief account of its origin cannot be unacceptable. We give it as narrated by Giovanni Florentino.—"There formerly resided in Germany two wealthy and well-born individuals, whose names were Guelfe and Ghibelline, very near neighbours, and greatly attached to each other. Returning together one day from the chase, there unfortunately arose some difference of opinion as to the merits of one of their hounds, which was maintained on both sides so very warmly, that from being almost inseparable friends and companions, they became each other's deadliest enemies. The division increasing, both sides collected parties of followers to annoy each other. The neighbouring lords and barons divided, according to their motives, either with the Guelf or the Ghibelline, and many serious affrays took place, and several persons fell victims to the feud. Ghibelline, being hard pressed, sought assistance from Frederick the First, the reigning emperor; upon which Guelfe applied to the pope, Honorius II., who was then at variance with the emperor. It was thus that the apostolic see became connected with the Guelfs, and the emperor with the Ghibellines; and it was thus that a vile hound became the origin of a deadly hate between two nobles;" nor this alone, for it became the foundation of a national quarrel that deluged the principal cities of Italy with blood. We have seen how the feud was introduced into the city of Florence. Its introduction into Pistoia was in the following manner.

he has a great knowledge of languages; although, if we may trust a lady's judgment on such a point, he has sacrificed to these aerial triumphs the acquirement of any very profound knowledge. Such an opinion is certainly not inconsistent with ordinary experience; for we believe it has seldom been observed of persons having a great aptitude for the attainment of languages, that they are also remarkable for mental power. Indeed, the study of languages, if pursued beyond moderate limits, produces paralysis of the mind.

Bologna derives celebrity from its school of painting, which numbers many illustrious names. The first academy of art in Bologna was opened by Franco Bolognese, one of the early followers of Giotto. But the greatest epoch of this school was led on by the three Caracci, who introduced a style of painting entirely new, and overthrew many of the venerated and long established maxims of art. To these masters, and to their pupils, Domenichino and Guido, the school of Bologna is chiefly indebted for its fame. Our limited space forbids us to dwell upon the merits of these painters, or to attempt an enumeration of their works. The churches of Bologna teem with their labours, and the Gallery of the Academy is a treasury of art of which the most laboured description could convey no adequate idea. To name only a few of the paintings: In the Gallery are found the Madonna and Child of Ludovico Caracci; the Communion of St. Jerome, by Agostino Caracci; the Martyrdom of St. Agnes, by Domenichino; the Madonna della Pietà of Guido, and his Massacre of the Innocents; the Magdalen of Guercino; the Santa Cecilia of Raphael; and the Madonna and Child of Parmegiano. In the church of San Stefano is the Saint Ursula of Simon of Bologna; the cathedral possesses the celebrated painting of the Annunciation, the last work of Ludovico Caracci; and the church of St. Bartolommeo contains the Nativity by Agostino Caracci. But it is hopeless to attempt even an indication of the leading works of art existing in the palaces, churches, and public institutions at Bologna.

The streets in Bologna are narrow, and the exterior of the public buildings is by no means

---

In that city flourished a noble family, named the Cancellieri, the offspring of one father by two wives. A division arose between the brothers in consequence of a rivalry in the affections of a lovely and enchanting girl; and the family separated into two parties, the offspring of the first wife taking the title of Bianchi, and the brothers of the second marriage that of Negri, or Neri. In a skirmish that followed, the Neri sustained a defeat, whereupon they sent their relative, the rival of the Bianchi, to offer terms and entreat forgiveness. The latter would listen to no accommodation, but satiated their vengeance by chopping off the right hand of the youth. This cruel action raised the indignation of the whole city, which then became implicated in the family quarrel. The citizens endeavoured to avert the coming evil by an appeal to the Florentines, who caused the partisans on both sides to be sent to Florence. But this had no other effect than to transfer the bloody feuds of the Bianchi and the Neri to Florence, where the former sided with the Ghibellines, and the latter with the Guelphs. The Bianchi with their Florentine adherents subsequently returned to Pistoia, and drove the Guelphic favourers of the Neri into exile.

The incident alluded to in our text, which served to foment the national quarrel in Bologna was this. Bonifazio Giaremei sought and won the affections of Imelda Lambertazzi. The brothers of Imelda having found the lovers in company with each other, dragged Bonifazio from their sister's presence and dispatched him with a poisoned dagger. Imelda afterwards returned to her lover, and endeavoured to restore him by sucking the poison from the wound, but failed in the generous effort, and sacrificed her own life. The families instantly declared war against each other, and the Great Piazza was a scene of battle and bloodshed for forty days. It was not until six years afterwards that a reconciliation was accomplished, when these families and their adherents once more met on the scene of their first struggle to exchange the kiss of peace.

proportioned to the fame and to the opulence of the city. The cathedral is comparatively a modern edifice, its original dating back no farther than 1605. The exterior is in the Roman, and the interior in the Corinthian style. The church of San Petronio presents an imposing appearance, but the most interesting circumstance connected with it is the *meridian* of Cassini, which is traced on its pavement.* An arcade of the extraordinary length of three miles, conducts to the church of the Madonna di S. Luca. This remarkable work was raised by the voluntary contributions of persons of every class in Bologna, for the purpose of accommodating in all seasons and in all weather, the crowds who flock to pay their devotions to the Virgin. At the annual fête of the Madonna the arcade presents an exciting scene, in which, however, little of the solemnity of a religious festival is observable.

Two brick towers, the Torre Asinelli and the Torre Garisenda, attract the traveller's attention by their slenderness and height, and yet more by their inclination from the perpendicular. In this last respect they resemble the tower of Pisa, and the cause of inclination is generally admitted to be the same in both cases, namely, a sinking of the earth. The towers of Bologna do not incline in the same direction, but towards each other; and the Torre Garisenda has the greatest inclination of the two.

The situation of Bologna offers very few points whence a favourable view of the city can be obtained. Our engraving exhibits it as seen from the descent of the hill of San Michael in Bosco. In this view, the cathedral, and other striking objects, including the leaning towers, form the most conspicuous features.†

---

* This meridian was originally drawn by Ignatio Danti, but Cassini, in 1653, conceived the idea of extending and correcting it, a task which he completed in two years. The results of this scientific achievement furnished more correct tables of the sun than had previously existed, by which the quantities of parallax and refraction were determined with an exactness unknown before. The son of this celebrated man followed up his father's labours, and by a remeasurement of the meridian discovered the true figure of the earth. Other branches of the Cassini family advanced the elements of geographical science to a high degree of perfection.

† There is a facetious novel by Giovanni Fiorentino, relating to a Bolognese student, which is worthy of mention, since it suggested to Shakspeare several of the most amusing scenes in "The Merry Wives of Windsor." The incidents of the novel, in brief, are these:—The student entreats his tutor to instruct him in the art of making love, a proposition to which the worthy professor, who esteems himself an adept in this branch of the humanities, readily assents. The scholar makes rapid progress under his teacher, but unfortunately, and quite unknowingly, chooses the professor's wife as his subject—to speak surgically. The amusement of the novel turns on the dilemmas of the poor professor, who can scarcely restrain his jealousy, yet dares not come to an explanation. At length, when matters are tending to an awful crisis, the student becomes aware of his position and makes a sudden retreat to Rome, having discovered that he has been "learning too much at other people's expense." The fertile imagination of our great dramatic poet has given a ten-fold interest to the incidents of the novel. In the latter, the student, who has been endeavouring to obtain the lady's love, is hastily hidden from the eyes of the professor under a heap of linen; but is remained for Shakspeare to invent all the humours of the buck-basket. The student effects his ultimate escape from the professor by a mere act of audacity on the part of his wife; but does not, like "the old woman of Brentford," receive in retiring the dramatic justice of "Master Ford's" cudgel.

FERRARA.

GLOOMY remains of departed grandeur are now the principal features of the ducal city of the house of Este, a princely family of distinguished lineage, from which the royalty of Britain traces a direct descent. "People talk," says a captivating writer, "of a city of the dead, and the phrase is very poetically strong, but it will not do for Ferrara; and yet, beyond all comparison, Ferrara has the saddest aspect to my fancy that ever city presented. It is not dead, for there are human beings still living and moving about in its melancholy, desolate-looking streets; but it looks like the last, ragged, rotten, remnant of a worn out world, struggling as it were for vital breath, and very nearly breathing its last sigh." Yet, despite of its gloom and desolation, Ferrara presents attractions such as few cities in Italy can offer; there Ariosto laughed, and Tasso groaned; and there "Parasina" and her paramour expiated their great offence, for which—such are human sympathies—they have been immortalized by the poet. But more of these anon.

Ferrara has no classical history. Its origin is referred to the fifth century; but nothing of interest is recorded concerning it until its association with the house of Este, in the twelfth century. This family, in the person of its representative, Azzo of Este, established its authority in Ferrara by an act of violence. Marchesella, the only descendant of the Adelardi, who had long exercised the chief authority amongst the Ferrarese, was forcibly seized by Azzo, who by marriage with her secured the recognition of his sovereignty. He transmitted the government to his son, Azzo VI., who, in 1208, received homage from the citizens, and power to nominate his successor. Thus Ferrara presented the first example of a free Italian city surrendering its liberty to a lord, and became the first of those principalities into which Italy was soon after divided.

The descendants of the house of Este came to be acknowledged as hereditary princes, holding generally of the pope, though sometimes asserting their independence. In 1452, Paul II. gave to Borso d'Este the title of Duke of Ferrara. An historical incident, connected with the reign of this ducal sovereign, forms the subject of an interesting novel by Niccolo Granucci. A youth, named Polidoro, obtained the affections of the beautiful Ortensia, to whose charms a host of admirers were paying homage. At one of their secret meetings the lover prevailed upon his mistress to receive a ring as a pledge of his love, and the seal of their betrothment. Scarcely had he retired, before a rival suitor attempted a forcible entrance at Ortensia's window. The maiden seized a sword that hung in her apartment, and struck the intruder so violently that he fell to the ground mortally wounded. The cries and groans of the dying man brought the officers of justice to the spot, and they, in their search for the assassin, laid hands upon Polidoro, who still lingered near Ortensia's residence. The lover, fearing to compromise his mistress, urged nothing in his defence, and his silence being received as an acknowledgment of his guilt, he was sentenced to death. When Ortensia learned the danger in which her lover stood, she threw aside maidenly fear, and sought Duke Borso, to whom she related all the circumstances of the suitor's death, and besought pardon for the innocent Polidoro. The duke not only granted her reasonable request, but also interested himself to obtain the consent of the two families to the union of the lovers. This he effected; and when he joined the hands of Ortensia and Polidoro, he made this naïve remark to his courtiers, "I think she did well to put the other poor fellow first out of his pain; he could not have borne this."

The dukedom of Ferrara descended, in the sixteenth century, to Alfonso I., whose reign is rendered illustrious by its association with the lays of Ariosto. The immediate patron of the poet was the duke's brother, the Cardinal Ippolito, who after having been made a prince of the church by Alexander Borgia, when only thirteen years of age, distinguished himself through life by his vices and brutality. It is related of him, that on one occasion a lady repelled his advances by declaring that she preferred his brother Giulio's eyes to Ippolito's whole body; upon which the monstrous villain hired two ruffians to put out his brother's eyes, and he is even said to have been present whilst this act of cruelty was performed. We need not be surprised to learn that Ippolito proved an ungenerous patron. He appears to have retained Ariosto in no higher capacity than that of a jester and court drudge. When the poet presented to him his *Orlando Furioso*, he repaid its author with insult, couched in terms so disgustingly offensive as to be unfit for repetition.

Alfonso II. was the patron of Tasso, and the liberality of his patronage may be gathered from the biography of the poet (*Sorrento, page* 107). It must, however, be admitted that Tasso was an unruly *pet*, and perhaps Alfonso might have proved more generous, if the poet had shown more prudence. The extinction of the legitimate branch of the Este family, on the death of Alfonso II., enabled Clement VIII., in 1597, to attach Ferrara to the papal territory.

The visitor to Ferrara regards with great interest the naked desolation of the old ducal palace, in whose apartments Tasso breathed forth his eloquent verses, and, if fame speaks truly, excited passionate love in the breast of a princess. Since the publication of Byron's "Parisina," the ciceroni have determined all the localities of that tale of crime, and they lead the visitor from room to room with a precision that has too much the air of contrivance. A brief extract from Gibbon reveals all that needs be told relative to this revolting incident. "Under the reign of Nicholas III.," (early in the fifteenth century,) "Ferrara was polluted with a domestic tragedy. By the testimony of an attendant, and his own observation, the Marquis of Este discovered the incestuous loves of his wife Parasina, and Hugo his bastard son, a beautiful and valiant youth. They were beheaded in the castle by the sentence of a father and husband, who published his shame, and survived their execution."

The prison of Tasso in the Hospital of St. Anne, excites much sentimental commiseration. The dungeon in which he was at first confined is horrible enough, but the poet passed only a few months of his captivity there; and probably he would never have been consigned to this place, if his patron had not really believed him to be mad. It is not very long since, that chains, and stripes, and dungeon-gloom, were deemed necessary and wholesome coercion for maniacs; we must not, therefore, charge Alfonso with cruelty for treating a supposed lunatic according to ordinary rule; and, more especially, when we learn from Tasso himself, that at the end of eight months he was removed to an apartment in which he could walk about and *philosophize*. The house of the gay and light-hearted Ariosto, and the Public Library where his manuscripts,

together with his chair and inkstand, are exhibited to the worshippers of genius, form the third great point of attraction in Ferrara.

Ferrara obtained some eminence by its school of painting, founded and patronized by the Este family. In its palmy days this city contained nearly one hundred thousand inhabitants, but its population decreased rapidly after the death of Alfonso II.; and at the present time it scarcely exceeds one-fourth of its former strength. Ferrara is not wanting in churches, and public buildings, nor in remains of art, but there is an oppressive gloom pervading the place, and were it not for the stirring associations connected with its past history, few visitors would venture within its melancholy precincts.

PADUA.

FEW cities,—says Eustace, "can boast of an origin so ancient and so honourable, and not many can pretend to have enjoyed for so long a period so much glory and prosperity, as Padua." Its foundation is attributed to Antenor, a Trojan prince, and a relative of Priam, but upon no better authority than poetical tradition, and the discovery, in 1274, of an old sarcophagus, which the Paduans believe to be the tomb of Antenor, but which is considered by antiquaries to be a monument of some prince of the middle ages. There can be no question, however, regarding the antiquity of Padua, for we learn from Tacitus that the ancient Patavium was accustomed to celebrate its origin, and the name of its supposed founder, in annual games, said to have been instituted by Antenor; and Livy relates that a naumachia, exhibited annually on one of the rivers which water the town, perpetuated the memory of a signal victory obtained by the Paduans long before their union with Rome. When the city afterwards submitted to the genius of Rome, it was treated rather as a friendly ally than as a conquered province. It shared in all the privileges and honours of the capital; and in the days of Strabo, it reckoned five hundred Roman knights among its citizens, and could send into the field twenty thousand armed men. At this time, also, she was celebrated for commercial enterprise, and drew by her cloth and woollen manufactures no small portion of the tribute of the provinces from the Roman treasury. After having shared the glory of Rome, Padua partook of her disasters, and fell under the yoke of the barbarians. The city was held in succession by the Goths, the Lombards, the Franks, and the Germans, and during the long period of its vassalage its fortunes vibrated between the favour and the caprice of its wayward tyrants. To escape the vengeance of the Lombards, the remains of its ancient inhabitants fled to the Rialto, and formed a union with the Venetian republic, reserving to themselves the privileges of their own laws and institutions. The consideration that Venice was founded by citizens of Padua, who flying before Alaric and Attila, took refuge in the solitary isles of the Adriatic, might perhaps have reconciled the Paduans to partial submission, and prompted the Venetians to offer a generous union. We afterwards find Padua taking

PADUA.

place, as a free republic, beside the sister states of Verona, Vicenza, Ferrara, and Mantua. In the fifteenth century it was besieged by the Venetians, and after enduring great extremities yielded submission; and it continued thereafter in union with Venice until 1797, when this republic was dismembered by the French. After the fall of Napoleon, it became part of the Lombardo-Venetian dependency of Austria.*

Padua was once celebrated for learning and art; but its famous University has sunk in reputation, and in the department of art it can now only refer to the works of Cimabue, Giotto, and Andrea Mantegna. It still presents the aspect of an impressive city, containing public buildings, religious and civil, of great interest and of some beauty. The vast structure, on the left of our view, is the Palazzo della Ragione, upon which has been raised a town hall, the largest building of the kind in Europe. It is 200 feet long, 80 feet wide, and 80 feet high. The church of St. Anthony is a remarkable structure, with domes and minaret spires, giving it the appearance of a Turkish mosque. It is rich in sculpture, painting, and decorations, and contains a magnificent fresco of the Crucifixion. The University, of which the tower appears in our view, was founded by Frederick II., early in the thirteenth century. Under the government of Venice, this institution numbered six thousand students. The pseudo sarcophagus of Antenor stands at the corner of a street under a baldacchino, or stone canopy, and is worthy of observation as a monument of high antiquity. It was long affirmed that Livy was born at Padua, but it is now certain that this event occurred at Abano, a place within the Paduan territory. The good citizens, however, contend manfully for ancient honours, and still point out a house in the Strada di San Giovanni as having been the residence of Livy! They, moreover, possess the mortal remains of the historian, if the contents of a leaden coffin, discovered early in the fifteenth century, can be safely taken for them.

---

* The middle age history of Padua is full of horrors. In the thirteenth century, that execrable tyrant, Ezzelino Romano, carried his oppressive enormities so far, that Alexander IV. directed his legate, the Archbishop of Ravenna, to preach a crusade against him, as an accursed monster whom it was the duty of mankind to destroy. This tyrant was a Ghibelline, a creature of Frederick II.; had he been a Guelph, the pope might not have been so indignant at his atrocities, for the papal power had, on several occasions, creatures not less infamous than Ezzelino. The Venetians rose against him, in 1256, when Padua endured all the miseries of storm and pillage for seven days. Ezzelino, who was at that time absent from the city, charged the loss of the place against the Paduans themselves, and revenged himself by sacrificing, in various ways, eleven thousand citizens who formed part of his army. His only redeeming quality, consummate military skill, prolonged his fate; but he was ultimately hunted down, wounded, and taken prisoner by three Ghibelline chiefs, who had discovered by mutual revelations that he had treacherous designs against each of them. The death of this monster was in keeping with all the acts of his life. He refused surgical aid, tore the bandages from his wounds, and expired. Dante (*Inferno* xii. 110) has consigned this tyrant to the river of blood, in which are found all who have injured their neighbours. And the castle of Romano, the birth-place of Ezzelino, is thus alluded to by the same poet:—

> In that part
> Of the depraved Italian land, which lies
> Between Rialto and the fountain springs
> Of Brenta and Piava, there doth rise,
> Not to so lofty eminence, a hill,
> From whence erewhile a fire-brand did descend,
> That sorely smote the region.
>
> *Paradise*, ix. 25—31.

VENICE.

Ætius.   A race of heroes
Meet in the bosom of the Adriatic,
And change to seats of rest the unstable seas.
With many a bridge they join the scatter'd isles,
And with huge works repel the ocean's tide,
While from afar the wand'ring traveller
Sees mighty walls and marble domes arise,
Where vessels once have sailed.

Val. Who has not heard
Of fam'd Antenor's race? To us 'tis known,
That when the flames of war were kindled first
By Attila, they left their fields and towns,
And in the bosom of the sea maintain'd
Their threatened liberty; full well we know
What wide extent their rising city forms;
In future times what may we hope to view it,
Since thus its infant state?

Ætius. Cæsar, I trace
The seeds of mighty actions yet to come;
The subject seas shall fear this people's nod;
The rage of powerful kings they shall resist;
Shall bear to distant realms their spreading sails,
And Asia's purple tyrants strike with fear.

Metastasio. Ætius, Act 1, Scene 2.

JUSTICE did but restore the balance of her scales when she gave sentence against Venice. When this city first arose upon its hundred isles, it was the hallowed retreat of a beleagured people, unable to resist their barbarian enemies, yet daring to be free. Its after importance as a maritime republic, and the power and authority of its Doges, rendered it the rival of that mighty empire of which in its origin it was the remnant. Indeed it had features of greatness that admitted no comparison; its history was an illustrious isolation. But the luxury and vice that ever follow in the train of national wealth, corrupted her citizens; and universally acknowledged authority begat tyranny in the hearts of her nobles. Popular insurrections, and the mutual jealousies of the patricians, led to an inquisitorial form of government, and the establishment of a fearful council which condemned in secret, and from whose sentence there was no appeal. Then, "the Lion's Mouth," the general receptacle for accusations, gaped nightly for its victims; and nobles and private citizens daily disappeared, no one dared to ask, but all knew, whither. The vicious trembled, for they were esteemed dangerous; and the virtuous were in no less peril, for they were the objects of suspicion. Venice was self-doomed, long before her hour of overthrow arrived; and her catastrophe, when at length it came, excited no sympathy beyond poetical regrets and sentimental lamentations.

The ancient Venetia was a province of Cisalpine Gaul, and the Veneti proper were a people located in northern Italy, whose descendants became the founders of Venice. The Veneti long maintained a separate and independent existence; they afterwards entered into friendly alliance with Rome; and ultimately, in the time of Augustus, they and their country were identified with the population and territory of the empire. They appear no more as a distinct people until the fall of the empire, in the beginning of the fifth century, at which period the inhabitants of Patavium (now Padua), one of the cities of Venetia, fled before Alaric, and took refuge on the sand-banks and north-western shores of the Hadrian Gulf. It was not, however, until 452, when Attila and his Huns spread desolation over Italy, that numerous refugees from the different cities of the Veneti, established themselves permanently on the islands of the Lagune, or shallows, that border the whole Venetian coast.

> "A few, in fear
> Flying away from him whose boast it was,
> That the grass grew not where his horse had trod,
> Gave birth to Venice."

The first settlement was upon the Island of Rialto, where the Patavians had some time before established a commercial station; and the refugees being principally of the poorer classes, they gladly availed themselves of the existing buildings, content to follow the occupation of fishermen, and to enjoy freedom from the outrages of the barbarian invaders of the empire. The Rialto is the principal island of the Lagune, upon which in the eighth century arose the city of Venice. So early, however, as 421 the modern city may be said to have had its foundation in the erection of the Church of San Jacopo di Rialto, an ecclesiastical edifice that continues to be held in great veneration, and which is said to retain, after all its repairs and restorations, much of its original form and structure.

The ocean-refuge of the Veneti was first named "the Port of the Deserted City," a title at once expressive of thankfulness and regret. Before the towns on the mainland arose from their ashes, the foundations of an independent government had been laid in the new State. In 697, a chief magistrate was elected under the title of Doge, or Duke, whose office was for life, and in whom was vested an authority little less than absolute. An abuse of this unlimited power led to the assassination of the third Doge, and the temporary abolition of the ducal office, which five years afterwards was restored. The renewal of this office brought with it fresh abuses of authority, and the aid of Pepin was sought to carry the election of a popular Doge. This wily monarch gladly availed himself of the opportunity for reducing the power of the republic; but his designs were defeated by the boldness and patriotism of Angelo Participazio, who received a just recompence in his advancement to the ducal chair. The son of this prince succeeded him; and in his reign (827) "the Translation of St. Mark" took place. This event, which is associated with all the subsequent glories of Venice, was marked by an incident of an extremely ludicrous character. The remains of the Saint were reposing in a church at

Alexandria, at the time when some Venetian ships arrived in that port; and the captains of these ships prevailed upon the priests, who had the custody of the holy treasure, to deliver it into their hands. The transfer was both difficult and dangerous, owing to the attachment of the populace to their Saint; and the following ingenious expedient was adopted to convey the remains on board. The body was placed in a basket stuffed with herbs, and covered with joints of pork, and the porters who bore it made their way to the vessel by crying aloud, "Khanzir, Khanzir!" (pork, pork!) on hearing which every Mussulman hastily avoided contact with the forbidden flesh. The saintly remains are said to have preserved the ship, in circumstances of great peril, on its homeward voyage. On its arrival at Venice, the joy of the people knew no bounds. They had an ancient tradition that St. Mark, in his travels, once visited Aquileia, and also touched at the Hundred Isles, where a prophetic vision declared to him that his bones should one day repose upon them. The arrival of the remains was therefore regarded as a most auspicious omen. Venice was solemnly consigned to the protection of the Saint; his effigy, or that of his Lion, was blazoned on the standards and impressed upon the coin; and thenceforward the gathering cry of the armies of the Republic was "*Viva San Marco!*" Nearly two hundred and seventy years after this occurrence, the Saint indicated symptoms of displeasure and disappeared; but afterwards, to the joy of the city, he returned, to confer upon it additional benefits. In 901, the magnificent Church of St. Mark was raised, as the mausoleum of the Saint and the national temple of the Venetian state.

In the time of the doge, Candiano II., (932.) occurred the romantic incident of "the Brides of Venice." According to ancient usage, the marriages of the chief families were celebrated publicly, and the same day and hour witnessed the union of numerous betrothed. On the eve of the feast of the Purification, a bridal procession embarked for Olivolo, the residence of the Patriarch, and proceeded to the cathedral. The corsairs of Istria, watching their opportunity, rushed into the sacred edifice and carried off the brides with all their costly adornings. The Doge, who was present, hastily assembled his galleys, overtook the ravishers before they had cleared the shallows of the Lagune, slew them to a man, and brought back the maidens in triumph. The memory of this event was long preserved by an annual procession of Venetian women, on the eve of the Purification. The trunk-makers of Olivolo formed the greater part of the crew that rescued the brides, and to reward their bravery the Doge bade them demand some privilege. They requested an annual visit from the Doge. "What," said the prince, "if it should prove rainy?" To this they replied, "We will send you hats to cover your heads, and if you are thirsty we will give you drink." To commemorate the question and reply, the priest of Santa Maria annually presented to the Doge, on his visit to Olivolo, two flasks of wine, two oranges, and two hats. This ceremony formed part of the Marian Games which were afterwards, in the palmiest days of the republic, celebrated with so much pomp and magnificence. But we must not linger amidst the early romance of Venice.

In 991, the ducal seat was filled by Pietro Urseolo II., an enterprising prince, who opened up the avenues of commerce for the Venetians, by forming for them the most advantageous alliances; whilst he gave security to their maritime operations by the total overthrow of the Istriote pirates. An amusing instance is recorded of the luxury which, in the eleventh century, found its way to Venice. A female of Constantinople, who shared the crown of the Doge, banished plain water from her toilet, and used only the richest and most fragrant medicated preparations. She refused also to touch her meat except with a golden fork. This dainty fair one died of a lingering disease, and her sufferings were regarded by the people as a divine judgment, whence we may infer that lavish expenditure and indulgence were not at this period generally prevalent in Venice. The republic joined in the general Crusade against the Infidels; not so much from religious enthusiasm, as from motives of state policy. Her naval armament besieged and reduced Tyre and Ascalon, and well nigh annihilated the Saracen power. These successes awoke the jealousies of the Greeks; but Venice was then the undisputed mistress of the sea; and her fleet swept and desolated the coast of the Eastern empire. The doge, Dominico Michieli, returned to Venice, and after his death this epitaph was engraven upon his tomb, *Terror Græcorum jacet hic*—The terror of the Greeks lies here.

Towards the close of the eleventh century the Venetians took up the cause of Alexander III. against Frederick Barbarossa; and when the doge, Liani, returned to Venice in triumph, the pope met him as he landed, and presented him with a ring as a token of his espousal to the sea. Hence originated that imposing ceremony annually witnessed on the Adriatic, when the doge, in his gorgeous state galley, the Bucentaur, went forth in pomp and triumph to renew his first espousal, by dropping a golden ring into the bosom of his betrothed. And proud and significant was the greeting that he offered to his bride: "We wed thee with this ring, in token of our true and perpetual sovereignty." The ceremony is retained to this day; but the romance of the pageant fled, when the winged lion gave place to the eagle of Austria.

The Venetians date a proud period of their history from the close of the twelfth century, when Enrico Dandolo was elected to the ducal seat. If, however, we separate from the glories of this vaunted era, the spoils of war and the territorial additions obtained by the Venetians, there is little else to claim exalted admiration. Venice was solicited to equip a naval armament for the transport of the united forces of the Fourth Crusade. The Doge and the Council fixed the terms of the contract in the true spirit of merchants, and secured, in mercantile phrase, a safe transaction. Dandolo himself, though upwards of eighty years of age, went forth with his fleet, and for the purpose, as the sequel will show, of making the expedition subservient to the political advantages of the Venetian State. The pope (Innocent III.) sanctioned the crusade, and confirmed the treaty with Venice, upon the express condition that the allied powers should not direct their arms against Christian princes, unless compelled to do so by violence, or other unavoidable necessity, and in any case the consent of the papal see was first to be obtained. The Doge, however, taking advantage of a deficiency in the payments of the contract, diverted the expedition from its legitimate object before the day of embarkation, and prevailed upon the knights and barons to reduce the city of Lara, then under the protection of the King of Hungary. This was accordingly done: and the spoils of the city were equally divided between the Venetians and the French. Shortly after this transaction, Dandolo is said to have been bribed by the Sultan of Damascus to postpone or frustrate the original design of the expedition. Be this as it may, the fleet, in place of sailing for the Holy Land, invested and took the city of Constantinople; and in the subsequent partition of the Greek Empire, Venice obtained an extent of territory that added greatly to her maritime power. The allied forces seem to have directed their crusade against Art. Scarcely one of those monuments which had rendered Constantinople the wonder of nations, was thought worthy of preservation; and it is recorded of Dandolo, as an especial honour, that he had sufficient taste to appropriate and carry off the four horses of gilt bronze which afterwards graced the western porch of the basilica of St. Mark.

In 1289, the Inquisition was established in Venice; but rather as the antagonist, than the coadjutor of the Roman institution. Venice yielded, at any time, little more than a nominal obedience to the pope, and uniformly disregarded his authority when it interfered with her own interests or designs. She deemed it incompatible with her safety, that the heresies of the ducal state should be judged by the papal see; but instead of openly defying the pontiff's power, she established an ecclesiastical tribunal, resembling the Holy Office, which, although nominally under the authority of the church, was truly and actually controlled by the Doge and Council. Nothing could be done by this Inquisition without the consent of the Doge, and the knowledge of the Council, to whom everything was to be revealed; whilst no appeal was to be made to the pontiff either to confirm its proceedings or to annul its sentence. The design of the Venetian Inquisition seems to have been to strengthen the government, and to curb the authority of Rome.

At the opening of the fourteenth century, Venice had possessed herself of Ferrara, which was claimed by the pope as the property of the pontificate, and the refusal of the republic to yield it up, led to an open rupture with the papal see. The ducal territory was laid under interdict; and Venice for the first time was disturbed by the Guelph and Ghibelline factions. Nor was this all: the Italian States, and indeed the whole of Europe, regarded this conjuncture as a favourable moment for vengeance. The factories of the republic were pillaged, her merchandize was confiscated, her ships were seized, and her residents and mariners either killed or sold into slavery. The Venetians added to these evils by internal disorder. A conspiracy was formed for the assassination of the Doge; but the latter detected the approach of insurrection, and made the necessary preparations to meet it. When the conspirators had nearly approached the ducal palace, they found themselves suddenly confronted by a strong array of soldiery. After a bloody contest the insurgents were defeated; and the gibbet and the axe put a fearful and hideous period to the transaction. The success which had nearly attended this conspiracy led the government to devise measures for the prevention of a similar outbreak. And now it was that the famous COUNCIL OF TEN was instituted; a body invested with plenary inquisitorial authority, whose spies, present everywhere and seen nowhere, permitted nothing to escape observation, and who hourly carried to the Council a report of their surveillance. The machinery was so perfect in its details, and so secret in its operations, that not a thing could be done nor a word be spoken, in any way affecting the State, of which the Council did not receive a particular account; and the information was so privately obtained and conveyed, that the mysterious Ten could choose their time for action without exciting suspicion. The very name of the Council became a byword of terror. Its proceedings were never known, and its sentences were never promulgated; but thus much was known, that things of which the popular ear had heard nothing, were first published by the Ten, and that individuals daily disappeared from their accustomed places of resort, and were seen no more.

In 1354, Marino Faliero ascended the ducal seat. Byron's tragedy has rendered the name of this doge deeply interesting to the English reader; but the doge of the poet and the doge of history are two widely different persons. Byron wanted a hero, and he made one of Faliero, by justifying treasons which admit of no justification, and ennobling a character whose only remarkable lineaments were pride and ungovernable wrath. At the time when Faliero took his seat, the power of the oligarchy infringed the authority of the doge to such an extent that the latter was little more than an illustrious prisoner, the mere nominal head of the State.

bearing the whole weight of popular odium, yet so circumscribed in his functions as to have no control over the proceedings of the legislature. Faliero could not brook the indignities which he suffered; and an incident occurred shortly after his accession, that carried his fury beyond all bounds, and hurried him into that treason against his country which brought him to the block. The doge, though advanced in years, had married a young and beautiful wife. A gallant of the court who had been reproved by Faliero, vented his spleen by writing upon the back of the ducal chair a few words equally offensive to the doge and his wife. Faliero waited impatiently to hear the sentence which the Forty would pass upon the bold offender; and when he learned that it extended only to two months' imprisonment, and a twelvemonth's banishment from Venice, he could not contain his rage. At this juncture the prince met with Bertuccio Israello, admiral of the arsenal, who claimed from him redress for a blow which he received from one of the nobles. "What wouldst thou have me do for thee?" was his answer. "Think upon the shameful gibe which hath been written concerning me, and think on the manner in which they have punished that ribald, Michele Steno, who wrote it; and how the Council of XL. respect our person!" To this the admiral replied by divulging a conspiracy then on foot for the destruction of the oligarchy; and Faliero at length consented to be a partner in an insurrection to overthrow the State of which he was himself the head. For many nights successively the conspirators conferred with the doge *in the ducal palace*, and arranged with him the massacre of the entire aristocracy, and the dissolution of the existing government. The unprecedented boldness of the transaction veiled its proceedings. Government spies would scarcely seek for evidence of treason in the ducal chamber. The argus-eyed Council for once was at fault, and Venice was upon the verge of a revolution. It was only the evening before the day of insurrection (15th April, 1355,) that Beltramo of Bergamo, one of the conspirators, called upon his patron, Nicolo Lioni, and with a view to save his life, entreated him to remain at home on the morrow. The singularity of the request led to inquiry, and inquiry terminated in a revelation of the plot. Beltramo was immediately secured; instant measures were taken for the arrest of the criminals; and nothing remained but to award punishment to the offenders. The ringleaders were hanged; and Faliero, by sentence of the Council of Ten, was beheaded on the landing of the Giant's Stairs leading to the ducal residence. His name was erased from the Golden Book, and his portrait excluded from the Hall of the Great Council. The frame which ought to have contained his portrait remains to this day covered with a black veil, inscribed with these words: *Hic est locus Marini Faletro decapitati pro criminibus*—This is the place of Marino Faliero, beheaded for his offences.

We pass over a century and arrive at the reign of Francesco Foscari. This doge obtained the ducal honours with difficulty, continued to sustain them when they had become a wearisome burden, and at length surrendered them under circumstances of suffering and misery that scarcely have a parallel. In 1433, ten years after his accession, he wished to retire from authority, but the council refused his request, and even exacted from him an oath that he would never abdicate. He had already lost three out of four sons, and to Giacopo the survivor, he looked for the solace of his age, and the perpetuation of his name. He contracted a marriage for this son with the family of Contarini, and from that event drew an augury of future happiness. Within four years after his marriage, Giacopo was denounced to the Council of Ten, as having received presents from foreign princes. The unhappy son was extended upon the rack in the presence of his own parent; but the agonies of torture compelled no confession;

and his father pronounced the sentence which banished him for life to Napoli di Romania. Five years afterwards he was recalled from exile on suspicion of having instigated a domestic to murder Hermolao Donato, the chief of the Ten. Again he suffered the exquisite tortures of the rack, and persisting in a denial of his guilt, he was now banished to Candia. Notwithstanding his sufferings, he yearned for his native land, and addressed a letter to the duke of Milan, imploring his intercession with the Senate for remission of punishment. This letter was conveyed to the Council of Ten; and Giacopo was once more recalled to answer the crime of having solicited a foreign government for aid. For the third time a father was compelled to witness the agonies of a son; thirty times was the victim raised upon the cord; and when nature at length gave way, he was carried bleeding and insensible to the apartments of the Doge. He was sent back again to his Candian prison, but had scarcely reached it ere he expired. The dregs of the cup of affliction still remained for the unhappy father. That very Council which had extorted an oath from the Doge that he would never abdicate, now forcibly deposed him. He surrendered the ducal ensigns, and prepared to leave the palace; but when it was suggested to him that he should retire privately, the spirit of the old man revived, and he answered proudly, "By these steps I entered, by these I will retire;" then, leaning upon his brother's arm, he slowly descended the Giant's Stairs. On the fifth day after his deposition, he died; his death being occasioned by suppressed agitation on hearing the bell of the Campanile announce the election of his successor in office. The miseries of the Foscari are referred to the vengeance of Giacopo Loredano, whose father and uncle's deaths were attributed to them. Loredano had made an entry in his ledger debiting the elder Foscari with the murder of his relatives, and when the death of the old man was reported to him, he calmly turned up the entry, and wrote on the credit side—"*He has paid me.*" In the reign of Francisco Foscari, the Inquisition of State was established. It consisted of three members, "the invisible three," two chosen from the Council of Ten, and one from the Council of the Doge. No ecclesiastic, nor any person interested in the Court of Rome, was eligible for the office of State Inquisitor, even though he were one of the Ten. "The statutes of this fearful tribunal exceed every other product of human wickedness, in premeditated, deliberate, systematic, unmixed, undissembled flagitiousness." Enormities have been revealed that make the flesh creep, and the blood run cold; but these form a small part only of the foul deeds enacted by this horrible tribunal. Who shall compute the number of unhappy victims who on entering the ducal palace received the greeting of a smile, and were then conducted by the Bridge of Sighs to the State Dungeons, whence they returned no more!

At the close of the fifteenth century Venice had arrived at the period of her loftiest elevation. Her maritime stations extended from the Po to the eastern boundaries of the Mediterranean and the mouth of the Don; and in these she gathered and dispersed the merchandise of the entire known world. Her silk manufactures supplied the nations with their most costly attire. Spain and England contributed fleeces for her unrivalled cloths; and the flax of Lombardy formed the material of her linens. Her laboratories prepared the choicest chemical preparations; her glass-houses furnished mirrors for regal saloons, and beads for the naked African; and her printing press, established not more than fifteen years after the discovery of the art, gave an impulse to literature. At this period the celebrated Aldus Manutius, the inventor of the *Italic* letter, collected around him the most learned men of the age, and from the literary circle which he formed, emanated those choice specimens of typography whose excellence is still a theme of admiration. Such were a few of the resources of the city which the fishermen of the Rialto founded on the fall of elder Rome. The territory, during the lapse of a thousand years, had stretched from the Lagune, over the fairest provinces of Northern Italy; "and Venice swayed on the adjoining *terra firma*, the principality of Ravenna, Trevisano and its dependencies, Padua, Vicenza, Verona, Crema, Brescia, and Bergamo. Friuli connected her with Istria; Lara, Spoleto, and the Dalmatic Islands, with Albania; Zante and Corfu continued the chain to Greece and the Morea, and numerous islands in the Archipelago supplied the remaining links with Candia and Cyprus."

The commencement of the sixteenth century witnessed the formation of the League of Cambrai; a junction between the powers of France, Spain, and Germany, nominally directed to the adjustment of differences between Venice and the Duke of Gueldres, but in point of fact having no other object than the ruin of the Venetian republic. The French defeated the Venetians with great loss at Agnadello, and the news of the disaster spread terror throughout the ducal city. A single blow had shattered in pieces the goodly fabric of continental dominion which it had cost Venice the toll of a century to erect. But amidst the clamours and terrors of the populace, the Senate preserved its calmness and dignity. No available provision for the exigency was overlooked; and the most wise and determined measures were concerted for the defence of the Lagune. By a master-stroke of policy, the Senate released the endangered provinces from all obligation of fidelity, and left them at liberty to make such terms with their opponents as their individual circumstances might require: and by this means they secured their attachment to the republic, and the probability of re-union whenever the chances of war should take a favourable turn. Having obtained a reconciliation with the pope, Venice began to retrieve her losses, or at least to resist with some measure of success the offensive operations directed against her. She afterwards formed an alliance with France, and the peace of Cambrai, which followed, gave her time to prepare for a renewal of hostilities. In a subsequent war with the Turks, the Venetians were again worsted; and a cessation of arms was at length procured by the Council of Ten, who on this occasion assumed the most absolute authority, and gave plenary powers to their envoy, without entering into any communication with other branches of the government. For thirty years after the peace with Turkey, Venice enjoyed tranquillity; and this season of repose was favourable to the cultivation of the Arts. Palladio and Scamozzi adorned the ducal city with rich and imposing architecture; and the Florentine Sansovino erected the Mint, the Library of St. Mark, and the Procuratie Nuove, and sculptured the noble statues of Mars and Neptune which still guard the Giant's Stairs. At this period also the Venetian school of painting was brought to its height by Titian, Tintoretto, and Paolo Veronese, to whom were entrusted the design and execution of a brilliant series of historical pictures for the Hall of the Great Council. The only reward bestowed upon Titian was an appointment to a civic office, yielding no greater emolument than three hundred crowns annually; and even this trifling patent was encumbered with a condition at once laborious and humiliating, namely, that of painting a portrait of every doge who succeeded during his lifetime, for *eight crowns a head*. On the accession of Lorenzo Priuli in 1550, Titian, then in his seventy-ninth year, discontinued his task; nevertheless, he lived twenty years longer, painted many other pictures, and even at last fell a victim, not to any ordinary disorder, but to the plague.

We diverge from the general history of Venice to narrate briefly the story of Bianca Cappello.

whose early amour, and subsequent ambition and crimes, have been greedily seized upon by poets and novelists. In the reign of Nicolo Daponte (1578), Bartolommeo Cappello, a noble Venetian, had a daughter named Bianca, for whom it was his chief object to procure an alliance suitable to her great beauty and the dignity of her birth. The maiden, however, had fixed her affections on Pietro Buonaventuro, a Florentine youth who filled no higher station than that of cashier in the bank of the Salviati, not far from the Palazzo Cappelli. False keys and the aid of a governess procured for Bianca nightly egress from her father's palace; but the stolen interviews thus obtained with her lover, soon led to urgent necessity for flight, to avoid the wrath and vengeance of Bartolommeo, and to conceal the maiden's shame from the eyes of Venice. The lovers escaped by night in a gondola, and having reached *terra firma*, proceeded to Florence, where they besought protection of the young prince Francisco, son of Cosmo de' Medici. Francisco interposed in vain between the lovers and the relatives of Bianca; the latter was for ever renounced by her father, who even obtained an edict from the Council of Ten, by which a reward of two thousand ducats was offered for the head of Pietro. The young exiles had not long sojourned at Florence when Francisco became enamoured of Bianca; and scarcely had the prince completed his nuptials with Joanna of Austria, before he appointed Pietro his master of the robes, and established Bianca magnificently as his mistress. Pietro was shortly afterwards murdered in the streets, and probably by Francisco's orders. Bianca now ruled the prince according to her caprice, and even resorted to the superstitions of the time to confirm her dominion over him. Nor was she content with this; for knowing that Francisco was desirous of male issue, which his marriage bed had not produced, she feigned appearances that promised the realization of his wishes. At a suitable time she lodged in different quarters of the city three women at the eve of confinement, and adroitly presented to Francisco, as his son, the issue of one of these mothers. These women she afterwards removed out of the way by poison; and shortly after, a Bolognese lady, her confidante, was dismissed on a visit to her native city, and murdered on the road. This last victim survived long enough to reveal the transaction in which she had taken part, and the monstrous guilt of Bianca was thus made known to the Cardinal de' Medici, the brother of Francisco. Meantime the consort of the prince died in child-bed of grief; and the indignation of the Cardinal and the people threatened a separation between the guilty pair. But Bianca had obtained a power over Francisco which he vainly endeavoured to resist; and after having yielded to a private marriage with her, he at length boldly and openly presented her to the people as his bride. He dispatched an embassy to Venice to demand Bianca as a daughter of St. Mark. The Cappelli remembered no longer the dishonour of their relative; and the Ten forgot their denunciations of vengeance. The ambassadors were treated with high distinction, and on their return were accompanied by a deputation from Venice to assist at the second nuptials of Francisco and Bianca. But the ducal honours with which Bianca was invested were of brief duration. The Cardinal de' Medici partly through fear, and partly from disgust, concerted measures for her destruction. What these measures were is not known; but the means by which the Medici were accustomed to work in the pursuit of vengeance or ambition *are* known; and the sudden death of Francisco and Bianca, within a few hours of each other, favours the suspicion of their removal by poison. Bianca was interred privately in the crypt of San Lorenzo at Florence; her title of Grand Duchess was erased from all public documents, and in its room was substituted, *la pessima Bianca*—the vile Bianca.

We descend to the reign of Antonio Priuli (1618), in which occurred the conspiracy whose incidents are rendered familiar, though in a distorted form, by St. Real's romance, and the "Venice Preserved" of Otway. The romance is a travestie of history, intermixed with much irrelevant matter, the mere creation of the writer's brain; and Otway's coarse and boisterous tragedy is a poetical extravaganza, in which character is violated, not delineated; a drama for rabid sentimentalists who delight to contemplate pathetic villains and hysterical women. History affords but few particulars regarding the conspiracy. Sir Henry Wotton, who was the English ambassador at Venice in 1618, thus alludes to it in a general way: "The whole town is here at present in horror and confusion upon the discovering of a foul and fearful conspiracy of the French against this State; whereof no less than thirty have already suffered very condign punishment, between men strangled in prison, drowned in the silence of the night, and hanged in public view; and yet the bottom is invisible." The facts that can be gathered in detail are meagre. It appears that in the summer of 1617, Jacques Pierre, a Norman pirate, fled from the service of the Duke d'Ossuna of Spain, and found employment as a subordinate at the arsenal of Venice. Scarcely had he arrived in the Lagune, before he denounced himself as the chief agent of the Duke d'Ossuna and the Spanish ambassador, for the accomplishment of a plot to fire the city of Venice, to seize and massacre the nobles, to overthrow the existing government, and to transfer the State to the Spanish crown. For ten months he was allowed to communicate on the one hand with his complotters, and on the other with the Inquisition of State; but at the expiration of that term, he was seized by the Council of Ten, and drowned. The Ten had kept the depositions of Pierre secret; and it was not until three or four hundred Frenchmen and Spaniards had been delivered to the executioner, and the body of Renault, the companion of Pierre, was discovered, suspended by one foot on a gibbet, on the Piazzetta, that the people had any knowledge of the great peril that had been averted. An apocryphal account of the plot states that on the very eve of its explosion, Jaffier, one of the conspirators, touched by the magnificence of the Espousals of the Adriatic, which he had just witnessed, was shaken from his stern purpose, and revealed the conspiracy. Whilst, however, this last incident is beyond all question a figment, it is difficult to say how much of the previous narrative is true. We see a smile upon the face of our readers on the discovery that Belvidera's sorrows are all moonshine, that Jaffier is a phantom of the heat-oppressed brain, and the magnanimous Pierre a vulgar, piratical cut-throat, undignified even by crime.

Twenty years before the downfall of the republic, Venice had sunk into a modern Sybaris: her political influence was gone, her possessions had fallen from her, the national spirit was extinguished; she was content to be a general mart of pleasure, and a pandemonium of crime. Every day had its festival, whose pomp and circumstance formed the serious occupation of the nobles and people. The patricians were the presidents of gaming establishments, and the hired servants of the proprietors, who frequently were rich Jews. Shylock then fed fat the ancient grudge he owed them. A Venetian noble had now become so abject in mind, that no personal indignity could excite honourable resentment. When insulted, he confided his revenge to the arm of the hired assassin. The general use of masks emboldened both sexes, and all degrees, to indulge in the grossest depravity of behaviour. Courtezans had houses allotted them, and funds set apart for their use; and parents did not hesitate to barter their daughters for unhallowed gains.

"The Republic *has* lived," was the pithy exclamation of Napoleon, when, in 1797, he determined on the final overthrow of Venice. On the 12th May of the same year, the nobles prostrated their city at the feet of the French general, "and proclaimed that the most ancient government in the world, which had just completed the eleventh century of its sway, was no longer in existence." In the following year, the city was ceded to Austria, under whose dominion it remains. The ancient majesty of Venice is recalled, at the present day, by relics of former magnificence; and the latest period of its decline continues to be reflected in the censurable manners that still prevail in this once "glorious city in the sea."

> Before St. Mark still glow his steeds of brass,
> Their gilded collars glittering in the sun;
> But is not Doria's menace come to pass?
> Are they not bridled? Venice, lost and won,
> Her thirteen hundred years of glory done,
> Sinks, like a sea-weed, into whence she rose!
>
> *Childe Harold.*

THE RIALTO AND PONTE DI RIALTO.

The Rialto has been rendered a household word by Shakspeare, but it is not necessary that we should summon up Shylock the Jew, and "the gentle lady married to the Moor," since their association with the scene before us is familiar to young and old. The Rialto and the Ponte di Rialto take their names from the Isola di Rialto, the island whereon they are built. The Rialto is the Exchange, or place of concourse for the merchants; and the Ponte di Rialto, the celebrated bridge so often mentioned, is one of the links that connect the hundred isles of Venice. The buildings on the right of our view were erected after the fire of 1513, which laid nearly the whole city in ruins. The nearest structure, supported by arcades, is a portion of the Fabbrico Nuovo, and adjoining it is the Fabbrico Vecchio; the latter is now appropriated to the Imperial Tribunal of Justice, and the building beyond it, which interrupts the view of the Bridge, is the seat of the Imperial Tribunal of Appeal. Through the arcades of the Fabbrico Vecchio lies the approach to the Exchange. Sabellico, whose work on Venice was published in 1492, a few years before the great fire, says of the Exchange,—"There the merchants meet in a noble piazza, in which all the commercial affairs of the city, and that is to say of the world, are transacted. It is crowded, with scarcely any intervention, from morning to night. Yet in spite of the crowd, there is no bustle, no altercation, no struggling, no quarrel." The Bridge of the Rialto was originally constructed of wood. The present structure was built in the year 1591, by Antonio da Ponte. The Venetians regard it as the finest arch in the world, and endeavour to add to its distinction by attributing its design either to Palladio, or to Michael Angelo. It has three passages, of which the one in the centre is the widest; and on either side are rows of shops, occupied chiefly by jewellers and haberdashers. Beyond the Bridge, is seen the tower of the church of St. Salvadore. The large building on the left of the view, contains the Offices of the Excise and Finance. An edifice, anciently named the Fondaca di Tedeschi, was the commercial factory of the Germans in the thirteenth century, and prior to that period, the residence of the Signory of Venice. This old building was destroyed by fire in 1505, and the present structure, which is said to contain two hundred chambers, was erected on its site by Giovanni Giocondo of Verona. Giorgione was employed to paint the façade fronting the Great Canal, and the grand entrance was adorned by Titian, and the praises lavished on the latter were so ungrateful to the ear of Giorgione, that he ever after renounced all intimacy with his pupil.

BAPTISTERY OF ST. MARK

The Church of St. Mark, from its first foundation in the tenth century, until its final completion in 1111, was an object of especial regard to the Doges, who devoted themselves to its progress and adornment. Its excess of ornament, in columns and screens, statues, arabesques, and mosaics, destroys the impressive effect which its scale of grandeur and magnitude would otherwise have produced. It is difficult to describe its architecture. The original plan was a Greek cross, and the adornments are Byzantine, Syriac, and Gothic, with much that cannot be referred to any known type or style. The subdued light renders the interior very striking, although under a stronger illumination the elaborate ornaments would distract the eye, and produce a meretricious effect. San Marco is set with rich objects won by Venetian enterprise and valour. In the principal front, there are five hundred splendid columns of precious marbles, of various colours; some polygonal, some with Armenian and Syrian inscriptions deeply engraven, the whole presenting a multiform enigma to the mind. The character of the entire building is rich and strange, full of mystery and meaning.

The chapel of the Baptistery is enriched with mosaics of the eleventh and twelfth centuries, representing, amongst other subjects, the baptism of Christ. One of the bronze doors is said to have been brought from the basilica of St. Sophia, at Constantinople. The Benetier, or water vase, is a work in porphyry, of the fifteenth century. It is supported by an antique altar of Greek sculpture, ornamented with dolphins and tridents, the attributes of Neptune, which though not inappropriate to Venice, can by no stretch of fancy be construed into emblems of St. Mark. A statue of the Baptist in bronze, the work of Francisco Segala, is placed over the font. The chapel of the Baptistery contains the tomb of Andrea Dandolo, the last Doge who obtained the honour of interment in St. Mark's. He was "an intrepid warrior and a skilful politician, the friend of Petrarch, and the oldest historian of Venice, as his ancestor was the greatest hero."

DASSANO.

BASSANO is beautifully situated on the Brenta, at the foot of the Trentine Alps. The history of this place can be traced no farther back than to the thirteenth century, at which period it was a town of the Trevisano, a district under the government of the Ezzelini family. In the early part of the fourteenth century, it was included in an extensive principality possessed by the Della Scala; and in a few years afterwards it fell into the power of Venice. The Venetians lost possession in the war of Chiozza, but subsequently regained it, and they continued thenceforward to hold the place until the dismemberment of their republic by Napoleon. The battle of Bassano was the last great contest by which Napoleon endeavoured to sustain his power in Italy.

Bassano is seldom visited by tourists, owing to its not lying in the direct routes ordinarily taken by travellers; the beauty of its scenery might, notwithstanding, claim more extensive regard. The approach to the city, by the road from Trent to Venice, is so picturesque as to be scarcely rivalled even in Italy.

VICENZA.

THE history of Vicenza offers few events sufficiently remarkable to demand especial notice. As the ancient Vicentia, or Vicetia, it is classed amongst the municipal towns by Tacitus. On the fall of the empire it suffered from the barbarians; and at a subsequent period it incurred the displeasure of Frederick II. for its attachment to the Guelphic cause. After having for some time formed part of the Venetian territories on *terra firma*, it was apportioned by the League of Cambrai, to pope Julius II. The republic afterwards recovered possession, and Vicenza continued under the government of Venice until the French invasion in 1798. When the power of Napoleon was annihilated in Italy, this city, with its dependencies, was annexed to the Austrian territory.

VICENZA.

Vicenza owes its chief distinction to the fame of its architect, the celebrated Palladio, who flourished in the sixteenth century. Some of his most famous works adorn his native city; and amongst these may be named the Palazzo della Ragione, or Court of Justice, and the Palazzo Prefettizio, the house of the chief magistrate; both which edifices come immediately into the foreground of our view. The style of Palladio is marked by severity, and is formed from the ancient temples and the works of Vitruvius. Palladian architecture was introduced into England by Inigo Jones, whose works are worthy imitations of the Italian master; but since his time no one in this country seems to have imbibed the spirit of Palladio, for scarcely a single edifice constructed by the followers of Inigo Jones exhibits anything better than a servile copy of his style, and an evident ignorance of its capabilities. British architects, to the present day, appear to delight in incongruities, or if not so, they certainly want mental power and correct taste, since their most elaborate efforts are too frequently "a chaos of disjointed things." In our own city, and within the last five or six years, an architect of some pretensions supported the loggia of a public edifice, consisting of a heavy pediment and massive Corinthian columns, upon slender Ionic pillars! True, the latter were removed, and a solid rusticated basement substituted in their room; still, "we cannot but remember such things were, that were most *frightful* to us." "Can such things be, and overcome us like a summer's cloud, without our special wonder!"

Our view of Vicenza represents the Piazza de' Signori. In the centre are the two columns erected by the Venetians, who were accustomed to set up, in all the towns they conquered, the national pillars of the ducal city. The nearest building on the right hand is the Palazzo della Ragione, or more properly Palladio's façades, the interior Palazzo being an ancient gothic building, of the age of Theodoric, which Palladio restored and enlarged. These façades are considered the best works of the Italian architect. They consist of two noble loggie, tier above tier, the *uppermost* Ionic, and the *lower* Doric. The Campanile, adjoining the Palazzo della Ragione, is a graceful structure occupying an area of little more than twenty square feet, and rising to three hundred feet in height. On the left of our view, and opposite to the Palazzo before mentioned, is the Palazzo Prefettizio. This building is in the Corinthian style, and is a skilful adaptation of the Roman triumphal arch to a palatial residence.

Upon the festival of Corpus Christi, a singular pageant, named the *Rua*, is exhibited at Vicenza. It consists of an enormous car, sixty feet in height, formed of temples and pyramids, surrounded by a combination of wheels, upon which, as they revolve, men, women, and children maintain their equilibrium, whilst the car itself is hauled along by about an hundred men. Tradition refers the origin of this procession to the achievements of the knights, Bassano and Verlato, who relieved the city from the atrocities of the tyrant Ezzelino.

The *Sette commune*, or Seven Communes, are seen from Vicenza. These Alpine villages are regarded with great interest by the historian as the residence of a people who for two thousand years have kept themselves apart from the rest of the world. The Cimbri and Teutones, two tribes from the northern Chersonesus, invaded Italy in the year of Rome 640, and were defeated, and almost extirpated by Marius, in the neighbourhood of Verona. The few who escaped the vengeance of the conquerors, took refuge in the neighbouring mountains, and formed a little colony, which, either from its poverty, its insignificance, or its retired position, has remained undisturbed for nearly two thousand years. These people retain the tradition

of their origin, and though surrounded by Italians, still preserve their Teutonic language. Frederick IV. of Denmark visited this singular colony, discoursed with the inhabitants in Danish, and found their idiom perfectly intelligible.

BRESCIA.

AFTER the fall of the Roman empire, Brescia, which boasted its splendour and distinction under the Cæsars, suffered great severities at the hands of Alaric and Attila. It was afterwards conquered by the Lombards, from whom it passed to the Franks; and when the power of the latter people declined, it submitted to Otho I. of Saxony, from whom it received many privileges. It partook of the miseries of the Guelph and Ghibelline contest; and its entire middle age history is composed of records of suffering. In 1222, an earthquake overthrew the principal buildings, and destroyed a large number of the inhabitants; and this calamity was succeeded by all the horrors of pestilence and famine. The bishops, nobles, and people were constantly at variance; and to this perpetual cause of disquiet was added the successive occupation of its citadel by turbulent and ambitious neighbours. It was taken in succession by Ezzelino, the tyrant of Padua, by the Pallavicini of Cremona, the Torriani of Milan, and the Scaglieri of Verona; and it at length fell under the power of the Visconti of Milan, from whose intolerable tyranny it sought escape by submission to the Venetian republic. When the league of Cambrai was entered into for the overthrow of Venice, Brescia was captured by the French (1512), under their celebrated leader, Gaston de Foix. The citizens hoisted the standard of St. Mark, and drove out their oppressors; but the citadel remained in the hands of the enemy. Gaston de Foix advanced upon the city with an army of 12,000 men, the flower of the French chivalry, and summoned it to surrender, under a menace that if he were resisted not a single life should be spared. The citizens replied by a mortal defiance. The forlorn hope of the French was led by the famous chevalier Bayard, who on mounting the breast-work received a dangerous wound, and was carried from the scene of strife by two archers. The fall of Bayard, who was supposed to be mortally wounded, increased the fury of the assailants, and seven thousand defenders of the city were slain in the heat of the conflict. But the fearful outrages and atrocities that followed during the sack of the city have scarcely a parallel. Men, women, and children, to the number of forty-six thousand, were ferociously slaughtered; and "the flower of the French chivalry" paused in their work of blood, only to indulge in shameful barbarities and violence towards the weaker sex, or to satiate their avarice by the most capricious plunder. The booty was immense: ducats were counted by the handful, and cloth of gold was measured by the lance. The miseries of war were succeeded by famine and pestilence; and Brescia has not, to this day, fully recovered the loss of population she sustained in the opening of the sixteenth century.

DRESCIA.

Two incidents are recorded in connection with this memorable assault that deserve especial mention; the one, as an example of the brutal ferocity of the conquerors; and the other as a solitary redeeming feature in their conduct. As the crowds pressed forward to the churches to find a refuge from the soldiery, the latter inflicted five sabre-wounds on the skull and face of a child in the arms of its mother. This child survived, but in consequence of its wounds never acquired the faculty of speech, and hence obtained the name of *Tartaglia*,—the same Tartaglia who became one of the greatest mathematicians of the age, and to whom modern algebraical science is principally indebted. The other incident refers to the Chevalier Bayard. The archers who bore him from the assault, took him to the house of a noble family named Cigola, whose cowardly master had fled to a monastery, leaving his wife and daughters exposed to the brutality of the French soldiery. Bayard observed, amidst his own sufferings, the terror and distress of these ladies, and ordered a guard to be placed at the door of the house to secure its inmates from outrage and pillage. During two months both mother and daughters nursed him with woman's tenderness, and when at length he was sufficiently restored to dispense with their attentions, the mother offered him a casket containing two thousand five hundred ducats as a ransom for herself and children. Bayard raised her from her suppliant posture, and begged, as the only return for the protection his presence had afforded them, that she would permit him to bid adieu to her daughters. On their entrance, he presented each with a thousand ducats from the casket as a marriage portion, and directed that the remaining five hundred should be given to some poor nuns who had been pillaged. When he took his leave, one of the young ladies presented him with a pair of rich bracelets woven of her own hair, and the other proffered for his acceptance an embroidered purse. These the gallant knight accepted; he placed the bracelets on his arm and the purse on his sleeve, and declared that whilst he lived he would wear them for the honour of their donors. Although this incident is vaunted by the French historians in honour of their chivalry, it can in fact only be taken as a testimony to the character of the individual knight whom they have themselves separated from his compeers by the title of "*Chevalier sans peur et sans reproche*," —The Knight without fear and without disgrace.

Brescia returned in 1516 to the government of Venice. Its subsequent history records two awful visitations of the plague, the one in 1575, and the other in 1630; and in 1769, the explosion of a powder magazine destroyed all the buildings in its vicinity, and killed a great number of the citizens. It was in the latter year that the Brescians aided the French against Venice. Since 1814, the city has been subject to Austria. At the present day Brescia is a flourishing city containing 40,000 inhabitants. It is pleasantly situated, and prospects of great beauty are obtained from the neighbouring heights. Among the numerous Roman antiquities, the most remarkable is a recently exhumed temple, supposed to have been dedicated to Hercules by Vespasian, and whose portico bears strong resemblance to that of the Pantheon. A museum of antiquities has been founded in the temple, under the direction of Signor Girolamo Ioli, to whom the antiquarian world is indebted for the recovery of the temple itself. Brescia is remarkable for its two cathedrals; the Duomo Vecchio, said to have been built by the dukes of Lombardy; and the Duomo Nuovo, begun in 1604 from the designs of Giovanni Battista Lantana, but of which the cupola remained unfinished until 1825. The Brescian school of painting has produced works of great merit, but the glory of its members is absorbed in that of the Venetian school. The churches and palazzi are decorated with the paintings of

native artists, amongst whom we may name Alessandro Buonvicino, called also *Il Moretto*, the founder of the school; Ricchino, a pupil of Moretto; Gaudini, a pupil of Paul Veronese; and Sebastian Conca. The works of the latter, however, exhibit only the decline of art in Italy.

ROCCA D'ANFO.

LAGO D'IDRO.

IDRO, the ancient Edrum or Edrinus, is a small village at the southern extremity of the Lago d'Idro, or Lake of Idro. The road on the eastern side of the lake terminates at this village; but on the other side a carriage road from the Val Sabbia is continued above the precipices overhanging the lake, and passing Rocca d'Anfo, proceeds as far as Ladrone on the confines of the Tyrol. The Lago d'Idro lies out of the travelling route, and is little known except to the inhabitants of the district; but to the lover of the picturesque, it offers beauties of no mean character.

The illustrative view is rendered generally interesting from its being the battle-field upon which a fierce conflict took place between the French and Austrians, in July of 1790. Prior to this contest, the Austrians had checked the career of Napoleon, and even driven his troops triumphantly before them; but the results of the battle of Rocca d'Anfo changed the face of affairs, and restored success to the army of the French republic.

BERGAMO.

NOT a few of the cities of Italy are, in their history, "as like as one pea to another." After having enjoyed more or less celebrity under the republic or the empire of Rome, they experienced one common visitation from the barbarians, afterwards shared in the turbulence of the middle ages, and ultimately fell under the yoke of a foreign despot. Bergamo is included in this class; and the only distinctions that *individualize* it, are the tradition of its great antiquity, and the fact of its having been the birth-place and early residence of the father of Tasso.

There are not many objects of striking interest in Bergamo. Under the portico of the Palazzo Vecchio, is a statue of Tasso, in Carrara marble. One of the most remarkable buildings is the *Fiera*, a vast quadrangle, with three gates on each side, and courts and streets. An annual fair, which traces its origin to the year 913, is held in this place on the feast of St. Bartholomew. The Fiera contains six hundred shops; and during the fair of 1833, goods, of which one-third consisted of silk, were sold to the amount of more than one million sterling.

LOUVERE,

ON THE LAKE OF ISEO.

TRAVELLERS in Italy pursue the beaten track, from which they are rarely tempted to diverge, hence many retired scenes of great beauty never fall under their observation, and amongst these localities Louvere claims a distinguished place. This district was anciently inhabited by the Euganei, a people expelled from their native abodes by the Veneti. According to Pliny, they held at one time thirty-four towns in this neighbourhood, all of which were admitted to the rights of Latin cities by Augustus. Descending to the twelfth century, we find Louvere an arena of the Guelph and Ghibelline contest, that universal curse to the cities of Italy. From this period, however, we are to date the modern population of the district, which was previously but thinly inhabited. The exiles from other cities sought and found a refuge on the banks of the Lago d'Iseo from the fierce vengeance of party strife. Louvere afterwards suffered great extremities, when its inhabitants were opposed to Pandolfo Malatesta, the lord of Bergamo. This nobleman advanced upon the town, and took it; he then lighted a candle and commanded every resident to depart, on pain of death, before it was consumed.

Louvere was the residence of Lady Mary Wortley Montague, who in a letter to her daughter, the Countess of Bute, describes the condition of the town and neighbourhood a century ago.—
"This extraordinary spot of land is almost unknown to the rest of the world; and indeed does not seem to be destined by nature to be inhabited by human creatures; and I believe never would have been so without the cruel civil war between the Guelphs and Ghibellines. Before that time here were only the huts of a few fishermen, who came, at certain seasons, on account of the fine fish with which this lake abounds, particularly trouts, as large and red as salmon. The lake is different from any other I ever saw or read of, being the colour of the sea, rather deeper, tinged with green, which convinces me that the surrounding mountains are full of minerals, and, it may be, rich in mines yet undiscovered, as well as quarries of marble, from whence the churches and houses are ornamented, and even the streets paved, which, if polished and laid with art, would look like the finest mosaic work, being a variety of beautiful colours. I ought to retract the honourable title of street, none of them being broader than an alley, and impassable for any wheel-carriage except a wheel-barrow. This town, which is the largest of twenty-five that are built on the banks of the Lake of Iseo, is nearly two miles long, and the figure of a semicircle, and situated at the northern extremity. If it was a regular range

of building, it would appear magnificent, but being founded accidentally by those who sought a refuge from the violence of the times, it is a mixture of shops and palaces, gardens and houses, which ascend a mile high in a confusion which is not disagreeable. After this salutary water was found, and the purity of the air was experienced, many people of quality chose it for their summer residence, and embellished it with several fine edifices. It was populous and flourishing till that fatal plague which overran all Europe in the year 1620. It made a terrible ravage in this place; the poor were almost destroyed, and the rich deserted it. Since that time it has never recovered its former splendour; few of the nobility returned; it is now only frequented during the water-drinking season. Several of the ancient palaces are degraded into lodging-houses, and others stand empty in a ruinous condition; one of these I have bought."

Louvere is, in the present day, a flourishing little town, and is still improving. The late Count Luigi Tadini built a fine palace, with an extensive façade towards the lake, and formed a museum of natural history, and a gallery of paintings and statuary. The best inn in Louvere is the Canon d'Oro, kept by the *noble* family of Celeri. We marvel that this circumstance alone does not attract a certain class of rich *parvenus* to the locality. They delight to "gall the kibe" of aristocracy; and for the expenditure of a few ducats at the Casa Celeria, they might summon the representative of the Celeri to unstrap their portmanteaus, and give a polish—to their boots.

COMO.

THE people of Como claim a Greek origin, and pride themselves on a descent more ancient than that of Roman cities. After the fall of the empire, this place was held successively by the Goths, the Lombards, and the Franks. In the middle ages it espoused the Ghibelline interest, and was thus led into contests with its Guelphic neighbours, the Milanese, by whom it was taken and burned in 1127. It was gradually rebuilt, and regained its independence, but at length fell irrecoverably under the power of Milan, and took part in all the subsequent political vicissitudes of that city.

Como is the the birth-place of Pliny, whose villa on the neighbouring lake is one of the points of attraction to travellers; an intermitting spring establishes the identity of the locality beyond all dispute. Amongst other eminent citizens, the Comasques delight to enumerate Caninius Rufus and Caius Cecilius, early Latin poets; Paulus Jovius, the bishop and historian; Rezzonico, the poet; and the popes, Innocent XI. and Clement XIII. There is, however, one name connected with Como, which in many respects claims pre-eminent regard, namely, that of Volta, to whose discoveries electricity and modern chemistry are so much indebted.

The Cathedral of Como is deemed one of the finest ecclesiastical structures of the middle ages. It was founded in 1396, and built of marbles from the neighbouring quarries. The façade of white marble is broad and striking, and the interior derives grandeur from the capacity of its dome and nave, and the sombre and impressive character that prevails throughout. The church of St. Fedele, an ancient edifice, is also remarkable for the character of its architecture. The city, including its suburbs, is said to contain upwards of eighteen thousand inhabitants. It has several silk-works and manufactories of woollen cloths; and in literary and scientific associations, and educational institutions, it claims precedence over many of the more important cities of Italy.

Access to the Lake of Como has been greatly facilitated, in recent years, by the introduction of steamers on the lake, and the construction of admirable roads along its shores. The passage down the lake was formerly by a heavy, dangerous boat, which started in the evening from Gravedona, and stopped at the villages to collect passengers to the market of Como, which was reached with difficulty, in the morning, except when foul weather baffled the boatmen's skill, and exposed all on board to imminent peril. On reaching Como, the peasant was compelled to hasten his transactions to secure his return home the same evening. Now, however, he rests tranquilly till six or eight in the morning, reaches Como in time to manage his business leisurely, and arrives at his home, even if situated at the upper extremity of the lake, long before night-fall. So much for steam, which some romantic blockheads have blown up as an intruder upon the quiet lake, but which, so far as we can ascertain, has never blown up them in return; on the contrary, it has contributed to the picturesque of Lake Como, and blessed its villagers with advantages they never before enjoyed. The road on the shores of the lake is one of the finest works of modern engineering science. It is carried by a succession of terraces and galleries from village to village, and through scenes of the most striking beauty. As this road leads to Milan by Lecco, avoiding Como, travellers who desire to enjoy the scenery of that branch of the lake which leads from the promontory of Bellagio to Como, must make its tour in a steamer, or hire a boat to visit the villas and villages which occupy a thousand picturesque sites around its shores.

The Tower of Baradello, situated on a conical sand-stone hill, forms a remarkable feature in the scenery of Como. Originally erected by the Gauls, it became in different ages a stronghold of the power temporarily predominant. During the French possession of Italy, this tower was employed as a telegraphic station—a use to which it seems also to have been put in ancient times, by the display of coloured flags by day, and the lighting of fires at night. It appears, indeed, to have formed the centre of a system of telegraphic communication, as the ruins of other towers seemingly erected for a similar purpose still exist in the district. The hill and tower of Baradello are situated too far to the right to fall within the limits of our view.

VARESE.

FROM THE SACRO MONTE.

A BEAUTIFUL, extensive, and diversified prospect is obtained from the Sacro Monte, or Calvary, as it is sometimes named, a commanding eminence situated about two miles from the unimportant city of Varese. In the ascent from Varese, the traveller, after passing fifteen chapels, arrives at the church of the Madonna, on the summit of the Sacro Monte. The sanctity of this edifice makes it the resort of religious pilgrims, and the pilgrims of art are attracted thither by the beauty of its architecture and pictures. It has also its absurdities; one, a statue of the Virgin, attributed to St. Luke; and another, a dried crocodile, said to be the remains of a fearful dragon destroyed by the power of the Madonna.

From the Sacro Monte the traveller looks down upon the picturesque sites of the chapels which he passed in the ascent; and below them lie Varese, the surrounding villas, and a hundred campagnas and palaces. On the right is the lake of Varese, beyond it the lake of Monate, and still more distant, a part of the Lago Maggiore. The view is bounded, in this direction, by the Alps, which blend with the haze and indistinctness of the distant plains. The eye sweeps round the panorama, taking in the Alps, and the mountains which bound the lakes of Lugano and Como, together with the rich intervening country. Milan is said to be sometimes distinguishable in the view. The elevation from which the spectator surveys this prospect, is about two thousand feet above the lake of Varese.

The neighbourhood of Varese is associated with many historical recollections. It was at an early period a district of the Insubrian Gauls; and about 170 B.C. it fell, together with other territories of the Cisalpino Gauls, into the hands of the Romans. About sixty years later, the Cimbrians descended upon the country; and on the decline of Rome, the northern barbarians laid it waste, in their passage to the interior of Italy. The senseless battles of jarring creeds, and the conflict between the temporal and ecclesiastical powers, involved it in the common miseries of the dark ages. And still later, it suffered severely from the people of Como, who resented its attachment to their Milanese enemies. Its plains have been the arena of a thousand battles; and from the time of Bellovesus, the Gaul, B.C. 610, down to the French invasion at the close of the last century, it was a place of sacrifice where rapine and ambition offered up their hecatombs of victims.

The Lago di Varese, or lake of Varese, is of an oval form, about twelve miles in length, and six in breadth. Its banks slope gently to the verge of the water, and are covered with luxuriant vegetation. Fields of deep verdure, bordered by lofty trees; hills covered with thickets; villas shaded with pines and poplars; and villages encircled with vineyards, attract the traveller's regard wherever he turns his eye, and charm him by the combination of picturesque beauty which they present to his view.

MILAN.

FEW cities in Italy can rank with Milan, which has brought down to modern times a great part of its ancient celebrity, and preserved through nearly all the periods of its eventful history a happy mediocrity of fame and magnificence. The ancient Mediolanum, the original of Milan, was founded by the Insubrian Gauls, whilst Rome itself was in its infancy. In the reign of Tarquinius Priscus, or that of his successor Ancus Martius, it had gradually risen to be a city of some importance. And in the year of Rome 532 (A.D. 221), it was possessed of strength sufficient to withstand a Roman army, and required the united efforts of two consuls. M. Marcellus and C. Cornelius Scipio, to effect its capture. Under the Roman republic, it enjoyed tranquillity for many ages, increased in extent and opulence, improved in the polite arts, and became the seat of an academy honoured with the appellation of *Novæ Athenæ*—New Athens. When the Roman empire gave way, and even the imperial city, with all her lofty prerogatives of majesty and fame, saw her streets deserted, and her pomp withering under the influence of warring powers, Mediolanum flourished in population and splendour, and became, not indeed the nominal but oftentimes the real seat of empire. Decorated with temples and porticoes, baths and amphitheatres, and a general magnificence of architecture, it claimed, under the Valentinians, equality of rank with the best cities of the empire. But the invasion of Italy by Attila, in the time of Valentinian III., commenced an era of disasters, in which Mediolanum took its share. Attila visited it in his fury, and first plundered, then butchered its inhabitants. After him came the Goths, under Vitiges, who burned a great part of the city. Then followed the Lombards, by whom it was sacked, and afterwards abandoned to contempt and insignificance. It was restored to much of its former dignity by Charlemagne; and again suffered reverses under Barbarossa, who razed it to the ground, and even, it is said, passed the ploughshare over its ruins. But this same prince almost immediately assisted in its restoration, and thus laid the foundation of modern Milan. The prosperity of the new city is identified with the Visconti, a family descended from Visconti, archbishop and "Perpetual Lord of Milan," in 1276. In the fourteenth century, the representatives of this family ranked amongst the most powerful princes in Italy, and extended their authority over all Lombardy north of the Po, and over several cities and states south of that river. Unfortunately for Milan, and indeed for all Italy, the Visconti formed matrimonial connections with the dynasty of France, which, on the extinction of this family, laid claim to the Milanese territory. The battle of Pavia at length broke the French power in Italy, and secured the possession of Milan to Spain, and eventually to Austria, which retained it, with a few intervals till the invasion of Napoleon. On the expulsion of the French, Milan was again placed under Austrian rule. The campaign of 1859 effected its transfer to the Sardinian dynasty.

Milan is a great and splendid city, nearly eleven miles in circumference; but its general appearance, according to Eustace, does not correspond with its reputation, the streets being

neither uniformly wide nor regular, and the edifices of magnificence or beauty being few in number. Amongst the latter, the Duomo, or Cathedral, claims priority of notice, as the great point of attraction to visitors. This edifice is situated almost in the centre of the city, and occupies the site of the ancient Basilica which was destroyed by Attila. A second building was accidentally destroyed by fire in 1075, and a third was demolished by Barbarossa. The present structure, the fourth erection, was begun by Giovanni Galeazzo Visconti, on the 15th May 1386. Since the day when the foundation-stone was laid, scaffolds have always been standing in some part of the building. The octagon cupola was not vaulted till 1522; the three western divisions, or arches, of the nave were not completed till 1685; the central tower and spire were only finished in 1772; at a later period the slumbering works were revived by Napoleon; and the Austrian has since added his quota to the labours of nearly five centuries; still there is more to do, and a millennium, if not *the* millennium, seems destined to arrive before the sound of the mallet and chisel shall cease to be heard. The west front of the Duomo is universally execrated as the great flaw in the building, a mixture of Italianized Roman and Gothic unique in ugliness. Apart from this repulsive feature, the exterior is magnificently grand. Its snowy pinnacles, with their delicate tracery, and the multitude of statues equally white, with which it is decorated, rising towards the bright blue sky, look like some exquisite piece of sculpture executed in molten silver. With some incongruities, it possesses great excellence; every one views it with delight, and carries its image in his memory when he can no longer recal the features of other structures presented in his travels. The interior of the edifice has an air of lightness and elegance that offers a striking contrast to the heavy internal arrangement which characterises other celebrated ecclesiastical structures. The extreme slenderness of the clustered pillars which rise without intervention to the vault, permits the eye to range over the whole extent of the interior. The pillars are more than ninety feet in height; and the clustre does not exceed eight feet in diameter. These elegant shafts, with the lofty arches and lustrous walls, and the numberless niches all filled with marble figures, give the building an appearance that is novel even in Italy, and singularly majestic. In materials, the cathedral of Milan surpasses all other churches, the noblest of which are only lined and coated with marble, while this is entirely built, paved, vaulted, and roofed with the same substance, and that of the whitest and most resplendent kind. The most remarkable object in the interior of the Duomo is the subterranean chapel in which the body of San Carlo Borromeo reposes. This illustrious individual was archbishop of Milan about the middle of the sixteenth century. The course of his life is illustrated in a number of *alti-rilievi*, chased and wrought in silver gilt, which adorn the walls of the chapel. These represent the birth of San Carlo; his Presidency of the Provincial Council of Milan, in 1565, in which canons were enacted virtually protesting against the abuses of the Roman church; his distribution of his domain of Oria to the poor; his public administration of the sacrament during the great plague; the attempt to assassinate him; his death; and his reception into paradise. The body of the saint reposes in a shrine of rock crystal behind the high altar; it is stretched at full length, dressed in pontifical robes, with the crosier and mitre; but the face, disfigured by decay, contrasts hideously with the splendour of the vestments which cover the body. St. Ambrose is another name of interest connected with the Duomo, and more particularly with the Basilica Ambrosiana, where his remains are interred. It was at the door of this last edifice that he met the emperor Theodosius and refused him admission,—an incident rendered familiar by Vandyke's painting,

PAVIA.

We pass by the numerous edifices, lay and ecclesiastical, that might claim particular regard in a more extended page than ours, and briefly advert to two points of interest, the one the Ambrosian Library, and the other the Conaculum, or repository of the Last Supper, by Da Vinci. The library, founded by a member of the Borromeo family, contains about forty thousand volumes, and more than fifteen thousand manuscripts, and includes a gallery of pictures, statues, antiques, and medals. But the most unique treasure is a voluminous manuscript of Leonardi da Vinci, filled with sketches, which testifies that his genius ranged over all the sciences at pleasure, and shone with equal lustre in poetry, painting, architecture, and philosophy. The Cœnaculum, a name applied somewhat affectedly to the refectory of the Dominican convent, contains the last fading, fragile relics of Leonardo da Vinci's great masterpiece, the Last Supper. The original painting was executed in oil, a circumstance much to be regretted, for had it been a fresco its beauties might have come down to us unimpaired. At an early period the colour separated from the wall, curled, and peeled off; and to repair the ruin into which it had fallen artists were from time to time employed to re-paint portions of the composition. It is now in the last stage of decay, and those parts which bear the impress of Da Vinci's hand alone, are inappreciable except by the lover and student of art. One cannot suppress a feeling of indignation to read that the French soldiery amused themselves by firing at this painting, as at a target, directing an especial aim at the head of the Saviour. Nor is our indignation less to be told that *the door* cut through the painting was made by the monks for readiness of access to the refectory.

PAVIA.

PAVIA derives no celebrity from classical history. Under its ancient name of Ticinum a few allusions are made to it, merely sufficient to attest its existence in the republican and imperial ages of Rome. Between the sixth and eighth centuries its name was changed to Papia, afterwards softened by Italian euphony into Pavia. It became a considerable city under Theodoric and his successors, and the Lombard princes made it the capital of their dominions. The residence of the Lombardic sovereigns occupied the site of the present Castello, erected by Galeazzo Visconti between 1400 and 1409. In this building were preserved the treasures of literature and art collected by Giovanni Galeazzo, the friend and protector of Petrarch, consisting of manuscripts, armour, and natural curiosities.

Petrarch is lavish in his praise of Galeazzo's liberality and magnificence, but he fails to record the fact that his patron, in a fit of passion, hanged his architect after the completion of

the edifice. When the Castello was dismantled by Louis XII., its treasures were carried to France. Pavia is indebted to the Visconti for its principal buildings, the Duomo, the church of Santa Maria de Campanouva, and the covered bridge over the Ticino, and also for the restoration of its university. Their sovereignty, however, was a tyranny galling and oppressive to all who fell under its domination; and if their memory be not execrated in the present day, it is simply because the ocular and tangible witnesses of their liberality and magnificence are more obtrusive than the page of history which records their misdeeds. It is recorded of Pavia, that in her republican days she sent fifteen thousand men to the crusades, a number equal to half her present population. The citizens have on various occasions exhibited a degree of spirit near akin to that of the old Romans. More than once they repelled the French from their walls; and it was in the celebrated battle of Pavia that Francis I. "lost all but honour." In their last struggle with the French, the Pavians abated nothing of their wonted courage, but on that occasion, their good genius deserted them, and their city was compelled to admit a conqueror. The excesses committed by Napoleon's army will compare with the foulest atrocities of barbarian and mediæval times; and the massacre of Pavia stands in fearful relief amidst the scenes of blood and carnage by which the Achilles of France sought to revive the empire of Charlemagne.

Amongst the churches of Pavia, that of San Pietro in Cœlo Aureo is worthy of mention from its having been the resting place of Bŏethius, the author of the "Consolation of Philosophy," who flourished early in the sixth century. The edifice has been in ruins for many ages. The cicerconi point out amidst the square towers which continue to form the striking features of Pavia, the identical tower in which Bŏethius was confined by Theodoric; but that this is not the prison into which the Consul was thrown for his opposition to the Arians, is manifest from two facts: the tower of Bŏethius disappeared in 1584, and the one now substituted for it is neither known to occupy the same site, nor is it of sufficient age to claim identity with a structure of the fifth or sixth century. The cathedral contains the tomb of St. Augustine, a curious and interesting work, richly decorated with innumerable *bassi-rilievi*, and nearly one hundred statues, and bearing evidence of its having been executed in the latter part of the fourteenth century. It is said to have been removed hither when the church of San Pietro in Cœlo Aureo was destroyed; but there is an evident anachronism in the tradition, that renders the whole account of this tomb apocryphal.

At the distance of three or four miles from Pavia, is the church and convent of Certosa, founded by Galeazzo Visconti in 1306, to atone for the murder of his uncle, whose dominions he had usurped. This splendid edifice is situated in a noble park, and forms one of the most imposing pictures imaginable. The most celebrated sculptors in Italy are said to have been employed during three centuries in ornamenting the façade of the church. The interior is even more beautiful than the exterior. The rarest marbles, alabasters, mosaics, sculpture, carvings in ivory and busts in gold, silver, bronze, and pietro-dura, inlaid with precious gems, paintings, and gilding, are lavishly distributed all over it. A detailed description of the gorgeous splendour of this institution would carry us beyond our limits. Let it suffice to say that the monks of Certosa are lodged right royally.

The University of Pavia, founded by Charlemagne in 774, still numbers about sixteen hundred students, and the most celebrated names of Italy have dignified its professorships.

THE WALDENSIAN COLLEGE AT LA TORRE,

VAL LUCERNA, PIEDMONTE.

THE illustrative view represents the opening of the valley of Lucerna into the plains of the Po. The town of Lucerna is seen at the base of the distant mountains; that of La Torre is in a great measure concealed by the foreground. The interest of the view, apart from its picturesque features, centres in the Waldensian College, an edifice of no great pretensions in itself, but dignified by the purposes for which it was built.

The Waldenses go back to a much more remote antiquity than is usually assigned to them. Their name literally signifies the dwellers in the valleys, but its derivation has been sought in connection with the name of Peter Waldus, a rich citizen of Lyons, who formed a religious community in 1170, known by the appellation of the Lyonists, or the Poor Men of Lyons. The ancient Waldenses, and the Waldensians of the twelfth century, can be identified only in the similarity of their religious views, and their contendings for the pure and simple faith preached and enforced by the Apostles. The modern term Vaudois is derived from Valdo or Vaud, each of which is merely a variation of the name of Waldus. The application of this term to the inhabitants of the Piedmontese valleys is incorrect, since they ought to be regarded as descendants from the ancient native reformers of Italy. The early history of the Waldenses is enveloped in considerable obscurity, but their great antiquity is admitted even by their enemies. Rainerus the Dominican, an Inquisitor in the thirteenth century, says that their heresy "existed, according to some, from the time of Silvester, and according to others, from the days of the Apostles." The same writer, in conjunction with other two, affirms that the Waldenses dated their own origin and the defection of the Roman communion from the reign of Silvester, A. D. 314. Leo, who flourished in the reign of Constantine, they regarded as their founder. Romanism, at this period, ceased to be Christianity, and the inhabitants of the valleys left the unholy communion. Other testimony declares that the Waldenses multiplied wonderfully, and spread themselves throughout all the countries of Europe. We ought rather to say their *principles* spread far and wide, since the defenders of these principles in various countries were distinguished by as various appellations, such as Cathari, Leonists, Wickliffites, Bohemians, and Albigensians. Pius II. states, in his History of Bohemia, that the Waldenses rejected purgatory, image-worship, sacramental confession, extreme unction, invocation of saints, prayer for the dead, and the use of oil and chrism in baptism. Petavius represents them as opposed to the papal supremacy, indulgences, purgatory, fasts, festivals, and saint-invocation. They denied the doctrine of transubstantiation; declared the celibacy of the clergy to be unscriptural; reduced the sacraments to two, namely, Baptism and the Supper; and rejected the worship of the Virgin herself, affirming that remission of sins can be obtained through Christ alone. An enemy (Rainerus, before quoted) has testified to "their

sobriety, modesty, chastity, and temperance; and their aversion to taverns, balls, vanity, anger, scurrility, detraction, levity, swearing, and falsehood." It is further recorded of them, that "a boy could scarcely be found among them, but, if questioned on his religion, could, with readiness, give a reason for his faith. Tribute they paid with the utmost punctuality; and if prevented for a time by civil war, they discharged this debt on the return of peace." Here, then, we have a race of men upon whom judgment has been pronounced by their enemies and persecutors. Of what have they been guilty? Verily of this: They have been from the first corruption of the Church down to the present day, witnesses against error, and upholders of Apostolic doctrine; they have testified to their faith by works that are its natural result; they have delighted to make Christianity known, and to impress its requirements upon their youth as a reasonable service; and they have ever been obedient to the civil power, giving constantly unto Cæsar that which is Cæsar's, and to God that which is God's. But how were these Christian graces regarded by those who could not deny their existence? Rejection of error was accounted obstinate heresy; deep, fervent piety was branded as mere enthusiasm; holiness of life, as a cunning pretence; and the spread of truth, as an unhallowed warfare against the head of the church. Crusade upon crusade was sent forth against these unoffending people, and Rome did all that lay in her power to extirpate to the very roots the name and doctrines of the Waldenses, but a remnant was ever left to bear faithful witness; often cast down, but never destroyed, the Waldenses continue, to this day, to exhibit all the grandeur of truth and all the beauty of holiness. The persecution of the Waldenses has ever exhibited on the part of their oppressors a ruthless vengeance and a brutal ferocity; whilst their own defensive operations are marked by magnanimity, and—if we may use the expression—the very chivalry of the Cross. Cold and unsympathizing must that heart be, that does not glow at the remembrance of their expatriation, and their subsequent "glorious return" to the valleys they loved, under the guidance of Arnaud, their pastor and leader. It is satisfactory now to think that after enduring through so many ages an almost uninterrupted series of persecutions, the religious and political rights of this interesting community have at last come to be fully recognized by the state authorities. Subsequent to the accession of Charles Albert, in 1831, the restrictions and disabilities affecting the Waldenses had been gradually removed; and, on 17th February, 1848, a royal edict was issued, admitting them to a full participation in all civil and political privileges enjoyed by the other subjects of the Sardinian monarchy. This event was celebrated by rejoicings throughout all the Vaudois valleys, and by a grand demonstration in the city of Turin itself.

The Waldensian College at La Torre originated in a munificent donation entrusted to Dr. Gilly, an English clergyman. Before its erection, the Waldensian clergy were educated at Geneva. Dr. Gilly thought that the donation could not be better employed than in the building and endowment of an institution in which the Waldensian youth might receive a sound classical education, combined with orthodox theological instruction. In connection with the College, a branch institution has been established at Pomaretto, in the valley of St. Martin. The educational staff consists of four professors, and a rector, who also acts as a professor, a sixth professor conducting the Latin school at Pomarétto. The salary of each professor is 1000 francs per annum.

FORT BARD, VAL D'AOSTA.

FORT BARD is a citadel of great strength, seated on Mont Albaredo, a stupendous mass of rock which rises in one of the narrow gorges of the Val d'Aosta, the defile through which Italy is entered by the passes of St. Bernard. A position so strong by nature was obviously fitted for a point of defence; and we meet with early mention of the locality as an arena of contest in which a handful of men disputed the passage of a numerous host. According to tradition, Hannibal entered Italy by the Val d'Aosta, and there is evidence to show that this was the probable route of his descent. About 134 B.C. the Satassi, who then inhabited the valley, repulsed a Roman army, and compelled the legions to retreat with the loss of ten thousand men. These people were reduced in the time of Augustus, when the Romans built Augusta Prætoria (now Aosta) on the site of Cordele, the Salassian city. On the fall of the empire, Aosta was taken and sacked by the Lombards, who, in turn, were expelled by Charlemagne. In the tenth century the fortress was built to command all ingress and egress to and from the valley. After a protracted siege, this citadel was taken by Amadeus IV., in 1252; and since that period it has been in the possession of the Dukes of Savoy, or of the Kings of Sardinia.

The most interesting incident in the history of Fort Bard is connected with Napoleon's descent into Italy. In May, 1800, the French army, having passed the Great St. Bernard, attempted a passage through the Val d'Aosta. The reduction of Fort Bard had been represented to Napoleon as an easy affair; and great was his chagrin to find so serious an obstacle interrupting his path. He had already learned that the Austrian general was hastening to enclose him in the valley; and his soldiers were provided only with rations for a few days, with no possibility of receiving fresh supplies in their present position. Two days were lost in devising means for effecting the passage, when at length Berthier suggested that they should find or make a passage up the precipitous sides of Mont Albaredo. This was undertaken and accomplished in an incredibly short time, and a safe passage procured for the men; but the path was impracticable for the cannon and artillery waggons. Another assault was attempted, but with no better success than former ones. Marmont now proposed to strew the road with straw and manure, and after binding the wheels of the cannon with hay-bands, to take them at night under the guns of the Fort through the village of Bard. This manœuvre succeeded, not without discovery by the Austrian in command of the Fort, but without any serious loss. In less than a month after this bold exploit, the battle of Marengo was won, and the eagle of Napoleon spread its wings over Italy.

MURANO.

THE town of Murano is situated rather more than a mile north from Venice, on an island of the same name, which is the largest in the Lagoons, and nearly forms the extremity of the long chain which, stretching from north to south, affords, with the assistance of art, an effectual barrier against the surges of the stormy Adriatic. The island, formed partly by alluvial deposits brought down from the mainland by rivers, and partly by low banks of sand thrown up by the waves, is almost devoid of natural beauty; but wherever the eye wanders from it, whether to the south, where the queen of the sea is seen rising in majesty, or to the north, where an Alpine chain terminates, and seems to encircle the horizon, the view is equally interesting and magnificent.

The town of Murano appears to have been founded at an early period of the Venetian republic, and gradually acquired so much importance that, while continuing to be a dependency of Venice, it was erected into a separate municipality, and governed by its own Podesta. In the fifteenth century it had a population estimated at 30,000; and from the number and grandeur, both of its public buildings and private palaces, was regarded as a kind of miniature Venice. Its mere proximity to this celebrated city, of which it may be considered a suburb, perhaps accounts for the rapid progress it had made; but it had a source of prosperity within itself, and in virtue of it claims to have been the principal artificer of its own greatness.

Toward the close of the dark ages, when Europe awoke from its slumber, and literature, science, and art began to revive, the Venetians occupied a foremost place, and took the lead in almost all the great commercial marts of the then known world, in consequence, not only of their vast maritime resources, but of the unrivalled excellence of several of their domestic industrial products. One of the most beautiful, if not the most useful of these, was glass; and in it the inhabitants of Murano, where the only Venetian glass-works existed, continued for centuries to enjoy an unquestioned and most lucrative monopoly; both the East and West looking to them for their principal supplies. It does not seem that there was anything in the locality of Murano peculiarly favourable to the manufacture; but having somehow or other become acquainted with the secrets of the art, or it may be re-invented them, the glass-makers endeavoured to perpetuate the monopoly by studiously concealing their more important processes. A monopoly thus maintained by secrets which must, of necessity, have been known to thousands, was very precarious; and it is interesting to see how anxious the Venetian government was to prevent foreign countries from entering into competition with them, and thereby endangering one of their most important sources of trade and revenue. One of the most obvious means was encouragement; and accordingly Baron Von Lowhen, in his *Analysis of Nobility in its Origin*, states, that the Senate, to encourage the men engaged in the glass-works to remain in Murano, made them all burgesses of Venice, and allowed nobles to marry their daughters, giving to the issue of such marriages all the privileges of noble birth. It would have been well if the government had been satisfied with encouragement; but, according to Daru, one of the statutes of the state inquisition contained the following atrocious clauses:—" If any workman or artizan carry his art to a foreign country, to the prejudice of the republic, he shall be ordered to return ; if he do not obey, his nearest relations shall be imprisoned, that his regard for them may induce him to come back. If he return, the past shall be forgiven, and employment shall be provided for him at Venice. If, in despite of the imprisonment of his relations, he persevere in his absence, an emissary shall be employed to despatch him; and after his death his relations shall be set at liberty."

Encouragement might have succeeded, but this determination to maintain a monopoly by having recourse, if necessary, to the dagger of an assassin, was a revolting outrage on humanity, and could not but prove a failure. France, which had long been anxiously labouring to succeed in one important branch of the art, that of making mirrors, effected her object about the middle of the seventeenth century, by securing the services of workmen who had learned it at Murano; Bohemia soon became a successful competitor in another important branch ; new discoveries followed, by which several of the boasted Venetian processes were superseded ; and in almost every country of Europe, and in none more than in our own island, numerous competitors arose, with whom the glass-makers of Murano, hampered as they were by their connection with a declining republic, have found it hopeless to contend. The works, however, continued to be carried on with spirit, and had not lost their celebrity about the middle of the seventeenth century, when they were visited by the celebrated John Evelyn, who thus speaks of them:—" I passed over to Murano, famous for the best glasses of the world, where having viewed their furnaces and seen their work, I made a collection of divers curiosities and glasses which I sent for England by long sea." The only glass-works which Murano now possesses, are two establishments, confined almost exclusively to the humble department of making glass-beads.

With the loss of its manufacture, its prosperity was at an end ; many of its finer buildings have perished by violence or gradual decay, and the population has dwindled down to about 5000. But independent of the interest which justly attaches to it as the cradle of one of the most beautiful creations of human skill, Murano possesses several structures well deserving of notice for their architecture, their venerable antiquity, and the treasures of art which, notwithstanding ruthless French spoliation, they still retain. Among these, the first place is due to the Duomo, or church of San Donato, said to have been built in the ninth century, though the date marked on the beautiful mosaic pavement is 1140, and many parts have been unfortunately modernized. It presents a mixture of Greek and Moorish styles, considered by some a very fine specimen of semi-Byzantine. The exterior of its east end consists of two curious tiers of arches, and the interior of the same part has an air of gloomy grandeur, though the beauty of its columns of fine Greek marble is concealed by a permanent covering of damask. The only paintings of any interest are portraits of a Podesta and his wife, dated 1310, and considered the earliest known specimens of the Venetian school. The church of San Pietro is remarkable only for its paintings and wood carvings. Among the former, are a Virgin enthroned by Gian Bellino, and a St. Jerome in the desert by Paolo Veronese; and among the latter is a baptism of Christ by J. Tintoretto. The church, Degli Angeli, contains a fine altar piece by Pordenone, and pieces by Pennacchi, Peranda, Salviatte, Palma, and D. Tintoretto. Paintings by Paolo Veronese, and Zelotti, and sculptures by Vittoria adorn the Trevisan Palace.

POZZUOLI.

POZZUOLI, situated in a district not more remarkable for the political and social, than for the physical revolutions which it has undergone, is built on a promontory near the centre of the beautiful Bay of Baiæ, which adjoins the western part of the Bay of Naples. The excellent shelter which it enjoys early marked it out as an advantageous site for a harbour, and it was accordingly taken possession of for this purpose by the Greeks, who had settled outside the bay, and there built the city of Cumæ. Not satisfied with its natural advantages, they had recourse to art, and built a mole of such massive structure, that the storms of more than two thousand years have spent their force without completely destroying it. The formation of the harbour was naturally followed by the gradual erection of a town, which received the name of Dicæarchia, and became prosperous from the traffic which it carried on both with Cumæ, of which it was considered the port, and with various other settlements along the coast. In course of time, as the Romans extended their conquests, Dicæarchia became so completely Latin, that it exchanged its Greek name for that of Puteoli, which was given to it, according to some, from the number of little wells or springs which it contained, and, according to others, from the *putor*, or stench of the sulphurous vapours exhaled from the numerous volcanic caves and fissures in its vicinity.

After the Roman conquests had embraced the greater part both of the East and West, Puteoli became a great commercial emporium. At the same time, its importance was not exclusively commercial. The mildness of its climate, and the beauties of its scenery, made it the favourite resort of the wealthiest and most distinguished citizens of Rome, and magnificent piles of building, not confined to the solid land, but carried out into the sea, from which their foundations had been gained by enormous expenditure, rose up on every side. It was here also that the apostle Paul terminated his eventful voyage when on his way to Rome; the last portion of it being from Syracuse, whence he sailed, two days previous to his arrival at Puteoli, in a ship of Alexandria, whose sign was Castor and Pollux.

In the general barbarism which accompanied the fall of the Roman empire, Puteoli once more changed its name, and became Pozzuoli. Its situation has never allowed it to sink into absolute insignificance. It still contains about 10,000 inhabitants; and, though, on the whole, indifferently built, possesses, among other public buildings, a cathedral, occupying the site and built mostly out of the ancient materials of a temple which was dedicated to Augustus.

The ancient ruins include the remains of an amphitheatre, and of a still more interesting building, which bears the name of the temple of Serapis, though there is reason to believe, both from its structure and the rigid proscription of the worship of that Egyptian deity at the date ascribed to it, that it was not a temple, but a kind of public bathing establishment. It was not discovered till 1750, when the tops of three pillars, which had remained concealed by bushes among the alluvium of the shore, were perceived, and led to an excavation, which showed that the pillars were still standing on their original pedestals, and formed part of a splendid edifice. The pavement was nearly entire, and the original plan of the whole building could be distinctly traced. Its body had consisted of a quadrangle, 70 feet in diameter, and its roof had been supported by forty six noble columns, twenty-four of granite, and the rest of marble. Unfortunately the work of spoliation immediately commenced, and soon little more of the building remained than the three pillars which had originally attracted attention to it. These, considered merely as architectural remains, are of no great value; but their surface contains a record of the deepest interest, engraved in most legible characters, though not by human hand. Each of the pillars consists of a single block of marble, and immediately above the pedestal, for the height of 12 feet, is smooth and uninjured; but the next 9 feet are pierced in all directions by the Lithodomus, a species of marine perforating bivalve. The Lithodomi live only in water, and hence it is perfectly obvious that the pillars, where perforated, must have been beneath its surface. The ground occupied by the temple must, therefore, have subsided at least 21 feet; namely, the 12 feet at the bottom uninjured by the Lithodomi, probably because protected from them by a covering of debris, and the 9 feet which they have perforated. The perforations are again far above the surface, and hence the subsidence must at some period have been followed by a corresponding rise, bringing the ground back nearly to its original state. The date of the subsidence is not easily traced, but that of the rise appears to be historically fixed to have taken place on 29th September, 1538, when, after a number of earthquakes, continued at intervals during two years, the earth suddenly opened, and threw up in a few hours, partly on the site of the Lucrine Lake, a hill with a base of 8000 and a height of 440 feet. This hill, called Monte Nuovo, forms a most striking object in the scenery of Pozzuoli.

TURIN.

THE capital of the new kingdom of Italy, presents few objects to interest the antiquary or the historian; in this respect contrasting remarkably with many other Italian cities. It derives its name from the Taurini, a Transalpine nation, by whom the surrounding country was in early times colonized, and who, along with the other Ligurian tribes, were ultimately brought under subjection to the Romans, who founded here a city, which occupied the site of modern Turin, and in honour of Augustus named it *Augusta Taurinorum.* In the decline of the Empire it shared the fate of Rome and other cities of the West, and was taken and plundered by the Goths under their king, the celebrated Alaric. To guard against the recurrence of similar disasters, it was surrounded with walls and fortified, but these defences were unable to shield it from the violence of the Lombards, who next became its masters. On the establishment of a universal monarchy by Charlemagne, Turin passed under his sovereignty, and was bestowed by him in feudal tenure on the bishops of the diocese, who governed it for a considerable period, some of them with great tyranny. It afterwards became incorporated with the territories of the Marquises of Susa, and on the heiress of that house allying herself with the Count of Savoy, Turin and its dependencies were conveyed by her with her other patrimonial estates to her husband.

The traveller who has descended into Italy by the pass of Mont Cenis, cannot fail to be most favourably impressed both by the position and the general aspect of the city of Turin. It is situated

TURIN.

nearly in the centre of Piedmont, 72 miles from Milan, and 118 from Genoa, at the confluence of a small stream, the Dora Riparia or Soaina, with the Po, which even at this early stage of its course has become a deep and rapid river. The plain on which the city stands is bounded on the north and west by the giant masses of the snow-capped Alps, among whose summits that of Mont Cenis towers aloft in silent majesty; on the south by the Collina di Torino, a beautiful range of low hills dotted with villas and gardens; and to the east it extends away in unbroken continuity to the horizon, forming the commencement of the great plain of North Italy, a very garden of fertility and loveliness, that stretches from the Alps to the Apennines and to the shores of the Adriatic. The approach to the city from the west is by a magnificent avenue of trees, the longest probably in Europe, which commencing at the town of Rivoli leads thence to Turin, forming a noble vista, to which the dome of the church of the Superga forms a fitting and picturesque termination. Nor are these pleasing impressions dissipated on a nearer acquaintance with the city. The elegance and regularity of its buildings—with the cleanliness and straightness of the streets—will bear comparison with the finest capitals of modern Europe; whilst the mingled sublimity and beauty of the surrounding country impart to it an aspect which few other large cities can rival. Its total want of suburbs never fails to strike the stranger with surprise, who thus passes at once from the open country to the busy town.

The town was formerly encircled by fortifications as well as suburbs, but both have now disappeared, the only vestige remaining of the former being the citadel, now almost abandoned, and its outworks razed. This stronghold, built by Emanuele Filiberto in 1565, is the earliest specimen of regular fortification in Europe. The destruction of the fortifications of the town was mainly the work of the French, who held possession of Turin from 1801 to 1814. Their places have been supplied by gardens, public walks, and splendid rows of houses. Among the first of these may be mentioned the Ripari gardens, a favourite place of resort, and forming a boulevard encircling the city from east to south. The Dora Riparia is crossed by two, and the Po by three bridges. The principal bridge over the Po was erected in 1810, under the government of the French, in room of an ancient bridge of thirteen arches, then taken down, which had existed from the beginning of the fifteenth century. It consists of five elliptic arches, and is seen in the middle distance of the engraving. Napoleon was so highly pleased with this bridge that he used to speak of it as one of the grandest monuments of his sovereignty. The piazze or public squares of Turin are thirteen in number, the principal, though not the handsomest, being the Piazza Castello, so called from the ancient castle of the Dukes of Savoy, which stands in its centre. It is surrounded in great part by arcades, and has on its north side the royal palace, and on its east the grand theatre. The Piazza di San Carlo is the finest square in Turin. In this piazza stands the bronze equestrian statue of Emanuele Filiberto, by Baron Marochetti, of whose works it is perhaps the finest.

The oldest ecclesiastical structure in the city is the Cathedral or Duomo, founded in 1498 and completed in 1505, on the site of an older edifice erected by Agilulph, king of the Lombards. It is in the Renaissance style, but has been much altered, and is not remarkable in regard to architecture. Behind the cathedral, and communicating with it, and also communicating with the royal palace, is the chapel of the Santo Sudario, considered the master-piece of Guarini. Its cupola is original and elegant in design, being composed of a series of arched ribs, from the summits of which others spring in succession, thus forming a species of dome, the light being admitted through the various perforations of the arches. In recesses around this chapel are placed fine marble monuments of the most renowned members of the house of Savoy. Many of the other churches are remarkable for the splendour of their decorations, and among them may be noticed that of San Agostino, erected in 1551, and distinguished by its monuments of many eminent public men; La Gran Madri di Dio, opposite the bridge over the Po, a building in imitation of the Pantheon at Rome, seen on the right of our view; La Consolata, so called from possessing a picture of the Virgin which claims a miraculous origin; and the churches of San Filippo and the Santissima Trinita, the former the largest, and the latter one of the most beautiful sacred edifices in Turin. None of these churches however are specially distinguished for architectural merit, and contain few works of art by the great masters. Though not within the town, reference must here be made to the splendid church of La Superga, which occupies a steep and elevated position at five miles' distance, commanding the finest possible view of the city and surrounding country. It was erected in fulfilment of a vow made by Victor Amadeus II., in 1706, when looking down with Prince Eugene from the heights of the Collina upon his capital invested by the forces of Louis XIV.; he vowed, if success should crown his arms, to found a church to the Virgin; and the subsequent victory of Turin and raising of the siege were interpreted by him as an answer to his prayers, and commemorated by the erection of La Superga. It is a magnificent structure, the work of Juvara, somewhat after the model of St. Peter's at Rome, and has a fine portico of eight red and white marble columns, and a most sumptuously decorated interior. Previously to 1821 it was the burial-place of the royal family.

Among the palaces of Turin the first place is due to the royal palace in the Piazza Castello, a building of unpretending appearance externally, but fitted up in the interior with great magnificence, and containing an extensive library, in which many valuable letters and manuscripts are preserved. There is also in the palace a fine collection of ancient armour, called the Armeria Regia, which being open to the public forms one of the principal sights of Turin. The apartments occupied by the Senate are in the ancient castle in the centre of the Piazza del Castello, known as the Palazzo Madama, which also contains the royal picture-gallery, a good collection of works of art. In the Palazzo Carignano, a highly decorated but somewhat fantastic building, the Chamber of Deputies holds its sittings. In the Palazzo dell' Academia Reale delle Scienze are several museums of natural history, antiquities, &c., of considerable importance.

The University of Turin is an extensive and magnificent edifice. It was founded in 1405, but the present buildings belong to the last century. The court is surrounded with a double tier of arcades, under which is a valuable collection of ancient sculptures, bas-reliefs, and inscribed marbles, many of them obtained from the ruins of the ancient Roman town of Industria, situated eighteen miles from Turin, and discovered in 1744. An extensive library is attached to the institution, which contains forty-seven professorial chairs, and has an average attendance of nearly 2000 students.

Like the other Italians the Turinese are enthusiastic lovers of music, and the Teatro Reale, or Teatro dell' Opera, is among the finest in Northern Italy, vying even with the famed La Scala at Milan. It was erected after the design and under the superintendence of Count Benedetto Alfieri, a distant relative of the celebrated tragic author of that name, and is capable of accommodating 2500 persons. There are also the Teatro Carignano, where the first tragedy of Alfieri was performed in public; the Teatro d'Angennes; the Teatro Nazionale, and other theatres, including two of *fantoccini* or *marionettes*, of which the Piedmontese claim to be the inventors.

As a place of resort for strangers, Turin cannot be said to have as yet found much favour, partly owing to its want of archaeological and artistic attractions, and partly also from the severity of the climate, which in winter is apt to be foggy, and is frequently extremely cold. At other seasons, however, the air is remarkably balmy and salubrious. The population numbers about 180,000.

MODENA.

ALTHOUGH now possessing few relics of ancient times, Modena (the *Mutina* of the Romans) claims an antiquity not much inferior to that of Rome herself, being previous to the Christian era one of the most flourishing cities in Gallia Cispadana. Situated on the Æmilian Way, between Parma and Bononia, it appears to have been originally founded by the Etruscans, from whom it was conquered by the Romans about the commencement of the third century B.C. At this period it was a considerable place, and strongly fortified; on the occasion of a sudden inroad of the Gauls, the triumvirs who had been appointed to organize the newly established colony of Placentia were constrained to take refuge within the walls of Mutina, where they were effectually shielded from the barbarians. It does not appear, however, to have been regularly settled as a colony till about B.C. 183, when, along with Parma, it was formally invested with this character, received an accession of 2000 immigrants, and its inhabitants were admitted to the honours and privileges of Roman citizens. Not long afterwards the town and adjoining territory were ravaged by the Ligurians; but these were speedily repulsed with great slaughter by the consul C. Claudius, and the colonists re-established in Mutina. From this time its prosperity rapidly increased. During the civil war after the death of Cæsar, it played an important part, and is noted for the siege which it sustained under Brutus against the blockading forces of Mark Antony. After various battles fought in its vicinity between the troops of the latter and the army sent by the senate to the assistance of Brutus, Antony found himself compelled to raise the siege. The various events connected with this stage in its history are referred to by Suetonius, under the title of *Bellum Mutinense*. Its importance and splendour at this period are attested by Cicero, who styles it "*firmissima et splendidissima populi Romani colonia*," and also by Appian and Mela, who refer to it as distinguished for opulence. The wool and wine produced in the adjoining territory were famous, and within the city were extensive manufactures of pottery and woollen stuffs. Towards the end of the fourth century it first began to decline, sharing the general fate of the western territories of the Roman empire, and in A.D. 452 was laid waste by Attila, king of the Huns. Though it partly recovered from these disasters, it was only to relapse into a state of gradual decay, in which it reached so low an ebb, that by the tenth century the city had become little more than a heap of ruins, and the adjoining country, from its irrigating streams being choked up and neglected, a desolate and impassable morass. In the course of a century or two, however, from this time, its fortunes began again to revive; and under its modern name of Modena, it ultimately became the flourishing capital of one of the republics of mediæval Italy. Having its safety endangered by the conflicting factions of the Guelfs and Ghibellines, it threw itself into the arms of the family of Este, and in 1288 elected as its sovereign Obizzo II., Marquis of Este, in the possession of whose house, with the exception of a short period of independence in the fourteenth century, it remained for upwards of five hundred years. In 1598, Pope Clement VIII. wrested the duchy of Ferrara from Duke Cæsar, and the family of Este then transferred its residence to Modena. The descendants of Cæsar, as Dukes of Modena and Reggio, maintained their independence till 1796. In that year the reigning duke, Ercole III., was compelled by the invasion of the French to abandon his dominions, which were united with the Papal legations of Bologna and Ferrara to form the Cispadane republic. On the overthrow of Napoleon, his grandson Francis was invested by the

MODENA.

congress of Vienna with the duchy of Modena, under the title of Francis IV. He also succeeded to the duchy of Massa Carrara, and the territory of Lunigiana on the death of his mother, Maria Beatrice of Este, in 1829. The policy of government adopted by him was like that of most of the restored sovereigns, extremely arbitrary and coercive; and though temporarily checked by the popular outbreaks of 1821 and 1831, it was only resumed with greater violence on the suppression of the liberal party. Francis IV. died in 1846, and was succeeded by his son Francis Ferdinand V., whose sway was at first characterised by greater mildness than that of his father. To quell the agitation, however, for political reform, he too resorted to arbitrary and persecuting measures, and in 1848 entered, along with the Duke of Parma, into a treaty with Austria, whereby that power was authorized to occupy their territories in the event of any insurrection. In 1850 the Jesuits were reinstated in all their former possessions and privileges. The support afforded by the French emperor, Louis Napoleon, to Sardinia, and his implied favourable views to the cause of Italian independence, infused in 1859 a fresh spirit of resistance to tyranny into the Modenese, and in consequence of the disturbance that ensued, the duke, in that year, finally abandoned his dominions. They were subsequently annexed, with the other territories of Central Italy, by a popular vote, to the sovereignty of Victor Emanuel, and now form part of the kingdom of Italy.

The city of Modena is very pleasantly situated in a low but fertile plain between the Secchia and Panaro, and on the banks of a canal which connects it with these rivers. It is surrounded by walls, of no great strength indeed, but their ramparts afford a fine promenade, and present splendid views of the Apennines and the surrounding country. The citadel with its esplanade occupies nearly a third of the whole town, which is in general built with great regularity, with clean and spacious streets, lined frequently with rows of elegant arcades. Among the public buildings may be mentioned first the Duomo or Cathedral, a fine Romanesque structure, adorned in front with many curious sculptures, and having a lofty bell-tower, in which is preserved the famous wooden bucket, now sadly worm-eaten, that was taken by the Modenese from the Bolognese in the affray of Rapolino, on 15th November, 1325, and forms the subject of Tassoni's serio-comic poem, *La Secchia rapita* (The Rape of the Bucket). It is seen towards the left centre of our view. The church of S. Agostino, recently restored, is also a fine edifice, and contains in a side-chapel the remarkable group by Begarelli, in *terra cotta*, of the Taking Down from the Cross, which called forth the enthusiastic admiration of Michael Angelo. The ducal palace, a splendid building, originally commenced in the seventeenth century, and greatly enlarged by the father of the present ex-duke, is represented in the centre of the view, towards the right. It contains a large and good collection of paintings, though many which formerly adorned it have been transferred by purchase to the Dresden Gallery. It possesses also a library, the *Biblioteca Estense*, rich in valuable manuscripts, and distinguished by ranking among its curators of former times the celebrated names of Zaccaria, Tiraboschi, and Muratori. There are no other buildings of great importance. With the exception of some woollen and silk manufactures, the trade and commerce of Modena is very inconsiderable, the inhabitants depending chiefly for their support on agriculture, and, previous to the late revolution, in supplying the demands occasioned by the presence of a court. The poets Molza and Tassoni, the archæologist Muratori, and the anatomist Fallopius, were natives of this city. The population is little upwards of 30,000.

www.ingramcontent.com/pod-product-compliance
Lightning Source LLC
Chambersburg PA
CBHW050848300426
44111CB00010B/1181